BAI 103L, Business Computing Lab

Using Excel 2013

Custom Edition for University of Dayton

Elizabeth Eisner Reding | Lynn Wermers | Dave Belden

CENGAGE Learning

Australia • Brazil • Japan • Korea • Mexico • Singapore • Spain • United Kingdom • United States

BAI 103L, Business Computing Lab
Using Excel 2013
Custom Edition for University of Dayton

Senior Manager, Student Engagement:

Linda deStefano

Janey Moeller

Manager, Student Engagement:

Julie Dierig

Marketing Manager:

Rachael Kloos

Manager, Production Editorial:

Kim Fry

Manager, Intellectual Property Project Manager:

Brian Methe

Senior Manager, Production and Manufacturing:

Donna M. Brown

Manager, Production:

Terri Daley

Printed in the United States of America

Microsoft® Excel® 2013-Illustrated Complete
Elizabeth Eisner Reding | Lynn Wermers

Library of Congress Control Number: 2013937388

Computer Concepts - Illustrated Essentials, Fourth Edition
Dave Belden

Library of Congress Control Number: 2013936572

ISBN-13: 978-1-305-29097-6

ISBN-10:

WCN: 01-100-101

Cengage Learning

5191 Natorp Boulevard
Mason, Ohio 45040
USA

Cengage Learning is a leading provider of customized learning solutions with office locations around the globe, including Singapore, the United Kingdom, Australia, Mexico, Brazil, and Japan. Locate your local office at:
international.cengage.com/region.

Cengage Learning products are represented in Canada by Nelson Education, Ltd.
For your lifelong learning solutions, visit **www.cengage.com/custom.**
Visit our corporate website at **www.cengage.com.**

Computer Concepts

ILLUSTRATED - Fourth Edition

Essentials

Dave Belden

Australia • Brazil • Japan • Korea • Mexico • Singapore • Spain • United Kingdom • United States

Printed in the United States of America
1 2 3 4 5 6 7 19 18 17 16 15 14 13

Contents

Preface

Welcome to *Computer Concepts—Illustrated Essentials, Fourth Edition.* This book has a unique design: Each concept is presented on two facing pages, with details on the left and illustrations on the right. The layout makes it easy to learn a skill without having to read a lot of text and flip pages to see an illustration.

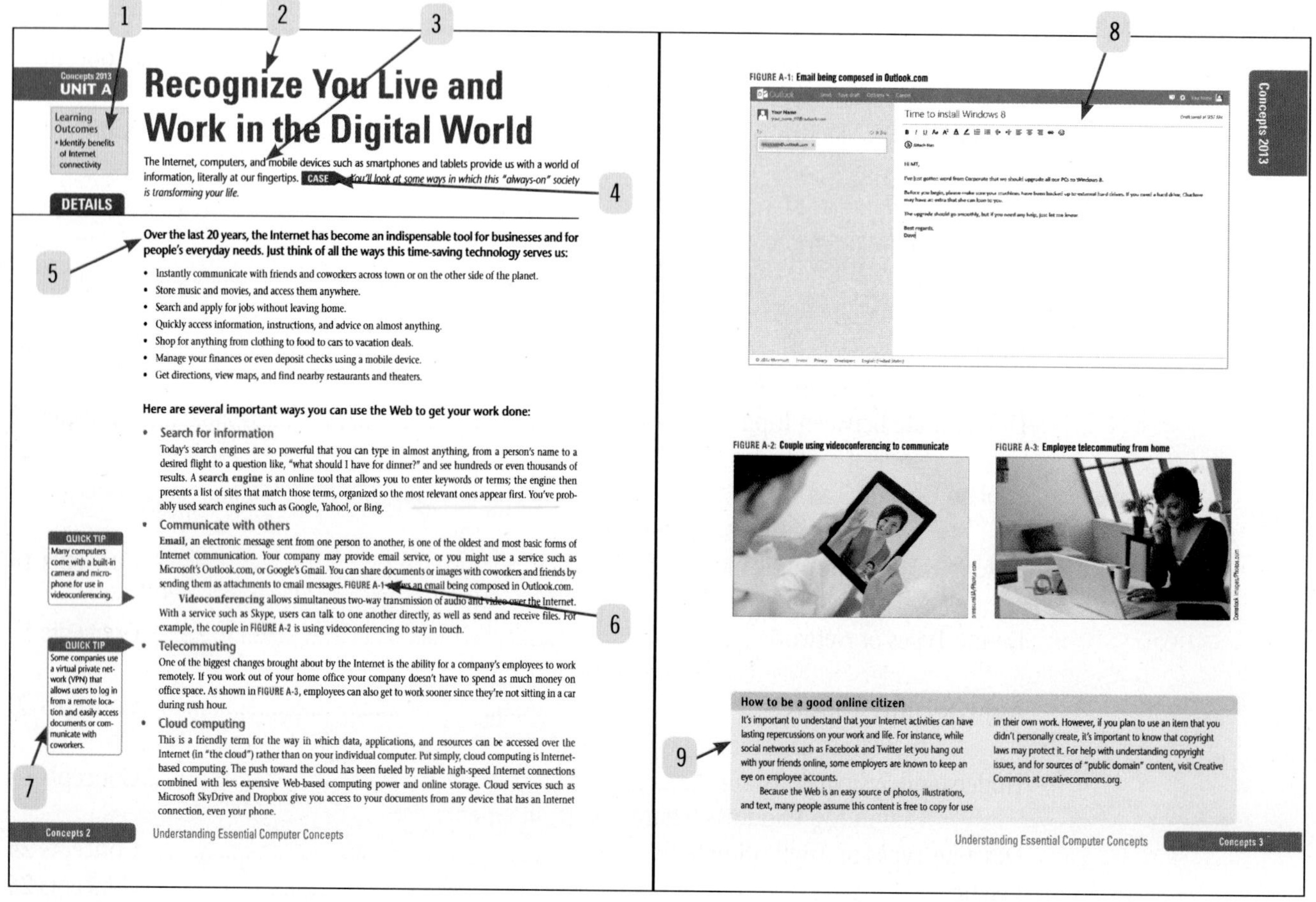

1 2 3 4 5 6 7 8 9

Concepts 2013
UNIT A

Learning Outcomes
• Identify benefits of Internet connectivity

Recognize You Live and Work in the Digital World

The Internet, computers, and mobile devices such as smartphones and tablets provide us with a world of information, literally at our fingertips. **CASE** *You'll look at some ways in which this "always-on" society is transforming your life.*

DETAILS

Over the last 20 years, the Internet has become an indispensable tool for businesses and for people's everyday needs. Just think of all the ways this time-saving technology serves us:

- Instantly communicate with friends and coworkers across town or on the other side of the planet.
- Store music and movies, and access them anywhere.
- Search and apply for jobs without leaving home.
- Quickly access information, instructions, and advice on almost anything.
- Shop for anything from clothing to food to cars to vacation deals.
- Manage your finances or even deposit checks using a mobile device.
- Get directions, view maps, and find nearby restaurants and theaters.

Here are several important ways you can use the Web to get your work done:

- Search for information

  Today's search engines are so powerful that you can type in almost anything, from a person's name to a desired flight to a question like, "what should I have for dinner?" and see hundreds or even thousands of results. A **search engine** is an online tool that allows you to enter keywords or terms; the engine then presents a list of sites that match those terms, organized so the most relevant ones appear first. You've probably used search engines such as Google, Yahoo!, or Bing.

- Communicate with others

  Email, an electronic message sent from one person to another, is one of the oldest and most basic forms of Internet communication. Your company may provide email service, or you might use a service such as Microsoft's Outlook.com, or Google's Gmail. You can share documents or images with coworkers and friends by sending them as attachments to email messages. FIGURE A-1 shows an email being composed in Outlook.com.

  Videoconferencing allows simultaneous two-way transmission of audio and video over the Internet. With a service such as Skype, users can talk to one another directly, as well as send and receive files. For example, the couple in FIGURE A-2 is using videoconferencing to stay in touch.

- Telecommuting

  One of the biggest changes brought about by the Internet is the ability for a company's employees to work remotely. If you work out of your home office your company doesn't have to spend as much money on office space. As shown in FIGURE A-3, employees can also get to work sooner since they're not sitting in a car during rush hour.

- Cloud computing

  This is a friendly term for the way in which data, applications, and resources can be accessed over the Internet (in "the cloud") rather than on your individual computer. Put simply, cloud computing is Internet-based computing. The push toward the cloud has been fueled by reliable high-speed Internet connections combined with less expensive Web-based computing power and online storage. Cloud services such as Microsoft SkyDrive and Dropbox give you access to your documents from any device that has an Internet connection, even your phone.

QUICK TIP
Many computers come with a built-in camera and microphone for use in videoconferencing.

QUICK TIP
Some companies use a virtual private network (VPN) that allows users to log in from a remote location and easily access documents or communicate with coworkers.

Concepts 2 Understanding Essential Computer Concepts

Concepts 2013

FIGURE A-1: Email being composed in Outlook.com

FIGURE A-2: Couple using videoconferencing to communicate

FIGURE A-3: Employee telecommuting from home

How to be a good online citizen

It's important to understand that your Internet activities can have lasting repercussions on your work and life. For instance, while social networks such as Facebook and Twitter let you hang out with your friends online, some employers are known to keep an eye on employee accounts.

Because the Web is an easy source of photos, illustrations, and text, many people assume this content is free to copy for use in their own work. However, if you plan to use an item that you didn't personally create, it's important to know that copyright laws may protect it. For help with understanding copyright issues, and for sources of "public domain" content, visit Creative Commons at creativecommons.org.

Understanding Essential Computer Concepts Concepts 3

1. New! Learning Outcomes box lists measurable learning goals for which a student is accountable in that lesson.
2. Each two-page lesson focuses on a single concept.
3. Introduction briefly explains why the lesson concept is important.
4. A case scenario puts learning in context.
5. Explanations guide students through each conceptual topic.
6. New! Figure references are now in red bold to help students refer back and forth between the text and images.
7. Tips and troubleshooting advice, right where you need it–next to the conceptual topic itself.
8. New! Larger images with green callouts keep students on track as they read.
9. Clues to Use yellow boxes provide useful information related to the lesson topic.

This book is an ideal learning tool for a wide range of learners—the "rookies" will find the clean design easy to follow and focused with only essential information presented, and the "hotshots" will appreciate being able to move quickly through the lessons to find the information they need without reading a lot of text. The design also makes this a great reference after the course is over! See the illustration on the left to learn more about the pedagogical and design elements of a typical lesson.

What's New in this Edition

- **Coverage** — Helps students of all levels learn essential computer concepts—examining different types of computer systems, and understanding input and output, memory, storage, security and applications software.
- **New! Learning Outcomes** — Each lesson displays a green Learning Outcomes box that lists knowledge-based learning goals for which students are accountable. Each Learning Outcome maps to a variety of learning activities and assessments. (See the *New! Learning Outcomes* section on page vi for more information.)
- **New! Updated Design** — This edition features many new design improvements to engage students—including larger lesson screenshots and images with green callouts and a refreshed Unit Opener page.

Assignments

This book includes a wide variety of high quality assignments you can use for practice and assessment. Assignments include:

- **Concepts Review** — Multiple choice, matching, and identification questions.
- **Independent Challenges** — Case projects requiring critical thinking and application of the unit skills. The Independent Challenges increase in difficulty. The first one in each unit provides the most hand-holding; the subsequent ones provide less guidance and require more critical thinking and independent problem solving.

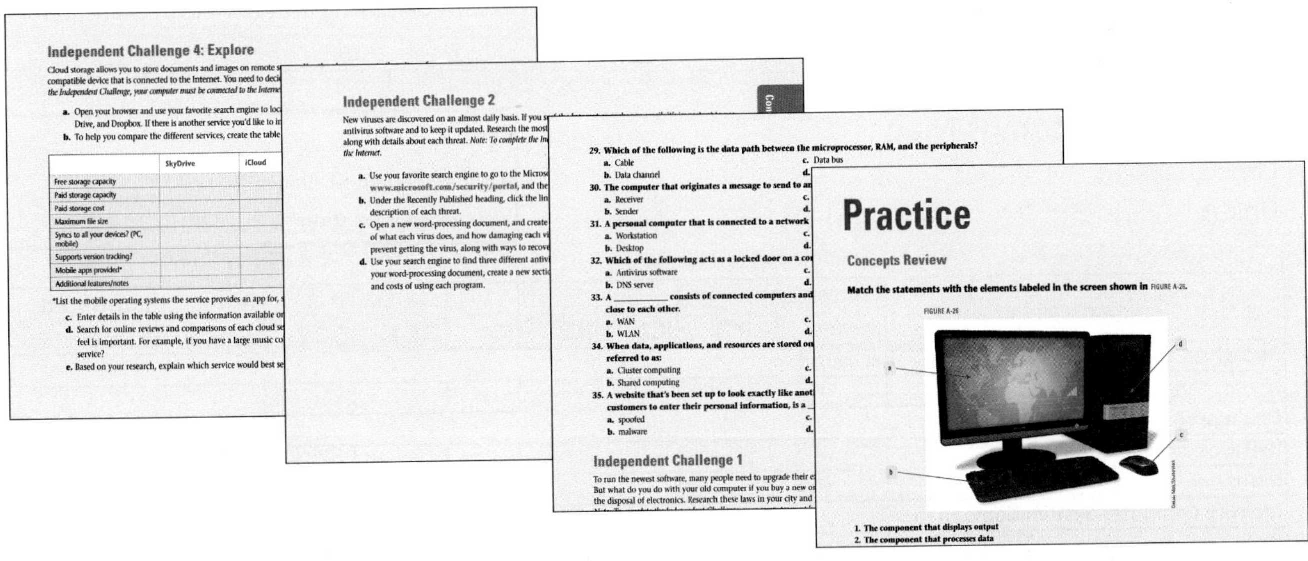

New! Learning Outcomes

Every 2-page lesson in this book now contains a green **Learning Outcomes box** that states the learning goals for that lesson.

- **What is a learning outcome?** A learning outcome states what a student is expected to know or be able to do after completing a lesson. Each learning outcome is knowledge-based and is *measurable.* Learning outcomes map to learning activities and assessments.
- **How do students benefit from learning outcomes?** Learning outcomes tell students exactly what knowledge they are *accountable* for learning in that lesson. This helps students study more efficiently and effectively and makes them more active learners.
- **How do instructors benefit from learning outcomes?** Learning outcomes provide clear, measurable learning goals that map to various high-quality learning activities and assessments. A **Learning Outcomes Map**, available for each unit in this book, maps every learning outcome to the learning activities and assessments shown below.

Learning Outcomes
- Define hardware and software
- Define mother-board and processor
- Define input and output

Learning Outcomes Map to These Learning Activities:

- **Book lessons:** Overview of one key concept presented in a two-page learning format.

Learning Outcomes Map to These Assessments:

1. **End-of-Unit Exercises: Concepts Review** (screen identification, matching, multiple choice); **Skills Review** (hands-on review of each lesson); **Independent Challenges** (hands-on, case-based review of specific skills); **Visual Workshop** (activity that requires student to build a project by looking at a picture of the final solution).
2. **Exam View Test Banks:** Objective-based questions you can use for online or paper testing.

Learning Outcomes Map

A **Learning Outcomes Map**, contained in the Instructor Resources, provides a listing of learning activities and assessments for each learning outcome in the book.

Learning Outcomes Map

Concepts 2013

Unit A

KEY:
IC=Independent Challenge
VW=Visual Workshop

	Concepts Review	IC1	IC2	IC3	IC4	EIC 1	EIC 2	Test Bank	Illustrated Video
Recognize You Live and Work in the Digital World									
Identify benefits of Internet connectivity	✓	✓		✓	✓			✓	
Distinguish Types of Computers									
Define a computer	✓			✓				✓	
Distinguish Types of Computers	✓	✓		✓				✓	
Identify Computer System Components									
Define hardware and software	✓			✓				✓	
Define motherboard and processor	✓								
Define inpu	✓								

Instructor Resources

This book comes with a wide array of high-quality technology-based, teaching tools to help you teach and to help students learn. The following teaching tools are available for download at our Instructor Companion Site. Simply search for this text at *login.cengage.com*. An instructor login is required.

- **New! Learning Outcomes Map** — A detailed grid for each unit (in Excel format) shows the learning activities and assessments that map to each learning outcome in that unit.
- **Instructor's Manual** — Available as an electronic file, the Instructor's Manual includes lecture notes with teaching tips for each unit.
- **Sample Syllabus** — Prepare and customize your course easily using this sample course outline.
- **PowerPoint Presentations** — A slide deck is provided that covers the the topics from the book that you can use in lectures, distribute to your students, or customize to suit your course.
- **Figure Files** — The figures in the text are provided on the Instructor Resources site to help you illustrate key topics or concepts. You can use these to create your own slide shows or learning tools.
- **Solutions Document** — This document outlines the solutions for the end-of-unit Concepts Review and Independent Challenges. An Annotated Solution File and Grading Rubric accompany each file and can be used together for efficient grading.
- **ExamView Test Banks** — ExamView is a powerful testing software package that allows you to create and administer printed, computer (LAN-based), and Internet exams. Our ExamView test banks include questions that correspond to the concepts covered in this text, enabling students to generate detailed study guides that include page references for further review. The computer-based and Internet testing components allow students to take exams at their computers, and also save you time by grading each exam automatically.

COURSECASTS **Learning on the Go. Always Available...Always Relevant.**

Our fast-paced world is driven by technology. You know because you are an active participant—always on the go, always keeping up with technological trends, and always learning new ways to embrace technology to power your life. Let CourseCasts, hosted by Ken Baldauf of Florida State University, be your guide into weekly updates in this ever-changing space. These timely, relevant podcasts are produced weekly and are available for download at http://coursecasts.course.com or directly from iTunes (search by CourseCasts). CourseCasts are a perfect solution to getting students (and even instructors) to learn on the go!

Tell Us What You Think!

We want to hear from you! Please email your questions, comments, and suggestions to the Illustrated Series team at: **illustratedseries@cengage.com**

Acknowledgements

Author Acknowledgements

Enormous thanks to Marjorie Hunt for this project, to everyone in production, and to Christina Kling-Garrett for shepherding us all. Special thanks to Marj Hopper for her wry humor, keen eye, and always finding the perfect simple solution. And extra thanks to MT for her support, patience, and feedback.

-Dave Belden

Advisory Board Acknowledgements

We thank our Illustrated Advisory Board who gave us their opinions and guided our decisions as we developed all of the new editions for Microsoft Office 2013.

Merlin Amirtharaj, Stanly Community College
Londo Andrews, J. Sargeant Reynolds Community College
Rachelle Hall, Glendale Community College
Terri Helfand, Chaffey Community College
Sheryl Lenhart, Terra Community College
Dr. Jose Nieves, Lord Fairfax Community College

Coming Soon: MindTap

MindTap is a fully online, highly personalized learning experience built upon Cengage Learning content. MindTap combines student learning tools—readings, multimedia, activities and assessments—into a singular Learning Path that guides students through their course. Instructors personalize the experience by customizing authoritative Cengage Learning content and learning tools, including the ability to add SAM trainings, assessments, and projects into the Learning Path via a SAM app that integrates into the MindTap framework seamlessly with Learning Management Systems. Available in 2014.

Understanding Essential Computer Concepts

CASE Computers are essential tools in almost all kinds of activity in virtually every type of business. In this unit, you'll learn about computers and their components. You'll learn about input and output, how a computer processes data and stores information, how information is transmitted, and ways to secure that information.

Unit Objectives

After completing this unit, you will be able to:

- Recognize you live and work in the digital world
- Distinguish types of computers
- Identify computer system components
- Compare types of memory
- Summarize types of storage media
- Differentiate between input devices
- Explain output devices
- Describe data communications
- Define types of networks
- Assess security threats
- Understand system software
- Describe types of application software

Files You Will Need

No files needed.

©theromb/Shutterstock

Learning Outcomes
- Identify benefits of Internet connectivity

Recognize You Live and Work in the Digital World

The Internet, computers, and mobile devices such as smartphones and tablets provide us with a world of information, literally at our fingertips. **CASE** *You'll look at some ways in which this "always-on" society is transforming your life.*

DETAILS

Over the last 20 years, the Internet has become an indispensable tool for businesses and for people's everyday needs. Just think of all the ways this time-saving technology serves us:

- Instantly communicate with friends and coworkers across town or on the other side of the planet.
- Store music and movies, and access them anywhere.
- Search and apply for jobs without leaving home.
- Quickly access information, instructions, and advice on almost anything.
- Shop for anything from clothing to food to cars to vacation deals.
- Manage your finances or even deposit checks using a mobile device.
- Get directions, view maps, and find nearby restaurants and theaters.

Here are several important ways you can use the Web to get your work done:

- **Search for information**

  Today's search engines are so powerful that you can type in almost anything, from a person's name to a desired flight to a question like, "what should I have for dinner?" and see hundreds or even thousands of results. A **search engine** is an online tool that allows you to enter keywords or terms; the engine then presents a list of sites that match those terms, organized so the most relevant ones appear first. You've probably used search engines such as Google, Yahoo!, or Bing.

- **Communicate with others**

  Email, an electronic message sent from one person to another, is one of the oldest and most basic forms of Internet communication. Your company may provide email service, or you might use a service such as Microsoft's Outlook.com, or Google's Gmail. You can share documents or images with coworkers and friends by sending them as attachments to email messages. **FIGURE A-1** shows an email being composed in Outlook.com.

  Videoconferencing allows simultaneous two-way transmission of audio and video over the Internet. With a service such as Skype, users can talk to one another directly, as well as send and receive files. For example, the couple in **FIGURE A-2** is using videoconferencing to stay in touch.

QUICK TIP
Many computers come with a built-in camera and microphone for use in videoconferencing.

- **Telecommuting**

  One of the biggest changes brought about by the Internet is the ability for a company's employees to work remotely. If you work out of your home office your company doesn't have to spend as much money on office space. As shown in **FIGURE A-3**, employees can also get to work sooner since they're not sitting in a car during rush hour.

QUICK TIP
Some companies use a virtual private network (VPN) that allows users to log in from a remote location and easily access documents or communicate with coworkers.

- **Cloud computing**

  This is a friendly term for the way in which data, applications, and resources can be accessed over the Internet (in "the cloud") rather than on your individual computer. Put simply, cloud computing is Internet-based computing. The push toward the cloud has been fueled by reliable high-speed Internet connections combined with less expensive Web-based computing power and online storage. Cloud services such as Microsoft SkyDrive and Dropbox give you access to your documents from any device that has an Internet connection, even your phone.

FIGURE A-1: Email being composed in Outlook.com

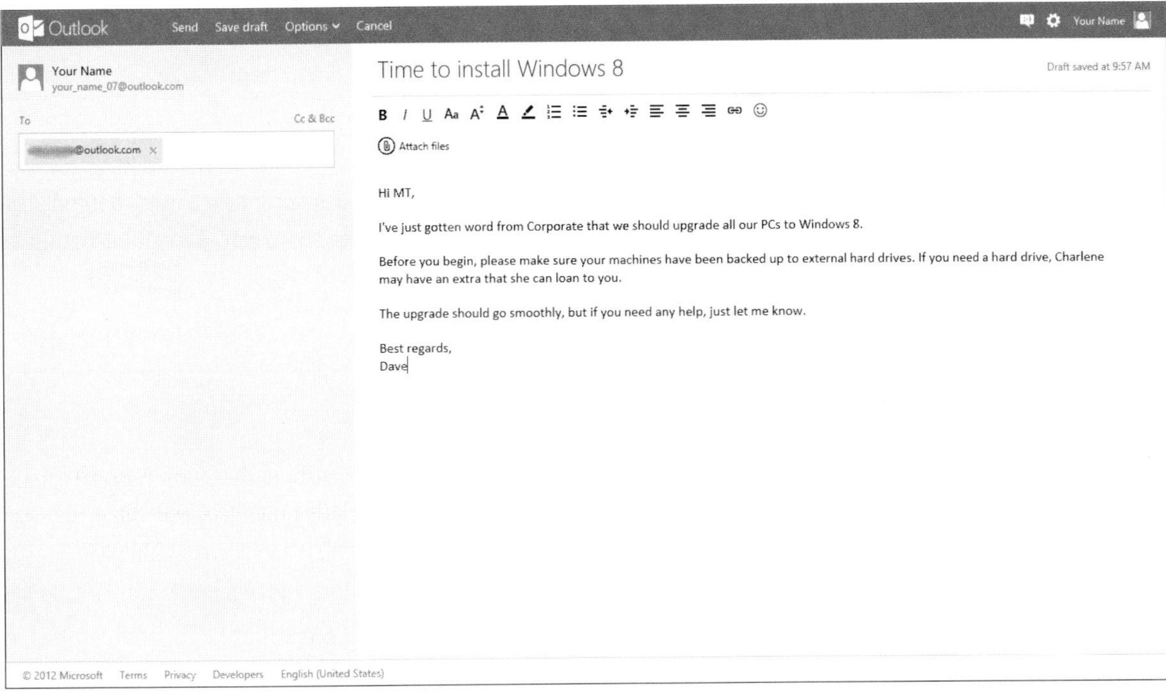

FIGURE A-2: Couple using videoconferencing to communicate

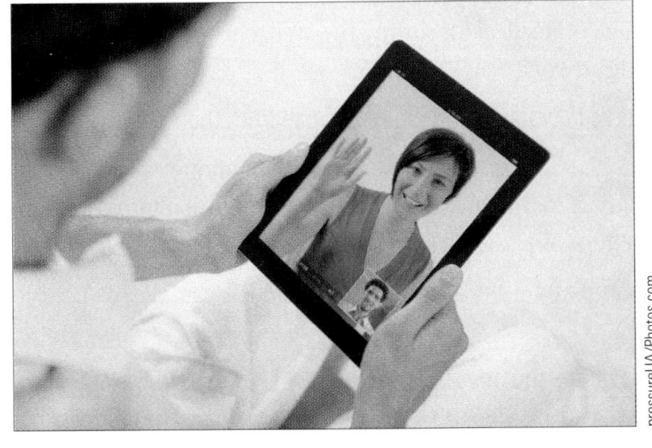

pressureUA/Photos.com

FIGURE A-3: Employee telecommuting from home

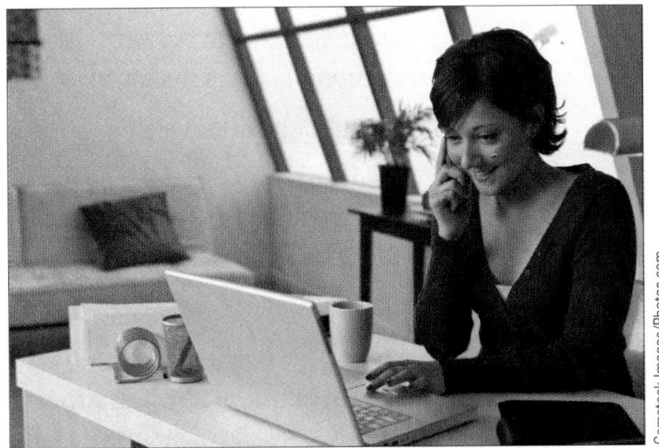

Comstock Images/Photos.com

How to be a good online citizen

It's important to understand that your Internet activities can have lasting repercussions on your work and life. For instance, while social networks such as Facebook and Twitter let you hang out with your friends online, some employers are known to keep an eye on employee accounts.

Because the Web is an easy source of photos, illustrations, and text, many people assume this content is free to copy for use in their own work. However, if you plan to use an item that you didn't personally create, it's important to know that copyright laws may protect it. For help with understanding copyright issues, and for sources of "public domain" content, visit Creative Commons at creativecommons.org.

Distinguish Types of Computers

Learning Outcomes
- Define a computer
- Distinguish types of computers

A **computer** is an electronic device that accepts information and instructions from a user, manipulates the information according to the instructions, displays the information in some way, and stores the information for later retrieval. Computers are classified by their size, speed, and capabilities. **CASE** *You'll look at the most common types of computers.*

DETAILS

The following list describes various types of computers:

QUICK TIP
In common usage, the term "PC" refers to personal computers running the Microsoft Windows operating system. Computers sold by Apple run the Mac (short for "Macintosh") operating system, and are referred to as Macs.

- **Personal computers (PCs)** are typically used by a single user at home or in the office. Personal computers are used for general computing tasks such as word processing, manipulating numbers, working with images or video, exchanging email, and accessing the Internet. The following are types of personal computers:
  - **Desktop computers** are designed to remain in one location and require a constant source of electricity. **FIGURE A-4** shows a desktop computer's monitor, CPU, keyboard, and mouse.
  - **Laptop computers** like the one shown in **FIGURE A-5** have a hinged lid that contains the computer's display and a lower portion that contains the keyboard. Laptops can be powered by rechargeable batteries, and they easily slip into a bag or briefcase. (**Notebook computers** are very similar, but are generally smaller and less powerful than laptops.)
  - **Subnotebook computers**, sometimes called **ultraportable computers** or **netbooks**, are very small and light, and are primarily designed to allow users to access the Internet and check email.
  - **Tablets** are thin computers that do not have an external keyboard or a mouse. To interact with a tablet, the user touches the screen or uses a stylus. Tablets are ideal for surfing the Web, checking email, reading electronic books, watching video, and creating artwork. See **FIGURE A-5**.
- **Handheld computers** are small computers that usually have more limited capabilities than traditional PCs.
  - **Smartphones**, like the one shown in **FIGURE A-5**, are used to make and receive phone calls, maintain an address book and calendar, send email, connect to the Internet, play music, and take photos or video. They can also perform some of the same functions as a traditional PC, such as word processing.
  - **MP3 players** are primarily used to store and play music, although some models can also be used to play digital movies or television shows.
- **Mainframe computers** and **supercomputers** like the one shown in **FIGURE A-6** are used by large businesses, government agencies, and in science and education. They provide centralized storage and processing, and can manipulate tremendous amounts of data.

FIGURE A-4: Desktop computer

Mmaxer/Shutterstock

FIGURE A-5: Laptop computer, smartphone, and tablet

Daboost/Shutterstock

FIGURE A-6: Supercomputer

senticus/iStockphoto.com

Computers are more personal than ever

Technology is constantly evolving and improving, which means that computer hardware becomes smaller and more powerful. For example, today's desktop PCs are far more powerful than the mainframe computers of a few decades ago, and current handheld smartphones are more capable than the first laptops. As the lines between types of devices become less distinct, consumers may need fewer devices to accomplish their tasks.

Identify Computer System Components

Learning Outcomes
- Define hardware and software
- Define mother-board and processor
- Define input and output

A **computer system** includes computer hardware and software. **Hardware** refers to the physical components of a computer. **Software** refers to the intangible components of a computer system, particularly the **programs**, or data routines, that the computer uses to perform a specific task. **CASE** *You'll look at how computers work and describe the main components of a computer system.*

DETAILS

The following list provides an overview of computer system components and how they work:

The design and construction of a computer is referred to as its **architecture** or **configuration**. The technical details about each hardware component are called **specifications**. For example, a computer system might be configured to include a printer; a specification for that printer might be a print speed of eight pages per minute or the ability to print in color.

The hardware and the software of a computer system work together to process data. **Data** refers to the numbers, words, figures, sounds, and graphics that describe people, events, things, and ideas. Modifying data is referred to as **processing**.

Processing tasks occur on the **motherboard**, the main electronic component inside the computer. See **FIGURE A-7**. The motherboard is a **circuit board**, which is a rigid piece of insulating material with **circuits**—electrical paths—that control specific functions. Motherboards typically contain the following processing hardware:

- The **microprocessor**, also called the **processor** or the **central processing unit (CPU)**, consists of transistors and electronic circuits on a silicon chip (an integrated circuit embedded in semiconductor material). The processor is mounted on the motherboard and is responsible for executing instructions. It is the "brain" of the computer. **FIGURE A-8** shows where the CPU sits in the flow of information through a computer.
- **Cards** are removable circuit boards that are inserted into slots in the motherboard to expand the capabilities of the computer. For example, a sound card translates digital audio information into analog sounds the human ear can hear.

Input is the data or set of instructions you give to a computer. You use an **input device**, such as a keyboard or a mouse, to enter data and issue commands. **Commands** are input instructions that tell the computer how to process data. For example, if you want to enhance the color of a photo in a graphics program, you input the appropriate commands that instruct the computer to modify the data in the image.

Output is the result of the computer processing the input you provide. Output can take many different forms, including printed documents, pictures, audio, and video. Computers produce output using **output devices**, such as a monitor or printer. The output you create using a computer may be stored inside the computer itself or on an external storage device, such as a DVD.

The computer itself takes care of the processing functions, but it needs additional components, called **peripheral devices**, to accomplish the input, output, and storage functions. You'll learn more about these devices later in this unit.

FIGURE A-7: Motherboard

FIGURE A-8: Flow of information through a computer system

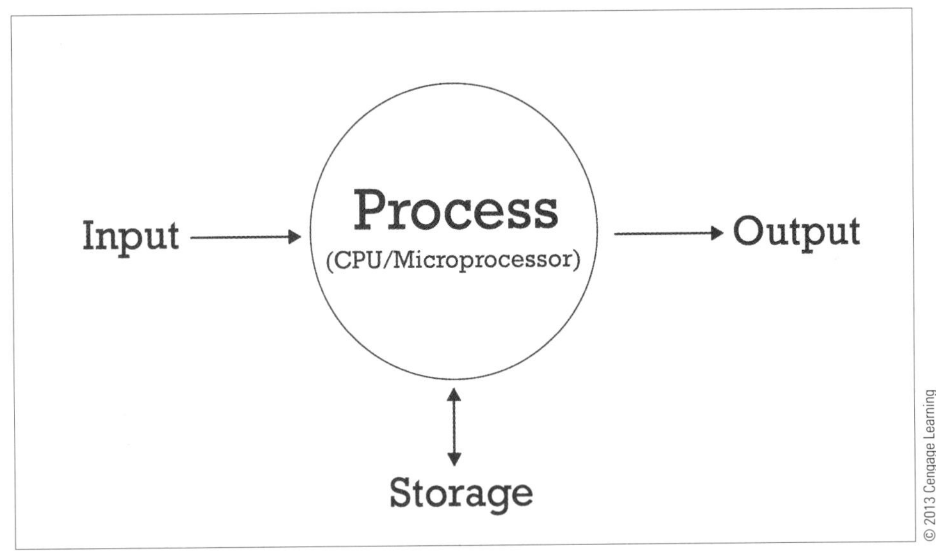

About microprocessor speeds

How fast a computer can process instructions depends partially on the speed of the microprocessor. Among other factors, the speed of the microprocessor is determined by its clock speed, word size, and whether it is single or multicore. **Clock speed** is measured in **megahertz (MHz)**, millions of cycles per second, or in **gigahertz (GHz)**, billions of cycles per second. **Word size** refers to the number of bits—the smallest unit of information in a computer—that are processed at one time; for example, a 32-bit processor processes 32 bits at a time. A computer with a large word size can process faster than a computer with a small word size. Most PCs sold today come with 64-bit processors. Finally, a **dual-core processor**, which has two processors on a single chip, can process information up to twice as fast as a **single-core processor**. Likewise, a **quad-core processor**, with four processors on a chip, processes information up to four times as fast as a single-core processor. Other multicore processors, such as hexacore and octacore, are also available.

Compare Types of Memory

Learning Outcomes
- Define memory
- Distinguish types of memory

One of the most important components of personal computer hardware is the **memory**, which stores instructions and data. **CASE** *You'll explore the different types of memory found in a typical computer: random access memory, cache memory, virtual memory, read-only memory, and complementary metal oxide semiconductor memory.*

DETAILS

Types of memory include the following:

QUICK TIP
When the computer is off, RAM is empty.

Random access memory (RAM) holds information only while the computer is on. Whenever you're using a computer, the microprocessor temporarily loads the necessary programs and data into RAM so it can quickly access them. The information present in RAM can be accessed in a different sequence from which it was stored, hence its name. RAM typically consists of chips mounted on cards that are plugged into the motherboard.

- RAM is considered **volatile memory** or **temporary memory** because it's constantly changing or being refreshed. RAM is cleared when the computer is turned off.
- Most personal computers use **synchronous dynamic random access memory (SDRAM)**, which allows faster access to data by synchronizing with the clock speed of the computer's system bus.
- **Memory capacity** is the amount of data the computer can handle at any given time and is usually measured in gigabytes. For example, a computer that has 4 GB of RAM has the capacity to temporarily use more than four billion bits of data at one time.

QUICK TIP
You can often add more RAM to a computer by installing additional memory cards on the motherboard. You cannot add ROM; it is permanently installed on the motherboard.

Cache memory, sometimes called **RAM cache** or **CPU cache**, is special, high-speed memory located on or near the microprocessor itself. Cache memory sits between the CPU and relatively slow RAM and stores frequently accessed and recently accessed data and commands.

Virtual memory is space on the computer's storage devices (usually the hard disk drive) that simulates additional RAM. It enables programs to run as if your computer had more RAM by moving data and commands from RAM to the computer's permanent storage device and swapping in the new data and commands. Virtual memory, however, is much slower than RAM.

Read-only memory (ROM), also known as **firmware**, is a chip on the motherboard that permanently stores the **BIOS (basic input/output system)**. The BIOS is activated when you turn on the computer; it initializes the motherboard, recognizes any devices connected to the computer, and starts the boot process. The **boot process**, or **booting up**, includes loading the operating system software and preparing the computer so you can begin working.

- ROM never changes, and it remains intact when the computer is turned off; it is therefore called **nonvolatile memory** or **permanent memory**.
- Some computers allow ROM to be reprogrammed via a **firmware update**, which allows a manufacturer to fix bugs and add features.

Complementary metal oxide semiconductor (**CMOS**, pronounced "SEE-moss") **memory** is a chip on the motherboard that stores the date, time, and system parameters. Often referred to as **semipermanent memory**, a small rechargeable battery powers CMOS so its contents are saved when the computer is turned off. **FIGURE A-9** shows the basic relationships between the different types of computer memory.

FIGURE A-9: Relationships between types of computer memory

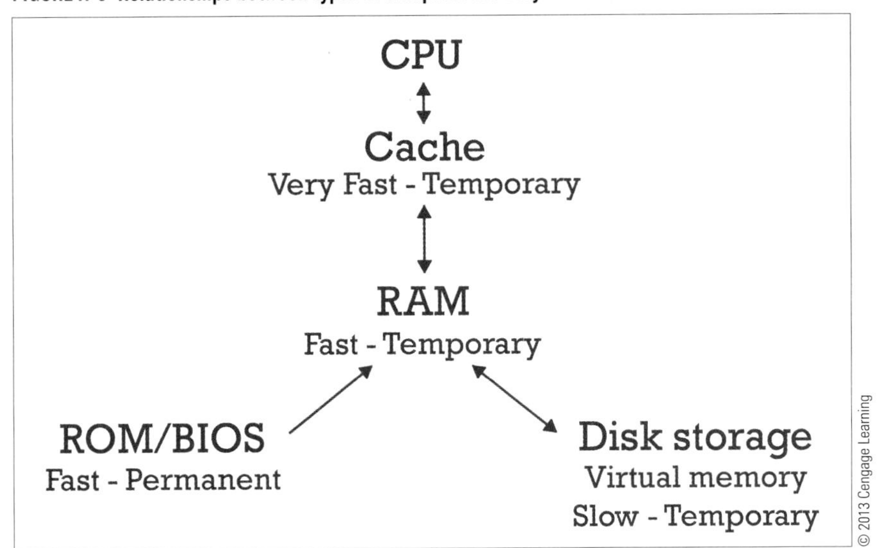

Upgrading RAM

One of the easiest ways to make your computer run faster is to add more RAM. The more RAM a computer has, the more instructions and data can be stored there. You can often add more RAM to a computer by installing additional memory cards on the motherboard, as shown in **FIGURE A-10**. Currently, you can buy from 512 MB to 16 GB RAM cards, and usually, you can add more than one card. Check your computer's specifications to see what size RAM cards the slots on your motherboard will accept. Note that if your computer has a 32-bit processor, it can't use more than 4 GB of RAM, even if the computer has places to plug in more cards.

FIGURE A-10: Installing RAM on a motherboard

Summarize Types of Storage Media

Learning Outcomes
- Define storage media
- Distinguish types of storage media

Since RAM retains data only while the power is on, your computer must have a more permanent storage option. As **FIGURE A-11** shows, a storage device receives data from RAM and stores it on a storage medium, some of which are described below. The data can later be read back to RAM to use again. All data and programs are stored as files. A computer **file** is a named collection of stored data. An **executable file** is a type of computer file that contains the instructions that tell a computer how to perform a specific task; for instance, the files that are used when the computer starts are executable. Another type of computer file is a **data file**. This is the kind of file you create when you use software. For instance, a report that you write with a word-processing program is data, and it must be saved as a data file if you want to access it later. **CASE** *You'll explore some common types of storage media.*

DETAILS

The types of storage media are discussed below:

Magnetic storage devices use various patterns of magnetization to store data on a magnetized surface. The most common type of magnetic storage device is the **hard disk drive (HDD)**, also called a **hard disk** or a **hard drive**. It contains several spinning platters on which a magnetic head writes and reads data. Most personal computers come with an internal hard drive on which the operating system, programs, and files are all stored. You can also purchase external hard drives for additional storage and for backing up your computer.

QUICK TIP
Optical storage devices, such as CDs and DVDs, are much more durable than magnetic storage media.

Optical storage devices use laser technology to store data in the form of tiny pits or bumps on the reflective surface of a spinning polycarbonate disc. To access the data, a laser illuminates the data path while a read head interprets the reflection.

- Originally developed to store audio recordings, the **CD (compact disc)** was later adapted for data storage; the **CD-ROM** then became the first standard optical storage device available for personal computers. One CD can store 700 MB of data.
- A **DVD** is the same physical size as a CD, but it can store between 4.7 and 15.9 GB of data, depending on whether the data is stored on one or two sides of the disc, and how many layers of data each side contains.
- **Blu-ray** discs store 25 GB of data per layer. They are used for storing high-definition video.

QUICK TIP
There is only one way to insert a flash drive, so if you're having problems inserting the drive into the slot, turn the drive over and try again.

Flash memory (also called **solid state storage**) is similar to ROM except that it can be written to more than once. Small **flash memory cards** are used in digital cameras, handheld computers, video game consoles, and many other devices.

- A popular type of flash memory is a **USB flash drive**, also called a **USB drive** or a **flash drive**. See **FIGURE A-12**.
- USB drives are available in a wide range of capacities, from one to 512 GB. They are popular for use as a secondary or backup storage device.
- USB drives plug directly into the USB port of a personal computer where the device is recognized as another disk drive. The location varies with the brand and model of computer you're using, but USB ports are usually found on the front, back, or side of a computer.

A **solid-state drive (SSD)** is based on flash memory, but is intended as a replacement for a traditional hard disk drive. Per gigabyte, SSDs are still more expensive than hard drives, but use less power and offer much faster data access and increased reliability.

FIGURE A-11: Storage devices and RAM

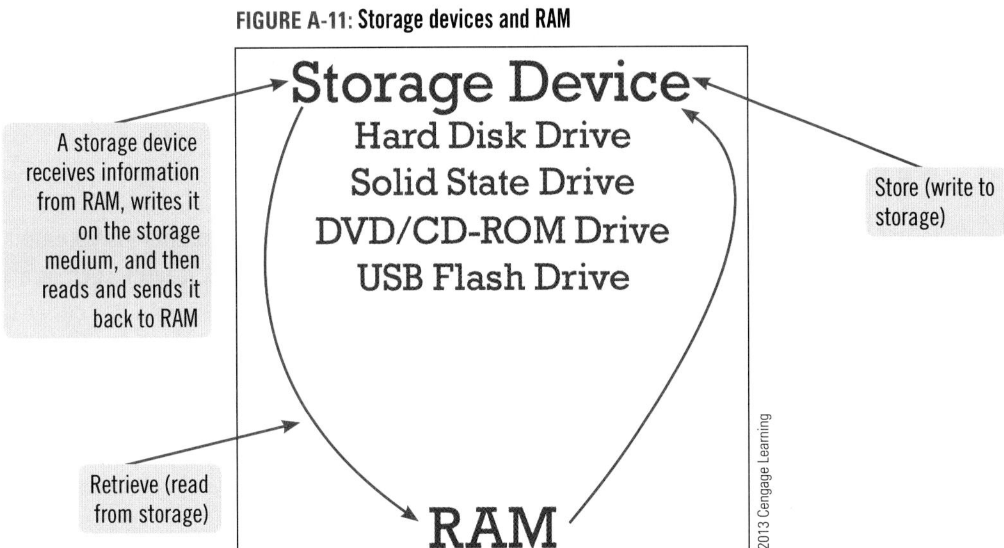

FIGURE A-12: USB flash drive being inserted into a laptop

Rewriting on optical storage

CDs that you buy with software or music already on them are CD-ROMs (compact disc read-only memory)—you can read from them, but you cannot record additional data onto them. To store data on a CD, you need to record it on a **CD-R (compact disc recordable)** or **CD-RW (compact disc rewritable)** drive and a CD-R or CD-RW disc. On a CD-R, after the data is recorded, you cannot erase or modify it, but you can add new data to the disc, as long as the disc has not been finalized. In contrast, you can rerecord a CD-RW. Recordable DVD drives are also available. As with CDs, you can buy a DVD to which you can record only once, or a rewritable DVD to which you can record and then rerecord data. Recordable DVDs come in two formats, **DVD-R** and **DVD+R**, and likewise rerecordable DVDs come in two formats, **DVD-RW** and **DVD+RW**. DVD drives on new computers are capable of reading from and writing to both -RW and +RW DVDs and CDs, as well as DVDs with two layers. **BD-R** are Blu-ray discs that you can record to once, and **BD-RE** are Blu-ray discs that you can record to multiple times. You need a Blu-ray drive to use Blu-ray discs.

Concepts 2013
UNIT A

Differentiate Between Input Devices

Learning Outcomes
- Define input device
- Identify various input devices

To accomplish a task, a computer first needs to receive the data and commands you input. In a typical personal computer system, you provide this information using an **input device** such as a keyboard or a mouse. Most input devices are hardware peripherals that connect to a computer either with cables or wirelessly. Wired devices typically connect with a USB cable, or using a specialized connector. Most wireless input devices connect using radio frequency technology, while some use the same infrared technology found in a television remote control. **CASE** *You'll look at some common input devices.*

DETAILS

There are many types of input devices, as described below:

QUICK TIP
You may also be able to avoid repetitive motion injuries by taking frequent breaks from computer work and by carefully stretching your hands, wrists, and arms.

The most frequently used input device is a **keyboard**, which allows you to input text and issue commands by typing. The keyboard on the right in **FIGURE A-13** is a standard keyboard, but the keyboard on the left is **ergonomic**, meaning that it has been designed to fit the natural placement of your hands and may reduce the risk of repetitive-motion injuries. Many keyboards have additional shortcut keys that are programmed to issue frequently used commands.

Another common input device is a **pointing device**, which controls the **pointer**—a small arrow or other symbol—on the screen. Pointing devices are used to select commands and manipulate text or graphics on the screen.

- The most popular pointing device for a desktop computer is a **mouse**, such as the one shown on the left in **FIGURE A-14**. You control the pointer by sliding the mouse across a surface, and this motion is tracked by either a roller ball or by infrared or laser light. A mouse usually has two or more buttons used for clicking objects on the screen. A mouse might also have a **scroll wheel** that you roll to scroll through the page or pages on your screen.
- A **trackball**, shown in the middle of **FIGURE A-14**, is similar to a mouse except that the rolling ball is on the top and you control the movement of the pointer by moving only the ball.
- Laptop computers are usually equipped with a touch pad like the one shown on the right in **FIGURE A-14**. A **touch pad**, also called a **track pad**, detects the motion of your fingers. Buttons are usually located at the bottom of the touch pad, but many also allow you to click by simply tapping the pad.

QUICK TIP
Tablets and smartphones typically feature a "virtual keyboard" for inputting text.

A **touch screen** like the one in **FIGURE A-15** accepts commands from your fingers (or a stylus), while it simultaneously displays the output. Touch screens are found on ATMs, smartphones, and tablets. Many newer desktop computers running the Microsoft Windows 8 operating system also have hardware that supports touch-screen technology.

A **microphone** can be used to record sound or communicate with others using audio or video conferencing software. Some computers have **voice-recognition software** that allows you to input data and commands with a microphone.

A **scanner** is a device that captures the image on a photograph or piece of paper and stores it digitally. If you scan a text document, you can use **optical character recognition (OCR)** software to translate it into text that can be edited in a word-processing program. If you scan a photo, it can be saved as an image file.

FIGURE A-13: Ergonomic keyboard and standard keyboard

Dmitry Melnikov/Shutterstock

pav197lin/Shutterstock

FIGURE A-14: Personal computer pointing devices: mouse, trackball, and touchpad

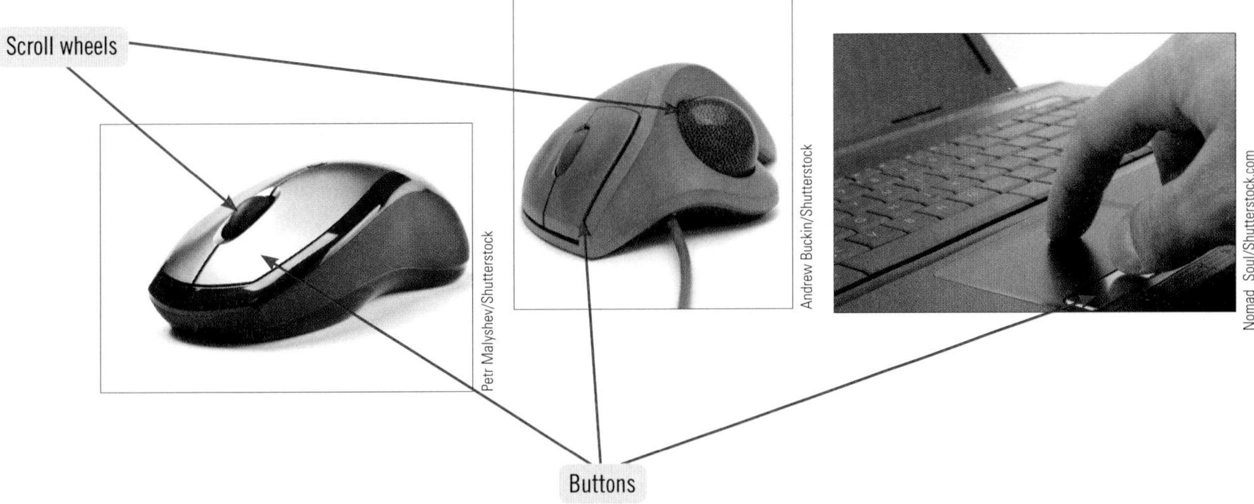

Petr Malyshev/Shutterstock
Andrew Buckin/Shutterstock
Nomad_Soul/Shutterstock.com

FIGURE A-15: Touchscreen

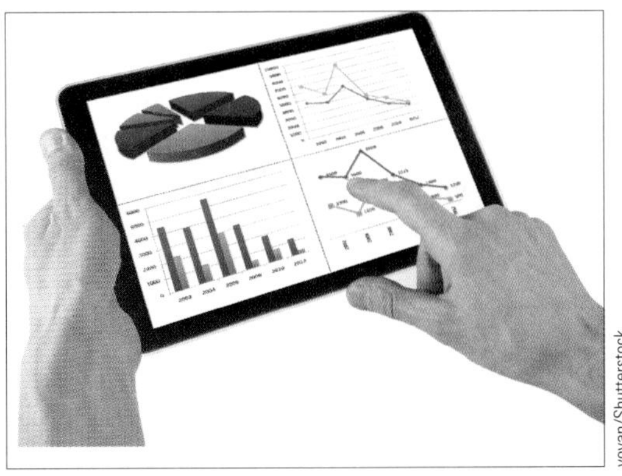
vovan/Shutterstock

Understanding assistive devices

Advances in **computer accessibility** mean that people with physical impairments or disabilities can use computers. For example, people who cannot use their arms or hands to operate a mouse may be able to use foot, head, or eye movements to control a specialized assistive device. Those with poor vision can use keyboards with large keys, screen enlargers that increase the size of objects on a monitor, or screen readers that speak on-screen content aloud. Brain-computer interface technology may soon allow you to control a computer with your thoughts.

Explain Output Devices

Learning Outcomes
- Define output device
- Identify different output devices

An **output device** is any hardware peripheral that communicates the results of data processing. **CASE** *You'll explore the most commonly used output devices: monitors, printers, and speakers.*

DETAILS

Output devices are described below:

The **monitor**, sometimes called the **display** or simply the **screen**, uses video technology to display the output from a computer.

- The **flat panel monitor** shown in **FIGURE A-16** uses **LCD (liquid crystal display)** technology to create an image by modulating light within a layer of liquid crystal. LCD monitors require a backlight for illumination. Older monitors typically use a fluorescent backlight, while newer ones use **LED (light emitting diode)** technology, which is more energy efficient.
- Monitor **screen size** is the diagonal measurement from one corner of the screen to the other. In general, monitors on desktop computers range in size from 15" to 30", whereas monitors on laptop computers range in size from 10" to 20".
- A monitor's screen is divided into a matrix of small dots called **pixels. Display resolution** is the number of pixels the monitor displays in each dimension, typically expressed as width x height. Common standard resolutions range from 640 x 480 to 2560 x 1440.
- To display graphics, a computer must have a **graphics card**, also called a **video display adapter** or **video card**, or a built-in **graphics processor** (sometimes called a **built-in graphics card**). The graphics card or processor controls the signals the computer sends to the monitor.

A **printer** produces a paper copy, often called a **hard copy**, of the text and graphics processed by a computer. Print quality, or resolution, is measured by the number of **dots per inch (dpi)** that a printer can produce. The speed of a printer is determined by how many **pages per minute (ppm)** it can output.

- **LED printers** and **laser printers**, like the one shown on the left in **FIGURE A-17**, are popular for business use because they produce high-quality output quickly and reliably. Each type uses its light source to temporarily transfer an image onto a rotating drum, which attracts a powdery substance called **toner**. The toner is then transferred from the drum onto paper. Laser and LED printers typically feature print resolutions of 600 to 1200 DPI and can print in black and white or color. However, they're generally better at producing sharp text and simple graphics than they are at printing clear photographs.
- **Inkjet printers**, such as the one shown on the right in **FIGURE A-17**, are popular for home and small business use. These printers spray ink onto paper, producing quality comparable to that of a laser printer, though at much slower speeds. Inkjets can also print on a wide variety of paper types, though use of plain paper may result in fuzzy text. Most inkjets sold today print in color, and they excel at producing photos with smooth color, especially when using special glossy photo paper.

Speakers (and **headphones**) allow you to hear sounds generated by your computer. Speakers can be separate peripheral devices, or they can be built into the computer case or monitor. For speakers to work, a sound card must be installed on the motherboard. The sound card converts the digital data in an audio file into analog sound that can be played through the speakers.

FIGURE A-16: LCD monitor

Roberts/Shutterstock

FIGURE A-17: Laser printer and inkjet printer

MalDix/Shutterstock

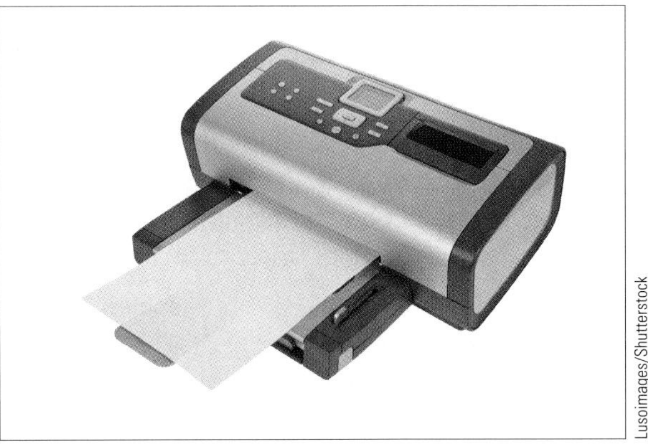

Lusoimages/Shutterstock

About multifunction printers

A **multifunction printer (MFP)** saves office space by combining several devices into one. Most small office/home office (SOHO) MFPs can print, scan, copy, and fax documents. Some MFPs also feature camera card readers and photo printing; this allows the user to print photos quickly without first loading them into a PC. MFPs can be made available to a network when connected to a computer or server. Some MFPs can also connect to a network wirelessly.

Describe Data Communications

Learning Outcomes
- Define data communications terms
- Identify PC slots and ports

Data communications is the transmission of data from one computer to another or to a peripheral device. The computer that originates the message is the **sender**. The message is sent over some type of **channel**, such as a telephone or coaxial cable, or wirelessly. The computer or device at the message's destination is the **receiver**. The rules that establish an orderly transfer of data between the sender and the receiver are called **protocols**. A **device driver**, or simply **driver**, handles the transmission protocols between a computer and its peripheral devices. A driver is a computer program that can establish communication because it understands the characteristics of your computer and of the device. **CASE** *You'll look at some common ways that computers communicate.*

DETAILS

The following describes some of the ways that computers communicate:

The path along which data travels between the microprocessor, RAM, and peripherals is called the **data bus**.

QUICK TIP
An internal peripheral device such as a hard disk drive or CD drive may plug directly into the motherboard, or it may have an attached controller card.

An external peripheral device must have a corresponding **expansion port** and **cable** that connect it to the computer. Inside the computer, each port connects to a **controller card**, sometimes called an **expansion card** or **interface card**. These cards plug into connectors on the motherboard called **expansion slots** or **slots**. Personal computers can have several types of ports, including parallel, serial, USB, MIDI, Ethernet, and Thunderbolt. **FIGURE A-18** shows the ports on one desktop computer.

A **USB (Universal Serial Bus) port** is a high-speed serial port that allows multiple connections at the same port. The device you install must have a **USB connector**, which is a small rectangular plug. When you plug the USB connector into the USB port, the computer recognizes the device and allows you to use it immediately. USB flash storage devices plug into USB ports. For most USB devices, power is supplied via the port, so there's no need for an extra power supply or cables.

An **Ethernet port**, which resembles a telephone jack, allows data to be transmitted at high speeds over a **local area network (LAN)**. You can use Ethernet to connect to another computer, to a LAN, or to a modem. A **modem** (short for modulator-demodulator) is a device that connects your computer to the Internet via a standard telephone jack or cable connection.

Monitors are connected to computers through HDMI, DVI, or VGA ports. Both **HDMI (high-definition multimedia interface)** and **DVI (digital video interface)** digitally transmit both video and audio. The older **VGA (video graphics array)** only allows analog transmission of video.

FIGURE A-18: Computer expansion ports

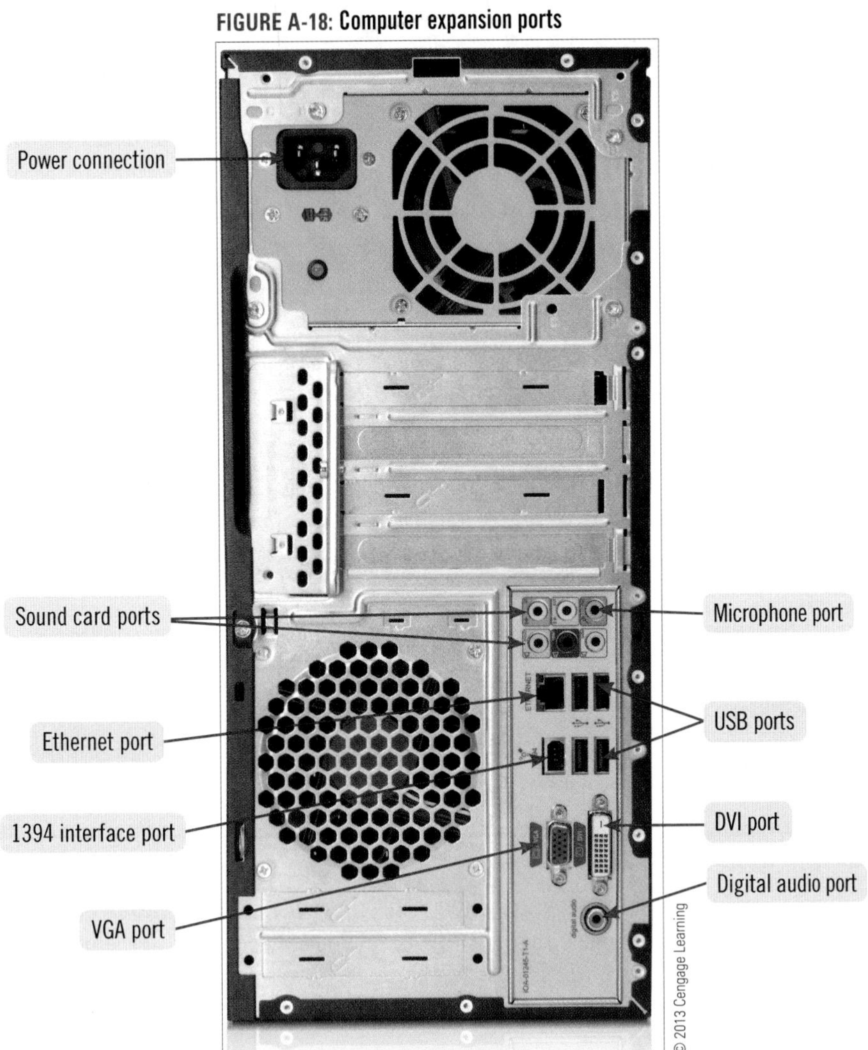

How computers represent and interpret data

A computer sees the world as a series of **binary digits or bits**. A bit can hold one of two numerical values: 1 for "on" or 0 for "off." You might think of bits as miniature light switches. Of course, a single bit doesn't hold much information, so eight of them are combined to form a **byte**, which can be used to represent 256 values. Integer value 1 equals 00000001 (only 1 bit is "flipped" on), while the byte that represents 255 is 11111111 (all the bits are flipped on). A **kilobyte (KB** or **K)** is 1024 bytes, or about a thousand bytes. A **megabyte (MB)** is 1,048,576 bytes (about a million bytes). A **gigabyte (GB)** is about a billion bytes, and a **terabyte (TB)** is about a trillion bytes.

Define Types of Networks

Learning Outcomes
- Define networking terms
- Identify network types

A network connects one computer to other computers and peripheral devices, enabling you to share data and resources with others. There is a wide a variety of network types; however, any type of network has some basic characteristics and requirements that you should know. **CASE** *You'll look at the components that make up some different types of networks.*

DETAILS

Components of networks and the types of networks are described below:

To connect with a network via Ethernet, a computer must have a **network interface card (NIC)** that creates a communications channel between the computer and the network. Most desktop PCs come with a NIC built-in, and an Ethernet cable is used to make the connection to a router or modem. A **router** is a device that controls traffic between network components.

QUICK TIP
The World Wide Web, a subset of the Internet, is a huge database of information stored on network servers.

Network software is also essential, establishing the communications protocols that will be observed on the network and controlling the data "traffic flow."

Some networks have one or more computers, called **servers**, that act as the central storage location for programs and provide mass storage for most of the data used on the network. A network with a server and computers dependent on the server is called a **client/server network**. The dependent computers are the clients.

When a network does not have a server, all the computers are essentially equal, with programs and data distributed among them. This is called a **peer-to-peer network**.

A personal computer that is not connected to a network is called a **stand-alone computer**. When it is connected to the network, it becomes a **workstation**. Any device connected to the network, from computers to printers to routers, is called a **node**. FIGURE A-19 illustrates a typical network configuration.

In a **local area network (LAN)**, the nodes are located relatively close to one another, usually in the same building.

A **wide area network (WAN)** is more than one LAN connected together. The **Internet** is the largest example of a WAN.

In a **wireless local area network (WLAN)**, devices communicate using radio waves instead of wires. **Wi-Fi** (short for **wireless fidelity**) is the term created by the nonprofit Wi-Fi Alliance to describe networks connected using a standard radio frequency established by the Institute of Electrical and Electronics Engineers (IEEE). Most Wi-Fi routers can transmit over distances of up to about 200 feet; a technique called **bridging** can be used to increase this range by using multiple routers.

A **personal area network (PAN)** allows two or more devices located close to each other to communicate directly via cables or wirelessly. A PAN can also be used to share one device's Internet connection with another.

Infrared technology uses infrared light waves to "beam" data from one device to another. The devices must be compatible, and they must have their infrared ports pointed at each other to communicate. This is also the technology used in TV remote controls.

Bluetooth uses short range radio waves (up to about 30 feet) to connect devices wirelessly to one another or to the Internet. Bluetooth is often used to connect wireless headsets to cell phones or computers, and for connecting some wireless pointing devices and keyboards.

FIGURE A-19: Typical network configuration

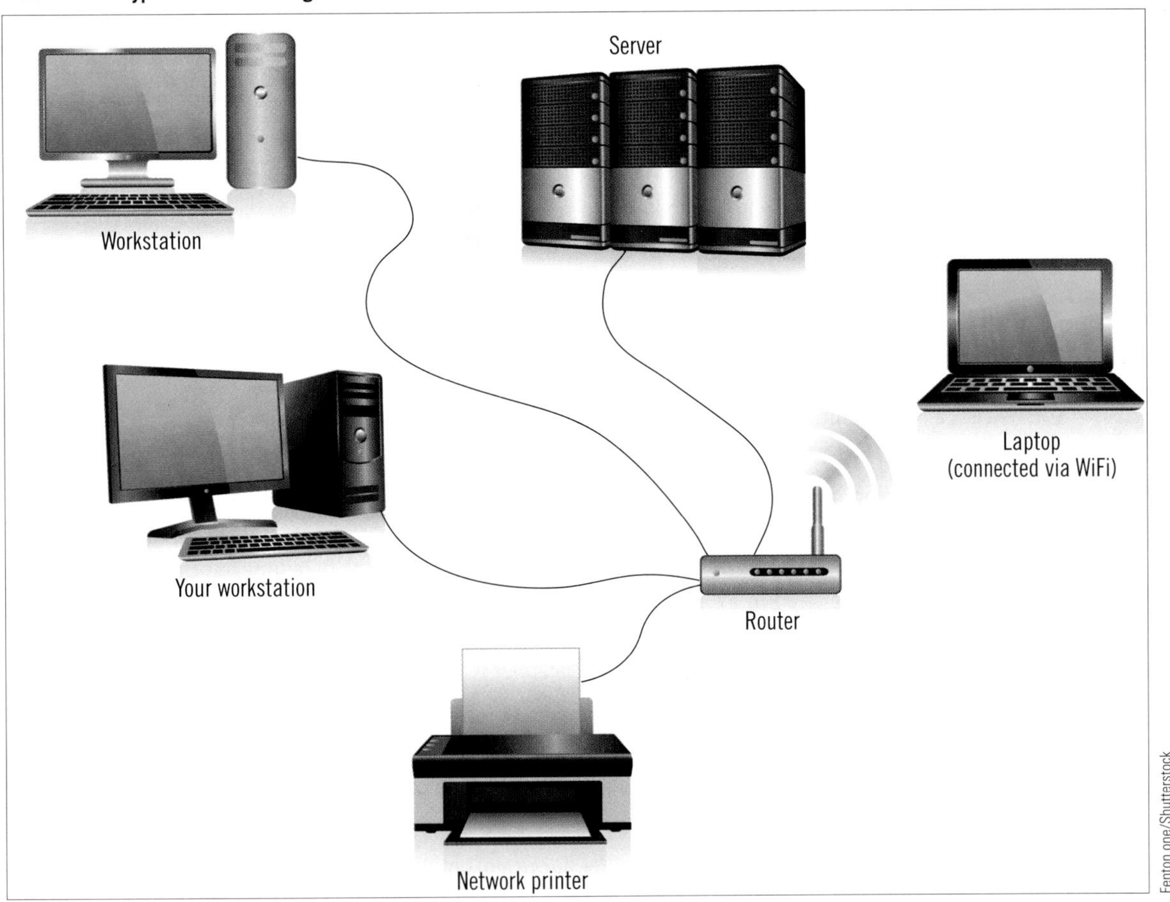

Understanding telecommunications

Telecommunications means communicating over a relatively long distance using a phone line or other data conduit. To make this connection, you must use a modem, a device that converts the digital signals that your computer outputs into analog signals that can travel over ordinary phone lines or cable lines. Many desktops and laptops come with a built-in 56K modem that can send and receive about 56,000 **bits per second (bps)** over a phone line. This is slow by modern standards, so many people opt for a high-speed connection using **DSL (digital subscriber line)**, which also operates over a phone line, or using a cable connection. If you go this route, you may need to purchase or rent an external DSL or cable modem. DSL and cable modems typically connect to a computer's **NIC (network interface card)** via an Ethernet cable. High-speed connections are often called **broadband connections.**

Assess Security Threats

Learning Outcomes
- Define types of security threats
- Establish importance of good security

Once a computer is connected to a network, it is essential that it be protected against the threat of someone stealing information or causing malicious damage. **Security** refers to the steps a computer user takes to prevent unauthorized use of or damage to a computer. **CASE** *You'll look at how important it is to be vigilant about keeping your computers secure and you'll review ways to do this.*

DETAILS

QUICK TIP
Some specific types of viruses are called worms; another type is a Trojan horse. Antivirus software usually protects against both types.

QUICK TIP
Adware is software installed with another program, often with the user's permission, that generates advertising revenue for the program's creator by displaying ads.

Malware is a broad term that describes any program designed to cause harm or transmit information without the permission of the computer owner.

Unscrupulous programmers deliberately construct harmful programs, called **viruses**, which instruct your computer to perform destructive activities, such as erasing a disk drive. Some viruses are more annoying than destructive, but some can be harmful, erasing data or causing your hard disk to require reformatting. **Antivirus software**, sometimes referred to as **virus protection software**, searches executable files for sequences of characters that may cause harm, and then disinfects files by erasing or disabling those commands. **FIGURE A-20** shows the dialog box that appears when Windows Defender is scanning a computer for potential threats.

Spyware is software that secretly gathers information from your computer and then sends this data to the company or person that created it. Spyware may be installed by a virus, though it may also be installed along with other software without the user's permission or knowledge. **Anti-spyware software** can detect these programs and delete them.

A **firewall** is like a locked door on your computer. It prevents other computers on the Internet from accessing your computer and prevents programs on it from accessing the Internet without your permission.

- A hardware firewall provides strong protection against incoming threats. Many routers come with built-in firewalls.
- Software firewalls, which are installed directly on your computer, track all incoming and outgoing traffic. If a program that never previously accessed the Internet attempts to do so, the user is notified and can choose to forbid access. There are several free software firewall packages available.

Criminals are relentlessly searching for new and aggressive ways of accessing computer users' personal information and passwords.

- A **spoofed** site is a website that's been set up to look exactly like another website, with the intention of convincing customers to enter their personal information. For example, a criminal site developer might create a **URL** (address on the Web) that looks similar to the URL of a legitimate site such as a bank's. If a customer isn't paying attention, he or she may inadvertently enter information such as credit card numbers, Social Security numbers, or passwords. Once a thief has this information, it can be used to steal the customer's money or identity. **FIGURE A-21** shows the alert displayed in the Internet Explorer browser when a known spoofed site is visited.
- **Phishing** refers to the practice of sending email to customers or potential customers of a legitimate website encouraging them to click a link in the email. When clicked, the user's **browser** (the software program used to access websites) displays a spoofed site where the user is asked to provide personal information.
- A **DNS server** is one of the many computers distributed around the world that's responsible for directing Internet traffic. Using a practice called **pharming**, a criminal can sometimes break into a DNS server and redirect any attempts to access a particular website to the criminal's spoofed site.

QUICK TIP
If you suspect you've received a phishing message, don't click any links in the email. Instead, open your browser and type the correct URL into the address bar.

FIGURE A-20: Windows Defender scan in progress

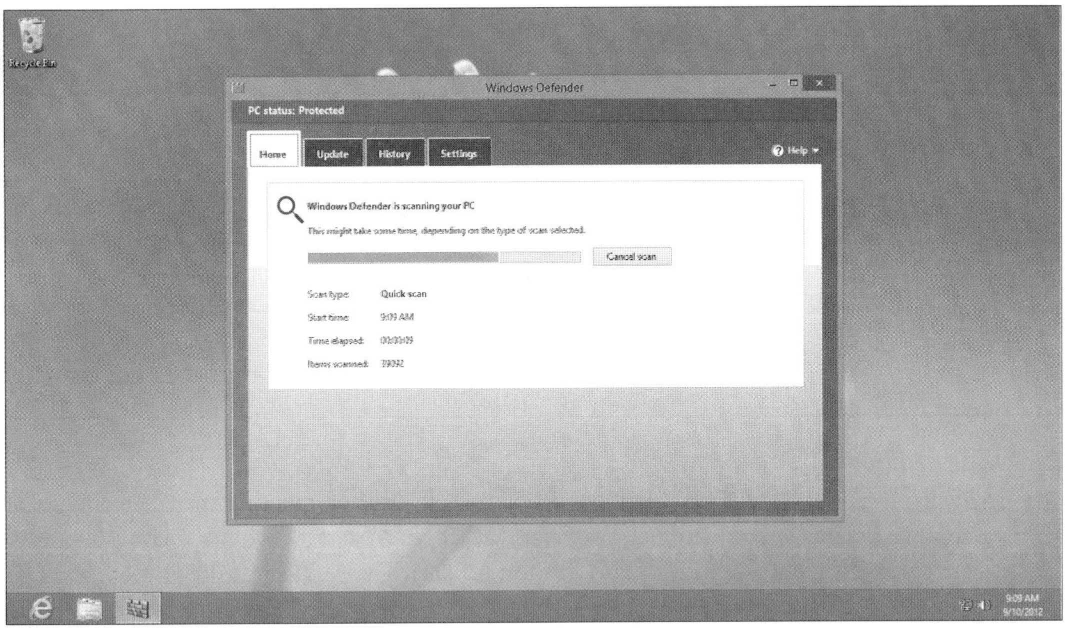
Windows Defender
PC status: Protected
Home
Update
History
Settings
Help
Windows Defender is scanning your PC
This might take some time, depending on the type of scan selected.
Cancel scan
Scan type: Quick scan
Start time: 9:09 AM
9:09 AM
9/10/2012

FIGURE A-21: Internet Explorer browser when visiting a known spoofed site

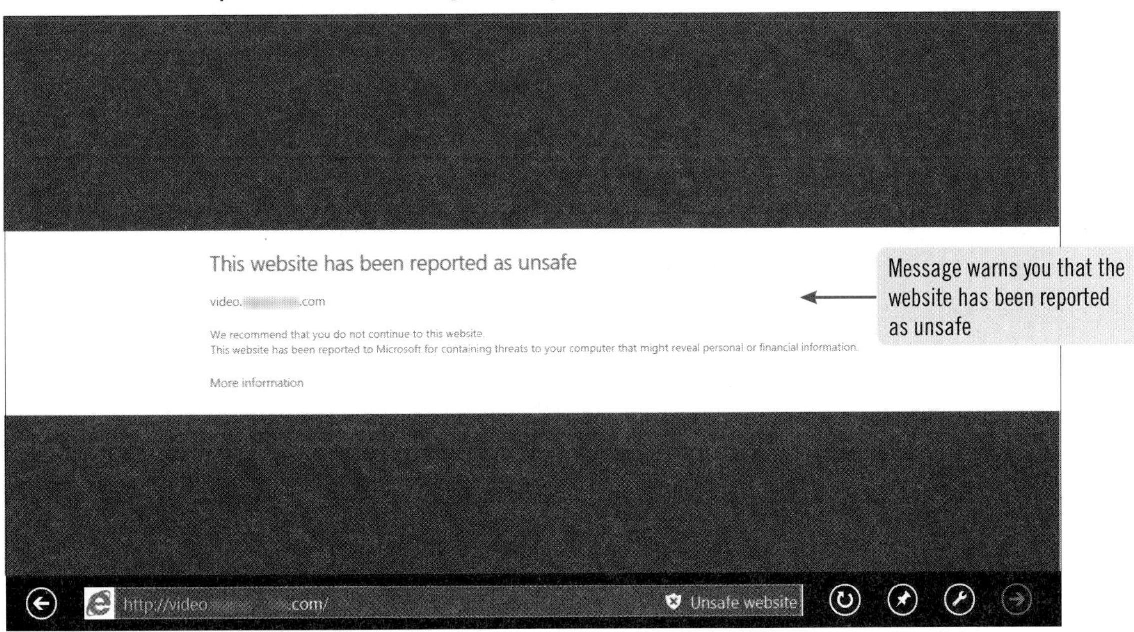
This website has been reported as unsafe
We recommend that you do not continue to this website.
This website has been reported to Microsoft for containing threats to your computer that might reveal personal or financial information.
More information
Unsafe website
Message warns you that the website has been reported as unsafe

Protecting information with passwords

You can protect data on your computer by using passwords. You can set up multiple user accounts on your computer and require that users sign in with a username and password before they can use it. This is known as **logging in** or **logging on.** You can also protect individual files on your computer so anyone who tries to access a file must type a password. Many websites, especially e-commerce and banking sites, require a username and password to access the information stored there. To prevent anyone from guessing your passwords, always create and use strong passwords. A **strong password** consists of at least eight characters of upper- and lowercase letters and numbers. Avoid using easy to obtain personal information in your passwords, such as birthdays and addresses, and always create different passwords that are unique to each website you use.

Understand System Software

Learning Outcomes
- Define system software
- Identify types of system software

The term *software* often refers to a single program, but it can also refer to a collection of programs and data that are packaged together. **System software** allocates system resources, manages storage space, maintains security, and detects equipment failure. It provides the basic platform for running specialized application software, which you'll learn about in the next lesson. CASE *You'll look at the components of system software and how they help the computer perform its basic operating tasks.*

DETAILS

The components of system software are described below:

System software (see **FIGURE A-22**) manages the fundamental operations of your computer, such as loading programs and data into memory, executing programs, saving data to storage devices, displaying information on the monitor, and transmitting data through a port to a peripheral device. There are four basic types of system software: operating systems, utility software, device drivers, and programming languages.

QUICK TIP

As part of its security responsibilities, your computer's operating system may require you to enter a username and password, or it may scan the computer to protect against viruses.

- The **operating system** manages the system resources of a computer so programs run properly. A **system resource** is any part of the computer system, including memory, storage devices, and the microprocessor. The operating system controls basic data **input and output**, or **I/O**, which is the flow of data from the microprocessor to memory to peripherals and back again.
- The operating system also manages the files on your storage devices. It opens and saves files, tracks every part of every file, and lets you know if any part of a file is missing.
- The operating system is always on the lookout for equipment failure. Each electronic circuit is checked periodically, and the user is notified whenever a problem is detected.
- Microsoft Windows, used on many personal computers, and OS X, used exclusively on Apple's Macintosh computers, are referred to as **operating environments** because they provide a **graphical user interface** (**GUI**, pronounced "goo-ey") that acts as a liaison between the user and all of the computer's hardware and software. **FIGURE A-23** shows the Start screen on a computer using Microsoft Windows 8.

Utility software helps analyze, optimize, configure, and maintain a computer. Examples of utilities include anti-virus software, backup tools, and disk tools that allow you to analyze a hard drive or compress data to save space.

As you learned in the discussion of hardware ports, device drivers handle the transmission protocol between a computer and its peripherals. When you add a new device to a computer, the installation process typically involves loading a driver that updates the computer's configuration.

While most of us have no contact with them, it's important to know that computer **programming languages** allow a programmer to write instructions, or code, that a computer can understand. Programmers typically write software in a particular language and then compile the code to create a program that the computer then executes. Popular programming languages include C, C++, Objective-C, Java, and Visual Basic/Basic.

FIGURE A-22: Relationships between system software and other system components

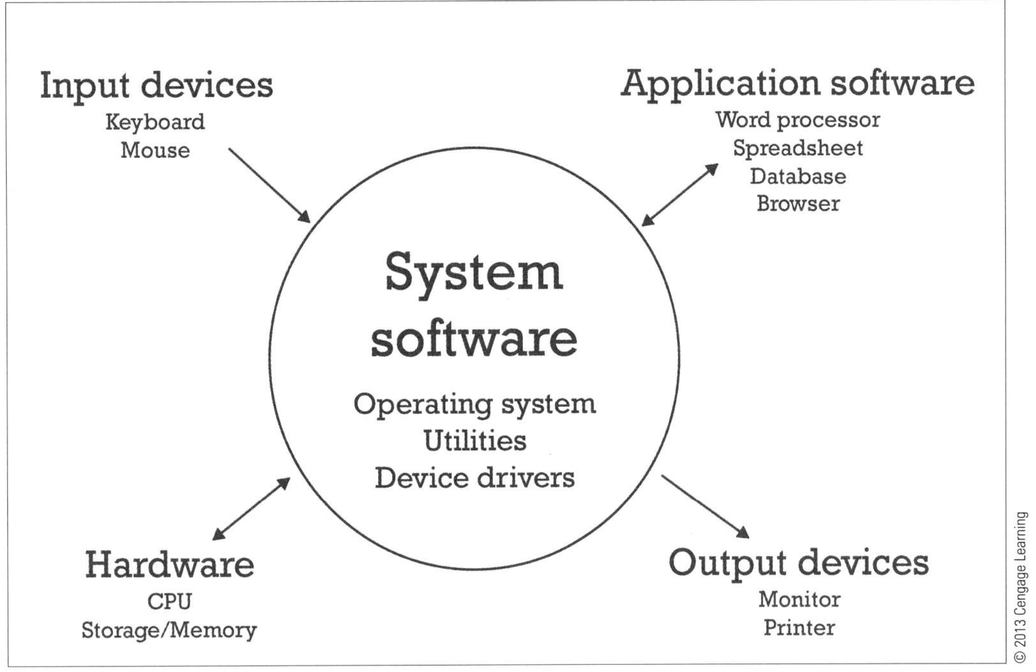

FIGURE A-23: Windows 8 Start screen

Examining Windows 8 hardware requirements

Windows 8, the newest version of the Windows operating system, requires a computer with at least a 1 GHz processor, 1 GB of RAM for the 32-bit version or 2 GB of RAM for the 64-bit version, a DirectX 9 graphics processor, 128 MB of specialized graphics RAM, and 16 GB of available space for the 32-bit version or 20 GB for the 64-bit version. Keep in mind that these are the minimum recommendations. To prevent your computer from slowing to a crawl, you should consider upgrading the amount of RAM and the processor speed.

Describe Types of Application Software

Learning Outcomes
- Define application software
- Identify types of application software

Application software enables you to perform specific tasks such as writing letters, creating presentations, analyzing statistics, creating graphics, enhancing photos, and much more. **CASE** *You'll look at some of the most common application software.*

DETAILS

QUICK TIP
To duplicate or move text, document production software allows you to perform copy-and-paste and cut-and-paste operations.

QUICK TIP
In Excel, a workbook is a file made up of multiple worksheets. The terms spreadsheet and worksheet are often used interchangeably.

Typical application software includes the following:

- **Document production software**, which includes word-processing software (such as Microsoft Word) and desktop publishing software (Microsoft Publisher), allows you to write and format text documents. As shown in **FIGURE A-24**, these tools offer automatic **spell checking** to help you avoid common grammar and spelling errors. You can also customize the look of a document by changing its **font** (the design of the typeface in which text is set) or by adding color, images, and **clip art**, simple drawings that are included as collections with many software packages.

- **Spreadsheet software** is a numerical analysis tool that displays data in a grid of **cells** arranged in columns and rows. This grid is called a **worksheet**. You can type data into the worksheet's cells, and then enter mathematical formulas that reference that data. **FIGURE A-25** shows a typical worksheet in Microsoft Excel that includes a simple calculation along with a graph that represents the data in the spreadsheet.

- **Database management software**, such as Microsoft Access, lets you collect and manage data. A **database** is a collection of information organized in a uniform format of fields and records. A **field** contains one piece of information, such as a person's first name. A **record** contains multiple fields and can therefore store a person's full name and address. The online catalog of books at a library is a database that contains one record for each book; each record contains fields that identify the title, the author, and the subjects under which the book is classified.

- **Presentation software** allows you to create a visual slide show to accompany a lecture, demonstration, or training session. In Microsoft PowerPoint, each presentation slide can contain text, illustrations, diagrams, charts, audio, and video. Slide shows can be projected in front of an audience, delivered over the Web, or transmitted to remote computers. To supplement a presentation, you can print audience handouts for quick reference.

- **Multimedia authoring software** allows you to record and manipulate digital image files, audio files, and video files. There are several types of multimedia authoring software: **Graphics software**, such as Microsoft Paint, lets you create illustrations, diagrams, graphs, and charts. **Photo-editing software** allows you to manipulate digital photos; you can make images brighter, add special effects, add other images, or crop photos to include only important parts of the image. Examples of photo-editing software include Windows Live Photo Gallery and Adobe Photoshop. **Video-editing software**, such as Windows Live Movie Maker or Adobe Premiere, allows you to edit video by clipping it, adding captions and a soundtrack, or rearranging clips.

- **Information management software** helps you schedule appointments, manage your address book, and create to-do lists. Microsoft Outlook is email software that includes information management components such as a contact list and a calendar. Some information management software allows you to synchronize information between a smartphone and your computer.

- **Website creation and management software** allows you to build websites and mobile apps using technologies that include **HTML (Hypertext Markup Language)** and **CSS (Cascading Style Sheets)**, the primary languages of Web design. Two popular tools, Adobe Dreamweaver and Microsoft Expression Web, allow you to see how the site will appear as you create it.

FIGURE A-24: Automatic spell checking in Microsoft Word

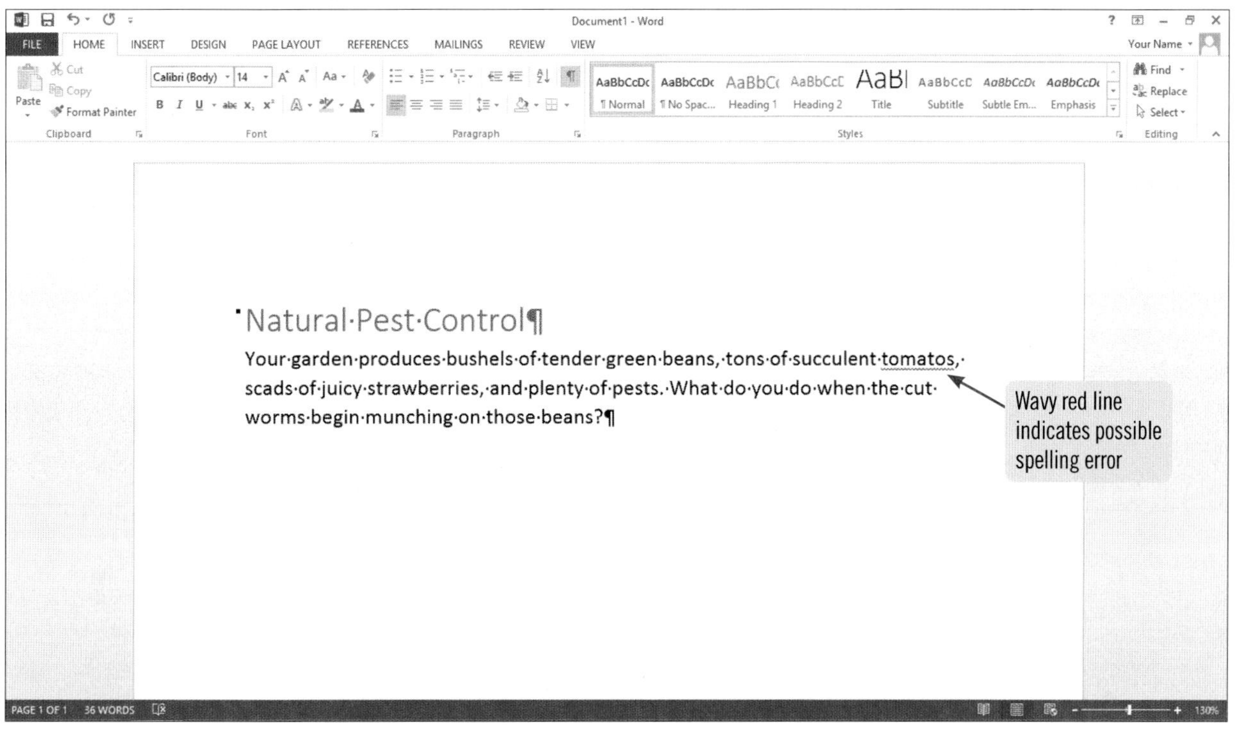

FIGURE A-25: Editing a worksheet in Microsoft Excel

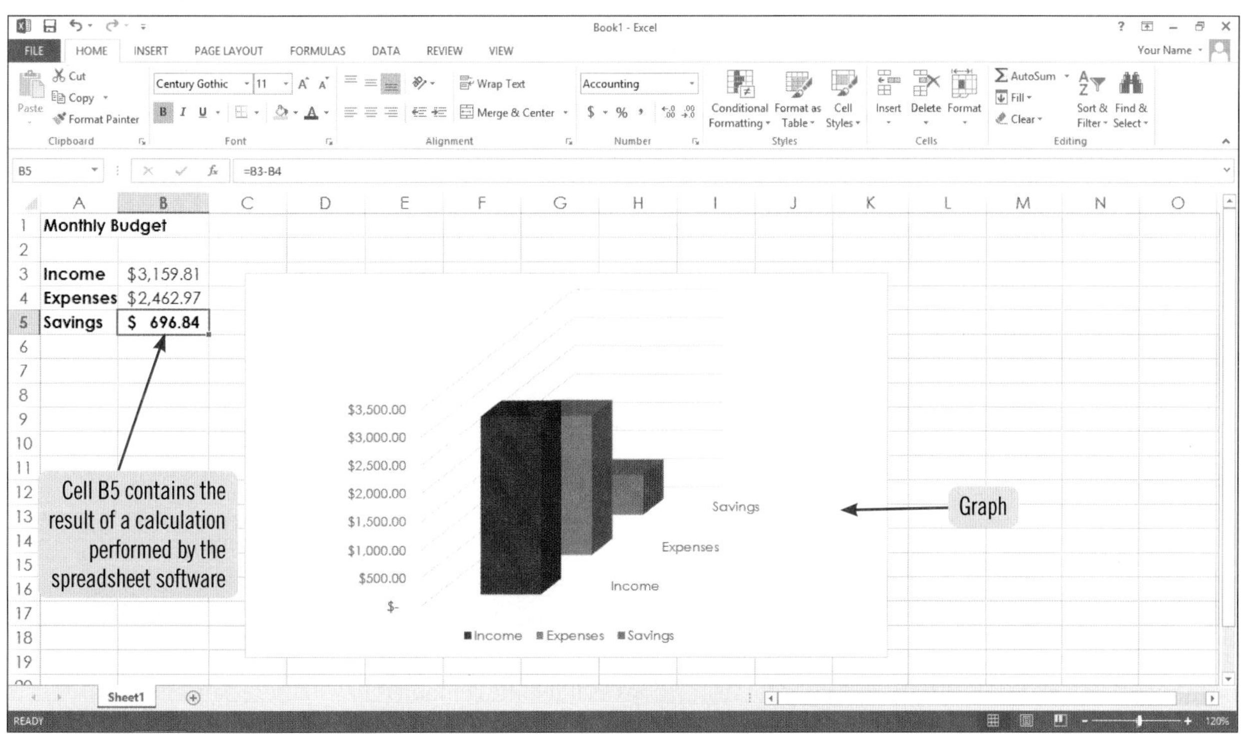

Practice

Concepts Review

Match the statements with the elements labeled in the screen shown in FIGURE A-26.

FIGURE A-26

Oleksiy Mark/Shutterstock

1. **The component that displays output**
2. **The component that processes data**
3. **The component that is used to enter text**
4. **The component you use to point to items on the screen**

Match each term with the statement that best describes it.

5. **Commands**
6. **Spyware**
7. **Virtual memory**
8. **RAM**
9. **Hard disk**
10. **Expansion slot**
11. **Server**
12. **SSD**
13. **Operating system**
14. **Database**

- **a.** Software that allocates resources, manages storage space, maintains security, and controls I/O
- **b.** Space on the computer's storage devices that simulates additional RAM
- **c.** Location on the motherboard into which a controller card for a peripheral device is inserted
- **d.** A collection of information stored on one or more computers organized in a uniform format of records and fields
- **e.** Based on flash memory and intended as a replacement for a traditional hard disk drive
- **f.** Input instructions that tell the computer how to process data
- **g.** Temporarily holds data and programs while the computer is on
- **h.** A program that tracks a user's Internet usage without the user's permission
- **i.** Magnetic storage media that is usually sealed in a case inside the computer
- **j.** A computer on a network that acts as the central storage location for programs and data used on the network

Select the best answer from the list of choices.

15. Which one of the following would not be considered a personal computer?

a. Desktop
b. Laptop
c. Mainframe
d. Tablet

16. The intangible components of a computer system, including the programs, are called:

a. Software
b. Peripherals
c. Hardware
d. RAM

17. What part of the computer is responsible for executing instructions to process information?

a. ROM
b. Card
c. Processor
d. Motherboard

18. What are the technical details about each hardware component called?

a. Configuration
b. Architecture
c. Circuits
d. Specifications

19. Keyboards, monitors, and printers are all examples of which of the following?

a. Peripheral devices
b. Input devices
c. Output devices
d. Data communications

20. Which of the following is a pointing device that allows you to control the pointer by moving the entire device around on a desk?

a. Scroll wheel
b. Touch pad
c. Trackball
d. Mouse

21. To display graphics, a computer needs a monitor and a:

a. Graphics card or graphics processor
b. Sound card
c. Network card (NIC)
d. USB cable

22. What do you call each 1 or 0 used in the representation of computer data?

a. A quark
b. A bit
c. A kilobyte
d. A byte

23. What is a megabyte?

a. About a million bits
b. About a million bytes
c. One-half a gigabyte
d. 10 kilobytes

24. Which of the following permanently stores the set of instructions that the computer uses to activate the software that controls the processing function when you turn the computer on?

a. ROM
b. RAM
c. The hard disk
d. CPU cache

25. Which of the following is space on the computer's storage devices that simulates additional RAM?

a. Solid-state memory
b. Cache memory
c. Virtual memory
d. Volatile memory

26. Which of the following is considered volatile or temporary memory?

a. ROM
b. CD-ROM
c. The hard disk
d. RAM

27. Which of the following is not a permanent storage medium?

a. Hard disk
b. RAM
c. DVD
d. CD-ROM

28. The transmission protocol between a computer and its peripheral devices is handled by a:

a. Driver
b. Channel
c. Controller card
d. Data bus

29. **Which of the following is the data path between the microprocessor, RAM, and the peripherals?**
   - **a.** Cable
   - **b.** Data channel
   - **c.** Data bus
   - **d.** Motherboard

30. **The computer that originates a message to send to another computer is called the:**
   - **a.** Receiver
   - **b.** Sender
   - **c.** Channel
   - **d.** Server

31. **A personal computer that is connected to a network is called a:**
   - **a.** Workstation
   - **b.** Desktop
   - **c.** Laptop
   - **d.** Channel

32. **Which of the following acts as a locked door on a computer?**
   - **a.** Antivirus software
   - **b.** DNS server
   - **c.** Firewall
   - **d.** Browser

33. **A ____________ consists of connected computers and peripheral devices that are located relatively close to each other.**
   - **a.** WAN
   - **b.** WLAN
   - **c.** PAN
   - **d.** LAN

34. **When data, applications, and resources are stored on servers rather than on users' computers, it is referred to as:**
   - **a.** Cluster computing
   - **b.** Shared computing
   - **c.** Leased computing
   - **d.** Cloud computing

35. **A website that's been set up to look exactly like another website, with the intention of convincing customers to enter their personal information, is a ____________ site.**
   - **a.** spoofed
   - **b.** malware
   - **c.** pharmed
   - **d.** phished

Independent Challenge 1

To run the newest software, many people need to upgrade their existing computer system or purchase a brand new one. But what do you do with your old computer if you buy a new one? Most municipalities have enacted laws regulating the disposal of electronics. Research these laws in your city and state, and write a brief report describing them.
Note: To complete the Independent Challenge, your computer must be connected to the Internet.

- **a.** Start your browser, go to your favorite search engine, and then search for information about laws regarding the disposal of electronics in your city and state. Try searching your city's official website for the information, or use **electronics disposal laws** followed by your city name as a search term and then repeat that search using your state's name.
- **b.** Open each website that you find in a separate browser tab or window.
- **c.** Read the information on each website. Can some components be thrown away? Are there laws that apply only to display monitors? Are the laws different for individuals and businesses? Does the size of the business matter? Are manufacturers or resellers required to accept used components they manufactured or sold?
- **d.** Search for organizations you can donate your computer to. How do these organizations promise to protect your privacy? Can you take a deduction on your federal income tax for your donation?
- **e.** Write a short report describing your findings. Include the URLs for all relevant websites. (*Hint*: If you are using a word processor to write your report, you can copy the URLs from your browser and paste them into the document. Drag to select the entire URL in the Address or Location bar in your browser. Right-click the selected text, then click Copy on the shortcut menu. Position the insertion point in the document where you want the URL to appear, then press [Ctrl][V] to paste it.)

Independent Challenge 2

New viruses are discovered on an almost daily basis. If you surf the Internet or exchange email, it's important to use antivirus software and to keep it updated. Research the most current virus threats, and create a table that lists them along with details about each threat. *Note: To complete the Independent Challenge, your computer must be connected to the Internet.*

a. Use your favorite search engine to go to the Microsoft Malware Protection Center (MMPC) at **www.microsoft.com/security/portal**, and then read about the MMPC and its mission.

b. Under the Recently Published heading, click the links to the five most recent threats, and then read the description of each threat.

c. Open a new word-processing document, and create a table that lists each virus threat, including a description of what each virus does, and how damaging each virus is (the alert level). Also note any steps you can take to prevent getting the virus, along with ways to recover an infected computer.

d. Use your search engine to find three different antivirus programs that can be installed on your computer. In your word-processing document, create a new section that lists the programs you found. Include the benefits and costs of using each program.

Independent Challenge 3

You've decided to buy a new desktop computer to run Windows 8 and Microsoft Office 2013. *Note: To complete the Independent Challenge, your computer must be connected to the Internet.*

a. To help you organize your search, create the table shown below.

	Your Requirements	Computer Retailer 1	Computer Retailer 2	Computer Retailer 3
Windows 8 (Edition)				
Office 2013 (Edition)				
Brand of computer				
Processor (brand and speed)				
RAM (amount)				
Video RAM (amount)				
Hard disk/SSD (size)				
Monitor (type and size)				
Printer (type and speed)				
Antivirus software				
Firewall (software or router with built-in fire-wall)				
System price				
Additional costs				
Total price				

Independent Challenge 3 (continued)

b. Decide which edition of Windows 8 you want, and enter it in the Your Requirements column of the table. To read a description of the available editions, go to **www.microsoft.com** and search the site for information about the different editions (Windows 8, Windows 8 Pro, and Windows RT).

c. Research the hardware requirements for running the edition of Windows 8 you selected. Search the Microsoft website again for the minimum and recommended hardware requirements for running Windows 8.

d. Decide which edition of Office 2013 you want, and enter it in the first column of the table. Search the Microsoft website to find a description of the software included with each edition of Office 2013, and then search for the hardware requirements for running the edition of Office 2013 that you chose. If necessary, change the hardware requirements in the table.

e. Research the cost of your new computer system. To begin, visit local stores, look at advertisements, or search the Web for computer retailers. Most retailers sell complete systems that come with all the necessary hardware, an operating system, and additional software already installed. In the Computer Retailer 1 column of the table, fill in the specifications for the system you chose. If any item listed as a minimum requirement is not included with the system you chose, determine the cost of adding that item and enter the price in the table. Repeat this process with systems from two other retailers, entering the specifications in the Computer Retailer 2 and Computer Retailer 3 columns.

f. If the system you chose does not come with a printer, search the Web for an inexpensive color inkjet printer.

g. If the system you chose does not come with antivirus software, search the Web for the cost, if any, of an antivirus software package. Make sure you look up reviews of the package you chose. Decide whether to purchase this software or download a free one, and enter this cost in the table.

h. If you decide you need a router with a built-in firewall, search the Web for the price of one. Enter this information in the table.

i. Determine the total cost for each of the three systems in your table. If the costs exceed your budget, think about items you can downgrade. Can you get a less expensive printer or share someone else's printer? Would a less expensive monitor still provide the room you need to work? On the other hand, if the total costs come in under your budget, you may be able to upgrade your system; perhaps you can afford a larger monitor with better resolution or a better mouse or keyboard.

Independent Challenge 4: Explore

Cloud storage allows you to store documents and images on remote servers. You then have access to these items from any compatible device that is connected to the Internet. You need to decide which cloud service is best for you. *Note: To complete the Independent Challenge, your computer must be connected to the Internet.*

a. Open your browser and use your favorite search engine to locate the sites for Microsoft SkyDrive, Apple iCloud, Google Drive, and Dropbox. If there is another service you'd like to investigate, include it as well (e.g., Amazon Cloud Drive).

b. To help you compare the different services, create the table shown below.

	SkyDrive	**iCloud**	**Google Drive**	**Dropbox**
Free storage capacity				
Paid storage capacity				
Paid storage cost				
Maximum file size				
Syncs to all your devices? (PC, mobile)				
Supports version tracking?				
Mobile apps provided*				
Additional features/notes				

*List the mobile operating systems the service provides an app for, such as Android, iPhone/iPad, or Windows Phone.

c. Enter details in the table using the information available on each service's website.

d. Search for online reviews and comparisons of each cloud service, and note any additional information that you feel is important. For example, if you have a large music collection on your computer, is it compatible with each service?

e. Based on your research, explain which service would best serve your needs and why.

Glossary

Adware Software installed with another program that generates advertising revenue for the program's creator by displaying targeted ads to the program's user.

American Standard Code for Information Interchange *See* ASCII.

Analog signal A continuous wave signal (sound wave) that can traverse ordinary phone lines.

Anti-spyware software Software that detects and removes spyware.

Antivirus software Software that searches executable files for the sequences of characters that may cause harm and disinfects the files by erasing or disabling those commands. *Also called* virus protection software.

Application software Software that enables you to perform specific computer tasks, such as document production, spreadsheet calculations, database management, and presentation preparation.

Architecture The design and construction of a computer. *Also called* configuration.

ASCII (American Standard Code for Information Interchange) The number system that personal computers use to represent character data.

Attachment A file sent along with an email message.

BD-R A Blu-ray disc on which you can record data once.

BD-RE A Blu-ray disc on which you can record data as on a BD-R, and then delete or re-record data on it as needed.

BIOS Stands for basic input/output system, the set of instructions stored in ROM that the computer uses to check its components to ensure they are working and to activate the software that provides the basic functionality of the computer when you turn on the computer.

Binary digit (bit) The representation of data as a 1 or 0.

Bit *See* binary digit.

Bits per second (bps) The unit of measurement for the speed of data transmission.

Bluetooth A wireless technology standard that allows electronic devices to use short range radio waves to communicate with one another or connect to the Internet; the radio waves can be transmitted around corners and through walls.

Blu-ray A disc used for storing high-definition video that stores 25 GB of data per layer.

Boot process The set of events that occurs between when you turn on the computer and when you can begin to use the computer.

Boot up The act of turning on the computer.

Bps *See* bits per second.

Bridging Using multiple rounters to increase the range of a Wi-Fi signal.

Broadband connection A high-speed connection to the Internet.

Browser Software that you use to navigate the World Wide Web and display information on websites.

Built-in graphics card *See* graphics processor.

Byte A series of eight bits.

Cable Plastic-enclosed wires that attach a peripheral device to a computer port.

Cache memory Special high-speed memory chips on the motherboard or CPU that store frequently-accessed and recently-accessed data and commands; *also called* RAM cache or CPU cache.

Card A removable circuit board that is inserted into a slot in the motherboard to expand the capabilities of the motherboard.

Cascading Style Sheets *See* CSS (Cascading Style Sheets).

CD (compact disc) Optical storage device that can store 700 MB of data.

CD-R (compact disc recordable) A CD on which you can record data with a laser that changes the reflectivity of a dye layer on the blank disk, creating dark spots on the disk's surface that represent the data; once data is recorded, you cannot erase or modify it.

CD-ROM (compact disc read-only memory) A CD that contains software or music when you purchase it, but you cannot record additional data on it.

CD-RW (compact disc rewritable) A CD on which you can record data as on a CD-R, and then delete or re-record data on it as needed.

Cell The intersection of a row and a column in a worksheet.

Central processing unit (CPU) *See* microprocessor.

Channel The medium, such as telephone or coaxial cable, over which a message is sent in data communications.

Chip An integrated circuit embedded in semiconductor material.

Circuit A path along which an electric current travels.

Circuit board A rigid piece of insulating material with circuits on it that control specific functions.

Client A computer networked to and dependent on a server.

Client/server network A network with a server and computers dependent on the server.

Clip art Simple drawings that are included as collections with many software packages.

Clock speed The pulse of the processor measured in megahertz or gigahertz.

Cloud computing When data, applications, and resources are stored on servers accessed over the Internet or a company's internal network rather than on users' computers.

CMOS *See* complementary metal oxide semiconductor memory.

Command Input that instructs the computer how to process data.

Compact disc read-only memory *See* CD-ROM.

Compact disc recordable *See* CD-R.

Compact disc *See* CD.

Compact disc rewritable *See* CD-RW.

Complementary metal oxide semiconductor (CMOS) memory A chip installed on the motherboard powered by a battery whose content changes every time you add or remove hardware on your computer system and that is activated during the boot process so it can identify where essential software is stored. *Also called* semipermanent memory.

Computer An electronic device that accepts input, processes data, displays output, and stores data for retrieval later.

Computer accessibility Technology that allows people with physical impairments or disabilities to use computers.

Computer system A computer, its peripheral devices, and software.

Configuration *See* architecture.

Controller card A card that plugs into a slot on the motherboard and connects to a port to provide an electrical connection to a peripheral device. *Also called* expansion card or interface card.

Copy-and-paste operation The feature in document production software that allows you to duplicate selected words and objects somewhere else in the document.

CPU *See* microprocessor.

CPU cache *See* cache memory.

CSS (Cascading Style Sheets) In web design, the language and techniques for styling HTML pages.

Cut-and-paste operation The feature in document production software that allows you to delete words and objects from one place in a document and place them somewhere else.

Data The words, numbers, figures, sounds, and graphics that describe people, events, things, and ideas.

Data bus The path between the microprocessor, RAM, and the peripherals along which communication travels.

Data communications The transmission of data from one computer to another or to a peripheral device via a channel using a protocol.

Data file A file created by a user, usually with software, such as a report that you write with a word processing program.

Database A collection of information stored on one or more computers organized in a uniform format of records and fields.

Database management software Used to collect and manage data.

Desktop computer A personal computer designed to sit compactly on a desk.

Device driver System software that handles the transmission protocol between a computer and its peripheral devices. *Also called* driver.

Digital signal A stop-start signal that your computer outputs.

Digital subscriber line *See* DSL.

Display *See* monitor.

Display resolution The number of pixels that a monitor displays. *See* pixels per inch (PPI).

DNS server A computer responsible for directing Internet traffic.

Document production software Word processing or desktop publishing software to help you write and format documents, including changing fonts and checking spelling.

Dots per inch (DPI) Determines quality of a printer's output. A higher number generally indicates higher quality.

Driver *See* device driver.

DSL (digital subscriber line) High-speed connection over phone lines.

Dual-core processor A CPU that has two processors on the chip.

DVD An optical storage device that can store up to 15.9 GB of data.

DVD+R, DVD-R A DVD on which you can record data once.

DVD+RW, DVD-RW A DVD on which you can record data as on a DVD-R, and then delete or re-record data on it as needed.

DVI (digital video interface) port Digitally transmits video.

Email An electronic message sent from one person to another over the Internet.

Ergonomic Designed to fit the natural placement of the body to reduce the risk of repetitive-motion injuries.

Ethernet port A port used to connect computers in a LAN or sometimes directly to the Internet; it allows for high-speed data transmission.

Executable file A file that contains instructions that tell a computer how to perform a specific task, such as the files used during the boot process.

Expansion card *See* controller card.

Expansion port The interface between a cable and a controller card. *Also called* port.

Expansion slot An electrical connector on the motherboard into which a card is plugged. *Also called* slot.

Field A piece of information in a record.

File A named collection of stored data.

FireWire A standard for transferring information between digital devices developed by Apple Computer company and the Institute of Electrical and Electronics Engineers (IEEE); was standardized as IEEE 1394 interface.

Firewall Hardware or software that prevents other computers on the Internet from accessing a computer or prevents a program on a computer from accessing the Internet.

Firmware *See* read-only memory (ROM).

Firmware update Allows ROM to be re-programmed with bug fixes or new features.

Flash drive *See* USB flash drive.

Flash memory Memory that is similar to ROM except that it can be written to more than once. *Also called* solid state storage.

Flash memory card A small, portable card encased in hard plastic to which data can be written and rewritten.

Flat panel monitor A lightweight monitor that takes up little room on the desktop and uses LCD technology to create the image on screen.

Font The design of the typeface in which text is set.

GB *See* gigabyte.

GHz *See* gigahertz.

Gigabyte (GB) 1,073,741,824 bytes, or about one billion bytes.

Gigahertz (GHz) One billion cycles per second.

Graphical user interface (GUI) A computer environment in which the user manipulates graphics, icons, and dialog boxes to execute commands.

Graphics card A card installed on the motherboard that controls the signals the computer sends to the monitor. *Also called* video display adapter or video card.

Graphics display A monitor that is capable of displaying graphics by dividing the screen into a matrix of pixels.

Graphics processor A processor that controls the signals the computer sends to the monitor. *Also called* built-in graphics card.

Graphics software Software that allows you to create illustrations, diagrams, graphs, and charts.

GUI *See* graphical user interface.

Handheld computer A small computer designed to fit in the palm of your hand; generally has fewer capabilities than a personal computer.

Hard copy A printed copy of computer output.

Hard disk *See* hard disk drive (HDD).

Hard disk drive (HDD) A magnetic storage device that contains several magnetic oxide-covered metal platters that are usually sealed in a case inside the computer. *Also called* hard disk or hard drive.

Hard drive *See* hard disk drive (HDD).

Hardware The physical components of a computer.

HDMI (high-definition multimedia interface) port A port that digitally transmits video and audio.

Headphones Worn over one's ears, allow you to hear sounds generated by your computer. *See also* speakers.

HTML (HyperText Markup Language) The primary code language used to create web pages.

I/O *See* input and output.

IEEE 1394 interface *See* FireWire.

Information management software Software that keeps track of schedules, appointments, contacts, and "to-do" lists.

Infrared technology A wireless technology; devices communicate with one another using infrared light waves; the devices must be positioned so that the infrared ports are pointed directly at one another.

Inkjet printer A printer that sprays ink onto paper and produces output whose quality is comparable to that of a laser printer.

Input The data or instructions you type into the computer.

Input and output (I/O) The flow of data from the microprocessor to memory to peripherals and back again.

Input device A hardware peripheral, such as a keyboard or a mouse, that you use to enter data and issue commands to the computer.

Interface card *See* controller card.

Internet The largest network in the world.

K *See* kilobyte.

KB *See* kilobyte.

Keyboard The most frequently used input device; consists of three major parts: the main keyboard, the keypads, and the function keys.

Kilobyte (KB or K) 1,024 bytes, or approximately one thousand bytes.

LAN *See* local area network.

Laptop computer *See* notebook computer.

Laser printer A printer that produces high-quality output quickly and efficiently by transferring a temporary laser image onto paper with toner.

LCD (liquid crystal display) A display technology that creates images by manipulating light within a layer of liquid crystal.

LED (light emitting diode) monitor A flat-panel monitor that uses LEDs to provide backlight.

LED printer Similar to a laser printer, produces high-quality output quickly and efficiently by using light to transfer a temporary image onto paper with toner.

Liquid crystal display *See* LCD.

Local area network (LAN) A network in which the computers and peripheral devices are located relatively close to each other, generally in the same building, and are usually connected with cables.

Log in/log on To sign in with a user name and password before being able to use a computer.

Magnetic storage device Uses various patterns of magnetization to store data on a magnetized surface.

Mainframe computer A computer used by larger business and government agencies that provides centralized storage, processing, and management for large amounts of data.

Malware A broad term that describes any program intended to cause harm or convey information to others without the owner's permission.

MB *See* megabyte.

Megabyte (MB) 1,048,576 bytes, or about one million bytes.

Megahertz (MHz) One million cycles per second.

Memory A set of storage locations on the main circuit board that store instructions and data.

Memory capacity The amount of data that the device can handle at any given time.

MHz *See* megahertz.

Microphone Used to record sound or communicate with others using audio or video conferencing software.

Microprocessor A silicon chip, located on the motherboard, that is responsible for executing instructions to process data; *also called* processor or central processing unit (CPU).

Mini notebook computer *See* subnotebook computer.

Modem Stands for modulator-demodulator; a device that converts the digital signals from your computer into analog signals that can traverse ordinary phone lines, and then converts analog signals back into digital signals at the receiving computer.

Monitor The TV-like peripheral device that displays the output from the computer.

Motherboard The main circuit board of the computer on which processing tasks occur.

Mouse A pointing device that has a rolling ball on its underside and two or more buttons for clicking commands; you control the movement of the pointer by moving the entire mouse around on your desk.

MP3 player A hand-held computer used primarily to play and store music; can also play digital movies, and FM radio stations, and access the Internet and email.

Multifunction printer (MFP) Combines several devices into one. Most MFPs can print, scan, copy, and fax documents.

Multimedia authoring software Allows you to record digital sound files, video files, and animations to be included in presentations.

Netbook A type of subnotebook computer primarily designed to allow users to access the Internet and check email. *See also* slate computer.

Network Two or more computers that share data and resources and which are connected to each other and to peripheral devices.

Network interface card (NIC) The card in a computer on a network that creates a communications channel between the computer and the network.

Network software Establishes the communications protocols to be observed on the network and controls the "traffic flow" as data travels through the network.

NIC *See* network interface card.

Node Any device connected to a network.

Nonvolatile memory *See* read-only memory.

Notebook computer A small, lightweight computer designed for portability. *Also called* laptop computer.

Operating environment An operating system that provides a graphical user interface, such as Microsoft Windows and the MAC OS.

Operating system Software that allocates system resources, manages storage space, maintains security, detects equipment failure, and controls basic input and output.

Optical character recognition (OCR) Software that translates a scanned text document into text that can be edited in a word processing program.

Optical storage device Uses laser technology to store data as tiny pits on the surface of a spinning polycarbonate disc. To access the data, a laser illuminates the data path while a read head interprets the reflection.

Output The result of the computer processing input.

Output device A device, such as a monitor or printer, that displays output.

Pages per minute (ppm) The unit of measurement for the speed of laser and inkjet printers.

PAN *See* personal area network.

PC *See* personal computer.

Peer-to-peer network A network in which all the computers essentially are equal, and programs and data are distributed among them.

Peripheral device The components of a computer that accomplish its input, output, and storage functions.

Permanent memory *See* read-only memory.

Personal area network (PAN) A network in which two or more devices communicate directly with each other.

Personal computer (PC) A computer typically used by a single user in the home or office for general computing tasks such as word processing, working with photographs or graphics, e-mail, and Internet access.

Pharm To break into a DNS server and redirect any attempts to access a particular website to a spoofed site.

Phish To send e-mails to customers or potential customers of a legitimate website asking them to click a link in the e-mail and then verify their personal information; the link leads to a spoofed site.

Photo editing software Allows you to manipulate digital photos.

Pixel One of the small dots in a matrix into which a graphics display is divided.

Pixels per inch (PPI) The number of pixels that a monitor can fit within one square inch. Higher PPI generally produces higher quality images. *See* display resolution.

Pointer A small arrow or symbol on the screen controlled by a pointing device.

Pointing device A device, such as a mouse or trackball, that controls the pointer.

Port *See* expansion port.

ppm *See* pages per minute.

Presentation software Allows you to display or project graphics and other information, print for quick reference, or transmit to remote computers.

Printer The peripheral computer component that produces a hard copy of the text or graphics processed by the computer.

Processing Modifying data in a computer.

Processor *See* microprocessor.

Program Instructions the computer uses to perform a specific task.

Programming language Software used to write computer instructions.

Protocol The set of rules that establishes the orderly transfer of data between the sender and the receiver in data communications.

PS/2 port A port through which a keyboard or a mouse is connected.

Quad-core processor A CPU with four processors on the chip.

RAM *See* random access memory.

RAM cache *See* cache memory.

Random access memory (RAM) Chips on cards plugged into the motherboard to temporarily hold programs and data while the computer is turned on. *Also called* volatile memory or temporary memory.

Read-only memory (ROM) A chip on the motherboard that is prerecorded with and permanently stores the set of instructions that the computer uses when you turn it on. *Also called* nonvolatile memory or permanent memory.

Receiver The computer or peripheral at the message's destination in data communications.

Record A collection of data items in a database.

Resolution *See* display resolution.

ROM *See* read-only memory.

Router A device that controls traffic between network components and usually has a built-in firewall.

Scanner A device that captures the image on a photograph or piece of paper and stores it digitally.

Screen *See* monitor.

Screen size The diagonal measurement from one corner of the screen to the other.

Scroll wheel A wheel on a mouse you roll to scroll the page on screen.

SDRAM *See* synchronous dynamic RAM.

Search engine An online tool that allows you to enter keywords or terms; the engine then presents a list of sites that match those terms.

Security The steps a computer owner takes to prevent unauthorized use of or damage to the computer.

Semipermanent memory *See* complementary metal oxide semiconductor memory.

Sender The computer that originates the message in data communications.

Server A computer on a network that is the central storage location for programs and provides mass storage for most data used on the network.

Single-core processor A CPU with one processor on the chip.

Slate computer A thin computer mainly used to read electronic books, view video, and access the Internet; does not have an external keyboard or mouse; instead users touch the screen or use a stylus to accomplish tasks.

Slot *See* expansion slot.

Smartphone A handheld computer used to make phone calls; maintain an address book, electronic appointment book, calculator, and notepad; send email; connect to the Internet; play music; take photos; and perform some functions of a PC, such as word processing.

Software The intangible components of a computer system, particularly the programs that the computer needs to perform a specific task.

Solid state storage *See* flash memory.

Solid state drive (SDD) Based on flash memory and intended as a replacement for a traditional hard disk drive. Though still more expensive than hard drives, SSDs use less power while offering much faster data access and increased reliability.

Speakers Allow you to hear sounds generated by your computer. Can be separate peripheral devices, or can be built into the computer.

Specifications The technical details about a hardware component.

Spell check The feature in document production software that helps you avoid typographical and grammatical errors.

Spoof To create a website that looks exactly like another legitimate site on the web but steals the information people enter.

Spreadsheet *See* worksheet.

Spreadsheet software Software that helps you analyze numerical data.

Spyware Software that tracks a computer user's Internet usage and sends this data back to the company or person that created it, usually without the computer user's permission or knowledge.

Standalone computer A personal computer not connected to a network.

Strong password A string of at least eight characters of upper and lowercase letters and numbers.

Subnotebook computers Notebook computers that are smaller and lighter than ordinary notebooks. *Also called* ultraportable computer and mini notebook.

Supercomputer The largest and fastest type of computer, used by large corporations and government agencies for processing a tremendous volume of data.

Synchronous dynamic RAM (SDRAM) RAM synchronized with the clock speed of the CPU's bus for faster access to its contents.

System resource Any part of the computer system, including memory, storage devices, and the microprocessor, that can be used by a computer program.

System software A collection of programs and data that helps the computer carry out its basic operating tasks.

Tablet A computer designed for portability that includes the capability of recognizing ordinary handwriting on the screen.

TB *See* terabyte.

Telecommunications The transmission of data over a comparatively long distance using a phone line.

Temporary memory *See* random access memory.

Terabyte (TB) 1,024 GB, or approximately one trillion bytes.

Toner A powdery substance used by laser printers to transfer a laser image onto paper.

Touch pad A touch-sensitive device on a laptop computer that you drag your finger over to control the pointer; buttons for clicking commands are located in front of the touch pad.

Touchscreen A display that shows you output and allows you to touch it with your finger or a stylus to input commands.

Trackball A pointing device with a rolling ball on the top side and buttons for clicking commands; you control the movement of the pointer by moving the ball.

Track pad *See* touch pad.

Ultraportable computer *See* subnotebook computer.

Universal Serial Bus port *See* USB port.

URL An address on the web.

USB (Universal Serial Bus) port A high-speed port to which you can connect a device with a USB connector to have the computer recognize the device and allow you to use it immediately.

USB connector A small, rectangular plug attached to a peripheral device and that you connect to a USB port.

USB drive *See* USB flash drive.

USB flash drive A popular type of flash memory. *Also called* USB drive or flash drive.

Utility software Helps analyze, optimize, configure, and maintain a computer. Examples include anti-virus software, backup tools, and disk tools to allow you to analyze a hard drive or compress data to save space.

VGA (video graphics array) port Transmits analog video.

Video card *See* graphics card.

Video display adapter *See* graphics card.

Video editing software Software that allows you to edit video by clipping it, adding captions or a soundtrack, or rearranging clips.

Virtual memory Space on the computer's storage devices that simulates additional RAM.

Virus A harmful program that instructs a computer to perform destructive activities, such as erasing a disk drive; variants are called worms and Trojan horses.

Virus protection software *See* antivirus software.

Voice recognition software Allows you to input data and commands by speaking into a microphone.

Volatile memory *See* random access memory.

WAN *See* wide area network.

Web *See* World Wide Web.

Web browser *See* browser.

Website creation and management software Allows you to create and manage websites and *see* what the web pages will look like as you create them.

Wi-Fi *See* wireless fidelity.

Wide area network (WAN) A network that connects one or more LANs.

WiMAX (Worldwide Interoperability for Microwave Access) A standard of wireless communication by the IEEE that allows computers to communicate wirelessly over many miles; signals are transmitted from WiMAX towers to a WiMAX receiver.

Wireless fidelity The term created by the nonprofit Wi-Fi Alliance to describe networks connected using a standard radio frequency established by the Institute of Electrical and Electronics Engineers (IEEE); frequently referred to as Wi-Fi.

Wireless local area network (WLAN) A LAN connected using high frequency radio waves rather than cables.

WLAN *See* wireless local area network.

Word size The amount of data processed by a microprocessor at one time.

Workbook In Microsoft Excel, a file made up of multiple worksheets.

Worksheet In spreadsheet software, a grid of columns and rows that create cells at their intersection; you type data and formulas into cells.

Workstation A computer that is connected to a network.

Worldwide Interoperability for Microwave Access *See* WiMAX.

World Wide Web (Web) A huge database of information that is stored on network servers in places that allow public access.

Index

M

N

O

P

Q

R

S

T

U

V

W

Microsoft® Excel® 2013

ILLUSTRATED

Brief Introductory Complete

Brief Contents

Windows 8

Excel 2013

Contents

Windows 8

Excel 2013

Understanding File Management

CASE Now that you are familiar with the Windows 8 operating system, your new employer has asked you to become familiar with **file management**, or how to create, save, locate and delete the files you create with Windows application programs. You begin by reviewing how files are organized on your computer, and then begin working with files you create in the WordPad app.

Unit Objectives

After completing this unit, you will be able to:

- Understand files and folders
- Create and save a file
- Explore the files and folders on your computer
- Change file and folder views
- Open, edit, and save files
- Copy files
- Move and rename files
- Search for files, folders, and programs
- Delete and restore files

Files You Will Need

No files needed.

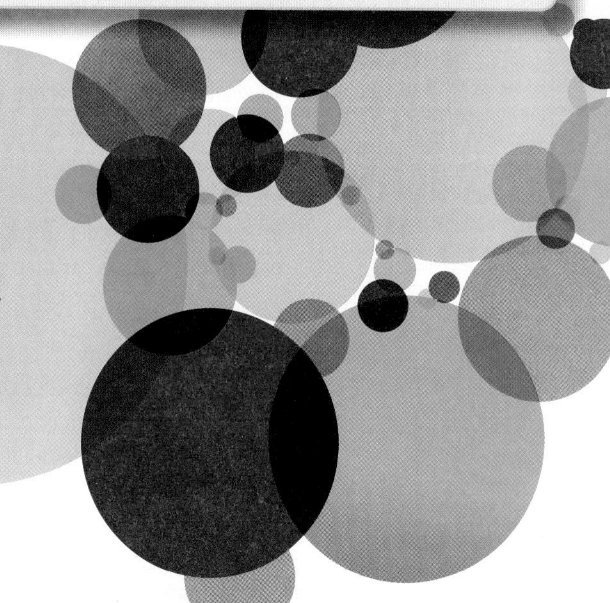

Understand Files and Folders

Learning Outcomes
- Analyze a file hierarchy
- Examine files and folders

As you work with computer programs, you create and save files, such as letters, drawings, or budgets. When you save files, you usually save them inside folders to help keep them organized. The files and folders on your computer are organized in a **file hierarchy**, a system that arranges files and folders in different levels, like the branches of a tree. FIGURE B-1 shows a sample file hierarchy. CASE *You decide to use folders and files to organize the information on your computer.*

DETAILS

Use the following guidelines as you organize files using your computer's file hierarchy:

- **Use folders and subfolders to organize files**

  As you work with your computer, you can add folders to your hierarchy and name them to help you organize your work. As you've learned, folders are storage areas in which you can group related files. You should give folders unique names that help you easily identify them. You can also create **subfolders**, which are folders that are inside other folders. Windows 8 comes with several existing folders, such as My Documents, My Music, My Pictures, and My Videos, that you can use as a starting point.

- **View and manage files in File Explorer**

  You can view and manage your computer contents using a built-in program called **File Explorer**, shown in FIGURE B-2. A File Explorer window is divided into **panes**, or sections. The **Navigation pane** on the left side of the window shows the folder structure on your computer. When you click a folder in the Navigation pane, you see its contents in the **File list** on the right side of the window. To open File Explorer from the desktop, click the File Explorer button on the taskbar. To open it from the Start screen, begin typing File Explorer, and when you see the program name on the Apps screen, press [Enter].

QUICK TIP
The program name "File Explorer" doesn't appear in the title bar. Instead, you'll see the current folder name.

- **Understand file addresses**

  A window also contains an **Address bar**, an area just below the Ribbon that shows the address, or location, of the files that appear in the File list. An **address** is a sequence of folder names, separated by the ▸ symbol, which describes a file's location in the file hierarchy. An address shows the folder with the highest hierarchy level on the left and steps through each hierarchy level toward the right; this is sometimes called a **path**. For example, the My Documents folder might contain subfolders named Work and Personal. If you clicked the Personal folder in the File list, the Address bar would show My Documents ▸ Personal. Each location between the ▸ symbols represents a level in the file hierarchy. The same path appears in the window's title bar, but instead of ▸ between the hierarchy levels, you see the backslash symbol (\ ). If you see a file path written out, you'll most likely see it with backslashes. For example, in Figure B-1, if you wanted to write the path to the Honolulu Sunset photo file, you would write My Documents\Quest Specialty Travel\Photos\Honolulu Sunset.jpg. File addresses might look complicated if they may have many levels, but they are helpful because they always describe the exact location of a file or folder in a file hierarchy.

QUICK TIP
Remember that in the Address bar you single-click a folder or subfolder to show its contents, but in the File list you double-click it.

- **Navigate up and down using the Address bar and File list**

  You can use the Address bar and the File list to move up or down in the hierarchy one or more levels at a time. To **navigate up** in your computer's hierarchy, you can click a folder or subfolder name to the left of the current folder name in the Address bar. For example, in FIGURE B-2, you can move up in the hierarchy one level by clicking once on Users in the Address bar. Then the File list would show the subfolders and files inside the Users folder. To **navigate down** in the hierarchy, double-click a subfolder in the File list. The path in the Address bar then shows the path to that subfolder.

- **Navigate up and down using the Navigation pane**

  You can also use the Navigation pane to navigate among folders. Move the mouse pointer over the Navigation pane, then click the small triangles to the left of a folder name to show ▷ or hide ◢ the folder's contents under the folder name. Subfolders appear indented under the folders that contain them, showing that they are inside that folder.

FIGURE B-1: Sample file hierarchy

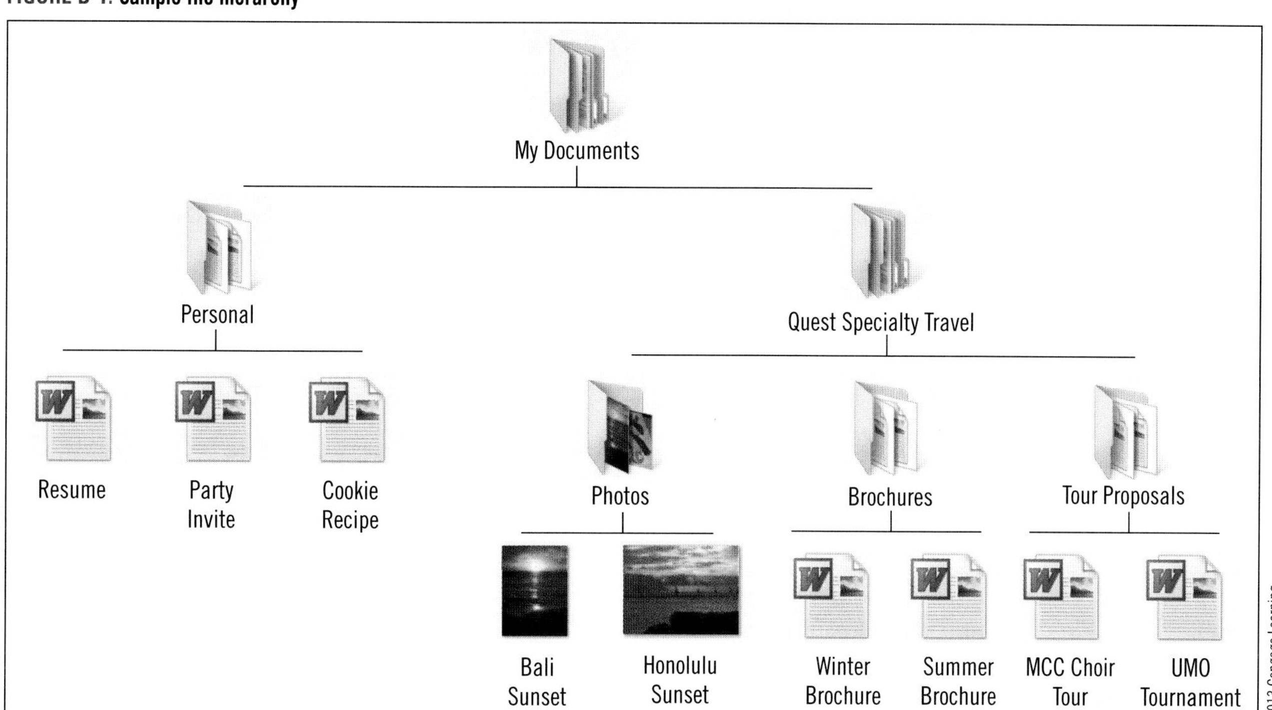

FIGURE B-2: File Explorer window

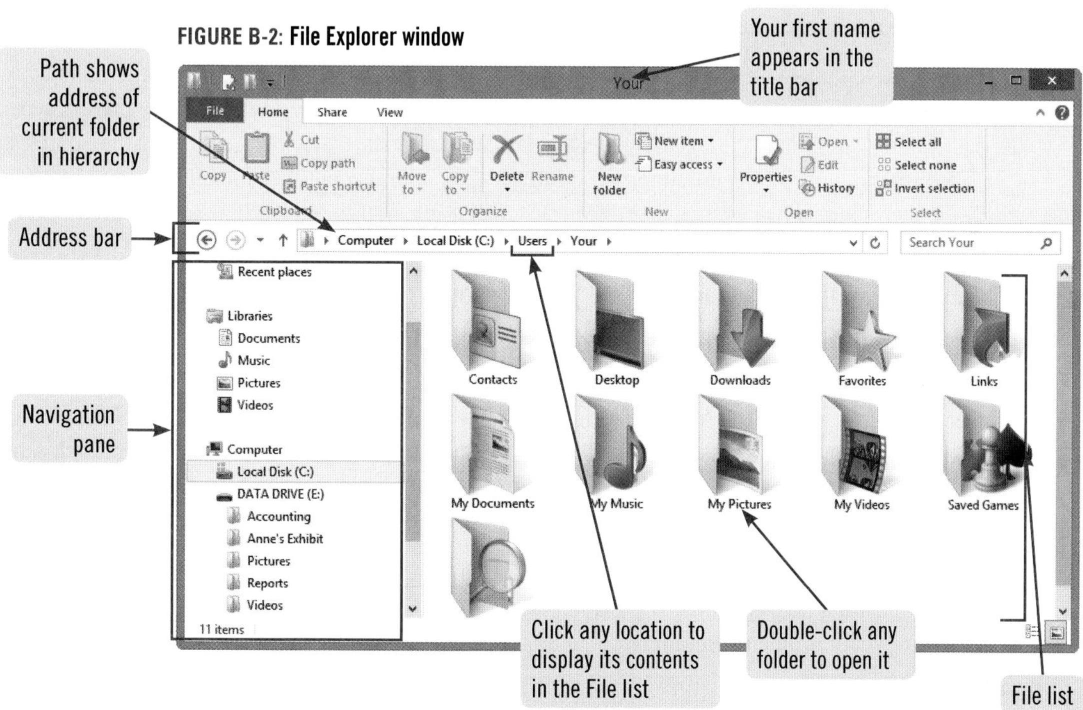

Plan your file organization

As you manage your files, you should plan how you want to organize them. First, identify the types of files you work with, such as images, music, and documents. Think about the content, such as personal, business, clients, or projects. Then think of a folder organization that will help you find them later. For example, you can use subfolders in the My Pictures folder to separate family photos from business photos or to group them by location or by month. In the My Documents folder, you might group personal files in one subfolder and business files in another subfolder. Then create additional subfolders to further separate sets of files. You can always move files among folders and rename folders. You should periodically reevaluate your folder structure to make sure it continues to meet your needs.

Windows 8
UNIT B

Create and Save a File

Learning Outcomes:
- Start WordPad
- Create a file
- Save a file

After you start a program and create a new file, the file exists only in your computer's **random access memory (RAM)**, a temporary storage location. RAM contains information only when your computer is on. When you turn off your computer, it automatically clears the contents of RAM. So you need to save a new file onto a storage device that permanently stores the file so you can open, change, and use it later. One important storage device is your computer's hard drive built into your computer. Another popular option is a **USB flash drive**, a small, portable storage device. CASE *You create a document, then save it.*

STEPS

1. **At the Start screen, type word**
   Available apps with "word" in their names are listed. See **FIGURE B-3**.
2. **Click WordPad, then maximize the WordPad window if necessary**
   Near the top of the WordPad window you see the Ribbon containing command buttons, similar to those you used in Paint in Unit A. The Home tab appears in front. A new, blank document appears in the document window. The blinking insertion point shows you where the next character you type will appear.
3. **Type New Tours, then press [Enter] twice, type Thailand, press [Enter], type New Zealand, press [Enter], type Canada, press [Enter] twice, then type your name**
   See **FIGURE B-4**.
4. **Click the File tab, then click Save**
   The first time you save a file using the Save button, the Save As dialog box opens. You use this dialog box to name the file and choose a storage location for it. The Save As dialog box has many of the same elements as a File Explorer window, including an Address bar, a Navigation pane, and a File list. Below the Address bar, the **toolbar** contains command buttons you can click to perform actions. In the Address bar, you can see the Documents library (which includes the My Documents folder) is the **default**, or automatically selected, storage location. But you can easily change it.
5. **Plug your USB flash drive into a USB port on your computer, if necessary**
6. **In the Navigation pane scroll bar, click the down scroll arrow as needed to see Computer and any storage devices listed under it**
   Under Computer, you see the storage locations available on your computer, such as Local Disk (C:) (your hard drive) and Removable Disk (F:) (your USB drive name and letter might differ). These storage locations are like folders in that you can open them and store files in them.
7. **Click the name for your USB flash drive**
   The files and folders on your USB drive, if any, appear in the File list. The Address bar shows the location where the file will be saved, which is now Computer ▶ Removable Disk (F:) (or the name of your drive). You need to give your document a meaningful name so you can find it later.
8. **Click in the File name text box to select the default name Document.rtf, type New Tours, compare your screen to FIGURE B-5, then click Save**
   The document is saved as a file on your USB flash drive. The filename New Tours.rtf appears in the title bar. The ".rtf" at the end of the filename is the file extension that Windows 8 added automatically. A **file extension** is a three- or four-letter sequence, preceded by a period, which identifies a file to your computer, in this case **Rich Text Format**. The WordPad program creates files in RTF format.
9. **Click the Close button on the WordPad window**
   The WordPad program closes. Your New Tours document is now saved in the location you specified.

TROUBLE
If you make a typing mistake, press [Backspace] to delete the character to the left of the insertion point.

QUICK TIP
On a laptop computer, the USB port is on the left or right side of your computer.

TROUBLE
If you don't have a USB flash drive, you can save the document in the My Documents folder or ask your instructor which storage location is best.

TROUBLE
If your Save As dialog box does not show the .rtf file extension, click Cancel, open File Explorer, click the View tab, then in the Show/hide group, click the File name extensions check box to select it.

FIGURE B-3: Results list

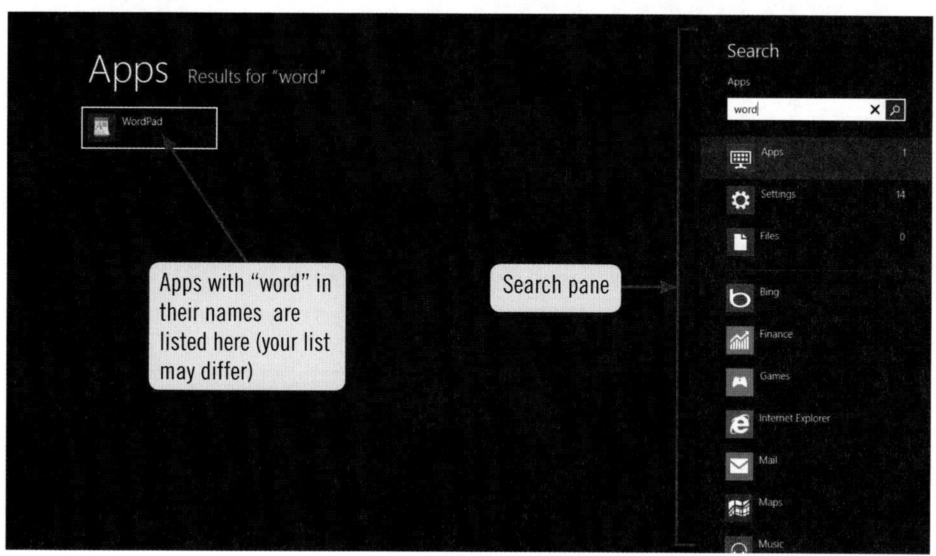

FIGURE B-4: New document in WordPad

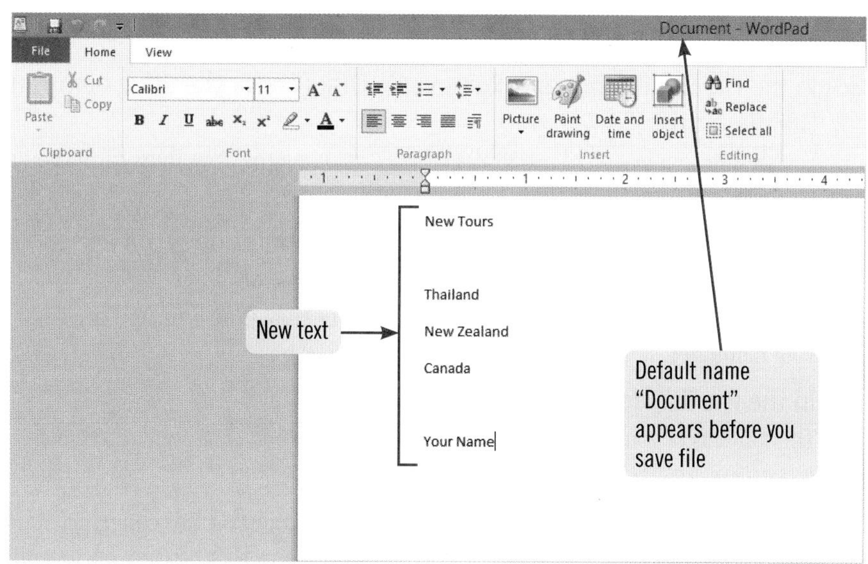

FIGURE B-5: Save As dialog box

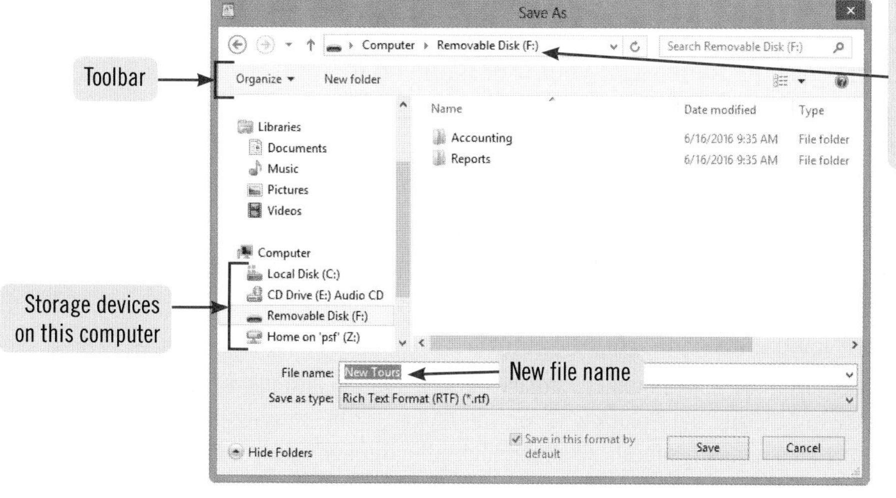

Windows 8
UNIT B

Learning Outcomes:
- Navigate to file storage locations
- Open folders

Explore the Files and Folders on Your Computer

In a File Explorer window, you can navigate through your computer contents using the File list, the Address bar, and the Navigation pane. Examining your computer and its existing folder and file structure helps you decide where to save files as you work with Windows 8 apps. **CASE** *In preparation for organizing documents at your new job, you look at the files and folders on your computer.*

STEPS

1. **If you see the Start screen, click the Desktop tile to display the Windows 8 desktop**

2. **On the taskbar, click the File Explorer button, then in the File Explorer Navigation pane, click Computer**

   Your computer's storage devices appear in a window, as shown in **FIGURE B-6**. These include hard drives; devices with removable storage, such as CD and DVD drives or USB flash drives; portable devices such as personal digital assistants (PDAs); and any network storage locations. A colored bar shows you how much space has been taken up on your hard drive. You decide to move down a level in your computer's hierarchy and see what is on your USB flash drive.

> **TROUBLE**
> If you don't see the colored bar, click the View tab, then click Tiles in the Layout group.

3. **In the File list, double-click Removable Disk (F:) (or the drive name and letter for your USB flash drive)**

   You see the contents of your USB flash drive, including the New Tours.rtf file you saved in the last lesson. You decide to navigate one level up in the file hierarchy.

> **TROUBLE**
> If you do not have a USB flash drive, click the Documents library in the Navigation pane instead.

4. **In the Address bar, click Computer, or if Computer does not appear, click the far-left list arrow in the Address bar, then click Computer**

   You return to the Computer window showing your storage devices. You decide to look at the contents of your hard drive.

5. **In the File list, double-click Local Disk (C:)**

   The contents of your hard drive appear in the File list.

6. **In the File list, double-click the Users folder**

   The Users folder contains a subfolder for each user account on this computer. You might see a folder with your user account name on it. Each user's folder contains that person's documents. User folder names are the names that were used to log in when your computer was set up. When a user logs in, the computer allows that user access to the folder with the same user name. If you are using a computer with more than one user, you might not have permission to view other users' folders. There is also a Public folder that any user can open.

7. **Double-click the folder with your user name on it**

   Depending on how your computer is set up, this folder might be labeled with your name; however, if you are using a computer in a lab or a public location, your folder might be called Student or Computer User or something similar. You see a list of folders, such as My Documents, My Music, and others. See **FIGURE B-7**.

8. **Double-click My Documents in the File list**

   In the Address bar, the path to the My Documents folder is Computer ▶ Local Disk (C:) ▶ Users ▶ *Your User Name* ▶ My Documents.

> **QUICK TIP**
> In the Address bar, you can click ▶ to the right of a folder name to see a list of its subfolders; if the folder is open, its name appears in bold in the list.

9. **In the Navigation pane, click Computer**

   You once again see your computer's storage devices. You can also move up one level at a time in your file hierarchy by clicking the Up arrow on the toolbar, or by pressing [Backspace] on your keyboard. See **TABLE B-1** for a summary of techniques for navigating through your computer's file hierarchy.

FIGURE B-6: Computer window showing storage devices

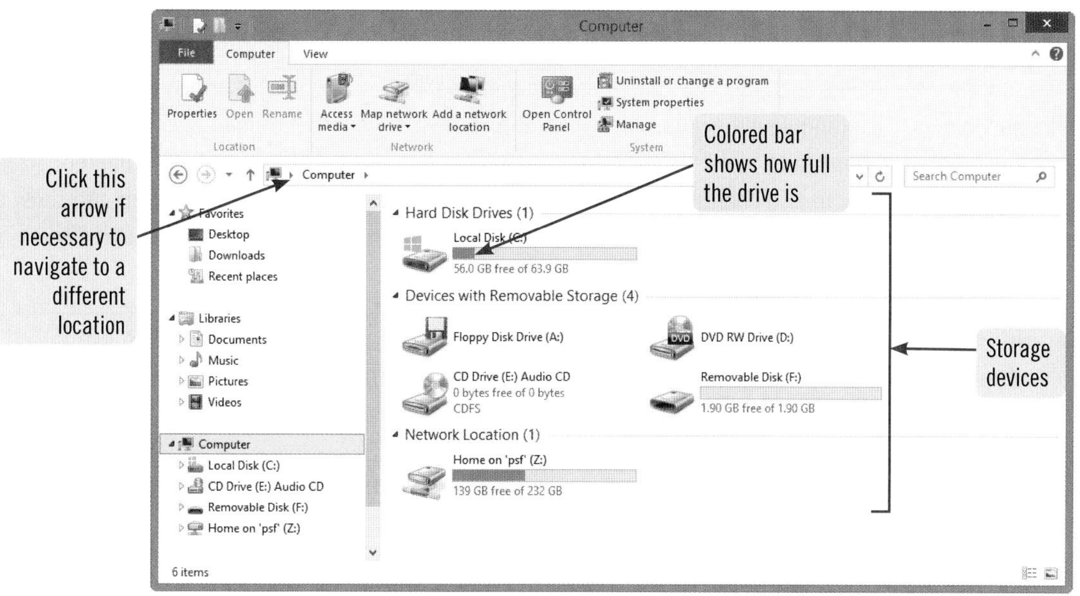

FIGURE B-7: Your user name folder

Path to your user name folder contents

Step 8

Your user name folder contents may differ

TABLE B-1: Navigating your computer's file hierarchy

to do this	Navigation pane	Address bar	File list	keyboard
Move up in hierarchy	Click a drive or folder name	Click an item to the left of ▶ or Click the **Up to** arrow ↑		Press **[Backspace]**
Move down in hierarchy	Click a drive or folder name that is indented from the left	Click an item to the right of ▶	Double-click a folder	Press ↑ or ↓ to select a folder, then press **[Enter]** to open the selected folder
Return to previously viewed location		Click the **Back to** button ← or **Forward to** button →		

Change File and Folder Views

Learning Outcomes:
- View files as large icons
- Sort files
- Preview files

As you view your folders and files, you can customize your **view**, which is a set of appearance choices for files and folders. Changing your view does not affect the content of your files or folders, only the way they appear. You can choose from eight different **layouts** to display your folders and files as different sized icons, or as a list. You can also change the order in which the folders and files appear. You can also show a preview of a file in the window. **CASE** *You experiment with different views of your folders and files.*

STEPS

1. **In the File Explorer window's Navigation pane, click Local Disk (C:), in the File list double-click Users, then double-click the folder with your user name**
   You opened your user name folder, which is inside the Users folder.
2. **Click the View tab on the Ribbon, then click the More button in the Layout group**
   The list of available layouts appears, as shown in **FIGURE B-8**.
3. **Click Extra large icons in the Layout list**
   In this view, the folder items appear as very large icons in the File list. This layout is especially helpful for image files, because you can see what the pictures are without opening each one.
4. **On the View tab, in the Layout list, point to the other layouts while watching the appearance of the File list, then click Details**
   In Details view, shown in **FIGURE B-9**, you can see each item's name, the date it was modified, and its file type. It shows the size of any files in the current folder, but it does not show sizes for folders.
5. **Click the Sort by button in the Current view group**
   The Sort by menu lets you **sort**, or reorder, your files and folders according to several criteria.
6. **Click Descending if it is not already selected**
   Now the folders are sorted in reverse alphabetical order.
7. **Click Removable Disk (F:) (or the location where you store your Data Files) in the Navigation pane, then click the New Tours.rtf filename in the File list**
8. **Click the Preview pane button in the Panes group on the View tab if necessary**
   A preview of the selected New Tours.rtf file you created earlier in this unit appears in the Preview pane on the right side of the screen. The WordPad file is not open, but you can still see the file's contents. See **FIGURE B-10**.
9. **Click the Preview pane button again to close the pane, then click the window's Close button**

QUICK TIP
You can scroll up and down in the Layout group to see views that are not currently visible.

QUICK TIP
Clicking Favorites in the Navigation pane displays folders you use frequently; to add a folder or location to Favorites, display it in the File list, then drag it to the Favorites list.

Snapping Windows 8 apps

If your machine has a screen resolution of 1366 × 768 or higher, you can use snapping to view two Windows 8 apps side by side. Go to the Start screen and open the first app, then return to the Start screen and open the second app. Point to the upper-left corner of the screen until you can see a small square representing the first app, right-click the square, then click Snap left or Snap right. (Or you can drag the square to the right or left side of the screen.) One app then occupies one third of the screen and the other taking up two thirds of the screen. See **FIGURE B-11**.

FIGURE B-11: Using snapping to view Weather and SkyDrive apps

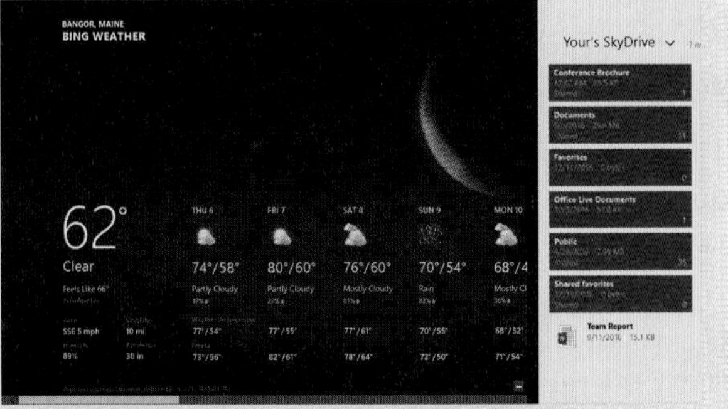

FIGURE B-8: Layout options for viewing folders and files

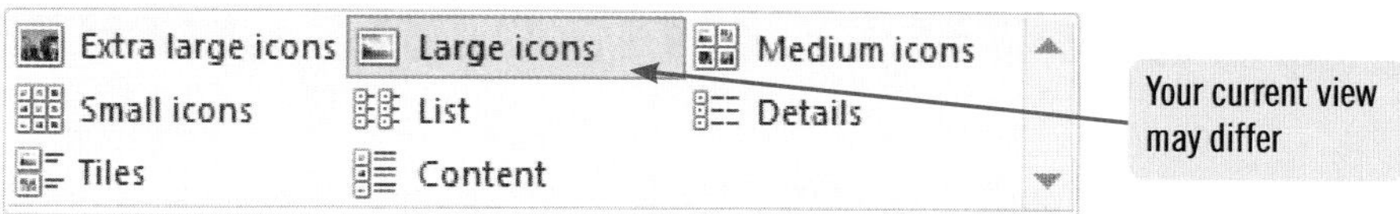

FIGURE B-9: Your user name folder contents in Details view

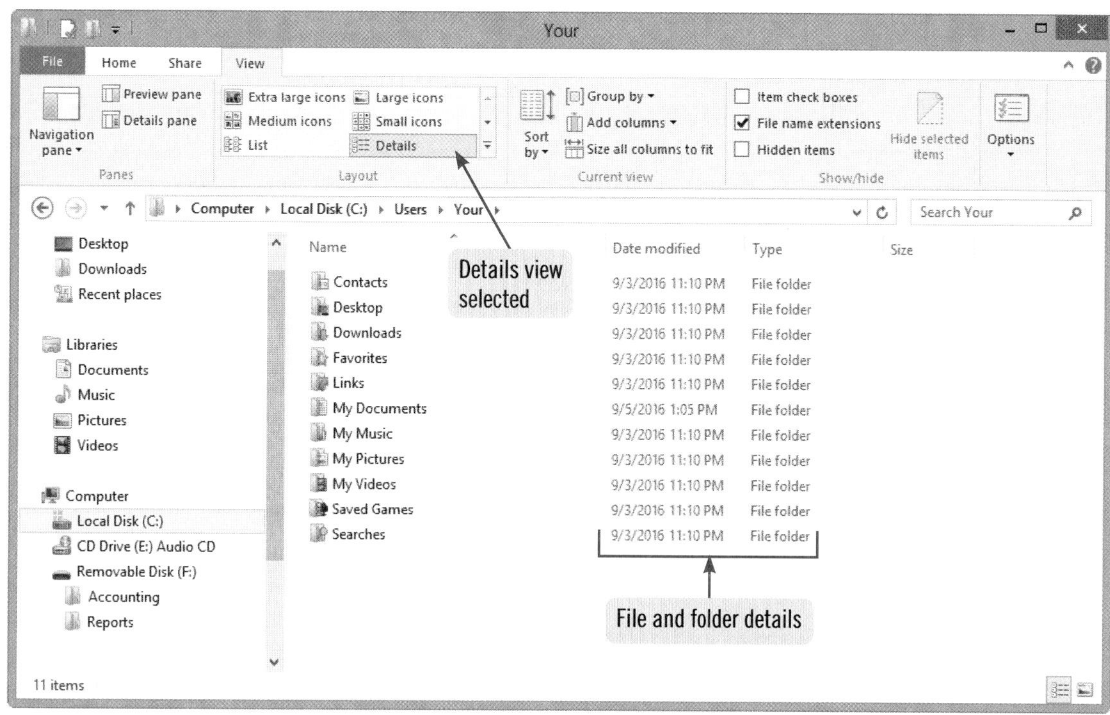

FIGURE B-10: Preview of selected New Tours.rtf file

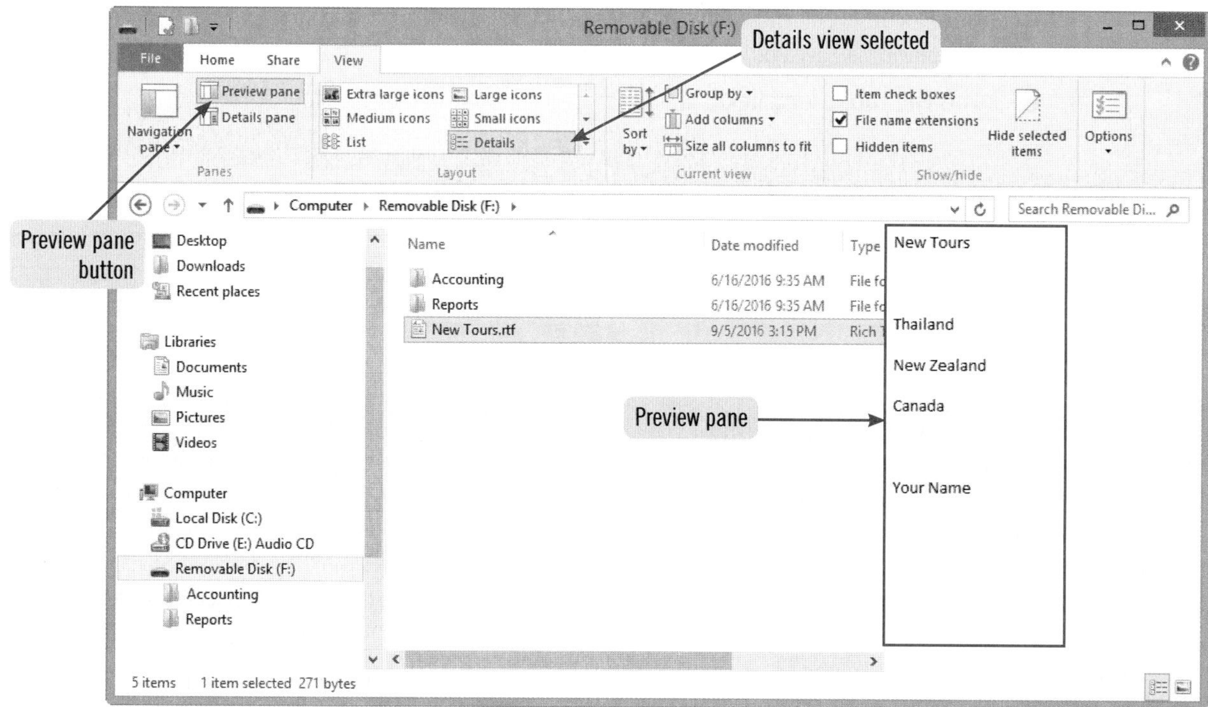

Open, Edit, and Save Files

Learning Outcomes:
- Open a file
- Edit a file
- Save a file

Once you have created a file and saved it with a name to a storage location, you can easily open it and **edit** (make changes to) it. For example, you might want to add or delete text or add a picture. Then you save the file again so the file contains your latest changes. Usually you save a file with the same filename and in the same location as the original, which replaces the existing file with the most up-to-date version. To save a file you have changed, you use the Save command. **CASE** *You need to complete the list of new tours, so you need to open the new Tours file you created earlier.*

STEPS

QUICK TIP
You can also press the Windows key to switch between the Start screen and the desktop. However, if you have a Windows 8 app open, it's best to click the Desktop tile on the Start screen.

1. **Point to the lower-left corner of the screen, then click the Start thumbnail to display the Start screen**
2. **Begin typing wordpad, then click the WordPad program if it is not selected or, if it is, simply press [Enter]**
   The WordPad program opens on the desktop.
3. **Click the File tab, then click Open**
   The Open dialog box opens. It contains a Navigation pane and a File list like the Save As dialog box and the File Explorer window.
4. **Scroll down in the Navigation pane if necessary until you see Computer and the list of computer drives, then click Removable Disk (F:) (or the location where you store your Data Files)**
   The contents of your USB flash drive (or the file storage location you chose) appear in the File list, as shown in **FIGURE B-12**.

QUICK TIP
You can also double-click a file in the File list to open a file.

5. **Click New Tours.rtf in the File list, then click Open**
   The document you created earlier opens.
6. **Click to the right of the last "a" in Canada, press [Enter], then type Greenland**
   The edited document includes the text you just typed. See **FIGURE B-13**.

QUICK TIP
To save changes to a file, you can also click the Save button on the Quick Access toolbar (on the left side of the title bar).

7. **Click the File tab, then click Save, as shown in FIGURE B-14**
   WordPad saves the document with your most recent changes, using the filename and location you specified when you previously saved it. When you save an existing file, the Save As dialog box does not open.
8. **Click the File tab, then click Exit**

Comparing Save and Save As

The WordPad menu has two save command options—Save and Save As. The first time you save a file, the Save As dialog box opens (whether you choose Save or Save As). Here you can select the drive and folder where you want to save the file and enter its filename. If you edit a previously saved file, you can save the file to the same location with the same filename using the Save command. The Save command updates the stored file using the same location and filename without opening the Save As dialog box. In some situations, you might want to save a copy of the existing document using a different filename or in a different storage location. To do this, open the document, click the Save As command on the File tab, navigate to the location where you want to save the copy if necessary, and/or edit the name of the file.

FIGURE B-12: Navigating in the Open dialog box

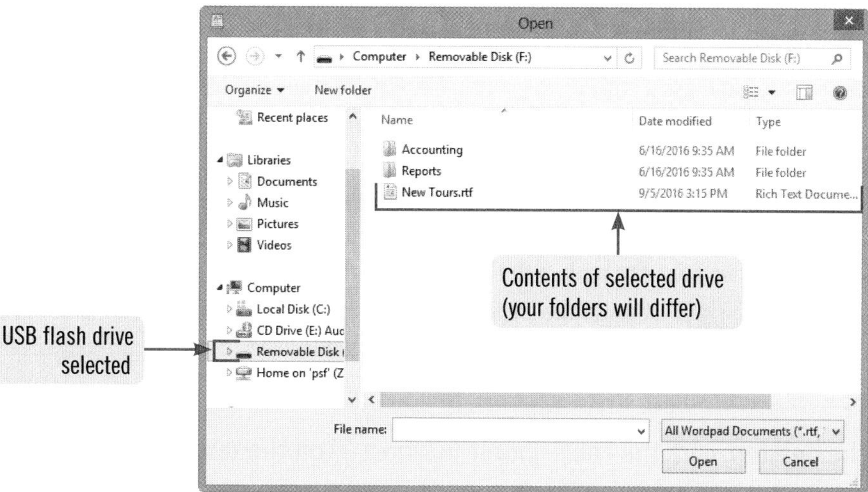

FIGURE B-13: Edited document

FIGURE B-14: Saving the updated document

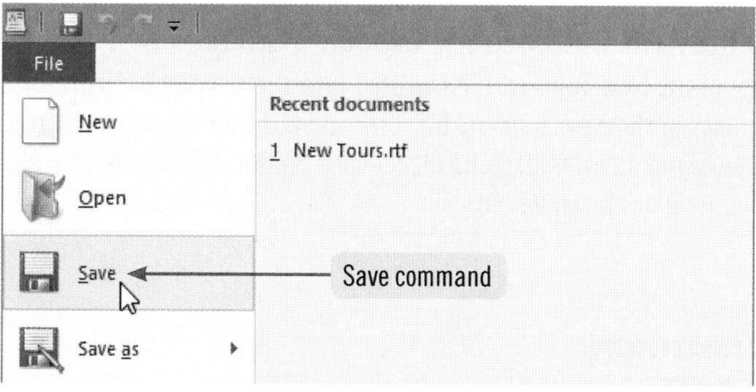

Using cloud storage

Many users store their files on special file storage locations on the World Wide Web, known as **cloud storage** locations. Examples of cloud storage locations include **Microsoft SkyDrive** and **DropBox**. By storing files in the cloud, your files are automatically updated when you make changes to them on your computer, and you can access them from different devices, including laptops, tablets, and smartphones. Microsoft Office programs such as Word and Excel show SkyDrive as a storage location when you open or save a file, making cloud storage a convenient option.

Copy Files

Learning Outcomes:
- Create a new folder
- Copy and paste a file

Sometimes you need to make a copy of an existing file. For example, you might want to put a copy on a USB flash drive so you can open the file on another machine or share it with a friend or colleague. Or you might want to create a copy as a **backup**, or replacement, in case something happens to your original file. You can copy files and folders using the Copy command and then place the copy in another location using the Paste command. You cannot have two copies of a file with the same name in the same folder. If you try to do this, Windows 8 asks you if you want to replace the first one, and then gives you a chance to give the second copy a different name. CASE *You want to create a backup copy of the New Tours document that you can store in a folder for company newsletter items. First you need to create the folder, then you can copy the file.*

STEPS

1. **On the desktop, click the File Explorer button on the taskbar**
2. **In the Navigation pane, click Removable Disk (F:) (or the drive name and letter that represents the location where you store your Data Files)**
   First you create the new folder you plan to use for storing newsletter-related files.
3. **If you don't see the Ribbon, double-click the Home tab to open the Ribbon**
4. **In the New group on the Home tab, click the New folder button**
   A new folder appears in the File list, with its default name, New folder, selected.
5. **Type Newsletter Items, then press [Enter]**
   Because the folder name was selected, the text you typed, Newsletter Items, replaced it. Pressing [Enter] confirmed your entry, and the folder is now named Newsletter Items.
6. **In the File list, click the New Tours.rtf document you saved earlier, then click the Copy button in the Clipboard group, as shown in FIGURE B-15**
   When you use the Copy command, Windows 8 places a duplicate copy of the file in an area of your computer's random access memory called the **clipboard**, ready to paste, or place, in a new location. Copying and pasting a file leaves the file in its original location.
7. **In the File list, double-click the Newsletter Items folder**
   The folder opens. Nothing appears in the File list because the folder currently is empty.
8. **Click the Paste button in the Clipboard group**
   A copy of the New Tours.rtf file is pasted into the Newsletter Items folder. See FIGURE B-16. You now have two copies of the New Tours.rtf file: one on your USB flash drive in the main folder, and another in your new Newsletter Items folder. The file remains on the clipboard until you end your Windows session or place another item on the clipboard.

QUICK TIP
You can also create a new folder by clicking the New Folder button on the Quick Access toolbar (on the left side of the title bar).

QUICK TIP
You can also copy a file by right-clicking the file in the File list and then clicking Copy, or you can use the keyboard by pressing and holding [Ctrl], pressing [C], then releasing both keys.

QUICK TIP
To paste using the keyboard, press and hold [Ctrl] and press [V], then release both keys.

TABLE B-2: Selected Send to menu commands

menu option	use to
Compressed (zipped) folder	Create a new compressed (smaller) file with a .zip file extension
Desktop (create shortcut)	Create a shortcut (link) for the file on the desktop
Documents	Copy the file to the Documents library
Fax recipient	Send a file to a fax recipient
Mail recipient	Create an e-mail with the file attached to it (only if you have an e-mail program on your computer)
DVD RW Drive (D:)	Copy the file to your computer's DVD drive
Removable Disk (F:)	Copy the file to a removable disk drive (F:) (your drive letter may differ)

FIGURE B-15: Copying a file

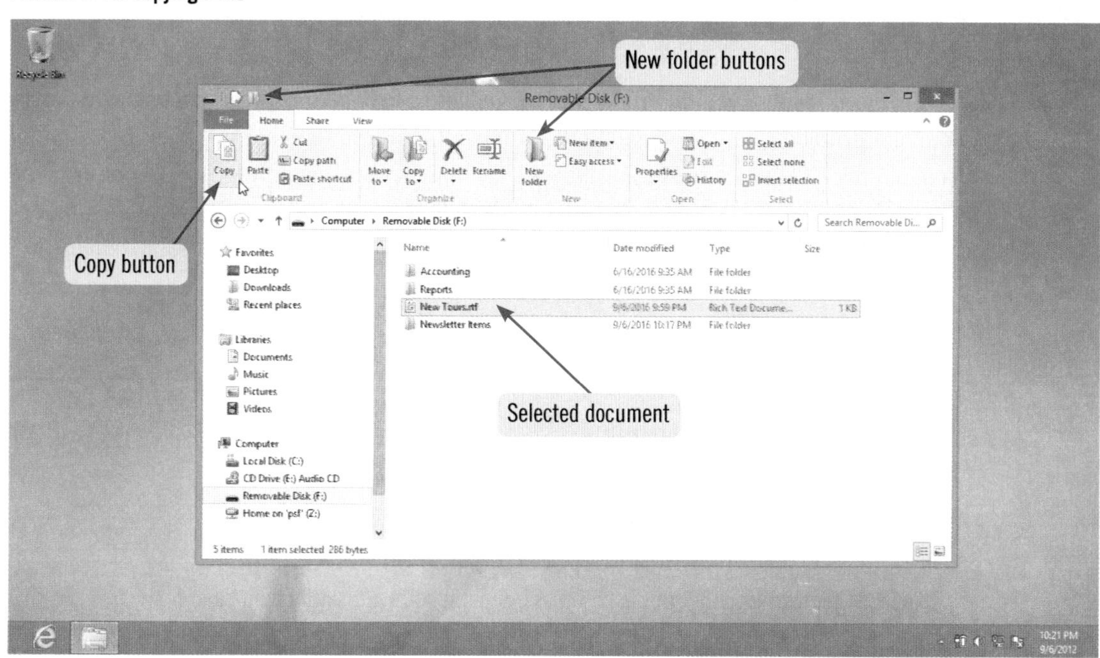

FIGURE B-16: Duplicate file pasted into Newsletter Items folder

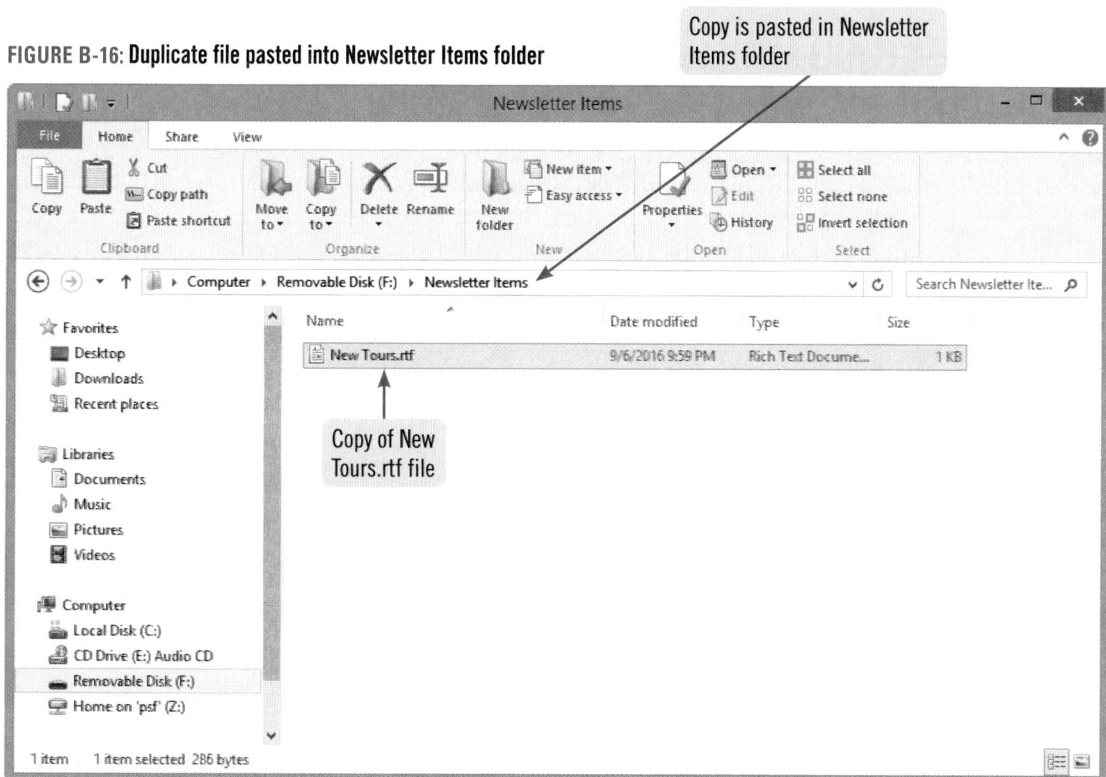

Copying files using Send to

You can also copy and paste a file using the Send to command. In File Explorer, right-click the file you want to copy, point to Send to, then in the shortcut menu, click the name of the device you want to send a copy of the file to. This leaves the original file on your hard drive and creates a copy on the external device. You can send a file to a compressed file, the desktop, a mail recipient, your Documents library, or a drive on your computer. See **TABLE B-2**.

Move and Rename Files

Learning Outcomes:
- Cut and paste a file
- Rename a file

As you work with files, you might need to move files or folders to another location. You can move one or more files or folders at a time, and you can move them to a different folder on the same drive or to a different drive. When you **move** a file, the file is transferred to the new location, and unlike copying it no longer exists in its original location. You can move a file using the Cut and Paste commands. Before or after you move a file, you might find that you want to change its name. You can easily rename it to make the name more descriptive or accurate. **CASE** *You decide to move your original New Tours.rtf document to your Documents library. After you move it, you edit the filename so it better describes the file contents.*

STEPS

QUICK TIP
You can also cut a file by right-clicking it in the File list, then clicking Cut, or by clicking it, pressing and holding [Ctrl] on the keyboard, pressing [X], then releasing both keys.

QUICK TIP
You can also paste a file by right-clicking an empty area in the File list and then clicking Paste, or by pressing and holding [Ctrl] on the keyboard, pressing [V], then releasing both keys.

1. **In the Address bar, click Removable Disk (F:) (or the drive name and letter for your USB flash drive)**
2. **Click the New Tours.rtf document to select it**
3. **Click the Cut button in the Clipboard group on the Ribbon**
   The icon representing the cut file becomes lighter in color, indicating you have cut it, as shown in **FIGURE B-17**.
4. **In the Navigation Pane, under Libraries, click Documents**
   You navigated to your Documents Library.
5. **Click the Paste button in the Clipboard group**
   The New Tours.rtf document appears in your Documents library and remains selected. See **FIGURE B-18**. Documents you paste into your Documents library are automatically stored in your My Documents folder. The filename could be clearer, to help you remember that it contains a list of new tours.
6. **With the New Tours.rtf file selected, click the Rename button in the Organize group**
   The filename is highlighted. The file extension isn't highlighted because that part of the filename identifies the file to WordPad and should not be changed. If you deleted or changed the file extension, WordPad would be unable to open the file. You decide to add the word "List" to the end of the original filename.
7. **Move the I pointer after the "s" in "Tours", click to place the insertion point, press [Spacebar], type List as shown in FIGURE B-19, then press [Enter]**
   You changed the name of the pasted file in the Documents library. The filename now reads New Tours List.rtf.
8. **Close the window**

Using Windows 8 libraries

The Navigation pane contains not only files and folders, but also libraries. A **library** gathers file and folder locations from different locations on your computer and displays them in one location. For example, you might have pictures in several different folders on your storage devices. You can add these folder locations to your Pictures library. Then when you want to see all your pictures, you open your Pictures library instead of several different folders. The picture files stay in their original locations, but their names appear in the Pictures library. A library is not a folder that stores files, but rather a way of viewing similar types of documents that you have stored in multiple locations on your computer. **FIGURE B-20** shows the four libraries that come with Windows 8: Documents, Music, Pictures, and Videos. To help you distinguish between library locations and actual folder locations, library names differ from actual folder names. For example, the My Documents folder is on your hard drive, but the library name is Documents. If you save a document to the Documents library, it is automatically saved to your My Documents folder.

FIGURE B-20: Libraries that come with Windows 8

FIGURE B-17: Cutting a file

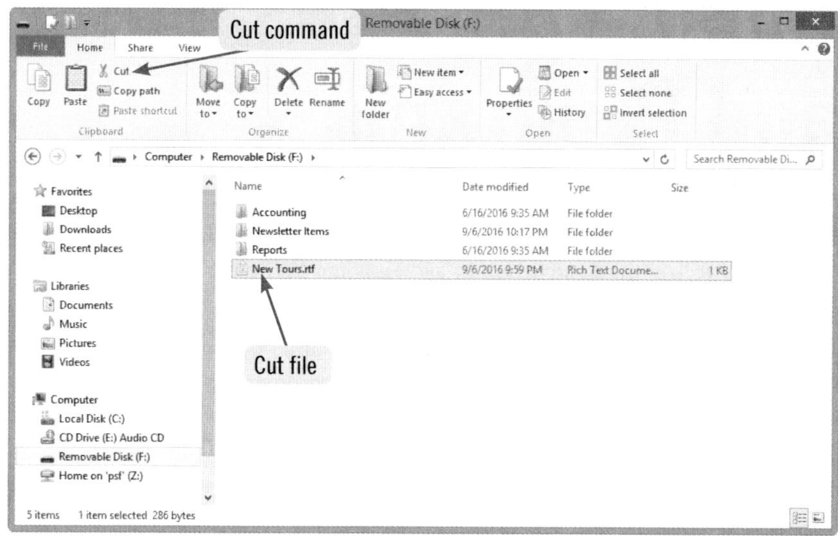

FIGURE B-18: Pasted file in Documents library

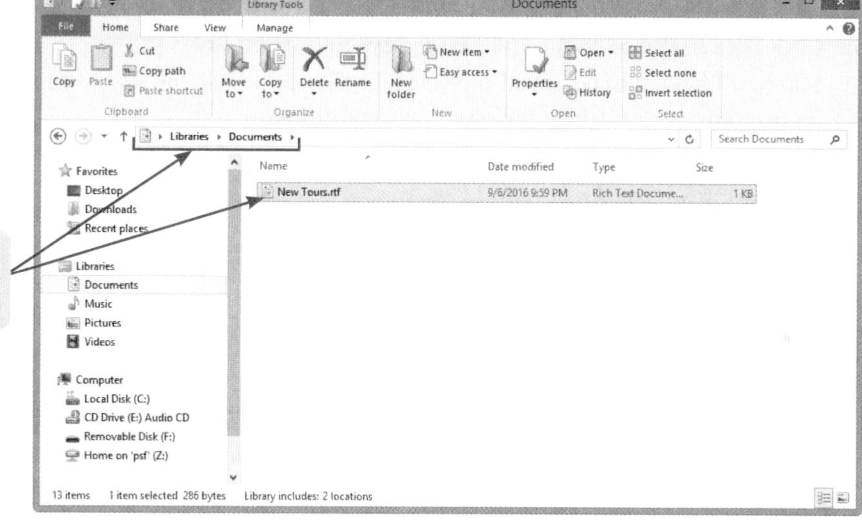

FIGURE B-19: Renaming a file

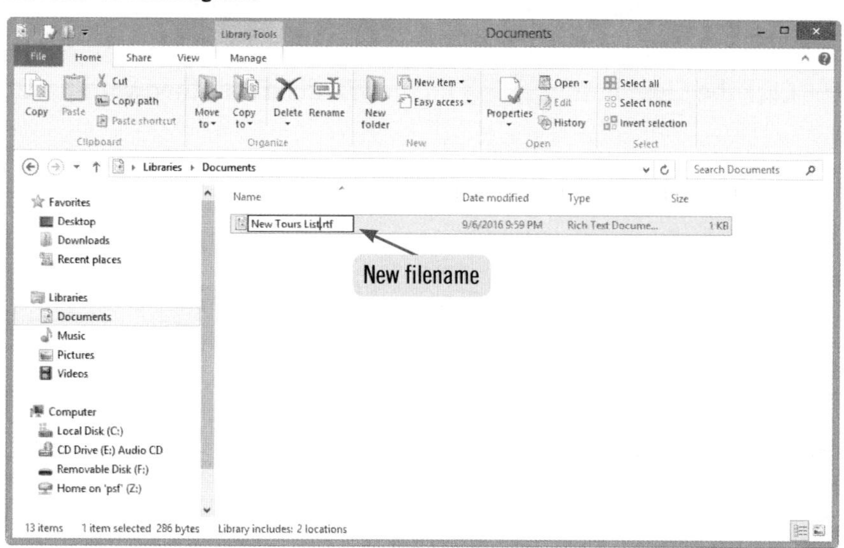

Search for Files, Folders, and Programs

Learning Outcomes:
- Search for a file
- Open a found file

Windows Search helps you quickly find any program, folder, or file. You can search from the Start screen using the Charms bar to locate applications, settings, or files. To search a particular location on your computer, you can use the Search box in File Explorer. You enter search text by typing one or more letter sequences or words that help Windows identify the item you want. The search text you type is called your **search criteria.** Your search criteria can be a filename, part of a filename, or any other text. CASE *You want to locate the New Tours.rtf document so you can print it for a colleague.*

STEPS

1. **Move the pointer to the lower-left corner of the screen, then click the Start thumbnail**
   The Start screen opens.
2. **Point to the upper-right corner of the screen, then point to and click the Search charm**
   A listing of the apps on your computer appears, along with a Search pane on the right side of the screen. See FIGURE B-21. You can search for Apps, Settings, or Files. Apps is selected by default.
3. **Click Files in the Search panel, type new tour, then press [Enter]**
   Your New Tours List.rtf document appears under Files. By default, the Search charm finds only files located on your computer hard drive, not on any external drives.
4. **Point to the New Tours List.rtf file**
   The path in the ScreenTip, C:\Users\Your Name\My Documents, indicates the found file is in the My Documents folder on the C: drive, as shown in FIGURE B-22.
5. **Press [Windows key] twice to display the desktop**
6. **Click the File Explorer button on the taskbar, then click Computer in the Navigation pane**
7. **Click in the Search box to the right of the Address bar, type new tour, then press [Enter]**
   Windows searches your computer for files that contain the words "new tour". A green bar in the Address bar indicates the progress of your search. After a few moments, your search results, shown in FIGURE B-23, appear. Windows found both the renamed file, New Tours List.rtf, in your My Documents folder, and the original New Tours.rtf document on your removable drive, in the Newsletter Items folder.
8. **Double-click the New Tours.rtf document on your removable flash drive**
   The file opens in WordPad or in another word-processing program on your computer that reads RTF files.
9. **Click the Close button on the WordPad (or other word-processor) window**

QUICK TIP
To immediately open File search in the Search charm, press [Windows key] [F].

QUICK TIP
If you navigated to a specific folder in your file hierarchy, Windows would search that folder and any subfolders below it.

QUICK TIP
Windows search is not case-sensitive, meaning that you can type upper- or lowercase letters when you search, and obtain the same results.

Using the Search Tools tab in File Explorer

The **Search Tools tab** appears in the Ribbon as soon as you click the Search text box, and it lets you narrow your search criteria. Use the commands in the Location group to specify a particular search location. The Refine group lets you limit the search to files modified after a certain date, or to files of a particular kind, size, type, or other property. The Options group lets you repeat previous searches, save searches, and open the folder containing a found file. See FIGURE B-24.

FIGURE B-24: Search Tools tab

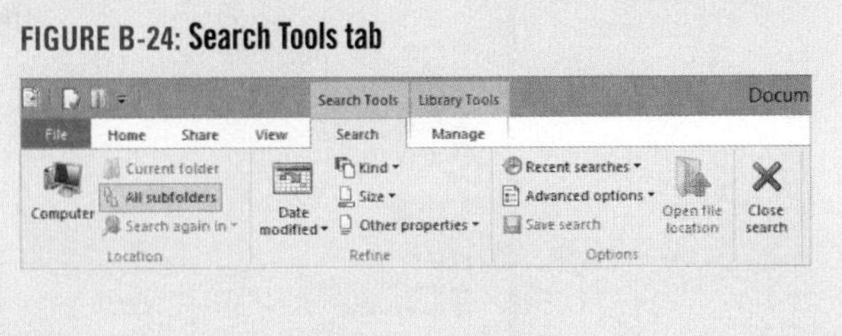

FIGURE B-21: Apps screen and search pane

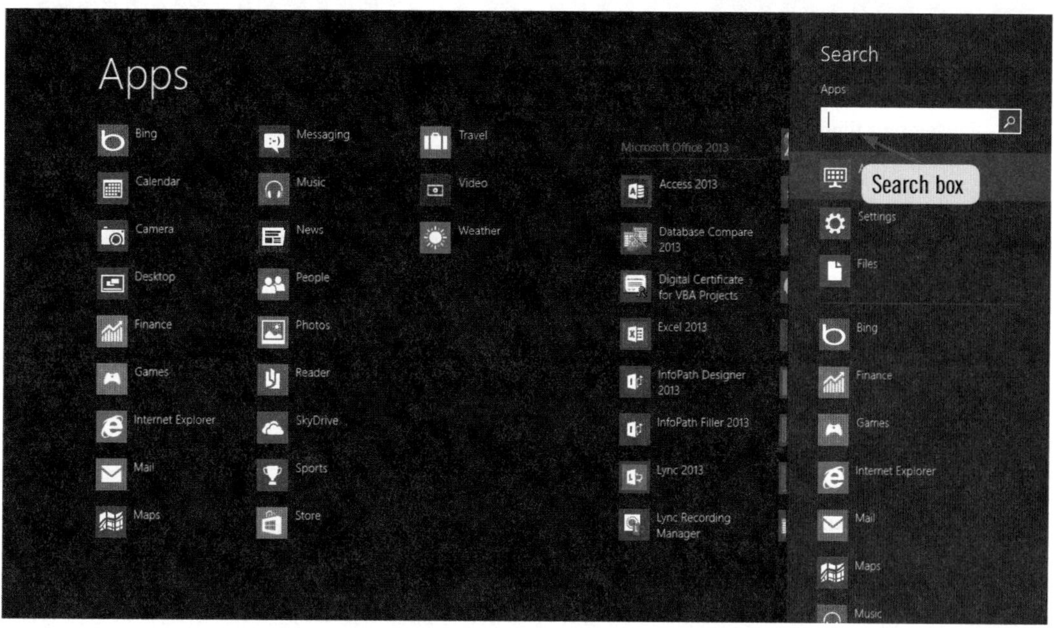

FIGURE B-22: Viewing the location of a found file

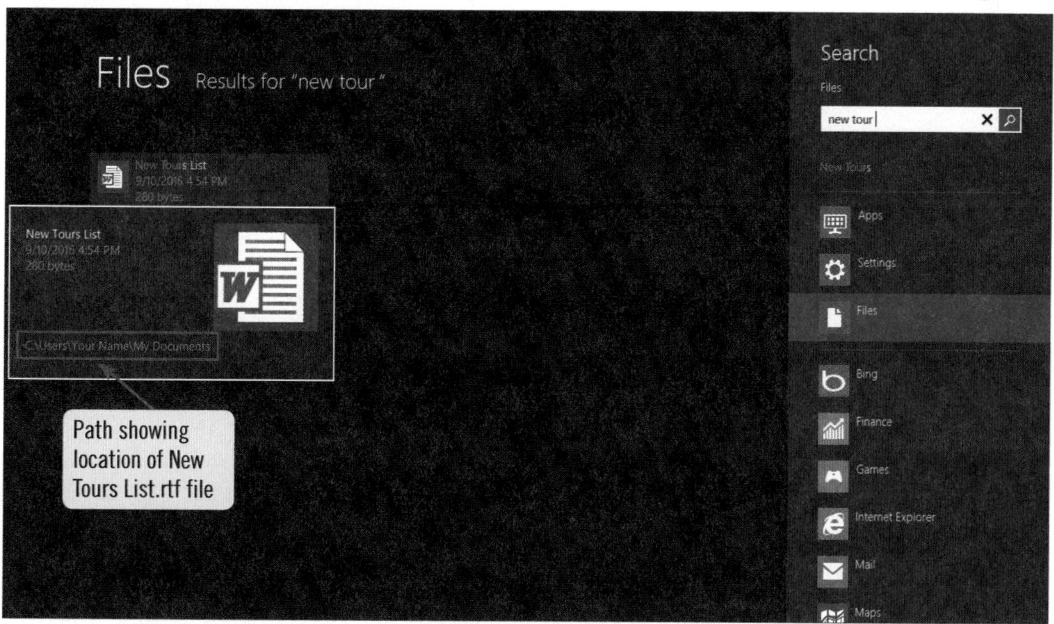

FIGURE B-23: Search results in File Explorer

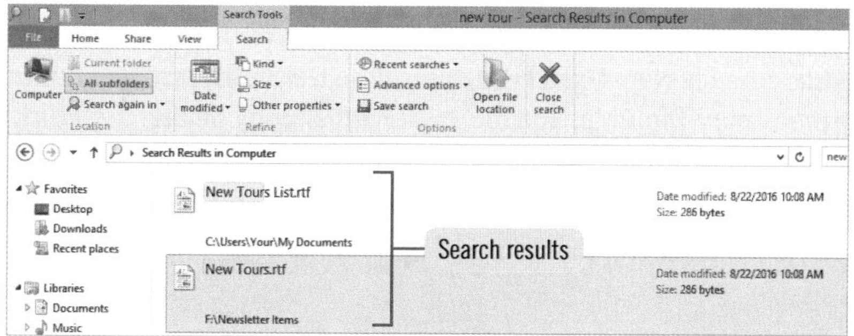

Windows 8

Delete and Restore Files

Learning Outcomes:
- Delete a file
- Restore a file
- Empty the Recycle Bin

If you no longer need a folder or file, you can delete (or remove) it from the storage device. By regularly deleting files and folders you no longer need and emptying the Recycle Bin, you free up valuable storage space on your computer. Windows 8 places folders and files you delete from your hard drive in the Recycle Bin. If you delete a folder, Windows 8 removes the folder as well as all files and subfolders stored in it. If you later discover that you need a deleted file or folder, you can restore it to its original location, as long as you have not yet emptied the Recycle Bin. Emptying the Recycle Bin permanently removes deleted folders and files from your computer. However, files and folders you delete from a removable drive, such as a USB flash drive, do not go to the Recycle Bin. They are immediately and permanently deleted and cannot be restored. CASE *You decide to delete the New Tours document, but later you change your mind about this.*

STEPS

1. **Click the Documents library in the File Explorer Navigation pane**
   Your Documents library opens, along with the Library Tools Manage tab on the Ribbon.

> **QUICK TIP**
> The Library Tools Manage tab becomes available on the Ribbon whenever a Library location is open. You can use it to change the locations the Library represents, as well as other related options.

2. **Click New Tours List.rtf to select it, then click the Delete list arrow in the Organize group on the Library Tools Manage tab; if the Show recycle confirmation command does not have a check mark next to it, click Show recycle confirmation (or if it does have a check mark, click the Delete list arrow again to close the menu)**
   Selecting the Show recycle confirmation command tells Windows that whenever you click the Delete button, you want to see a confirmation dialog box before Windows deletes the file. That way you can change your mind if you want, before deleting the file.
3. **Click the Delete button**
   The Delete File dialog box opens so you can confirm the deletion, as shown in FIGURE B-25.
4. **Click Yes**
   You deleted the file. Because the file was stored on your computer and not on a removable drive, it was moved to the Recycle Bin.

> **QUICK TIP**
> If the Recycle Bin icon does not contain crumpled paper, then it is empty.

5. **Click the Minimize button on the window's title bar, examine the Recycle Bin icon, then double-click the Recycle Bin icon on the desktop**
   The Recycle Bin icon appears to contain crumpled paper, indicating that it contains deleted folders and/or files. The Recycle Bin window displays any previously deleted folders and files, including the New Tours List.rtf file.
6. **Click the New Tours List.rtf file to select it, then click the Restore the selected items button in the Restore group on the Recycle Bin Tools Manage tab, as shown in FIGURE B-26**
   The file returns to its original location and no longer appears in the Recycle Bin window.
7. **In the Navigation pane, click the Documents library**
   The Documents library window contains the restored file. You decide to permanently delete this file.
8. **Click the file New Tours List.rtf, click the Delete list arrow in the Organize group on the Library Tools Manage tab, click Permanently delete, then click Yes in the Delete File dialog box**

> **QUICK TIP**
> Another way to delete a file completely is to select the file, press and hold [Shift], then press [Delete]; if you click Yes in the message box that opens, Windows 8 deletes the file without sending it to the Recycle Bin. Use caution, because you cannot restore the file.

9. **Minimize the window, double-click the Recycle Bin, notice that the New Tours List.rtf file is no longer there, then close all open windows**

FIGURE B-25: Delete File dialog box

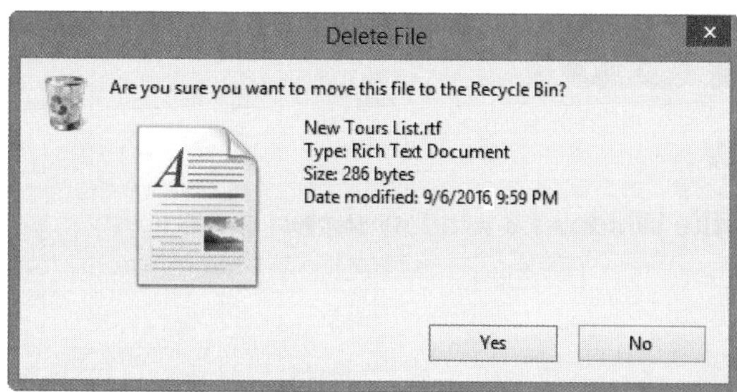

FIGURE B-26: Restoring a file from the Recycle Bin

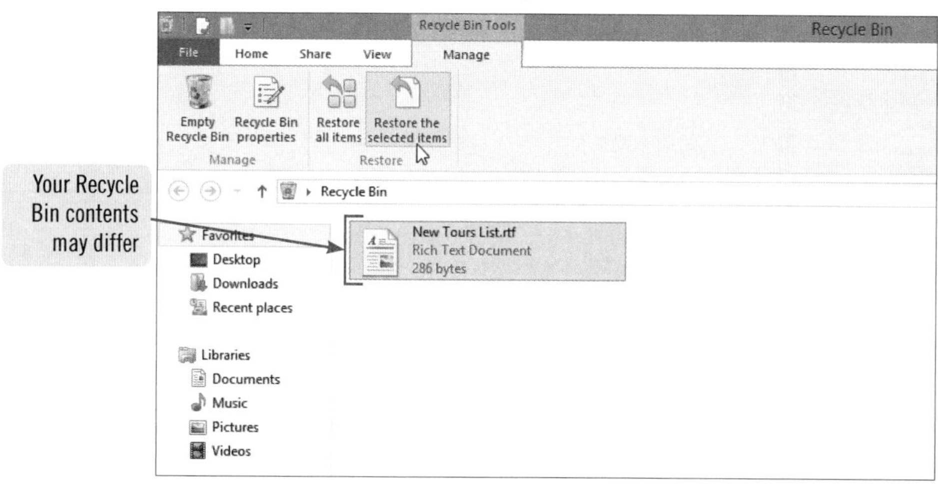

More techniques for selecting and moving files

To select a group of items that are next to each other in a window, click the first item in the group, press and hold [Shift], then click the last item in the group. Both items you click and all the items between them become selected. To select files that are not next to each other, click the first file, press and hold [Ctrl], then click the other items you want to select as a group. Then you can copy, cut, or delete the group of files or folders you selected. **Drag and drop** is a technique in which you use your pointing device to drag a file or folder into a different folder and then drop it, or let go of the mouse button, to place it in that folder. Using drag and drop does not copy your file to the clipboard. If you drag and drop a file to a folder on a different drive, Windows 8 *copies the file.* However, if you drag and drop a file to a folder on the same drive, Windows 8 *moves* the file into that folder instead. See **FIGURE B-27**. If you want to move a file to another drive, hold down [Shift] while you drag and drop. If you want to copy a file to another folder on the same drive, hold down [Ctrl] while you drag and drop.

FIGURE B-27: Moving a file using drag and drop

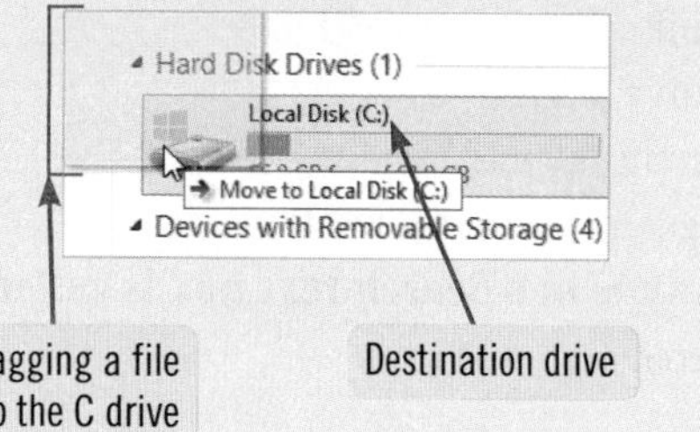

Practice

Concepts Review

Label the elements of the Windows 8 window shown in FIGURE B-28.

FIGURE B-28

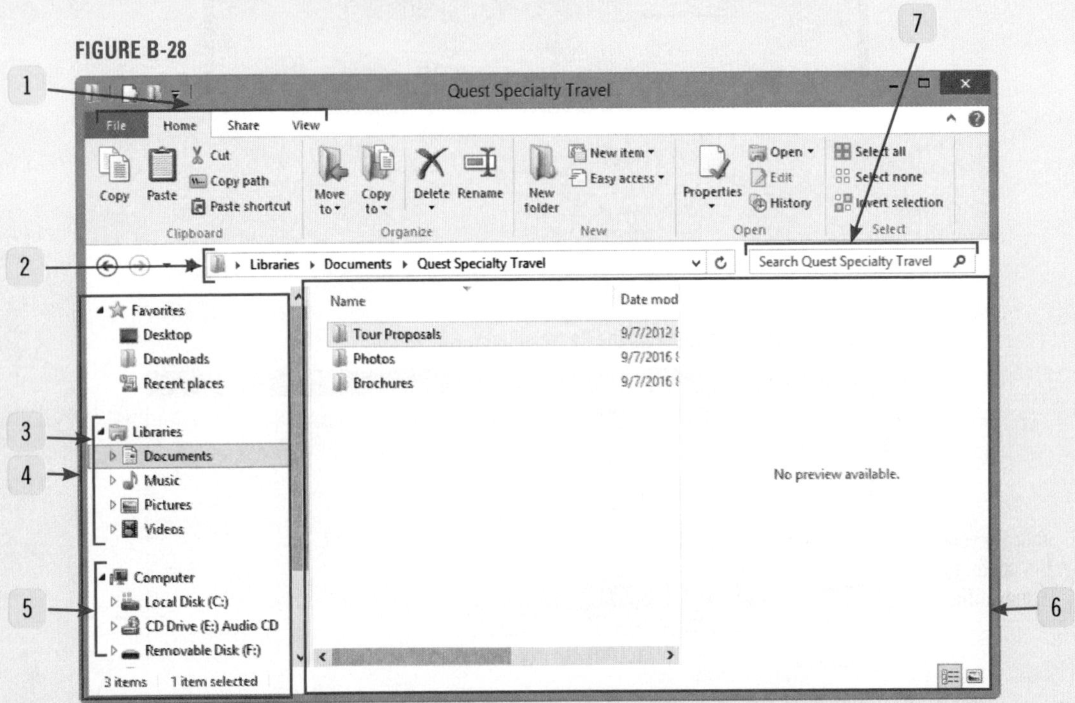

Match each term with the statement that best describes it.

8. File management
9. File extension
10. Address bar
11. Path
12. Library
13. File hierarchy

a. An area above the Files list that contains a path
b. Structure of files and folders organized in different levels
c. A series of locations separated by small triangles or backslashes that describes a file's location in the file hierarchy
d. Skills that help you organize your files and folders
e. A three- or four-letter sequence, preceded by a period, that identifies the type of file
f. Gathers files and folders from different computer locations

Select the best answer from the list of choices.

14. Which part of a window lets you see a file's contents without opening the file?

a. File list
b. Preview pane
c. Navigation pane
d. Address bar

15. When you move a file:

a. It remains in its original location.
b. It is no longer in its original location.
c. It is copied to another location.
d. It is no longer in your file hierarchy.

16. The text you type in a Search text box is called:

a. Search criteria.
b. RAM.
c. Sorting.
d. Clipboard.

17. Which of the following is not a visible section in a File Explorer window?

a. Address bar
b. File list
c. Navigation pane
d. Clipboard

18. The way your files appear in the Files list is determined by the:

a. Path.
b. View.
c. Subfolder.
d. Criterion.

19. When you copy a file, it is automatically placed in the:

a. Preview pane.
b. My Documents folder.
c. Hierarchy.
d. Clipboard.

20. After you delete a file from your hard disk, it is automatically placed in the:

a. USB flash drive.
b. Clipboard.
c. Recycle Bin.
d. Search box.

Skills Review

1. Understand files and folders.

a. Create a file hierarchy for a property management business. The business manages three apartment buildings and two private homes. Activities include renting the properties and managing maintenance and repair. How would you organize your folders and files using a file hierarchy of at least three levels? How would you use folders and subfolders to keep the documents related to these activities distinct and easy to navigate? Draw a diagram and write a short paragraph explaining your answer.

b. Use tools in the File Explorer window to create the folder hierarchy in the My Documents folder on your computer.

2. Create and save a file.

a. Connect your USB flash drive to a USB port on your computer, then open WordPad from the Start screen.

b. Type **Tour Marketing Plan** as the title, then start a new line.

c. Type your name, then press [Enter] twice.

d. Create the following list:

Airline co-marketing
Email blasts
Web ads
Adult education partnership

e. Save the WordPad file with the filename **Tour Marketing Plan.rtf** on your USB flash drive.

f. View the filename in the WordPad title bar, then close WordPad.

3. Explore the files and folders on your computer.

a. Open a File Explorer window.

b. Use the Navigation pane to navigate to your USB flash drive or another location where you store your Data Files.

c. Use the Address bar to navigate to Computer.

d. Use the File list to navigate to your local hard drive (C:).

e. Use the File list to open the Users folder, and then open the folder that represents your user name.

f. Open the My Documents folder. (*Hint:* The path is Computer\Local Disk (C:) \Users \Your User Name\ My Documents.)

g. Use the Navigation pane to navigate back to your Computer contents.

4. Change file and folder views.

a. Navigate to your USB flash drive using the method of your choice.

b. Use the View tab to view its contents as large icons.

c. View the drive contents in the seven other views.

d. Sort the items on your USB flash drive by date modified in ascending order.

e. Open the Preview pane, then view the selected item's preview.

f. Close the Preview pane.

Skills Review (continued)

5. **Open, edit, and save files.**
   a. Open WordPad.
   b. Use the Open dialog box to open the Tour Marketing Plan.rtf document you created.
   c. After the text "Adult education partnership," add a line with the text **Travel conventions**.
   d. Save the document and close WordPad.
6. **Copy files.**
   a. In the File Explorer window, navigate to your USB flash drive if necessary.
   b. Copy the Tour Marketing Plan.rtf document.
   c. Create a new folder named **Marketing** on your USB flash drive or the location where you store your Data Files (*Hint:* Use the Home tab), then open the folder.
   d. Paste the document copy in the new folder.
7. **Move and rename files.**
   a. Navigate to your USB flash drive or the location where you store your Data Files.
   b. Select the Tour Marketing Plan.rtf document located there, then cut it.
   c. Navigate to your Documents library, then paste the file there.
   d. Rename the file **Tour Marketing Plan - Backup.rtf**.
8. **Search for files, folders, and programs.**
   a. Go to the Start screen, and use the Search charm to search for a file using the search text **backup**.
   b. Point to the found file, and notice its path.
   c. Open the Tour Marketing Plan - Backup document from the search results, then close WordPad. (*Hint:* Closing the program automatically closes any open documents.)
   d. Open a File Explorer window, click in the Search box, then use the Data Modified button on the Search Tools Search tab to find a file modified today. (*Hint:* Click the Date Modified button, then click Today.)
   e. Open the found document from the File list, then close WordPad.
9. **Delete and restore files.**
   a. Navigate to your Documents library.
   b. Verify that your Delete preference is Show recycle confirmation, then delete the Tour Marketing Plan Backup.rtf file.
   c. Open the Recycle Bin, and restore the document to its original location.
   d. Navigate to your Documents library, then move the Tour Marketing Plan-Backup.rtf file to your USB flash drive.

Independent Challenge 1

To meet the needs of pet owners in your town, you have opened a pet-sitting business named CritterCare. Customers hire you to care for their pets in their own homes when the pet owners go on vacation. To promote your new business, your Web site designer asks you to give her selling points to include in a Web ad.

a. Connect your USB flash drive to your computer, if necessary.
b. Create a new folder named **CritterCare** on your USB flash drive or the location where you store your Data Files.
c. In the CritterCare folder, create two subfolders named **Print Ads** and **Web site**.
d. Use WordPad to create a short paragraph or list that describes three advantages of your business. Use CritterCare as the first line, followed by the paragraph or list. Include an address and a phone number. Below the paragraph, type your name.
e. Save the WordPad document with the filename **Selling Points.rtf** in the Web site folder, then close the document and exit WordPad.
f. Open a File Explorer window, then navigate to the Web site folder.
g. View the contents in at least three different views, then choose the view option that you prefer.
h. Copy the Selling Points.rtf file, then paste a copy in the Document library.
i. Rename the copied file **Selling Points Backup.rtf**.
j. Close the folder.

Independent Challenge 2

As a freelance editor for several international publishers, you depend on your computer to meet critical deadlines. Whenever you encounter a computer problem, you contact a computer consultant who helps you resolve the problem. This consultant has asked you to document, or keep records of, your computer's current settings.

a. Connect your USB flash drive to your computer, if necessary.
b. Open the Computer window so you can view information on your drives and other installed hardware.
c. View the window contents using three different views, then choose the one you prefer.
d. Open WordPad and create a document with the title **My Hardware Documentation** and your name on separate lines.
e. List the names of the hard drive (or drives), devices with removable storage, and any other hardware devices installed on the computer you are using. Also include the total size and amount of free space on your hard drive(s) and removable storage drive(s). (*Hint:* If you need to check the Computer window for this information, use the taskbar button for the Computer window to view your drives, then use the WordPad taskbar button to return to WordPad.)
f. Save the WordPad document with the filename **My Hardware Documentation** on your USB flash drive or the location where you store your Data Files.
g. Close WordPad, then preview your document in the Preview pane.

Independent Challenge 3

You are an attorney at Garcia, Buck, and Sato, a large law firm. You participate in your firm's community outreach program by speaking at career days in area high schools. You teach students about career opportunities available in the field of law. You want to create a folder structure on your USB flash drive to store the files for each session.

a. Connect your USB flash drive to your computer, then open the window for your USB flash drive or the location where you store your Data Files.
b. Create a folder named **Career Days**.
c. In the Career Days folder, create a subfolder named **Nearwater High**, then open the folder.
d. Close the Nearwater High folder window.
e. Use WordPad to create a document with the title **Career Areas** and your name on separate lines, and the following list of items:
   Current Opportunities:
   Attorney
   Paralegal
   Police Officer
   Judge
f. Save the WordPad document with the filename **Careers.rtf** in the Nearwater High folder. (*Hint:* After you switch to your USB flash drive in the Save As dialog box, open the Career Days folder, then open the Nearwater High folder before saving the file.)
g. Close WordPad.
h. Open WordPad and the Careers document again, add **Court Reporter** to the bottom of the list, then save the file and close WordPad.
i. Using pencil and paper, draw a diagram of your new folder structure.
j. Use the Search method of your choice to search for the Careers document, then open the file, to search your computer using the search criterion **car**. Locate the Careers.rtf document in the list, then use the link to open the file.
k. Close the file.

Independent Challenge 4: Explore

Think of a hobby or volunteer activity that you do now, or one that you would like to start. You will use your computer to help you manage your plans or ideas for this activity.

a. Using paper and pencil, sketch a folder structure with at least two subfolders to contain your documents for this activity.
b. Connect your USB flash drive to your computer, then open the window for your USB flash drive.
c. Create the folder structure for your activity, using your sketch as a reference.
d. Think of at least three tasks that you can do to further your work in your chosen activity.
e. Go to the Windows 8 Start screen, click the Store app tile and scroll to explore the available app categories. Choose a category that might relate to your activity, and click the Top Free tile to see if any of these apps might help you. Click an app name to read its description. (*Note:* You do not need to install any apps.)
f. Close the Store app by dragging its top border to the bottom of the screen.
g. Start a new WordPad document. Add the title **Next Steps** at the top of the page and your name on the next line.
h. Below your name, list the three tasks, then write a paragraph on how Windows 8 apps might help you accomplish your tasks. Save the file in one of the folders created on your USB flash drive, with the title **To Do.rtf**.
i. Close WordPad, then open a File Explorer window for the folder where you stored the document.
j. Create a copy of the file, place the copied file in your documents library, then rename this file with a name you choose.
k. Delete the copied file from your Documents library.
l. Open the Recycle Bin window, then restore the copied file to the Documents library.

Visual Workshop

Create the folder structure shown in FIGURE B-29 on your USB flash drive (or in another location if requested by your instructor). As you work, use WordPad to prepare a short summary of the steps you followed to create the folder structure. Add your name to the document, then save it as **Customer Support.rtf** on your USB Flash drive or the location where you store your Data Files.

FIGURE B-29

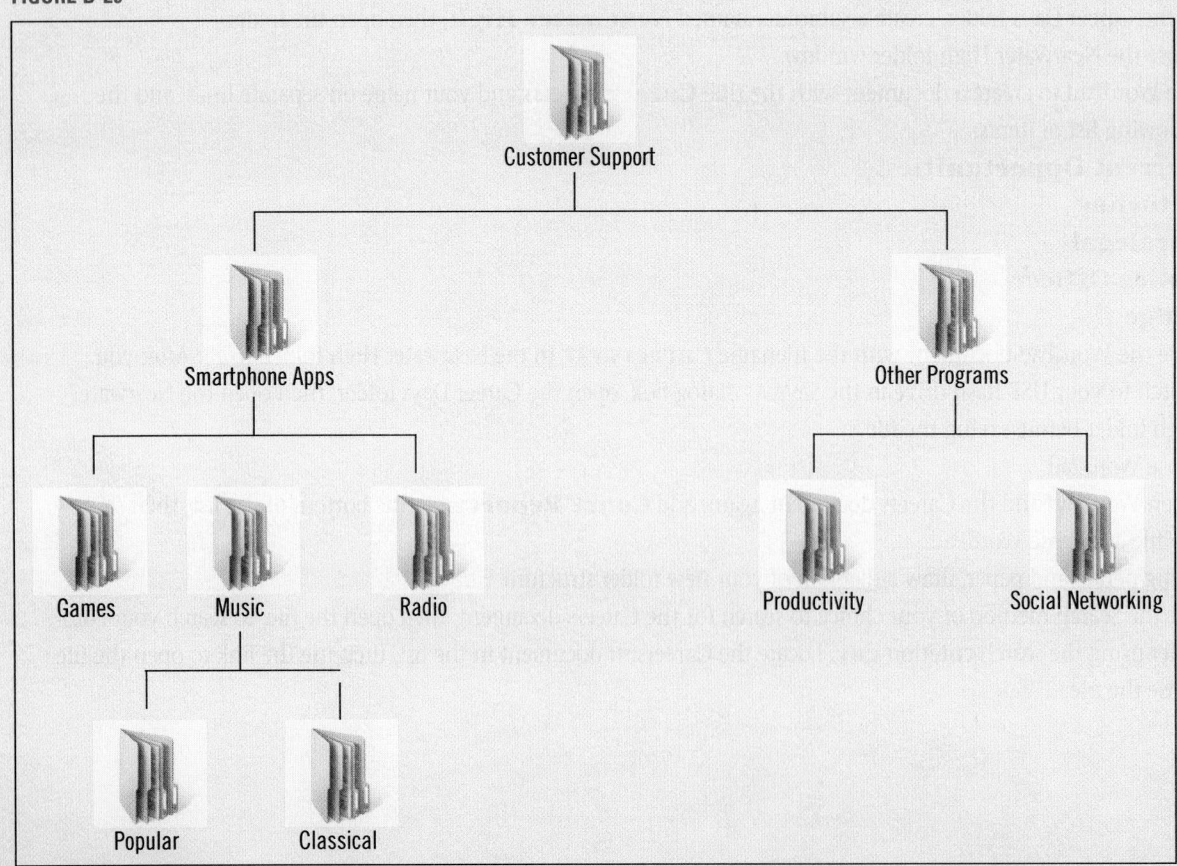

Getting Started with Excel 2013

CASE You have been hired as an assistant at Quest Specialty Travel (QST), a company offering tours that immerse travelers in regional culture. You report to Grace Wong, the vice president of finance. As Grace's assistant, you create worksheets to analyze data from various divisions of the company, so you can help her make sound decisions on company expansion and investments.

Unit Objectives

After completing this unit, you will be able to:

- Understand spreadsheet software
- Identify Excel 2013 window components
- Understand formulas
- Enter labels and values and use the AutoSum button
- Edit cell entries
- Enter and edit a simple formula
- Switch worksheet views
- Choose print options

Files You Will Need

EX A-1.xlsx
EX A-2.xlsx
EX A-3.xlsx
EX A-4.xlsx
EX A-5.xlsx

©Katerina Havelkova/Shutterstock

Learning Outcomes
- Describe the uses of Excel
- Define key spreadsheet terms

Understand Spreadsheet Software

Microsoft Excel is the electronic spreadsheet program within the Microsoft Office suite. An **electronic spreadsheet** is an application you use to perform numeric calculations and to analyze and present numeric data. One advantage of a spreadsheet program over pencil and paper is that your calculations are updated automatically, so you can change entries without having to manually recalculate. **TABLE A-1** shows some of the common business tasks people accomplish using Excel. In Excel, the electronic spreadsheet you work in is called a **worksheet**, and it is contained in a file called a **workbook**, which has the file extension .xlsx. **CASE** *At Quest Specialty Travel, you use Excel extensively to track finances and manage corporate data.*

DETAILS

When you use Excel, you have the ability to:

QUICK TIP
You can also use the **Quick Analysis tool** to easily create charts and other elements that help you visualize how data is distributed.

- **Enter data quickly and accurately**
  With Excel, you can enter information faster and more accurately than with pencil and paper. **FIGURE A-1** shows a payroll worksheet created using pencil and paper. **FIGURE A-2** shows the same worksheet created using Excel. Equations were added to calculate the hours and pay. You can use Excel to recreate this information for each week by copying the worksheet's structure and the information that doesn't change from week to week, then entering unique data and formulas for each week.

- **Recalculate data easily**
  Fixing typing errors or updating data is easy in Excel. In the payroll example, if you receive updated hours for an employee, you just enter the new hours and Excel recalculates the pay.

- **Perform what-if analysis**
  The ability to change data and quickly view the recalculated results gives you the power to make informed business decisions. For instance, if you're considering raising the hourly rate for an entry-level tour guide from $12.50 to $15.00, you can enter the new value in the worksheet and immediately see the impact on the overall payroll as well as on the individual employee. Any time you use a worksheet to ask the question "What if?" you are performing **what-if analysis**. Excel also includes a Scenario Manager where you can name and save different what-if versions of your worksheet.

- **Change the appearance of information**
  Excel provides powerful features, such as the Quick Analysis tool, for making information visually appealing and easier to understand. Format text and numbers in different fonts, colors, and styles to make it stand out.

- **Create charts**
  Excel makes it easy to create charts based on worksheet information. Charts are updated automatically in Excel whenever data changes. The worksheet in **FIGURE A-2** includes a 3-D pie chart.

- **Share information**
  It's easy for everyone at QST to collaborate in Excel using the company intranet, the Internet, or a network storage device. For example, you can complete the weekly payroll that your boss, Grace Wong, started creating. You can also take advantage of collaboration tools such as shared workbooks, so that multiple people can edit a workbook simultaneously.

QUICK TIP
The **flash fill** feature makes it easy to fill a range of text based on existing examples. Simply type [Ctrl][E] if Excel correctly matches the information you want and it will be entered in a cell for you.

- **Build on previous work**
  Instead of creating a new worksheet for every project, it's easy to modify an existing Excel worksheet. When you are ready to create next week's payroll, you can open the file for last week's payroll, save it with a new filename, and modify the information as necessary. You can also use predesigned, formatted files called **templates** to create new worksheets quickly. Excel comes with many templates that you can customize.

FIGURE A-1: Traditional paper worksheet

Quest Specialty Travel
Trip Advisor Division Payroll Calculator

Name	Hours	O/T Hrs	Hrly Rate	Reg Pay	O/T Pay	Gross Pay
Brueghel, Pieter	40	4	16.50	660–	132–	792–
Cortona, Livia	35	0	11–	385–	0–	385–
Klimt, Gustave	40	2	13–	520–	52–	572–
Le Pen, Jean-Marie	29	0	15–	435–	0–	435–
Martinez, Juan	37	0	13–	481–	0–	461–
Mioshi, Keiko	39	0	20.50	799.50	0–	799.50
Sherwood, Burton	40	0	16.50	660–	0–	660–
Strano, Riccardo	40	8	16–	640–	256–	896–
Wadsworth, Alicia	40	5	13–	520–	130–	650–
Yamamoto, Johji	38	0	15–	570–	0–	570–

FIGURE A-2: Excel worksheet

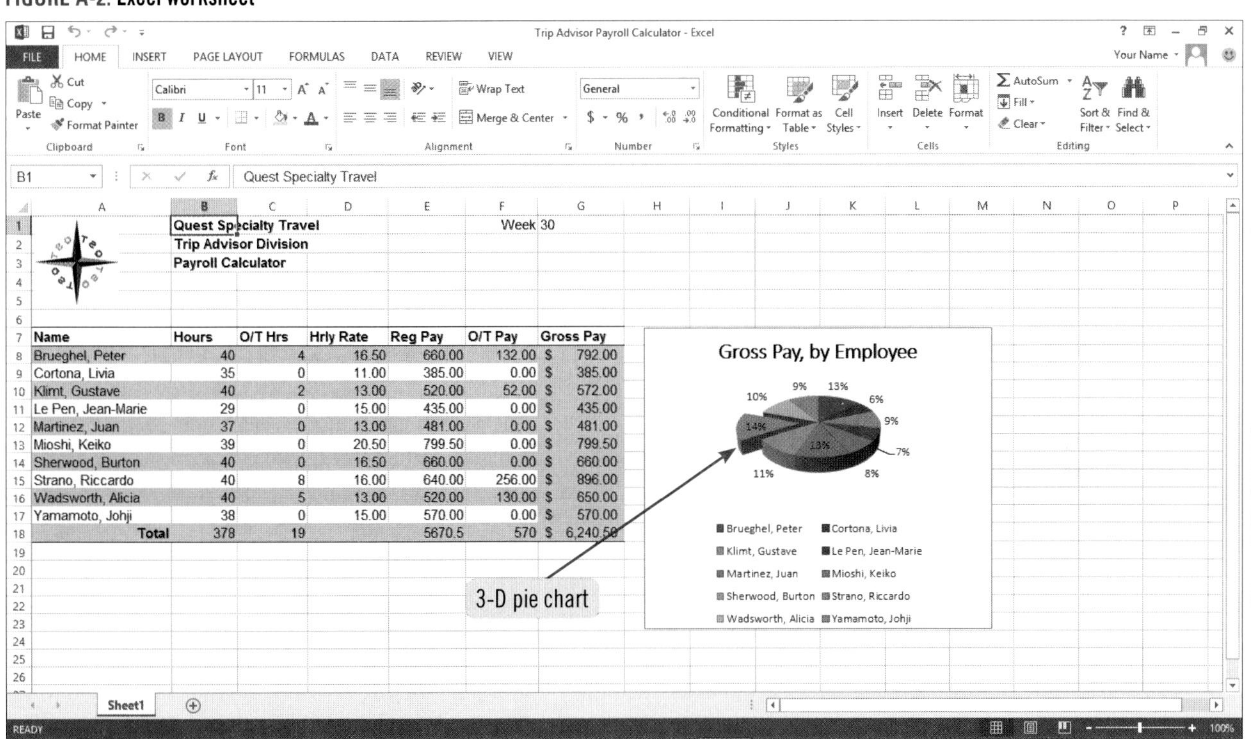

TABLE A-1: Business tasks you can accomplish using Excel

you can use spreadsheets to	by
Perform calculations	Adding formulas and functions to worksheet data; for example, adding a list of sales results or calculating a car payment
Represent values graphically	Creating charts based on worksheet data; for example, creating a chart that displays expenses
Generate reports	Creating workbooks that combine information from multiple worksheets, such as summarized sales information from multiple stores
Organize data	Sorting data in ascending or descending order; for example, alphabetizing a list of products or customer names, or prioritizing orders by date
Analyze data	Creating data summaries and short lists using PivotTables or AutoFilters; for example, making a list of the top 10 customers based on spending habits
Create what-if data scenarios	Using variable values to investigate and sample different outcomes, such as changing the interest rate or payment schedule on a loan

Excel 2013
UNIT A

Learning Outcomes
- Open and save an Excel file
- Identify Excel window elements

Identify Excel 2013 Window Components

To start Excel, Microsoft Windows must be running. Similar to starting any program in Office, you can use the Start screen thumbnail on the Windows taskbar, the Start button on your keyboard, or you may have a shortcut on your desktop you prefer to use. If you need additional assistance, ask your instructor or technical support person. **CASE** *You decide to start Excel and familiarize yourself with the worksheet window.*

STEPS

QUICK TIP
For more information on starting a program or opening and saving a file, see the unit "Getting Started with Microsoft Office 2013."

1. **Start Excel, click Open Other Workbooks on the navigation bar, click Computer, then click Browse to open the Open dialog box**
2. **In the Open dialog box, navigate to the location where you store your Data Files, click EX A-1.xlsx, click Open**

   The file opens in the Excel window.
3. **Click the FILE tab, click Save As on the navigation bar, click Computer, then click Browse to open the Save As dialog box**

TROUBLE
If you don't see the extension .xlsx on the filenames in the Save As dialog box, don't worry; Windows can be set up to display or not to display the file extensions.

4. **In the Save As dialog box, navigate to the location where you store your Data Files if necessary, type EX A-Trip Advisor Payroll Calculator in the File name text box, then click Save**

   Using FIGURE A-3 as a guide, identify the following items:
   - The **Name box** displays the active cell address. "A1" appears in the Name box.
   - The **formula bar** allows you to enter or edit data in the worksheet.
   - The **worksheet window** contains a grid of columns and rows. Columns are labeled alphabetically and rows are labeled numerically. The worksheet window can contain a total of 1,048,576 rows and 16,384 columns. The intersection of a column and a row is called a **cell**. Cells can contain text, numbers, formulas, or a combination of all three. Every cell has its own unique location or **cell address**, which is identified by the coordinates of the intersecting column and row. The column and row indicators are shaded to make identifying the cell address easy.
   - The **cell pointer** is a dark rectangle that outlines the cell you are working in. This cell is called the **active cell**. In FIGURE A-3, the cell pointer outlines cell A1, so A1 is the active cell. The column and row headings for the active cell are highlighted, making it easier to locate.
   - **Sheet tabs** below the worksheet grid let you switch from sheet to sheet in a workbook. By default, a workbook file contains one worksheet—but you can have as many as 255, in a workbook. The New sheet button to the right of Sheet 1 allows you to add worksheets to a workbook. **Sheet tab scrolling buttons** let you navigate to additional sheet tabs when available.
   - You can use the **scroll bars** to move around in a worksheet that is too large to fit on the screen at once.
   - The **status bar** is located at the bottom of the Excel window. It provides a brief description of the active command or task in progress. **The mode indicator** in the lower-left corner of the status bar provides additional information about certain tasks.
5. **Click cell A4**

   Cell A4 becomes the active cell. To activate a different cell, you can click the cell or press the arrow keys on your keyboard to move to it.

QUICK TIP
The button that displays in the bottom-right corner of a range is the Quick Analysis tool.

6. **Click cell B5, press and hold the mouse button, drag to cell B14, then release the mouse button**

   You selected a group of cells and they are highlighted, as shown in FIGURE A-4. A selection of two or more cells such as B5:B14 is called a **range**; you select a range when you want to perform an action on a group of cells at once, such as moving them or formatting them. When you select a range, the status bar displays the average, count (or number of items selected), and sum of the selected cells as a quick reference.

FIGURE A-3: Open workbook

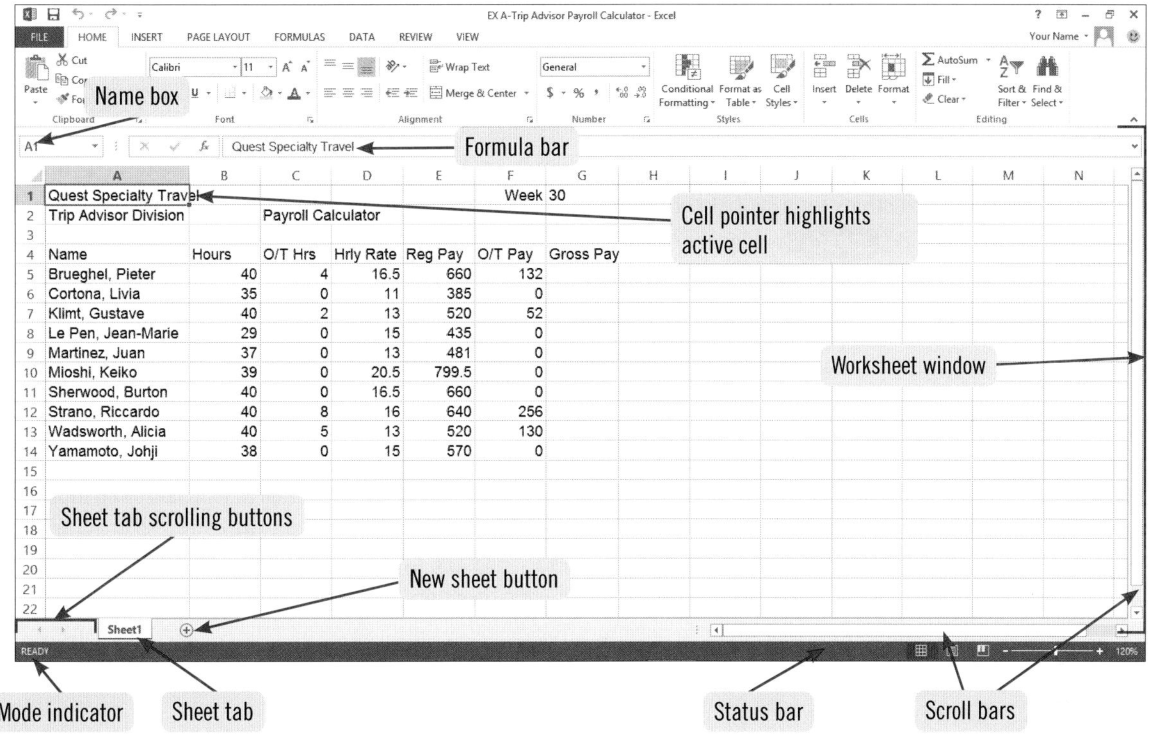

FIGURE A-4: Selected range

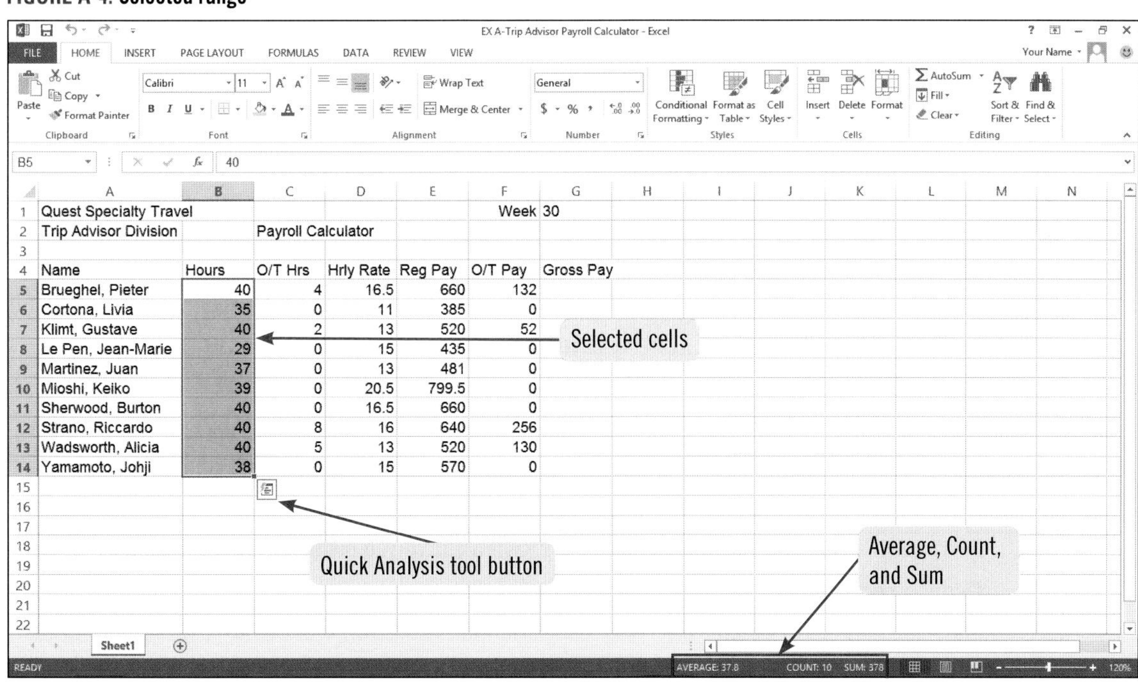

Using SkyDrive and Web Apps

If you have a free Microsoft account, you can save your Excel files to SkyDrive, a free cloud-based service from Microsoft. When you save files to SkyDrive, you can access them on other devices–such as a tablet or smart phone. SkyDrive is available as an app on smart phones, which makes access very easy. You can open files to view them on any device and you can even make edits to them using **Office Web Apps**, which are simplified versions of the apps found in the Office 2013 suite. Because the Web Apps are online, they take up no computer disk space, and you can use them on any Internet-connected device. You can find more information in the "Working in the Cloud" appendix.

Understand Formulas

Learning Outcomes
- Explain how a formula works
- Identify Excel arithmetic operators

Excel is a truly powerful program because users at every level of mathematical expertise can make calculations with accuracy. To do so, you use formulas. A **formula** is an equation in a worksheet. You use formulas to make calculations as simple as adding a column of numbers, or as complex as creating profit-and-loss projections for a global corporation. To tap into the power of Excel, you should understand how formulas work. **CASE** *Managers at QST use the Trip Advisor Payroll Calculator workbook to keep track of employee hours prior to submitting them to the Payroll Department. You'll be using this workbook regularly, so you need to understand the formulas it contains and how Excel calculates the results.*

STEPS

1. **Click cell E5**

   The active cell contains a formula, which appears on the formula bar. All Excel formulas begin with the equal sign (=). If you want a cell to show the result of adding 4 plus 2, the formula in the cell would look like this: =4+2. If you want a cell to show the result of multiplying two values in your worksheet, such as the values in cells B5 and D5, the formula would look like this: =B5*D5, as shown in **FIGURE A-5**. While you're entering a formula in a cell, the cell references and arithmetic operators appear on the formula bar. See **TABLE A-2** for a list of commonly used arithmetic operators. When you're finished entering the formula, you can either click the Enter button on the formula bar or press [Enter].

2. **Click cell F5**

   An example of a more complex formula is the calculation of overtime pay. At QST, overtime pay is calculated at twice the regular hourly rate times the number of overtime hours. The formula used to calculate overtime pay for the employee in row 5 is:

   O/T Hrs times (2 times Hrly Rate)

   In the worksheet cell, you would enter: =C5*(2*D5), as shown in **FIGURE A-6**. The use of parentheses creates groups within the formula and indicates which calculations to complete first—an important consideration in complex formulas. In this formula, first the hourly rate is multiplied by 2, because that calculation is within the parentheses. Next, that value is multiplied by the number of overtime hours. Because overtime is calculated at twice the hourly rate, managers are aware that they need to closely watch this expense.

DETAILS

In creating calculations in Excel, it is important to:

- **Know where the formulas should be**

  An Excel formula is created in the cell where the formula's results should appear. This means that the formula calculating Gross Pay for the employee in row 5 will be entered in cell G5.

- **Know exactly what cells and arithmetic operations are needed**

  Don't guess; make sure you know exactly what cells are involved before creating a formula.

- **Create formulas with care**

  Make sure you know exactly what you want a formula to accomplish before it is created. An inaccurate formula may have far-reaching effects if the formula or its results are referenced by other formulas, as shown in the payroll example in **FIGURE A-6**.

- **Use cell references rather than values**

  The beauty of Excel is that whenever you change a value in a cell, any formula containing a reference to that cell is automatically updated. For this reason, it's important that you use cell references in formulas, rather than actual values, whenever possible.

- **Determine what calculations will be needed**

  Sometimes it's difficult to predict what data will be needed within a worksheet, but you should try to anticipate what statistical information may be required. For example, if there are columns of numbers, chances are good that both column and row totals should be present.

FIGURE A-5: Viewing a formula

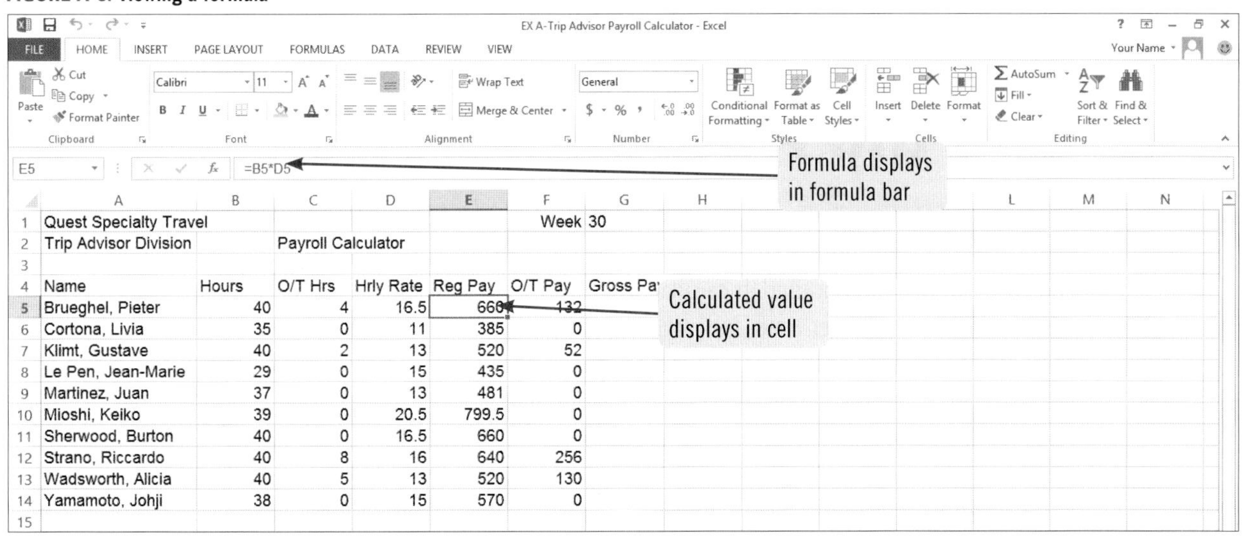

FIGURE A-6: Formula with multiple operators

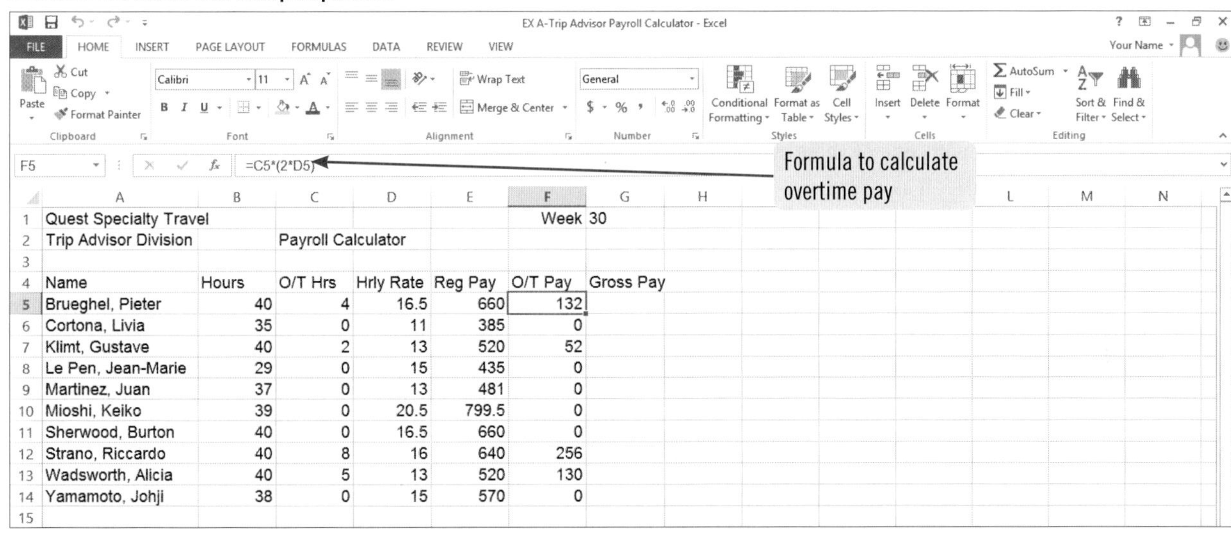

TABLE A-2: Excel arithmetic operators

operator	purpose	example
+	Addition	=A5+A7
-	Subtraction or negation	=A5-10
*	Multiplication	=A5*A7
/	Division	=A5/A7
%	Percent	=35%
^ (caret)	Exponent	=6^2 (same as 6^2)

Excel 2013
UNIT A

Learning Outcomes
- Build formulas with the AutoSum button
- Copy formulas with the fill handle

Enter Labels and Values and Use the AutoSum Button

To enter content in a cell, you can type in the formula bar or directly in the cell itself. When entering content in a worksheet, you should start by entering all the labels first. **Labels** are entries that contain text and numerical information not used in calculations, such as "2012 Sales" or "Travel Expenses". Labels help you identify data in worksheet rows and columns, making your worksheet easier to understand. **Values** are numbers, formulas, and functions that can be used in calculations. To enter a calculation, you type an equal sign (=) plus the formula for the calculation; some examples of an Excel calculation are "=2+2" and "=C5+C6". Functions are Excel's built-in formulas; you learn more about them in the next unit. **CASE** *You want to enter some information in the Trip Advisor Payroll Calculator workbook, and use a very simple function to total a range of cells.*

STEPS

1. **Click cell A15, then click in the formula bar**
   Notice that the **mode indicator** on the status bar now reads "Edit," indicating you are in Edit mode. You are in Edit mode any time you are entering or changing the contents of a cell.

QUICK TIP
If you change your mind and want to cancel an entry in the formula bar, click the Cancel button on the formula bar.

2. **Type Totals, then click the Enter button on the formula bar**
   Clicking the Enter button accepts the entry. The new text is left-aligned in the cell. Labels are left-aligned by default, and values are right-aligned by default. Excel recognizes an entry as a value if it is a number or it begins with one of these symbols: +, -, =, @, #, or $. When a cell contains both text and numbers, Excel recognizes it as a label.
3. **Click cell B15**
   You want this cell to total the hours worked by all the trip advisors. You might think you need to create a formula that looks like this: =B5+B6+B7+B8+B9+B10+B11+B12+B13+B14. However, there's an easier way to achieve this result.
4. **Click the AutoSum button in the Editing group on the HOME tab on the Ribbon**
   The SUM function is inserted in the cell, and a suggested range appears in parentheses, as shown in **FIGURE A-7**. A **function** is a built-in formula; it includes the **arguments** (the information necessary to calculate an answer) as well as cell references and other unique information. Clicking the AutoSum button sums the adjacent range (that is, the cells next to the active cell) above or to the left, although you can adjust the range if necessary by selecting a different range before accepting the cell entry. Using the SUM function is quicker than entering a formula, and using the range B5:B14 is more efficient than entering individual cell references.

QUICK TIP
You can create formulas in a cell even before you enter the values to be calculated; the results will be recalculated as soon as the data is entered.

5. **Click on the formula bar**
   Excel calculates the total contained in cells B5:B14 and displays the result, 378, in cell B15. The cell actually contains the formula =SUM(B5:B14), and the result is displayed.
6. **Click cell C13, type 6, then press [Enter]**
   The number 6 replaces the cell's contents, the cell pointer moves to cell C14, and the value in cell F13 changes.

QUICK TIP
You can also press [Tab] to complete a cell entry and move the cell pointer to the right.

7. **Click cell C18, type Average Gross Pay, then press [Enter]**
   The new label is entered in cell C18. The contents appear to spill into the empty cells to the right.
8. **Click cell B15, position the pointer on the lower-right corner of the cell (the fill handle) so that the pointer changes to +, drag the + to cell G15, then release the mouse button**
   Dragging the fill handle across a range of cells copies the contents of the first cell into the other cells in the range. In the range B15:G15, each filled cell now contains a function that sums the range of cells above, as shown in **FIGURE A-8**.
9. **Save your work**

FIGURE A-7: Creating a formula using the AutoSum button

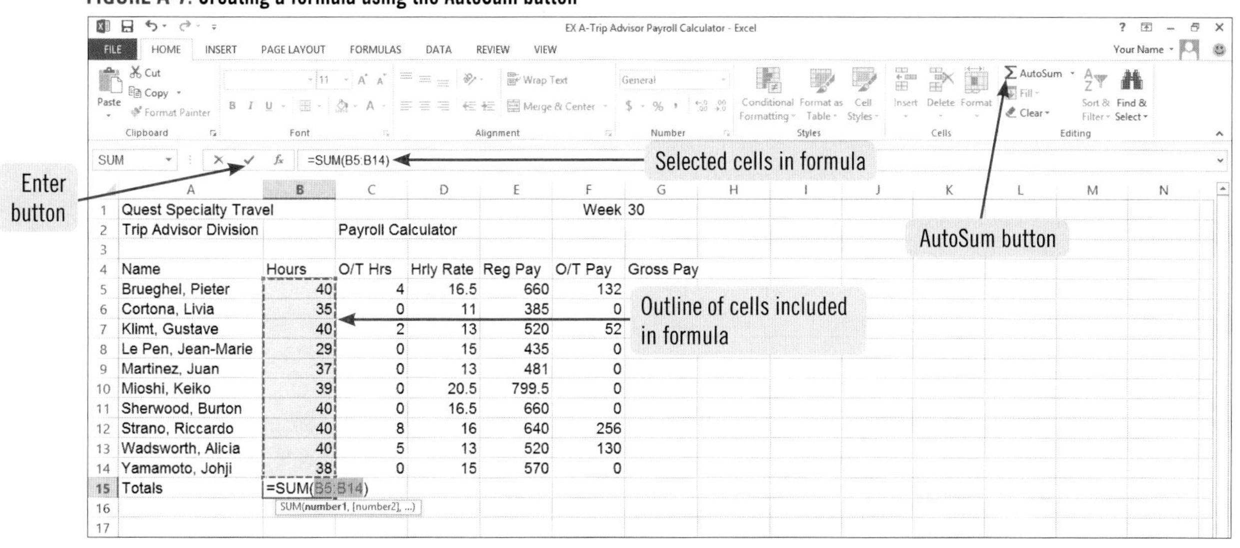

FIGURE A-8: Results of copied SUM functions

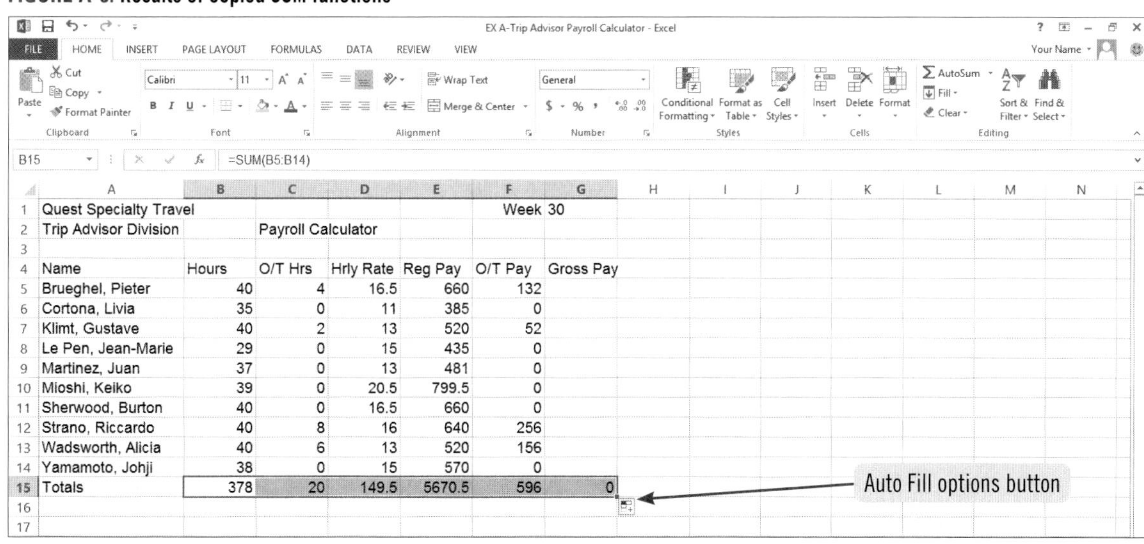

Excel 2013

Navigating a worksheet

With over a million cells available in a worksheet, it is important to know how to move around in, or **navigate**, a worksheet. You can use the arrow keys on the keyboard ↑, ↓, → or ← to move one cell at a time, or press [Page Up] or [Page Down] to move one screen at a time. To move one screen to the left press [Alt][Page Up]; to move one screen to the right press [Alt][Page Down]. You can also use the mouse pointer to click the desired cell. If the desired cell is not visible in the worksheet window, use the scroll bars or use the Go To command by clicking the Find & Select button in the Editing group on the HOME tab on the Ribbon. To quickly jump to the first cell in a worksheet press [Ctrl][Home]; to jump to the last cell, press [Ctrl][End].

Excel 2013
UNIT A

Edit Cell Entries

Learning Outcomes
- Edit cell entries in the formula bar
- Edit cell entries in the cell

You can change, or **edit**, the contents of an active cell at any time. To do so, double-click the cell, click in the formula bar, or just start typing. Excel switches to Edit mode when you are making cell entries. Different pointers, shown in **TABLE A-3**, guide you through the editing process. **CASE** *You noticed some errors in the worksheet and want to make corrections. The first error is in cell A5, which contains a misspelled name.*

STEPS

1. **Click cell A5, then click to the right of P in the formula bar**
   As soon as you click in the formula bar, a blinking vertical line called the **insertion point** appears on the formula bar at the location where new text will be inserted. See **FIGURE A-9**. The mouse pointer changes to I when you point anywhere in the formula bar.

2. **Press [Delete], then click the Enter button ✓ on the formula bar**
   Clicking the Enter button accepts the edit, and the spelling of the employee's first name is corrected. You can also press [Enter] or [Tab] to accept an edit. Pressing [Enter] to accept an edit moves the cell pointer down one cell, and pressing [Tab] to accept an edit moves the cell pointer one cell to the right.

> **QUICK TIP**
> On some keyboards, you might need to press an [F Lock] key to enable the function keys.

3. **Click cell B6, then press [F2]**
   Excel switches to Edit mode, and the insertion point blinks in the cell. Pressing [F2] activates the cell for editing directly in the cell instead of the formula bar. Whether you edit in the cell or the formula bar is simply a matter of preference; the results in the worksheet are the same.

> **QUICK TIP**
> The Undo button allows you to reverse up to 100 previous actions, one at a time.

4. **Press [Backspace], type 8, then press [Enter]**
   The value in the cell changes from 35 to 38, and cell B7 becomes the active cell. Did you notice that the calculations in cells B15 and E15 also changed? That's because those cells contain formulas that include cell B6 in their calculations. If you make a mistake when editing, you can click the Cancel button ✕ on the formula bar *before* pressing [Enter] to confirm the cell entry. The Enter and Cancel buttons appear only when you're in Edit mode. If you notice the mistake *after* you have confirmed the cell entry, click the Undo button ↶ on the Quick Access toolbar.

> **QUICK TIP**
> You can use the keyboard to select all cell contents by clicking to the right of the cell contents in the cell or formula bar, pressing and holding [Shift], then pressing [Home].

5. **Click cell A9, then double-click the word Juan in the formula bar**
   Double-clicking a word in a cell selects it. When you selected the word, the Mini toolbar automatically displayed.

6. **Type Javier, then press [Enter]**
   When text is selected, typing deletes it and replaces it with the new text.

7. **Double-click cell C12, press [Delete], type 4, then click ✓**
   Double-clicking a cell activates it for editing directly in the cell. Compare your screen to **FIGURE A-10**.

8. **Save your work**
   Your changes to the workbook are saved.

Recovering unsaved changes to a workbook file

You can use Excel's AutoRecover feature to automatically save (Autosave) your work as often as you want. This means that if you suddenly lose power or if Excel closes unexpectedly while you're working, you can recover all or some of the changes you made since you saved it last. (Of course, this is no substitute for regularly saving your work: this is just added insurance.) To customize the AutoRecover settings, click the FILE tab, click Options, then click Save. AutoRecover lets you decide how often and into which location it should Autosave files. When you restart Excel after losing power, a Document Recovery pane opens and provides access to the saved and Autosaved versions of the files that were open when Excel closed. You can also click the FILE tab, click Open on the navigation bar, then click any file in the Recent Workbooks list to open Autosaved workbooks.

FIGURE A-9: Worksheet in Edit mode

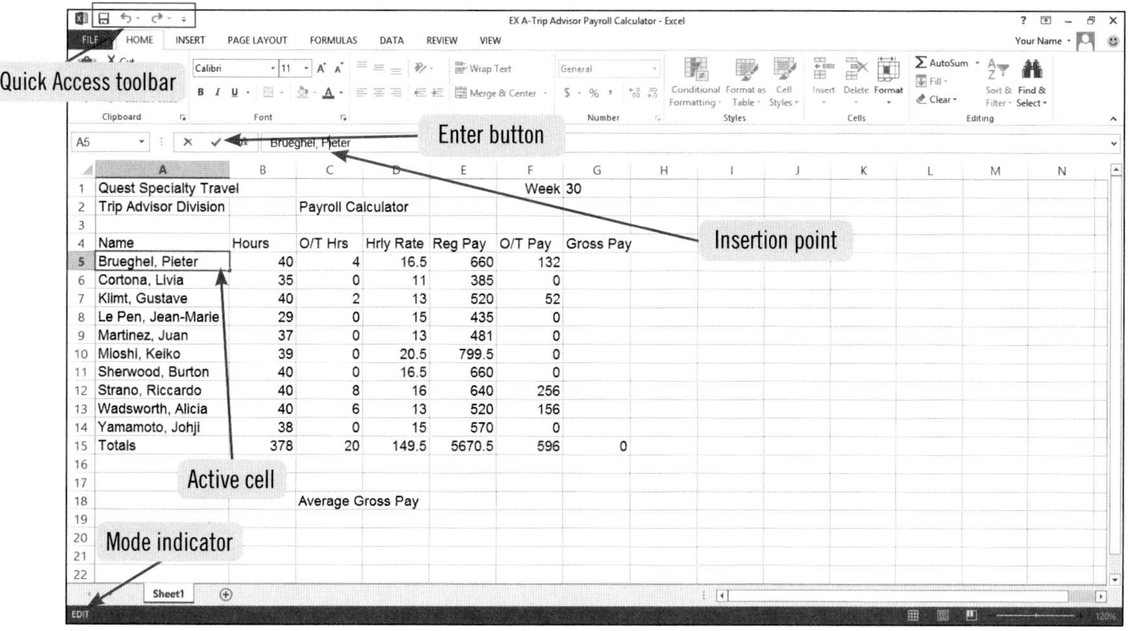

FIGURE A-10: Edited worksheet

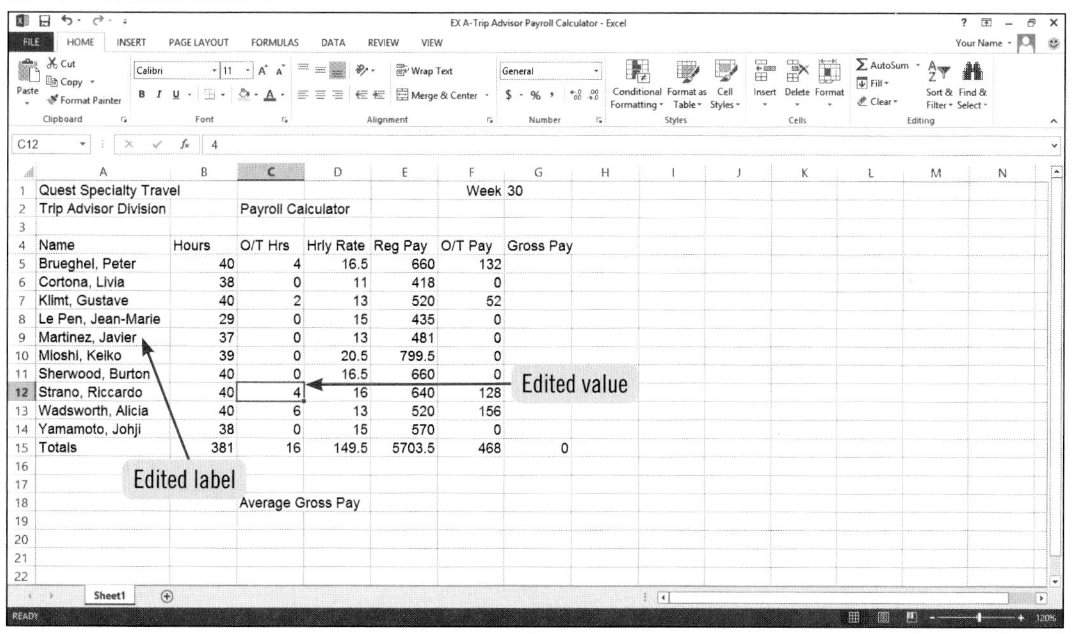

TABLE A-3: Common pointers in Excel

name	pointer	use to	visible over the
Normal	[arrow pointer]	Select a cell or range; indicates Ready mode	Active worksheet
Fill handle	+	Copy cell contents to adjacent cells	Lower-right corner of the active cell or range
I-beam	I	Edit cell contents in active cell or formula bar	Active cell in Edit mode or over the formula bar
Move	[move pointer]	Change the location of the selected cell(s)	Perimeter of the active cell(s)
Copy	[copy pointer]	Create a duplicate of the selected cell(s)	Perimeter of the active cell(s) when [Ctrl] is pressed
Column resize	[resize pointer]	Change the width of a column	Border between column heading indicators

Enter and Edit a Simple Formula

Learning Outcomes
- Enter a formula
- Use cell references to create a formula

You use formulas in Excel to perform calculations such as adding, multiplying, and averaging. Formulas in an Excel worksheet start with the equal sign (=), also called the **formula prefix**, followed by cell addresses, range names, values, and **calculation operators**. Calculation operators indicate what type of calculation you want to perform on the cells, ranges, or values. They can include **arithmetic operators**, which perform mathematical calculations (see TABLE A-2 in the "Understand Formulas" lesson); **comparison operators**, which compare values for the purpose of true/false results; **text concatenation operators**, which join strings of text in different cells; and **reference operators**, which enable you to use ranges in calculations. **CASE** *You want to create a formula in the worksheet that calculates gross pay for each employee.*

STEPS

1. **Click cell G5**
   This is the first cell where you want to insert the formula. To calculate gross pay, you need to add regular pay and overtime pay. For employee Peter Brueghel, regular pay appears in cell E5 and overtime pay appears in cell F5.

2. **Type =, click cell E5, type +, then click cell F5**
   Compare your formula bar to **FIGURE A-11**. The blue and red cell references in cell G5 correspond to the colored cell outlines. When entering a formula, it's a good idea to use cell references instead of values whenever you can. That way, if you later change a value in a cell (if, for example, Peter's regular pay changes to 690), any formula that includes this information reflects accurate, up-to-date results.

QUICK TIP
You can reference a cell in a formula either by typing the cell reference or clicking the cell in the worksheet; when you click a cell to add a reference, the Mode indicator changes to "Point."

3. **Click the Enter button ✓ on the formula bar**
   The result of the formula =E5+F5, 792, appears in cell G5. This same value appears in cell G15 because cell G15 contains a formula that totals the values in cells G5:G14, and there are no other values at this time.

4. **Click cell F5**
   The formula in this cell calculates overtime pay by multiplying overtime hours (C5) times twice the regular hourly rate (2*D5). You want to edit this formula to reflect a new overtime pay rate.

5. **Click to the right of 2 in the formula bar, then type .5 as shown in FIGURE A-12**
   The formula that calculates overtime pay has been edited.

6. **Click ✓ on the formula bar**
   Compare your screen to **FIGURE A-13**. Notice that the calculated values in cells G5, F15, and G15 have all changed to reflect your edits to cell F5.

7. **Save your work**

Understanding named ranges

It can be difficult to remember the cell locations of critical information in a worksheet, but using cell names can make this task much easier. You can name a single cell or range of contiguous, or touching, cells. For example, you might name a cell that contains data on average gross pay "AVG_GP" instead of trying to remember the cell address C18. A named range must begin with a letter or an underscore. It cannot contain any spaces or be the same as a built-in name, such as a function or another object (such as a different named range) in the workbook. To name a range, select the cell(s) you want to name, click the Name box in the formula bar, type the name you want to use, then press [Enter]. You can also name a range by clicking the FORMULAS tab, then clicking the Define Name button in the Defined Names group. Type the new range name in the Name text box in the New Name dialog box, verify the selected range, then click OK. When you use a named range in a formula, the named range appears instead of the cell address. You can also create a named range using the contents of a cell already in the range. Select the range containing the text you want to use as a name, then click the Create from Selection button in the Defined Names group. The Create Names from Selection dialog box opens. Choose the location of the name you want to use, then click OK.

FIGURE A-11: Simple formula in a worksheet

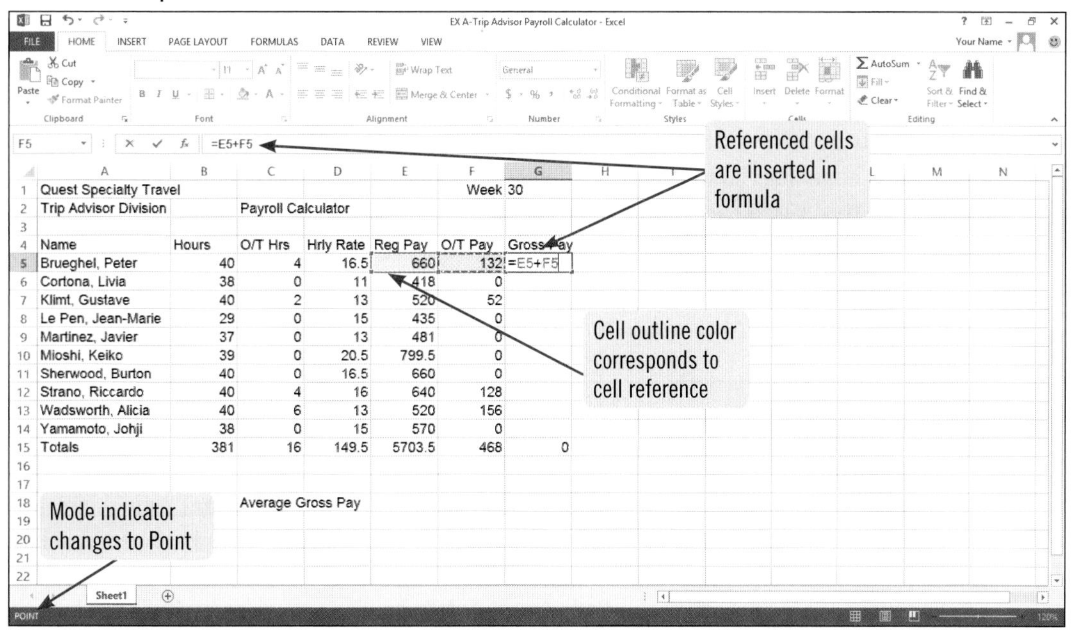

FIGURE A-12: Edited formula in a worksheet

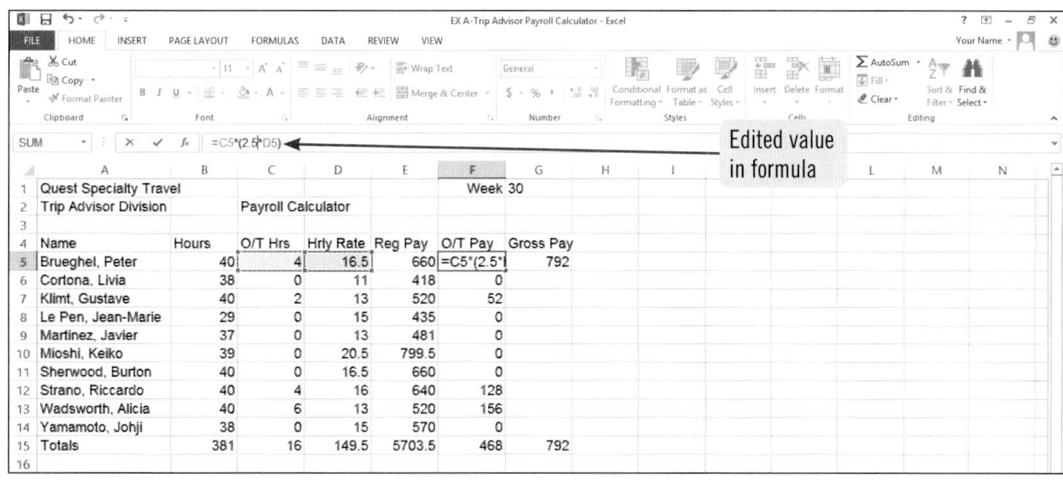

FIGURE A-13: Edited formula with changes

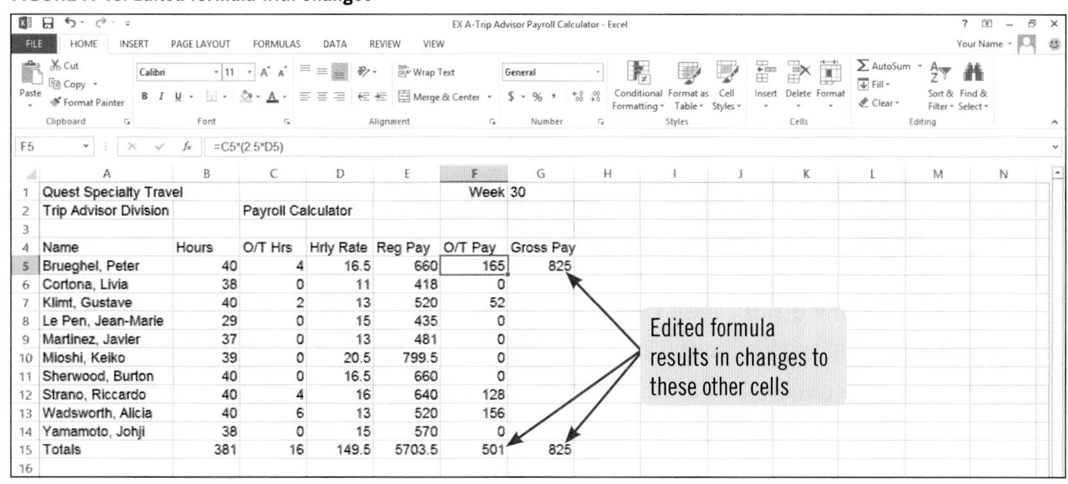

Excel 2013

Switch Worksheet Views

Learning Outcomes
- Change worksheet views
- Create a header/footer
- Select a range

You can change your view of the worksheet window at any time, using either the VIEW tab on the Ribbon or the View buttons on the status bar. Changing your view does not affect the contents of a worksheet; it just makes it easier for you to focus on different tasks, such as entering content or preparing a worksheet for printing. The VIEW tab includes a variety of viewing options, such as View buttons, zoom controls, and the ability to show or hide worksheet elements such as gridlines. The status bar offers fewer View options but can be more convenient to use. **CASE** *You want to make some final adjustments to your worksheet, including adding a header so the document looks more polished.*

STEPS

QUICK TIP
Although a worksheet can contain more than a million rows and thousands of columns, the current document contains only as many pages as necessary for the current project.

1. **Click the VIEW tab on the Ribbon, then click the Page Layout button in the Workbook Views group**
   The view switches from the default view, Normal, to Page Layout view. **Normal view** shows the worksheet without including certain details like headers and footers, or tools like rulers and a page number indicator; it's great for creating and editing a worksheet, but may not be detailed enough when you want to put the finishing touches on a document. **Page Layout view** provides a more accurate view of how a worksheet will look when printed, as shown in **FIGURE A-14**. The margins of the page are displayed, along with a text box for the header. A footer text box appears at the bottom of the page, but your screen may not be large enough to view it without scrolling. Above and to the left of the page are rulers. Part of an additional page appears to the right of this page, but it is dimmed, indicating that it does not contain any data. A page number indicator on the status bar tells you the current page and the total number of pages in this worksheet.

2. **Move the pointer over the header *without clicking***
   The header is made up of three text boxes: left, center, and right. Each text box is outlined in green as you pass over it with the pointer.

QUICK TIP
You can change header and footer information using the Header & Footer Tools Design tab that opens on the Ribbon when a header or footer is active. For example, you can insert the date by clicking the Current Date button in the Header & Footer Elements group, or insert the time by clicking the Current Time button.

3. **Click the left header text box, type Quest Specialty Travel, click the center header text box, type Trip Advisor Payroll Calculator, click the right header text box, then type Week 30**
   The new text appears in the text boxes, as shown in **FIGURE A-15**. You can also press the [Tab] key to advance from one header box to the next.

4. **Select the range A1:G2, then press [Delete]**
   The duplicate information you just entered in the header is deleted from cells in the worksheet.

5. **Click the VIEW tab if necessary, click the Ruler check box in the Show group, then click the Gridlines check box in the Show group**
   The rulers and the gridlines are hidden. By default, gridlines in a worksheet do not print, so hiding them gives you a more accurate image of your final document.

6. **Click the Page Break Preview button on the status bar**
   Your view changes to Page Break Preview, which displays a reduced view of each page of your worksheet, along with page break indicators that you can drag to include more or less information on a page.

QUICK TIP
Once you view a worksheet in Page Break Preview, the page break indicators appear as dotted lines after you switch back to Normal view or Page Layout view.

7. **Drag the pointer from the bottom page break indicator to the bottom of row 20**
   See **FIGURE A-16**. When you're working on a large worksheet with multiple pages, sometimes you need to adjust where pages break; in this worksheet, however, the information all fits comfortably on one page.

8. **Click the Page Layout button in the Workbook Views group, click the Ruler check box in the Show group, then click the Gridlines check box in the Show group**
   The rulers and gridlines are no longer hidden. You can show or hide VIEW tab items in any view.

9. **Save your work**

FIGURE A-14: Page Layout view

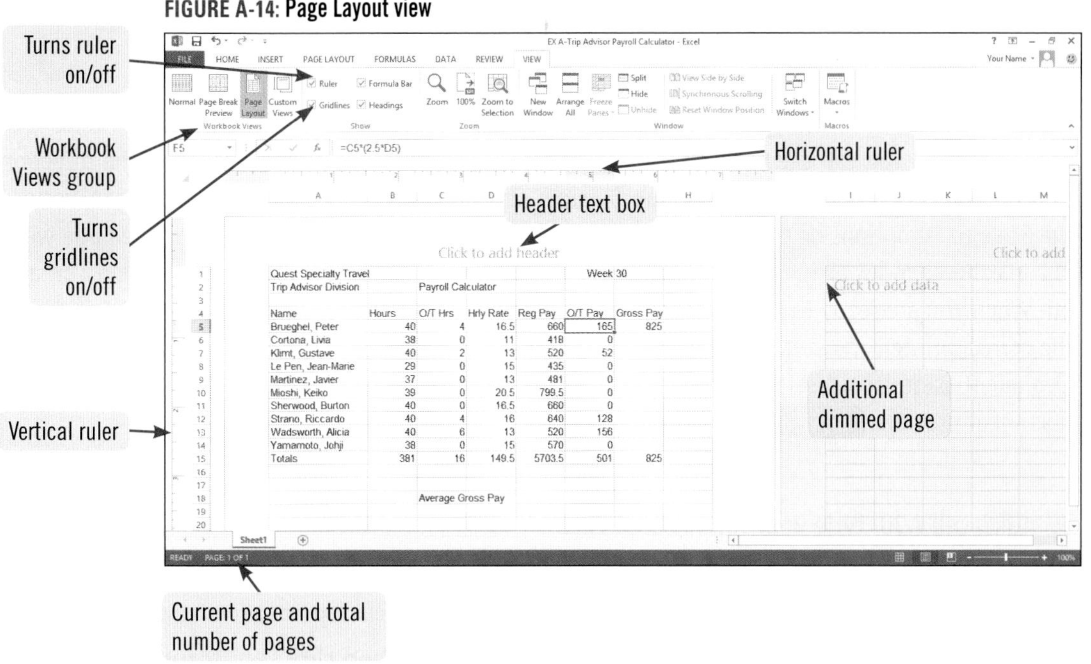

FIGURE A-15: Header text entered

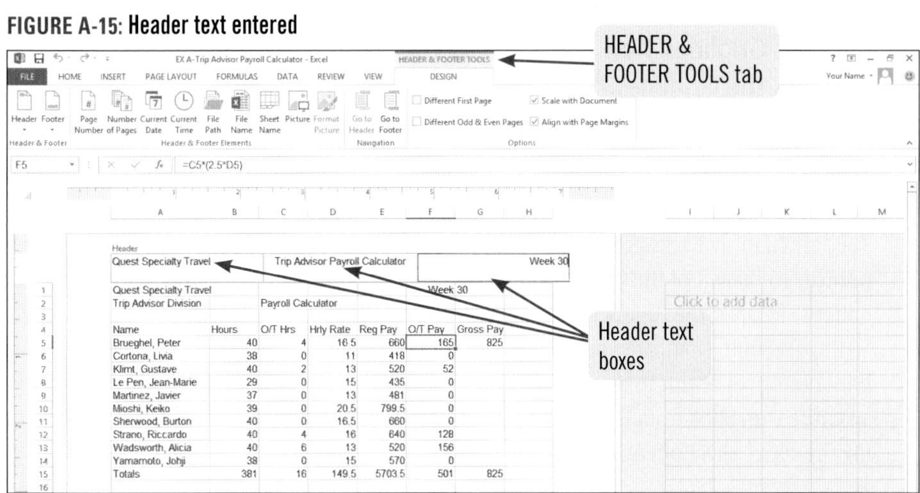

FIGURE A-16: Page Break Preview

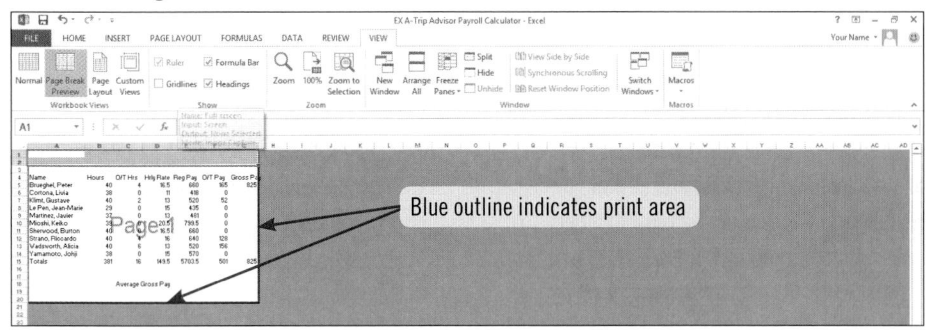

Excel 2013

Choose Print Options

Learning Outcomes
- Change the page orientation
- Hide/view gridlines when printing
- Preview and print a worksheet

Before printing a document, you may want to review it using the PAGE LAYOUT tab to fine-tune your printed output. You can use tools on the PAGE LAYOUT tab to adjust print orientation (the direction in which the content prints across the page), paper size, and location of page breaks. You can also use the Scale to Fit options on the PAGE LAYOUT tab to fit a large amount of data on a single page without making changes to individual margins, and to turn gridlines and column/row headings on and off. When you are ready to print, you can set print options such as the number of copies to print and the correct printer, and you can preview your document in Backstage view using the FILE tab. You can also adjust page layout settings from within Backstage view and immediately see the results in the document preview. **CASE** *You are ready to prepare your worksheet for printing.*

STEPS

1. **Click cell A20, type your name, then click ✓**
2. **Click the PAGE LAYOUT tab on the Ribbon**

   Compare your screen to **FIGURE A-17**. The solid outline indicates the default **print area**, the area to be printed.

QUICK TIP
You can use the Zoom slider on the status bar at any time to enlarge your view of specific areas of your worksheet.

3. **Click the Orientation button in the Page Setup group, then click Landscape**

   The paper orientation changes to **landscape**, so the contents will print across the length of the page instead of across the width.
4. **Click the Orientation button in the Page Setup group, then click Portrait**

   The orientation returns to **portrait**, so the contents will print across the width of the page.
5. **Click the Gridlines View check box in the Sheet Options group on the PAGE LAYOUT tab, click the Gridlines Print check box to select it if necessary, then save your work**

   Printing gridlines makes the data easier to read, but the gridlines will not print unless the Gridlines Print check box is checked.

QUICK TIP
To change the active printer, click the current printer in the Printer section in Backstage view, then choose a different printer.

6. **Click the FILE tab, then click Print on the navigation bar**

   The Print tab in Backstage view displays a preview of your worksheet exactly as it will look when it is printed. To the left of the worksheet preview, you can also change a number of document settings and print options. To open the Page Setup dialog box and adjust page layout options, click the Page Setup link in the Settings section. Compare your preview screen to **FIGURE A-18**. You can print from this view by clicking the Print button, or return to the worksheet without printing by clicking the Back button. You can also print an entire workbook from the Backstage view by clicking the Print button in the Settings section, then selecting the active sheet or entire workbook.

QUICK TIP
If the Quick Print button appears on the Quick Access Toolbar, you can print your worksheet using the default settings by clicking it.

7. **Compare your settings to FIGURE A-18, then click the Print button**

   One copy of the worksheet prints.
8. **Submit your work to your instructor as directed, then exit Excel**

Printing worksheet formulas

Sometimes you need to keep a record of all the formulas in a worksheet. You might want to do this to see exactly how you came up with a complex calculation, so you can explain it to others. To prepare a worksheet to show formulas rather than results when printed, open the workbook containing the formulas you want to print. Click the FORMULAS tab, then click the Show Formulas button in the Formula Auditing group to select it. When the Show Formulas button is selected, formulas rather than resulting values are displayed in the worksheet on screen and when printed. (The Show Formulas button is a *toggle*: click it again to hide the formulas.)

FIGURE A-17: Worksheet with Portrait orientation

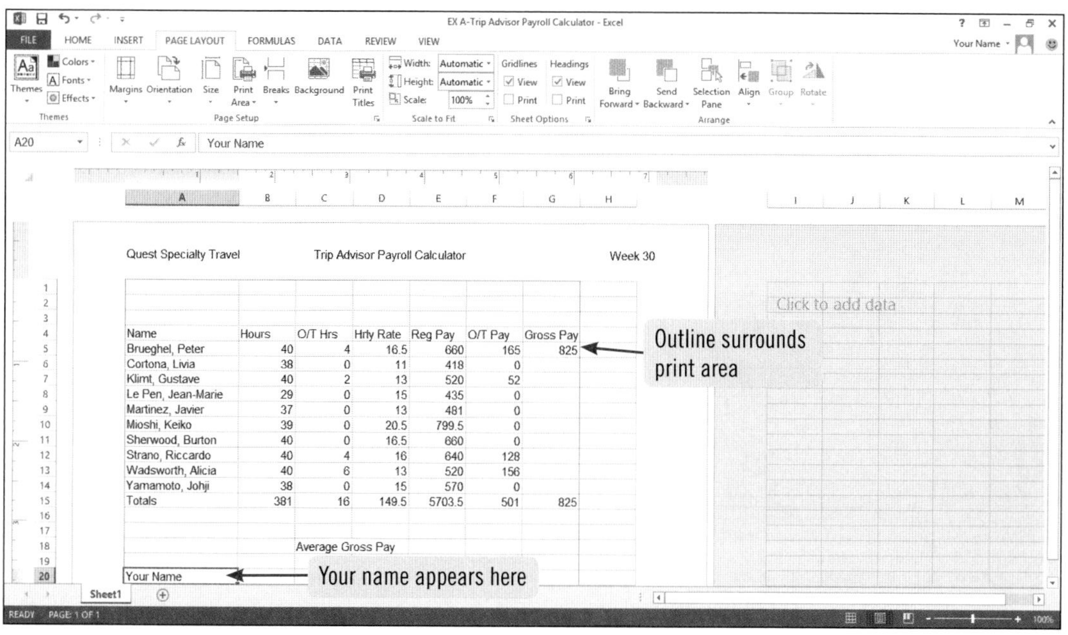

FIGURE A-18: Worksheet in Backstage view

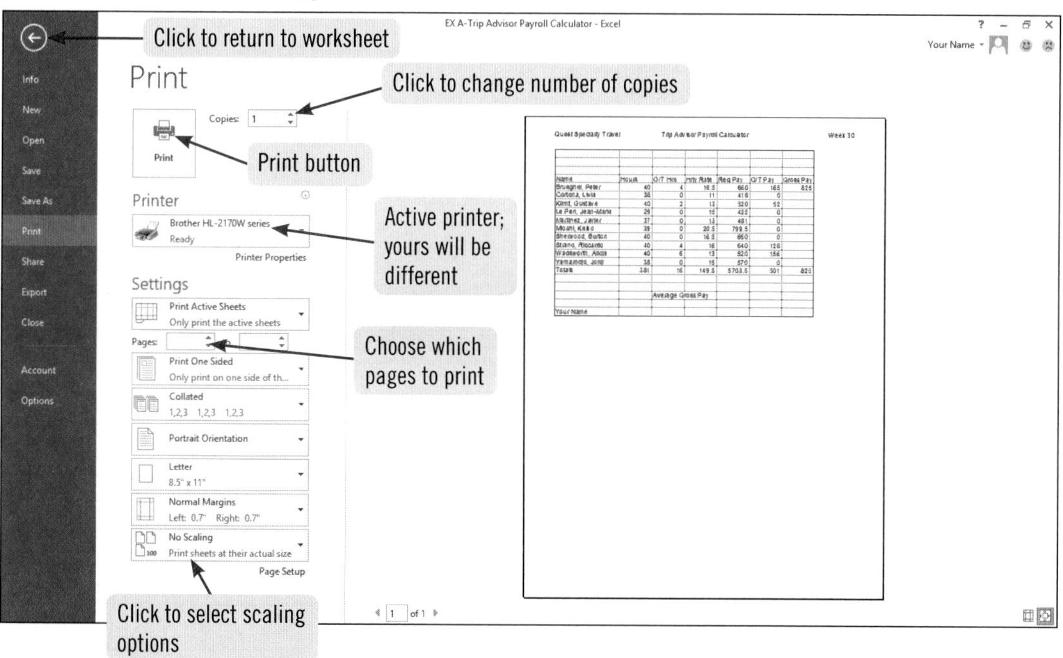

Scaling to fit

If you have a large amount of data that you want to fit to a single sheet of paper, but you don't want to spend a lot of time trying to adjust the margins and other settings, you have several options. You can easily print your work on a single sheet by clicking the No Scaling list arrow in the Settings section on the Print button in Backstage view, then clicking Fit Sheet on One Page. Another method for fitting worksheet content onto one page is to click the PAGE LAYOUT tab, then change the Width and Height settings in the Scale to Fit group each to 1 Page. You can also use the Fit to option in the Page Setup dialog box to fit a worksheet on one page. To open the Page Setup dialog box, click the dialog box launcher in the Scale to Fit group on the PAGE LAYOUT tab, or click the Page Setup link on the Print tab in Backstage view. Make sure the Page tab is selected in the Page Setup dialog box, then click the Fit to option button.

Practice

Put your skills into practice with **SAM Projects**! SAM Projects for this unit can be found online. If you have a SAM account, go to www.cengage.com/sam2013 to download the most recent Project Instruction and Start Files.

Concepts Review

Label the elements of the Excel worksheet window shown in FIGURE A-19.

FIGURE A-19

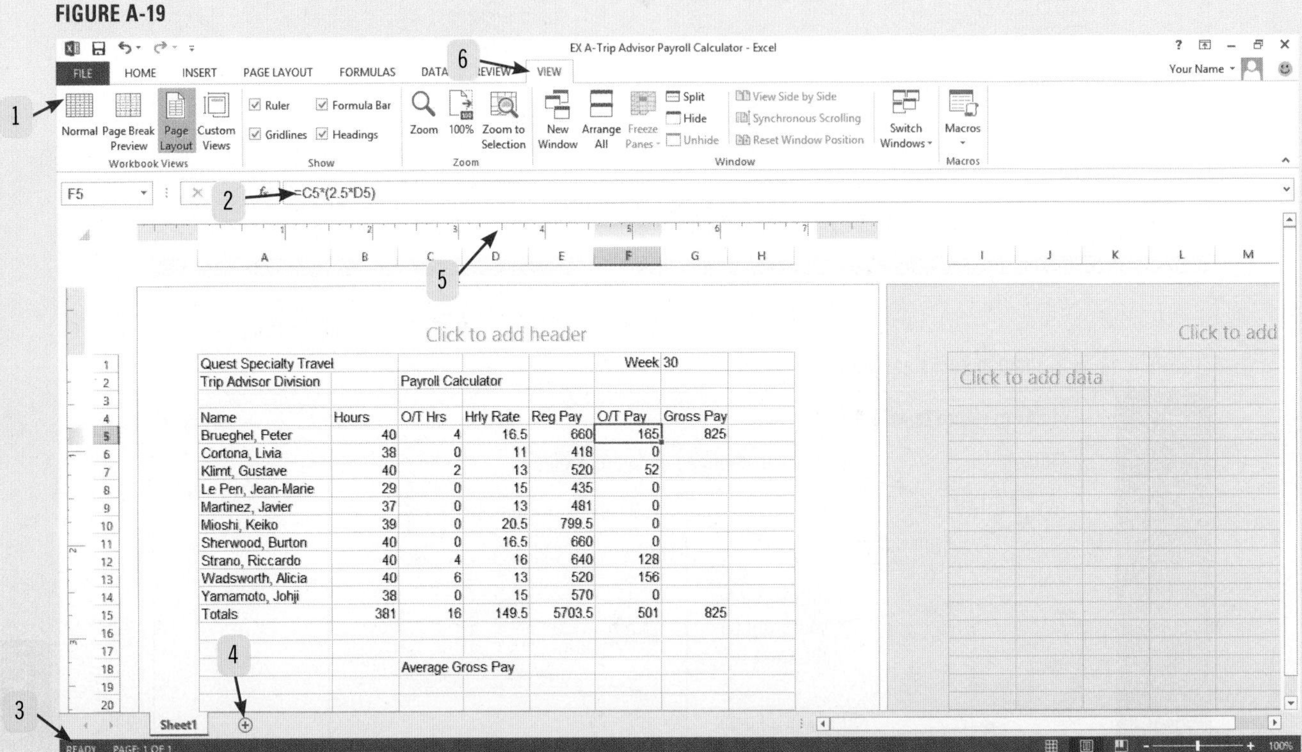

Match each term with the statement that best describes it.

7. Cell	**a.** Part of the Excel program window that displays the active cell address
8. Orientation	**b.** Default view in Excel
9. Normal view	**c.** Direction in which contents of page will print
10. Formula prefix	**d.** Equal sign preceding a formula
11. Workbook	**e.** File consisting of one or more worksheets
12. Name box	**f.** Intersection of a column and a row

Select the best answer from the list of choices.

13. The maximum number of worksheets you can include in a workbook is:

a. 3.

b. 250.

c. 255.

d. Unlimited.

14. Which feature could be used to print a very long worksheet on a single sheet of paper?

a. Show Formulas

b. Scale to fit

c. Page Break Preview

d. Named Ranges

15. Using a cell address in a formula is known as:

a. Formularizing.

b. Prefixing.

c. Cell referencing.

d. Cell mathematics.

16. A selection of multiple cells is called a:

a. Group.

b. Range.

c. Reference.

d. Package.

17. In which area can you see a preview of your worksheet?

a. Page Setup

b. Backstage view

c. Printer Setup

d. VIEW tab

18. Which worksheet view shows how your worksheet will look when printed?

a. Page Layout

b. Data

c. Review

d. View

19. Which key can you press to switch to Edit mode?

a. [F1]

b. [F2]

c. [F4]

d. [F6]

20. In which view can you see the header and footer areas of a worksheet?

a. Normal view

b. Page Layout view

c. Page Break Preview

d. Header/Footer view

21. Which view shows you a reduced view of each page of your worksheet?

a. Normal

b. Page Layout

c. Thumbnail

d. Page Break Preview

Skills Review

1. Understand spreadsheet software.

a. What is the difference between a workbook and a worksheet?

b. Identify five common business uses for electronic spreadsheets.

c. What is what-if analysis?

2. Identify Excel 2013 window components.

a. Start Excel.

b. Open the file EX A-2.xlsx from the location where you store your Data Files, then save it as **EX A-Weather Statistics**.

c. Locate the formula bar, the Sheet tabs, the mode indicator, and the cell pointer.

3. Understand formulas.

a. What is the average high temperature of the listed cities? (*Hint*: Select the range B5:G5 and use the status bar.)

b. What formula would you create to calculate the difference in altitude between Atlanta and Phoenix? Enter your answer (as an equation) in cell D13.

Skills Review (continued)

4. Enter labels and values and use the AutoSum button.

- **a.** Click cell H8, then use the AutoSum button to calculate the total snowfall.
- **b.** Click cell H7, then use the AutoSum button to calculate the total rainfall.
- **c.** Save your changes to the file.

5. Edit cell entries.

- **a.** Use [F2] to correct the spelling of SanteFe in cell G3 (the correct spelling is Santa Fe).
- **b.** Click cell A17, then type your name.
- **c.** Save your changes.

6. Enter and edit a simple formula.

- **a.** Change the value 41 in cell C8 to **52**.
- **b.** Change the value 37 in cell D6 to **35.4**.
- **c.** Select cell J4, then use the fill handle to copy the formula in cell J4 to cells J5:J8.
- **d.** Save your changes.

7. Switch worksheet views.

- **a.** Click the VIEW tab on the Ribbon, then switch to Page Layout view.
- **b.** Add the header **Average Annual Weather Statistics** to the center header text box.
- **c.** Add your name to the right header box.
- **d.** Delete the contents of cell A17.
- **e.** Delete the contents of cell A1.
- **f.** Save your changes.

8. Choose print options.

- **a.** Use the PAGE LAYOUT tab to change the orientation to Portrait.
- **b.** Turn off gridlines by deselecting both the Gridlines View and Gridlines Print check boxes (if necessary) in the Sheet Options group.
- **c.** Scale the worksheet so all the information fits on one page. If necessary, scale the worksheet so all the information fits on one page. (*Hint*: Click the Width list arrow in the Scale to Fit group, click 1 page, click the Height list arrow in the Scale to Fit group, then click 1 page.) Compare your screen to **FIGURE A-20**.
- **d.** Preview the worksheet in Backstage view, then print the worksheet.
- **e.** Save your changes, submit your work to your instructor as directed, then close the workbook and exit Excel.

FIGURE A-20

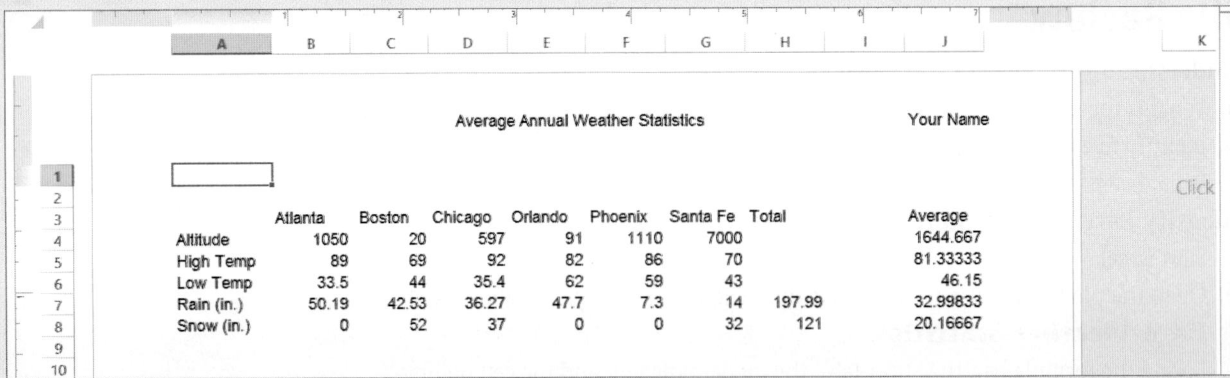

Independent Challenge 1

A local executive relocation company has hired you to help them make the transition to using Excel in their office. They would like to list their properties in a workbook. You've started a worksheet for this project that contains labels but no data.

a. Open the file EX A-3.xlsx from the location where you store your Data Files, then save it as **EX A-Property Listings**.
b. Enter the data shown in **TABLE A-4** in columns A, C, D, and E (the property address information should spill into column B).

TABLE A-4

Property Address	Price	Bedrooms	Bathrooms
1507 Pinon Lane	525000	4	2.5
32 Zanzibar Way	325000	3	4
60 Pottery Lane	475500	2	2
902 Excelsior Drive	310000	4	3

c. Use Page Layout view to create a header with the following components: the title **Property Listings** in the center and your name on the right.
d. Create formulas for totals in cells C6:E6.
e. Save your changes, then compare your worksheet to **FIGURE A-21**.
f. Submit your work to your instructor as directed.
g. Close the worksheet and exit Excel.

FIGURE A-21

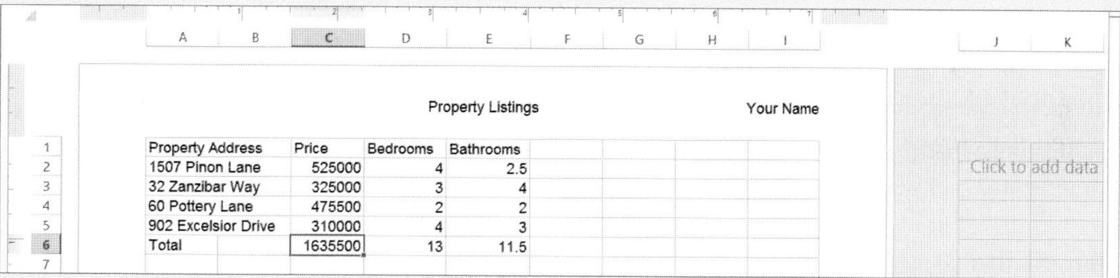

Independent Challenge 2

You are the General Manager for Prestige Import Motors, a small auto parts supplier. Although the company is just five years old, it is expanding rapidly, and you are continually looking for ways to save time. You recently began using Excel to manage and maintain data on inventory and sales, which has greatly helped you to track information accurately and efficiently.

a. Start Excel.
b. Save a new workbook as **EX A-Prestige Import Motors** in the location where you store your Data Files.
c. Switch to an appropriate view, then add a header that contains your name in the left header text box and the title **Prestige Import Motors** in the center header text box.

Independent Challenge 2 (continued)

d. Using **FIGURE A-22** as a guide, create labels for at least seven car manufacturers and sales for three months. Include other labels as appropriate. The car make should be in column A and the months should be in columns B, C, and D. A Total row should be beneath the data, and a Total column should be in column E.

FIGURE A-22

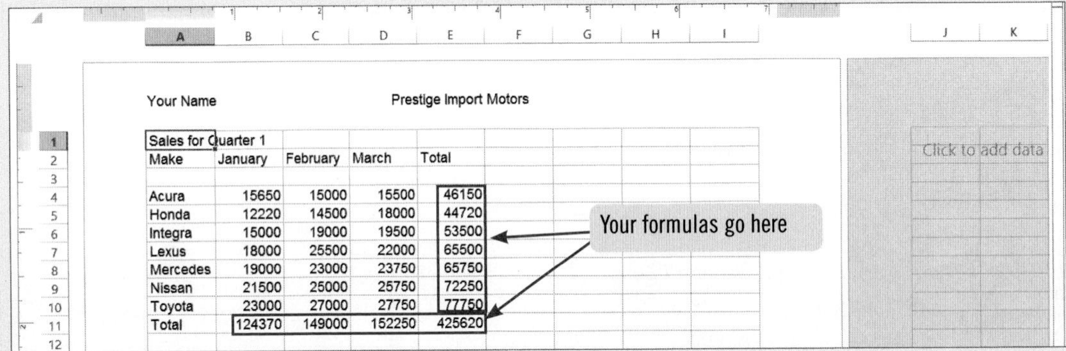

Your Name | Prestige Import Motors

Sales for Quarter 1				
Make	January	February	March	Total
Acura	15650	15000	15500	46150
Honda	12220	14500	18000	44720
Integra	15000	19000	19500	53500
Lexus	18000	25500	22000	65500
Mercedes	19000	23000	23750	65750
Nissan	21500	25000	25750	72250
Toyota	23000	27000	27750	77750
Total	124370	149000	152250	425620

e. Enter values of your choice for the monthly sales for each make.

f. Add formulas in the Total column to calculate total quarterly sales for each make. Add formulas at the bottom of each column of values to calculate the total for that column. Remember that you can use the AutoSum button and the fill handle to save time.

g. Save your changes, preview the worksheet in Backstage view, then submit your work to your instructor as directed.

h. Close the workbook and exit Excel.

Independent Challenge 3

This Independent Challenge requires an Internet connection.

Your office is starting a branch in Paris, and you think it would be helpful to create a worksheet that can be used to convert Fahrenheit temperatures to Celsius, to help employees who are unfamiliar with this type of temperature measurement.

a. Start Excel, then save a blank workbook as **EX A-Temperature Conversions** in the location where you store your Data Files.

b. Create column headings using **FIGURE A-23** as a guide. (*Hint*: You can widen column B by clicking cell B1, clicking the Format button in the Cells group on the HOME tab, then clicking AutoFit Column Width.)

c. Create row labels for each of the seasons.

d. In the appropriate cells, enter what you determine to be a reasonable indoor temperature for each season.

e. Use your Web browser to find out the conversion rate for Fahrenheit to Celsius. (*Hint*: Use your favorite search engine to search on a term such as **temperature conversion formula**.)

f. In the appropriate cells, create a formula that calculates the conversion of the Fahrenheit temperature you entered into a Celsius temperature.

g. In Page Layout View, add your name and the title **Temperature Conversions** to the header.

h. Save your work, then submit your work to your instructor as directed.

i. Close the file, then exit Excel.

Independent Challenge 3 (continued)

FIGURE A-23

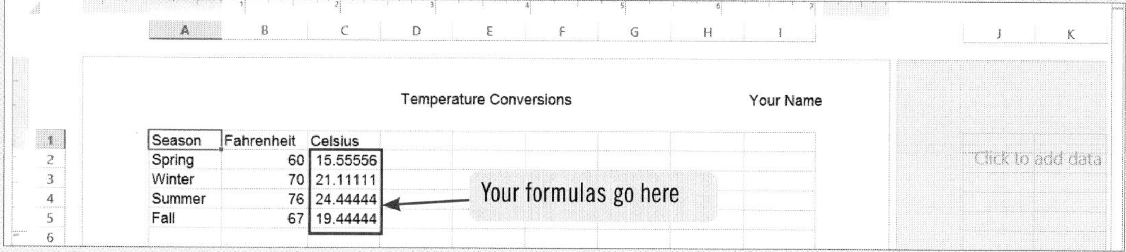

Independent Challenge 4: Explore

You've been asked to take over a project started by a co-worker whose Excel skills are not as good as your own. The assignment was to create a sample invoice for a prospective client. The invoice will include personnel, supplies, and sales tax. Your predecessor started the project, including layout and initial calculations, but she has not made good use of Excel features and has made errors in her calculations. Complete the worksheet by correcting the errors and improving the design. Be prepared to discuss what is wrong with all the items in the worksheet that you change.

a. Start Excel, open the file EX A-4.xlsx from the location where you store your Data Files, then save it as **EX A-Sample Invoice**.

b. There is an error in cell E5: please use the Help feature to find out what is wrong. If you need additional assistance, search Help on *overview of formulas*.

c. Correct the error in the formula in cell E5, then copy the corrected formula into cells E6:E7.

d. Correct the error in the formula in cell E11: then copy the corrected formula into cells E12 and E13.

e. Cells E8 and E14 each contain incorrect formulas. Cell E8 should contain a formula that calculates the total personnel expense and cell E14 should calculate the total supplies used.

f. Cell F17 should contain a formula that adds the Invoice subtotal (total personnel and total supplies).

g. Cell F18 should calculate the sales tax by multiplying the Subtotal (F17) and the sales tax (cell B18).

h. The Invoice Total (cell F19) should contain a formula that adds the Invoice subtotal (cell F17) and Sales tax (cell F18).

i. Switch to the Page Layout view and make the following changes to the Header: Sample Invoice for Week 22 (in the left header box), Client ABC (in the center header box), and your name (in the right header box).

j. Delete the contents of A1:A2, switch to the Normal view, then compare your worksheet to **FIGURE A-24**.

k. Save your work.

FIGURE A-24

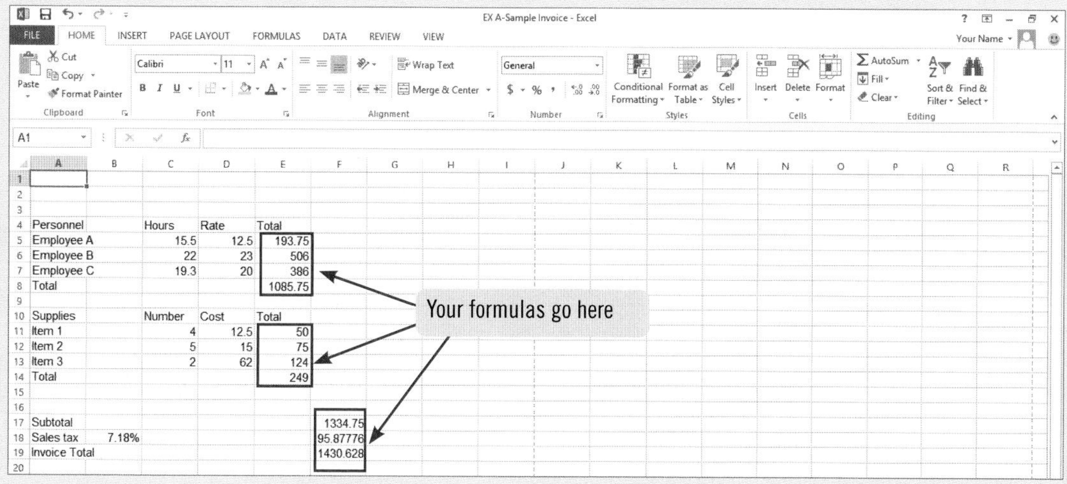

Visual Workshop

Open the file EX A-5.xlsx from the location where you store your Data Files, then save it as **EX A-Inventory Items**. Using the skills you learned in this unit, modify your worksheet so it matches **FIGURE A-25**. Enter formulas in cells D4 through D13 and in cells B14 and C14. Use the AutoSum button and fill handle to make entering your formulas easier. Add your name in the left header text box, then print one copy of the worksheet with the formulas displayed.

FIGURE A-25

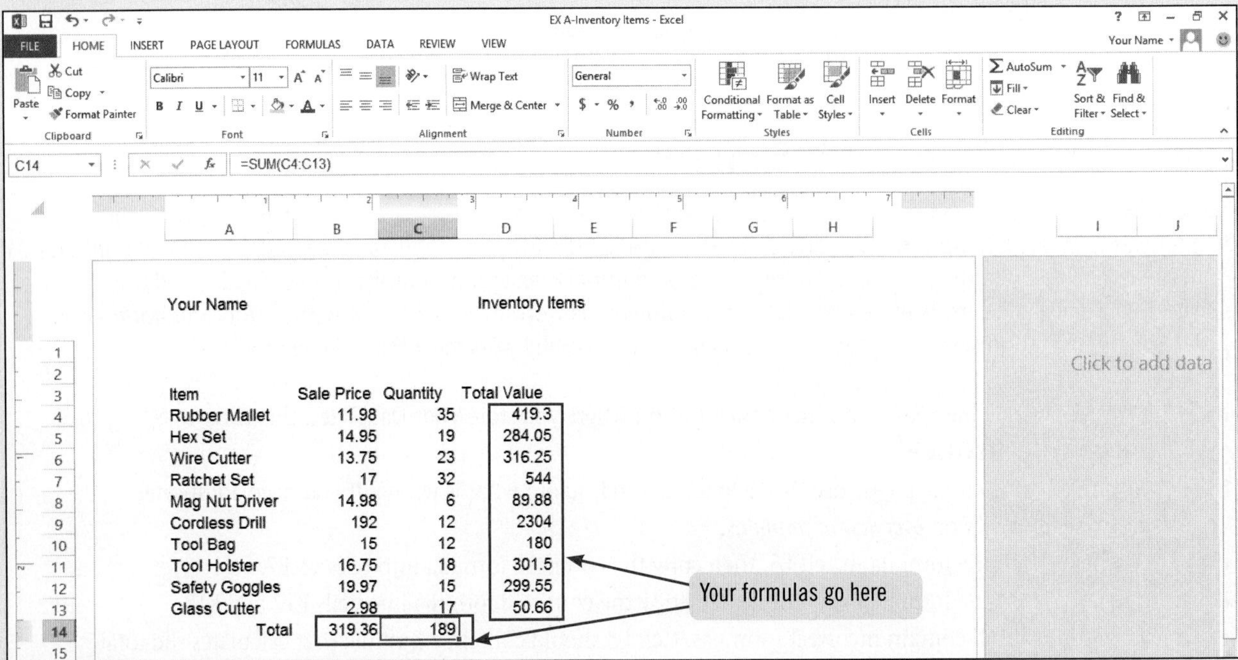

Working with Formulas and Functions

CASE Grace Wong, vice president of finance at Quest Specialty Travel, needs to analyze tour expenses for the current year. She has asked you to prepare a worksheet that summarizes this expense data and includes some statistical analysis. She would also like you to perform some what-if analysis, to see what quarterly expenses would look like with various projected increases.

Unit Objectives

After completing this unit, you will be able to:

- Create a complex formula
- Insert a function
- Type a function
- Copy and move cell entries
- Understand relative and absolute cell references
- Copy formulas with relative cell references
- Copy formulas with absolute cell references
- Round a value with a function

Files You Will Need

EX B-1.xlsx
EX B-2.xlsx
EX B-3.xlsx
EX B-4.xlsx

©Katerina Havelkova/Shutterstock

Create a Complex Formula

Learning Outcomes
- Create a complex formula by pointing
- Use the fill handle and Auto Fill

A **complex formula** is one that uses more than one arithmetic operator. You might, for example, need to create a formula that uses addition and multiplication. In formulas containing more than one arithmetic operator, Excel uses the standard **order of precedence** rules to determine which operation to perform first. You can change the order of precedence in a formula by using parentheses around the part you want to calculate first. For example, the formula =4+2*5 equals 14, because the order of precedence dictates that multiplication is performed before addition. However, the formula =(4+2)*5 equals 30, because the parentheses cause 4+2 to be calculated first. CASE *You want to create a formula that calculates a 20% increase in tour expenses.*

STEPS

1. **Start Excel, open the file EX B-1.xlsx from the location where you store your Data Files, then save it as EX B-Tour Expense Analysis**
2. **Select the range B4:B11, click the Quick Analysis tool, then click the Totals tab**
   The Totals tab in the Quick Analysis tool displays commonly used functions, as seen in **FIGURE B-1**.
3. **Click the AutoSum button in the Quick Analysis tool**
   The newly calculated value displays in cell B12 and has a darker appearance than the figures in the selected range.
4. **Click cell B12, then drag the fill handle to cell E12**
   The formula in cell B12 is copied to cells C12:E12. The copied cells have the same dark appearance as that of cell B12.

QUICK TIP
When the mode indicator on the status bar says "Point," cells you click are added to the formula.

5. **Click cell B14, type =, click cell B12, then type +**
   In this first part of the formula, you are using a reference to the total expenses for Quarter 1.
6. **Click cell B12, then type *.2**
   The second part of this formula adds a 20% increase (B12*.2) to the original value of the cell (the total expenses for Quarter 1).
7. **Click the Enter button on the formula bar**
   The result, 41789.556, appears in cell B14.
8. **Press [Tab], type =, click cell C12, type +, click cell C12, type *.2, then click**
   The result, 41352.912, appears in cell C14.

QUICK TIP
You can also copy the formulas by selecting the range C14:E14, clicking the Fill button in the Editing group on the HOME tab, then clicking Right.

9. **Drag the fill handle from cell C14 to cell E14**
   The calculated values appear in the selected range, as shown in **FIGURE B-2**. Dragging the fill handle on a cell copies the cell's contents or continues a series of data (such as Quarter 1, Quarter 2, etc.) into adjacent cells. This option is called **Auto Fill**.
10. **Save your work**

Using Apps for Office to improve worksheet functionality

Excel has more functionality than simple and complex math computations. Using the Apps for Office feature (found in the Apps group in the INSERT tab), you can insert an app into your worksheet that accesses the web and adds functionality to your work. Many of the available apps are free and can be used to create an email, appointment, meeting, contact, or task, or be a reference source, such as the Mini Calendar and Date Picker. When you click the Apps for Office button, you'll see any Recently Used Apps. Click See All to display the featured apps and to go to the Office store to view available apps. When you find an app you want, make sure you're logged in to Office.com (you may need to log in again), click the app, click Add, then follow the prompts to download the app. Click the Apps for Office button, click See All, click the app you just added, then click Insert. The app will display as an embedded object in your worksheet and will also appear in the Recently Used Apps palette when you click the Apps for Office button.

FIGURE B-1: Totals tab in the Quick Analysis tool

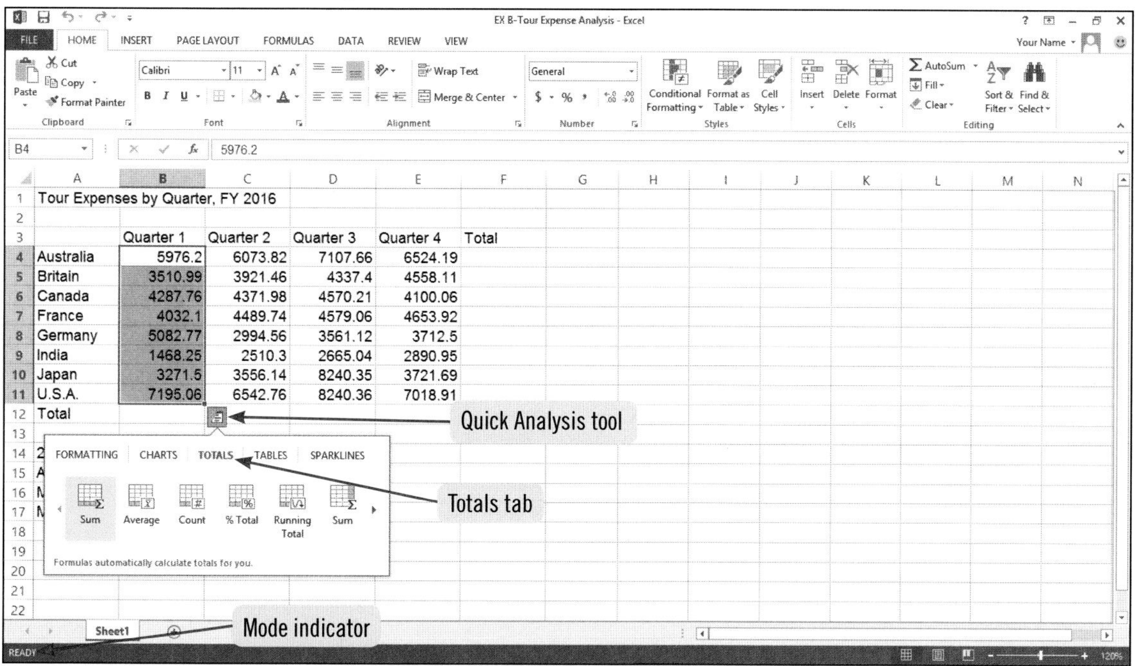

FIGURE B-2: Complex formulas in worksheet

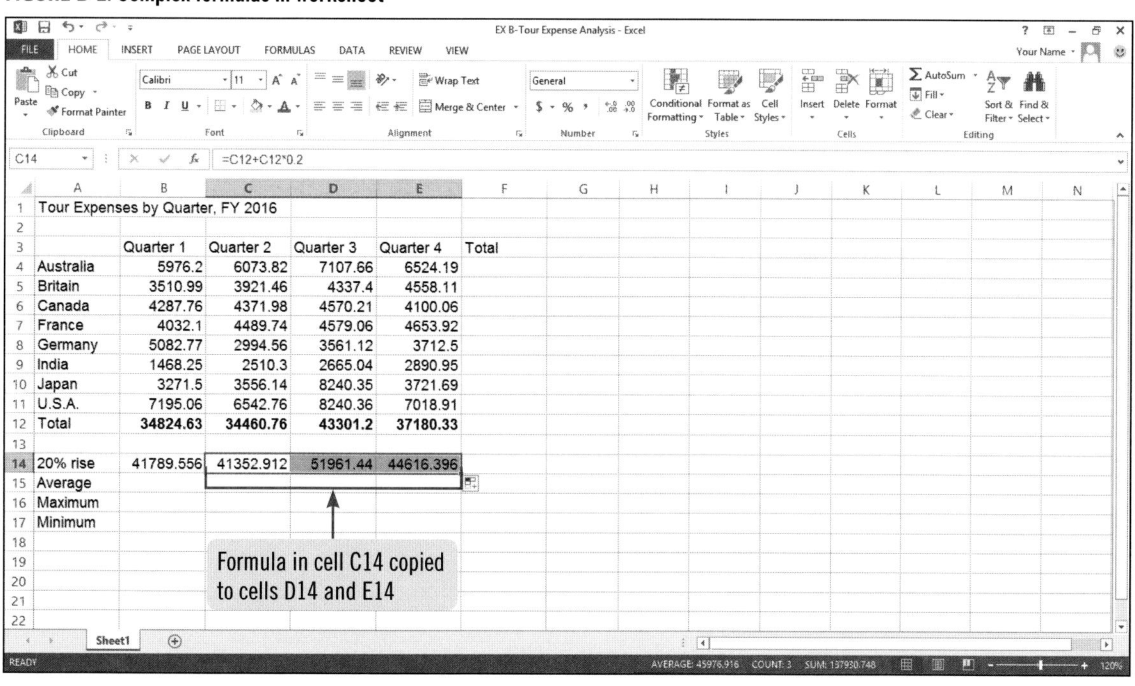

Reviewing the order of precedence

When you work with formulas that contain more than one operator, the order of precedence is very important because it affects the final value. If a formula contains two or more operators, such as 4+.55/4000*25, Excel performs the calculations in a particular sequence based on the following rules: Operations inside parentheses are calculated before any other operations. Reference operators (such as ranges) are calculated first. Exponents are calculated next, then any multiplication and division—progressing from left to right. Finally, addition and subtraction are calculated from left to right. In the example 4+.55/4000*25, Excel performs the arithmetic operations by first dividing .55 by 4000, then multiplying the result by 25, then adding 4. You can change the order of calculations by using parentheses. For example, in the formula (4+.55)/4000*25, Excel would first add 4 and .55, then divide that amount by 4000, then finally multiply by 25.

Insert a Function

Learning Outcomes
- Use the Insert Function button
- Select a range for use in a function
- Select a function from the AutoSum list arrow

Functions are predefined worksheet formulas that enable you to perform complex calculations easily. You can use the Insert Function button on the formula bar to choose a function from a dialog box. You can quickly insert the SUM function using the AutoSum button on the Ribbon, or you can click the AutoSum list arrow to enter other frequently used functions, such as AVERAGE. You can also use the Quick Analysis tool to calculate commonly used functions. Functions are organized into categories, such as Financial, Date & Time, and Statistical, based on their purposes. You can insert a function on its own or as part of another formula. For example, you have used the SUM function on its own to add a range of cells. You could also use the SUM function within a formula that adds a range of cells and then multiplies the total by a decimal. If you use a function alone, it always begins with an equal sign (=) as the formula prefix. **CASE** *You need to calculate the average expenses for the first quarter of the year, and decide to use a function to do so.*

STEPS

QUICK TIP
When using the Insert Function button or the AutoSum list arrow, it is not necessary to type the equal sign (=); Excel adds it as necessary.

QUICK TIP
To learn about a function, click it in the Select a function list. The arguments and format required for the function appear below the list.

QUICK TIP
When selecting a range, remember to select all the cells between and including the two references in the range.

1. **Click cell B15**

   This is the cell where you want to enter the calculation that averages expenses per country for the first quarter. You want to use the Insert Function dialog box to enter this function.

2. **Click the Insert Function button on the formula bar**

   An equal sign (=) is inserted in the active cell and in the formula bar, and the Insert Function dialog box opens, as shown in **FIGURE B-3**. In this dialog box, you specify the function you want to use by clicking it in the Select a function list. The Select a function list initially displays recently used functions. If you don't see the function you want, you can click the Or select a category list arrow to choose the desired category. If you're not sure which category to choose, you can type the function name or a description in the Search for a function field. The AVERAGE function is a statistical function, but you don't need to open the Statistical category because this function already appears in the Most Recently Used category.

3. **Click AVERAGE in the Select a function list if necessary, read the information that appears under the list, then click OK**

   The Function Arguments dialog box opens, in which you define the range of cells you want to average.

4. **Click the Collapse button in the Number1 field of the Function Arguments dialog box, select the range B4:B11 in the worksheet, then click the Expand button in the Function Arguments dialog box**

   Clicking the Collapse button minimizes the dialog box so you can select cells in the worksheet. When you click the Expand button, the dialog box is restored, as shown in **FIGURE B-4**. You can also begin dragging in the worksheet to automatically minimize the dialog box; after you select the desired range, the dialog box is restored.

5. **Click OK**

   The Function Arguments dialog box closes, and the calculated value is displayed in cell B15. The average expenses per country for Quarter 1 is 4353.0788.

6. **Click cell C15, click the AutoSum list arrow in the Editing group on the HOME tab, then click Average**

   A ScreenTip beneath cell C15 displays the arguments needed to complete the function. The text "number1" is shown in boldface type, telling you that the next step is to supply the first cell in the group you want to average. You want to average a range of cells.

7. **Select the range C4:C11 in the worksheet, then click the Enter button on the formula bar**

   The average expenses per country for the second quarter appears in cell C15.

8. **Drag the fill handle from cell C15 to cell E15**

   The formula in cell C15 is copied to the rest of the selected range, as shown in **FIGURE B-5**.

9. **Save your work**

FIGURE B-3: Insert Function dialog box

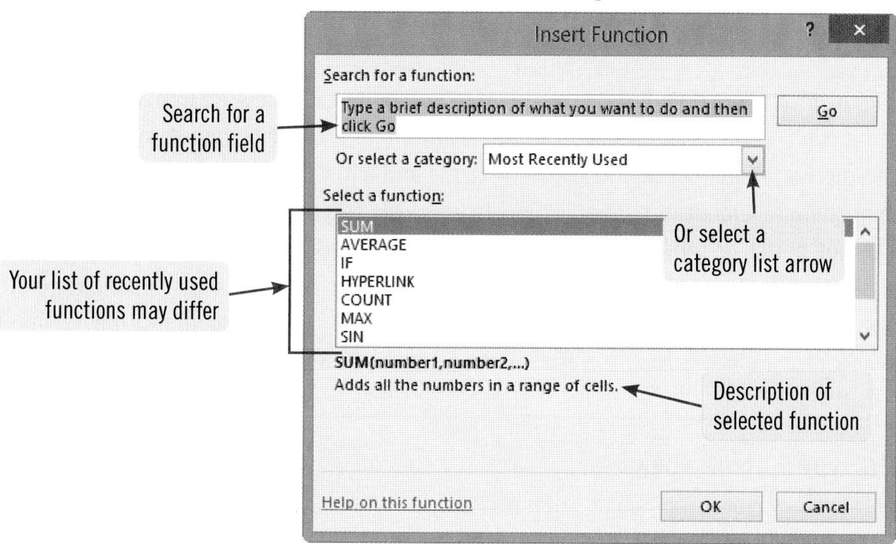

FIGURE B-4: Expanded Function Arguments dialog box

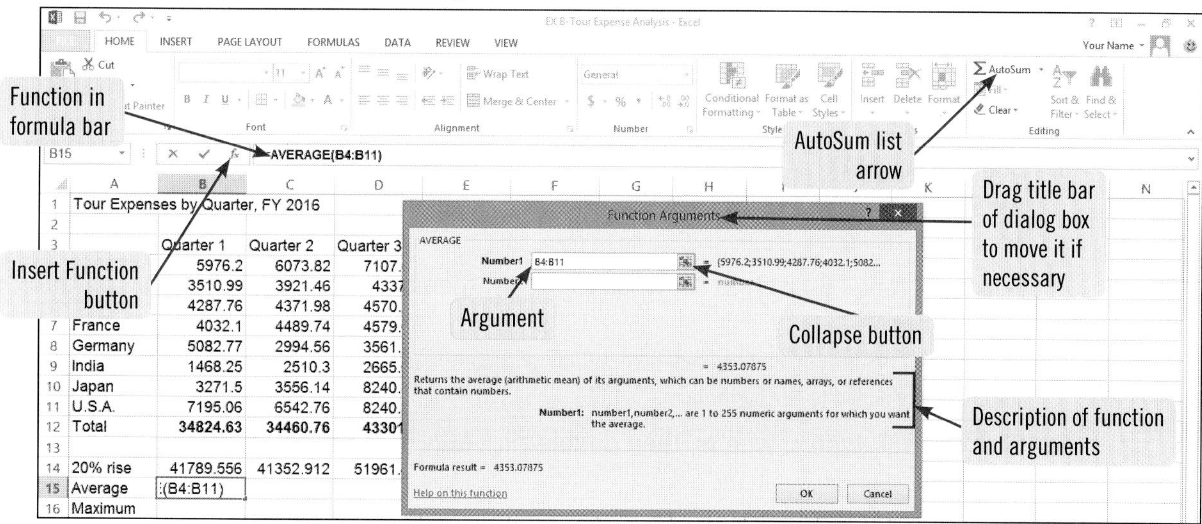

FIGURE B-5: Average functions used in worksheet

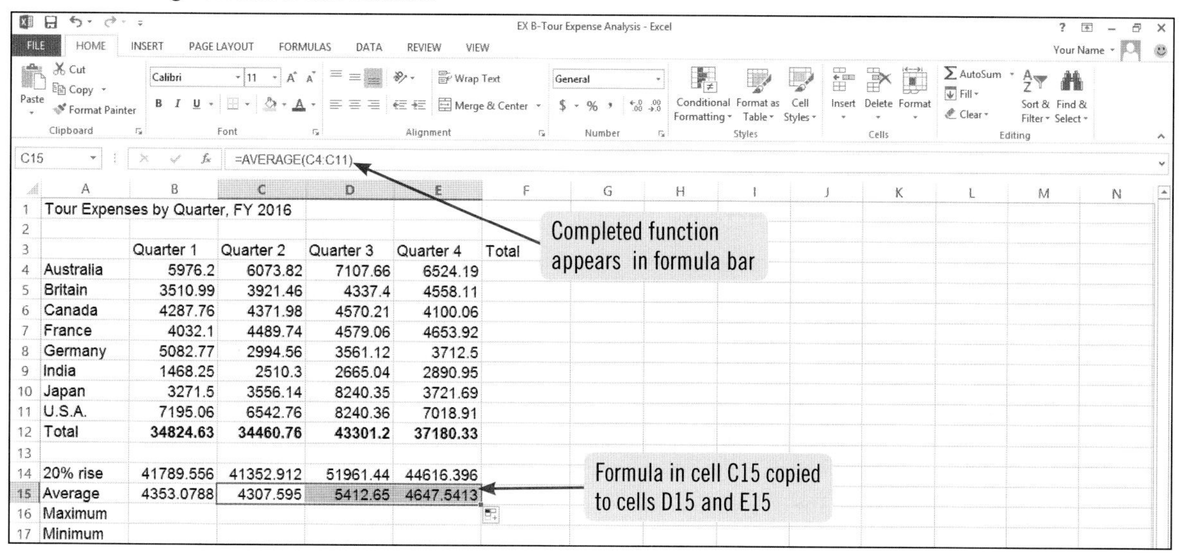

	A	B	C	D	E	F
1	Tour Expenses by Quarter, FY 2016					
2						
3		Quarter 1	Quarter 2	Quarter 3	Quarter 4	Total
4	Australia	5976.2	6073.82	7107.66	6524.19	
5	Britain	3510.99	3921.46	4337.4	4558.11	
6	Canada	4287.76	4371.98	4570.21	4100.06	
7	France	4032.1	4489.74	4579.06	4653.92	
8	Germany	5082.77	2994.56	3561.12	3712.5	
9	India	1468.25	2510.3	2665.04	2890.95	
10	Japan	3271.5	3556.14	8240.35	3721.69	
11	U.S.A.	7195.06	6542.76	8240.36	7018.91	
12	Total	**34824.63**	**34460.76**	**43301.2**	**37180.33**	
13						
14	20% rise	41789.556	41352.912	51961.44	44616.396	
15	Average	4353.0788	4307.595	5412.65	4647.5413	
16	Maximum					
17	Minimum					

Type a Function

Learning Outcomes
- Select a function by typing
- Use AutoComplete to copy formulas

In addition to using the Insert Function dialog box, the AutoSum button, or the AutoSum list arrow on the Ribbon to enter a function, you can manually type the function into a cell and then complete the arguments needed. This method requires that you know the name and initial characters of the function, but it can be faster than opening several dialog boxes. Experienced Excel users often prefer this method, but it is only an alternative, not better or more correct than any other method. Excel's Formula AutoComplete feature makes it easier to enter function names by typing, because it suggests functions depending on the first letters you type. **CASE** *You want to calculate the maximum and minimum quarterly expenses in your worksheet, and you decide to manually enter these statistical functions.*

STEPS

1. **Click cell B16, type =, then type m**
   Because you are manually typing this function, it is necessary to begin with the equal sign (=). The Formula AutoComplete feature displays a list of function names beginning with "M" beneath cell B16. Once you type an equal sign in a cell, each letter you type acts as a trigger to activate the Formula AutoComplete feature. This feature minimizes the amount of typing you need to do to enter a function and reduces typing and syntax errors.
2. **Click MAX in the list**
   Clicking any function in the Formula AutoComplete list opens a ScreenTip next to the list that describes the function.
3. **Double-click MAX**
   The function is inserted in the cell, and a ScreenTip appears beneath the cell to help you complete the formula. See **FIGURE B-6**.
4. **Select the range B4:B11, as shown in FIGURE B-7, then click the Enter button ✓ on the formula bar**
   The result, 7195.06, appears in cell B16. When you completed the entry, the closing parenthesis was automatically added to the formula.
5. **Click cell B17, type =, type m, then double-click MIN in the list of function names**
   The MIN function appears in the cell.
6. **Select the range B4:B11, then press [Enter]**
   The result, 1468.25, appears in cell B17.
7. **Select the range B16:B17, then drag the fill handle from cell B17 to cell E17**
   The maximum and minimum values for all of the quarters appear in the selected range, as shown in **FIGURE B-8**.
8. **Save your work**

Using the COUNT and COUNTA functions

When you select a range, a count of cells in the range that are not blank appears in the status bar. For example, if you select the range A1:A5 and only cells A1, A4 and A5 contain data, the status bar displays "Count: 3." To count nonblank cells more precisely, or to incorporate these calculations in a worksheet, you can use the COUNT and COUNTA functions. The COUNT function returns the number of cells in a range that contain numeric data, including numbers, dates, and formulas. The COUNTA function returns the number of cells in a range that contain any data at all, including numeric data, labels, and even a blank space. For example, the formula =COUNT(A1:A5) returns the number of cells in the range that contain numeric data, and the formula =COUNTA(A1:A5) returns the number of cells in the range that are not empty. If you use the COUNT functions in the Quick Analysis tool, the calculation is entered in the cell immediately beneath the selected range.

FIGURE B-6: MAX function in progress

13					
14	20% rise	41789.556	41352.912	51961.44	44616.396
15	Average	4353.0788	4307.595	5412.65	4647.5413
16	Maximum	=MAX(			
17	Minimum	MAX(number1, [number2], ...)			

FIGURE B-7: Completing the MAX function

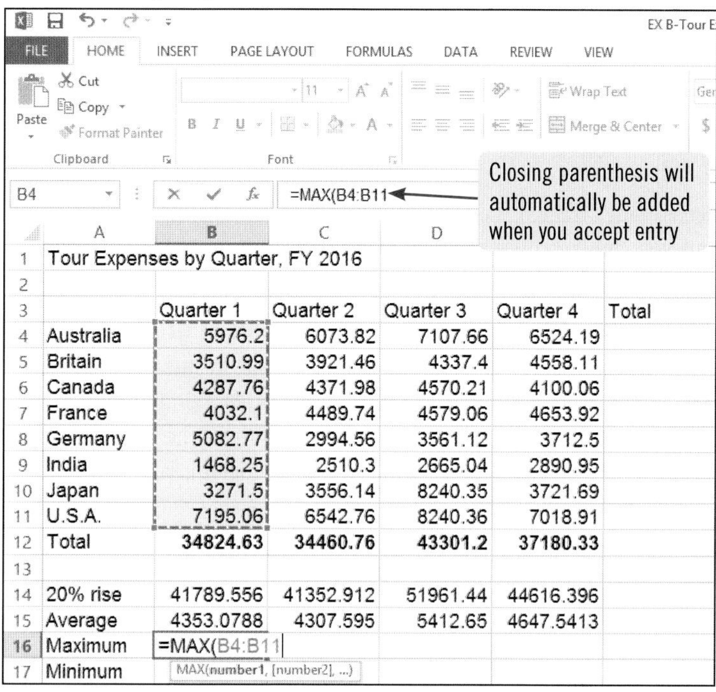

	A	B	C	D	E	F
1	Tour Expenses by Quarter, FY 2016					
2						
3		Quarter 1	Quarter 2	Quarter 3	Quarter 4	Total
4	Australia	5976.2	6073.82	7107.66	6524.19	
5	Britain	3510.99	3921.46	4337.4	4558.11	
6	Canada	4287.76	4371.98	4570.21	4100.06	
7	France	4032.1	4489.74	4579.06	4653.92	
8	Germany	5082.77	2994.56	3561.12	3712.5	
9	India	1468.25	2510.3	2665.04	2890.95	
10	Japan	3271.5	3556.14	8240.35	3721.69	
11	U.S.A.	7195.06	6542.76	8240.36	7018.91	
12	Total	**34824.63**	**34460.76**	**43301.2**	**37180.33**	
13						
14	20% rise	41789.556	41352.912	51961.44	44616.396	
15	Average	4353.0788	4307.595	5412.65	4647.5413	
16	Maximum	=MAX(B4:B11				
17	Minimum	MAX(number1, [number2], ...)				

FIGURE B-8: Completed MAX and MIN functions

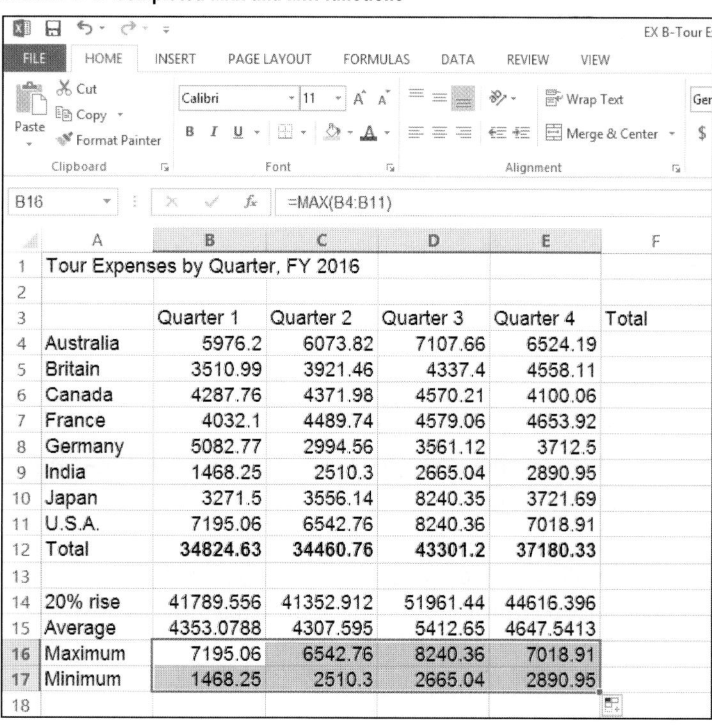

	A	B	C	D	E	F
1	Tour Expenses by Quarter, FY 2016					
2						
3		Quarter 1	Quarter 2	Quarter 3	Quarter 4	Total
4	Australia	5976.2	6073.82	7107.66	6524.19	
5	Britain	3510.99	3921.46	4337.4	4558.11	
6	Canada	4287.76	4371.98	4570.21	4100.06	
7	France	4032.1	4489.74	4579.06	4653.92	
8	Germany	5082.77	2994.56	3561.12	3712.5	
9	India	1468.25	2510.3	2665.04	2890.95	
10	Japan	3271.5	3556.14	8240.35	3721.69	
11	U.S.A.	7195.06	6542.76	8240.36	7018.91	
12	Total	**34824.63**	**34460.76**	**43301.2**	**37180.33**	
13						
14	20% rise	41789.556	41352.912	51961.44	44616.396	
15	Average	4353.0788	4307.595	5412.65	4647.5413	
16	Maximum	7195.06	6542.76	8240.36	7018.91	
17	Minimum	1468.25	2510.3	2665.04	2890.95	
18						

Copy and Move Cell Entries

Learning Outcomes
- Copy a range to the Clipboard
- Paste a Clipboard entry
- Empty cell contents
- Copy cell contents

There are three ways you can copy or move cells and ranges (or the contents within them) from one location to another: the Cut, Copy, and Paste buttons on the HOME tab on the Ribbon; the fill handle in the lower-right corner of the active cell or range; or the drag-and-drop feature. When you copy cells, the original data remains in the original location; when you cut or move cells, the original data is deleted from its original location. You can also cut, copy, and paste cells or ranges from one worksheet to another. **CASE** *In addition to the 20% rise in tour expenses, you also want to show a 30% rise. Rather than retype this information, you copy and move the labels in these cells.*

STEPS

QUICK TIP
To cut or copy selected cell contents, activate the cell, then select the characters within the cell that you want to cut or copy.

1. **Select the range B3:E3, then click the Copy button in the Clipboard group on the HOME tab**
   The selected range (B3:E3) is copied to the **Clipboard**, a temporary Windows storage area that holds the selections you copy or cut. A moving border surrounds the selected range until you press [Esc] or copy an additional item to the Clipboard.
2. **Click the dialog box launcher in the Clipboard group**
   The Office Clipboard opens in the Clipboard task pane, as shown in **FIGURE B-9**. When you copy or cut an item, it is cut or copied both to the Clipboard provided by Windows and to the Office Clipboard. Unlike the Windows Clipboard, which holds just one item at a time, the Office Clipboard contains up to 24 of the most recently cut or copied items from any Office program. Your Clipboard task pane may contain more items than shown in the figure.

QUICK TIP
Once the Office Clipboard contains 24 items, the oldest existing item is automatically deleted each time you add an item.

3. **Click cell B19, then click the Paste button in the Clipboard group**
   A copy of the contents of range B3:E3 is pasted into the range B19:E19. When pasting an item from the Office Clipboard or Clipboard into a worksheet, you only need to specify the upper-left cell of the range where you want to paste the selection. Notice that the information you copied remains in the original range B3:E3; if you had cut instead of copied, the information would have been deleted from its original location once it was pasted.
4. **Press [Delete]**
   The selected cells are empty. You have decided to paste the cells in a different row. You can repeatedly paste an item from the Office Clipboard as many times as you like, as long as the item remains in the Office Clipboard.

QUICK TIP
You can also close the Office Clipboard pane by clicking the dialog box launcher in the Clipboard group.

5. **Click cell B20, click the first item in the Office Clipboard, then click the Close button on the Clipboard task pane**
   Cells B20:E20 contain the copied labels.
6. **Click cell A14, press and hold [Ctrl], point to any edge of the cell until the pointer changes to the copy pointer, drag cell A14 to cell A21, release the mouse button, then release [Ctrl]**
   The copy pointer continues to appear as you drag, as shown in **FIGURE B-10**. When you release the mouse button, the contents of cell A14 are copied to cell A21.
7. **Click to the right of 2 in the formula bar, press [Backspace], type 3, then press [Enter]**
8. **Click cell B21, type =, click cell B12, type *1.3, click the Enter button on the formula bar, then save your work**
   This new formula calculates a 30% increase of the expenses for Quarter 1, though using a different method from what you previously used. Anything you multiply by 1.3 returns an amount that is 130% of the original amount, or a 30% increase. Compare your screen to **FIGURE B-11**.

FIGURE B-9: Copied data in Office Clipboard

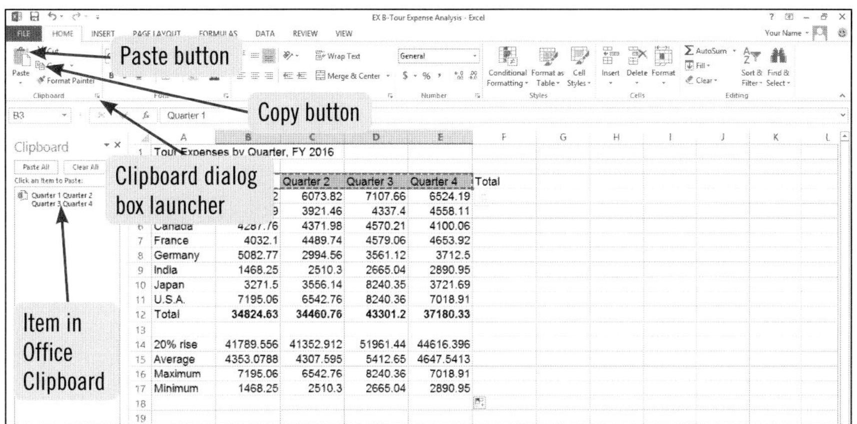

FIGURE B-10: Copying cell contents with drag-and-drop

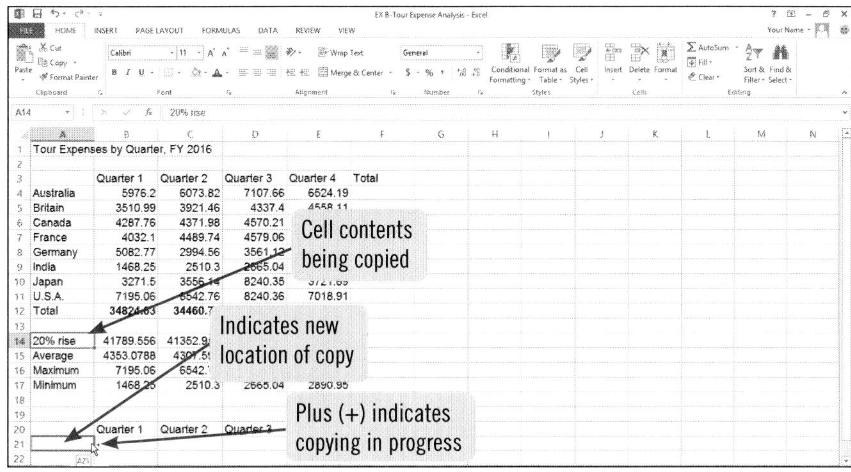

FIGURE B-11: Formula entered to calculate a 30% increase

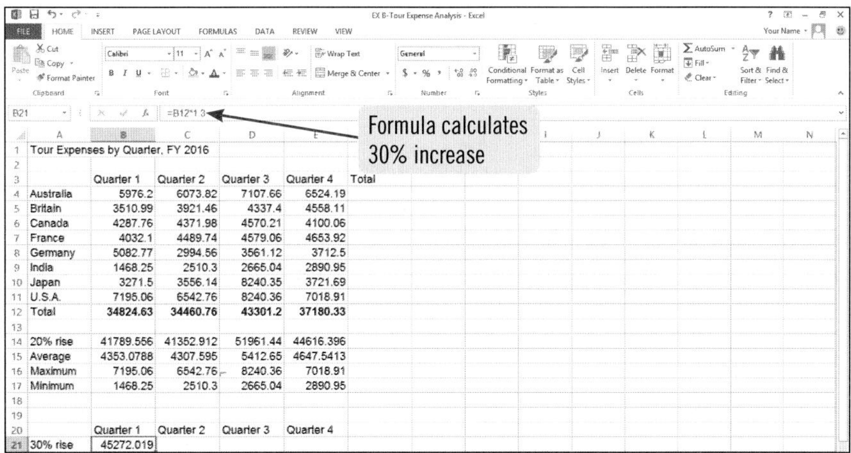

Inserting and deleting selected cells

As you add formulas to your workbook, you may need to insert or delete cells. When you do this, Excel automatically adjusts cell references to reflect their new locations. To insert cells, click the Insert list arrow in the Cells group on the HOME tab, then click Insert Cells. The Insert dialog box opens, asking if you want to insert a cell and move the current active cell down or to the right of the new one. To delete one or more selected cells, click the Delete list arrow in the Cells group, click Delete Cells, and in the Delete dialog box, indicate which way you want to move the adjacent cells. When using this option, be careful not to disturb row or column alignment that may be necessary to maintain the accuracy of cell references in the worksheet. Click the Insert button or Delete button in the Cells group to insert or delete a single cell.

Understand Relative and Absolute Cell References

Learning Outcomes
- Identify cell referencing
- Identify when to use absolute or relative cell references

As you work in Excel, you may want to reuse formulas in different parts of a worksheet to reduce the amount of data you have to retype. For example, you might want to include a what-if analysis in one part of a worksheet showing a set of sales projections if sales increase by 10%. To include another analysis in another part of the worksheet showing projections if sales increase by 50%, you can copy the formulas from one section to another and simply change the "1" to a "5". But when you copy formulas, it is important to make sure that they refer to the correct cells. To do this, you need to understand the difference between relative and absolute cell references. **CASE** *You plan to reuse formulas in different parts of your worksheets, so you want to understand relative and absolute cell references.*

DETAILS

Consider the following when using relative and absolute cell references:

- **Use relative references when you want to preserve the relationship to the formula location**

  When you create a formula that references another cell, Excel normally does not "record" the exact cell address for the cell being referenced in the formula. Instead, it looks at the relationship that cell has to the cell containing the formula. For example, in **FIGURE B-12**, cell F5 contains the formula: =SUM(B5:E5). When Excel retrieves values to calculate the formula in cell F5, it actually looks for "the four cells to the left of the formula," which in this case is cells B5:E5. This way, if you copy the cell to a new location, such as cell F6, the results will reflect the new formula location, and will automatically retrieve the values in cells B6, C6, D6, and E6. These are **relative cell references**, because Excel is recording the input cells *in relation to* or *relative to* the formula cell.

  In most cases, you want to use relative cell references when copying or moving, so this is the Excel default. In **FIGURE B-12**, the formulas in F5:F12 and in B13:F13 contain relative cell references. They total the "four cells to the left of" or the "eight cells above" the formulas.

- **Use absolute cell references when you want to preserve the exact cell address in a formula**

  There are times when you want Excel to retrieve formula information from a specific cell, and you don't want the cell address in the formula to change when you copy it to a new location. For example, you might have a price in a specific cell that you want to use in all formulas, regardless of their location. If you use relative cell referencing, the formula results would be incorrect, because Excel would use a different cell every time you copy the formula. Therefore you need to use an **absolute cell reference**, which is a reference that does not change when you copy the formula.

  You create an absolute cell reference by placing a $ (dollar sign) in front of both the column letter and the row number of the cell address. You can either type the dollar sign when typing the cell address in a formula (for example, "=C12*$B$16"), or you can select a cell address on the formula bar and then press [F4] and the dollar signs are added automatically. **FIGURE B-13** shows formulas containing both absolute and relative references. The formulas in cells B19 to E26 use absolute cell references to refer to a potential sales increase of 50%, shown in cell B16.

FIGURE B-12: Formulas containing relative references

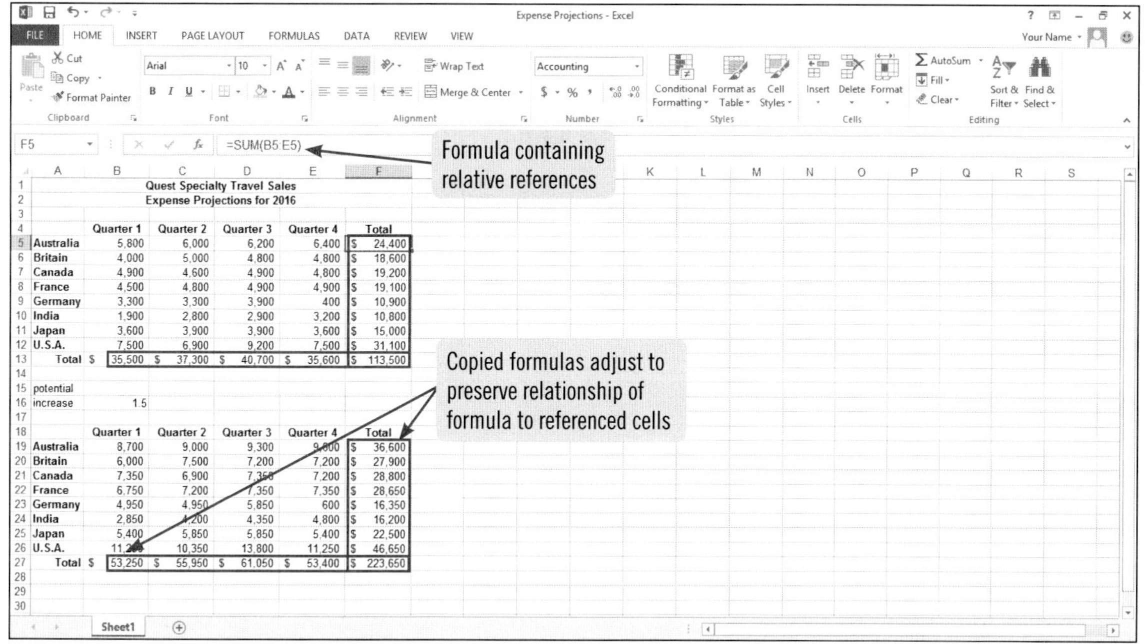

Formula containing relative references
Copied formulas adjust to preserve relationship of formula to referenced cells

FIGURE B-13: Formulas containing absolute and relative references

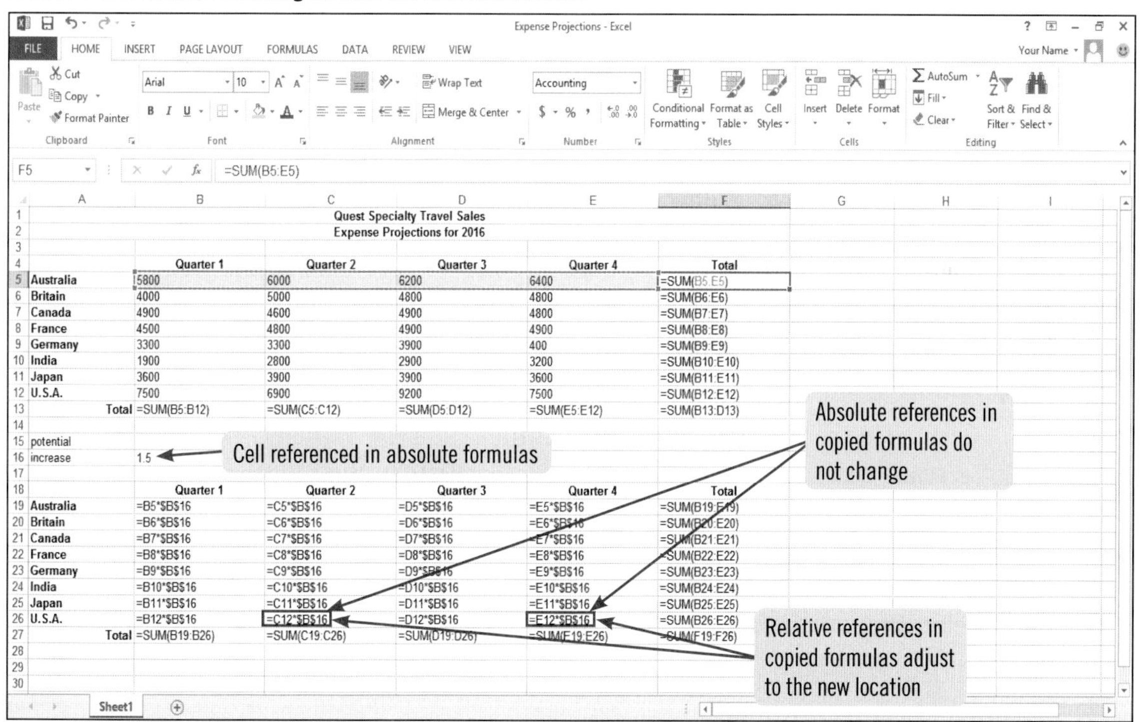

Cell referenced in absolute formulas
Absolute references in copied formulas do not change
Relative references in copied formulas adjust to the new location

Excel 2013

Using a mixed reference

Sometimes when you copy a formula, you want to change the row reference, but keep the column reference the same. This type of cell referencing combines elements of both absolute and relative referencing and is called a **mixed reference**. For example, when copied, a formula containing the mixed reference C$14 would change the column letter relative to its new location, but not the row number. In the mixed reference $C14, the column letter would not change, but the row number would be updated relative to its location. Like an absolute reference, a mixed reference can be created by pressing the [F4] function key with the cell reference selected. With each press of the [F4] key, you cycle through all the possible combinations of relative, absolute, and mixed references (C14, $C$14, C$14, and $C14).

Excel 2013
UNIT B

Learning Outcomes
- Copy and Paste formulas with relative cell references
- Examine Auto Fill and Paste Options
- Use the Fill button

Copy Formulas with Relative Cell References

Copying and moving a cell allows you to reuse a formula you've already created. Copying cells is usually faster than retyping the formulas in them and helps to prevent typing errors. If the cells you are copying contain relative cell references and you want to maintain the relative referencing, you don't need to make any changes to the cells before copying them. **CASE** *You want to copy the formula in cell B21, which calculates the 30% increase in quarterly expenses for Quarter 1, to cells C21 through E21. You also want to create formulas to calculate total expenses for each tour country.*

STEPS

1. **Click cell B21, if necessary, then click the Copy button in the Clipboard group on the HOME tab**
   The formula for calculating the 30% expense increase during Quarter 1 is copied to the Clipboard. Notice that the formula =B12*1.3 appears in the formula bar, and a moving border surrounds the active cell.

2. **Click cell C21, then click the Paste button** ***(not the list arrow)*** **in the Clipboard group**
   The formula from cell B21 is copied into cell C21, where the new result of 44798.988 appears. Notice in the formula bar that the cell references have changed, so that cell C12 is referenced in the formula. This formula contains a relative cell reference, which tells Excel to substitute new cell references within the copied formulas as necessary. This maintains the same relationship between the new cell containing the formula and the cell references within the formula. In this case, Excel adjusted the formula so that cell C12—the cell reference nine rows above C21—replaced cell B12, the cell reference nine rows above B21.

> **QUICK TIP**
> To paste only specific components of a copied cell or range, click the Paste list arrow in the Clipboard group, then click Paste Special. You can selectively copy formats, formulas, values, comments, validation rules, transpose columns and rows, paste a link, or add, subtract, multiply, or divide using the Paste Special dialog box.

3. **Drag the fill handle from cell C21 to cell E21**
   A formula similar to the one in cell C21 now appears in cells D21 and E21. After you use the fill handle to copy cell contents, the **Auto Fill Options button** appears, as seen in **FIGURE B-14**. You can use the Auto Fill Options button to fill the cells with only specific elements of the copied cell if you wish.

4. **Click cell F4, click the AutoSum button in the Editing group, then click the Enter button on the formula bar**

5. **Click in the Clipboard group, select the range F5:F6, then click the Paste button**
   See **FIGURE B-15**. After you click the Paste button, the **Paste Options button** appears, which you can use to paste only specific elements of the copied selection if you wish. The formula for calculating total expenses for tours in Britain appears in the formula bar. You would like totals to appear in cells F7:F11. The Fill button in the Editing group can be used to copy the formula into the remaining cells.

6. **Select the range F6:F11**

7. **Click the Fill button in the Editing group, then click Down**
   The formulas containing relative references are copied to each cell. Compare your worksheet to **FIGURE B-16**.

8. **Save your work**

FIGURE B-14: Formula copied using the fill handle

	A	B	C	D	E
19					
20		Quarter 1	Quarter 2	Quarter 3	Quarter 4
21	30% rise	45272.019	44798.988	56291.56	48334.429
22					

AutoFill Options button

FIGURE B-15: Formulas pasted in the range F5:F6

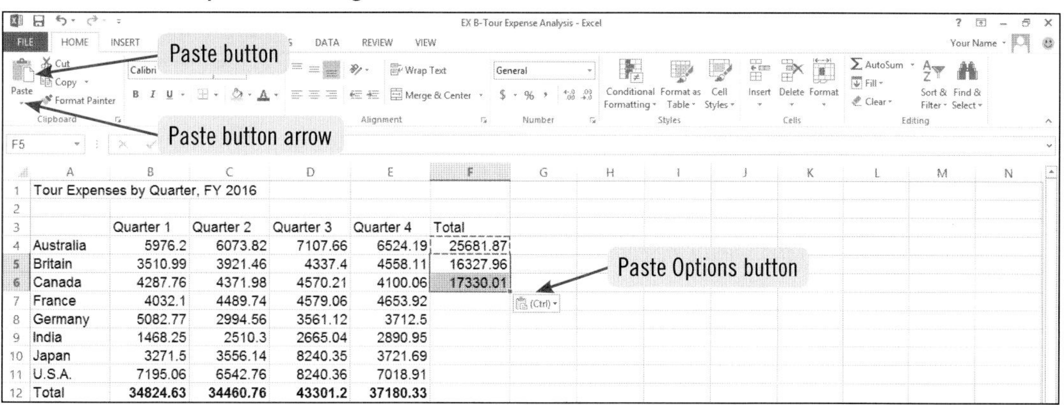

	A	B	C	D	E	F
1	Tour Expenses by Quarter, FY 2016					
2						
3		Quarter 1	Quarter 2	Quarter 3	Quarter 4	Total
4	Australia	5976.2	6073.82	7107.66	6524.19	25681.87
5	Britain	3510.99	3921.46	4337.4	4558.11	16327.96
6	Canada	4287.76	4371.98	4570.21	4100.06	17330.01
7	France	4032.1	4489.74	4579.06	4653.92	
8	Germany	5082.77	2994.56	3561.12	3712.5	
9	India	1468.25	2510.3	2665.04	2890.95	
10	Japan	3271.5	3556.14	8240.35	3721.69	
11	U.S.A.	7195.06	6542.76	8240.36	7018.91	
12	Total	34824.63	34460.76	43301.2	37180.33	

FIGURE B-16: Formula copied using Fill Down

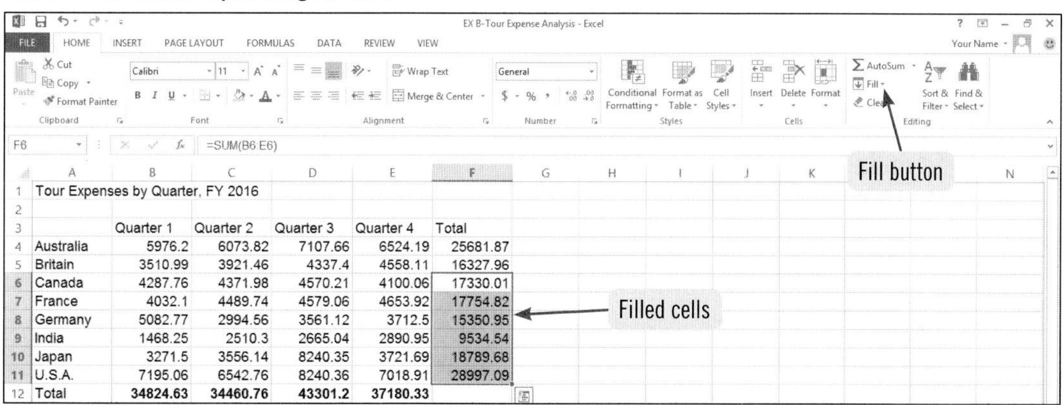

	A	B	C	D	E	F
1	Tour Expenses by Quarter, FY 2016					
2						
3		Quarter 1	Quarter 2	Quarter 3	Quarter 4	Total
4	Australia	5976.2	6073.82	7107.66	6524.19	25681.87
5	Britain	3510.99	3921.46	4337.4	4558.11	16327.96
6	Canada	4287.76	4371.98	4570.21	4100.06	17330.01
7	France	4032.1	4489.74	4579.06	4653.92	17754.82
8	Germany	5082.77	2994.56	3561.12	3712.5	15350.95
9	India	1468.25	2510.3	2665.04	2890.95	9534.54
10	Japan	3271.5	3556.14	8240.35	3721.69	18789.68
11	U.S.A.	7195.06	6542.76	8240.36	7018.91	28997.09
12	Total	34824.63	34460.76	43301.2	37180.33	

Using Paste Preview

You can selectively copy formulas, values, or other choices using the Paste list arrow, and you can see how the pasted contents will look using the Paste Preview feature. When you click the Paste list arrow, a gallery of paste option icons opens. When you point to an icon, a preview of how the content will be pasted using that option is shown in the worksheet. Options include pasting values only, pasting values with number formatting, pasting formulas only, pasting formatting only, pasting transposed data so that column data appears in rows and row data appears in columns, and pasting with no borders (to remove any borders around pasted cells).

Using Auto Fill options

When you use the fill handle to copy cells, the Auto Fill Options button appears. Auto Fill options differ depending on what you are copying. If you had selected cells containing a series (such as "Monday" and "Tuesday") and then used the fill handle, you would see options for continuing the series (such as "Wednesday" and "Thursday") or for simply pasting the copied cells. Clicking the Auto Fill Options button opens a list that lets you choose from the following options: Copy Cells, Fill Series (if applicable), Fill Formatting Only, Fill Without Formatting, or Flash Fill. Choosing Copy Cells means that the cell's contents and its formatting will be copied. The Fill Formatting Only option copies only the formatting attributes, but not cell contents. The Fill Without Formatting option copies the cell contents, but no formatting attributes. Copy Cells is the default option when using the fill handle to copy a cell, so if you want to copy the cell's contents and its formatting, you can ignore the Auto Fill Options button. The Flash Fill option allows you to create customized fill ranges on the fly, such as 2, 4, 6, 8, 10 by entering at least two values in a pattern: Excel automatically senses the pattern.

Copy Formulas with Absolute Cell References

Learning Outcomes
- Create an absolute cell reference
- Use the fill handle to copy absolute cell references

When copying formulas, you might want one or more cell references in the formula to remain unchanged in relation to the formula. In such an instance, you need to apply an absolute cell reference before copying the formula to preserve the specific cell address when the formula is copied. You create an absolute reference by placing a dollar sign ($) before the column letter and row number of the address (for example, $A$1). **CASE** *You need to do some what-if analysis to see how various percentage increases might affect total expenses. You decide to add a column that calculates a possible increase in the total tour expenses, and then change the percentage to see various potential results.*

STEPS

1. **Click cell G1, type Change, then press [Enter]**
2. **Type 1.1, then press [Enter]**

   You store the increase factor that will be used in the what-if analysis in this cell (G2). The value 1.1 can be used to calculate a 10% increase: anything you multiply by 1.1 returns an amount that is 110% of the original amount.
3. **Click cell H3, type What if?, then press [Enter]**
4. **In cell H4, type =, click cell F4, type *, click cell G2, then click the Enter button ✓ on the formula bar**

   The result, 28250.1, appears in cell H4. This value represents the total annual expenses for Australia if there is a 10% increase. You want to perform a what-if analysis for all the tour countries.
5. **Drag the fill handle from cell H4 to cell H11**

   The resulting values in the range H5:H11 are all zeros, which is not the result you wanted. Because you used relative cell addressing in cell H4, the copied formula adjusted so that the formula in cell H5 is =F5*G3. Because there is no value in cell G3, the result is 0, an error. You need to use an absolute reference in the formula to keep the formula from adjusting itself. That way, it will always reference cell G2.
6. **Click cell H4, press [F2] to change to Edit mode, then press [F4]**

   When you press [F2], the range finder outlines the arguments of the equation in blue and red. The insertion point appears next to the G2 cell reference in cell H4. When you press [F4], dollar signs are inserted in the G2 cell reference, making it an absolute reference. See **FIGURE B-17**.
7. **Click ✓, then drag the fill handle from cell H4 to cell H11**

   Because the formula correctly contains an absolute cell reference, the correct values for a 10% increase appear in cells H4:H11. You now want to see what a 20% increase in expenses looks like.
8. **Click cell G2, type 1.2, then click ✓**

   The values in the range H4:H11 change to reflect the 20% increase. Compare your worksheet to **FIGURE B-18**.
9. **Save your work**

QUICK TIP
Before you copy or move a formula, always check to see if you need to use an absolute cell reference.

QUICK TIP
When changing a cell reference to an absolute reference, make sure the reference is selected or the insertion point is next to it in the cell before pressing [F4].

FIGURE B-17: Absolute reference created in formula

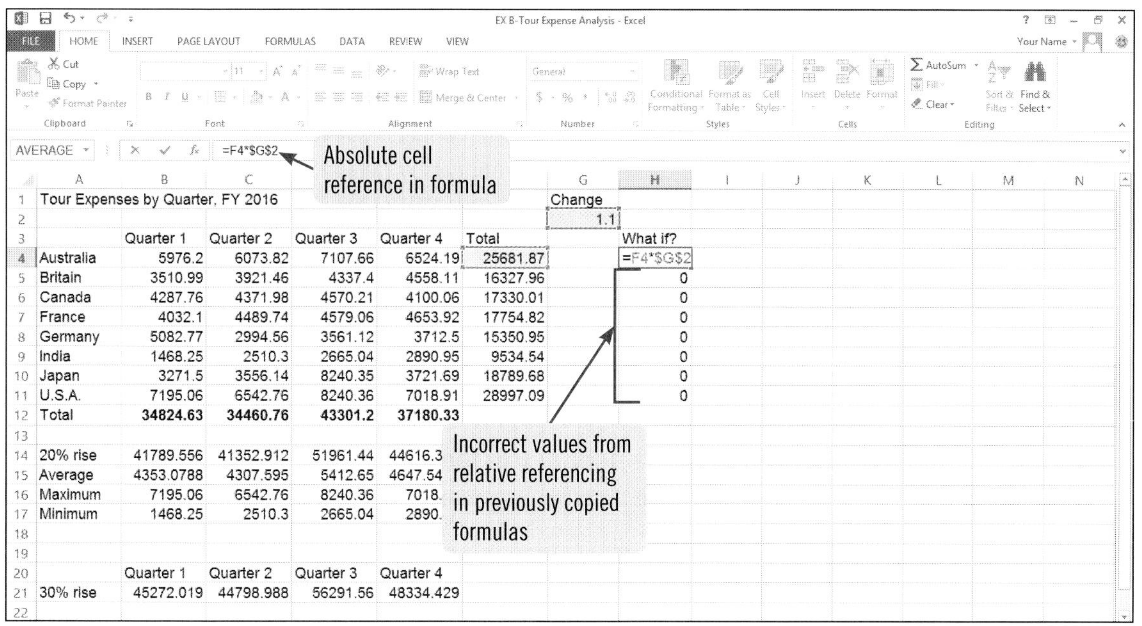

FIGURE B-18: What-if analysis with modified change factor

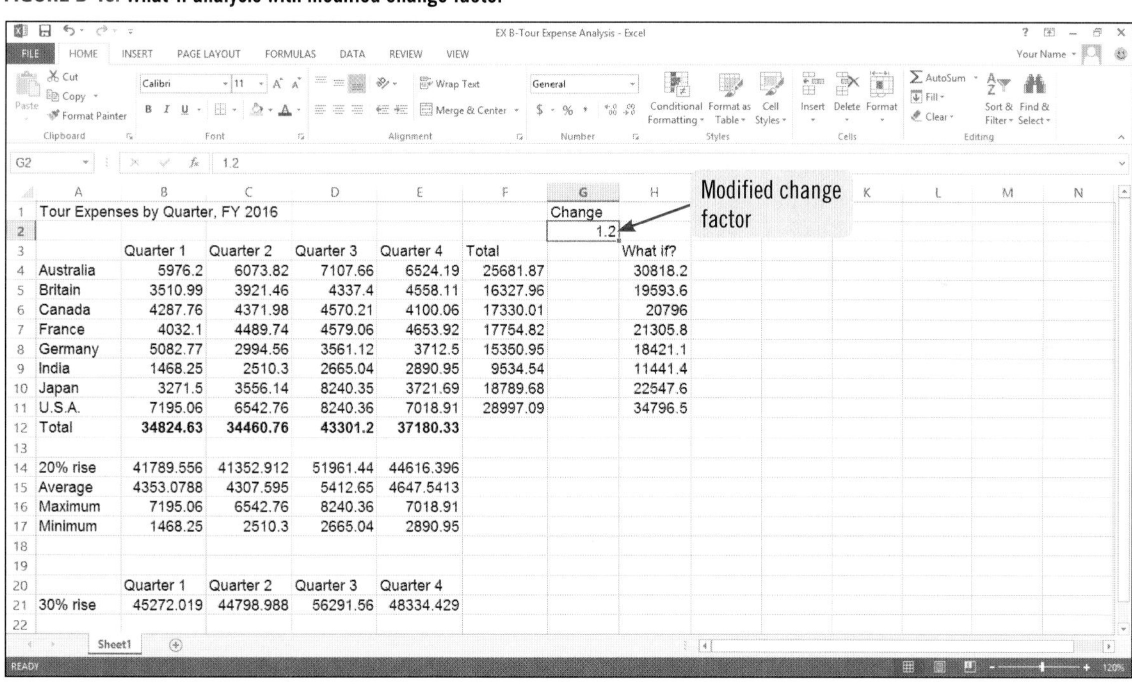

Excel 2013

Using the fill handle for sequential text or values

Often, you need to fill cells with sequential text: months of the year, days of the week, years, or text plus a number (Quarter 1, Quarter 2,...). For example, you might want to create a worksheet that calculates data for every month of the year. Using the fill handle, you can quickly and easily create labels for the months of the year just by typing "January" in a cell. Drag the fill handle from the cell containing "January" until you have all the monthly labels you need. You can also easily fill cells with a date sequence by dragging the fill handle on a single cell containing a date. You can fill cells with a number sequence (such as 1, 2, 3,...) by dragging the fill handle on a selection of two or more cells that contain the sequence. To create a number sequence using the value in a single cell, press and hold [Ctrl] as you drag the fill handle of the cell. As you drag the fill handle, Excel automatically extends the existing sequence into the additional cells. (The content of the last filled cell appears in the ScreenTip.) To examine all the fill series options for the current selection, click the Fill button in the Editing group on the HOME tab, then click Series to open the Series dialog box.

Excel 2013
UNIT B

Round a Value with a Function

Learning Outcomes
- Use Formula AutoComplete to insert a function
- Copy an edited formula

The more you explore features and tools in Excel, the more ways you'll find to simplify your work and convey information more efficiently. For example, cells containing financial data are often easier to read if they contain fewer decimal places than those that appear by default. You can round a value or formula result to a specific number of decimal places by using the ROUND function. **CASE** *In your worksheet, you'd like to round the cells showing the 20% rise in expenses to show fewer digits; after all, it's not important to show cents in the projections, only whole dollars. You want Excel to round the calculated value to the nearest integer. You decide to edit cell B14 so it includes the ROUND function, and then copy the edited formula into the other formulas in this row.*

STEPS

1. **Click cell B14, then click to the right of = in the formula bar**
   You want to position the function at the beginning of the formula, before any values or arguments.

QUICK TIP
In the Insert Function dialog box, the ROUND function is in the Math & Trig category.

2. **Type RO**
   Formula AutoComplete displays a list of functions beginning with RO beneath the formula bar.
3. **Double-click ROUND in the functions list**
   The new function and an opening parenthesis are added to the formula, as shown in **FIGURE B-19**. A few additional modifications are needed to complete your edit of the formula. You need to indicate the number of decimal places to which the function should round numbers and you also need to add a closing parenthesis around the set of arguments that comes after the ROUND function.

TROUBLE
If you have too many or too few parentheses, the extraneous parenthesis is displayed in red, or a warning dialog box opens with a suggested solution to the error.

4. **Press [END], type ,0), then click the Enter button ✓ on the formula bar**
   The comma separates the arguments within the formula, and 0 indicates that you don't want any decimal places to appear in the calculated value. When you complete the edit, the parentheses at either end of the formula briefly become bold, indicating that the formula has the correct number of open and closed parentheses and is balanced.
5. **Drag the fill handle from cell B14 to cell E14**
   The formula in cell B14 is copied to the range C14:E14. All the values are rounded to display no decimal places. Compare your worksheet to **FIGURE B-20**.
6. **Scroll down so row 25 is visible, click cell A25, type your name, then click ✓ on the formula bar**
7. **Save your work, preview the worksheet in Backstage view, then submit your work to your Instructor as directed**
8. **Exit Excel**

FIGURE B-19: ROUND function added to an existing formula

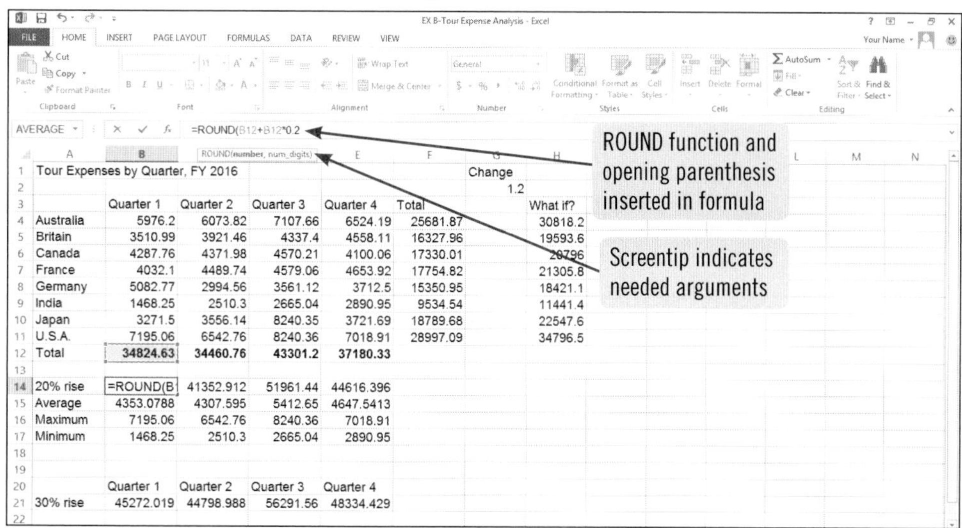

FIGURE B-20: Completed worksheet

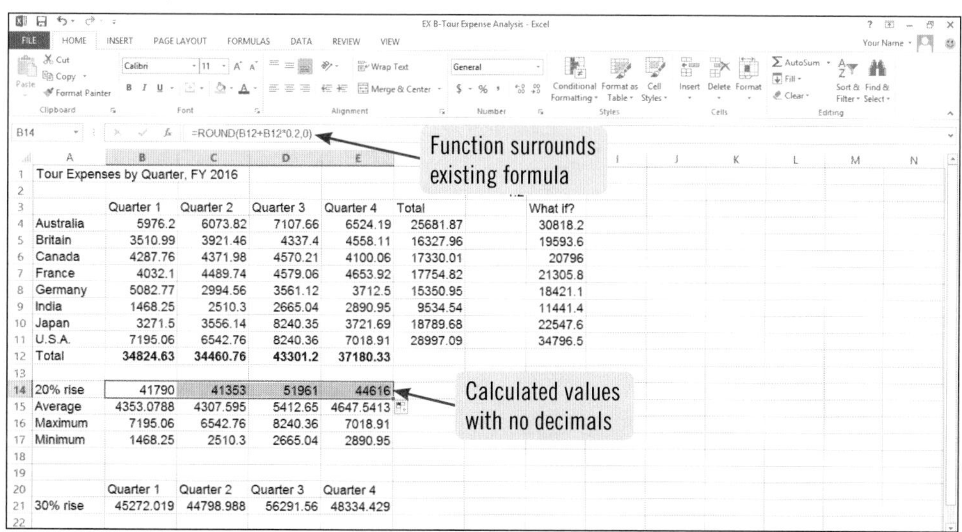

Creating a new workbook using a template

Excel **templates** are predesigned workbook files intended to save time when you create common documents such as balance sheets, budgets, or time cards. Templates contain labels, values, formulas, and formatting, so all you have to do is customize them with your own information. Excel comes with many templates, and you can also create your own or find additional templates on the Web. Unlike a typical workbook, which has the file extension .xlsx, a template has the extension .xltx. To create a workbook using a template, click the FILE tab, then click New on the navigation bar. The New pane in Backstage view lists templates available through Office.com. The Blank workbook template is selected by default and is used to create a blank workbook with no content or special formatting. A preview of the selected template appears in a separate window on top of the New pane. To select a template, click one of the selections in the New pane, then click Create. **FIGURE B-21** shows an Office.com template. (Your list of templates may differ.) When you click Create, a new workbook is created based on the template; when you save the new file in the default format, it has the regular .xlsx extension. To save a workbook of your own as a template, open the Save As dialog box, click the Save as type list arrow, then change the file type to Excel Template.

FIGURE B-21: EXPENSE TRENDS template selected in Backstage view

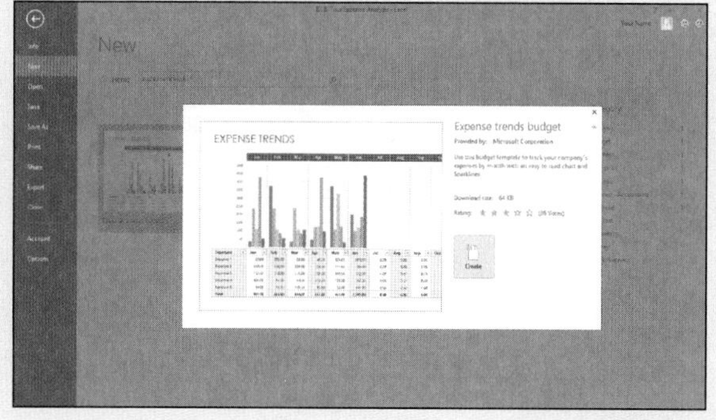

Excel 2013

Practice

Put your skills into practice with **SAM Projects**! SAM Projects for this unit can be found online. If you have a SAM account, go to www.cengage.com/sam2013 to download the most recent Project Instruction and Start Files.

Concepts Review

Label each element of the Excel worksheet window shown in FIGURE B-22.

FIGURE B-22

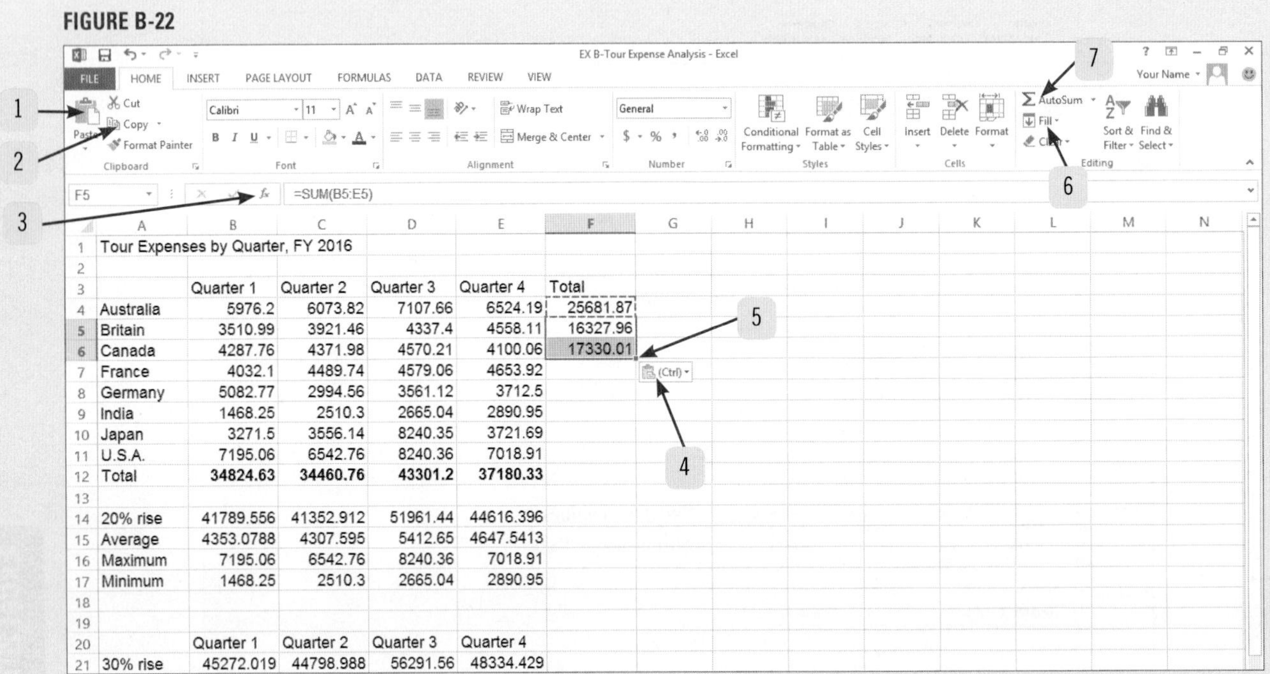

	A	B	C	D	E	F
1	Tour Expenses by Quarter, FY 2016					
2						
3		Quarter 1	Quarter 2	Quarter 3	Quarter 4	Total
4	Australia	5976.2	6073.82	7107.66	6524.19	25681.87
5	Britain	3510.99	3921.46	4337.4	4558.11	16327.96
6	Canada	4287.76	4371.98	4570.21	4100.06	17330.01
7	France	4032.1	4489.74	4579.06	4653.92	
8	Germany	5082.77	2994.56	3561.12	3712.5	
9	India	1468.25	2510.3	2665.04	2890.95	
10	Japan	3271.5	3556.14	8240.35	3721.69	
11	U.S.A.	7195.06	6542.76	8240.36	7018.91	
12	Total	**34824.63**	**34460.76**	**43301.2**	**37180.33**	
13						
14	20% rise	41789.556	41352.912	51961.44	44616.396	
15	Average	4353.0788	4307.595	5412.65	4647.5413	
16	Maximum	7195.06	6542.76	8240.36	7018.91	
17	Minimum	1468.25	2510.3	2665.04	2890.95	
18						
19						
20		Quarter 1	Quarter 2	Quarter 3	Quarter 4	
21	30% rise	45272.019	44798.988	56291.56	48334.429	

Match each term or button with the statement that best describes it.

8. **Fill handle**
9. **[Delete]**
10. **Dialog box launcher**
11. **Formula AutoComplete**
12. **Drag-and-drop method**

a. Clears the contents of selected cells

b. Item on the Ribbon that opens a dialog box or task pane

c. Lets you move or copy data from one cell to another without using the Clipboard

d. Displays an alphabetical list of functions from which you can choose

e. Lets you copy cell contents or continue a series of data into a range of selected cells

Select the best answer from the list of choices.

13. What type of cell reference changes when it is copied?

- **a.** Circular
- **b.** Absolute
- **c.** Relative
- **d.** Specified

14. What type of cell reference is C$19?

- **a.** Relative
- **b.** Absolute
- **c.** Mixed
- **d.** Certain

15. Which key do you press to copy while dragging and dropping selected cells?

- **a.** [Alt]
- **b.** [Ctrl]
- **c.** [F2]
- **d.** [Tab]

16. You can use any of the following features to enter a function *except*:

- **a.** Insert Function button.
- **b.** Formula AutoComplete.
- **c.** AutoSum list arrow.
- **d.** Clipboard.

17. Which key do you press to convert a relative cell reference to an absolute cell reference?

- **a.** [F2]
- **b.** [F4]
- **c.** [F5]
- **d.** [F6]

Skills Review

1. Create a complex formula.

- **a.** Open the file EX B-2.xlsx from the location where you store your Data Files, then save it as **EX B-Baking Supply Company Inventory**.
- **b.** Select the range B4:B8, click the Totals tab in the Quick Analysis tool, then click the AutoSum button.
- **c.** Use the fill handle to copy the formula in cell B9 to cells C9:E9
- **d.** In cell B11, create a complex formula that calculates a 30% decrease in the total number of cases of cake pans.
- **e.** Use the fill handle to copy this formula into cell C11 through cell E11.
- **f.** Save your work.

2. Insert a function.

- **a.** Use the AutoSum list arrow to create a formula in cell B13 that averages the number of cases of cake pans in each storage area.
- **b.** Use the Insert Function button to create a formula in cell B14 that calculates the maximum number of cases of cake pans in a storage area.
- **c.** Use the AutoSum list arrow to create a formula in cell B15 that calculates the minimum number of cases of cake pans in a storage area.
- **d.** Save your work.

3. Type a function.

- **a.** In cell C13, type a formula that includes a function to average the number of cases of pie pans in each storage area. (*Hint*: Use Formula AutoComplete to enter the function.)
- **b.** In cell C14, type a formula that includes a function to calculate the maximum number of cases of pie pans in a storage area.
- **c.** In cell C15, type a formula that includes a function to calculate the minimum number of cases of pie pans in a storage area.
- **d.** Save your work.

Skills Review (continued)

4. Copy and move cell entries.

- **a.** Select the range B3:F3.
- **b.** Copy the selection to the Clipboard.
- **c.** Open the Clipboard task pane, then paste the selection into cell B17.
- **d.** Close the Clipboard task pane, then select the range A4:A9.
- **e.** Use the drag-and-drop method to copy the selection to cell A18. (*Hint*: The results should fill the range A18:A23.)
- **f.** Save your work.

5. Understand relative and absolute cell references.

- **a.** Write a brief description of the difference between relative and absolute references.
- **b.** List at least three situations in which you think a business might use an absolute reference in its calculations. Examples can include calculations for different types of worksheets, such as time cards, invoices, and budgets.

6. Copy formulas with relative cell references.

- **a.** Calculate the total in cell F4.
- **b.** Use the Fill button to copy the formula in cell F4 down to cells F5:F8.
- **c.** Select the range C13:C15.
- **d.** Use the fill handle to copy these cells to the range D13:F15.
- **e.** Save your work.

7. Copy formulas with absolute cell references.

- **a.** In cell H1, enter the value **1.575**.
- **b.** In cell H4, create a formula that multiplies F4 and an absolute reference to cell H1.
- **c.** Use the fill handle to copy the formula in cell H4 to cells H5 and H6.
- **d.** Use the Copy and Paste buttons to copy the formula in cell H4 to cells H7 and H8.
- **e.** Change the amount in cell H1 to **2.5**.
- **f.** Save your work.

8. Round a value with a function.

- **a.** Click cell H4.
- **b.** Edit this formula to include the ROUND function showing zero decimal places.
- **c.** Use the fill handle to copy the formula in cell H4 to the range H5:H8.
- **d.** Enter your name in cell A25, then compare your work to **FIGURE B-23**.
- **e.** Save your work, preview the worksheet in Backstage view, then submit your work to your instructor as directed.
- **f.** Close the workbook, then exit Excel.

FIGURE B-23

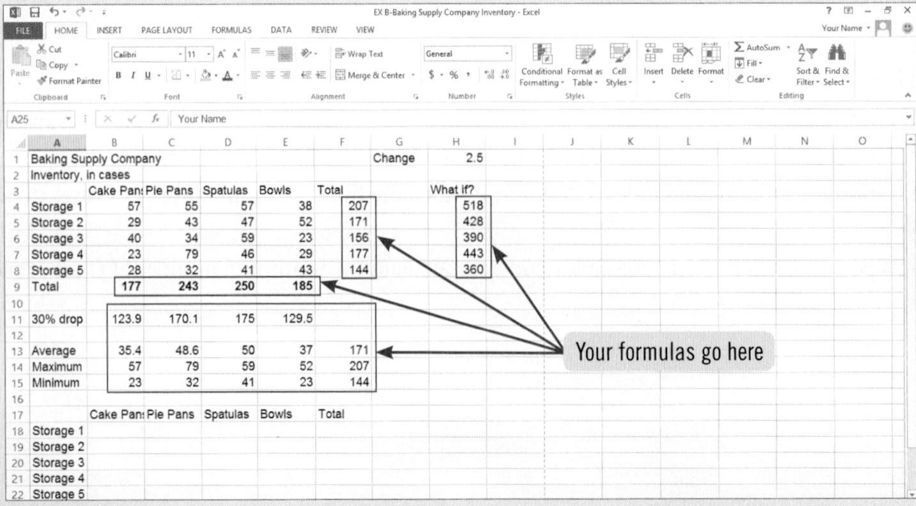

Independent Challenge 1

You are thinking of starting a small express oil change service center. Before you begin, you need to evaluate what you think your monthly expenses will be. You've started a workbook, but need to complete the entries and add formulas.

a. Open the file EX B-3.xlsx from the location where you store your Data Files, then save it as **EX B-Express Oil Change Expenses**.

b. Make up your own expense data, and enter it in cells B4:B10. (Monthly sales are already included in the worksheet.)

c. Create a formula in cell C4 that calculates the annual rent.

d. Copy the formula in cell C4 to the range C5:C10.

e. Move the label in cell A15 to cell A14.

f. Create formulas in cells B11 and C11 that total the monthly and annual expenses.

g. Create a formula in cell C13 that calculates annual sales.

h. Create a formula in cell B14 that determines whether you will make a profit or loss, then copy the formula into cell C14.

i. Copy the labels in cells B3:C3 to cells E3:F3.

j. Type **Projected Increase** in cell G1, then type **.2** in cell H2.

k. Create a formula in cell E4 that calculates an increase in the monthly rent by the amount in cell H2. You will be copying this formula to other cells, so you'll need to use an absolute reference.

l. Create a formula in cell F4 that calculates the increased annual rent expense based on the calculation in cell E4.

m. Copy the formulas in cells E4:F4 into cells E5:F10 to calculate the remaining monthly and annual expenses.

n. Create a formula in cell E11 that calculates the total monthly expenses, then copy that formula to cell F11.

o. Copy the contents of cells B13:C13 into cells E13:F13.

p. Create formulas in cells E14 and F14 that calculate profit/loss based on the projected increase in monthly and annual expenses.

q. Change the projected increase to **.17**, then compare your work to the sample in **FIGURE B-24**.

r. Enter your name in a cell in the worksheet.

s. Save your work, preview the worksheet in Backstage view, submit your work to your instructor as directed, close the workbook, and exit Excel. Print Gridlines/Headings

FIGURE B-24

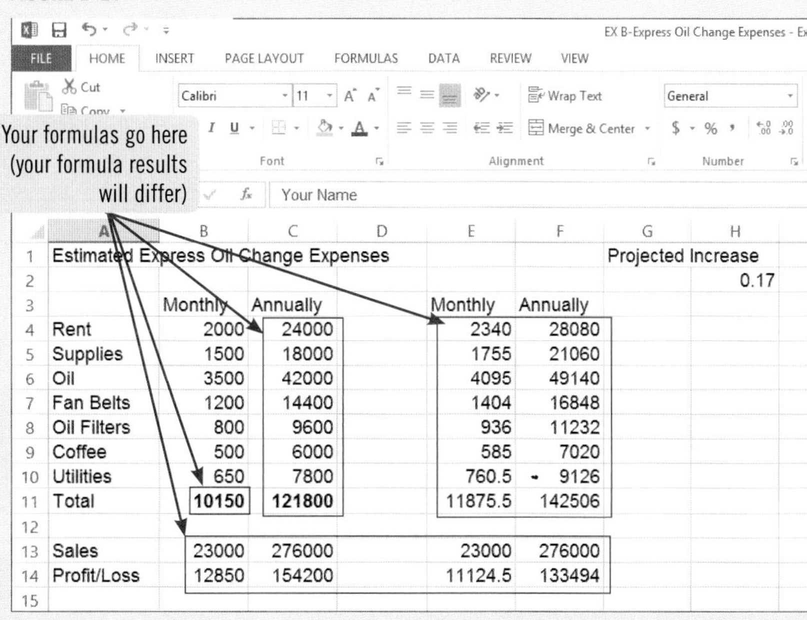

Excel 2013

Independent Challenge 2

The Dog Days Daycare Center is a small, growing pet care center that has hired you to organize its accounting records using Excel. The owners want you to track the company's expenses. Before you were hired, one of the bookkeepers began entering last year's expenses in a workbook, but the analysis was never completed.

a. Start Excel, open the file EX B-4.xlsx from the location where you store your Data Files, then save it as **EX B-Dog Days Daycare Center Finances**. The worksheet includes labels for functions such as the average, maximum, and minimum amounts of each of the expenses in the worksheet.
b. Think about what information would be important for the bookkeeping staff to know.
c. Using the Quick Analysis tool, create a formula in the Quarter 1 column that uses the SUM function, then copy that formula into the Total row for the remaining Quarters.
d. Use the SUM function to create formulas for each expense in the Total column.
e. Create formulas for each expense and each quarter in the Average, Maximum, and Minimum columns and rows using the method of your choice.
f. Compare your worksheet to the sample shown in **FIGURE B-25**.
g. Enter your name in cell A25, then save your work.
h. Preview the worksheet, then submit your work to your instructor as directed.
i. Close the workbook and exit Excel.

FIGURE B-25

	A	B	C	D	E	F	G	H	I
1	Dog Days Daycare Center								
2									
3	Operating Expenses for 2016								
4									
5	Expense	Quarter 1	Quarter 2	Quarter 3	Quarter 4	Total	Average	Maximum	Minimum
6	Rent	9240	9240	9240	9240	36960	9240	9240	9240
7	Utilities	9000	7982	7229	8096	32307	8076.75	9000	7229
8	Payroll	23456	26922	25876	29415	105669	26417.3	29415	23456
9	Insurance	8550	8194	8225	8327	33296	8324	8550	8194
10	Education	3000	3081	6552	4006	16639	4159.75	6552	3000
11	Inventory	29986	27115	25641	32465	115207	28801.8	32465	25641
12	Total	**83232**	**82534**	**82763**	**91549**				
13									
14	Average	13872	13755.7	13793.8	15258.2				
15	Maximum	29986	27115	25876	32465				
16	Minimum	3000	3081	6552	4006				

Your formulas go here

Independent Challenge 3

As the accounting manager of a locally owned business, it is your responsibility to calculate accrued sales tax payments on a monthly basis and then submit the payments to the state government. You've decided to use an Excel workbook to make these calculations.

a. Start Excel, then save a new, blank workbook to the drive and folder where you store your Data Files as **EX B-Sales Tax Calculations**.

b. Decide on the layout for all columns and rows. The worksheet will contain data for six stores, which you can name by store number, neighborhood, or another method of your choice. For each store, you will calculate total sales tax based on the local sales tax rate. You'll also calculate total tax owed for all six stores.

c. Make up sales data for all six stores.

d. Enter the rate to be used to calculate the sales tax, using your own local rate.

e. Create formulas to calculate the sales tax owed for each store. If you don't know the local tax rate, use **6.5%**.

f. Create a formula to total all the accrued sales tax.

g. Use the ROUND function to eliminate any decimal places in the sales tax figures for each store and the total due.

h. Add your name to the header, then compare your work to the sample shown in **FIGURE B-26**.

i. Save your work, preview the worksheet, and submit your work to your instructor as directed.

j. Close the workbook and exit Excel.

FIGURE B-26

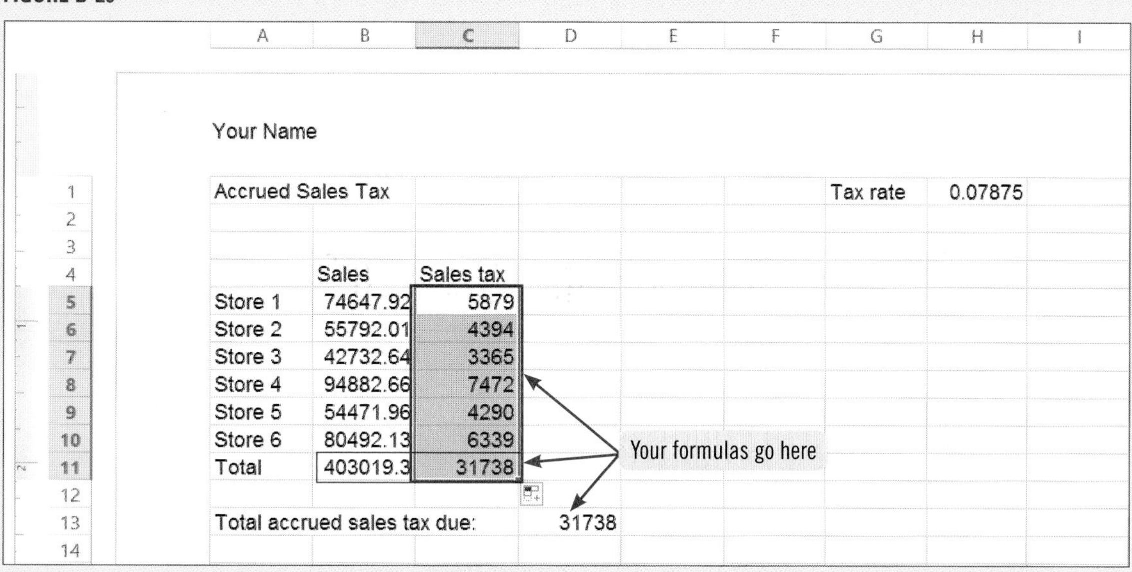

Excel 2013

Independent Challenge 4: Explore

Since your recent promotion at work, you have started thinking about purchasing a home. As you begin the round of open houses and realtors' listings, you notice that there are many fees associated with buying a home. Some fees are based on a percentage of the purchase price, and others are a flat fee; overall, they seem to represent a substantial amount above the purchase prices you see listed. You've seen five houses so far that interest you; one is easily affordable, and the remaining four are all nice, but increasingly more expensive. Although you will be financing the home, the bottom line is still important to you, so you decide to create an Excel workbook to figure out the real cost of buying each one.

a. Find out the typical cost or percentage rate of at least three fees that are usually charged when buying a home and taking out a mortgage. (*Hint*: If you have access to the Internet you can research the topic of home buying on the Web, or you can ask friends about standard rates or percentages for items such as title insurance, credit reports, and inspection fees.)

b. Start Excel, then save a new, blank workbook to the location where you store your Data Files as **EX B-Home Purchase Costs**.

c. Create labels and enter data for at least three homes. If you enter this information across the columns in your worksheet, you should have one column for each house, with the purchase price in the cell below each label. Be sure to enter a different purchase price for each house.

d. Create labels for the Fees column and for an Amount or Rate column. Enter the information for each of the fees you have researched.

e. In each house column, enter formulas that calculate the fee for each item. The formulas (and use of absolute or relative referencing) will vary depending on whether the charges are a flat fee or based on a percentage of the purchase price. Make sure that the formulas for items that are based on a percentage of the purchase price (such as the fees for the Title Insurance Policy, Loan Origination, and Underwriter) contain absolute references.

Independent Challenge 4: Explore (continued)

f. Total the fees for each house, then create formulas that add the total fees to the purchase price. A sample of what your workbook might look like is shown in **FIGURE B-27**.
g. Enter a title for the worksheet in the header.
h. Enter your name in the header, save your work, preview the worksheet, then submit your work to your instructor as directed.
i. Close the file and exit Excel.

FIGURE B-27

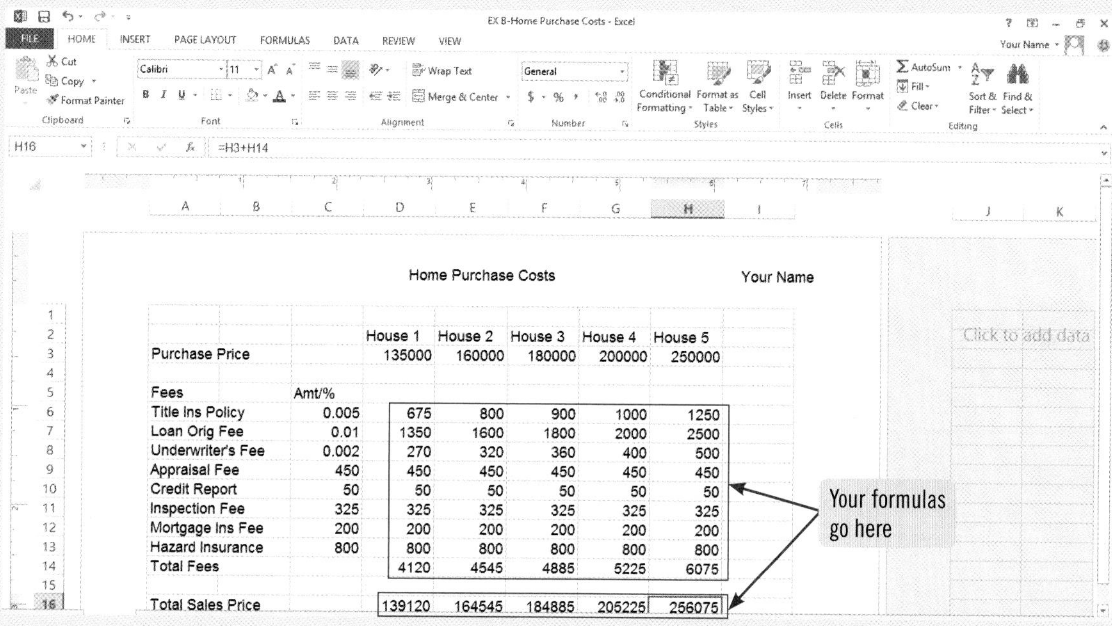

	A	B	C	D	E	F	G	H
1								
2				House 1	House 2	House 3	House 4	House 5
3	Purchase Price			135000	160000	180000	200000	250000
4								
5	Fees		Amt/%					
6	Title Ins Policy		0.005	675	800	900	1000	1250
7	Loan Orig Fee		0.01	1350	1600	1800	2000	2500
8	Underwriter's Fee		0.002	270	320	360	400	500
9	Appraisal Fee		450	450	450	450	450	450
10	Credit Report		50	50	50	50	50	50
11	Inspection Fee		325	325	325	325	325	325
12	Mortgage Ins Fee		200	200	200	200	200	200
13	Hazard Insurance		800	800	800	800	800	800
14	Total Fees			4120	4545	4885	5225	6075
15								
16	Total Sales Price			139120	164545	184885	205225	256075

Excel 2013

Visual Workshop

Create the worksheet shown in **FIGURE B-28** using the skills you learned in this unit. Save the workbook as **EX B-Expense Analysis** to the location where you store your Data Files. Enter your name and worksheet title in the header as shown, hide the gridlines, preview the worksheet, and then submit your work to your instructor as directed. (*Hint:* Change the Zoom factor to 100% by clicking the Zoom out button twice.)

FIGURE B-28

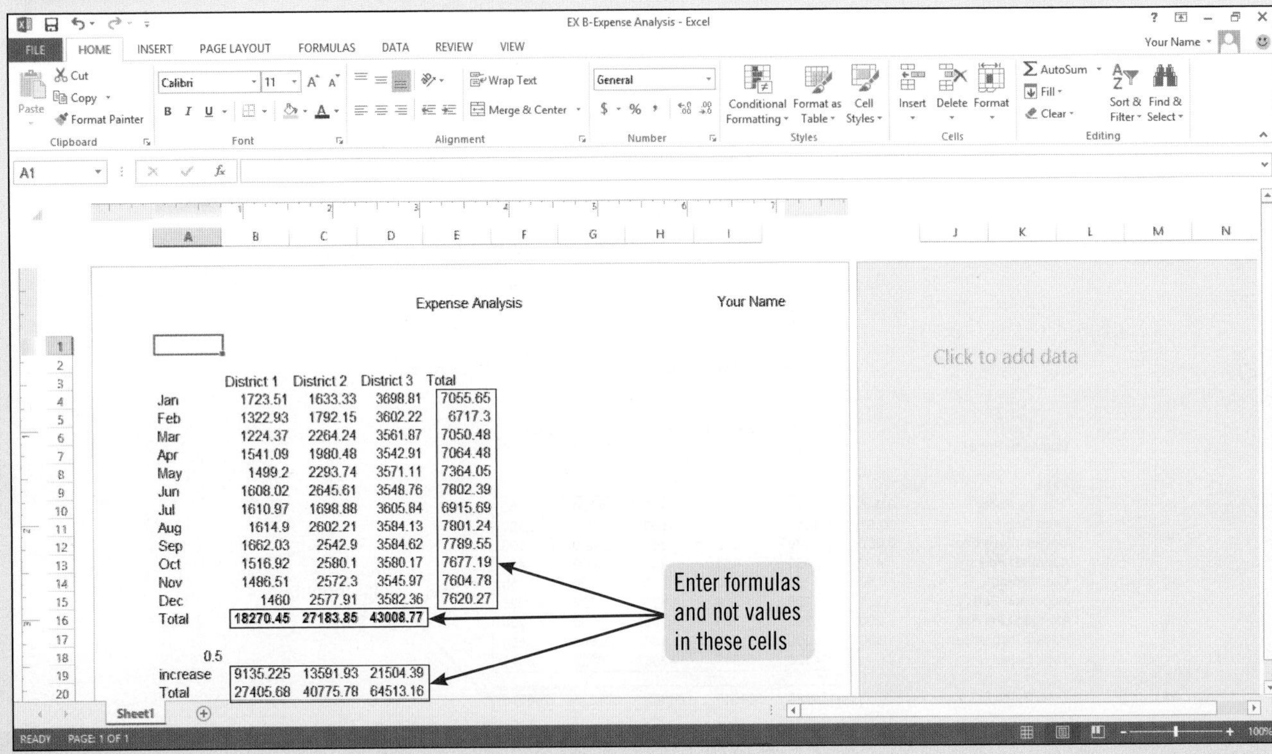

Formatting a Worksheet

CASE The corporate marketing managers at QST have requested data from all QST locations for advertising expenses incurred during the first quarter of this year. Grace Wong has created a worksheet listing this information. She asks you to format the worksheet to make it easier to read and to call attention to important data.

Unit Objectives

After completing this unit, you will be able to:

- Format values
- Change font and font size
- Change font styles and alignment
- Adjust the column width
- Insert and delete rows and columns
- Apply colors, patterns, and borders
- Apply conditional formatting
- Rename and move a worksheet
- Check spelling

Files You Will Need

EX C-1.xlsx
EX C-2.xlsx
EX C-3.xlsx
EX C-4.xlsx
EX C-5.xlsx

©Katerina Havelkova/Shutterstock

Excel 2013
UNIT C

Format Values

Learning Outcomes
- Format a number
- Format a date
- Increase/decrease decimals

The **format** of a cell determines how the labels and values look—for example, whether the contents appear boldfaced, italicized, or with dollar signs and commas. Formatting changes only the appearance of a value or label; it does not alter the actual data in any way. To format a cell or range, first you select it, then you apply the formatting using the Ribbon, Mini toolbar, or a keyboard shortcut. You can apply formatting before or after you enter data in a cell or range. **CASE** *Grace has provided you with a worksheet that details advertising expenses, and you're ready to improve its appearance and readability. You start by formatting some of the values so they are displayed as currency, percentages, and dates.*

STEPS

1. **Start Excel, open the file EX C-1.xlsx from the location where you store your Data Files, then save it as EX C-QST Advertising Expenses**

   This worksheet is difficult to interpret because all the information is crowded and looks the same. In some columns, the contents appear cut off because there is too much data to fit given the current column width. You decide not to widen the columns yet, because the other changes you plan to make might affect column width and row height. The first thing you want to do is format the data showing the cost of each ad.

> **QUICK TIP**
> You can use a different type of currency, such as Euros or British pounds, by clicking the Accounting Number Format list arrow, then clicking a different currency type.

2. **Select the range D4:D32, then click the Accounting Number Format button $ in the Number group on the HOME tab**

   The default Accounting **number format** adds dollar signs and two decimal places to the data, as shown in **FIGURE C-1**. Formatting this data in Accounting format makes it clear that its values are monetary values. Excel automatically resizes the column to display the new formatting. The Accounting and Currency number formats are both used for monetary values, but the Accounting format aligns currency symbols and decimal points of numbers in a column.

> **QUICK TIP**
> Select any range of contiguous cells by clicking the upper-left cell of the range, pressing and holding [Shift], then clicking the lower-right cell of the range. Add a column to the selected range by continuing to hold down [Shift] and pressing →; add a row by pressing ↓.

3. **Select the range F4:H32, then click the Comma Style button , in the Number group**

   The values in columns F, G, and H display the Comma Style format, which does not include a dollar sign but can be useful for some types of accounting data.

4. **Select the range J4:J32, click the Number Format list arrow, click Percentage, then click the Increase Decimal button in the Number group**

   The data in the % of Total column is now formatted with a percent sign (%) and three decimal places. The Number Format list arrow lets you choose from popular number formats and shows an example of what the selected cell or cells would look like in each format (when multiple cells are selected, the example is based on the first cell in the range). Each time you click the Increase Decimal button, you add one decimal place; clicking the button twice would add two decimal places.

5. **Click the Decrease Decimal button in the Number group twice**

   Two decimal places are removed from the percentage values in column J.

6. **Select the range B4:B31, then click the dialog box launcher in the Number group**

   The Format Cells dialog box opens with the Date category already selected on the Number tab.

7. **Select the first 14-Mar-12 format in the Type list box as shown in FIGURE C-2, then click OK**

   The dates in column B appear in the 14-Mar-12 format. The second 14-Mar-12 format in the list (visible if you scroll down the list) displays all days in two digits (it adds a leading zero if the day is only a single-digit number), while the one you chose displays single-digit days without a leading zero.

> **QUICK TIP**
> Make sure you examine formatted data to confirm that you have applied the appropriate formatting; for example, dates should not have a currency format, and monetary values should not have a date format.

8. **Select the range C4:C31, right-click the range, click Format Cells on the shortcut menu, click 14-Mar in the Type list box in the Format Cells dialog box, then click OK**

   Compare your worksheet to **FIGURE C-3**.

9. **Press [Ctrl][Home], then save your work**

FIGURE C-1: Accounting number format applied to range

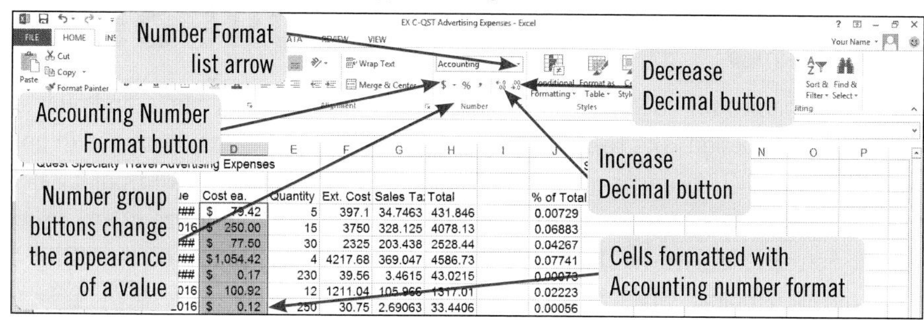

FIGURE C-2: Format Cells dialog box

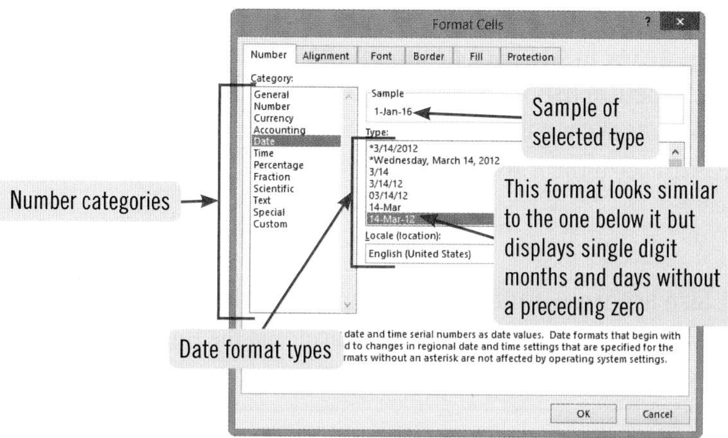

FIGURE C-3: Worksheet with formatted values

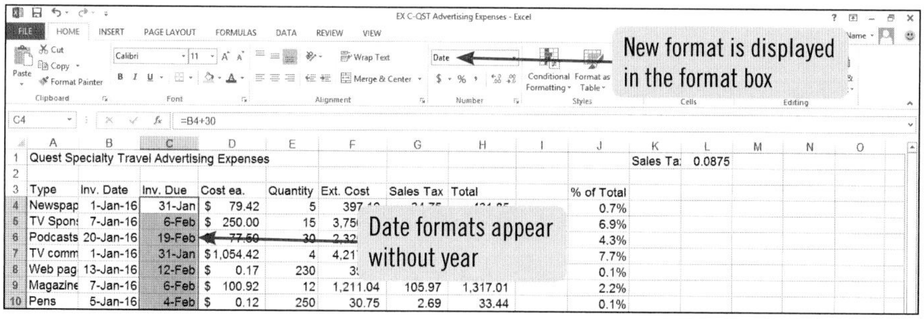

New format is displayed in the format box

Date formats appear without year

Formatting as a table

Excel includes 60 predefined **table styles** to make it easy to format selected worksheet cells as a table. You can apply table styles to any range of cells that you want to format quickly, or even to an entire worksheet, but they're especially useful for those ranges with labels in the left column and top row, and totals in the bottom row or right column. To apply a table style, select the data to be formatted or click anywhere within the intended range (Excel can automatically detect a range of cells filled with data), click the Format as Table button in the Styles group on the HOME tab, then click a style in the gallery, as shown in **FIGURE C-4**. Table styles are organized in three categories: Light, Medium, and Dark. Once you click a style, Excel asks you to confirm the range selection, then applies the style. Once you have formatted a range as a table, you can use Live Preview to preview the table in other styles by pointing to any style in the Table Styles gallery.

FIGURE C-4: Table Styles gallery

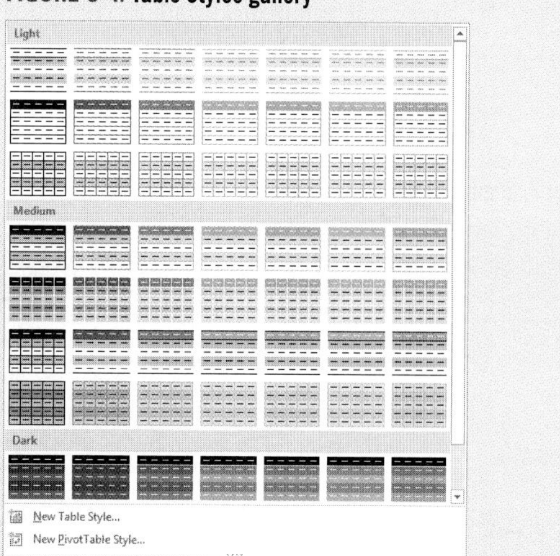

Change Font and Font Size

Learning Outcomes
- Change a font
- Change a font size
- Use the Mini toolbar

A **font** is the name for a collection of characters (letters, numbers, symbols, and punctuation marks) with a similar, specific design. The **font size** is the physical size of the text, measured in units called points. A **point** is equal to 1/72 of an inch. The default font and font size in Excel is 11-point Calibri. TABLE C-1 shows several fonts in different font sizes. You can change the font and font size of any cell or range using the Font and Font Size list arrows. The Font and Font Size list arrows appear on the HOME tab on the Ribbon and on the Mini toolbar, which opens when you right-click a cell or range. **CASE** *You want to change the font and font size of the labels and the worksheet title so that they stand out more from the data.*

STEPS

QUICK TIP When you point to an option in the Font or Font Size list, Live Preview shows the selected cells with the option temporarily applied.

1. **Click the Font list arrow in the Font group on the HOME tab, scroll down in the Font list to see an alphabetical listing of the fonts available on your computer, then click Times New Roman, as shown in FIGURE C-5**
   The font in cell A1 changes to Times New Roman. Notice that the font names on the list are displayed in the font they represent.

QUICK TIP You can format an entire row by clicking the row indicator button to select the row before formatting (or select an entire column by clicking the column indicator button before formatting).

2. **Click the Font Size list arrow in the Font group, then click 20**
   The worksheet title appears in 20-point Times New Roman, and the Font and Font Size list boxes on the HOME tab display the new font and font size information.

3. **Click the Increase Font Size button A^ in the Font group twice**
   The font size of the title increases to 24 point.

4. **Select the range A3:J3, right-click, then click the Font list arrow on the Mini toolbar**
   The Mini toolbar includes the most commonly used formatting tools, so it's great for making quick formatting changes.

QUICK TIP To quickly move to a font in the Font list, type the first few characters of its name.

5. **Scroll down in the Font list and click Times New Roman, click the Font Size list arrow on the Mini toolbar, then click 14**
   The Mini toolbar closes when you move the pointer away from the selection. Compare your worksheet to FIGURE C-6. Notice that some of the column labels are now too wide to appear fully in the column. Excel does not automatically adjust column widths to accommodate cell formatting; you have to adjust column widths manually. You'll learn to do this in a later lesson.

6. **Save your work**

TABLE C-1: Examples of fonts and font sizes

font	12 point	24 point
Calibri	Excel	Excel
Playbill	Excel	Excel
Comic Sans MS	Excel	Excel
Times New Roman	Excel	Excel

FIGURE C-5: Font list

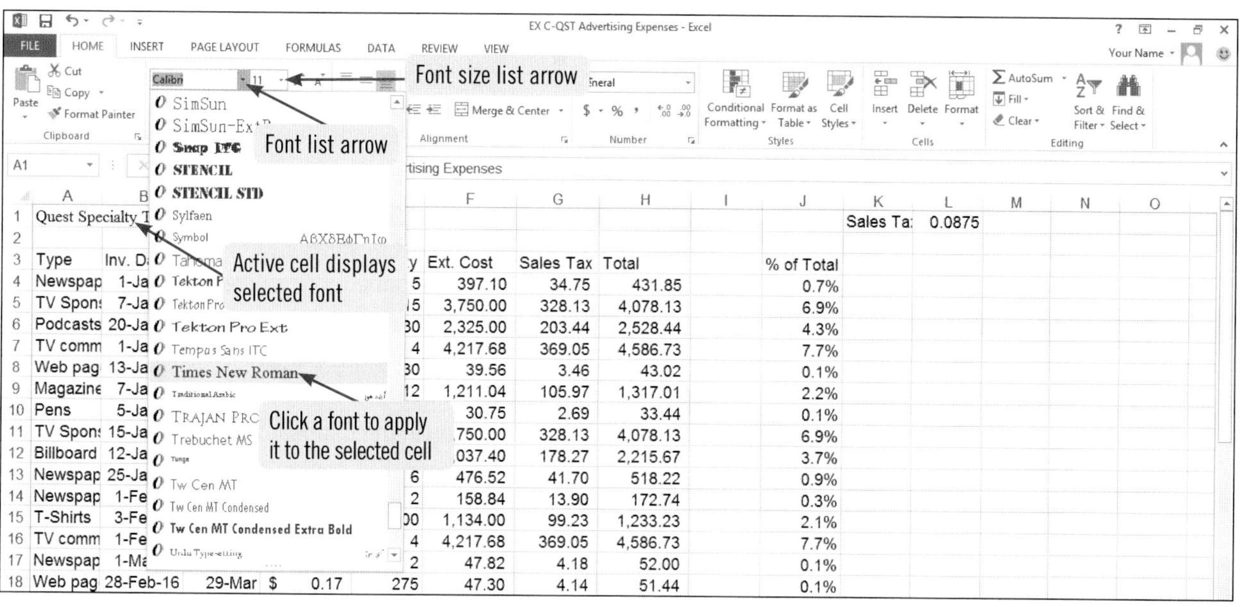

FIGURE C-6: Worksheet with formatted title and column labels

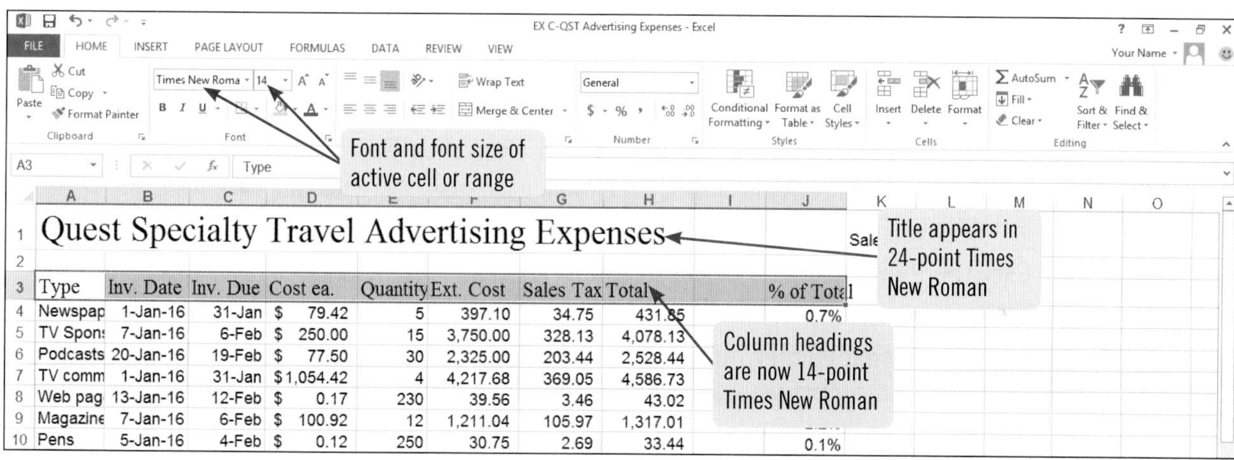

Inserting and adjusting online pictures and other images

You can illustrate your worksheets using online pictures and other images. Office.com makes many photos and animations available for your use. To add a picture to a worksheet, click the Online Pictures button in the Illustrations group on the INSERT tab. The Insert Pictures window opens. Here you can search for online pictures (or Clip Art) in Office.com, through the Bing search engine, or on your SkyDrive by typing one or more **keywords** (words related to your subject) in the appropriate Search text box, then click [Enter]. For example, pictures that relate to the keyword house in a search of Office.com appear in the Office.com window, as shown in **FIGURE C-7**. When you double-click the image you want in the window, the image is inserted at the location of the active cell. To add images on your computer (or computers on your network) to a worksheet, click the INSERT tab on the Ribbon, then click the Pictures button in the Illustrations group. Navigate to the file you want, then click Insert. To resize an image, drag any corner sizing handle. To move an image, point inside the clip until the pointer changes to ✥, then drag it to a new location.

FIGURE C-7: Results of Online Picture search

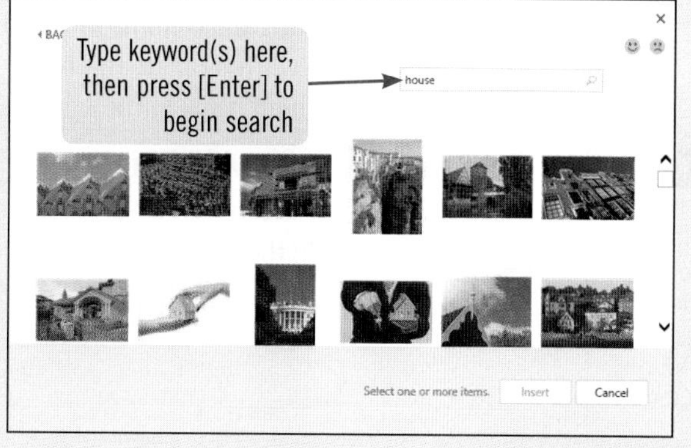

Change Font Styles and Alignment

Learning Outcomes
- Apply formatting
- Use the Format Painter
- Change cell alignment

Font styles are formats such as bold, italic, and underlining that you can apply to affect the way text and numbers look in a worksheet. You can also change the **alignment** of labels and values in cells to position them in relation to the cells' edges—such as left-aligned, right-aligned, or centered. You can apply font styles and alignment options using the HOME tab, the Format Cells dialog box, or the Mini toolbar. See **TABLE C-2** for a description of common font style and alignment buttons that are available on the HOME tab and the Mini toolbar. Once you have formatted a cell the way you want it, you can "paint" or copy the cell's formats into other cells by using the Format Painter button in the Clipboard group on the HOME tab. This is similar to using copy and paste, but instead of copying cell contents, it copies only the cell's formatting. **CASE** *You want to further enhance the worksheet's appearance by adding bold and underline formatting and centering some of the labels.*

STEPS

1. **Press [Ctrl][Home], then click the Bold button B in the Font group on the HOME tab**
   The title in cell A1 appears in bold.

QUICK TIP
You can use the following keyboard shortcuts to format a selected cell or range: [Ctrl][B] to bold, [Ctrl][I] to italicize, and [Ctrl][U] to underline.

2. **Click cell A3, then click the Underline button U in the Font group**
   The column label is now underlined, though this may be difficult to see with the cell selected.
3. **Click the Italic button I in the Font group, then click B**
   The heading now appears in boldface, underlined, italic type. Notice that the Bold, Italic, and Underline buttons in the Font group are all selected.

QUICK TIP
Overuse of any font style and random formatting can make a workbook difficult to read. Be consistent and add the same formatting to similar items throughout a worksheet or in related worksheets.

4. **Click the Italic button I to deselect it**
   The italic font style is removed from cell A3, but the bold and underline font styles remain.
5. **Click the Format Painter button in the Clipboard group, then select the range B3:J3**
   The formatting in cell A3 is copied to the rest of the column labels. To paint the formats on more than one selection, double-click the Format Painter button to keep it activated until you turn it off. You can turn off the Format Painter by pressing [Esc] or by clicking . You decide the title would look better if it were centered over the data columns.
6. **Select the range A1:H1, then click the Merge & Center button in the Alignment group**
   The Merge & Center button creates one cell out of the eight cells across the row, then centers the text in that newly created, merged cell. The title "Quest Specialty Travel Advertising Expenses" is centered across the eight columns you selected. To split a merged cell into its original components, select the merged cell, then click the Merge & Center button to deselect it. The merged and centered text might look awkward now, but you'll be changing the column widths shortly. Occasionally, you may find that you want cell contents to wrap within a cell. You can do this by selecting the cells containing the text you want to wrap, then clicking the Wrap Text button in the Alignment group on the HOME tab on the Ribbon.

QUICK TIP
To clear all formatting from a selected range, click the Clear button in the Editing group on the HOME tab, then click Clear Formats.

7. **Select the range A3:J3, right-click, then click the Center button on the Mini toolbar**
   Compare your screen to **FIGURE C-8**. Although they may be difficult to read, notice that all the headings are centered within their cells.
8. **Save your work**

FIGURE C-8: Worksheet with font styles and alignment applied

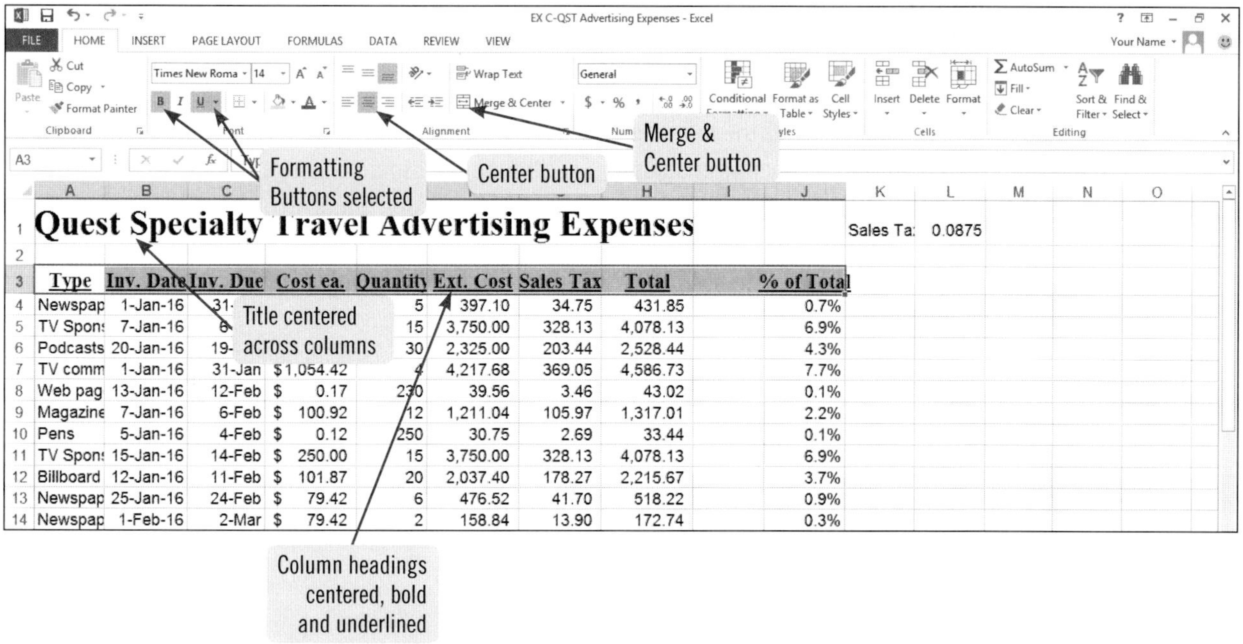

Formatting Buttons selected

Center button

Merge & Center button

Title centered across columns

Column headings centered, bold and underlined

TABLE C-2: Common font style and alignment buttons

button	description
B	Bolds text
I	Italicizes text
U	Underlines text
	Centers text across columns, and combines two or more selected, adjacent cells into one cell
	Aligns text at the left edge of the cell
	Centers text horizontally within the cell
	Aligns text at the right edge of the cell
	Wraps long text into multiple lines

Excel 2013

Rotating and indenting cell entries

In addition to applying fonts and font styles, you can rotate or indent data within a cell to further change its appearance. You can rotate text within a cell by altering its alignment. To change alignment, select the cells you want to modify, then click the dialog box launcher in the Alignment group to open the Alignment tab of the Format Cells dialog box. Click a position in the Orientation box or type a number in the Degrees text box to rotate text from its default horizontal orientation, then click OK. You can indent cell contents using the Increase Indent button in the Alignment group, which moves cell contents to the right one space, or the Decrease Indent button, which moves cell contents to the left one space.

Adjust the Column Width

Learning Outcomes
- Change a column width by dragging
- Resize a column with AutoFit
- Change the width of multiple columns

As you format a worksheet, you might need to adjust the width of one or more columns to accommodate changes in the amount of text, the font size, or font style. The default column width is 8.43 characters, a little less than 1". With Excel, you can adjust the width of one or more columns by using the mouse, the Format button in the Cells group on the HOME tab, or the shortcut menu. Using the mouse, you can drag or double-click the right edge of a column heading. The Format button and shortcut menu include commands for making more precise width adjustments. **TABLE C-3** describes common column formatting commands. **CASE** *You have noticed that some of the labels in columns A through J don't fit in the cells. You want to adjust the widths of the columns so that the labels appear in their entirety.*

STEPS

1. **Position the mouse pointer on the line between the column A and column B headings until it changes to ↔**
   See **FIGURE C-9**. The **column heading** is the box at the top of each column containing a letter. Before you can adjust column width using the mouse, you need to position the pointer on the right edge of the column heading for the column you want to adjust. The cell entry "TV commercials" is the widest in the column.

2. **Click and drag the ↔ to the right until the column displays the "TV commercials" cell entries fully (approximately 15.29 characters, 1.23", or 112 pixels)**
   As you change the column width, a ScreenTip is displayed listing the column width. In Normal view, the ScreenTip lists the width in characters and pixels; in Page Layout view, the ScreenTip lists the width in inches and pixels.

> **QUICK TIP**
> If "#######" appears after you adjust a column of values, the column is too narrow to display the values completely; increase the column width until the values appear.

3. **Position the pointer on the line between columns B and C until it changes to ↔, then double-click**
   Double-clicking the right edge of a column heading activates the **AutoFit** feature, which automatically resizes the column to accommodate the widest entry in the column. Column B automatically widens to fit the widest entry, which is the column label "Inv. Date".

4. **Use AutoFit to resize columns C, D, and J**

5. **Select the range E5:H5**
   You can change the width of multiple columns at once, by first selecting either the column headings or at least one cell in each column.

6. **Click the Format button in the Cells group, then click Column Width**
   The Column Width dialog box opens. Column width measurement is based on the number of characters that will fit in the column when formatted in the Normal font and font size (in this case, 11 pt Calibri).

> **QUICK TIP**
> If an entire column rather than a column cell is selected, you can change the width of the column by right-clicking the column heading, then clicking Column Width on the shortcut menu.

7. **Drag the dialog box by its title bar if its placement obscures your view of the worksheet, type 11 in the Column width text box, then click OK**
   The widths of columns E, F, G, and H change to reflect the new setting. See **FIGURE C-10**.

8. **Save your work**

FIGURE C-9: Preparing to change the column width

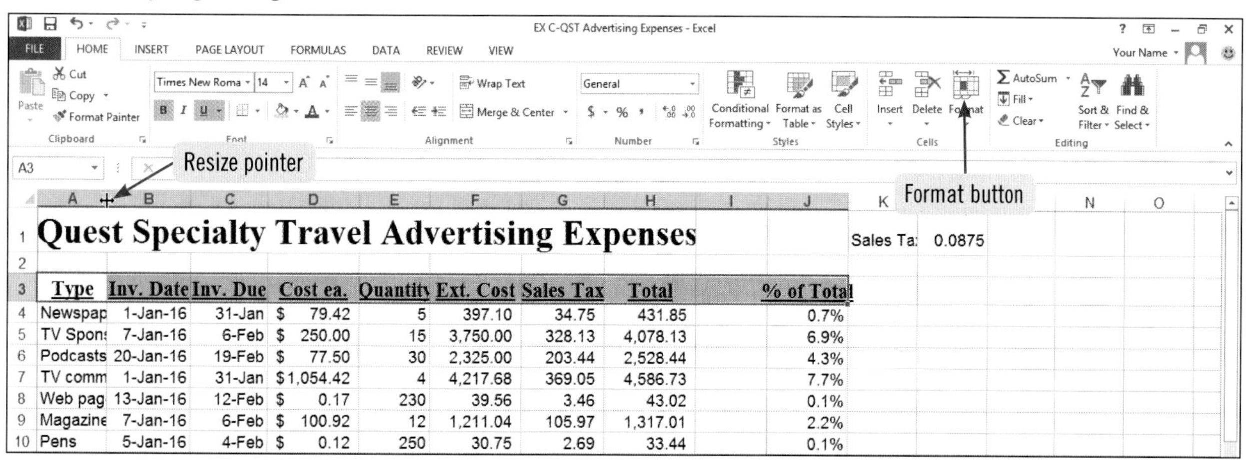

FIGURE C-10: Worksheet with column widths adjusted

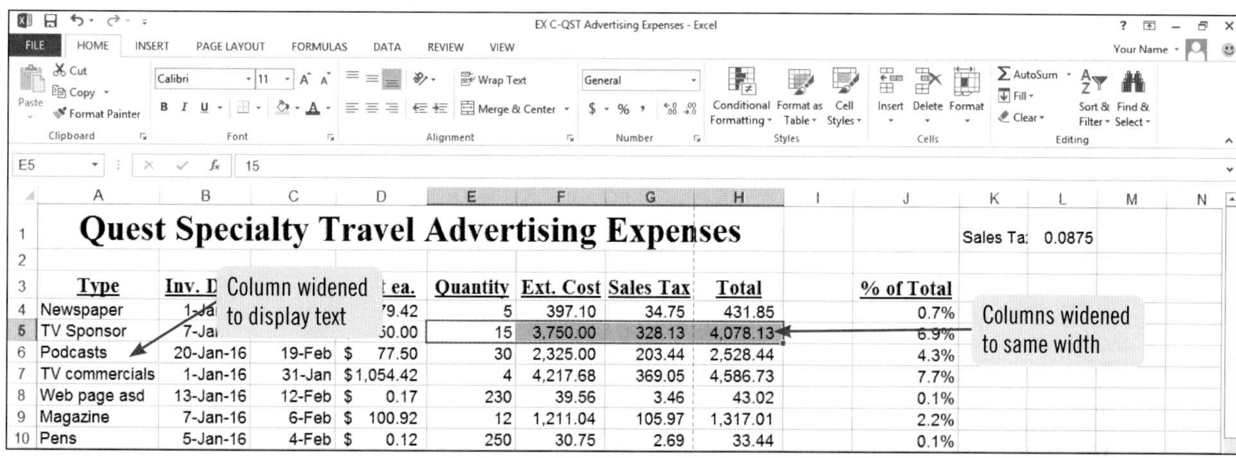

Excel 2013

TABLE C-3: Common column formatting commands

command	description	available using
Column Width	Sets the width to a specific number of characters	Format button; shortcut menu
AutoFit Column Width	Fits to the widest entry in a column	Format button; mouse
Hide & Unhide	Hides or displays hidden column(s)	Format button; shortcut menu
Default Width	Resets column to worksheet's default column width	Format button

Changing row height

Changing row height is as easy as changing column width. Row height is calculated in points, the same units of measure used for fonts. The row height must exceed the size of the font you are using. Normally, you don't need to adjust row heights manually, because row heights adjust automatically to accommodate font size changes. If you format something in a row to be a larger point size, Excel adjusts the row to fit the largest point size in the row. However, you have just as many options for changing row height as you do column width. Using the mouse, you can place the ╪ pointer on the line dividing a row heading from the heading below, and then drag to the desired height; double-clicking the line AutoFits the row height where necessary. You can also select one or more rows, then use the Row Height command on the shortcut menu, or click the Format button on the HOME tab and click the Row Height or AutoFit Row Height command.

Excel 2013
UNIT C

Insert and Delete Rows and Columns

Learning Outcomes
- Use the Insert dialog box
- Use column and row heading buttons to insert and delete

As you modify a worksheet, you might find it necessary to insert or delete rows and columns to keep your worksheet current. For example, you might need to insert rows to accommodate new inventory products or remove a column of yearly totals that are no longer necessary. When you insert a new row, the row is inserted above the cell pointer and the contents of the worksheet shift down from the newly inserted row. When you insert a new column, the column is inserted to the left of the cell pointer and the contents of the worksheet shift to the right of the new column. To insert multiple rows, select the same number of row headings as you want to insert before using the Insert command. **CASE** *You want to improve the overall appearance of the worksheet by inserting a row between the last row of data and the totals. Also, you have learned that row 27 and column J need to be deleted from the worksheet.*

STEPS

QUICK TIP
To insert a single row or column, right-click the row heading immediately below where you want the new row, or right-click the column heading to the right of where you want the new column, then click Insert on the shortcut menu.

QUICK TIP
If you inadvertently click the Delete list arrow instead of the button itself, click Delete Sheet Rows in the menu that opens.

QUICK TIP
After inserting or deleting rows or columns in a worksheet, be sure to proof formulas that contain relative cell references.

1. **Right-click cell A32, then click Insert on the shortcut menu**
   The Insert dialog box opens. See **FIGURE C-11**. You can choose to insert a column or a row; insert a single cell and shift the cells in the active column to the right; or insert a single cell and shift the cells in the active row down. An additional row between the last row of data and the totals will visually separate the totals.
2. **Click the Entire row option button, then click OK**
   A blank row appears between the Billboard data and the totals, and the formula result in cell E33 has not changed. The Insert Options button appears beside cell A33. Pointing to the button displays a list arrow, which you can click and then choose from the following options: Format Same As Above (the default setting, already selected), Format Same As Below, or Clear Formatting.
3. **Click the row 27 heading**
   All of row 27 is selected, as shown in **FIGURE C-12**.
4. **Click the Delete button in the Cells group; *do not click the list arrow***
   Excel deletes row 27, and all rows below it shift up one row. You must use the Delete button or the Delete command on the shortcut menu to delete a row or column; pressing [Delete] on the keyboard removes only the *contents* of a selected row or column.
5. **Click the column J heading**
   The percentage information is calculated elsewhere and is no longer necessary in this worksheet.
6. **Click the Delete button in the Cells group**
   Excel deletes column J. The remaining columns to the right shift left one column.
7. **Use AutoFit to resize columns F and H, then save your work**

FIGURE C-11: Insert dialog box

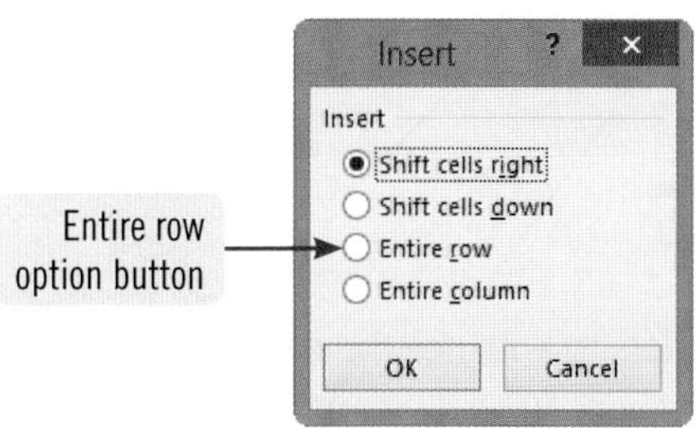

FIGURE C-12: Worksheet with row 27 selected

	A	B	C	D	E	F	G	H	I	J	K	L	M	N
15	T-Shirts	3-Feb-16	4-Mar	$ 5.67	200	1,134.00	99.23	1,233.23		2.1%				
16	TV commercials	1-Feb-16	2-Mar	$1,054.42	4	4,217.68	369.05	4,586.73		7.7%				
17	Newspaper	1-Mar-16	31-Mar	$ 23.91	2	47.82	4.18	52.00		0.1%				
18	Web page ads	28-Feb-16	29-Mar	$ 0.17	275	47.30	4.14	51.44		0.1%				
19	Magazine	27-Feb-16	28-Mar	$ 100.92	12	1,211.04	105.97	1,317.01		2.2%				
20	Podacsts	22-Feb-16	23-Mar	$ 77.50	30	2,325.00	203.44	2,528.44		4.3%				
21	TV Sponsor	1-Feb-16	2-Mar	$ 250.00	30	7,500.00	656.25	8,156.25		13.8%				
22	Newspaper	25-Feb-16	26-Mar	$ 79.42	6	476.52	41.70	518.22		0.9%				
23	W	ar-16	9-Apr	$ 0.17	275	47.30	4.14	51.44		0.1%				
24	T	eb-16	16-Mar	$ 250.00	25	6,250.00	546.88	6,796.88		11.5%				
25	Pens	15-Mar-16	14-Apr	$ 0.12	250	30.75	2.69	33.44		0.1%				
26	TV commercials	1-Mar-16	31-Mar	$1,054.44	4	4,217.76	369.05	4,586.81		7.7%				
27	Hats	20-Mar-16	19-Apr	$ 7.20	250	1,800.00	157.50	1,957.50		3.3%				
28	Podcasts	20-Mar-16	19-Apr	$ 75.50	30	2,265.00	198.19	2,463.19		4.2%				
29	Newspaper	2	-Apr	$ 79.42	2	158.84	13.90	172.74		0.3%				
30	Podcasts	2	-Apr	$ 77.50	30	2,325.00	203.44	2,528.44		4.3%				
31	Billboard	28-Mar-16	27-Apr	$ 101.87	20	2,037.40	178.27	2,215.67		3.7%				
32														
33					2034	########	4,767.46	########		100.0%				

Hiding and unhiding columns and rows

When you don't want data in a column or row to be visible, but you don't want to delete it, you can hide the column or row. To hide a selected column, click the Format button in the Cells group on the HOME tab, point to Hide & Unhide, then click Hide Columns. A hidden column is indicated by a dark green vertical line in its original position. This green line disappears when you click elsewhere in the worksheet. You can display a hidden column by selecting the columns on either side of the hidden column, clicking the Format button in the Cells group, pointing to Hide & Unhide, and then clicking Unhide Columns. (To hide or unhide one or more rows, substitute Hide Rows and Unhide Rows for the Hide Columns and Unhide Columns commands.)

Adding and editing comments

Much of your work in Excel may be in collaboration with teammates with whom you share worksheets. You can share ideas with other worksheet users by adding comments within selected cells. To include a comment in a worksheet, click the cell where you want to place the comment, click the REVIEW tab on the Ribbon, then click the New Comment button in the Comments group. You can type your comments in the resizable text box that opens containing the computer user's name. A small, red triangle appears in the upper-right corner of a cell containing a comment. If comments are not already displayed in a workbook, other users can point to the triangle to display the comment. To see all worksheet comments, as shown in **FIGURE C-13**, click the Show All Comments button in the Comments group. To edit a comment, click the cell containing the comment, then click the Edit Comment button in the Comments group. To delete a comment, click the cell containing the comment, then click the Delete button in the Comments group.

FIGURE C-13: Comments displayed in a worksheet

20	Podcasts	22-Feb-16	23-Mar	iPodAds	$ 75.50
21	TV Sponsor	1-Feb-16	2-Mar	Food Networ	
22	Newspaper	25-Feb-16	26-Mar	Village Read	
23	Web page ads	10-Mar-16	9-Apr	Advertising C	
24	TV Sponsor	15-Feb-16	16-Mar	Food Networ	
25	Pens	15-Mar-16	14-Apr	Mass Appeal, Inc.	$ 0.12
26	TV commercial	1-Mar-16	31-Mar	Discovery Channel	
27	Podcasts	20-Mar-16	19-Apr	iPodAds	
28	Newspaper	1-Apr-16	1-May	University Vc	
29	Podcasts	10-Apr-16	10-May	iPodAds	
30	Billboard	28-Mar-16	27-Apr	Advertising Concepts	$ 101.87
31					
32					$5,166.04
33					
34					

Excel 2013

Apply Colors, Patterns, and Borders

Learning Outcomes
- Use Live Preview to apply color to cells
- Format cells using the shortcut menu
- Apply a border and pattern to a cell

You can use colors, patterns, and borders to enhance the overall appearance of a worksheet and make it easier to read. You can add these enhancements by using the Borders, Font Color, and Fill Color buttons in the Font group on the HOME tab of the Ribbon and on the Mini toolbar, or by using the Fill tab and the Border tab in the Format Cells dialog box. You can open the Format Cells dialog box by clicking the dialog box launcher in the Font, Alignment, or Number group on the HOME tab, or by right-clicking a selection, then clicking Format Cells on the shortcut menu. You can apply a color to the background of a cell or a range or to cell contents (such as letters and numbers), and you can apply a pattern to a cell or range. You can apply borders to all the cells in a worksheet or only to selected cells to call attention to selected information. To save time, you can also apply **cell styles**, predesigned combinations of formats. **CASE** *You want to add a pattern, a border, and color to the title of the worksheet to give the worksheet a more professional appearance.*

STEPS

1. **Select cell A1, click the Fill Color list arrow in the Font group, then hover the pointer over the Turquoise, Accent 2 color (first row, sixth column from the left)**
   See **FIGURE C-14**. Live Preview shows you how the color will look *before* you apply it. (Remember that cell A1 spans columns A through H because the Merge & Center command was applied.)
2. **Click the Turquoise, Accent 2 color**
   The color is applied to the background (or fill) of this cell. When you change fill or font color, the color on the Fill Color or Font Color button changes to the last color you selected.
3. **Right-click cell A1, then click Format Cells on the shortcut menu**
   The Format Cells dialog box opens.
4. **Click the Fill tab, click the Pattern Style list arrow, click the 6.25% Gray style (first row, sixth column from the left), then click OK**
5. **Click the Borders list arrow in the Font group, then click Thick Bottom Border**
   Unlike underlining, which is a text-formatting tool, borders extend to the width of the cell, and can appear at the bottom of the cell, at the top, on either side, or on any combination of the four sides. It can be difficult to see a border when the cell is selected.
6. **Select the range A3:H3, click the Font Color list arrow in the Font group, then click the Blue, Accent 1 color (first Theme color row, fifth column from the left) on the palette**
   The new color is applied to the labels in the selected range.
7. **Select the range J1:K1, click the Cell Styles button in the Styles group, click the Neutral cell style (first row, fourth column from the left) in the gallery, then AutoFit column J**
   The font and color change in the range is shown in **FIGURE C-15**.
8. **Save your work**

QUICK TIP
Use fill colors and patterns sparingly. Too many colors can be distracting or make it hard to see which information is important.

QUICK TIP
You can also create custom cell borders. Click the Borders list arrow in the Font group, click More Borders, then click the individual border buttons to apply the borders you want to the selected cell(s).

FIGURE C-14: Live Preview of fill color

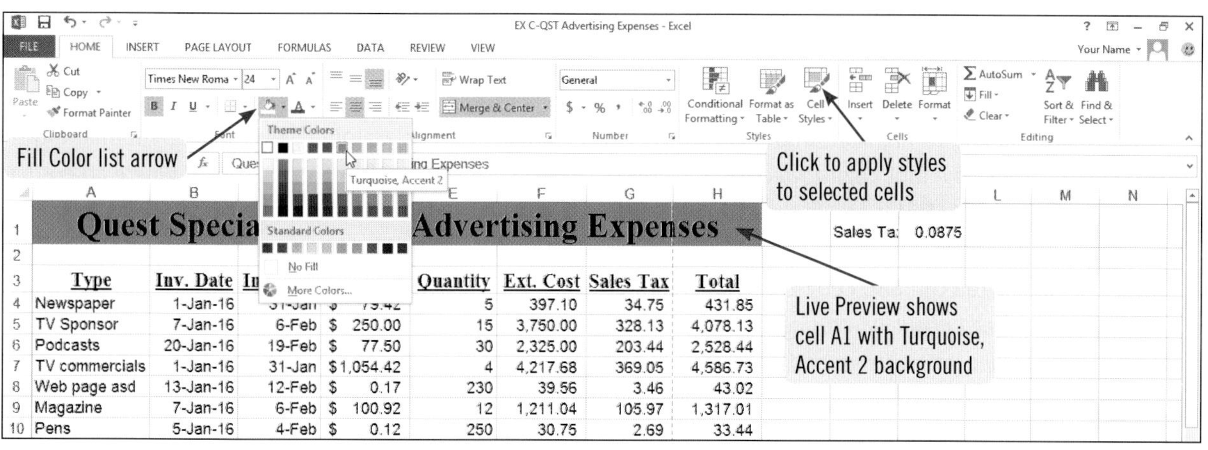

FIGURE C-15: Worksheet with color, patterns, border, and cell style applied

	A	B	C	D	E	F	G	H
1	Quest Specialty Travel Advertising Expenses							
2								
3	Type	Inv. Date	Inv. Due	Cost ea.	Quantity	Ext. Cost	Sales Tax	Total
4	Newspaper	1-Jan-16	31-Jan	$ 79.42	5	397.10	34.75	431.85
5	TV Sponsor	7-Jan-16	6-Feb	$ 250.00	15	3,750.00	328.13	4,078.13
6	Podcasts	20-Jan-16	19-Feb	$ 77.50	30	2,325.00	203.44	2,528.44
7	TV commercials	1-Jan-16	31-Jan	$1,054.42	4	4,217.68	369.05	4,586.73
8	Web page asd	13-Jan-16	12-Feb	$ 0.17	230	39.56	3.46	43.02
9	Magazine	7-Jan-16	6-Feb	$ 100.92	12	1,211.04	105.97	1,317.01
10	Pens	5-Jan-16	4-Feb	$ 0.12	250	30.75	2.69	33.44
11	TV Sponsor	15-Jan-16	14-Feb	$ 250.00	15	3,750.00	328.13	4,078.13
12	Billboard	12-Jan-16	11-Feb	$ 101.87	20	2,037.40	178.27	2,215.67
13	Newspaper	25-Jan-16	24-Feb	$ 79.42	6	476.52	41.70	518.22
14	Newspaper	1-Feb-16	2-Mar	$ 79.42	2	158.84	13.90	172.74
15	T-Shirts	3-Feb-16	4-Mar	$ 5.67	200	1,134.00	99.23	1,233.23
16	TV commercials	1-Feb-16	2-Mar	$1,054.42	4	4,217.68	369.05	4,586.73

Sales Tax 0.0875

Excel 2013

Working with themes and cell styles

Using themes and cell styles makes it easier to ensure that your worksheets are consistent. A **theme** is a predefined set of formats that gives your Excel worksheet a professional look. Formatting choices included in a theme are colors, fonts, and line and fill effects. To apply a theme, click the Themes button in the Themes group on the PAGE LAYOUT tab to open the Themes gallery, as shown in **FIGURE C-16**, then click a theme in the gallery. **Cell styles** are sets of cell formats based on themes, so they are automatically updated if you change a theme. For example, if you apply the 20% - Accent1 cell style to cell A1 in a worksheet that has no theme applied, the fill color changes to light blue with no pattern, and the font changes to Constantia. If you change the theme of the worksheet to Ion Boardroom, cell A1's fill color changes to red and the font changes to Century Gothic, because these are the new theme's associated formats.

FIGURE C-16: Themes gallery

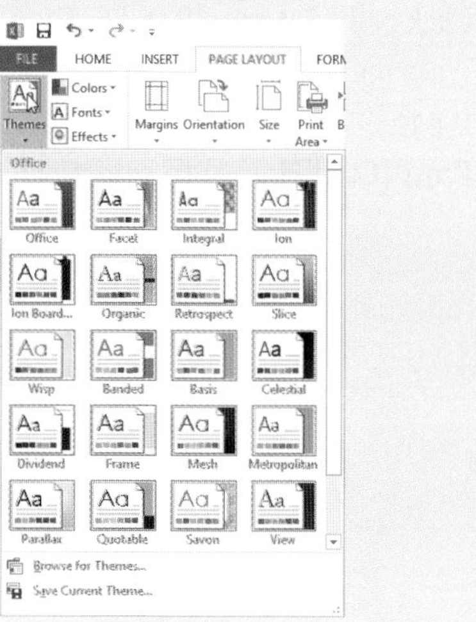

Apply Conditional Formatting

Learning Outcomes
- Create conditional formatting in a range
- Change formatting and parameters in conditional formatting

So far, you've used formatting to change the appearance of different types of data, but you can also use formatting to highlight important aspects of the data itself. For example, you can apply formatting that changes the font color to red for any cells where ad costs exceed $100 and to green where ad costs are below $50. This is called **conditional formatting** because Excel automatically applies different formats to data if the data meets conditions you specify. The formatting is updated if you change data in the worksheet. You can also copy conditional formats the same way you copy other formats. **CASE** *Grace is concerned about advertising costs exceeding the yearly budget. You decide to use conditional formatting to highlight certain trends and patterns in the data so that it's easy to spot the most expensive advertising.*

STEPS

QUICK TIP
You can also use the Quick Analysis tool to create data bars, but with fewer choices.

1. **Select the range H4:H30, click the Conditional Formatting button in the Styles group on the HOME tab, point to Data Bars, then point to the Light Blue Data Bar (second row, second from left)**

   Data bars are colored horizontal bars that visually illustrate differences between values in a range of cells. Live Preview shows how this formatting will appear in the worksheet, as shown in **FIGURE C-17**.

QUICK TIP
You can apply an Icon Set to a selected range by clicking the Conditional Formatting button in the Styles group, then pointing to Icon Sets; icons appear within the cells to illustrate differences in values.

2. **Point to the Green Data Bar (first row, second from left), then click it**
3. **Select the range F4:F30, click the Conditional Formatting button in the Styles group, then point to Highlight Cells Rules**

   The Highlight Cells Rules submenu displays choices for creating different formatting conditions. For example, you can create a rule for values that are greater than or less than a certain amount, or between two amounts.

4. **Click Between on the submenu**

   The Between dialog box opens, displaying input boxes you can use to define the condition and a default format (Light Red Fill with Dark Red Text) selected for cells that meet that condition. Depending on the condition you select in the Highlight Cells Rules submenu (such as "Greater Than" or "Less Than"), this dialog box displays different input boxes. You define the condition using the input boxes and then assign the formatting you want to use for cells that meet that condition. Values used in input boxes for a condition can be constants, formulas, cell references, or dates.

QUICK TIP
To define custom formatting for data that meets the condition, click Custom Format at the bottom of the with list, and then use the Format Cells dialog box to set the formatting to be applied.

5. **Type 2000 in the first text box, type 4000 in the second text box, click the with list arrow, click Light Red Fill, compare your settings to FIGURE C-18, then click OK**

   All cells with values between 2000 and 4000 in column F appear with a light red fill.

6. **Click cell F7, type 3975.55, then press [Enter]**

   When the value in cell F7 changes, the formatting also changes because the new value meets the condition you set. Compare your results to **FIGURE C-19**.

7. **Press [Ctrl][Home] to select cell A1, then save your work**

FIGURE C-17: Previewing data bars in a range

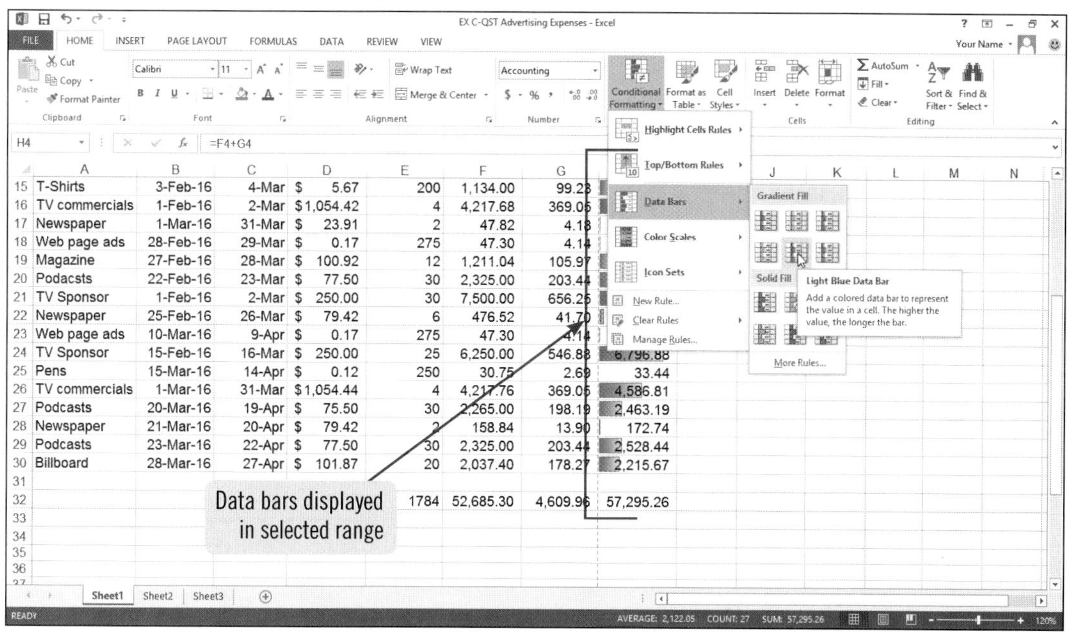

FIGURE C-18: Between dialog box

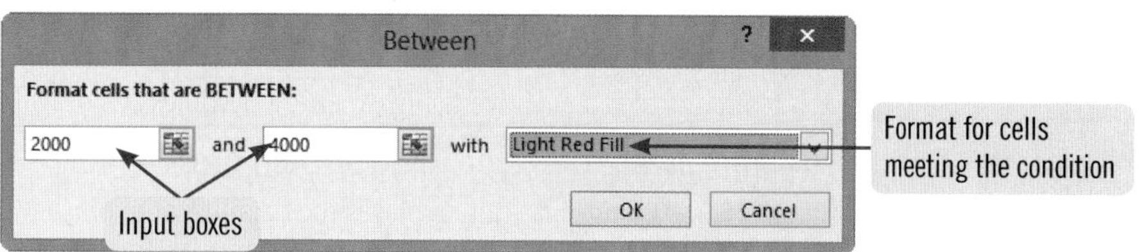

FIGURE C-19: Worksheet with conditional formatting

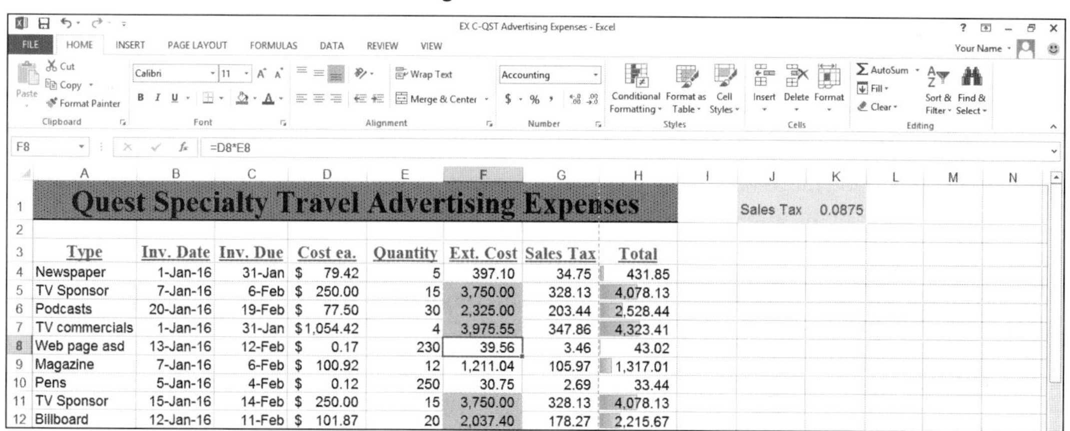

Managing conditional formatting rules

If you create a conditional formatting rule and then want to change the condition to reflect a different value or format, you don't need to create a new rule; instead, you can modify the rule using the Rules Manager. Select the cell(s) containing conditional formatting, click the Conditional Formatting button in the Styles group, then click Manage Rules. The Conditional Formatting Rules Manager dialog box opens. Select the rule you want to edit, click Edit Rule, and then modify the settings in the Edit the Rule Description area in the Edit Formatting Rule dialog box. To change the formatting for a rule, click the Format button in the Edit the Rule Description area, select the formatting styles you want the text to have, then click OK three times to close the Format Cells dialog box, the Edit Formatting Rule dialog box, and then the Conditional Formatting Rules Manager dialog box. The rule is modified, and the new conditional formatting is applied to the selected cells. To delete a rule, select the rule in the Conditional Formatting Rules Manager dialog box, then click the Delete Rule button.

Rename and Move a Worksheet

Learning Outcomes
- Rename a sheet
- Apply color to a sheet tab
- Reorder sheets in a workbook

By default, an Excel workbook initially contains one worksheet named Sheet1, although you can add sheets at any time. Each sheet name appears on a sheet tab at the bottom of the worksheet. When you open a new workbook, the first worksheet, Sheet1, is the active sheet. To move from sheet to sheet, you can click any sheet tab at the bottom of the worksheet window. The sheet tab scrolling buttons, located to the left of the sheet tabs, are useful when a workbook contains too many sheet tabs to display at once. To make it easier to identify the sheets in a workbook, you can rename each sheet and add color to the tabs. You can also organize them in a logical way. For instance, to better track performance goals, you could name each workbook sheet for an individual salesperson, and you could move the sheets so they appear in alphabetical order. **CASE** *In the current worksheet, Sheet1 contains information about actual advertising expenses. Sheet2 contains an advertising budget, and Sheet3 contains no data. You want to rename the two sheets in the workbook to reflect their contents, add color to a sheet tab to easily distinguish one from the other, and change their order.*

STEPS

QUICK TIP
You can also rename a sheet by right-clicking the tab, clicking Rename on the shortcut menu, typing the new name, then pressing [Enter].

QUICK TIP
To delete a sheet, click its tab, click the Delete list arrow in the Cells group, then click Delete Sheet. To insert a worksheet, click the New sheet button ⊕ to the right of the sheet tabs.

QUICK TIP
If you have more sheet tabs than are visible, you can move between sheets by using the tab scrolling buttons to the left of the sheet tabs: the Previous Worksheet button ◀ and the Next Worksheet button ▶.

1. **Click the Sheet2 tab**
   Sheet2 becomes active, appearing in front of the Sheet1 tab; this is the worksheet that contains the budgeted advertising expenses. See **FIGURE C-20**.
2. **Click the Sheet1 tab**
   Sheet1, which contains the actual advertising expenses, becomes active again.
3. **Double-click the Sheet2 tab, type Budget, then press [Enter]**
   The new name for Sheet2 automatically replaces the default name on the tab. Worksheet names can have up to 31 characters, including spaces and punctuation.
4. **Right-click the Budget tab, point to Tab Color on the shortcut menu, then click the Bright Green, Accent 4, Lighter 40% color (fourth row, third column from the right) as shown in FIGURE C-21**
5. **Double-click the Sheet1 tab, type Actual, then press [Enter]**
   Notice that the color of the Budget tab changes depending on whether it is the active tab; when the Actual tab is active, the color of the Budget tab changes to the green tab color you selected. You decide to rearrange the order of the sheets, so that the Budget tab is to the left of the Actual tab.
6. **Click the Budget tab, hold down the mouse button, drag it to the left of the Actual tab, as shown in FIGURE C-22, then release the mouse button**
   As you drag, the pointer changes to the sheet relocation pointer, and a small, black triangle just above the tabs shows the position the moved sheet will be in when you release the mouse button. The first sheet in the workbook is now the Budget sheet. See **FIGURE C-23**. You can move multiple sheets by pressing and holding [Shift] while clicking the sheets you want to move, then dragging the sheets to their new location.
7. **Click the Actual sheet tab, click the Page Layout button on the status bar to open Page Layout view, enter your name in the left header text box, then click anywhere in the worksheet to deselect the header**
8. **Click the PAGE LAYOUT tab on the Ribbon, click the Orientation button in the Page Setup group, then click Landscape**
9. **Right-click the Sheet3 tab, click Delete on the shortcut menu, press [Ctrl][Home], then save your work**

FIGURE C-20: Sheet tabs in workbook

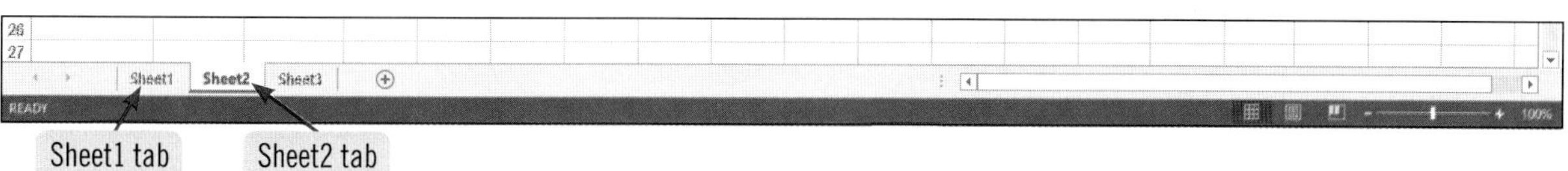

FIGURE C-21: Tab Color palette

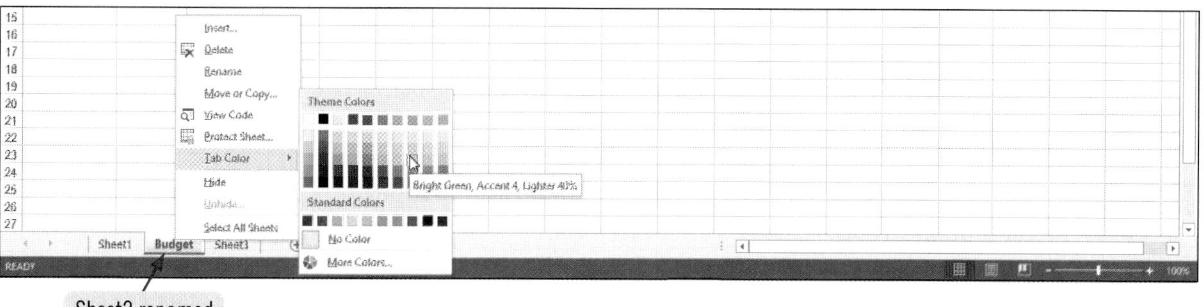

FIGURE C-22: Moving the Budget sheet

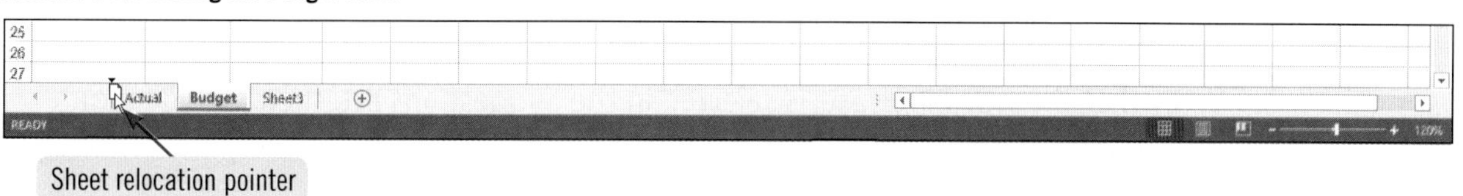

FIGURE C-23: Reordered sheets

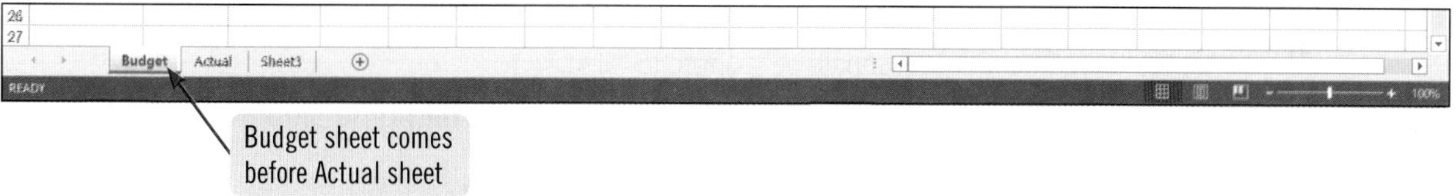

Excel 2013

Copying, Adding, and Deleting worksheets

There are times when you may want to copy a worksheet. For example, a workbook might contain a sheet with Quarter 1 expenses, and you want to use that sheet as the basis for a sheet containing Quarter 2 expenses. To copy a sheet within the same workbook, press and hold [Ctrl], drag the sheet tab to the desired tab location, release the mouse button, then release [Ctrl]. A duplicate sheet appears with the same name as the copied sheet followed by "(2)" indicating it is a copy. You can then rename the sheet to a more meaningful name. To copy a sheet to a different workbook, both the source and destination workbooks must be open. Select the sheet to copy or move, right-click the sheet tab, then click Move or Copy in the shortcut menu. Complete the information in the Move or Copy dialog box. Be sure to click the Create a copy check box if you are copying rather than moving the worksheet. Carefully check your calculation results whenever you move or copy a worksheet. You can add multiple worksheets to a workbook by clicking the HOME tab on the Ribbon, pressing and holding [Shift], then clicking the number of existing worksheet tabs that correspond with the number of sheets you want to add, clicking the Insert list arrow in the Cells group on the HOME tab, then clicking Insert Sheet. You can delete multiple worksheets from a workbook by clicking the HOME tab on the Ribbon, pressing and holding [Shift], clicking the sheet tabs of the worksheets you want to delete, clicking the Delete list arrow in the Cells group on the HOME tab, then clicking Delete Sheet.

Check Spelling

Learning Outcomes
- Describe how spell checking works
- Change the spelling using a suggestion
- Replace a word using Find & Select

Excel includes a spell checker to help you ensure that the words in your worksheet are spelled correctly. The spell checker scans your worksheet, displays words it doesn't find in its built-in dictionary, and suggests replacements when they are available. To check all of the sheets in a multiple-sheet workbook, you need to display each sheet individually and run the spell checker for each one. Because the built-in dictionary cannot possibly include all the words that anyone needs, you can add words to the dictionary, such as your company name, an acronym, or an unusual technical term. Once you add a word or term, the spell checker no longer considers that word misspelled. Any words you've added to the dictionary using Word, Access, or PowerPoint are also available in Excel. **CASE** *Before you distribute this workbook to Grace and the marketing managers, you check its spelling.*

STEPS

QUICK TIP
The Spelling dialog box lists the name of the language currently being used in its title bar.

1. **Click the REVIEW tab on the Ribbon, then click the Spelling button in the Proofing group**
   The Spelling: English (U.S.) dialog box opens, as shown in **FIGURE C-24**, with "asd" selected as the first misspelled word in the worksheet, and with "ads" selected in the Suggestions list as a possible replacement. For any word, you have the option to Ignore this case of the flagged word, Ignore All cases of the flagged word, Change the word to the selected suggestion, Change All instances of the flagged word to the selected suggestion, or add the flagged word to the dictionary using Add to Dictionary.
2. **Click Change**
   Next, the spell checker finds the word "Podacsts" and suggests "Podcasts" as an alternative.
3. **Verify that the word Podcasts is selected in the Suggestions list, then click Change**
   When no more incorrect words are found, Excel displays a message indicating that the spell check is complete.
4. **Click OK**
5. **Click the HOME tab, click Find & Select in the Editing group, then click Replace**
   The Find and Replace dialog box opens. You can use this dialog box to replace a word or phrase. It might be a misspelling of a proper name that the spell checker didn't recognize as misspelled, or it could simply be a term that you want to change throughout the worksheet. Grace has just told you that each instance of "Billboard" in the worksheet should be changed to "Sign."
6. **Type Billboard in the Find what text box, press [Tab], then type Sign in the Replace with text box**
   Compare your dialog box to **FIGURE C-25**.
7. **Click Replace All, click OK to close the Microsoft Excel dialog box, then click Close to close the Find and Replace dialog box**
   Excel has made two replacements.
8. **Click the FILE tab, click Print on the navigation bar, click the No Scaling setting in the Settings section on the Print tab, then click Fit Sheet on One Page**
9. **Click the Return button to return to your worksheet, save your work, submit it to your instructor as directed, close the workbook, then exit Excel**
   The completed worksheet is shown in **FIGURE C-26**.

Emailing a workbook

You can send an entire workbook from within Excel using your installed email program, such as Microsoft Outlook. To send a workbook as an email message attachment, open the workbook, click the FILE tab, then click Share on the navigation bar. With the Email option selected in the Share section in Backstage view, click Send as Attachment in the right pane. An email message opens in your default email program with the workbook automatically attached; the filename appears in the Attached field. Complete the To and optional Cc fields, include a message if you wish, then click Send.

FIGURE C-24: Spelling: English (U.S.) dialog box

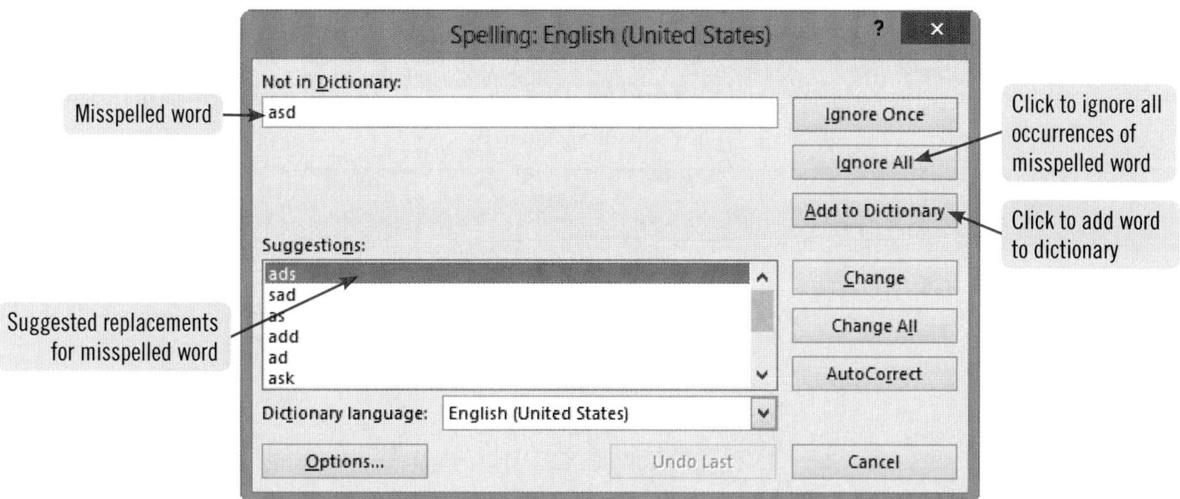

FIGURE C-25: Find and Replace dialog box

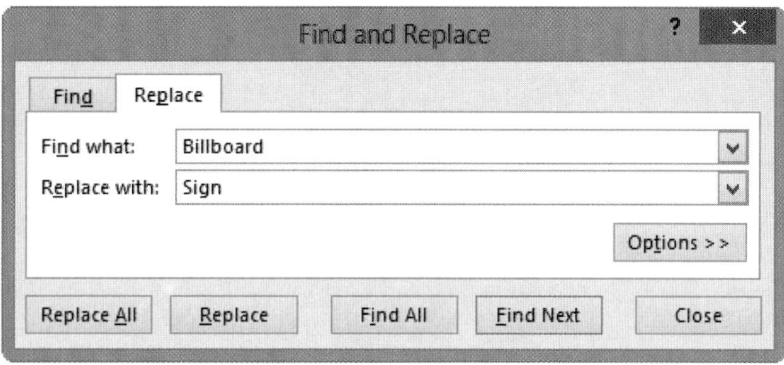

FIGURE C-26: Completed worksheet

Your Name

Quest Specialty Travel Advertising Expenses

Sales Tax

Type	Inv. Date	Inv. Due	Cost ea.	Quantity	Ext. Cost	Sales Tax	Total
Newspaper	1-Jan-16	31-Jan	$ 79.42	5	397.10	34.75	431.85
TV Sponsor	7-Jan-16	6-Feb	$ 250.00	15	3,750.00	328.13	4,078.13
Podcasts	20-Jan-16	19-Feb	$ 77.50	30	2,325.00	203.44	2,528.44
TV commercials	1-Jan-16	31-Jan	$ 1,054.42	4	3,975.55	347.86	4,323.41
Web page ads	13-Jan-16	12-Feb	$ 0.17	230	39.56	3.46	43.02
Magazine	7-Jan-16	6-Feb	$ 100.92	12	1,211.04	105.97	1,317.01
Pens	5-Jan-16	4-Feb	$ 0.12	250	30.75	2.69	33.44
TV Sponsor	15-Jan-16	14-Feb	$ 250.00	15	3,750.00	328.13	4,078.13
Sign	12-Jan-16	11-Feb	$ 101.87	20	2,037.40	178.27	2,215.67
Newspaper	25-Jan-16	24-Feb	$ 79.42	6	476.52	41.70	518.22
Newspaper	1-Feb-16	2-Mar	$ 79.42	2	158.84	13.90	172.74
T-Shirts	3-Feb-16	4-Mar	$ 5.67	200	1,134.00	99.23	1,233.23
TV commercials	1-Feb-16	2-Mar	$ 1,054.42	4	4,217.68	369.05	4,586.73
Newspaper	1-Mar-16	31-Mar	$ 23.91	2	47.82	4.18	52.00
Web page ads	28-Feb-16	29-Mar	$ 0.17	275	47.30	4.14	51.44
Magazine	27-Feb-16	28-Mar	$ 100.92	12	1,211.04	105.97	1,317.01
Podcasts	22-Feb-16	23-Mar	$ 77.50	30	2,325.00	203.44	2,528.44
TV Sponsor	1-Feb-16	2-Mar	$ 250.00	30	7,500.00	656.25	8,156.25
Newspaper	25-Feb-16	26-Mar	$ 79.42	6	476.52	41.70	518.22
Web page ads	10-Mar-16	9-Apr	$ 0.17	275	47.30	4.14	51.44
TV Sponsor	15-Feb-16	16-Mar	$ 250.00	25	6,250.00	546.88	6,796.88
Pens	15-Mar-16	14-Apr	$ 0.12	250	30.75	2.69	33.44
TV commercials	1-Mar-16	31-Mar	$ 1,054.44	4	4,217.76	369.05	4,586.81
Podcasts	20-Mar-16	19-Apr	$ 75.50	30	2,265.00	198.19	2,463.19
Newspaper	21-Mar-16	20-Apr	$ 79.42	2	158.84	13.90	172.74
Podcasts	23-Mar-16	22-Apr	$ 77.50	30	2,325.00	203.44	2,528.44
Sign	28-Mar-16	27-Apr	$ 101.87	20	2,037.40	178.27	2,215.67
			$ 5,304.30	1784	52,443.17	4,588.78	57,031.95

Excel 2013

Practice

Put your skills into practice with **SAM Projects!** SAM Projects for this unit can be found online. If you have a SAM account, go to www.cengage.com/sam2013 to download the most recent Project Instruction and Start Files.

Concepts Review

Label each element of the Excel worksheet window shown in FIGURE C-27.

FIGURE C-27

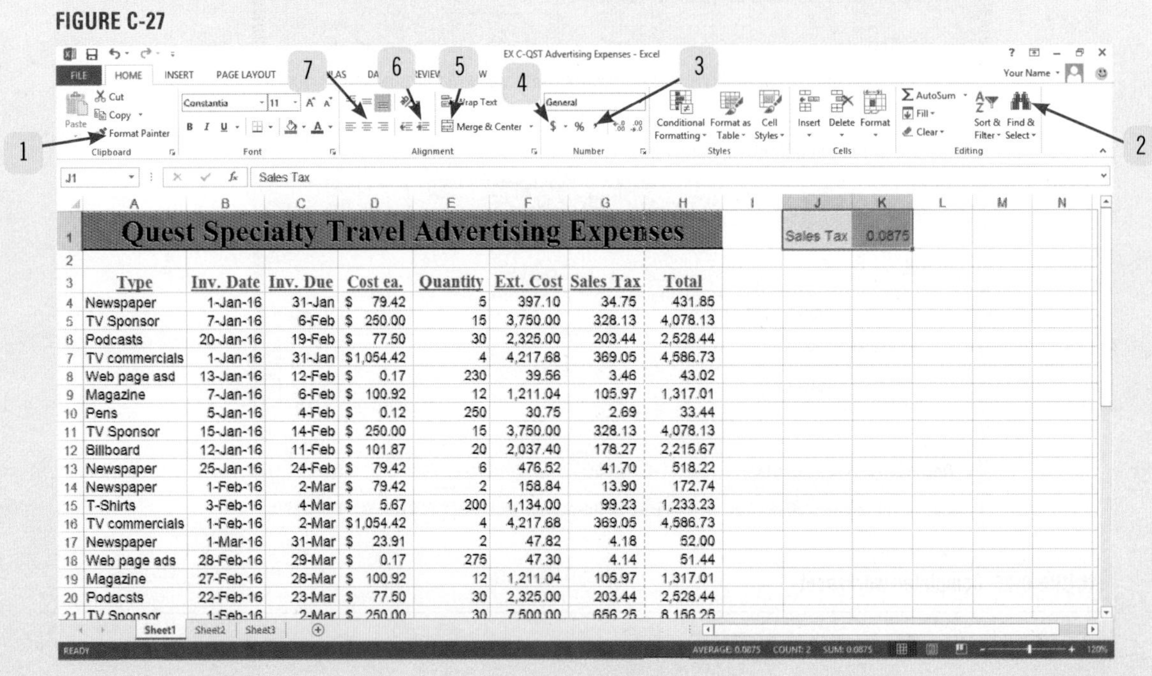

Match each command or button with the statement that best describes it.

8. Conditional formatting	**a.** Checks for apparent misspellings in a worksheet
9. $	**b.** Adds dollar signs and two decimal places to selected data
10. Spelling button	**c.** Centers cell contents over multiple cells
11. [Ctrl][Home]	**d.** Changes formatting of a cell that meets a certain rule
12.	**e.** Moves cell pointer to cell A1
13.	**f.** Displays background color options for a cell

Select the best answer from the list of choices.

14. Which button increases the number of decimal places in selected cells?

- **a.** ←.0 .00
- **b.** .00 →.0
- **c.** [Decrease Indent button]
- **d.** [Increase Indent button]

15. What feature is used to delete a conditional formatting rule?

- **a.** Rules Reminder
- **b.** Conditional Formatting Rules Manager
- **c.** Condition Manager
- **d.** Format Manager

16. Which button removes the italic font style from selected cells?

- **a.** *I*
- **b.** **B**
- **c.** *I*
- **d.** U

17. Which button copies multiple formats from selected cells to other cells?

- **a.** [Redo button]
- **b.** [Dialog Box Launcher button]
- **c.** A
- **d.** [Format Painter button]

18. What is the name of the feature used to resize a column to accommodate its widest entry?

- **a.** AutoFormat
- **b.** AutoFit
- **c.** AutoResize
- **d.** AutoRefit

19. Which of the following is an example of Accounting number format?

- **a.** 5555
- **b.** $5,555.55
- **c.** 55.55%
- **d.** 5,555.55

Skills Review

1. Format values.

- **a.** Start Excel, open the file EX C-2.xlsx from the location where you store your Data Files, then save it as **EX C-Life Insurance Premiums**.
- **b.** Use the Sum function to enter a formula in cell B10 that totals the number of employees.
- **c.** Create a formula in cell C5 that calculates the monthly insurance premium for the accounting department. (*Hint*: Make sure you use the correct type of cell reference in the formula. To calculate the department's monthly premium, multiply the number of employees by the monthly premium in cell B14.)
- **d.** Copy the formula in cell C5 to the range C6:C10.
- **e.** Format the range C5:C10 using Accounting number format.
- **f.** Change the format of the range C6:C9 to the Comma Style.
- **g.** Reduce the number of decimals in cell B14 to 0 using a button in the Number group on the HOME tab.
- **h.** Save your work.

2. Change font and font sizes.

- **a.** Select the range of cells containing the column labels (in row 4).
- **b.** Change the font of the selection to Times New Roman.
- **c.** Increase the font size of the selection to 12 points.
- **d.** Increase the font size of the label in cell A1 to 14 points.
- **e.** Save your changes.

3. Change font styles and alignment.

- **a.** Apply the bold and italic font styles to the worksheet title in cell A1.
- **b.** Use the Merge & Center button to center the Life Insurance Premiums label over columns A through C.
- **c.** Apply the italic font style to the Life Insurance Premiums label.
- **d.** Add the bold font style to the labels in row 4.
- **e.** Use the Format Painter to copy the format in cell A4 to the range A5:A10.
- **f.** Apply the format in cell C10 to cell B14.
- **g.** Change the alignment of cell A10 to Align Right using a button in the Alignment group.

- **h.** Select the range of cells containing the column labels, then center them.
- **i.** Remove the italic font style from the Life Insurance Premiums label, then increase the font size to 14.
- **j.** Move the Life Insurance Premiums label to cell A3, then add the bold and underline font styles.
- **k.** Save your changes.

4. Adjust the column width.

- **a.** Resize column C to a width of 10.71 characters.
- **b.** Use the AutoFit feature to resize columns A and B.
- **c.** Clear the contents of cell A13 (do not delete the cell).
- **d.** Change the text in cell A14 to **Monthly Premium**, then change the width of the column to 25 characters.
- **e.** Save your changes.

5. Insert and delete rows and columns.

- **a.** Insert a new row between rows 5 and 6.
- **b.** Add a new department, **Charity**, in the newly inserted row. Enter **6** as the number of employees in the department.
- **c.** Copy the formula in cell C7 to C6.
- **d.** Add the following comment to cell A6: **New department**. Display the comment, then drag to move it out of the way, if necessary.
- **e.** Add a new column between the Department and Employees columns with the title **Family Coverage**, then resize the column using AutoFit.
- **f.** Delete the Legal row from the worksheet.
- **g.** Move the value in cell C14 to cell B14.
- **h.** Save your changes.

6. Apply colors, patterns, and borders.

- **a.** Add Outside Borders around the range A4:D10.
- **b.** Add a Bottom Double Border to cells C9 and D9 (above the calculated employee and premium totals).
- **c.** Apply the Aqua, Accent 5, Lighter 80% fill color to the labels in the Department column (do not include the Total label).
- **d.** Apply the Orange, Accent 6, Lighter 60% fill color to the range A4:D4.
- **e.** Change the color of the font in the range A4:D4 to Red, Accent 2, Darker 25%.
- **f.** Add a 12.5% Gray pattern style to cell A1.
- **g.** Format the range A14:B14 with a fill color of Dark Blue, Text 2, Lighter 40%, change the font color to White, Background 1, then apply the bold font style.
- **h.** Save your changes.

7. Apply conditional formatting.

- **a.** Select the range D5:D9, then create a conditional format that changes cell contents to green fill with dark green text if the value is between 150 and 275.
- **b.** Select the range C5:C9, then create a conditional format that changes cell contents to red text if the number of employees exceeds 10.
- **c.** Apply a purple gradient-filled data bar to the range C5:C9. (*Hint*: Click Purple Data Bar in the Gradient Fill section.)
- **d.** Use the Rules Manager to modify the conditional format in cells C5:C9 to display values greater than 10 in bold dark red text.
- **e.** Merge and center the title (cell A1) over columns A through D.
- **f.** Save your changes.

8. Rename and move a worksheet.

- **a.** Name the Sheet1 tab **Insurance Data**.
- **b.** Add a sheet to the workbook, then name the new sheet **Employee Data**.
- **c.** Change the Insurance Data tab color to Red, Accent 2, Lighter 40%.

d. Change the Employee Data tab color to Aqua, Accent 5, Lighter 40%.
e. Move the Employee Data sheet so it comes before (to the left of) the Insurance Data sheet.
f. Make the Insurance Data sheet active, enter your name in cell A20, then save your work.

9. **Check spelling.**
   a. Move the cell pointer to cell A1.
   b. Use the Find & Select feature to replace the Accounting label in cell A5 with Accounting/Legal.
   c. Check the spelling in the worksheet using the spell checker, and correct any spelling errors if necessary.
   d. Save your changes, then compare your Insurance Data sheet to **FIGURE C-28**.
   e. Preview the Insurance Data sheet in Backstage view, submit your work to your instructor as directed, then close the workbook and exit Excel.

FIGURE C-28

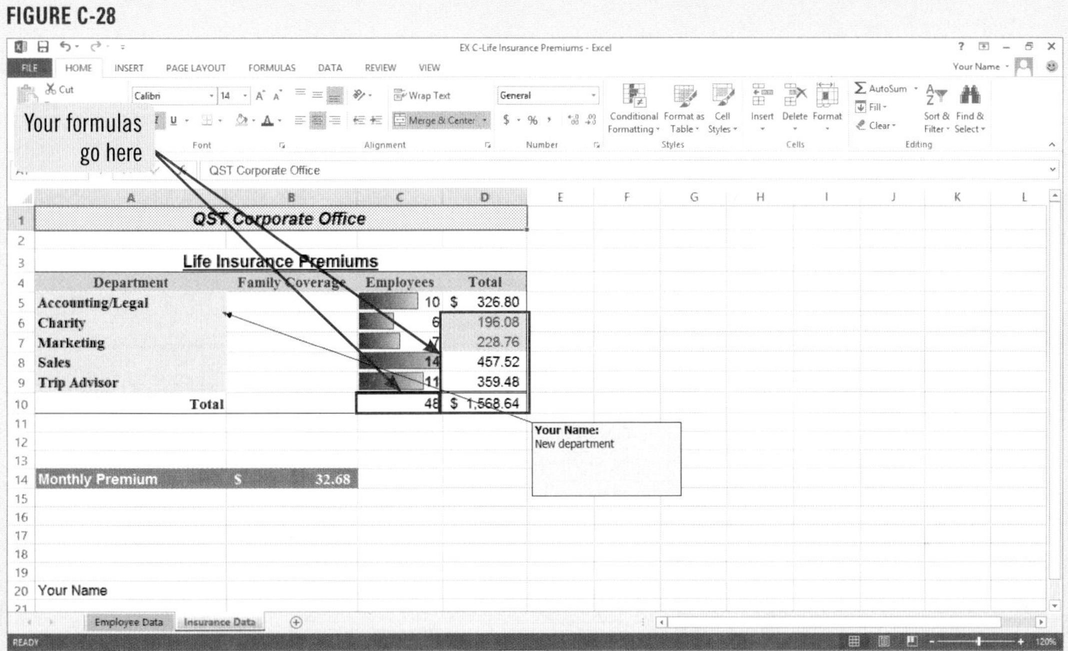

Independent Challenge 1

You run a freelance accounting business, and one of your newest clients is Pen & Paper, a small office supply store. Now that you've converted the store's accounting records to Excel, the manager would like you to work on an analysis of the inventory. Although more items will be added later, the worksheet has enough items for you to begin your modifications.

a. Start Excel, open the file EX C-3.xlsx from the location where you store your Data Files, then save it as **EX C-Pen & Paper Office Supply Inventory**.
b. Create a formula in cell E4 that calculates the value of the items in stock based on the price paid per item in cell B4. Format the cell in the Comma Style.
c. In cell F4, calculate the sale price of the items in stock using an absolute reference to the markup value shown in cell H1.
d. Copy the formulas created above into the range E5:F14; first convert any necessary cell references to absolute so that the formulas work correctly.
e. Apply bold to the column labels, and italicize the inventory items in column A.
f. Make sure all columns are wide enough to display the data and labels.
g. Format the values in the Sale Price column as Accounting number format with two decimal places.
h. Format the values in the Price Paid column as Comma Style with two decimal places.

Independent Challenge 1 (continued)

i. Add a row under #2 Pencils for **Digital cordless telephones**, price paid **53.45**, sold individually (**each**), with **23** on hand. Copy the appropriate formulas to cells E7:F7.

j. Verify that all the data in the worksheet is visible and formulas are correct. Adjust any items as needed, and check the spelling of the entire worksheet.

k. Use conditional formatting to apply yellow fill with dark yellow text to items with a quantity of less than 25 on hand.

l. Use an icon set of your choosing in the range D4:D15 to illustrate the relative differences between values in the range.

m. Add an outside border around the data in the Item column (*do not* include the Item column label).

n. Delete the row containing the Thumb tacks entry.

o. Enter your name in an empty cell below the data, then save the file. Compare your worksheet to the sample in **FIGURE C-29**.

p. Preview the worksheet in Backstage view, submit your work to your instructor as directed, close the workbook, then exit Excel.

FIGURE C-29

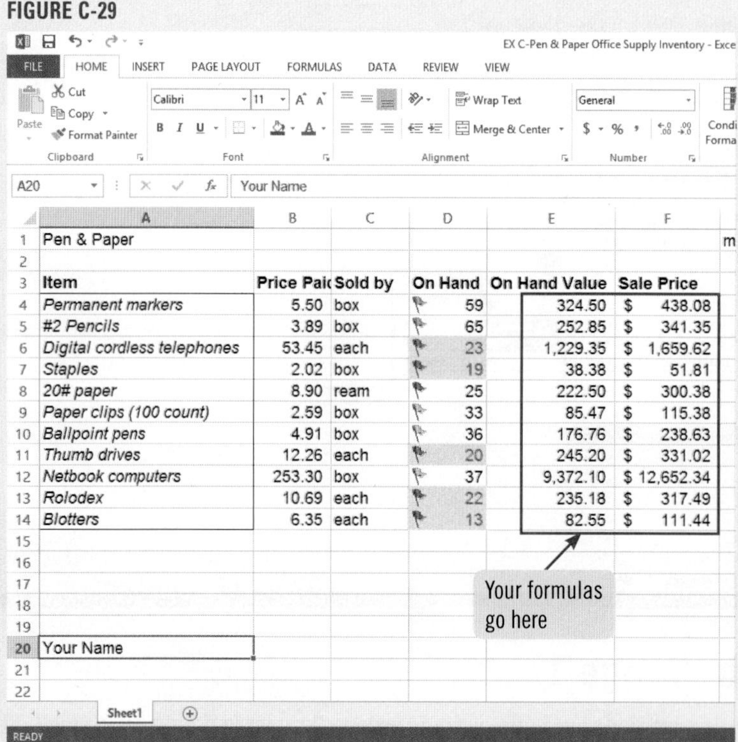

	A	B	C	D	E	F
1	Pen & Paper					
2						
3	Item	Price Paic	Sold by	On Hand	On Hand Value	Sale Price
4	Permanent markers	5.50	box	59	324.50	$ 438.08
5	#2 Pencils	3.89	box	65	252.85	$ 341.35
6	Digital cordless telephones	53.45	each	23	1,229.35	$ 1,659.62
7	Staples	2.02	box	19	38.38	$ 51.81
8	20# paper	8.90	ream	25	222.50	$ 300.38
9	Paper clips (100 count)	2.59	box	33	85.47	$ 115.38
10	Ballpoint pens	4.91	box	36	176.76	$ 238.63
11	Thumb drives	12.26	each	20	245.20	$ 331.02
12	Netbook computers	253.30	box	37	9,372.10	$ 12,652.34
13	Rolodex	10.69	each	22	235.18	$ 317.49
14	Blotters	6.35	each	13	82.55	$ 111.44
20	Your Name					

Independent Challenge 2

You volunteer several hours each week with the Assistance League of San Antonio, and you are in charge of maintaining the membership list. You're currently planning a mailing campaign to members in certain regions of the city. You also want to create renewal letters for members whose membership expires soon. You decide to format the list to enhance the appearance of the worksheet and make your upcoming tasks easier to plan.

a. Start Excel, open the file EX C-4.xlsx from the location where you store your Data Files, then save it as **EX C-San Antonio Assistance League**.

b. Remove any blank columns.

c. Create a conditional format in the Zip Code column so that entries greater than 78249 appear in light red fill with dark red text.

d. Make all columns wide enough to fit their data and labels. (*Hint*: You can use any method to size the columns.)

e. Use formatting enhancements, such as fonts, font sizes, font styles, and fill colors, to make the worksheet more attractive.

Independent Challenge 2 (continued)

f. Center the column labels.

g. Use conditional formatting so that entries for Year of Membership Expiration that are between 2017 and 2019 appear in green fill with bold black text. (*Hint*: Create a custom format for cells that meet the condition.)

h. Adjust any items as necessary, then check the spelling.

i. Change the name of the Sheet1 tab to one that reflects the sheet's contents, then add a tab color of your choice.

j. Enter your name in an empty cell, then save your work.

k. Preview the worksheet in Backstage view, make any final changes you think necessary, then submit your work to your instructor as directed. Compare your work to the sample shown in **FIGURE C-30**.

l. Close the workbook, then exit Excel.

FIGURE C-30

EX C-San Antonio Assistance League - Excel

A30 · Your Name

	A	B	C	D	E	F
2						Year
3			Number of	Year of Membership		2016
4	Member	Zip Code	Employees	Expiration	Code	
5	Candy's Candy Shop	78256	23	2020	3	
6	Chip Technology	78251	175	2021	3	
7	Computer Attic	78263	14	**2018**	2	
8	Deluxe Auto Shop	78245	17	**2017**	1	
9	Dental Associates	78287	15	**2018**	5	
10	Dr. Mary Terese	78263	12	2021	2	
11	Dunkin' Donuts	78278	10	**2018**	4	
12	Earl's Restaurant	78235	45	**2019**	3	
13	First Federal Bank	78267	36	2021	3	
14	Friendly Chevy	78286	17	2023	3	
15	From Office	78211	25	2022	5	
16	General Hospital	78225	538	2020	4	
17	Grande Table	78246	31	**2019**	4	
18	Holiday Inn	78221	75	**2018**	4	
19	Ken's Florist Shop	78241	10	**2017**	2	
20	Lisa's Photo Studio	78202	5	2020	4	
21	Meineke Muffler	78256	24	**2019**	1	
22	Midas Muffler	78221	22	2023	3	
23	Mill Shoppe	78205	165	2020	2	

Members, by zip code

READY

Independent Challenge 3

Prestige Press is a Boston-based publisher that manufactures children's books. As the finance manager for the company, one of your responsibilities is to analyze the monthly reports from the five district sales offices. Your boss, Joanne Bennington, has just asked you to prepare a quarterly sales report for an upcoming meeting. Because several top executives will be attending this meeting, Joanne reminds you that the report must look professional. In particular, she asks you to emphasize the company's surge in profits during the last month and to highlight the fact that the Northeastern district continues to outpace the other districts.

a. Plan a worksheet that shows the company's sales during the first quarter. Assume that all books are the same price. Make sure you include the following:
   - The number of books sold (units sold) and the associated revenues (total sales) for each of the five district sales offices. The five sales districts are Northeastern, Midwestern, Southeastern, Southern, and Western.
   - Calculations that show month-by-month totals for January, February, and March, and a 3-month cumulative total.
   - Calculations that show each district's share of sales (percent of Total Sales).
   - Labels that reflect the month-by-month data as well as the cumulative data.
   - Formatting enhancements such as data bars that emphasize the recent month's sales surge and the Northeastern district's sales leadership.

b. Ask yourself the following questions about the organization and formatting of the worksheet: What worksheet title and labels do you need, and where should they appear? How can you calculate the totals? What formulas can you copy to save time and keystrokes? Do any of these formulas need to use an absolute reference? How do you show dollar amounts? What information should be shown in bold? Do you need to use more than one font? Should you use more than one point size?

c. Start Excel, then save a new, blank workbook as **EX C-Prestige Press** to the location where you store your Data Files.

Independent Challenge 3 (continued)

d. Build the worksheet with your own price and sales data. Enter the titles and labels first, then enter the numbers and formulas. You can use the information in **TABLE C-4** to get started.

TABLE C-4

Prestige Press										
1st Quarter Sales Report										
		January		February		March		Total		
Office	Price	Units Sold	Sales	Units Sold	Sales	Units Sold	Sales	Units Sold	Sales	Total % of Sales
Northeastern										
Midwestern										
Southeastern										
Southern										
Western										

e. Add a row beneath the data containing the totals for each column.

f. Adjust the column widths as necessary.

g. Change the height of row 1 to 33 points.

h. Format labels and values to enhance the look of the worksheet, and change the font styles and alignment if necessary.

i. Resize columns and adjust the formatting as necessary.

j. Add data bars for the monthly Units Sold columns.

k. Add a column that calculates a 25% increase in total sales dollars. Use an absolute cell reference in this calculation. (*Hint*: Make sure the current formatting is applied to the new information.)

l. Delete the contents of cells J4:K4 if necessary, then merge and center cell I4 over column I:K.

m. Add a bottom double border to cells I10:L10.

n. Enter your name in an empty cell.

o. Check the spelling in the workbook, change to a landscape orientation, save your work, then compare your work to **FIGURE C-31**.

p. Preview the worksheet in Backstage view, then submit your work to your instructor as directed.

q. Close the workbook file, then exit Excel.

FIGURE C-31

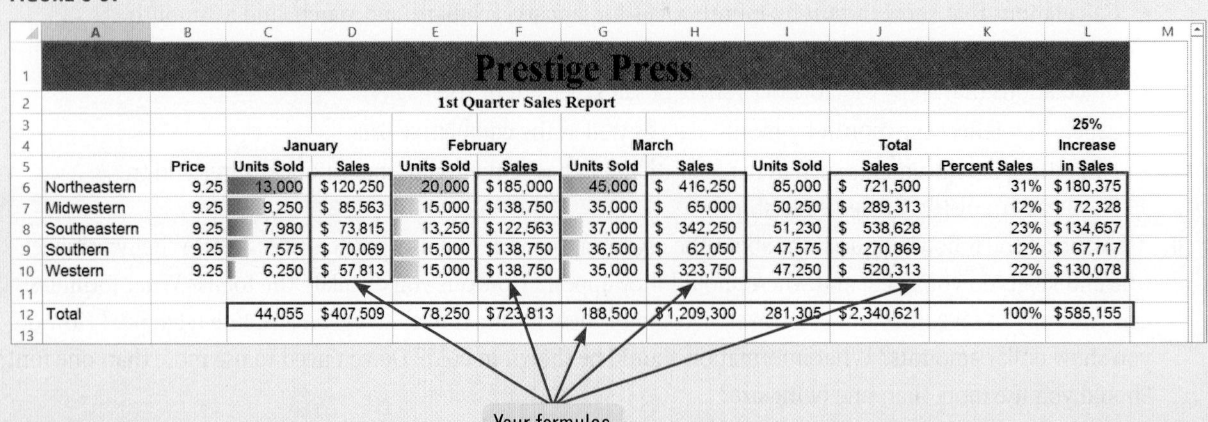

	A	B	C	D	E	F	G	H	I	J	K	L
1	Prestige Press											
2	1st Quarter Sales Report											
3												25%
4			January		February		March		Total			Increase
5		Price	Units Sold	Sales	Units Sold	Sales	Units Sold	Sales	Units Sold	Sales	Percent Sales	in Sales
6	Northeastern	9.25	13,000	$120,250	20,000	$185,000	45,000	$ 416,250	85,000	$ 721,500	31%	$180,375
7	Midwestern	9.25	9,250	$ 85,563	15,000	$138,750	35,000	$ 65,000	50,250	$ 289,313	12%	$ 72,328
8	Southeastern	9.25	7,980	$ 73,815	13,250	$122,563	37,000	$ 342,250	51,230	$ 538,628	23%	$134,657
9	Southern	9.25	7,575	$ 70,069	15,000	$138,750	36,500	$ 62,050	47,575	$ 270,869	12%	$ 67,717
10	Western	9.25	6,250	$ 57,813	15,000	$138,750	35,000	$ 323,750	47,250	$ 520,313	22%	$130,078
11												
12	Total		44,055	$407,509	78,250	$723,813	188,500	$1,209,300	281,305	$2,340,621	100%	$585,155
13												

Independent Challenge 4: Explore

This Independent Challenge requires an Internet connection.

You are saving money to take the international trip you have always dreamed about. You plan to visit seven different countries over the course of 2 months, and you have budgeted an identical spending allowance in each country. You want to create a worksheet that calculates the amount of native currency you will have in each country based on the budgeted amount. You want the workbook to reflect the currency information for each country.

a. Start Excel, then save a new, blank workbook as **EX C-World Tour Budget** to the location where you store your Data Files.
b. Add a title at the top of the worksheet.
c. Think of seven countries you would like to visit, then enter column and row labels for your worksheet. (*Hint*: You may wish to include row labels for each country, plus column labels for the country, the $1 equivalent in native currency, the total amount of native currency you'll have in each country, and the name of each country's monetary unit.)
d. Decide how much money you want to bring to each country (for example, $1,000), and enter that in the worksheet.
e. Use your favorite search engine to find your own information sources on currency conversions for the countries you plan to visit.
f. Enter the cash equivalent to $1 in U.S. dollars for each country in your list.
g. Create an equation that calculates the amount of native currency you will have in each country, using an absolute cell reference in the formula.
h. Format the entries in the column containing the native currency $1 equivalent as Number number format with three decimal places, and format the column containing the total native currency budget with two decimal places, using the correct currency number format for each country. (*Hint*: Use the Number tab in the Format cells dialog box; choose the appropriate currency number format from the Symbol list.)
i. Create a conditional format that changes the font style and color of the calculated amount in the $1,000 US column to light red fill with dark red text if the amount exceeds **1000** units of the local currency.
j. Merge and center the worksheet title over the column headings.
k. Add any formatting you want to the column headings, and resize the columns as necessary.
l. Add a background color to the title and change the font color if you choose.
m. Enter your name in the header of the worksheet.
n. Spell check the worksheet, save your changes, compare your work to **FIGURE C-32**, then preview the worksheet in Backstage view, and submit your work to your instructor as directed.
o. Close the workbook and exit Excel.

FIGURE C-32

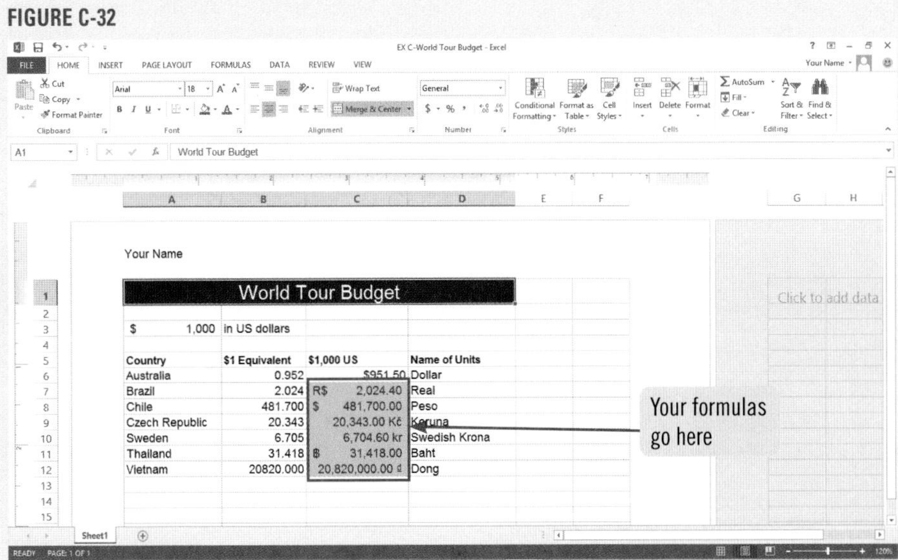

Visual Workshop

Open the file EX C-5.xlsx from the location where you store your Data Files, then save it as **EX C-Tip-Top Temps**. Use the skills you learned in this unit to format the worksheet so it looks like the one shown in **FIGURE C-33**. Create a conditional format in the Level column so that entries greater than 3 appear in light red fill with dark red text. Create an additional conditional format in the Review Cycle column so that any value equal to 3 appears in black fill with white bold text. Replace the Accounting department label with **Legal**. (*Hint*: The only additional font used in this exercise is 18-point Times New Roman in row 1.) Enter your name in the upper-right part of the header, check the spelling in the worksheet, save your changes, then submit your work to your instructor as directed. (*Hint*: Zoom out until the Zoom level is 100%.)

FIGURE C-33

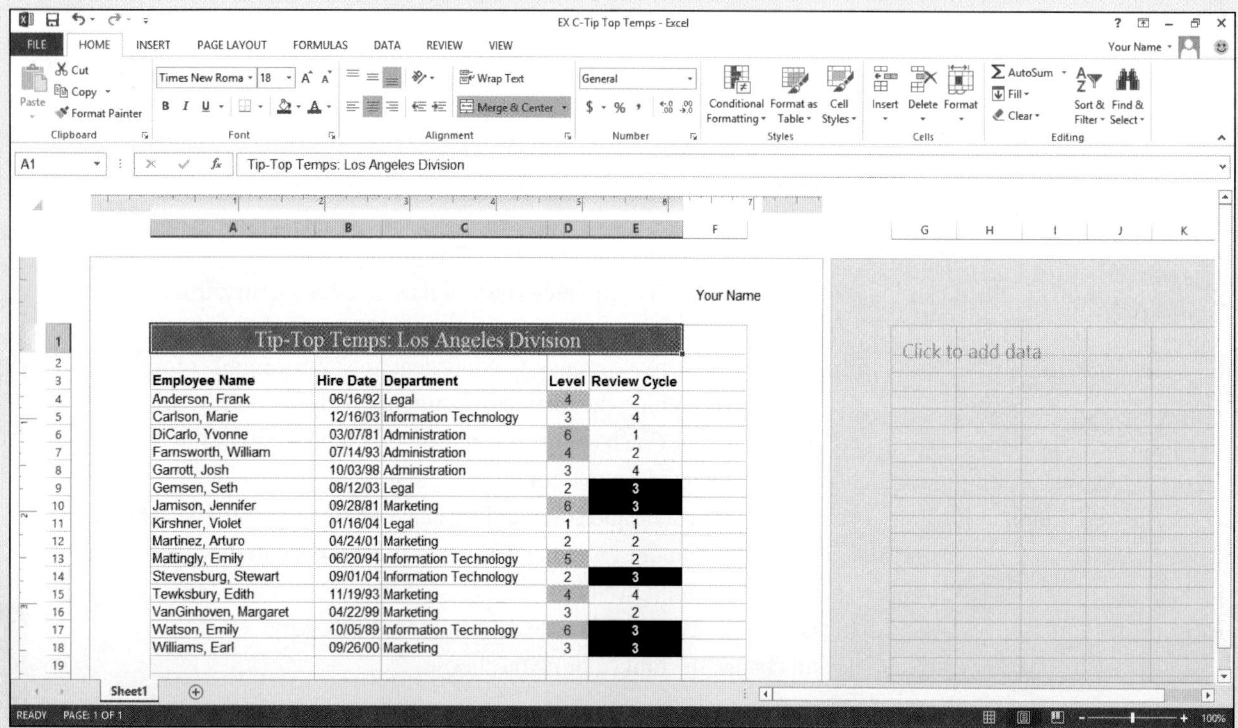

Your Name

Tip-Top Temps: Los Angeles Division

Employee Name	Hire Date	Department	Level	Review Cycle
Anderson, Frank	06/16/92	Legal	4	2
Carlson, Marie	12/16/03	Information Technology	3	4
DiCarlo, Yvonne	03/07/81	Administration	6	1
Farnsworth, William	07/14/93	Administration	4	2
Garrott, Josh	10/03/98	Administration	3	4
Gemsen, Seth	08/12/03	Legal	2	3
Jamison, Jennifer	09/28/81	Marketing	6	3
Kirshner, Violet	01/16/04	Legal	1	1
Martinez, Arturo	04/24/01	Marketing	2	2
Mattingly, Emily	06/20/94	Information Technology	5	2
Stevensburg, Stewart	09/01/04	Information Technology	2	3
Tewksbury, Edith	11/19/93	Marketing	4	4
VanGinhoven, Margaret	04/22/99	Marketing	3	2
Watson, Emily	10/05/89	Information Technology	6	3
Williams, Earl	09/26/00	Marketing	3	3

Working with Charts

CASE At the upcoming annual meeting, Grace Wong wants to emphasize spending patterns at Quest Specialty Travel. She asks you to create a chart showing the trends in company expenses over the past four quarters.

Unit Objectives

After completing this unit, you will be able to:

- Plan a chart
- Create a chart
- Move and resize a chart
- Change the chart design
- Change the chart format
- Format a chart
- Annotate and draw on a chart
- Create a pie chart

Files You Will Need

EX D-1.xlsx
EX D-2.xlsx
EX D-3.xlsx
EX D-4.xlsx
EX D-5.xlsx
EX D-6.xlsx

Plan a Chart

Learning Outcomes
- Prepare to create a chart
- Identify chart elements
- Explore common chart types

Before creating a chart, you need to plan the information you want your chart to show and how you want it to look. Planning ahead helps you decide what type of chart to create and how to organize the data. Understanding the parts of a chart makes it easier to format and to change specific elements so that the chart best illustrates your data. **CASE** *In preparation for creating the chart for Grace's presentation, you identify your goals for the chart and plan its layout.*

DETAILS

Use the following guidelines to plan the chart:

- **Determine the purpose of the chart, and identify the data relationships you want to communicate graphically**

  You want to create a chart that shows quarterly tour expenses for each country where Quest Specialty Travel provides tours. This worksheet data is shown in **FIGURE D-1**. You also want the chart to illustrate whether the quarterly expenses for each country increased or decreased from quarter to quarter.

- **Determine the results you want to see, and decide which chart type is most appropriate**

  Different chart types display data in distinctive ways. For example, a pie chart compares parts to the whole, so it's useful for showing what proportion of a budget amount was spent on tours in one country relative to what was spent on tours in other countries. A line chart, in contrast, is best for showing trends over time. To choose the best chart type for your data, you should first decide how you want your data displayed and interpreted. **TABLE D-1** describes several different types of charts you can create in Excel and their corresponding buttons on the INSERT tab on the Ribbon. Because you want to compare QST tour expenses in multiple countries over a period of four quarters, you decide to use a column chart.

- **Identify the worksheet data you want the chart to illustrate**

  Sometimes you use all the data in a worksheet to create a chart, while at other times you may need to select a range within the sheet. The worksheet from which you are creating your chart contains expense data for each of the past four quarters and the totals for the past year. You will need to use all the quarterly data contained in the worksheet except the quarterly totals.

- **Understand the elements of a chart**

  The chart shown in **FIGURE D-2** contains basic elements of a chart. In the figure, QST tour countries are on the horizontal axis (also called the **x-axis**) and expense dollar amounts are on the vertical axis (also called the **y-axis**). The horizontal axis is also called the **category axis** because it often contains the names of data groups, such as locations, months, or years. The vertical axis is also called the **value axis** because it often contains numerical values that help you interpret the size of chart elements. (3-D charts also contain a **z-axis**, for comparing data across both categories and values.) The area inside the horizontal and vertical axes is the **plot area**. The **tick marks**, on the vertical axis, and **gridlines** (extending across the plot area) create a scale of measure for each value. Each value in a cell you select for your chart is a **data point**. In any chart, a **data marker** visually represents each data point, which in this case is a column. A collection of related data points is a **data series**. In this chart, there are four data series (Quarter 1, Quarter 2, Quarter 3, and Quarter 4). Each is made up of column data markers of a different color, so a **legend** is included to make it easy to identify them.

FIGURE D-1: Worksheet containing expense data

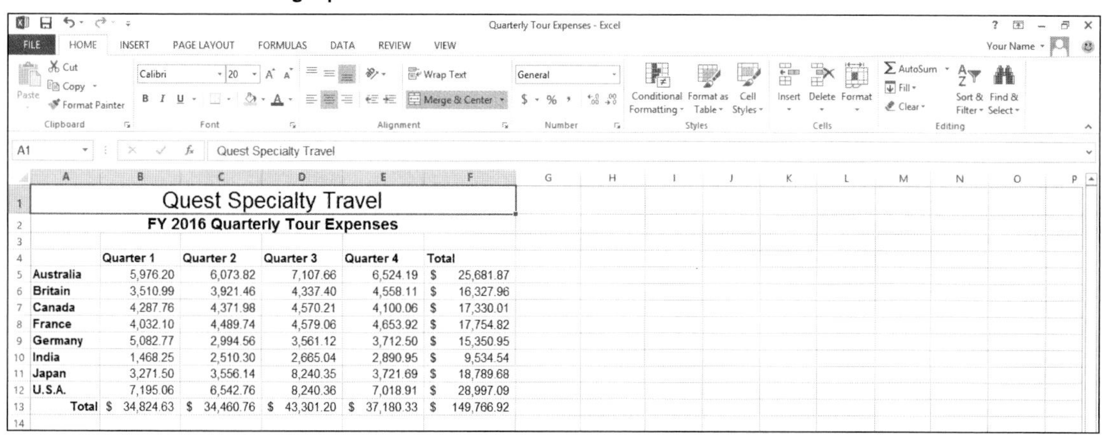

	Quarter 1	Quarter 2	Quarter 3	Quarter 4	Total
Quest Specialty Travel					
FY 2016 Quarterly Tour Expenses					
Australia	5,976.20	6,073.82	7,107.66	6,524.19	$ 25,681.87
Britain	3,510.99	3,921.46	4,337.40	4,558.11	$ 16,327.96
Canada	4,287.76	4,371.98	4,570.21	4,100.06	$ 17,330.01
France	4,032.10	4,489.74	4,579.06	4,653.92	$ 17,754.82
Germany	5,082.77	2,994.56	3,561.12	3,712.50	$ 15,350.95
India	1,468.25	2,510.30	2,665.04	2,890.95	$ 9,534.54
Japan	3,271.50	3,556.14	8,240.35	3,721.69	$ 18,789.68
U.S.A.	7,195.06	6,542.76	8,240.36	7,018.91	$ 28,997.09
Total	$ 34,824.63	$ 34,460.76	$ 43,301.20	$ 37,180.33	$ 149,766.92

FIGURE D-2: Chart elements

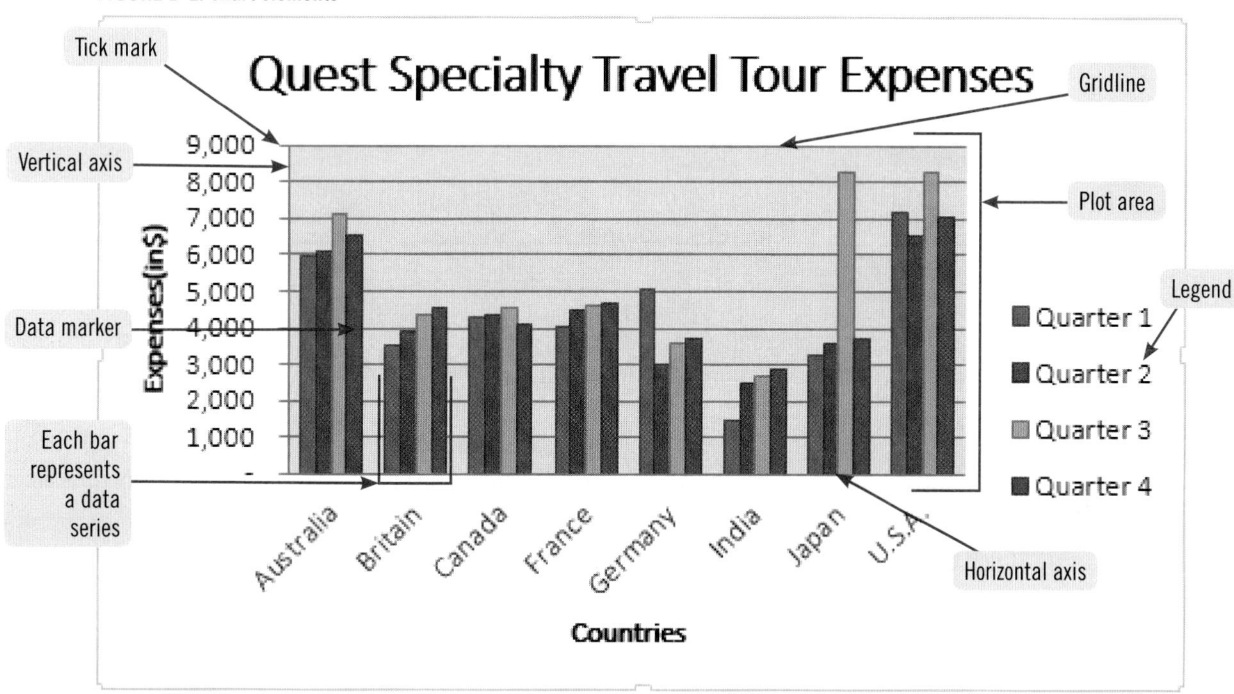

TABLE D-1: Common chart types

type	button	description
Column		Compares data using columns; the Excel default; sometimes referred to as a bar chart in other spreadsheet programs
Line		Compares trends over even time intervals; looks similar to an area chart, but does not emphasize total
Pie		Compares sizes of pieces as part of a whole; used for a single series of numbers
Bar		Compares data using horizontal bars; sometimes referred to as a horizontal bar chart in other spreadsheet programs
Area		Shows how individual volume changes over time in relation to total volume
Scatter		Compares trends over uneven time or measurement intervals; used in scientific and engineering disciplines for trend spotting and extrapolation

Create a Chart

Learning Outcomes
- Create a chart
- Switch a chart's columns/rows
- Add a chart title

To create a chart in Excel, you first select the range in a worksheet containing the data you want to chart. Once you've selected a range, you can use buttons on the INSERT tab on the Ribbon to create a chart based on the data in the range. **CASE** *Using the worksheet containing the quarterly expense data, you create a chart that shows how the expenses in each country varied across the quarters.*

STEPS

QUICK TIP
When charting data for a particular time period, make sure all series are for the same time period.

1. **Start Excel, open the file EX D-1.xlsx from the location where you store your Data Files, then save it as EX D-Quarterly Tour Expenses**

   You want the chart to include the quarterly tour expenses values, as well as quarter and country labels. You don't include the Total column and row because the figures in these cells would skew the chart.

2. **Select the range A4:E12, then click the Quick Analysis tool in the lower-right corner of the range**

   The Quick Analysis tool contains a tab that lets you quickly insert commonly used charts. The CHARTS tab includes buttons for each major chart type, plus a More Charts button for additional chart types, such as stock charts for charting stock market data.

QUICK TIP
To base a chart on data in nonadjacent ranges, press and hold [Ctrl] while selecting each range, then use the INSERT tab to create the chart.

3. **Click the CHARTS tab, verify that the Clustered Column is selected, as shown in FIGURE D-3, then click Clustered Column**

   The chart is inserted in the center of the worksheet, and two contextual CHART TOOLS tabs appear on the Ribbon: DESIGN, and FORMAT. On the DESIGN tab, which is currently in front, you can quickly change the chart type, chart layout, and chart style, and you can swap how the columns and rows of data in the worksheet are represented in the chart. When seen in the Normal view, three tools display to the right of the chart: these enable you to add, remove, or change chart elements, set a style and color scheme, and filter the results shown in a chart. Currently, the countries are charted along the horizontal x-axis, with the quarterly expense dollar amounts charted along the y-axis. This lets you easily compare the quarterly expenses for each country.

4. **Click the Switch Row/Column button in the Data group on the CHART TOOLS DESIGN tab**

   The quarters are now charted along the x-axis. The expense amounts per country are charted along the y-axis, as indicated by the updated legend. See **FIGURE D-4**.

5. **Click the Undo button on the Quick Access toolbar**

   The chart returns to its original design.

QUICK TIP
You can also triple-click to select the chart title text.

6. **Click the Chart Title placeholder to show the text box, click anywhere in the Chart Title text box, press [Ctrl][A] to select the text, type Quarterly Tour Expenses, then click anywhere in the chart to deselect the title**

   Adding a title helps identify the chart. The border around the chart and the chart's **sizing handles**, the small series of dots at the corners and sides of the chart's border, indicate that the chart is selected. See **FIGURE D-5**. Your chart might be in a different location on the worksheet and may look slightly different; you will move and resize it in the next lesson. Any time a chart is selected, as it is now, a blue border surrounds the worksheet data range on which the chart is based, a purple border surrounds the cells containing the category axis labels, and a red border surrounds the cells containing the data series labels. This chart is known as an **embedded chart** because it is inserted directly in the current worksheet and doesn't exist in a separate file. Embedding a chart in the current sheet is the default selection when creating a chart, but you can also embed a chart on a different sheet in the workbook, or on a newly created chart sheet. A **chart sheet** is a sheet in a workbook that contains only a chart that is linked to the workbook data.

7. **Save your work**

FIGURE D-3: CHARTS tab in Quick Analysis tool

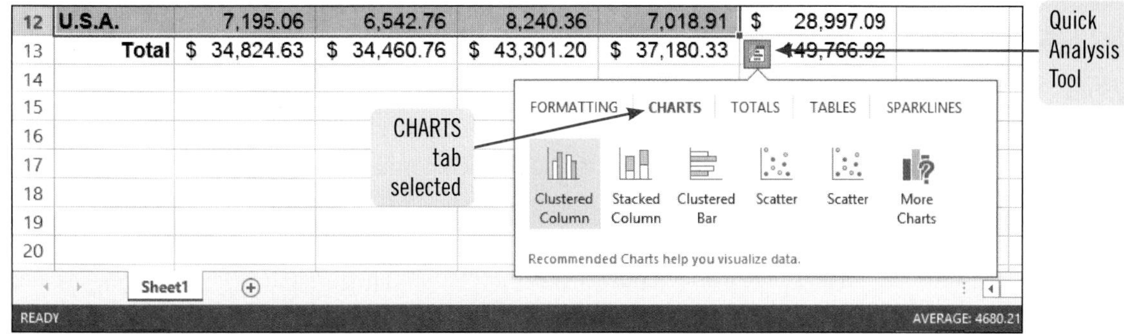

FIGURE D-4: Clustered Column chart with different presentation of data

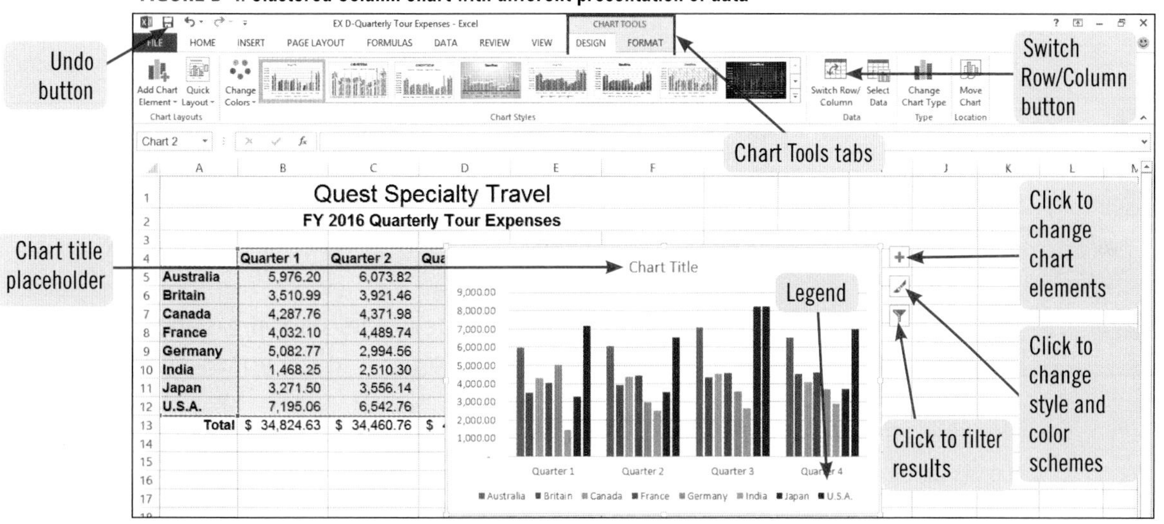

FIGURE D-5: Chart with rows and columns restored and title added

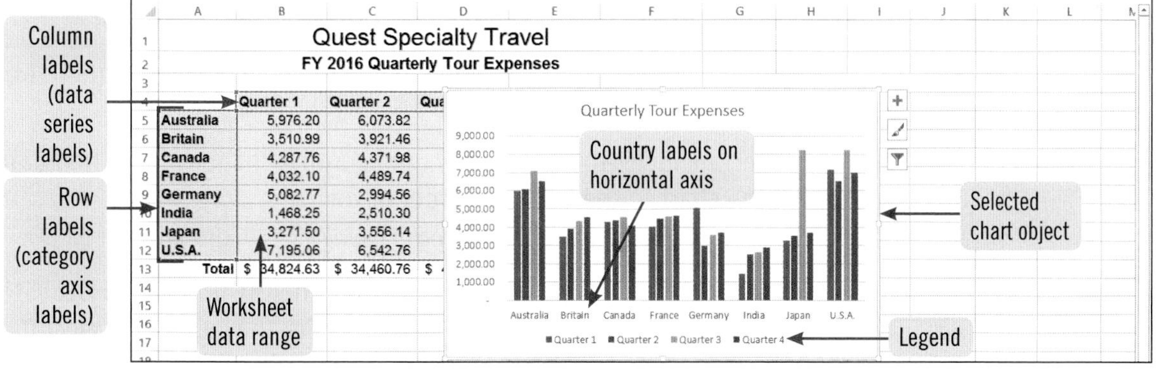

Creating sparklines

You can quickly create a miniature chart called a **sparkline** that serves as a visual indicator of data trends. You can create a sparkline by selecting a range of data, clicking the Quick Analysis tool, clicking the SPARKLINES tab, then clicking the type of sparkline you want. (The sparkline appears in the cell immediately adjacent to the selected range.) You can also select a range, click the INSERT tab, then click the Line, Column, or Win/Loss button in the Sparklines group. In the Create Sparklines dialog box that opens, enter the cell in which you want the sparkline to appear, then click OK.

FIGURE D-6 shows a sparkline created in a cell. Any changes to data in the range are reflected in the sparkline. To delete a selected sparkline from a cell, click the Clear button in the Group group on the SPARKLINE TOOLS DESIGN tab.

FIGURE D-6: Sparkline in a cell

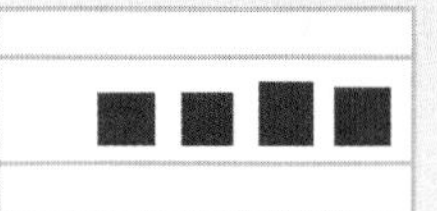

Excel 2013

Move and Resize a Chart

Learning Outcomes
- Reposition a chart
- Resize a chart
- Modify a legend
- Modify chart data

A chart is an **object**, or an independent element on a worksheet, and is not located in a specific cell or range. You can select an object by clicking it; sizing handles around the object indicate it is selected. (When a chart is selected in Excel, the Name box, which normally tells you the address of the active cell, tells you the chart number.) You can move a selected chart anywhere on a worksheet without affecting formulas or data in the worksheet. Any data changed in the worksheet is automatically updated in the chart. You can even move a chart to a different sheet in the workbook and it will still reflect the original data. You can resize a chart to improve its appearance by dragging its sizing handles. You can reposition chart objects (such as a title or legend) to predefined locations using commands using the Chart Elements button or the Add Chart Element button on the CHART TOOLS DESIGN tab, or you can freely move any chart object by dragging it or by cutting and pasting it to a new location. When you point to a chart object, the name of the object appears as a ScreenTip. **CASE** *You want to resize the chart, position it below the worksheet data, and move the legend.*

STEPS

QUICK TIP
To delete a selected chart, press [Delete].

1. **Make sure the chart is still selected, then position the pointer over the chart**
   The pointer shape ✥ indicates that you can move the chart. For a table of commonly used object pointers, refer to **TABLE D-2**.

TROUBLE
If you do not drag a blank area on the chart, you might inadvertently move a chart element instead of the whole chart; if this happens, undo the action and try again.

2. **Position ✥ on a blank area near the upper-left edge of the chart, press and hold the left mouse button, drag the chart until its upper-left corner is at the upper-left corner of cell A16, then release the mouse button**
   As you drag the chart, you can see the chart being dragged. When you release the mouse button, the chart appears in the new location.

3. **Scroll down so you can see the whole chart, position the pointer on the right-middle sizing handle until it changes to ⇔, then drag the right border of the chart to the right edge of column G**
   The chart is widened. See **FIGURE D-7**.

QUICK TIP
To resize a selected chart to an exact specification, click the CHART TOOLS FORMAT tab, then enter the desired height and width in the Size group.

4. **Position the pointer over the upper-middle sizing handle until it changes to ⇕, then drag the top border of the chart to the top edge of row 15**

5. **Position the pointer over the lower-middle sizing handle until it changes to ⇕, then drag the bottom border of the chart to the bottom border of row 26**
   You can move any object on a chart. You want to align the top of the legend with the top of the plot area.

QUICK TIP
You can move a legend to the right, top, left, or bottom of a chart by clicking Legend in the Add Chart Element button in the Chart Layouts group on the CHART TOOLS DESIGN tab, then clicking a location option.

6. **Click the Quick Layout button in the Chart Layouts group of the CHART TOOLS DESIGN tab, click Layout 1 (in the upper-left corner of the palette), click the legend to select it, press and hold [Shift], drag the legend up using ✥ so the dotted outline is approximately 1⁄4" above the top of the plot area, then release [Shift]**
   When you click the legend, sizing handles appear around it and "Legend" appears as a ScreenTip when the pointer hovers over the object. As you drag, a dotted outline of the legend border appears. Pressing and holding the [Shift] key holds the horizontal position of the legend as you move it vertically. Although the sizing handles on objects within a chart look different from the sizing handles that surround a chart, they function the same way.

7. **Click cell A12, type United States, click the Enter button ✓ on the formula bar, use AutoFit to resize column A, then save your work**
   The axis label changes to reflect the updated cell contents, as shown in **FIGURE D-8**. Changing any data in the worksheet modifies corresponding text or values in the chart. Because the chart is no longer selected, the CHART TOOLS tabs no longer appear on the Ribbon.

FIGURE D-7: Moved and resized chart

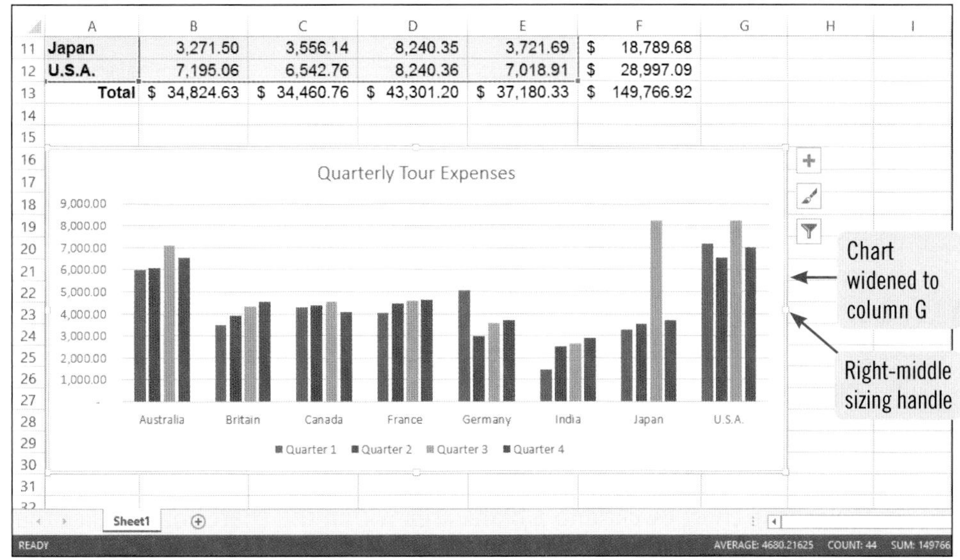

FIGURE D-8: Worksheet with modified legend and label

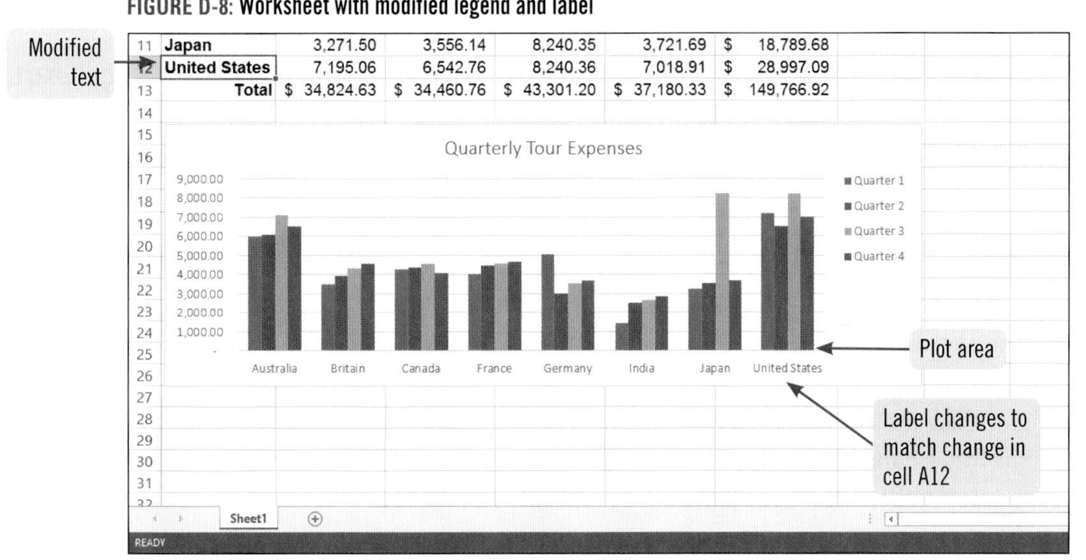

TABLE D-2: Common object pointers

name	pointer	use	name	pointer	use
Diagonal resizing	or	Change chart shape from corners	**I-beam**		Edit object text
Draw		Draw an object	**Move**		Move object
Horizontal resizing		Change object width	**Vertical resizing**		Change object height

Moving an embedded chart to a sheet

Suppose you have created an embedded chart that you decide would look better on a chart sheet or in a different worksheet. You can make this change without recreating the entire chart. To do so, first select the chart, click the CHART TOOLS DESIGN tab, then click the Move Chart button in the Location group. The Move Chart dialog box opens. To move the chart to its own chart sheet, click the New sheet option button, type a name for the new sheet if desired, then click OK. If the chart is already on its own sheet, click the Object in option button, select the worksheet to where you want to move it, then click OK.

Excel 2013
UNIT D

Change the Chart Design

Learning Outcomes
- Change the chart design
- Change the chart type
- Apply a chart style

Once you've created a chart, you can change the chart type, modify the data range and column/row configuration, apply a different chart style, and change the layout of objects in the chart. The layouts in the Chart Layouts group on the CHART TOOLS DESIGN tab offer arrangements of objects in your chart, such as its legend, title, or gridlines; choosing one of these layouts is an alternative to manually changing how objects are arranged in a chart. **CASE** *You discovered the data for Japan and the United States in Quarter 3 is incorrect. After the correction, you want to see how the data looks using different chart layouts and types.*

STEPS

1. **Click cell D11, type 4568.92, press [Enter], type 6107.09, then press [Enter]**
   In the chart, the Quarter 3 data markers for Japan and the United States reflect the adjusted expense figures. See **FIGURE D-9**.

QUICK TIP
You can see more layout choices by clicking the More button in the Chart Styles group.

2. **Select the chart by clicking a blank area within the chart border, click the CHART TOOLS DESIGN tab on the Ribbon, click the Quick Layout button in the Chart Layouts group, then click Layout 3**
   The legend moves to the bottom of the chart. You prefer the original layout.
3. **Click the Undo button on the Quick Access toolbar, then click the Change Chart Type button in the Type group**
   The Change Chart Type dialog box opens, as shown in **FIGURE D-10**. The left pane of the dialog box lists the available categories, and the right pane shows the individual chart types. A pale green border surrounds the currently selected chart type.
4. **Click Bar in the left pane of the Change Chart Type dialog box, confirm that the first Clustered Bar chart type is selected in the right pane, then click OK**
   The column chart changes to a clustered bar chart. See **FIGURE D-11**. You look at the bar chart, then decide to see how the data looks in a three-dimensional column chart.
5. **Click the Change Chart Type button in the Type group, click Column in the left pane of the Change Chart Type dialog box, click 3-D Clustered Column (fourth from the left in the top row) in the right pane, verify that the left-most 3-D chart is selected, then click OK**
   A three-dimensional column chart appears. You notice that the three-dimensional column format gives you a sense of volume, but it is more crowded than the two-dimensional column format.

QUICK TIP
If you plan to print a chart on a black-and-white printer, you may wish to apply a black-and-white chart style to your chart so you can see how the output will look as you work.

6. **Click the Change Chart Type button in the Type group, click Clustered Column (first from the left in the top row) in the right pane of the Change Chart Type dialog box, then click OK**
7. **Click the Style 3 chart style in the Chart Styles group**
   The columns change to lighter shades of color. You prefer the previous chart style's color scheme.
8. **Click on the Quick Access toolbar, then save your work**

Creating a combination chart

A **combination chart** is two charts in one; a column chart with a line chart, for example. This type of chart is helpful when charting dissimilar but related data. For example, you can create a combination chart based on home price and home size data, showing home prices in a column chart, and related home sizes in a line chart. Here a **secondary axis** (such as a vertical axis on the right side of the chart) would supply the scale for the home sizes. To create a combination chart, select all the data you want to plot, click Recommended Charts in the Charts group in the INSERT tab, click the All Charts tab, select Combo, supply the series information that conforms to the chart you want to create, then click OK. To change an existing chart to a combination chart, select the chart , then click Change Chart Type in the Type group on the CHART TOOLS DESIGN tab. Click Combo in the Change Chart Type dialog box, select the Secondary Axis box for each data series you want to plot, change the chart type to Line, then click OK.

FIGURE D-9: Worksheet with modified data

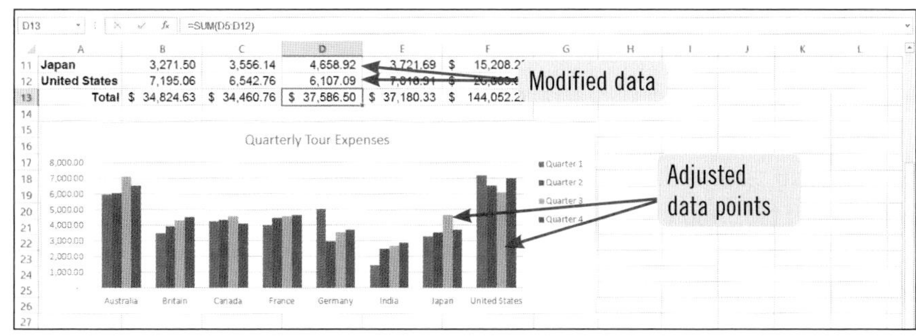

FIGURE D-10: Change Chart Type dialog box

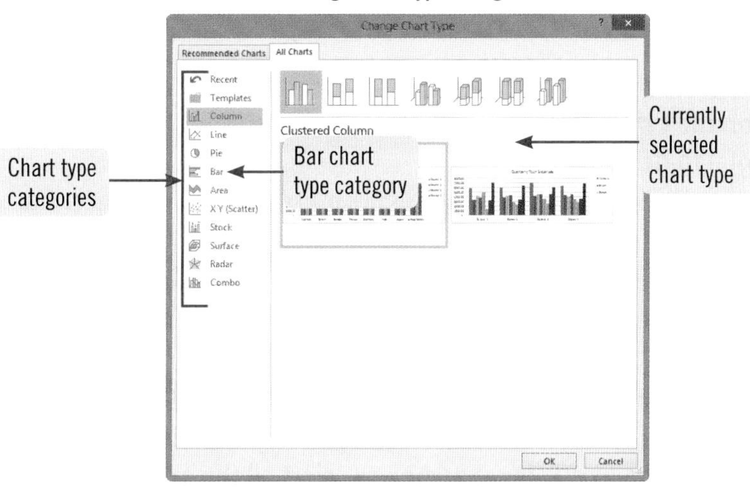

FIGURE D-11: Column chart changed to bar chart

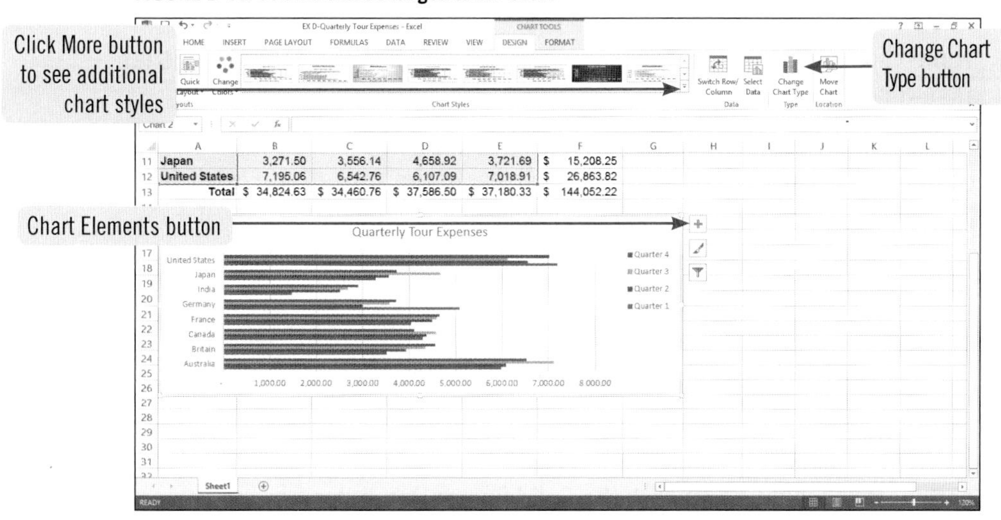

Working with a 3-D chart

Excel includes two kinds of 3-D chart types. In a true 3-D chart, a third axis, called the **z-axis**, lets you compare data points across both categories and values. The z-axis runs along the depth of the chart, so it appears to advance from the back of the chart. To create a true 3-D chart, look for chart types that begin with "3-D," such as 3-D Column. In a 3-D chart, data series can sometimes obscure other columns or bars in the same chart, but you can rotate the chart to obtain a better view. Right-click the chart, then click 3-D Rotation. The Format Chart Area pane opens with the 3-D Rotation category active. The 3-D Rotation options let you change the orientation and perspective of the chart area, plot area, walls, and floor. The 3-D Format category lets you apply three-dimensional effects to selected chart objects. (Not all 3-D Rotation and 3-D Format options are available on all charts.)

Change the Chart Format

Learning Outcomes
- Change the gridlines display
- Add axis titles
- Change the border color
- Add a shadow to an object

While the CHART TOOLS DESIGN tab contains preconfigured chart layouts you can apply to a chart, the Chart Elements button makes it easy to add, remove, and modify individual chart objects such as a chart title or legend. Using options on this shortcut menu (or using the Add Chart Element button on the CHART TOOLS DESIGN tab), you can also add text to a chart, add and modify labels, change the display of axes, modify the fill behind the plot area, create titles for the horizontal and vertical axes, and eliminate or change the look of gridlines. You can format the text in a chart object using the HOME tab or the Mini toolbar, just as you would the text in a worksheet. **CASE** *You want to change the layout of the chart by creating titles for the horizontal and vertical axes. To improve the chart's appearance, you'll add a drop shadow to the chart title.*

STEPS

1. **With the chart still selected, click the Add Chart Element button in the Chart Layouts group on the CHART TOOLS DESIGN tab, point to Gridlines, then click Primary Major Horizontal to deselect it**
   The gridlines that extend from the value axis tick marks across the chart's plot area are removed from the chart, as shown in **FIGURE D-12**.
2. **Click the Chart Elements button [+] in the upper-right corner *outside* the chart border, click the Gridlines arrow, click Primary Major Horizontal, click Primary Minor Horizontal, then click [+] to close the Chart Elements fly-out menu**
   Both major and minor gridlines now appear in the chart. **Major gridlines** represent the values at the value axis tick marks, and **minor gridlines** represent the values between the tick marks.
3. **Click [+], click the Axis Titles checkbox to select all the axis titles options, triple-click the vertical axis title on the chart, then type Expenses (in $)**
   Descriptive text on the category axis helps readers understand the chart.
4. **Triple-click the horizontal axis title on the chart, then type Tour Countries**
   The text "Tour Countries" appears on the horizontal axis, as shown in **FIGURE D-13**.
5. **Right-click the horizontal axis labels ("Australia", "Britain", etc.), click Font on the shortcut menu, click the Latin text font list arrow in the Font dialog box, click Times New Roman, click the Size down arrow, click until 8 is displayed, then click OK**
   The font of the horizontal axis labels changes to Times New Roman, and the font size decreases, making more of the plot area visible.
6. **With the horizontal axis labels still selected, click the HOME tab, click the Format Painter button in the Clipboard group, then click the area within the vertical axis labels**
7. **Right-click the Chart Title ("Quarterly Tour Expenses"), click Format Chart Title on the shortcut menu, click the BORDER arrow in the Format Chart Title pane to display the options if necessary, then click the Solid line option button in the Format Chart Title pane**
   A solid border will appear around the chart title with the default blue color.
8. **Click the Effects button in the Format Chart Title pane, click Shadow, click the Presets list arrow, click Offset Diagonal Bottom Right in the Outer group (first row, first from the left), click the Format Chart Title pane Close button [X], then save your work**
   A blue border with a drop shadow surrounds the title. Compare your work to **FIGURE D-14**.

QUICK TIP
You can move any title to a new position by clicking one of its edges, then dragging it.

QUICK TIP
You can also edit text in a chart or axis title by positioning the pointer over the selected title until it changes to I, clicking the title, then editing the text.

QUICK TIP
You can also apply a border to a selected chart object by clicking the Shape Outline list arrow on the CHART TOOLS FORMAT tab, and then selecting from the available options.

QUICK TIP
You can also apply a shadow to a selected chart object by clicking the Shadow arrow, then clicking a shadow effect.

FIGURE D-12: Gridlines removed from chart

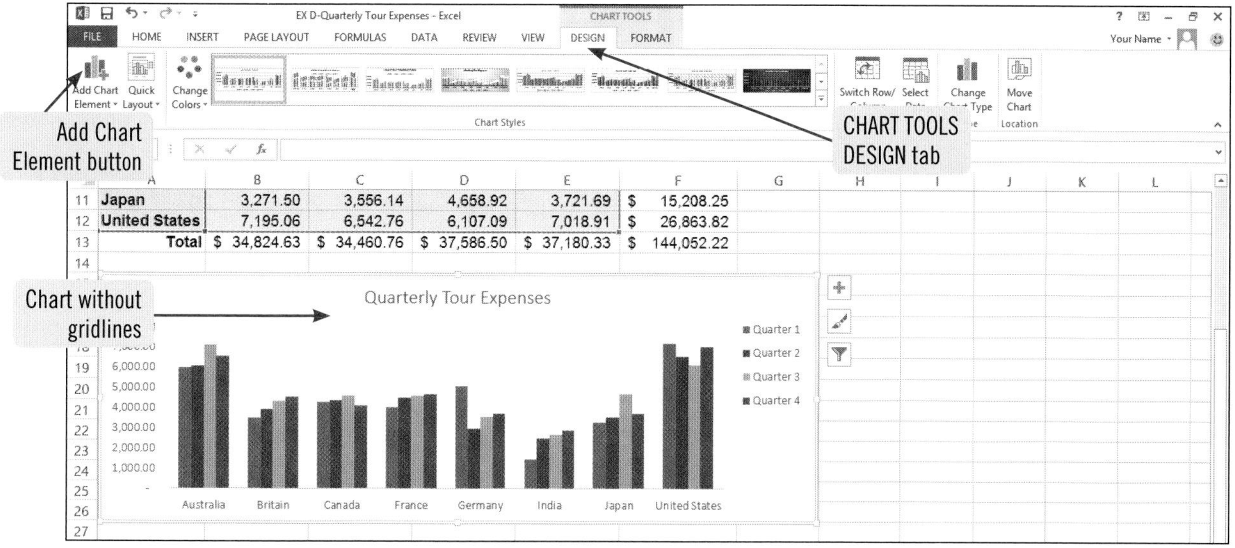

FIGURE D-13: Axis titles added to chart

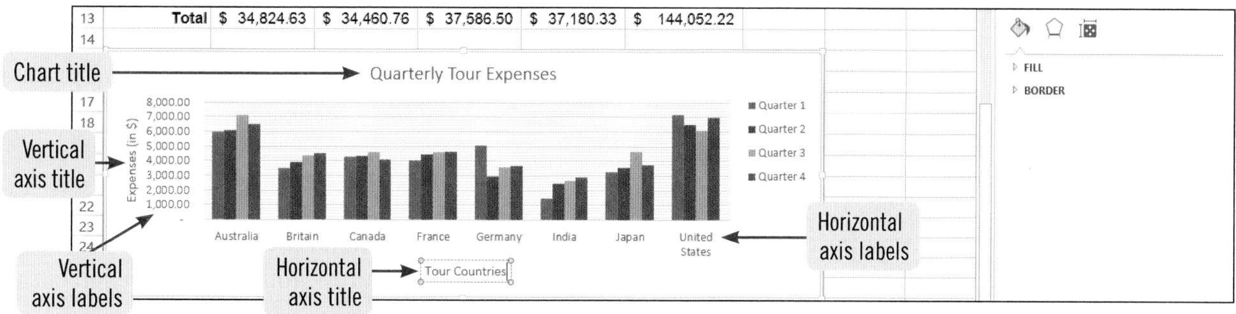

FIGURE D-14: Enhanced chart

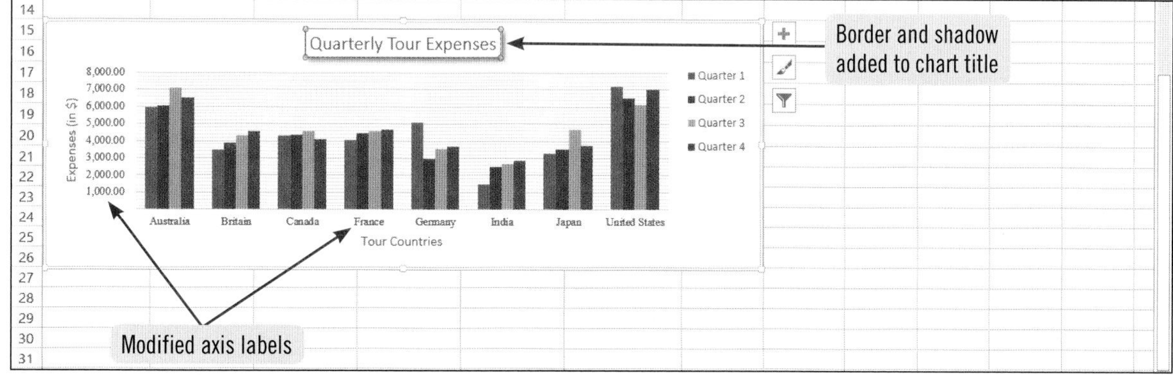

Adding data labels to a chart

There are times when your audience might benefit by seeing data labels on a chart. These labels appear next to the data markers in the chart and can indicate the series name, category name, and/or the value of one or more data points. Once your chart is selected, you can add this information to your chart by clicking the Chart Elements button in the upper-right corner outside the selected chart, clicking the Data Labels arrow, and then clicking a display option for the data labels. Once you have added the data labels, you can format them or delete individual data labels. To delete a data label, select it and then press [Delete].

Format a Chart

Learning Outcomes
- Change the fill of a data series
- Use Live Preview to see a new data series color
- Apply a style to a data series

Formatting a chart can make it easier to read and understand. Many formatting enhancements can be made using the CHART TOOLS FORMAT tab. You can change the fill color for a specific data series, or you can apply a shape style to a title or a data series using the Shape Styles group. Shape styles make it possible to apply multiple formats, such as an outline, fill color, and text color, all with a single click. You can also apply different fill colors, outlines, and effects to chart objects using arrows and buttons in the Shape Styles group. **CASE** *You want to use a different color for one data series in the chart and apply a shape style to another to enhance the look of the chart.*

STEPS

1. **With the chart selected, click the CHART TOOLS FORMAT tab on the Ribbon, then click any column in the Quarter 4 data series**
   The CHART TOOLS FORMAT tab opens, and handles appear on each column in the Quarter 4 data series, indicating that the entire series is selected.
2. **Click the Shape Fill list arrow in the Shape Styles group on the CHART TOOLS FORMAT tab**
3. **Click Orange, Accent 6 (first row, 10th from the left) as shown in FIGURE D-15**
   All the columns for the series become orange, and the legend changes to match the new color. You can also change the color of selected objects by applying a shape style.
4. **Click any column in the Quarter 3 data series**
   Handles appear on each column in the Quarter 3 data series.
5. **Click the More button on the Shape Styles gallery, then *hover the pointer* over the Moderate Effect – Olive Green, Accent 3 shape style (fifth row, fourth from the left) in the gallery, as shown in FIGURE D-16**
   Live Preview shows the data series in the chart with the shape style applied.
6. **Click the Subtle Effect – Olive Green, Accent 3 shape style (fourth row, fourth from the left) in the gallery**
   The style for the data series changes, as shown in **FIGURE D-17**.
7. **Save your work**

QUICK TIP
To apply a WordArt style to a text object (such as the chart title), select the object, then click a style in the WordArt Styles group on the CHART TOOLS FORMAT tab.

Previewing a chart

To print or preview just a chart, select the chart (or make the chart sheet active), click the FILE tab, then click Print on the navigation bar. To reposition a chart by changing the page's margins, click the Show Margins button in the lower-right corner of the Print tab to display the margins in the preview. You can drag the margin lines to the exact settings you want; as the margins change, the size and placement of the chart on the page changes too.

FIGURE D-15: New shape fill applied to data series

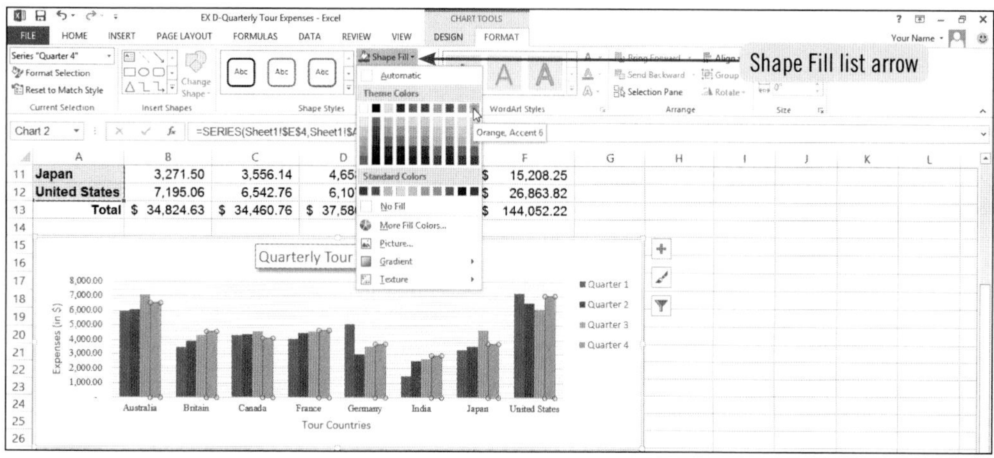

FIGURE D-16: Live Preview of new style applied to data series

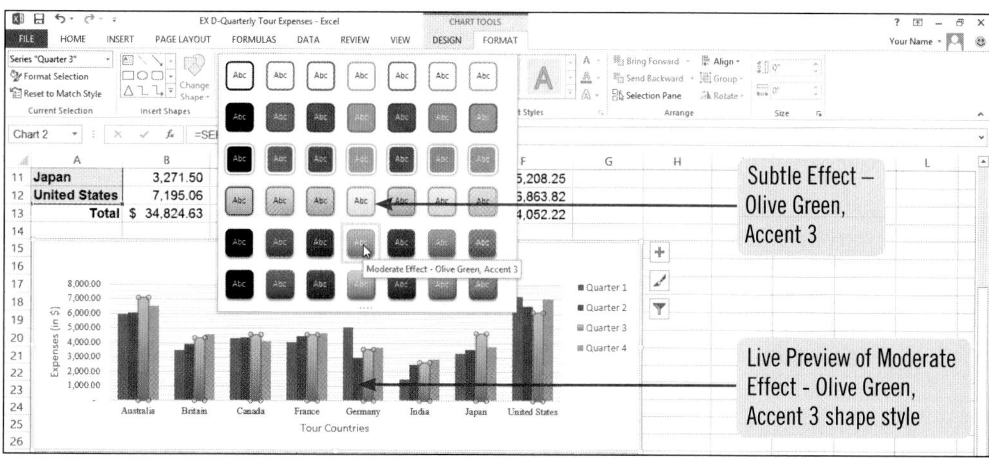

FIGURE D-17: Style of data series changed

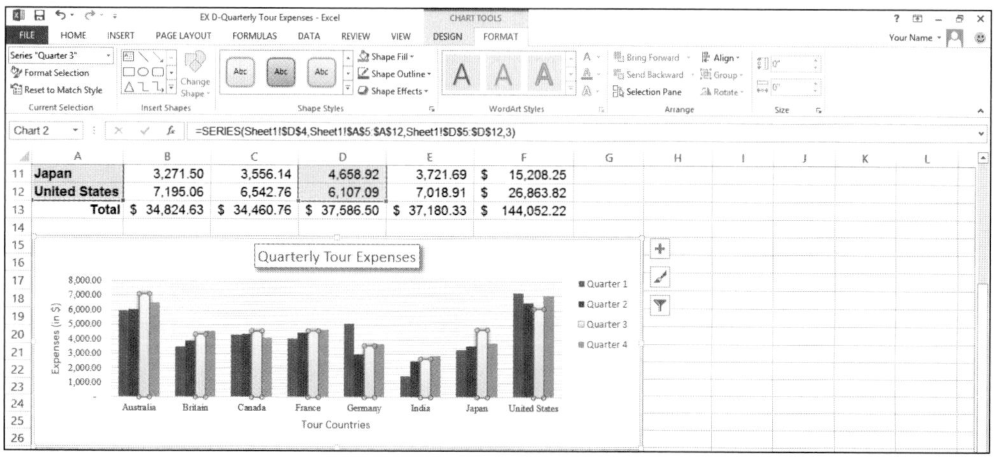

Excel 2013

Changing alignment and angle in axis labels and titles

The buttons on the CHART TOOLS DESIGN tab provide a few options for positioning axis labels and titles, but you can customize their position and rotation to exact specifications using the Format Axis pane or Format Axis Title pane. With a chart selected, right-click the axis text you want to modify, then click Format Axis or Format Axis Title on the shortcut menu. In the pane that is displayed, click the Size & Properties button, then select the appropriate Text layout option. You can also create a custom angle by clicking the Custom angle up and down arrows. When you have made the desired changes, close the pane.

Annotate and Draw on a Chart

Learning Outcomes
- Type text in a text box
- Draw an arrow on a chart
- Modify a drawn object

You can use text annotations and graphics to point out critical information in a chart. **Text annotations** are labels that further describe your data. You can also draw lines and arrows that point to the exact locations you want to emphasize. Shapes such as arrows and boxes can be added from the Illustrations group on the INSERT tab or from the Insert Shapes group on the CHART TOOLS FORMAT tab on the Ribbon. The INSERT group is also used to insert pictures into worksheets and charts. **CASE** *You want to call attention to the Germany tour expense decrease, so you decide to add a text annotation and an arrow to this information in the chart.*

STEPS

1. **Make sure the chart is selected with the CHART TOOLS FORMAT tab selected, click the Text Box button in the Insert Shapes group, then move the pointer over the worksheet**
   The pointer changes to ↓, indicating that you will insert a text box where you next click.

2. **Click to the right of the chart (anywhere *outside* the chart boundary)**
   A text box is added to the worksheet, and the DRAWING TOOLS FORMAT tab appears on the Ribbon so that you can format the new object. First you need to type the text.

3. **Type Great Improvement**
   The text appears in a selected text box on the worksheet, and the chart is no longer selected, as shown in **FIGURE D-18**. Your text box may be in a different location; this is not important, because you'll move the annotation in the next step.

4. **Point to an edge of the text box so that the pointer changes to , drag the text box into the chart to the left of the chart title, as shown in FIGURE D-19, then release the mouse button**
   The text box is a text annotation for the chart. You also want to add a simple arrow shape in the chart.

5. **Click the chart to select it, click the CHART TOOLS FORMAT tab, click the Arrow button in the Insert Shapes group, then move the pointer over the text box on the chart**
   The pointer changes to +, and the status bar displays "Click and drag to insert an AutoShape." When + is over the text box, black handles appear around the text in the text box. A black handle can act as an anchor for the arrow.

6. **Position + on the black handle to the right of the "t" in the word "improvement" (in the text box), press and hold the left mouse button, drag the line to the Quarter 2 column for the Germany category in the chart, then release the mouse button**
   An arrow points to the Quarter 2 expense for Germany, and the DRAWING TOOLS FORMAT tab displays options for working with the new arrow object. You can resize, format, or delete it just like any other object in a chart.

7. **Click the Shape Outline list arrow in the Shape Styles group, click the Automatic color, click the Shape Outline list arrow again, point to Weight, then click 1½ pt**
   Compare your finished chart to **FIGURE D-20**.

8. **Save your work**

QUICK TIP
You can also insert a text box by clicking the Text Box button in the Text group in the INSERT tab, then clicking in the worksheet.

QUICK TIP
To annotate a chart using a callout, click the Shapes button in the Illustrations group on the INSERT tab or the More button on the Insert Shapes group on the CHART TOOLS FORMAT tab, then click a shape in the Callouts category of the Shapes gallery.

FIGURE D-18: Text box added

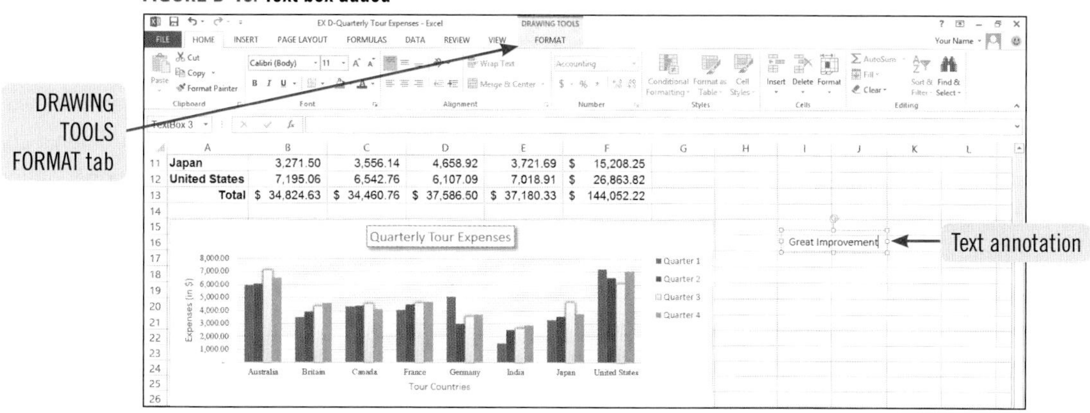

FIGURE D-19: Text annotation on the chart

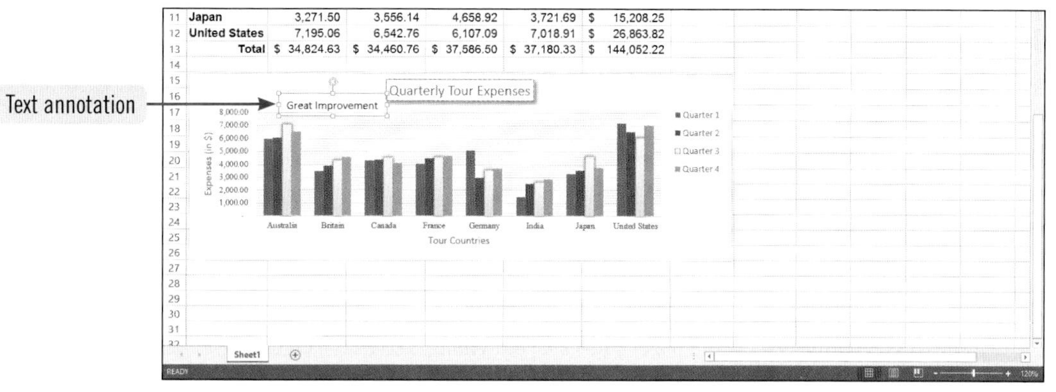

FIGURE D-20: Arrow shape added to chart

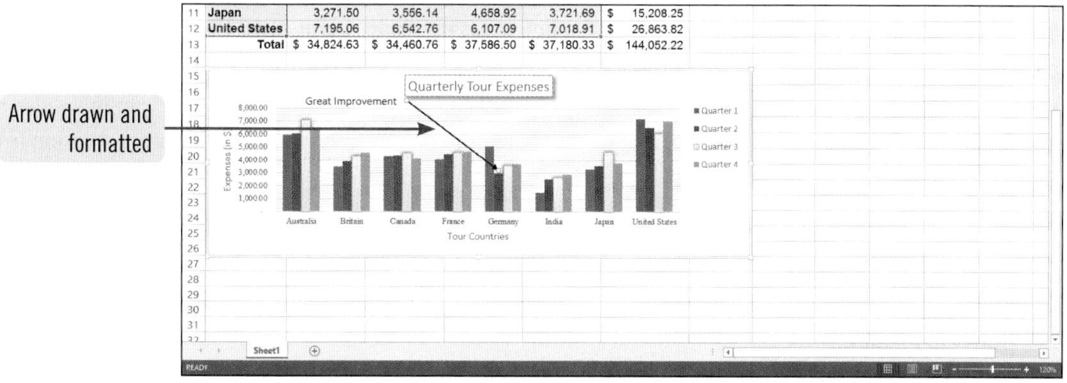

Adding SmartArt graphics

In addition to charts, annotations, and drawn objects, you can create a variety of diagrams using SmartArt graphics. **SmartArt graphics** are available in List, Process, Cycle, Hierarchy, Relationship, Matrix, and Pyramid categories. To insert SmartArt, click the Insert a SmartArt Graphic button in the Illustrations group on the INSERT tab to open the Choose a SmartArt Graphic dialog box. Click a SmartArt category in the left pane, then click the layout for the graphic in the right pane. The right pane shows a sample of the selected SmartArt layout, as shown in **FIGURE D-21**. The SmartArt graphic appears in the worksheet as an embedded object with sizing handles. Click the Text Pane button on the SmartArt Tools Design tab to open a text pane next to the graphic; you can enter text into the graphic using the text pane or by typing directly in the shapes in the diagram.

FIGURE D-21: Choose a SmartArt Graphic dialog box

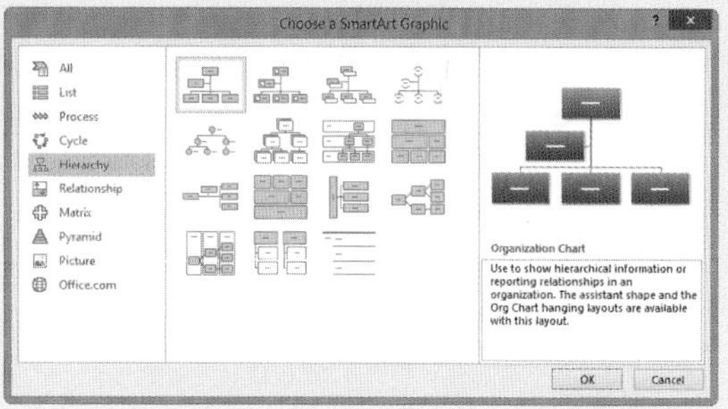

Create a Pie Chart

Learning Outcomes
- Create a pie chart
- Explode a pie chart slice

You can create multiple charts based on the same worksheet data. While a column chart may illustrate certain important aspects of your worksheet data, you may find you want to create an additional chart to emphasize a different point. Depending on the type of chart you create, you have additional options for calling attention to trends and patterns. For example, if you create a pie chart, you can emphasize one data point by **exploding**, or pulling that slice away from, the pie chart. When you're ready to print a chart, you can preview it just as you do a worksheet to check the output before committing it to paper. You can print a chart by itself or as part of the worksheet. **CASE** *At an upcoming meeting, Grace plans to discuss the total tour expenses and which countries need improvement. You want to create a pie chart she can use to illustrate total expenses. Finally, you want to fit the worksheet and the charts onto one worksheet page.*

STEPS

1. **Select the range A5:A12, press and hold [Ctrl], select the range F5:F12, click the INSERT tab, click the Insert Pie or Doughnut Chart button in the Charts group, then click 3-D Pie in the chart gallery**

   The new chart appears in the center of the worksheet. You can move the chart and quickly format it using a chart layout.

2. **Drag the chart so its upper-left corner is at the upper-left corner of cell G1, click the Quick Layout button in the Chart Layouts group of the CHART TOOLS DESIGN tab, then click Layout 2**

   The chart is repositioned on the page, and its layout changes so that a chart title is added, the percentages display on each slice, and the legend appears just below the chart title.

3. **Select the Chart Title text, then type Total Expenses, by Country**

4. **Click the slice for the India data point, click it again so it is the only slice selected, right-click it, then click Format Data Point**

   The Format Data Point pane opens, as shown in **FIGURE D-22**. You can use the Point Explosion slider to control the distance a pie slice moves away from the pie, or you can type a value in the Point Explosion text box.

> **TROUBLE**
> If the Format Data Series command appears on the shortcut menu instead of Format Data Point, double-click the slice you want to explode to make sure it is selected by itself, then right-click it again.

5. **Double-click 0 in the Point Explosion text box, type 40, then click the Close button ✖**

   Compare your chart to **FIGURE D-23**. You decide to preview the chart and data before you print.

6. **Click cell A1, switch to Page Layout view, type your name in the left header text box, then click cell A1**

   You decide the chart and data would fit better on the page if they were printed in landscape orientation.

7. **Click the PAGE LAYOUT tab, click the Orientation button in the Page Setup group, then click Landscape**

8. **Click the FILE tab, click Print on the navigation bar, click the No Scaling setting in the Settings section on the Print tab, then click Fit Sheet on One Page**

   The data and chart are positioned horizontally on a single page, as shown in **FIGURE D-24**. The printer you have selected may affect the appearance of your preview screen.

9. **Save and close the workbook, submit your work to your instructor as directed, then exit Excel**

FIGURE D-22: Format Data Point pane

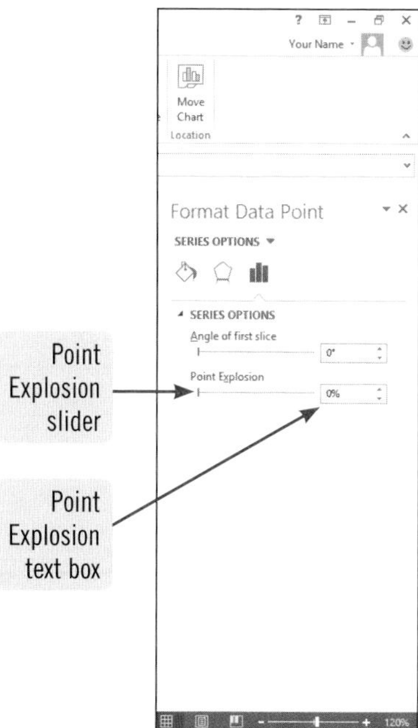

FIGURE D-23: Exploded pie slice

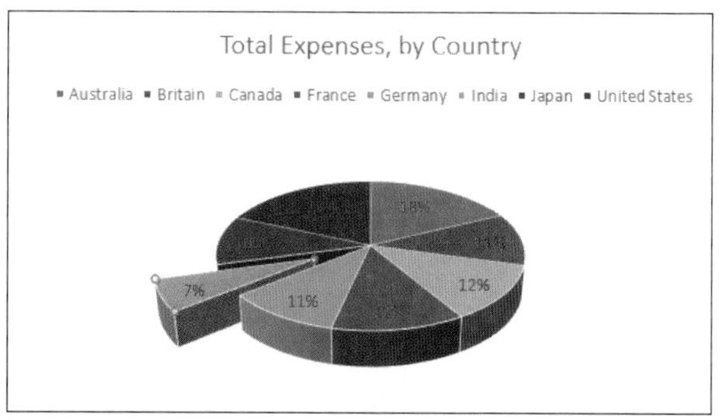

FIGURE D-24: Preview of worksheet with charts in Backstage view

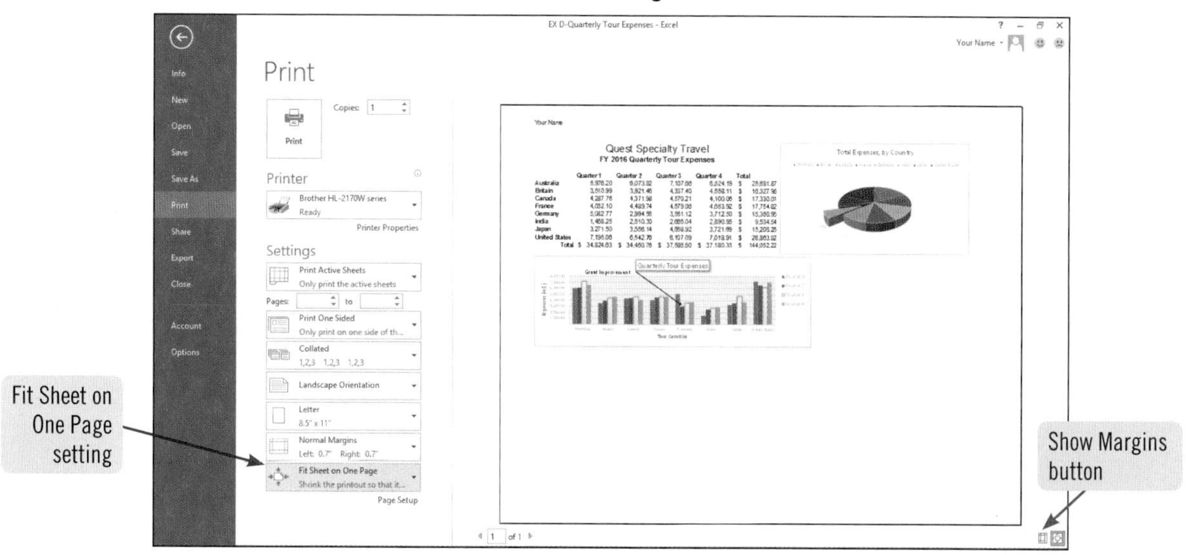

Practice

Put your skills into practice with **SAM Projects**! SAM Projects for this unit can be found online. If you have a SAM account, go to www.cengage.com/sam2013 to download the most recent Project Instruction and Start Files.

Concepts Review

Label each element of the Excel chart shown in FIGURE D-25.

FIGURE D-25

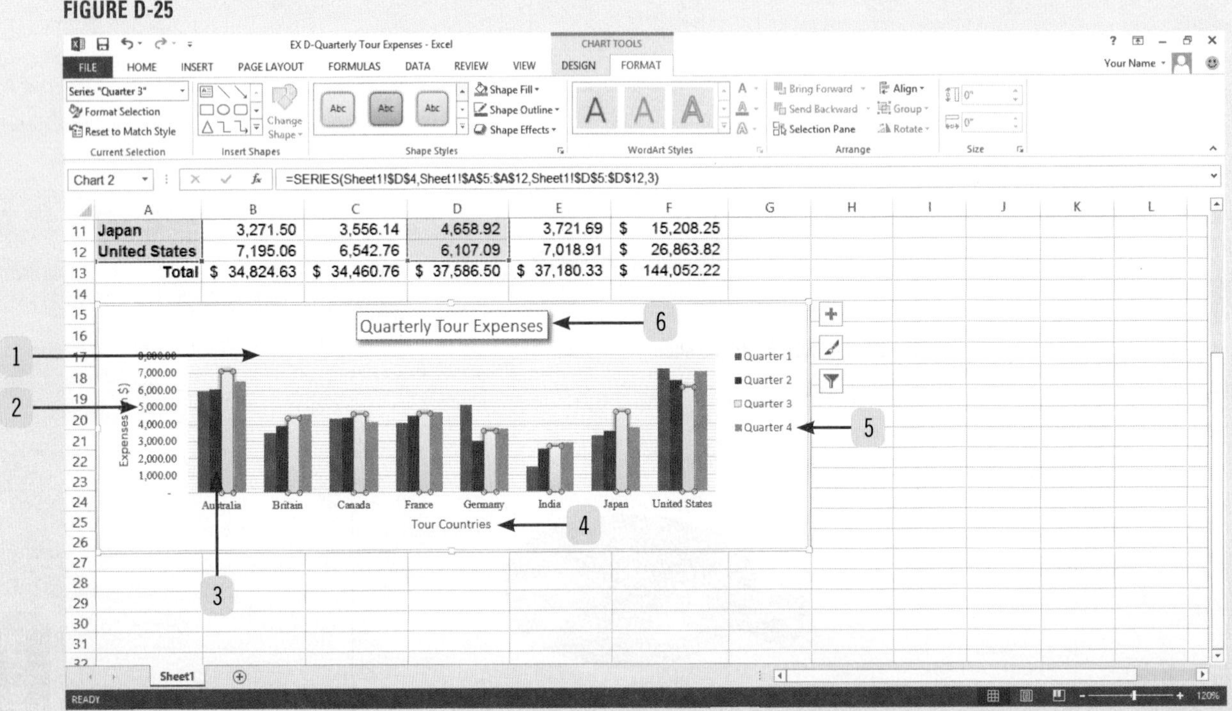

Match each chart type with the statement that best describes it.

7. Area
8. Line
9. Column
10. Combination
11. Pie

a. Displays a column and line chart using different scales of measurement
b. Compares trends over even time intervals
c. Compares data using columns
d. Compares data as parts of a whole
e. Shows how volume changes over time

Select the best answer from the list of choices.

12. Which tab appears only when a chart is selected?
- **a.** INSERT
- **b.** CHART TOOLS FORMAT
- **c.** REVIEW
- **d.** PAGE LAYOUT

13. Which is *not* an example of a SmartArt graphic?
- **a.** Sparkline
- **b.** Basic Matrix
- **c.** Organization Chart
- **d.** Basic Pyramid

14. How do you move an embedded chart to a chart sheet?
- **a.** Click a button on the CHART TOOLS DESIGN tab.
- **b.** Drag the chart to the sheet tab.
- **c.** Delete the chart, switch to a different sheet, then create a new chart.
- **d.** Use the Copy and Paste buttons on the Ribbon.

15. The object in a chart that identifies the colors used for each data series is a(n):
- **a.** Data marker.
- **b.** Data point.
- **c.** Organizer.
- **d.** Legend.

16. A collection of related data points in a chart is called a:
- **a.** Data series.
- **b.** Data tick.
- **c.** Cell address.
- **d.** Value title.

17. Which tab on the Ribbon do you use to create a chart?
- **a.** DESIGN
- **b.** INSERT
- **c.** PAGE LAYOUT
- **d.** FORMAT

Skills Review

1. Plan a chart.
- **a.** Start Excel, open the Data File EX D-2.xlsx from the location where you store your Data Files, then save it as **EX D-Departmental Software Usage**.
- **b.** Describe the type of chart you would use to plot this data.
- **c.** What chart type would you use to compare the number of Excel users in each department?

2. Create a chart.
- **a.** In the worksheet, select the range containing all the data and headings.
- **b.** Click the Quick Analysis tool.
- **c.** Create a Clustered Column chart, then add the chart title **Software Usage, by Department** above the chart.
- **d.** If necessary, click the Switch Row/Column button so the Department appears as the x-axis.
- **e.** Save your work.

Skills Review (continued)

3. **Move and resize a chart.**
   a. Make sure the chart is still selected, and close any open panes if necessary.
   b. Move the chart beneath the worksheet data.
   c. Widen the chart so it extends to the right edge of column H.
   d. Use the Quick Layout button in the CHART TOOLS DESIGN tab to move the legend to the right of the charted data. (*Hint*: Use Layout 1.)
   e. Resize the chart so its bottom edge is at the top of row 25.
   f. Save your work.
4. **Change the chart design.**
   a. Change the value in cell B3 to **15**. Observe the change in the chart.
   b. Select the chart.
   c. Use the Quick Layout button in the Chart Layouts group on the CHART TOOLS DESIGN tab to apply the Layout 10 layout to the chart, then undo the change.
   d. Use the Change Chart Type button on the CHART TOOLS DESIGN tab to change the chart to a Clustered Bar chart.
   e. Change the chart to a 3-D Clustered Column chart, then change it back to a Clustered Column chart.
   f. Save your work.
5. **Change the chart layout.**
   a. Use the CHART ELEMENTS button to turn off the primary major horizontal gridlines in the chart.
   b. Change the font used in the horizontal and vertical axes labels to Times New Roman.
   c. Turn on the primary major gridlines for both the horizontal and vertical axes.
   d. Change the chart title's font to Times New Roman if necessary, with a font size of 20.
   e. Insert **Departments** as the primary horizontal axis title.
   f. Insert **Number of Users** as the primary vertical axis title.
   g. Change the font size of the horizontal and vertical axis titles to 10 and the font to Times New Roman, if necessary.
   h. Change "Personnel" in the worksheet column heading to **Human Resources**, then AutoFit column E.
   i. Change the font size of the legend to 14.
   j. Add a solid line border in the default color and a (preset) Offset Diagonal Bottom Right shadow to the chart title.
   k. Save your work.
6. **Format a chart.**
   a. Make sure the chart is selected, then select the CHART TOOLS FORMAT tab, if necessary.
   b. Change the shape fill of the Excel data series to Dark Blue, Text 2.
   c. Change the shape style of the Excel data series to Subtle Effect – Orange, Accent 6.
   d. Save your work.
7. **Annotate and draw on a chart.**
   a. Make sure the chart is selected, then create the text annotation **Needs more users**.
   b. Position the text annotation so the word "Needs" is just below the word "Software" in the chart title.
   c. Select the chart, then use the CHART TOOLS FORMAT tab to create a 1½ pt weight dark blue arrow that points from the bottom center of the text box to the Excel users in the Design department.
   d. Deselect the chart.
   e. Save your work.

Skills Review (continued)

8. **Create a pie chart.**
   a. Select the range A1:F2, then create a 3-D Pie chart.
   b. Drag the 3-D pie chart beneath the existing chart.
   c. Change the chart title to **Excel Users**.
   d. Apply the Style 7 chart style to the chart, then apply Layout 6 using the Quick Layout button.
   e. Explode the Human Resources slice from the pie chart at **25%**.
   f. In Page Layout view, enter your name in the left section of the worksheet header.
   g. Preview the worksheet and charts in Backstage view, make sure all the contents fit on one page, then submit your work to your instructor as directed. When printed, the worksheet should look like **FIGURE D-26**.
   h. Save your work, close the workbook, then exit Excel.

FIGURE D-26

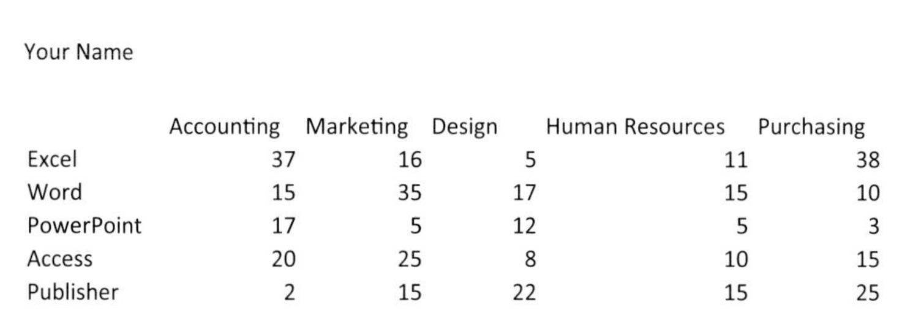

Your Name

	Accounting	Marketing	Design	Human Resources	Purchasing
Excel	37	16	5	11	38
Word	15	35	17	15	10
PowerPoint	17	5	12	5	3
Access	20	25	8	10	15
Publisher	2	15	22	15	25

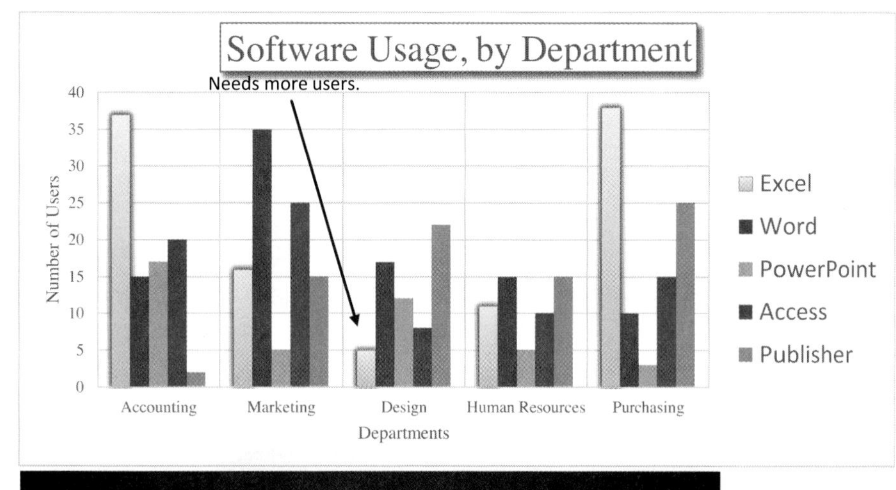

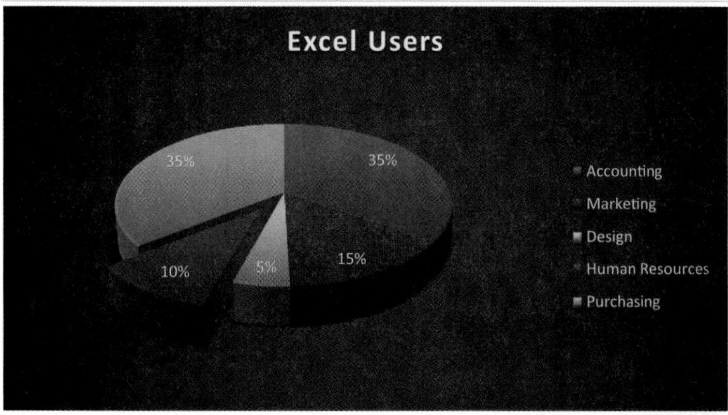

Excel 2013

Independent Challenge 1

You are the operations manager for the Tulsa Arts Alliance in Oklahoma. Each year the group applies to various state and federal agencies for matching funds. For this year's funding proposal, you need to create charts to document the number of productions in previous years.

a. Start Excel, open the file EX D-3.xlsx from the location where you store your Data Files, then save it as **EX D-Tulsa Arts Alliance**.

b. Take some time to plan your charts. Which type of chart or charts might best illustrate the information you need to display? What kind of chart enhancements do you want to use? Will a 3-D effect make your chart easier to understand?

c. Create a Clustered Column chart for the data.

d. Change at least one of the colors used in a data series.

e. Make the appropriate modifications to the chart to make it visually attractive and easier to read and understand. Include a legend to the right of the chart, and add chart titles and horizontal and vertical axis titles using the text shown in **TABLE D-3**.

TABLE D-3

title	text
Chart title	Tulsa Arts Alliance Events
Vertical axis title	Number of Events
Horizontal axis title	Types of Events

f. Create at least two additional charts for the same data to show how different chart types display the same data. Reposition each new chart so that all charts are visible in the worksheet. One of the additional charts should be a pie chart; the other is up to you.

g. Modify each new chart as necessary to improve its appearance and effectiveness. A sample worksheet containing three charts based on the worksheet data is shown in **FIGURE D-27**.

h. Enter your name in the worksheet header.

i. Save your work. Before printing, preview the worksheet in Backstage view, then adjust any settings as necessary so that all the worksheet data and charts print on a single page.

j. Submit your work to your instructor as directed.

k. Close the workbook, then exit Excel.

FIGURE D-27

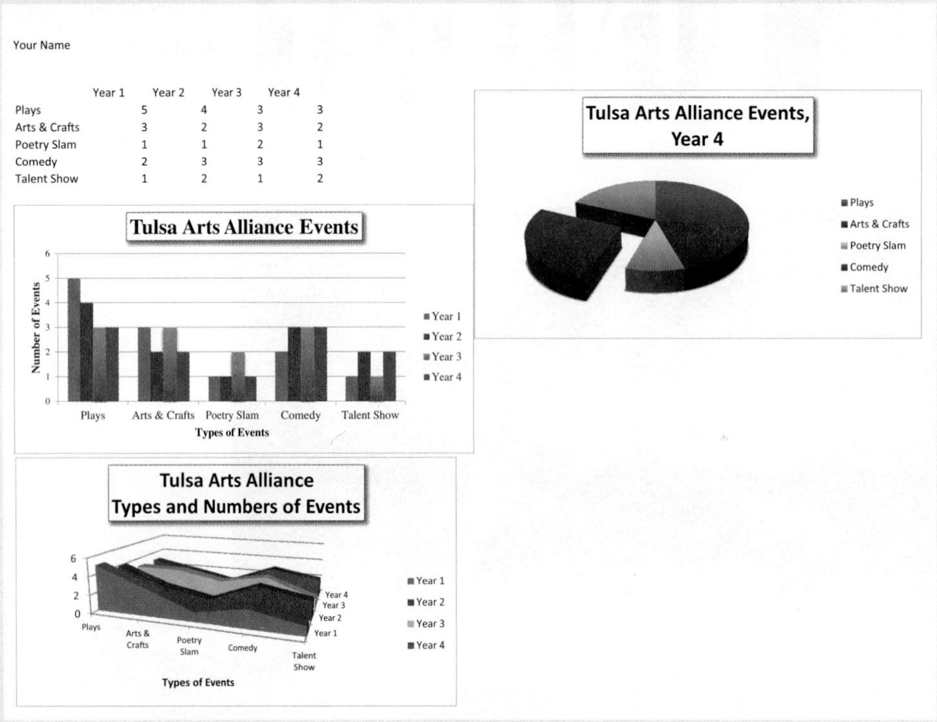

Independent Challenge 2

You work at Bark Bark Bark, a locally owned day spa for dogs. One of your responsibilities at the day spa is to manage the company's sales and expenses using Excel. Another is to convince the current staff that Excel can help them make daily operating decisions more easily and efficiently. To do this, you've decided to create charts using the previous year's operating expenses including rent, utilities, and payroll. The manager will use these charts at the next monthly meeting.

a. Start Excel, open the Data File EX D-4.xlsx from the location where you store your Data Files, then save it as **EX D-Bark Bark Bark Doggie Day Spa Analysis**.

b. Decide which data in the worksheet should be charted. What chart types are best suited for the information you need to show? What kinds of chart enhancements are necessary?

c. Create a 3-D Clustered Column chart in the worksheet showing the expense data for all four quarters. (*Hint*: The expense categories should appear on the x-axis. Do not include the totals.)

d. Change the vertical axis labels (Expenses data) so that no decimals are displayed. (*Hint*: Right-click the axis labels you want to modify, click Format Axis, click the Number category in the Format Axis pane, change the number of decimal places, then close the Format Axis pane.)

e. Using the sales data, create two charts on this worksheet that compare the sales amounts. (*Hint*: Move each chart to a new location on the worksheet, then deselect it before creating the next one.)

f. In one chart of the sales data, add data labels, then add chart titles as you see fit.

g. Make any necessary formatting changes to make the charts look more attractive, then enter your name in a worksheet cell.

h. Save your work.

i. Preview each chart in Backstage view, and adjust any items as needed. Fit the worksheet to a single page, then submit your work to your instructor as directed. A sample of a printed worksheet is shown in **FIGURE D-28**.

j. Close the workbook, then exit Excel.

FIGURE D-28

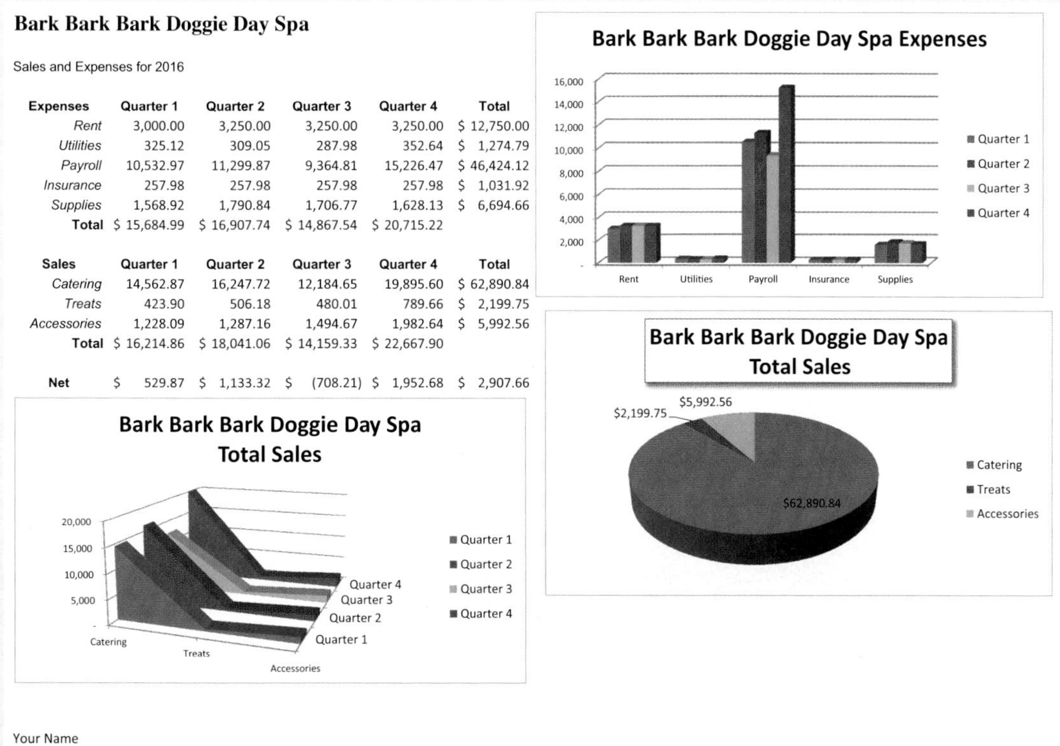

Bark Bark Bark Doggie Day Spa

Sales and Expenses for 2016

Expenses	Quarter 1	Quarter 2	Quarter 3	Quarter 4	Total
Rent	3,000.00	3,250.00	3,250.00	3,250.00	$ 12,750.00
Utilities	325.12	309.05	287.98	352.64	$ 1,274.79
Payroll	10,532.97	11,299.87	9,364.81	15,226.47	$ 46,424.12
Insurance	257.98	257.98	257.98	257.98	$ 1,031.92
Supplies	1,568.92	1,790.84	1,706.77	1,628.13	$ 6,694.66
Total	$ 15,684.99	$ 16,907.74	$ 14,867.54	$ 20,715.22	

Sales	Quarter 1	Quarter 2	Quarter 3	Quarter 4	Total
Catering	14,562.87	16,247.72	12,184.65	19,895.60	$ 62,890.84
Treats	423.90	506.18	480.01	789.66	$ 2,199.75
Accessories	1,228.09	1,287.16	1,494.67	1,982.64	$ 5,992.56
Total	$ 16,214.86	$ 18,041.06	$ 14,159.33	$ 22,667.90	
Net	$ 529.87	$ 1,133.32	$ (708.21)	$ 1,952.68	$ 2,907.66

Independent Challenge 3

You are working as an account representative at a magazine called *Creativity*. You have been examining the expenses incurred recently. The CEO wants to examine expenses designed to increase circulation and has asked you to prepare charts that can be used in this evaluation. In particular, you want to see how dollar amounts compare among the different expenses, and you also want to see how expenses compare with each other proportional to the total budget.

a. Start Excel, open the Data File EX D-5.xlsx from the location where you store your Data Files, then save it as **EX D-Creativity Magazine.**

b. Identify three types of charts that seem best suited to illustrate the data in the range A16:B24. What kinds of chart enhancements are necessary?

c. Create at least two different types of charts that show the distribution of circulation expenses. (*Hint*: Move each chart to a new location on the same worksheet.) One of the charts should be a 3-D pie chart.

d. In at least one of the charts, add annotated text and arrows highlighting important data, such as the largest expense.

e. Change the color of at least one data series in at least one of the charts.

f. Add chart titles and category and value axis titles where appropriate. Format the titles with a font of your choice. Apply a shadow to the chart title in at least one chart.

g. Add your name to a section of the header, then save your work.

h. Explode a slice from the 3-D pie chart.

i. Add a data label to the exploded pie slice.

j. Preview the worksheet in Backstage view. Adjust any items as needed. Be sure the charts are all visible on one page. Compare your work to the sample in **FIGURE D-29**.

k. Submit your work to your instructor as directed, close the workbook, then exit Excel.

FIGURE D-29

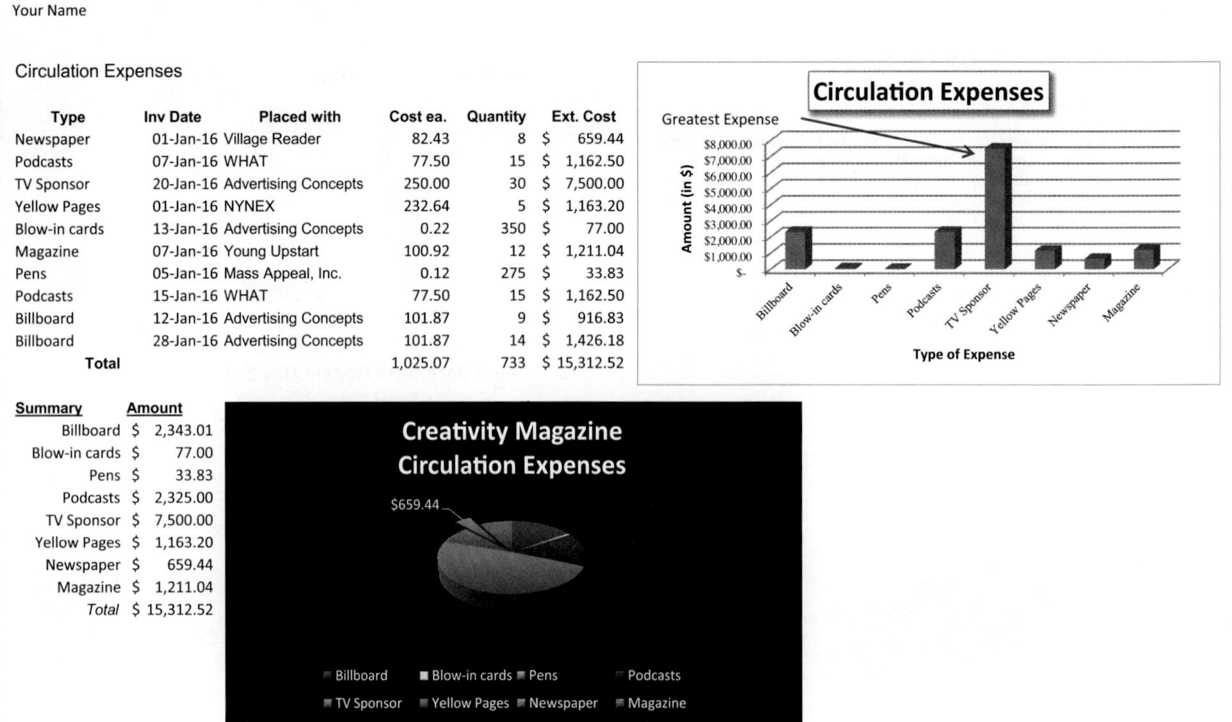

Your Name

Circulation Expenses

Type	Inv Date	Placed with	Cost ea.	Quantity	Ext. Cost
Newspaper	01-Jan-16	Village Reader	82.43	8	$ 659.44
Podcasts	07-Jan-16	WHAT	77.50	15	$ 1,162.50
TV Sponsor	20-Jan-16	Advertising Concepts	250.00	30	$ 7,500.00
Yellow Pages	01-Jan-16	NYNEX	232.64	5	$ 1,163.20
Blow-in cards	13-Jan-16	Advertising Concepts	0.22	350	$ 77.00
Magazine	07-Jan-16	Young Upstart	100.92	12	$ 1,211.04
Pens	05-Jan-16	Mass Appeal, Inc.	0.12	275	$ 33.83
Podcasts	15-Jan-16	WHAT	77.50	15	$ 1,162.50
Billboard	12-Jan-16	Advertising Concepts	101.87	9	$ 916.83
Billboard	28-Jan-16	Advertising Concepts	101.87	14	$ 1,426.18
Total			1,025.07	733	$ 15,312.52

Summary	Amount
Billboard	$ 2,343.01
Blow-in cards	$ 77.00
Pens	$ 33.83
Podcasts	$ 2,325.00
TV Sponsor	$ 7,500.00
Yellow Pages	$ 1,163.20
Newspaper	$ 659.44
Magazine	$ 1,211.04
Total	$ 15,312.52

Independent Challenge 4: Explore

This Independent Challenge requires an Internet connection.

A cash inheritance from a distant relative has finally been deposited in your bank account, and you have decided to purchase a home. You have a good idea where you'd like to live, and you decide to use the web to find out more about houses that are currently available.

- **a.** Start Excel, then save a new, blank workbook as **EX D-My Dream House** to the location where you save your Data Files.
- **b.** Decide on where you would like to live, and use your favorite search engine to find information sources on homes for sale in that area. (*Hint*: Try using realtor.com or other realtor-sponsored sites.)
- **c.** Determine a price range and features within the home. Find data for at least five homes that meet your location and price requirements, and enter them in the worksheet. See **TABLE D-4** for a suggested data layout.
- **d.** Format the data so it looks attractive and professional.
- **e.** Create any type of column chart using only the House and Asking Price data. Place it on the same worksheet as the data. Include a descriptive title.
- **f.** Change the colors in the chart using the chart style of your choice.
- **g.** Enter your name in a section of the header.
- **h.** Create an additional chart: a combo chart that plots the asking price on one axis and the size of the home on the other axis. (*Hint*: Use Help to get tips on how to chart with a secondary axis.)
- **i.** Save the workbook. Preview the worksheet in Backstage view and make adjustments if necessary to fit all of the information on one page. See **FIGURE D-30** for an example of what your worksheet might look like.
- **j.** Submit your work to your instructor as directed.
- **k.** Close the workbook, then exit Excel.

TABLE D-4

suggested data layout					
Location					
Price range					
	House 1	House 2	House 3	House 4	House 5
Asking price					
Bedrooms					
Bathrooms					
Year built					
Size (in sq. ft.)					

Excel 2013

FIGURE D-30

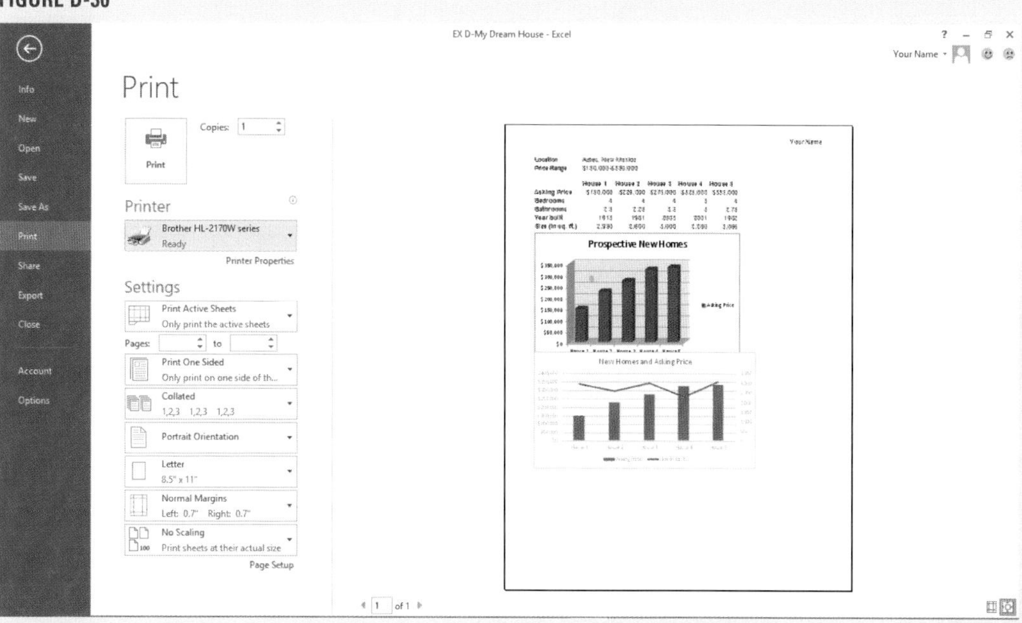

Visual Workshop

Open the Data File EX D-6.xlsx from the location where you store your Data Files, then save it as **EX D-Projected Project Expenses**. Format the worksheet data so it looks like **FIGURE D-31**, then create and modify two charts to match the ones shown in the figure. You will need to make formatting, layout, and design changes once you create the charts. (*Hint*: The shadow used in the 3-D pie chart title is made using the Outer Offset Diagonal Top Right shadow.) Enter your name in the left text box of the header, then save and preview the worksheet. Submit your work to your instructor as directed, then close the workbook and exit Excel.

FIGURE D-31

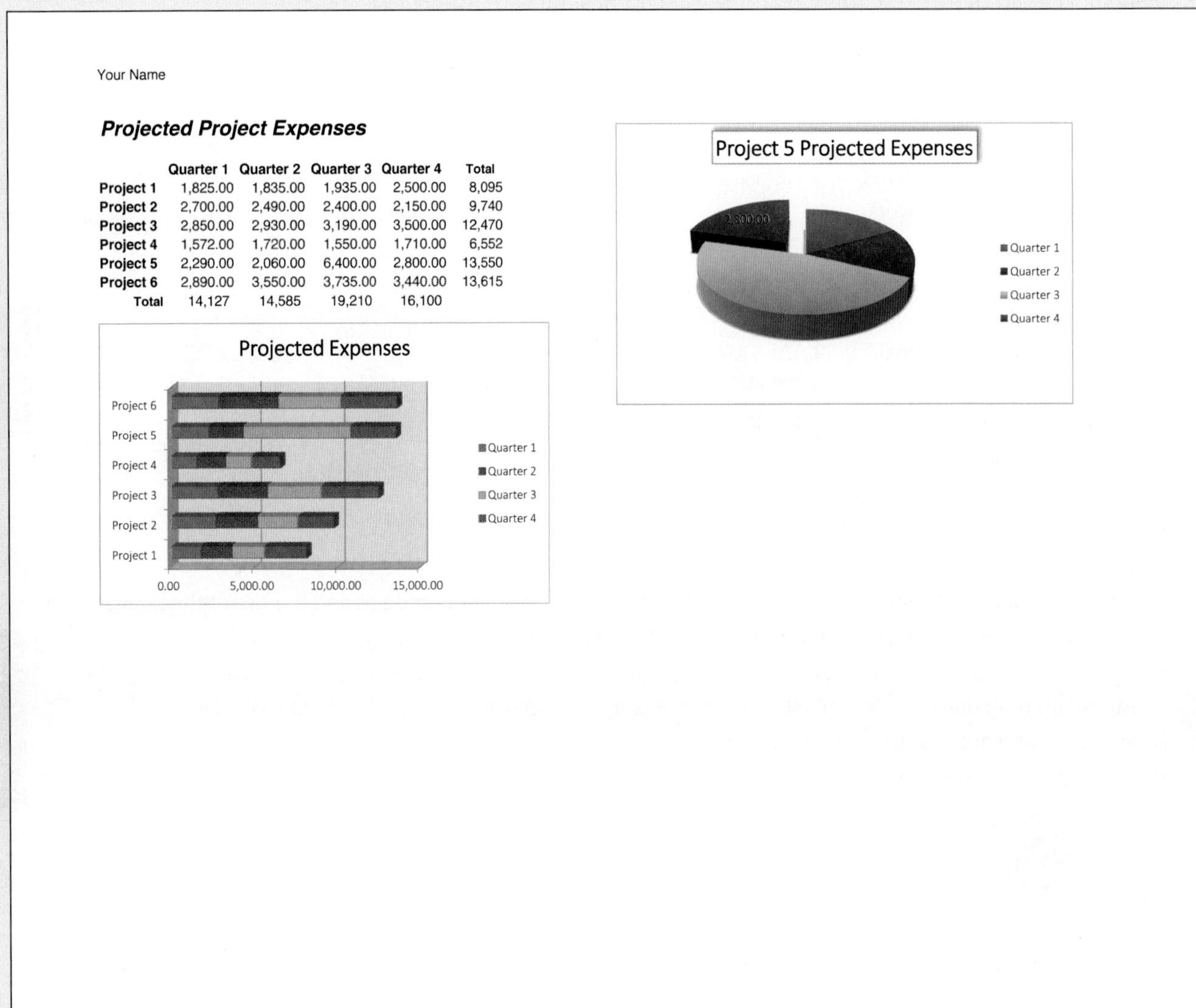

Your Name

Projected Project Expenses

	Quarter 1	Quarter 2	Quarter 3	Quarter 4	Total
Project 1	1,825.00	1,835.00	1,935.00	2,500.00	8,095
Project 2	2,700.00	2,490.00	2,400.00	2,150.00	9,740
Project 3	2,850.00	2,930.00	3,190.00	3,500.00	12,470
Project 4	1,572.00	1,720.00	1,550.00	1,710.00	6,552
Project 5	2,290.00	2,060.00	6,400.00	2,800.00	13,550
Project 6	2,890.00	3,550.00	3,735.00	3,440.00	13,615
Total	14,127	14,585	19,210	16,100	

Analyzing Data Using Formulas

CASE Kate Morgan, Quest's vice president of sales, uses Excel formulas and functions to analyze sales data for the U.S. region and to consolidate sales data from several worksheets. Because management is considering adding a new regional branch, Kate asks you to estimate the loan costs for a new office facility and to compare tour sales in the existing U.S. offices.

Unit Objectives

After completing this unit, you will be able to:

- Format data using text functions
- Sum a data range based on conditions
- Consolidate data using a formula
- Check formulas for errors
- Construct formulas using named ranges
- Build a logical formula with the IF function
- Build a logical formula with the AND function
- Calculate payments with the PMT function

Files You Will Need

EX E-1.xlsx
EX E-2.xlsx
EX E-3.xlsx
EX E-4.xlsx
EX E-5.xlsx
EX E-6.xlsx
EX E-7.xlsx

Excel 2013
UNIT E

Format Data Using Text Functions

Learning Outcomes
- Separate text data using Flash Fill
- Format text data using the PROPER function
- Format text data using the CONCATENATE function

Often, you need to import data into Excel from an outside source, such as another program or the Internet. Sometimes you need to reformat this data to make it understandable and attractive. Instead of handling these tasks manually in each cell, you can save time by using Excel text functions to perform these tasks automatically for a range of cell data. The Convert Text to Columns feature breaks data fields in one column into separate columns. The text function PROPER capitalizes the first letter in a string of text as well as any text following a space. You can use the CONCATENATE function to join two or more strings into one text string. **CASE** *Kate has received the U.S. sales representatives' data from the Human Resources Department. She asks you to use text formulas to format the data into a more useful layout.*

STEPS

1. **Start Excel, open the file EX E-1.xlsx from the location where you store your Data Files, then save it as EX E-Sales**
2. **On the Sales Reps sheet, click cell B4, type ramon silva, press [Tab], type new york, press [Tab], type 3, then click the Enter button on the Formula bar**

   You are manually separating the data in cell A4 into the adjacent cells as shown in **FIGURE E-1**. You will let Excel follow your pattern for the rows below using Flash Fill. **Flash Fill** uses worksheet data you have entered as an example to predict what should be entered into similar column cells.
3. **With cell D4 selected, click the DATA tab, then click the Flash Fill button in the Data Tools group**

   The years of service number is copied from cell D4 into the range D5:D15. You will use Flash Fill to fill in the names and cities.
4. **Click cell B4, click the Flash Fill button in the Data Tools group, click cell C4, then click the Flash Fill button again**

   The column A data is separated into columns B, C and D. You want to format the letters in the names and cities to the correct cases.
5. **Click cell E4, click the FORMULAS tab, click the Text button in the Function Library group, click PROPER, with the insertion point in the Text text box, click cell B4, then click OK**

   The name is copied from cell B4 to cell E4 with the correct uppercase letters for proper names. The remaining names and the cities are still in lowercase letters.
6. **Drag the fill handle to copy the formula in cell E4 to cell F4, then copy the formulas in cells E4:F4 into the range E5:F15**

   You want to format the years data to be more descriptive.
7. **Click cell G4, click the Text button in the Function Library group, click CONCATENATE, with the insertion point in the Text1 text box, click cell D4, press [Tab], with the insertion point in the Text2 text box, press [Spacebar], type Years, then click OK**
8. **Copy the formula in cell G4 into the range G5:G15, click cell A1, compare your work to FIGURE E-2, click the INSERT tab, click the Header & Footer button in the Text group, click the Go to Footer button in the Navigation group, enter your name in the center text box, click on the worksheet, scroll up and click cell A1, then click the Normal button in the status bar**
9. **Save your file, then preview the worksheet**

QUICK TIP
You can move the Function Arguments dialog box if it overlaps a cell or range that you need to click. You can also click the Collapse Dialog box button, select the cell or range, then click the Expand Dialog box button to return to the Function Arguments dialog box.

QUICK TIP
Excel automatically inserts quotation marks to enclose the space and the Years text.

FIGURE E-1: Worksheet with data separated into columns

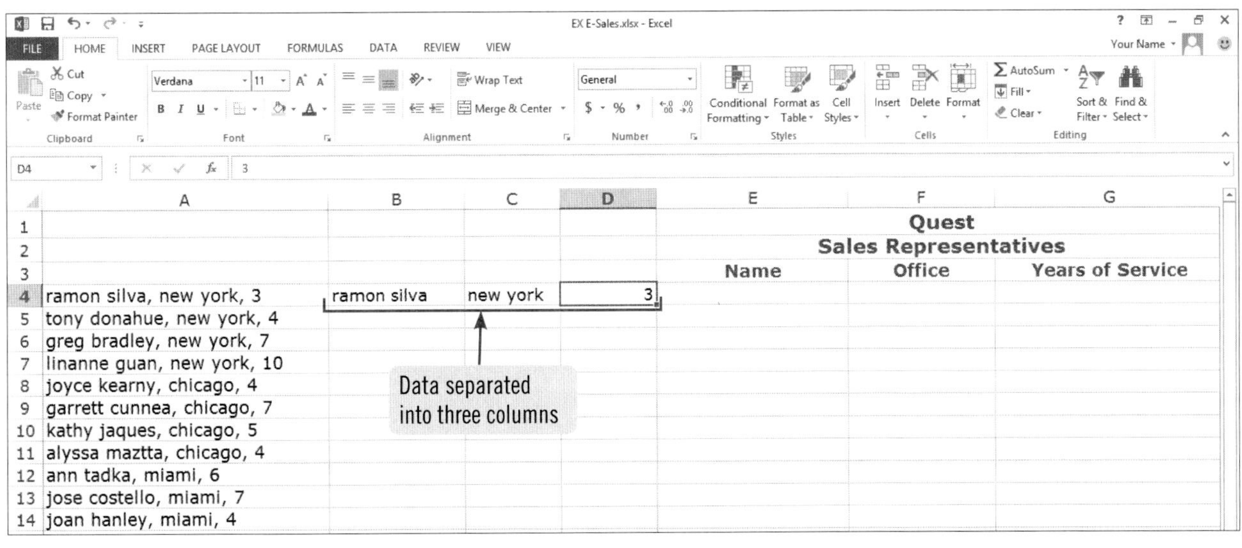

FIGURE E-2: Worksheet with data formatted in columns

	A	B	C	D	E	F	G
1						Quest	
2						Sales Representatives	
3					Name	Office	Years of Service
4	ramon silva, new york, 3	ramon silva	new york	3	Ramon Silva	New York	3 Years
5	tony donahue, new york, 4	tony donahue	new york	4	Tony Donahue	New York	4 Years
6	greg bradley, new york, 7	greg bradley	new york	7	Greg Bradley	New York	7 Years
7	linanne guan, new york, 10	linanne guan	new york	10	Linanne Guan	New York	10 Years
8	joyce kearny, chicago, 4	joyce kearny	chicago	4	Joyce Kearny	Chicago	4 Years
9	garrett cunnea, chicago, 7	garrett cunnea	chicago	7	Garrett Cunnea	Chicago	7 Years
10	kathy jaques, chicago, 5	kathy jaques	chicago	5	Kathy Jaques	Chicago	5 Years
11	alyssa maztta, chicago, 4	alyssa maztta	chicago	4	Alyssa Maztta	Chicago	4 Years
12	ann tadka, miami, 6	ann tadka	miami	6	Ann Tadka	Miami	6 Years
13	jose costello, miami, 7	jose costello	miami	7	Jose Costello	Miami	7 Years
14	joan hanley, miami, 4	joan hanley	miami	4	Joan Hanley	Miami	4 Years
15	spring zola, miami, 7	spring zola	miami	7	Spring Zola	Miami	7 Years

Excel 2013

Working with text in other ways

Other useful text functions include UPPER, LOWER, and SUBSTITUTE. The UPPER function converts text to all uppercase letters, the LOWER function converts text to all lowercase letters, and SUBSTITUTE replaces text in a text string. For example, if cell A1 contains the text string "Today is Wednesday", then =LOWER(A1) would produce "today is wednesday"; =UPPER(A1) would produce "TODAY IS WEDNESDAY"; and =SUBSTITUTE(A1, "Wednesday", "Tuesday") would result in "Today is Tuesday". You can separate text data stored in one column into multiple columns by clicking the DATA tab, clicking the Text to Columns button in the Data Tools group, and specifying the delimiter for your data. A **delimiter** is a separator, such as a space, comma, or semicolon, that should separate your data. Excel then separates your data into columns at the delimiter.

If you want to copy and paste data that you have formatted using text functions, you need to select Values Only from the Paste Options drop-down list to paste the cell values rather than the text formulas.

Sum a Data Range Based on Conditions

Learning Outcomes
- Count data using the COUNTIF function
- Total data using the SUMIF function
- Summarize data using the AVERAGEIF function

You can also use Excel functions to sum, count, and average data in a range based on criteria, or conditions, you set. The SUMIF function totals only the cells in a range that meet given criteria. The COUNTIF function counts cells and the AVERAGEIF function averages cells in a range based on a specified condition. The format for the SUMIF function appears in **FIGURE E-3**. **CASE** *Kate asks you to analyze the New York branch's January sales data to provide her with information about each tour.*

STEPS

1. **Click the NY sheet tab, click cell G7, click the FORMULAS tab, click the More Functions button in the Function Library group, point to Statistical, scroll down the list of functions if necessary, then click COUNTIF**

   You want to count the number of times Pacific Odyssey appears in the Tour column. The formula you use will say, in effect, "Examine the range I specify, then count the number of cells in that range that contain "Pacific Odyssey."" You will specify absolute addresses for the range so you can copy the formula.

2. **With the insertion point in the Range text box, select the range A6:A25, press [F4], press [Tab], with the insertion point in the Criteria text box, click cell F7, then click OK**

   Your formula as shown in the formula bar in **FIGURE E-4** asks Excel to search the range A6:A25, and where it finds the value shown in cell F7 (that is, when it finds the value "Pacific Odyssey"), add one to the total count. The number of Pacific Odyssey tours, 4, appears in cell G7. You want to calculate the total sales revenue for the Pacific Odyssey tours.

QUICK TIP
You can also sum, count, and average ranges with multiple criteria using the functions SUMIFS, COUNTIFS, and AVERAGEIFS.

3. **Click cell H7, click the Math & Trig button in the Function Library group, scroll down the list of functions, then click SUMIF**

   The Function Arguments dialog box opens. You want to enter two ranges and a criterion; the first range is the one where you want Excel to search for the criteria entered. The second range contains the corresponding cells that Excel will total when it finds the criterion you specify in the first range.

4. **With the insertion point in the Range text box, select the range A6:A25, press [F4], press [Tab], with the insertion point in the Criteria text box, click cell F7, press [Tab], with the insertion point in the Sum_range text box, select the range B6:B25, press [F4], then click OK**

   Your formula asks Excel to search the range A6:A25, and where it finds the value shown in cell F7 (that is, when it finds the value "Pacific Odyssey"), add the corresponding amounts from column B. The revenue for the Pacific Odyssey tours, $4,503, appears in cell H7. You want to calculate the average price paid for the Pacific Odyssey tours.

5. **Click cell I7, click the More Functions button in the Function Library group, point to Statistical, then click AVERAGEIF**

6. **With the insertion point in the Range text box, select the range A6:A25, press [F4], press [Tab], with the insertion point in the Criteria text box, click cell F7, press [Tab], with the insertion point in the Average_range text box, select the range B6:B25, press [F4], then click OK**

   The average price paid for the Pacific Odyssey tours, $1,126, appears in cell I7.

7. **Select the range G7:I7, drag the fill handle to fill the range G8:I10**

   Compare your results with those in **FIGURE E-5**.

TROUBLE
Follow the same steps that you used to add a footer to the Sales Reps worksheet in the previous lesson.

8. **Add your name to the center of the footer, save the workbook, then preview the sheet**

FIGURE E-3: Format of SUMIF function

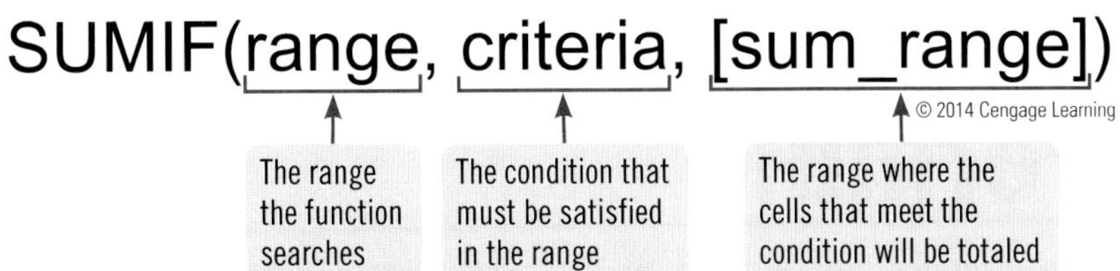

FIGURE E-4: COUNTIF function in the formula bar

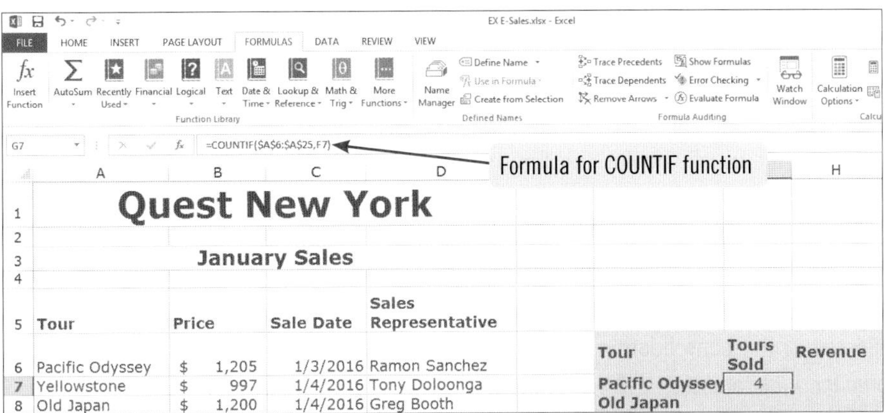

FIGURE E-5: Worksheet with conditional statistics

Tour	Tours Sold	Revenue	Average Price
Pacific Odyssey	4	$ 4,503	$ 1,126
Old Japan	5	$ 5,603	$ 1,121
Costa Rica	5	$ 9,016	$ 1,803
Yellowstone	6	$ 5,864	$ 977

Entering date and time functions

Microsoft Excel stores dates as sequential serial numbers and uses them in calculations. January 1, 1900 is assigned serial number 1 and numbers are represented as the number of days following that date. You can see the serial number of a date by using the DATE function. To see the serial number of January, 1, 2016, you would enter =DATE(2016,1,1). The result would be in date format, but if you format the cell as Number, then you will see the serial number of 42370 for this date. Because Excel uses serial numbers, you can perform calculations that include dates and times using the Excel date and time functions. To enter a date or time function, click the FORMULAS tab on the Ribbon, click the Date & Time button in the Function Library group, then click the Date or Time function you want. All of the date and time functions will be displayed as dates and times unless you change the formatting to Number to see the serial date or time. See **TABLE E-1** for some of the available Date and Time functions in Excel.

TABLE E-1: Date and Time functions

function	calculates the serial number of	example
TODAY	The current date	=TODAY()
NOW	The current date and time	=NOW()
DATE	A date you enter	=DATE(2016,1,2)
TIME	A time you enter	=TIME(0,0,2000)
YEAR	A year you enter	=YEAR(2016)
HOUR	An hour time you enter	=HOUR("15:30:30")
MINUTE	A time you enter	=MINUTE("15:30:30")

Consolidate Data Using a Formula

Learning Outcomes
- Consolidate data on multiple sheets using AutoSum
- Consolidate data on multiple sheets using 3-D references

When you want to summarize similar data that exists in different sheets or workbooks, you can **consolidate**, or combine and display, the data in one sheet. For example, you might have entered departmental sales figures on four different store sheets that you want to consolidate on one summary sheet, showing total departmental sales for all stores. Or, you may have quarterly sales data on separate sheets that you want to total for yearly sales on a summary sheet. The best way to consolidate data is to use cell references to the various sheets on a consolidation, or summary, sheet. Because they reference other sheets that are usually behind the summary sheet, such references effectively create another dimension in the workbook and are called **3-D references**, as shown in FIGURE E-6. You can reference, or **link** to, data in other sheets and in other workbooks. Linking to a worksheet or workbook is better than retyping calculated results from another worksheet or workbook because the data values that the calculated totals depend on might change. If you reference the values, any changes to the original values are automatically reflected in the consolidation sheet. **CASE** *Kate asks you to prepare a January sales summary sheet comparing the total U.S. revenue for the tours sold in the month.*

STEPS

1. **Click the US Summary Jan sheet tab**

   Because the US Summary Jan sheet (which is the consolidation sheet) will contain the reference to the data in the other sheets, the cell pointer must reside there when you begin entering the reference.

2. **Click cell B7, click the FORMULAS tab, click the AutoSum button in the Function Library group, click the NY sheet tab, press and hold [Shift] and click the Miami sheet tab, scroll up if necessary and click cell G7, then click the Enter button ✓ on the formula bar**

   The US Summary Jan sheet becomes active, and the formula bar reads =SUM(NY:Miami!G7), as shown in FIGURE E-7. "NY:Miami" references the NY, Chicago, and Miami sheets. The exclamation point (!) is an **external reference indicator**, meaning that the cells referenced are outside the active sheet; G7 is the actual cell reference you want to total in the external sheets. The result, 12, appears in cell B7 of the US Summary Jan sheet; it is the sum of the number of Pacific Odyssey tours sold and referenced in cell G7 of the NY, Chicago, and Miami sheets. Because the Revenue data is in the column to the right of the Tours Sold column on the NY, Chicago, and Miami sheets, you can copy the tours sold summary formula, with its relative addresses, into the cell that holds the revenue summary information.

3. **Drag the fill handle to copy the formula in cell B7 to cell C7, click the Auto Fill Options list arrow, then click the Fill Without Formatting option button**

   The result, $13,514, appears in cell C7 of the US Summary Jan sheet, showing the sum of the Pacific Odyssey tour revenue referenced in cell H7 of the NY, Chicago, and Miami sheets.

4. **In the US Summary Jan sheet, with the range B7:C7 selected, drag the fill handle to fill the range B8:C10**

   You can test a consolidation reference by changing one cell value on which the formula is based and seeing if the formula result changes.

5. **Click the Chicago sheet tab, edit cell A6 to read Pacific Odyssey, then click the US Summary Jan sheet tab**

   The number of Pacific Odyssey tours sold is automatically updated to 13, and the revenue is increased to $15,393, as shown in FIGURE E-8.

6. **Save the workbook, then preview the worksheet**

QUICK TIP
You can preview your worksheet with the worksheet gridlines and column and row headings for printing at a later time. On the PAGE LAYOUT tab, click the Print check boxes under Gridlines and Headings in the Sheet Options group.

FIGURE E-6: Consolidating data from three worksheets

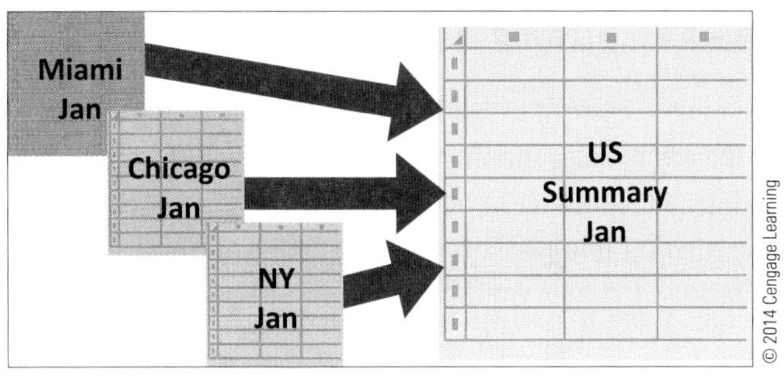

FIGURE E-7: Worksheet showing total Pacific Odyssey tours sold

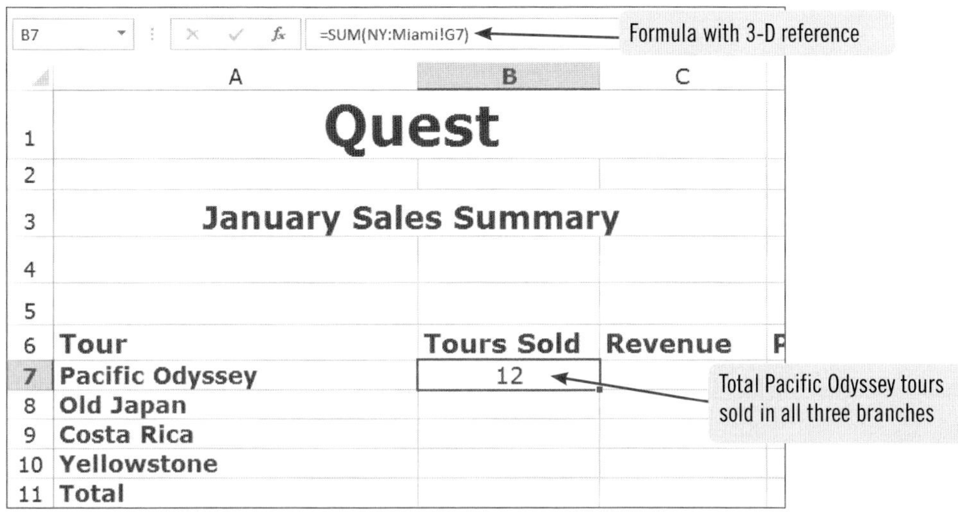

FIGURE E-8: US Summary Jan worksheet with updated totals

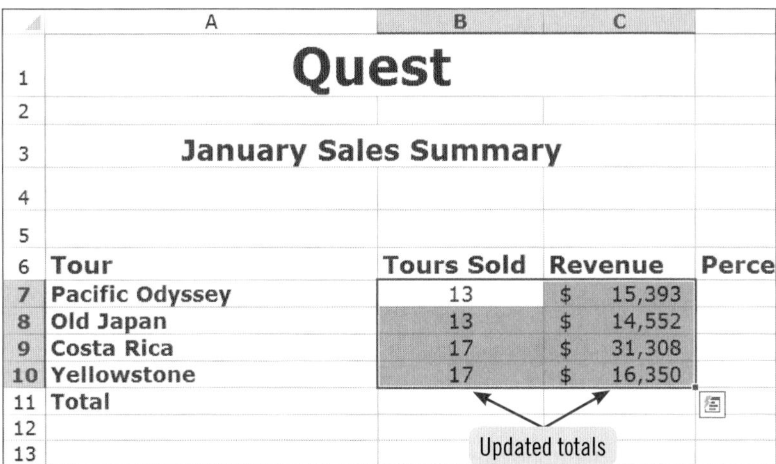

Quest
January Sales Summary
Tour
Tours Sold
Revenue
Perce
Pacific Odyssey
13
$ 15,393
Old Japan
13
$ 14,552
Costa Rica
17
$ 31,308
Yellowstone
17
$ 16,350
Total
Updated totals

Linking data between workbooks

Just as you can link data between cells in a worksheet and between sheets in a workbook, you can link workbooks so that changes made in referenced cells in one workbook are reflected in the consolidation sheet in the other workbook. To link a single cell between workbooks, open both workbooks, select the cell to receive the linked data, type the equal sign (=), select the cell in the other workbook containing the data to be linked, then press [Enter]. Excel automatically inserts the name of the referenced workbook in the cell reference. For example, if the linked data is contained in cell C7 of the Sales worksheet in the Product workbook, the cell entry reads =[Product.xlsx]Sales!$C$7. To perform calculations, enter formulas on the consolidation sheet using cells in the supporting sheets.

Check Formulas for Errors

Learning Outcomes
- Check for formula errors using IFERROR
- Display worksheet formulas

When formulas result in errors, Excel displays an error value based on the error type. See **TABLE E-2** for an explanation of the error values that might appear in worksheets. One way to check worksheet formulas for errors is to display the formulas on the worksheet rather than the formula results. You can also check for errors when entering formulas by using the IFERROR function. The IFERROR function simplifies the error-checking process for your worksheets. This function displays a message or value that you specify, rather than the one automatically generated by Excel, if there is an error in a formula. **CASE** *Kate asks you to use formulas to compare the tour revenues for January. You will use the IFERROR function to help catch formula errors.*

STEPS

1. **On the US Summary Jan sheet, click cell B11, click the FORMULAS tab, click the AutoSum button in the Function Library group, then click the Enter button ✓ on the formula bar**
   The number of tours sold, 60, appears in cell B11.
2. **Drag the fill handle to copy the formula in cell B11 into cell C11, click the Auto Fill options list arrow, then click the Fill Without Formatting option button**
   The tour revenue total of $77,603 appears in cell C11. You decide to enter a formula to calculate the percentage of revenue the Pacific Odyssey tour represents by dividing the individual tour revenue figures by the total revenue figure. To help with error checking, you decide to enter the formula using the IFERROR function.
3. **Click cell D7, click the Logical button in the Function Library group, click IFERROR, with the insertion point in the Value text box, click cell C7, type /, click cell C11, press [Tab], in the Value_if_error text box, type ERROR, then click OK**
   The Pacific Odyssey tour revenue percentage of 19.84% appears in cell D7. You want to be sure that your error message will be displayed properly, so you decide to test it by intentionally creating an error. You copy and paste the formula—which has a relative address in the denominator, where an absolute address should be used.

TROUBLE
You will fix the ERROR codes in cells D8:D10 in the next step.

4. **Drag the fill handle to copy the formula in cell D7 into the range D8:D10**
   The ERROR value appears in cells D8:D10, as shown in **FIGURE E-9**. The errors are a result of the relative address for C11 in the denominator of the copied formula. Changing the relative address of C11 in the copied formula to an absolute address of $C$11 will correct the errors.

QUICK TIP
You can also check formulas for errors using the buttons in the Formula Auditing group on the FORMULAS tab.

5. **Double-click cell D7, select C11 in the formula, press [F4], then ✓ click on the formula bar**
   The formula now contains an absolute reference to cell C11.
6. **Copy the corrected formula in cell D7 into the range D8:D10**
   The tour revenue percentages now appear in all four cells, without error messages, as shown in **FIGURE E-10**. You want to check all of your worksheet formulas by displaying them on the worksheet.

QUICK TIP
You can also display worksheet formulas by holding [Ctrl] and pressing [`].

7. **Click the Show Formulas button in the Formula Auditing group**
   The formulas appear in columns B, C, and D. You want to display the formula results again. The Show Formulas button works as a toggle, turning the feature on and off with each click.
8. **Click the Show Formulas button in the Formula Auditing group**
   The formula results appear on the worksheet.
9. **Add your name to the center section of the footer, save the workbook, preview the worksheet, close the workbook, then submit the workbook to your instructor**

FIGURE E-9: Worksheet with error codes

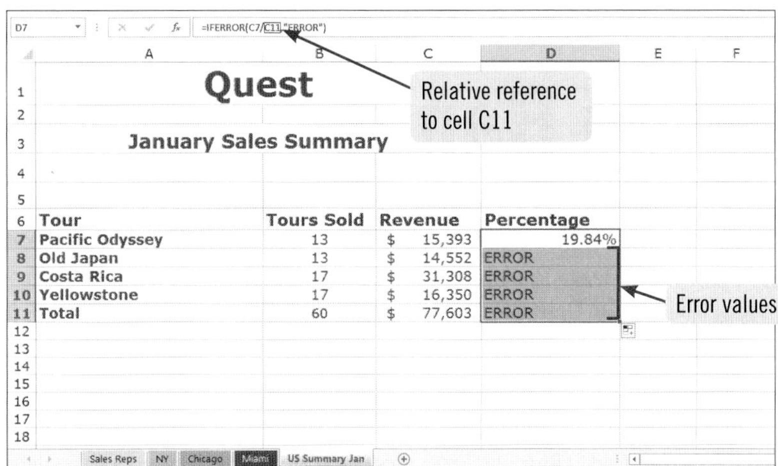

FIGURE E-10: Worksheet with tour percentages

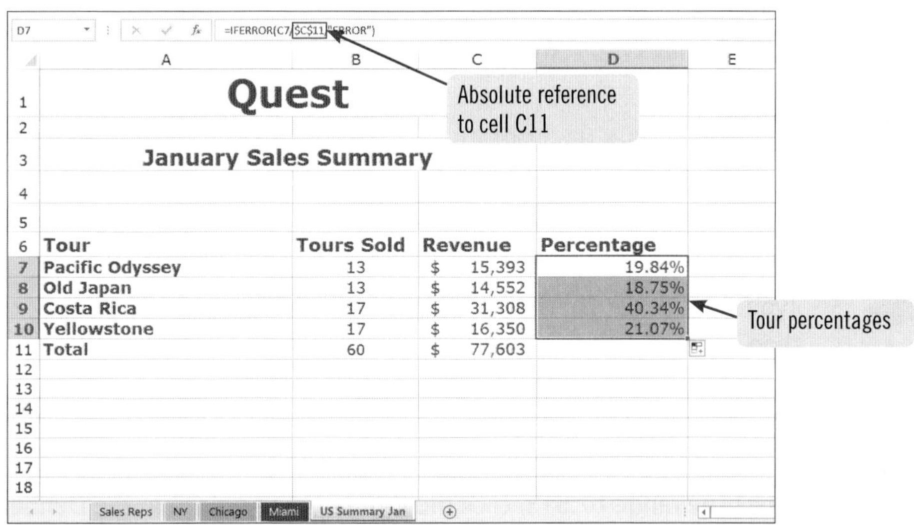

TABLE E-2: Understanding error values

error value	cause of error	error value	cause of error
#DIV/0!	A number is divided by 0	#NAME?	Formula contains text error
#NA	A value in a formula is not available	#NULL!	Invalid intersection of areas
#NUM!	Invalid use of a number in a formula	#REF!	Invalid cell reference
#VALUE!	Wrong type of formula argument or operand	#####	Column is not wide enough to display data

Correcting circular references

A cell with a circular reference contains a formula that refers to its own cell location. If you accidentally enter a formula with a circular reference, a warning box opens, alerting you to the problem. Click Help to open a Help window explaining how to find the circular reference. In simple formulas, a circular reference is easy to spot. To correct it, edit the formula to remove any reference to the cell where the formula is located.

If the circular reference is intentional, you can avoid this error by enabling the iteration feature. Excel then recalculates the formula for the number of times you specify. To enable iterative calculations, click the FILE tab on the Ribbon, click Options, click Formulas to view the options for calculations, click the Enable iterative calculation check box in the Calculation options group, enter the maximum number of iterations in the Maximum Iterations text box, enter the maximum amount of change between recalculation results in the Maximum Change text box, then click OK.

Construct Formulas Using Named Ranges

Learning Outcomes
- Assign names to cells
- Assign names to cell ranges
- Build formulas using names

To make your worksheet easier to follow, you can assign names to cells and ranges. Then you can use the names in formulas to make them easier to build and to reduce formula errors. For example, the formula "revenue-cost" is easier to understand than the formula "A5-A8". Cell and range names can use uppercase or lowercase letters as well as digits, but cannot have spaces. After you name a cell or range, you can define its **scope**, or the worksheets where you will be able to use it. When defining a name's scope, you can limit its use to a worksheet or make it available to the entire workbook. If you move a named cell or range, its name moves with it, and if you add or remove rows or columns to the worksheet the ranges are adjusted to their new position in the worksheet. When used in formulas, names become absolute cell references by default. **CASE** *Kate asks you to calculate the number of days before each tour departs. You will use range names to construct the formula.*

STEPS

QUICK TIP
You can also create range names by selecting a cell or range, typing a name in the Name Box, then pressing [Enter]. By default, its scope will be the workbook.

QUICK TIP
Because names cannot contain spaces, underscores are often used between words to replace spaces.

QUICK TIP
Named cells and ranges can be used as a navigational tool in a worksheet by selecting the name in the Name box.

1. **Open the file EX E-2.xlsx from the location where you store your Data Files, then save it as EX E-Tours**
2. **Click cell B4, click the FORMULAS tab if necessary, then click the Define Name button in the Defined Names group**
   The New Name dialog box opens, as shown in FIGURE E-11. You can give a cell that contains a date a name that will make it easier to build formulas that perform date calculations.
3. **Type current_date in the Name text box, click the Scope list arrow, click April Tours, then click OK**
   The name assigned to cell B4, current_date, appears in the Name Box. Because its scope is the April Tours worksheet, the range name current_date will appear on the name list only on that worksheet. You can also name ranges that contain dates.
4. **Select the range B7:B13, click the Define Name button in the Defined Names group, enter tour_date in the Name text box, click the Scope list arrow, click April Tours, then click OK**
   Now you can use the named cell and named range in a formula. The formula =tour_date–current_date is easier to understand than =B7-$B$4.
5. **Click cell C7, type =, click the Use in Formula button in the Defined Names group, click tour_date, type –, click the Use in Formula button, click current_date, then click the Enter button ✓ on the formula bar**
   The number of days before the Costa Rica tour departs, 9, appears in cell C7. You can use the same formula to calculate the number of days before the other tours depart.
6. **Drag the fill handle to copy the formula in cell C7 into the range C8:C13, then compare your formula results with those in FIGURE E-12**
7. **Save the workbook**

Consolidating data using named ranges

You can consolidate data using named cells and ranges. For example, you might have entered team sales figures using the names team1, team2, and team3 on different sheets that you want to consolidate on one summary sheet. As you enter the summary formula you can click the FORMULAS tab, click the Use in Formula button in the Defined Names group, and select the cell or range name.

FIGURE E-11: New Name dialog box

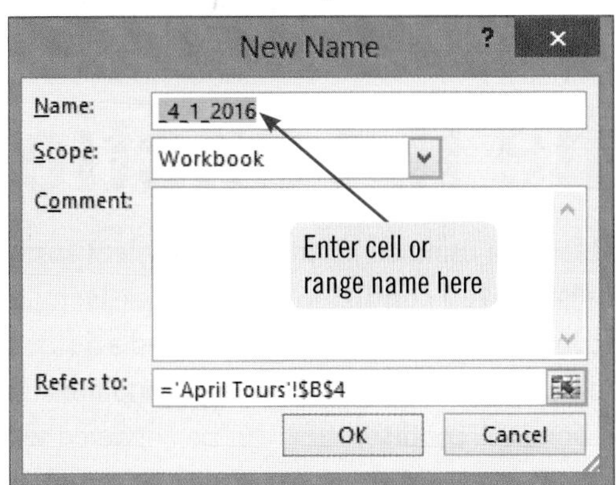

FIGURE E-12: Worksheet with days before departure

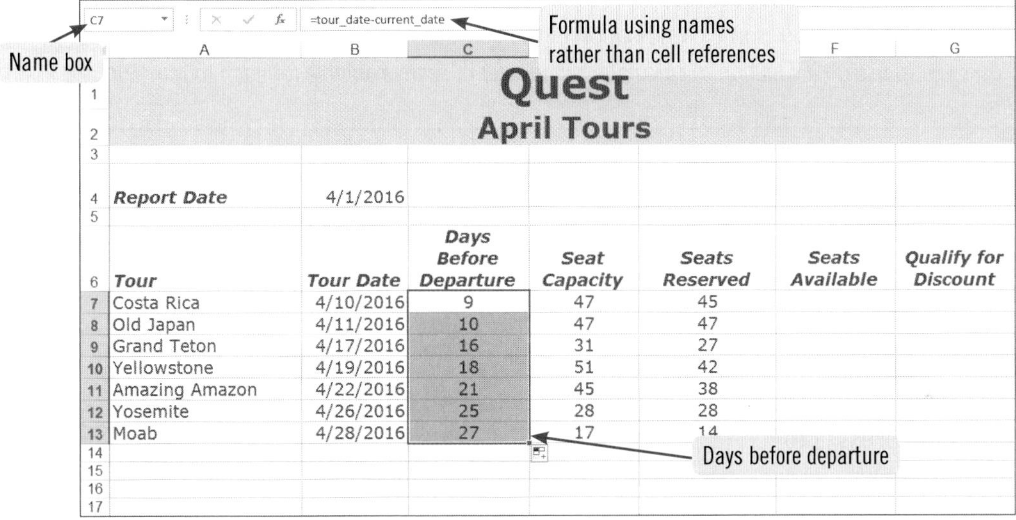

Managing workbook names

You can use the Name Manager to create, delete, and edit names in a workbook. Click the Name Manager button in the Defined Names group on the FORMULAS tab to open the Name Manager dialog box, shown in **FIGURE E-13**. Click the New button to create a new named cell or range, click Delete to remove a highlighted name, and click Filter to see options for displaying specific criteria for displaying names. Clicking Edit opens the Edit Name dialog box where you can change a highlighted cell name, edit or add comments, and change the cell or cells that the name refers to on the worksheet.

FIGURE E-13: Name Manager dialog box

Click to create new name

Click to change name

Click to delete name

Click to filter name

Excel 2013

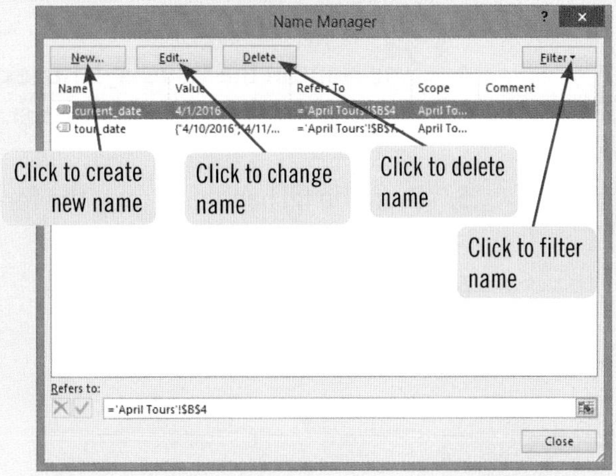

Build a Logical Formula with the IF Function

Learning Outcomes
- Build a logical formula using the IF function
- Apply comparison operators in a logical test

You can build a logical formula using an IF function. A **logical formula** makes calculations based on criteria that you create, called **stated conditions**. For example, you can build a formula to calculate bonuses based on a person's performance rating. If a person is rated a 5 (the stated condition) on a scale of 1 to 5, with 5 being the highest rating, he or she receives an additional 10% of his or her salary as a bonus; otherwise, there is no bonus. A condition that can be answered with a true or false response is called a **logical test**. The IF function has three parts, separated by commas: a condition or logical test, an action to take if the logical test or condition is true, and an action to take if the logical test or condition is false. Another way of expressing this is: IF(test_cond,do_this,else_this). Translated into an Excel IF function, the formula to calculate bonuses might look like this: IF(Rating=5,Salary*0.10,0). In other words, if the rating equals 5, multiply the salary by 0.10 (the decimal equivalent of 10%), then place the result in the selected cell; if the rating does not equal 5, place a 0 in the cell. When entering the logical test portion of an IF statement, you typically use some combination of the comparison operators listed in **TABLE E-3**. **CASE** *Kate asks you to use an IF function to calculate the number of seats available for each tour in April.*

STEPS

1. **Click cell F7, on the FORMULAS tab, click the Logical button in the Function Library group, then click IF**

   The Function Arguments dialog box opens. You want the function to calculate the seats available as follows: If the seat capacity is greater than the number of seats reserved, calculate the number of seats that are available (capacity minus number reserved), and place the result in cell F7; otherwise, place the text "None" in the cell.

2. **With the insertion point in the Logical_test text box, click cell D7, type >, click cell E7, then press [Tab]**

   The symbol (>) represents "greater than." So far, the formula reads "If the seating capacity is greater than the number of reserved seats,". The next part of the function tells Excel the action to take if the capacity exceeds the reserved number of seats.

3. **With the insertion point in the Value_if_true text box, click cell D7, type –, click cell E7, then press [Tab]**

   This part of the formula tells the program what you want it to do if the logical test is true. Continuing the translation of the formula, this part means "Subtract the number of reserved seats from the seat capacity." The last part of the formula tells Excel the action to take if the logical test is false (that is, if the seat capacity does not exceed the number of reserved seats).

4. **Type None in the Value_if_false text box, then click OK**

   The function is complete, and the result, 2 (the number of available seats), appears in cell F7, as shown in **FIGURE E-14**.

5. **Drag the fill handle to copy the formula in cell F7 into the range F8:F13**

   Compare your results with **FIGURE E-15**.

6. **Save the workbook**

QUICK TIP

You can nest IF functions to test several conditions in a formula. A nested IF function contains IF functions inside other IF functions to test these multiple conditions. The second IF statement is actually the value_if_false argument of the first IF statement.

FIGURE E-14: Worksheet with IF function

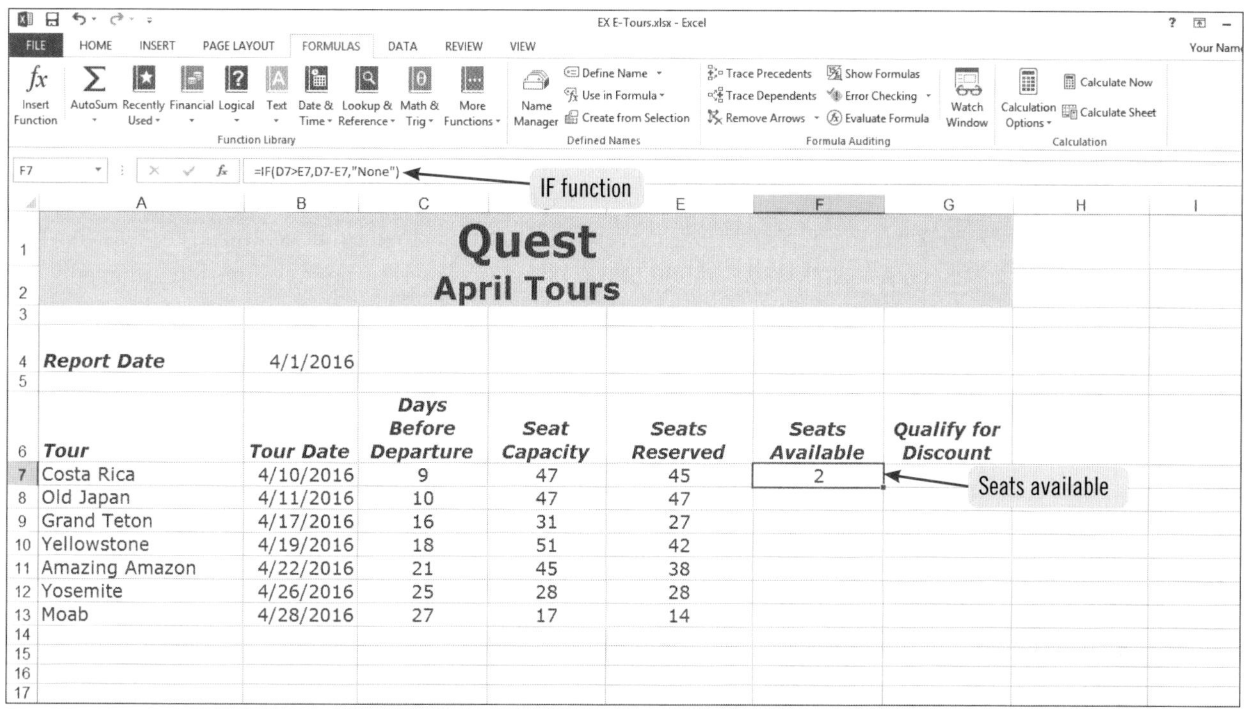

	A	B	C	D	E	F	G
1			Quest				
2			April Tours				
3							
4	***Report Date***	4/1/2016					
5							
6	***Tour***	***Tour Date***	***Days Before Departure***	***Seat Capacity***	***Seats Reserved***	***Seats Available***	***Qualify for Discount***
7	Costa Rica	4/10/2016	9	47	45	2	
8	Old Japan	4/11/2016	10	47	47		
9	Grand Teton	4/17/2016	16	31	27		
10	Yellowstone	4/19/2016	18	51	42		
11	Amazing Amazon	4/22/2016	21	45	38		
12	Yosemite	4/26/2016	25	28	28		
13	Moab	4/28/2016	27	17	14		

FIGURE E-15: Worksheet showing seats available

	A	B	C	D	E	F	G
1			Quest				
2			April Tours				
3							
4	***Report Date***	4/1/2016					
5							
6	***Tour***	***Tour Date***	***Days Before Departure***	***Seat Capacity***	***Seats Reserved***	***Seats Available***	***Qualify for Discount***
7	Costa Rica	4/10/2016	9	47	45	2	
8	Old Japan	4/11/2016	10	47	47	None	
9	Grand Teton	4/17/2016	16	31	27	4	
10	Yellowstone	4/19/2016	18	51	42	9	
11	Amazing Amazon	4/22/2016	21	45	38	7	
12	Yosemite	4/26/2016	25	28	28	None	
13	Moab	4/28/2016	27	17	14	3	

Seats available

TABLE E-3: Comparison operators

operator	meaning	operator	meaning
<	Less than	<=	Less than or equal to
>	Greater than	>=	Greater than or equal to
=	Equal to	<>	Not equal to

Build a Logical Formula with the AND Function

Learning Outcomes
- Select the AND function
- Apply logical tests using text

You can also build a logical function using the AND function. The AND function evaluates all of its arguments and **returns**, or displays, TRUE if every logical test in the formula is true. The AND function returns a value of FALSE if one or more of its logical tests is false. The AND function arguments can include text, numbers, or cell references. **CASE** *Kate wants you to analyze the tour data to find tours that qualify for discounting. You will use the AND function to check for tours with seats available and that depart within 21 days.*

STEPS

1. **Click cell G7, click the Logical button in the Function Library group, then click AND**
   The Function Arguments dialog box opens. You want the function to evaluate the discount qualification as follows: There must be seats available, and the tour must depart within 21 days.
2. **With the insertion point in the Logical1 text box, click cell F7, type < >, type "None", then press [Tab]**
   The symbol (<>) represents "not equal to." So far, the formula reads "If the number of seats available is not equal to None,"—in other words, if it is an integer. The next logical test checks the number of days before the tour departs.
3. **With the insertion point in the Logical2 text box, click cell C7, type <21, then click OK**
   The function is complete, and the result, TRUE, appears in cell G7, as shown in **FIGURE E-16**.
4. **Drag the fill handle to copy the formula in cell G7 into the range G8:G13**
   Compare your results with **FIGURE E-17**.
5. **Add your name to the center of the footer, save the workbook, then preview the worksheet**

TROUBLE
If you get a formula error, check to be sure that you typed the quotation marks around None.

Using the OR and NOT logical functions

The OR logical function has the same syntax as the AND function, but rather than returning TRUE if every argument is true, the OR function will return TRUE if any of its arguments are true. It will only return FALSE if all of its arguments are false. The NOT logical function reverses the value of its argument. For example NOT(TRUE) reverses its argument of TRUE and returns FALSE. This can be used in a worksheet to ensure that a cell is not equal to a particular value. See **TABLE E-4** for examples of the AND, OR, and NOT functions.

TABLE E-4: Examples of AND, OR, and NOT functions with cell values A1=10 and B1=20

function	formula	result
AND	=AND(A1>5,B1>25)	FALSE
OR	=OR(A1>5,B1>25)	TRUE
NOT	=NOT(A1=0)	TRUE

FIGURE E-16: Worksheet with AND function

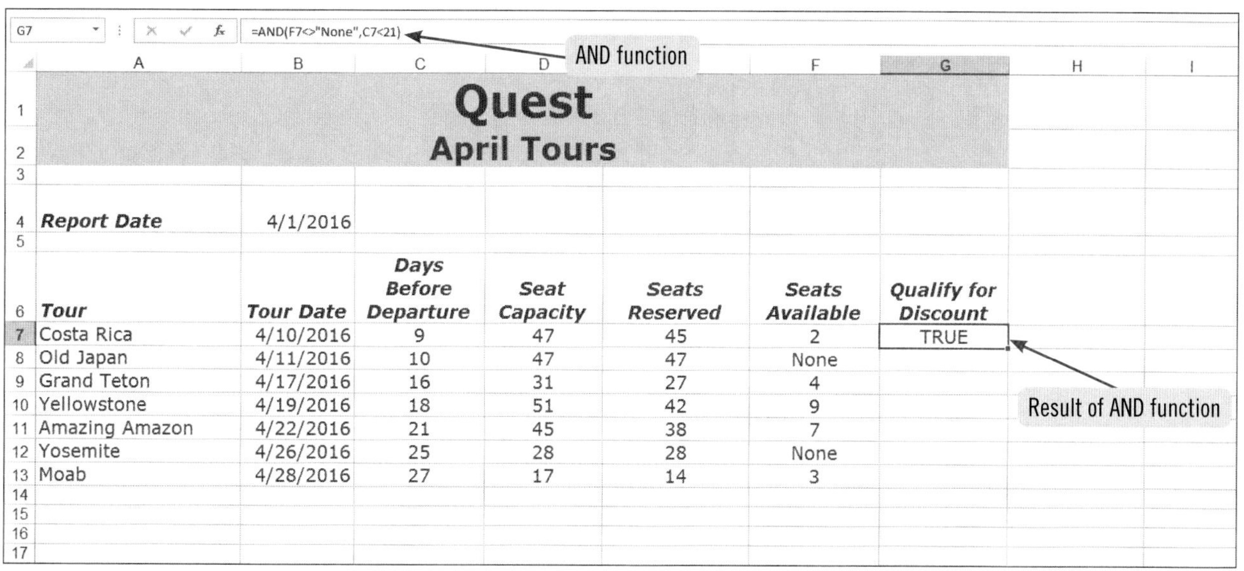

	A	B	C	D	E	F	G
1			Quest				
2			April Tours				
3							
4	***Report Date***	4/1/2016					
5							
6	***Tour***	***Tour Date***	***Days Before Departure***	***Seat Capacity***	***Seats Reserved***	***Seats Available***	***Qualify for Discount***
7	Costa Rica	4/10/2016	9	47	45	2	TRUE
8	Old Japan	4/11/2016	10	47	47	None	
9	Grand Teton	4/17/2016	16	31	27	4	
10	Yellowstone	4/19/2016	18	51	42	9	
11	Amazing Amazon	4/22/2016	21	45	38	7	
12	Yosemite	4/26/2016	25	28	28	None	
13	Moab	4/28/2016	27	17	14	3	

FIGURE E-17: Worksheet with discount status evaluated

G7 =AND(F7<>"None",C7<21)

	A	B	C	D	E	F	G
1			Quest				
2			April Tours				
3							
4	***Report Date***	4/1/2016					
5							
6	***Tour***	***Tour Date***	***Days Before Departure***	***Seat Capacity***	***Seats Reserved***	***Seats Available***	***Qualify for Discount***
7	Costa Rica	4/10/2016	9	47	45	2	TRUE
8	Old Japan	4/11/2016	10	47	47	None	FALSE
9	Grand Teton	4/17/2016	16	31	27	4	TRUE
10	Yellowstone	4/19/2016	18	51	42	9	TRUE
11	Amazing Amazon	4/22/2016	21	45	38	7	FALSE
12	Yosemite	4/26/2016	25	28	28	None	FALSE
13	Moab	4/28/2016	27	17	14	3	FALSE

Inserting an equation into a worksheet

If your worksheet contains formulas, you might want to place an equation on the worksheet to document how you arrived at your results. First create a text box to hold the equation: Click the INSERT tab, click the Text Box button in the Text group, then click on the worksheet location where you want the equation to appear. To place the equation in the text box, click the INSERT tab again, then click the Equation button in the Symbols group. When you see "Type equation here," you can build an equation by clicking the mathematical symbols in the Structures group of the EQUATION TOOLS DESIGN tab. For example, if you wanted to enter a fraction of 2/7, you click the Fraction button, choose the first option, click the top box, enter 2, press [Tab], enter 7, then click outside of the fraction. To insert the symbol x^2 into a text box, click the Script button in the Structures group of the EQUATION TOOLS DESIGN tab, click the first option, click in the lower-left box and enter "x", press [Tab], enter 2 in the upper-right box, then click to the right of the boxes to exit the symbol. You can also add built-in equations to a text box: On the EQUATION TOOLS DESIGN tab, click the Equation button in the Tools group, then select the equation. Built-in equations include the equation for the area of a circle, the binomial theorem, Pythagorean theorem, and the quadratic equation.

Excel 2013
UNIT E

Calculate Payments with the PMT Function

Learning Outcomes
- Calculate monthly payments using the PMT function
- Edit the PMT function to display payments as a positive value

PMT is a financial function that calculates the periodic payment amount for money borrowed. For example, if you want to borrow money to buy a car, and you know the principal amount, interest rate, and loan term, the PMT function can calculate your monthly payment. Say you want to borrow $20,000 at 6.5% interest and pay the loan off in 5 years. The Excel PMT function can tell you that your monthly payment will be $391.32. The main parts of the PMT function are PMT(rate, nper, pv). See **FIGURE E-18** for an illustration of a PMT function that calculates the monthly payment in the car loan example. **CASE** *For several months, QST's United States region has been discussing opening a new branch in San Francisco. Kate has obtained quotes from three different lenders on borrowing $359,000 to begin the expansion. She obtained loan quotes from a commercial bank, a venture capitalist, and an investment banker. She wants you to summarize the information using the Excel PMT function.*

STEPS

1. **Click the Loan sheet tab, click cell F5, click the FORMULAS tab, click the Financial button in the Function Library group, scroll down the list of functions, then click PMT**
2. **With the insertion point in the Rate text box, click cell D5 on the worksheet, type /12, then press [Tab]**

   You must divide the annual interest by 12 because you are calculating monthly, not annual, payments. You need to be consistent about the units you use for rate and nper. If you express nper as the number of monthly payments, then you must express the interest rate as a monthly rate.
3. **With the insertion point in the Nper text box, click cell E5; click the Pv text box, click cell B5, then click OK**

   The payment of ($6,990.84) in cell F5 appears in red, indicating that it is a negative amount. Excel displays the result of a PMT function as a negative value to reflect the negative cash flow the loan represents to the borrower. To show the monthly payment as a positive number, you can place a minus sign in front of the Pv cell reference in the function.
4. **Double-click cell F5 and edit it so it reads =PMT(D5/12,E5,-B5), then click the Enter button ✓ on the formula bar**

   A positive value of $6,990.84 now appears in cell F5, as shown in **FIGURE E-19**. You can use the same formula to generate the monthly payments for the other loans.
5. **With cell F5 selected, drag the fill handle to fill the range F6:F7**

   A monthly payment of $11,130.81 for the venture capitalist loan appears in cell F6. A monthly payment of $16,257.28 for the investment banker loan appears in cell F7. The loans with shorter terms have much higher monthly payments. But you will not know the entire financial picture until you calculate the total payments and total interest for each lender.
6. **Click cell G5, type =, click cell E5, type *, click cell F5, then press [Tab], in cell H5, type =, click cell G5, type –, click cell B5, then click ✓**
7. **Copy the formulas in cells G5:H5 into the range G6:H7, then click cell A1**

   You can experiment with different interest rates, loan amounts, or terms for any one of the lenders; the PMT function generates a new set of values automatically.
8. **Add your name to the center section of the footer, save the workbook, preview the worksheet, then submit the workbook to your instructor**

   Your worksheet appears as shown in **FIGURE E-20**.
9. **Close the workbook and exit Excel**

QUICK TIP
The Fv and Type arguments are optional: The argument Fv is the future value, or the total amount you want to obtain after all payments. If you omit it, Excel assumes you want to pay off the loan completely, so the default Fv is 0. The Type argument indicates when the payments are made; 0 is the end of the period, and 1 is the beginning of the period. The default is the end of the period.

QUICK TIP
You can use the keyboard shortcut of [Ctrl][Enter] rather than clicking the Enter button. This enters the formula and leaves the cell selected.

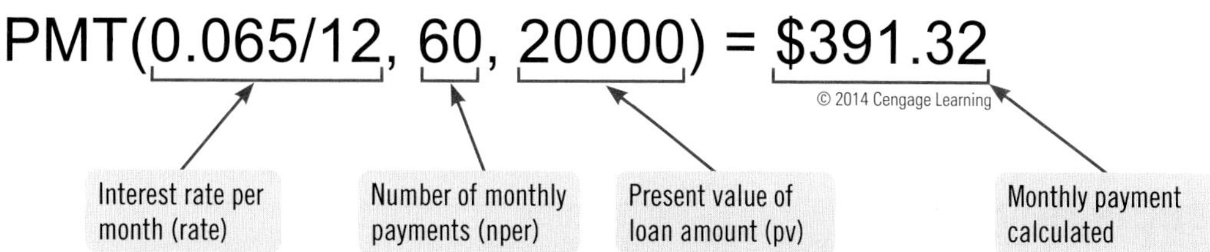

FIGURE E-18: Example of PMT function for car loan

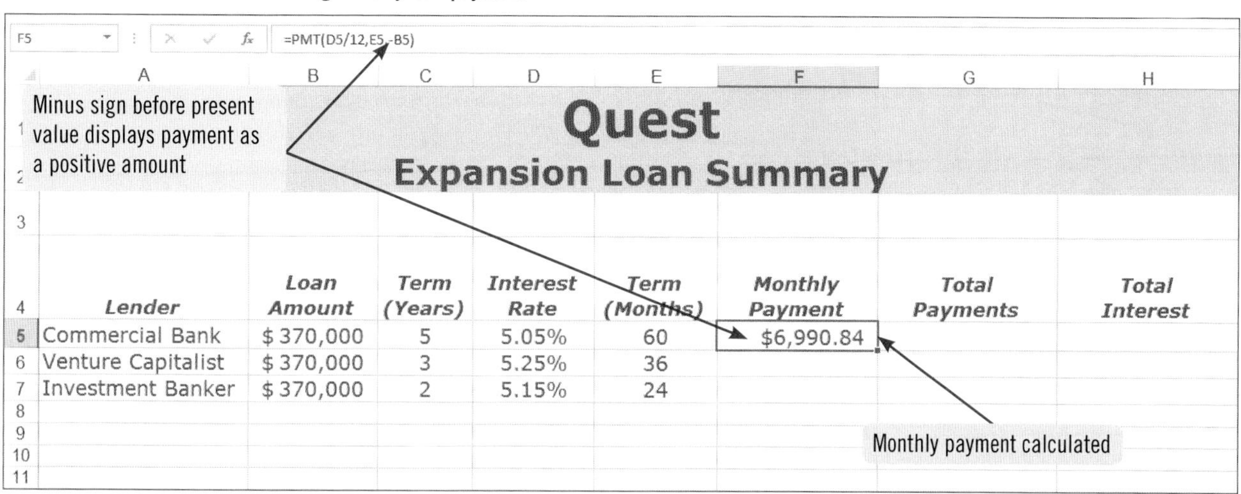

Lender	Loan Amount	Term (Years)	Interest Rate	Term (Months)	Monthly Payment	Total Payments	Total Interest
Commercial Bank	$ 370,000	5	5.05%	60	$6,990.84		
Venture Capitalist	$ 370,000	3	5.25%	36			
Investment Banker	$ 370,000	2	5.15%	24			

FIGURE E-19: PMT function calculating monthly loan payment

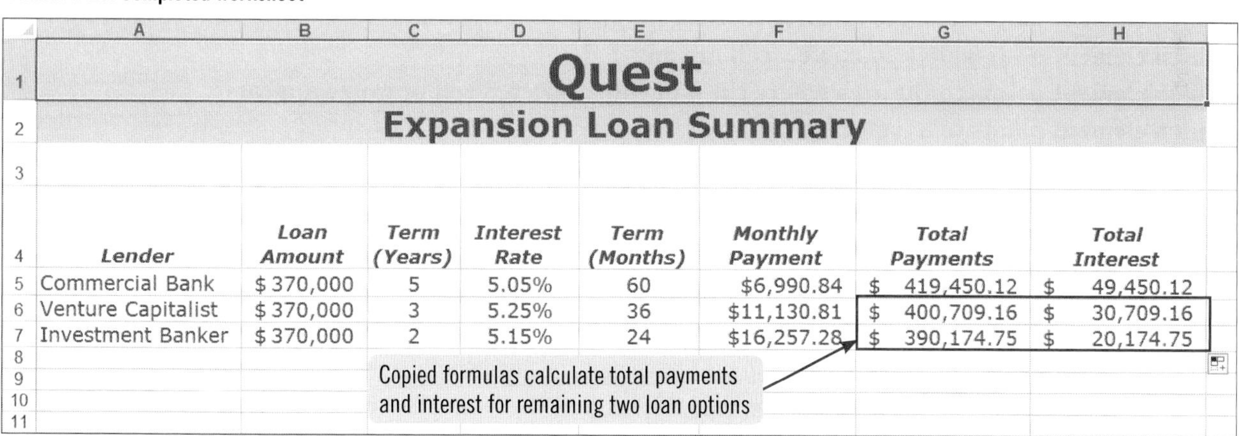

Lender	Loan Amount	Term (Years)	Interest Rate	Term (Months)	Monthly Payment	Total Payments	Total Interest
Commercial Bank	$ 370,000	5	5.05%	60	$6,990.84	$ 419,450.12	$ 49,450.12
Venture Capitalist	$ 370,000	3	5.25%	36	$11,130.81	$ 400,709.16	$ 30,709.16
Investment Banker	$ 370,000	2	5.15%	24	$16,257.28	$ 390,174.75	$ 20,174.75

FIGURE E-20: Completed worksheet

Calculating future value with the FV function

You can use the FV (Future Value) function to determine the amount of money a given monthly investment will amount to, at a given interest rate, after a given number of payment periods. The syntax is similar to that of the PMT function: FV(rate,nper,pmt,pv,type). The rate is the interest paid by the financial institution, the nper is the number of periods, and the pmt is the amount that you deposit. For example, suppose you want to invest $1,000 every month for the next 12 months into an account that pays 2% a year, and you want to know how much you will have at the end of 12 months (that is, its future value). You enter the function FV(.02/12,12,-1000), and Excel returns the value $12,110.61 as the future value of your investment. As with the PMT function, the units for the rate and nper must be consistent.

Practice

Put your skills into practice with **SAM Projects!** SAM Projects for this unit can be found online. If you have a SAM account, go to www.cengage.com/sam2013 to download the most recent Project Instruction and Start Files.

Concepts Review

FIGURE E-21

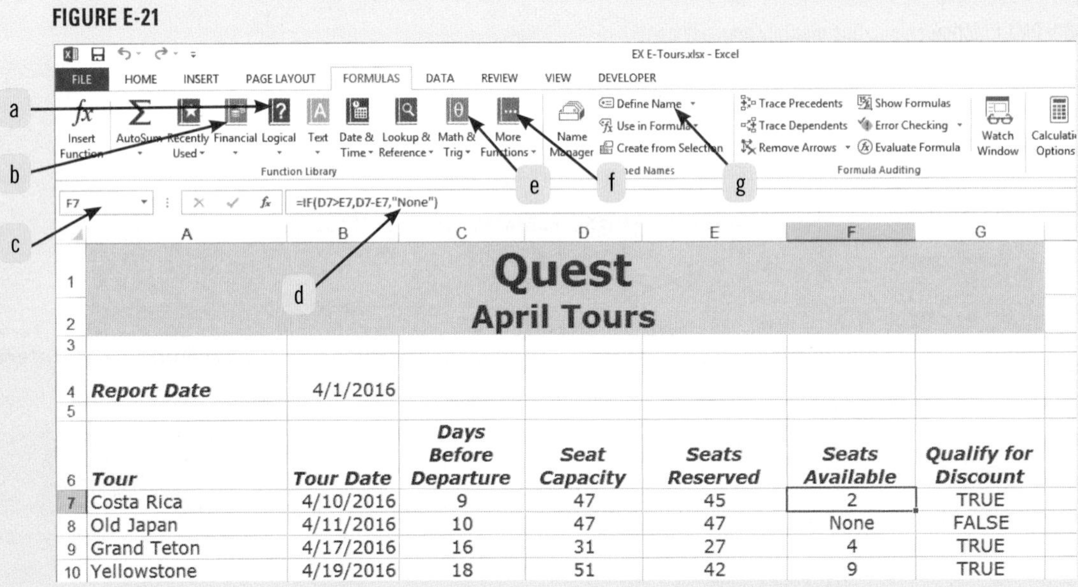

1. **Which element do you click to add a statistical function to a worksheet?**
2. **Which element do you click to name a cell or range?**
3. **Which element points to the area where the name of a selected cell or range appears?**
4. **Which element points to a logical formula?**
5. **Which element do you click to insert a PMT function into a worksheet?**
6. **Which element do you click to add a SUMIF function to a worksheet?**
7. **Which element do you click to add an IF function to a worksheet?**

Match each term with the statement that best describes it.

8. **PV**
9. **FV**
10. **PROPER**
11. **SUMIF**
12. **test_cond**

a. Function used to change the first letter of a string to uppercase
b. Function used to determine the future amount of an investment
c. Part of the PMT function that represents the loan amount
d. Part of the IF function that the conditions are stated in
e. Function used to conditionally total cells

Select the best answer from the list of choices.

13. **When you enter the rate and nper arguments in a PMT function, you must:**
    - **a.** Be consistent in the units used.
    - **b.** Multiply both units by 12.
    - **c.** Divide both values by 12.
    - **d.** Always use annual units.
14. **To express conditions such as less than or equal to, you can use a:**
    - **a.** Text formula.
    - **b.** Comparison operator.
    - **c.** PMT function.
    - **d.** Statistical function.

15. Which of the following statements is false?

a. When used in formulas, names become relative cell references by default.

b. Names cannot contain spaces.

c. Named ranges make formulas easier to build.

d. If you move a named cell or range, its name moves with it.

16. Which of the following is an external reference indicator in a formula?

a. &

b. :

c. !

d. =

17. When using text in logical tests, the text must be enclosed in:

a. " "

b. ( )

c. !

d. < >

18. Which function joins text strings into one text string?

a. Proper

b. Join

c. Combine

d. Concatenate

Skills Review

1. Format data using text functions.

a. Start Excel, open the file EX E-3.xlsx from the location where you store your Data Files, then save it as **EX E-Reviews**.

b. On the Managers worksheet, select cell B4 and use the Flash Fill button on the DATA tab to enter the names into column B.

c. In cell D2, enter the text formula to convert the first letter of the department in cell C2 to uppercase, then copy the formula in cell D2 into the range D3:D9.

d. In cell E2, enter the text formula to convert all letters of the department in cell C2 to uppercase, then copy the formula in cell E2 into the range E3:E9.

e. In cell F2, use the text formula to convert all letters of the department in cell C2 to lowercase, then copy the formula in cell F2 into the range F3:F9.

f. In cell G2, use the text formula to substitute "Human Resources" for "hr" if that text exists in cell F2. (*Hint*: In the Function Arguments dialog box, Text is F2, Old_text is "hr", and New_text is "Human Resources".) Copy the formula in cell G2 into the range G3:G9 to change the other cells containing "hr" to "Human Resources" and widen column G to fit the new entries. (The marketing and sales entries will not change because the formula searches for the text "hr".)

g. Save your work, then enter your name in the worksheet footer. Compare your screen to **FIGURE E-22**.

h. Display the formulas in the worksheet.

i. Redisplay the formula results.

FIGURE E-22

	A	B	C	D	E	F	G
1		Name	Department	Proper	Upper	Lower	Substitute
2	JohnSmith@company.com	John Smith	hr	Hr	HR	hr	Human Resources
3	PaulaJones@company.com	Paula Jones	sALES	Sales	SALES	sales	sales
4	LindaKristol@company.com	Linda Kristol	MarKeting	Marketing	MARKETING	marketing	marketing
5	AlMeng@company.com	Al Meng	hR	Hr	HR	hr	Human Resources
6	RobertDelgado@company.com	Robert Delgado	saLEs	Sales	SALES	sales	sales
7	HarryDegual@company.com	Harry Degual	saleS	Sales	SALES	sales	sales
8	JodyWilliams@company.com	Jody Williams	hR	Hr	HR	hr	Human Resources
9	MaryAbbott@company.com	Mary Abbott	MaRketing	Marketing	MARKETING	marketing	marketing
10							

2. Sum a data range based on conditions.

a. Make the HR sheet active.

b. In cell B20, use the COUNTIF function to count the number of employees with a rating of 5.

c. In cell B21, use the AVERAGEIF function to average the salaries of those with a rating of 5.

d. In cell B22, enter the SUMIF function that totals the salaries of employees with a rating of 5.

e. Format cells B21 and B22 with the Number format using commas and no decimals. Save your work, then compare your formula results to **FIGURE E-23**.

FIGURE E-23

17		
18	Department Statistics	
19	Top Rating	
20	Number	5
21	Average Salary	31,200
22	Total Salary	156,000
23		

Excel 2013

Skills Review (continued)

3. Consolidate data using a formula.

a. Make the Summary sheet active.

b. In cell B4, use the AutoSum function to total cell F15 on the HR and Accounting sheets.

c. Format cell B4 with the Accounting Number format with two decimal places.

d. Enter your name in the worksheet footer, then save your work. Compare your screen to **FIGURE E-24**.

e. Display the formula in the worksheet, then redisplay the formula results in the worksheet.

FIGURE E-24

	A	B
1	Payroll Summary	
2		
3		Salary
4	TOTAL	$ 566,035.00
5		

4. Check formulas for errors.

a. Make the HR sheet active.

b. In cell I6, use the IFERROR function to display "ERROR" in the event that the formula F6/F15 results in a formula error. (*Note*: This formula will generate an intentional error after the next step, which you will correct in a moment.)

c. Copy the formula in cell I6 into the range I7:I14.

d. Correct the formula in cell I6 by making the denominator, F15, an absolute address.

e. Copy the new formula in cell I6 into the range I7:I14, then save your work.

5. Construct formulas using named ranges.

a. On the HR sheet, name the range C6:C14 **review_date**, and limit the scope of the name to the HR worksheet.

b. In cell E6, enter the formula **=review_date+183**, using the Use in Formula button to enter the cell name.

c. Copy the formula in cell E6 into the range E7:E14.

d. Use the Name Manager to add a comment of **Date of last review** to the review_date name. (*Hint*: In the Name Manager dialog box, click the review_date name, then click Edit to enter the comment.) Save your work.

6. Build a logical formula with the IF function.

a. In cell G6, use the Function Arguments dialog box to enter the formula **=IF(D6=5,F6*0.05,0)**.

b. Copy the formula in cell G6 into the range G7:G14.

c. In cell G15, use AutoSum to total the range G6:G14.

d. Save your work.

7. Build a logical formula with the AND function.

a. In cell H6, use the Function Arguments dialog box to enter the formula **=AND(G6>0,B6>5)**.

b. Copy the formula in cell H6 into the range H7:H14.

c. Enter your name in the worksheet footer, save your work, then compare your worksheet to **FIGURE E-25**.

d. Make the Accounting sheet active.

e. In cell H6, indicate if the employee needs more development hours to reach the minimum of 5. Use the Function Arguments dialog box for the NOT function to enter **B6>=5** in the Logical text box. Copy the formula in cell H6 into the range H7:H14.

f. In cell I6, indicate if the employee needs to enroll in a quality class, as indicated by a rating less than 5 or having fewer than 5 development hours. Use the Function Arguments dialog box for the OR function to enter **D6<5** in the Logical1 text box and **B6<5** in the Logical2 text box. Copy the formula in cell I6 into the range I7:I14.

FIGURE E-25

	A	B	C	D	E	F	G	H	I
1	Human Resources Department								
2	Merit Pay								
3									
4									
5	Last Name	Professional Development Hours	Review Date	Rating	Next Review	Salary	Bonus	Pay Bonus	Percentage of Total
6	Brady	6	1/5/2016	2	7/6/2016	$ 19,740.00	$0.00	FALSE	7.17%
7	Case	8	4/1/2016	5	10/1/2016	$ 26,800.00	$1,340.00	TRUE	9.74%
8	Donnely	1	7/1/2016	4	12/31/2016	$ 33,400.00	$0.00	FALSE	12.13%
9	Hemsley	3	4/1/2016	5	10/1/2016	$ 25,500.00	$1,275.00	FALSE	9.26%
10	Kim	10	3/1/2016	5	8/31/2016	$ 37,500.00	$1,875.00	TRUE	13.62%
11	Maaley	7	5/1/2016	5	10/31/2016	$ 36,500.00	$1,825.00	TRUE	13.26%
12	Merry	10	6/1/2016	4	12/1/2016	$ 37,500.00	$0.00	FALSE	13.62%
13	Smith	7	1/1/2016	3	7/2/2016	$ 28,600.00	$0.00	FALSE	10.39%
14	Storey	3	7/1/2016	5	12/31/2016	$ 29,700.00	$1,485.00	FALSE	10.79%
15	Totals					$ 275,240.00	$7,800.00		

Skills Review (continued)

g. Enter your name in the worksheet footer, save your work, then compare your screen to **FIGURE E-26**.

8. Calculate payments with the PMT function.

a. Make the Loan sheet active.

b. In cell B9, determine the monthly payment using the loan information shown: Use the Function Arguments dialog box to enter the formula **=PMT(B5/12,B6,-B4)**.

c. In cell B10, enter a formula that multiplies the number of payments by the monthly payment.

d. In cell B11, enter the formula that subtracts the loan amount from the total payment amount, then compare your screen to **FIGURE E-27**.

e. Enter your name in the worksheet footer, save the workbook, then submit your workbook to your instructor.

f. Close the workbook, then exit Excel.

FIGURE E-26

Merit Pay

Last Name	Professional Development Hours	Review Date	Rating	Next Review	Salary	Bonus	Hours Required	Enroll in Quality Class
Allen	7	3/10/2016	5	9/9/2016	$ 21,645.00	$1,082.25	FALSE	FALSE
Green	1	5/1/2016	4	10/31/2016	$ 28,650.00	$0.00	TRUE	TRUE
LaFonte	6	8/1/2016	3	1/31/2017	$ 33,200.00	$0.00	FALSE	TRUE
Henley	7	6/1/2016	4	12/1/2016	$ 35,500.00	$0.00	FALSE	TRUE
Gosselin	9	3/8/2016	5	9/7/2016	$ 39,500.00	$1,975.00	FALSE	FALSE
Ramerez	5	5/1/2016	5	10/31/2016	$ 36,500.00	$1,825.00	FALSE	FALSE
Marton	10	6/1/2016	4	12/1/2016	$ 36,500.00	$0.00	FALSE	TRUE
Suille	6	1/1/2016	5	7/2/2016	$ 29,600.00	$1,480.00	FALSE	FALSE
Zen	6	9/15/2016	1	3/17/2017	$ 29,700.00	$0.00	FALSE	TRUE
Totals					$ 290,795.00	$ 6,362.25		

FIGURE E-27

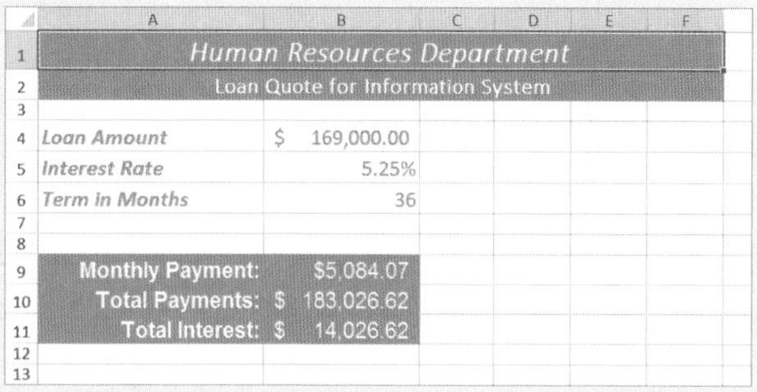

Human Resources Department

Loan Quote for Information System

Loan Amount	$ 169,000.00
Interest Rate	5.25%
Term in Months	36
Monthly Payment:	$5,084.07
Total Payments:	$ 183,026.62
Total Interest:	$ 14,026.62

Independent Challenge 1

As the accounting manager of International Insurance, a travel insurance company, you are reviewing the accounts payable information for your advertising accounts and prioritizing the overdue invoices for your collections service. You will analyze the invoices and use logical functions to emphasize priority accounts.

a. Start Excel, open the file EX E-4.xlsx from the location where you store your Data Files, then save it as **EX E-Accounts**.

b. Name the range B7:B13 **invoice_date**, and give the name a scope of the accounts payable worksheet.

c. Name the cell B4 **current_date**, and give the name a scope of the accounts payable worksheet.

d. Enter a formula using the named range invoice_date in cell E7 that calculates the invoice due date by adding 30 to the invoice date.

e. Copy the formula in cell E7 to the range E8:E13.

f. In cell F7, enter a formula using the named range invoice_date and the named cell current_date that calculates the invoice age by subtracting the invoice date from the current date.

g. Copy the formula in cell F7 to the range F8:F13.

h. In cell G7, enter an IF function that calculates the number of days an invoice is overdue, assuming that an invoice must be paid in 30 days. (*Hint*: The Logical_test should check to see if the age of the invoice is greater than 30, the Value_if_true should calculate the current date minus the invoice due date, and the Value_if_false should be 0.) Copy the IF function into the range G8:G13.

i. In cell H7, enter an AND function to prioritize the overdue invoices that are more than $1,000 for collection services. (*Hint*: The Logical1 condition should check to see if the number of days overdue is more than 0, and the Logical2 condition should check if the amount is more than 1,000.) Copy the AND function into the range H8:H13.

j. Use the Name Manager to name the range H7:H13 **Priority** and give the name a scope of the accounts payable worksheet. (*Hint*: In the Name Manager dialog box, click New to enter the range name.)

k. Enter your name in the worksheet footer, save the workbook, preview the worksheet, then submit the workbook to your instructor.

l. Close the workbook, then exit Excel.

Independent Challenge 2

You are an auditor with a certified public accounting firm. Be Green, an online seller of environmentally friendly home products, has contacted you to audit its first-quarter sales records. The management is considering expanding and needs its sales records audited to prepare the business plan. Specifically, they want to show what percent of annual sales each category represents. You will use a formula on a summary worksheet to summarize the sales for January, February, and March and to calculate the overall first-quarter percentage of the sales categories.

a. Start Excel, open the file EX E-5.xlsx from the location where you store your Data Files, then save it as **EX E-Products**.

b. In cell B10 of the Jan, Feb, and Mar sheets, enter the formulas to calculate the sales totals for the month.

c. For each month, in cell C5, create a formula calculating the percent of sales for the Compost Bins sales category. Use a function to display "**INCORRECT**" if there is a mistake in the formula. Verify that the percent appears with two decimal places. Copy this formula as necessary to complete the % of sales for all sales categories on all sheets. If any cells display "**INCORRECT**", fix the formulas in those cells.

d. In column B of the Summary sheet, use formulas to total the sales categories for the Jan, Feb, and Mar worksheets.

e. Enter the formula to calculate the first quarter sales total in cell B10 using the sales totals on the Jan, Feb, and Mar worksheets.

f. Calculate the percent of each sales category on the Summary sheet. Use a function to display **MISCALCULATION** if there is a mistake in the formula. Copy this formula as necessary. If any cells display **MISCALCULATION**, fix the formulas in those cells.

g. Enter your name in the Summary worksheet footer, save the workbook, preview the worksheet, then submit it to your instructor.

h. On the Products sheet, separate the product list in cell A1 into separate columns of text data. (*Hint*: With cell A1 as the active cell, use the Text to Columns button in the Data Tools group of the DATA tab. The products are delimited with commas.) Widen the columns as necessary. Use the second row to display the products with the first letter of each word in uppercase, as shown in **FIGURE E-28**.

i. Enter your name in the Products worksheet footer, save the workbook, preview the worksheet, then submit the workbook to your instructor.

FIGURE E-28

	A	B	C	D	E	F	G	H
1	compost bins	green furniture	shopping bags	solar education materials	natural hot tubs			
2	Compost Bins	Green Furniture	Shopping Bags	Solar Education Materials	Natural Hot Tubs			
3								

Independent Challenge 3

As the owner of Graphic Solutions, a Web and graphic design firm, you are planning to expand your business. Because you will have to purchase additional equipment and hire a new part-time designer, you decide to take out a $60,000 loan to finance your expansion expenses. You check three loan sources: the Small Business Administration (SBA), your local bank, and a consortium of investors. The SBA will lend you the money at 5.5% interest, but you have to pay it off in 3 years. The local bank offers you the loan at 6.75% interest over 4 years. The consortium offers you a 7% loan, but they require you to pay it back in 2 years. To analyze all three loan options, you decide to build a loan summary worksheet. Using the loan terms provided, build a worksheet summarizing your options.

a. Start Excel, open a new workbook, save it as **EX E-Loan**, then rename Sheet1 **Loan Summary**.

b. Using **FIGURE E-29** as a guide, enter labels and worksheet data for the three loan sources in columns A through D. Use the formatting of your choice.

FIGURE E-29

	A	B	C	D	E	F	G
1	Graphic Solutions						
2	Loan Options						
3							
4	Loan Source	Loan Amount	Interest Rate	# Payments	Monthly Payment	Total Payments	Total Interest
5	SBA	$ 60,000.00	5.50%	36	$ 1,811.75	$ 65,223.15	$ 5,223.15
6	Bank	$ 60,000.00	6.75%	48	$ 1,429.83	$ 68,631.63	$ 8,631.63
7	Investors	$ 60,000.00	7.00%	24	$ 2,686.35	$ 64,472.51	$ 4,472.51
8							
9							

Independent Challenge 3 (continued)

c. Enter the monthly payment formula for your first loan source (making sure to show the payment as a positive amount), copy the formula as appropriate, then name the range containing the monthly payment formulas **Monthly_Payment** with a scope of the workbook.
d. Name the cell range containing the number of payments **Number_Payments** with the scope of the workbook.
e. Enter the formula for total payments for your first loan source using the named ranges Monthly_Payment and Number_Payments, then copy the formula as necessary.
f. Name the cell range containing the formulas for Total payments **Total_Payments**. Name the cell range containing the loan amounts **Loan_Amount**. Each name should have the workbook as its scope.
g. Enter the formula for total interest for your first loan source using the named ranges Total_Payments and Loan_Amount, then copy the formula as necessary.
h. Format the worksheet using appropriate formatting, then enter your name in the worksheet footer.
i. Save the workbook, preview the worksheet and change it to landscape orientation on a single page, then submit the workbook to your instructor.
j. Close the workbook then exit Excel.

Independent Challenge 4: Explore

As the triathlon trainer at Total Fitness, you are using a weekly worksheet to log and analyze the training for each of your clients. As part of this training, you record daily running, biking, swimming, and weight training data and analyze it on a weekly basis.

a. Start Excel, open the file EX E-6.xlsx from the location where you store your Data Files, then save it as **EX E-Workout**.
b. Use SUMIF functions in cells G5:G8 to calculate the total minutes spent on each corresponding activity in cells F5:F8.
c. Use AVERAGEIF functions in cells H5:H8 to calculate the average number of minutes spent on each corresponding activity in cells F5:F8.
d. Use COUNTIF functions in cells I5:I8 to calculate the number of times each activity in cells F5:F8 was performed. (*Hint*: The Range of cells to count is $B$4:$B$15.)
e. Use the SUMIFS function in cell G9 to calculate the total number of minutes spent running outdoors.
f. Use the AVERAGEIFS function in cell H9 to calculate the average number of minutes spent running outdoors.
g. Use the COUNTIFS function in cell I9 to calculate the number of days spent running outdoors. Compare your worksheet to **FIGURE E-30** and adjust your cell formatting as needed to match the figure.
h. Enter your name in the worksheet footer, save the workbook, preview the worksheet, then submit it to your instructor.
i. Close the workbook, then exit Excel.

Excel 2013

FIGURE E-30

	A	B	C	D	E	F	G	H	I
1	Total Fitness								
2	Client Name: Kathy Howe								
3	Date	Activity	Minutes	Location		Week of January 2nd			
4	1/2/2016	Run	30	Gym		Activity	Total Minutes	Average Minutes	Number of Workouts
5	1/2/2016	Swim	40	Aquatics Center		Run	155	38.75	4
6	1/3/2016	Run	50	Outdoors		Swim	135	45.00	3
7	1/3/2016	Bike	35	Outdoors		Bike	90	30.00	3
8	1/4/2016	Run	35	Outdoors		Weights	60	30.00	2
9	1/4/2016	Weights	30	Gym		Run Outdoors	85	42.5	2
10	1/5/2016	Swim	50	Aquatics Center					
11	1/6/2016	Weights	30	Gym					
12	1/6/2016	Bike	30	Outdoors					
13	1/7/2016	Run	40	Gym					
14	1/7/2016	Swim	45	Aquatics Center					
15	1/8/2016	Bike	25	Gym					

Visual Workshop

Open the file EX E-7.xlsx from the location where you store your Data Files, then save it as **EX E-Summary**. Create the worksheet shown in **FIGURE E-31** using the data in columns B, C, and D along with the following criteria:

- The employee is eligible for a bonus if:
  - The employee has sales that exceed the sales quota.

    AND
  - The employee has a performance rating of six or higher.
- If the employee is eligible for a bonus, the bonus amount is calculated as two percent of the sales amount. Otherwise the bonus amount is 0. (*Hint*: Use an AND formula to determine if a person is eligible for a bonus, and use an IF formula to check eligibility and to enter the bonus amount.) Enter your name in the worksheet footer, save the workbook, preview the worksheet, then submit the worksheet to your instructor.

FIGURE E-31

	A	B	C	D	E	F	G
1	Westside Plumbing Supplies						
2	Bonus Pay Summary						
3	Last Name	Quota	Sales	Performance Rating	Eligible	Bonus Amount	
4	Adams	$135,000	$157,557	7	TRUE	$3,151	
5	Gurano	$90,774	$91,223	3	FALSE	$0	
6	Greely	$112,663	$100,307	9	FALSE	$0	
7	Hanlon	$149,335	$153,887	5	FALSE	$0	
8	Perez	$145,000	$151,228	8	TRUE	$3,025	
9	Medway	$130,000	$152,774	5	FALSE	$0	
10	Merkel	$152,885	$160,224	7	TRUE	$3,204	
11	Star	$98,000	$87,224	3	FALSE	$0	
12	Gonzalez	$90,000	$86,700	9	FALSE	$0	
13							
14							

Managing Data Using Tables

CASE Quest uses tables to analyze tour data. The vice president of sales, Kate Morgan, asks you to help her build and manage a table of 2016 tour information. You will help by planning and creating a table; adding, changing, finding, and deleting table information; sorting table data, and performing calculations with table data.

Unit Objectives

After completing this unit, you will be able to:

- Plan a table
- Create and format a table
- Add table data
- Find and replace table data
- Delete table data
- Sort table data
- Use formulas in a table
- Print a table

Files You Will Need

EX G-1.xlsx
EX G-2.xlsx
EX G-3.xlsx
EX G-4.xlsx
EX G-5.xlsx
EX G-6.xlsx

Plan a Table

Learning Outcomes
- Plan the data organization for a table
- Plan the data elements for a table

In addition to using Excel spreadsheet features, you can analyze and manipulate data in a table structure. An Excel **table** is an organized collection of rows and columns of similarly structured worksheet data. Tables are a convenient way to understand and manage large amounts of information. When planning a table, consider what information you want your table to contain and how you want to work with the data, now and in the future. As you plan a table, you should understand its most important components. A table is organized into rows called records. A **record** is a table row that contains data about an object, person, or other item. Records are composed of fields. **Fields** are columns in the table; each field describes a characteristic of the record, such as a customer's last name or street address. Each field has a **field name**, which is a column label, such as "Address," that describes its contents. Tables usually have a **header row** as the first row, which contains the field names. To plan your table, use the guidelines below. **CASE** *Kate asks you to compile a table of the 2016 tours. Before entering the tour data into an Excel worksheet, you plan the table contents.*

DETAILS

As you plan your table, use the following guidelines:

- **Identify the purpose of the table**
  The purpose of the table determines the kind of information the table should contain. You want to use the tours table to find all departure dates for a particular tour and to display the tours in order of departure date. You also want to quickly calculate the number of available seats for a tour.
- **Plan the structure of the table**
  In designing your table's structure, determine the fields (the table columns) you need to achieve the table's purpose. You have worked with the sales department to learn the type of information they need for each tour. **FIGURE G-1** shows a layout sketch for the table. Each row will contain one tour record. The columns represent fields that contain pieces of descriptive information you will enter for each tour, such as the name, departure date, and duration.
- **Plan your row and column structure**
  You can create a table from any contiguous range of cells on your worksheet. Plan and design your table so that all rows have similar types of information in the same column. A table should not have any blank rows or columns. Instead of using blank rows to separate table headings from data, use a table style, which will use formatting to make column labels stand out from your table data. **FIGURE G-2** shows a table, populated with data that has been formatted using a table style.
- **Document the table design**
  In addition to your table sketch, you should make a list of the field names to document the type of data and any special number formatting required for each field. Field names should be as short as possible while still accurately describing the column information. When naming fields it is important to use text rather than numbers because Excel could interpret numbers as parts of formulas. Your field names should be unique and not easily confused with cell addresses, such as the name D2. You want your tours table to contain eight field names, each one corresponding to the major characteristics of the 2016 tours. **TABLE G-1** shows the documentation of the field names in your table.

FIGURE G-1: Table layout sketch

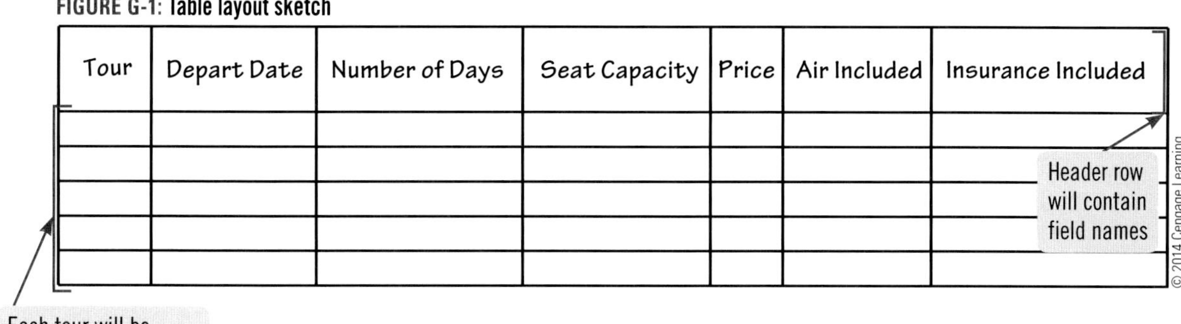

Tour
Depart Date
Number of Days
Seat Capacity
Price
Air Included
Insurance Included
Header row will contain field names
Each tour will be placed in a table row

FIGURE G-2: Formatted table with data

Header row contains field names

Records for each tour, organized by field name

	A	B	C	D	E	F	G	H
1	Tour	Depart Date	Number of Days	Seat Capacity	Seats Reserved	Price	Air Included	Insurance Included
2	Pacific Odyssey	1/12/2016	14	50	50	$ 2,255	Yes	No
3	Old Japan	1/13/2016	21	47	42	$ 1,984	Yes	No
4	Costa Rica	1/19/2016	10	31	28	$ 1,966	Yes	Yes
5	Yellowstone	1/21/2016	18	51	40	$ 1,850	Yes	Yes
6	Amazing Amazon	2/22/2016	14	43	39	$ 2,134	No	No
7	Hiking Patagonia	2/28/2016	7	20	15	$ 2,812	Yes	No
8	Pearls of the Orient	3/13/2016	14	45	15	$ 2,350	Yes	No
9	Silk Road Travels	3/19/2016	18	23	19	$ 2,110	Yes	Yes
10	Photographing France	3/20/2016	7	20	20	$ 1,755	Yes	Yes
11	Green Adventures in Ecuado	3/23/2016	18	25	22	$ 2,450	No	No
12	African National Parks	4/8/2016	30	12	10	$ 3,115	Yes	Yes
13	Experience Cambodia	4/11/2016	12	35	21	$ 2,441	Yes	No
14	Old Japan	4/15/2016	21	47	30	$ 1,900	Yes	No
15	Costa Rica	4/18/2016	10	30	20	$ 2,800	Yes	Yes
16	Yellowstone	4/20/2016	18	51	31	$ 1,652	Yes	Yes

TABLE G-1: Table documentation

field name	type of data	description of data
Tour	Text	Name of tour
Depart Date	Date	Date tour departs
Number of Days	Number with 0 decimal places	Duration of the tour
Seat Capacity	Number with 0 decimal places	Maximum number of people the tour can accommodate
Seats Reserved	Number with 0 decimal places	Number of reservations for the tour
Price	Accounting with 0 decimal places and $ symbol	Tour price (This price is not guaranteed until a 30% deposit is received)
Air Included	Text	Yes: Airfare is included in the price No: Airfare is not included in the price
Insurance Included	Text	Yes: Insurance is included in the price No: Insurance is not included in the price

Create and Format a Table

Learning Outcomes
- Create a table
- Format a table

Once you have planned the table structure, the sequence of fields, and appropriate data types, you are ready to create the table in Excel. After you create a table, a TABLE TOOLS DESIGN tab appears, containing a gallery of table styles. **Table styles** allow you to easily add formatting to your table by using preset formatting combinations of fill color, borders, type style, and type color. **CASE** *Kate asks you to build a table with the 2016 tour data. You begin by entering the field names. Then you enter the tour data that corresponds to each field name, create the table, and format the data using a table style.*

STEPS

TROUBLE
Don't worry if your field names are wider than the cells; you will fix this later.

QUICK TIP
Do not insert extra spaces at the beginning of a cell because it can affect sorting and finding data in a table.

QUICK TIP
You can also create a table using the shortcut key combination [Ctrl][T].

1. **Start Excel, open the file EX G-1.xlsx from the location where you store your Data Files, then save it as EX G-2016 Tours**
2. **Beginning in cell A1 of the Practice sheet, enter each field name in a separate column, as shown in FIGURE G-3**
   Field names are usually in the first row of the table.
3. **Enter the information from FIGURE G-4 in the rows immediately below the field names, leaving no blank rows**
   The data appears in columns organized by field name.
4. **Select the range A1:H4, click the Format button in the Cells group, click AutoFit Column Width, then click cell A1**
   Resizing the column widths this way is faster than double-clicking the column divider lines.
5. **With cell A1 selected, click the INSERT tab, click the Table button in the Tables group, in the Create Table dialog box verify that your table data is in the range $A$1:$H$4, and make sure My table has headers is checked as shown in FIGURE G-5, then click OK**
   The data range is now defined as a table. **Filter list arrows**, which let you display portions of your data, now appear next to each column header. When you create a table, Excel automatically applies a table style. The default table style has a dark blue header row and alternating gray and blue data rows. The TABLE TOOLS DESIGN tab appears, and the Table Styles group displays a gallery of table formatting options. You decide to choose a different table style from the gallery.
6. **Click the Table Styles More button, scroll to view all of the table styles, then move the mouse pointer over several styles without clicking**
   The Table Styles gallery on the TABLE TOOLS DESIGN tab has three style categories: Light, Medium, and Dark. Each category has numerous design types; for example, in some of the designs, the header row and total row are darker and the rows alternate colors. The available table designs use the current workbook theme colors so the table coordinates with your existing workbook content. If you select a different workbook theme and color scheme in the Themes group on the PAGE LAYOUT tab, the Table Styles gallery uses those colors. As you point to each table style, Live Preview shows you what your table will look like with the style applied. However, you only see a preview of each style; you need to click a style to apply it.
7. **Click Table Style Medium 24 to apply it to your table, then click cell A1**
   Compare your table to **FIGURE G-6**.

FIGURE G-3: Field names entered in row 1

	A	B	C	D	E	F	G	H
1	Tour	Depart Date	Number of Days	Seat Capacity	Seats Reserved	Price	Air Included	Insurance Included

FIGURE G-4: Three records entered in the worksheet

	A	B	C	D	E	F	G	H
1	Tour	Depart Date	Number of Days	Seat Capacity	Seats Reserved	Price	Air Included	Insurance Included
2	Pacific Odyssey	1/12/2016	14	50	40	2255	Yes	No
3	Old Japan	1/13/2016	21	47	42	1964	Yes	No
4	Costa Rica	1/19/2016	10	31	28	1833	Yes	Yes
5								

FIGURE G-5: Create Table dialog box

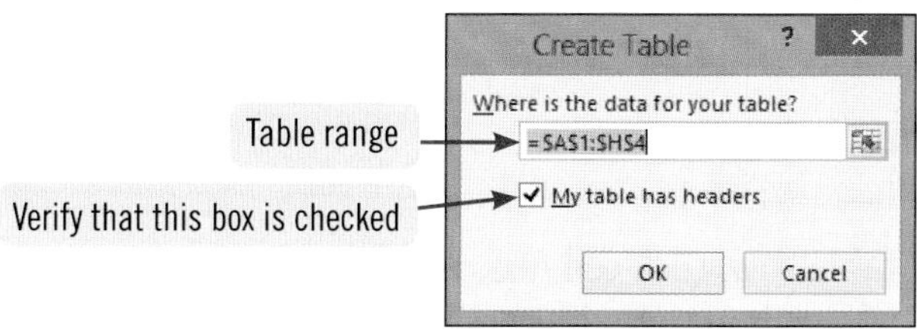

FIGURE G-6: Formatted table with three records

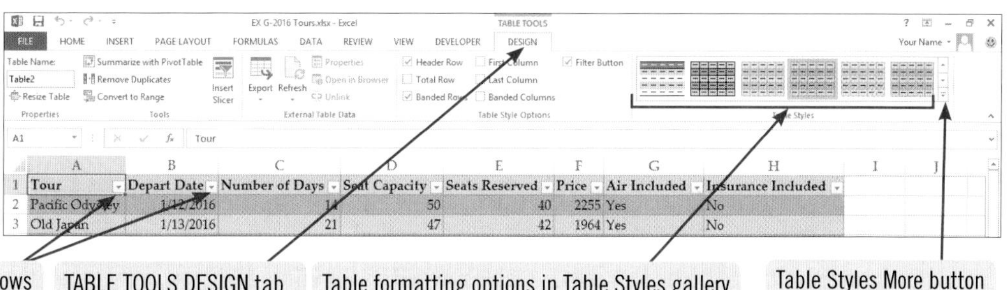

Changing table style options

You can change a table's appearance by using the check boxes in the Table Styles Options group on the TABLE TOOLS DESIGN tab, shown in **FIGURE G-7**. For example, you can turn on or turn off the following options: Header Row, which displays or hides the header row; Total Row, which calculates totals for each column; **banding**, which creates different formatting for adjacent rows and columns; and special formatting for first and last columns. Use these options to modify a table's appearance either before or after applying a table style. For example, if your table has banded rows, you can select the Banded Columns check box to change the table to be displayed with banded columns as well. Also, you may want to deselect the Header Row check box to hide a table's header row if a table will be included in a presentation where the header row repeats slide labels.

You can also create your own table style by clicking the Table Styles More button, then at the bottom of the Table Styles Gallery, clicking New Table Style. In the New Table Style dialog box, name the style in the Name text box, click a table element, then format selected table elements by clicking Format. You can also set a custom style as the default style for your tables by checking the Set as default table quick style for this document check box. You can click Clear at the bottom of the Table Styles gallery if you want to delete a table style from the currently selected table.

FIGURE G-7: Table Styles Options

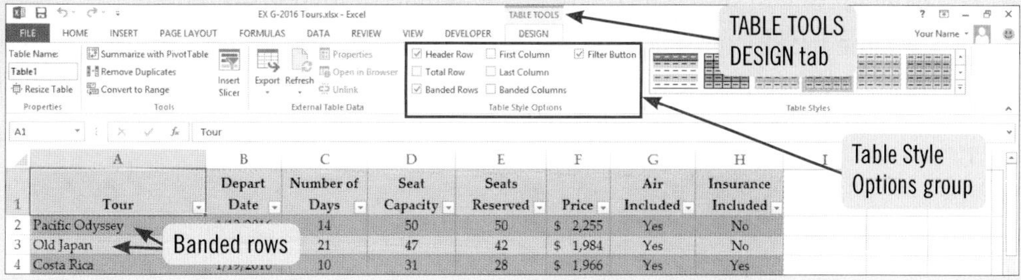

Add Table Data

Learning Outcomes
- Add fields to a table
- Add records to a table

You can add records to a table by typing data directly below the last row of the table. After you press [Enter], the new row becomes part of the table and the table formatting extends to the new data. When the active cell is the last cell of a table, you can add a new row by pressing [Tab]. You can also insert rows in any table location. If you decide you need additional data fields, you can add new columns to a table. You can also expand a table by dragging the sizing handle in a table's lower-right corner; drag down to add rows and drag to the right to add columns. **CASE** *After entering all of the 2016 tour data, Kate decides to offer two additional tours. She also wants the table to display the number of available seats for each tour and whether visas are required for the destination.*

STEPS

1. **Click the 2016 Tours sheet tab**
   The 2016 sheet containing the 2016 tour data becomes active.

2. **Scroll down to the last table row, click cell A65, enter the data for the new Pearls of the Orient tour, as shown below, then press [Enter]**

Pearls of the Orient	7/25/2016	14	50	0	$ 2,400	Yes	No

   As you scroll down, the table headers are visible at the top of the table as long as the active cell is inside the table. The new Pearls of the Orient tour is now part of the table. You want to enter a record about a new January tour above row 6.

3. **Scroll up to and click the inside left edge of cell A6 to select the table row data as shown in FIGURE G-8, click the Insert list arrow in the Cells group, then click Insert Table Rows Above**
   Clicking the left edge of the first cell in a table row selects the entire table row, rather than the entire worksheet row. A new blank row 6 is available for the new record.

4. **Click cell A6, then enter the Yellowstone record shown below**

Yellowstone	1/28/2016	18	51	0	$ 1,850	Yes	Yes

   The new Yellowstone tour is part of the table. You want to add a new field that displays the number of available seats for each tour.

5. **Click cell I1, enter the field name Seats Available, then press [Enter]**
   The new field becomes part of the table, and the header formatting extends to the new field as shown in **FIGURE G-9**. The AutoCorrect menu allows you to undo or stop the automatic table expansion, but in this case you decide to leave this feature on. You want to add another new field to the table to display tours that require visas, but this time you will add the new field by resizing the table.

QUICK TIP
You can also resize a table by clicking the TABLE TOOLS DESIGN tab, clicking the Resize Table button in the Properties group, selecting the new data range for the table, then clicking OK.

6. **Scroll down until cell I66 is visible, drag the sizing handle in the table's lower-right corner one column to the right to add column J to the table, as shown in FIGURE G-10**
   The table range is now A1:J66, and the new field name is Column1.

7. **Scroll up to and click cell J1, enter Visa Required, then press [Enter]**

8. **Click the INSERT tab, click the Header & Footer button in the Text group, enter your name in the center header text box, click cell A1, click the Normal button ▦ in the status bar, then save the workbook**

FIGURE G-8: Table row 6 selected

	Tour	Depart Date	Number of Days	Seat Capacity	Seats Reserved	Price	Air Included	Insurance Included
2	Pacific Odyssey	1/12/2016	14	50	50	$ 2,255	Yes	No
3	Old Japan	1/13/2016	21	47	42	$ 1,984	Yes	No
4	Costa Rica	1/19/2016	10	31	28	$ 1,966	Yes	Yes
5	Yellowstone	1/21/2016	18	51	40	$ 1,850	Yes	Yes
6	Amazing Amazon	2/22/2016	14	43	39	$ 2,134	No	No
7	Hiking Patagonia	2/28/2016	7	20	15	$ 2,812	Yes	No
8	Pearls of the Orient	3/13/2016	14	45	15	$ 2,350	Yes	No
9	Silk Road Travels	3/19/2016	18	23	19	$ 2,110	Yes	Yes
10	Photographing France	3/20/2016	7	20	20	$ 1,755	Yes	Yes
11	Green Adventures in Ecuado:	3/23/2016	18	25	22	$ 2,450	No	No
12	African National Parks	4/8/2016	30	12	10	$ 3,115	Yes	Yes

Row 6 selected

Place the pointer over the inside left edge of cell to select only the table row

FIGURE G-9: New table column

	A	B	C	D	E	F	G	H	I
1	Tour	Depart Date	Number of Days	Seat Capacity	Seats Reserved	Price	Air Included	Insurance Included	Seats Available
2	Pacific Odyssey	1/12/2016	14	50	50	$ 2,255	Yes	No	
3	Old Japan	1/13/2016	21	47	42	$ 1,984	Yes	No	
4	Costa Rica	1/19/2016	10	31	28	$ 1,966	Yes	Yes	
5	Yellowstone	1/21/2016	18	51	40	$ 1,850	Yes	Yes	
6	Yellowstone	1/28/2016	18	51	0	$ 1,850	Yes	Yes	
7	Amazing Amazon	2/22/2016	14	43	39	$ 2,134	No	No	
8	Hiking Patagonia	2/28/2016	7	20	15	$ 2,812	Yes	No	

New table column will show available seats for each tour

New record in row 6

FIGURE G-10: Resizing a table using the resizing handle

	Depart Da	Number of	Seat Capacit	Seats Reserv	Price	Air Include	Insurance In	Seats Avai	J	K
55	10/29/2016	14	18	8	$ 4,200	Yes	Yes			
56	10/31/2016	7	38	15	$ 1,900	Yes	No			
57	10/31/2016	12	40	2	$ 2,908	Yes	No			
58	11/18/2016	10	41	12	$ 2,200	Yes	Yes			
59	12/18/2016	10	50	21	$ 2,204	Yes	Yes			
60	12/18/2016	10	50	21	$ 2,204	Yes	Yes			
61	12/20/2016	14	15	1	$ 2,100	Yes	Yes			
62	12/20/2016	14	15	1	$ 2,100	Yes	Yes			
63	12/21/2016	14	50	10	$ 2,105	Yes	No			
64	12/30/2016	18	51	15	$ 2,922	Yes	Yes			
65	12/31/2016	21	47	4	$ 2,100	Yes	No			
66	7/25/2016	14	50	0	$ 2,400	Yes	No			

Drag sizing handle to add column J to table

Selecting table elements

When working with tables you often need to select rows, columns, and even the entire table. Clicking to the right of a row number, inside column A, selects the entire table row. You can select a table column by clicking the top edge of the header. Be careful not to click a column letter or row number, however, because this selects the entire worksheet row or column. You can select the table data by clicking the upper-left corner of the first table cell. When selecting a column or a table, the first click selects only the data in the column or table. If you click a second time, you add the headers to the selection.

Find and Replace Table Data

Learning Outcomes
- Find data in a table
- Replace data in a table

From time to time, you need to locate specific records in your table. You can use the Excel Find feature to search your table for the information you need. You can also use the Replace feature to locate and replace existing entries or portions of entries with information you specify. If you don't know the exact spelling of the text you are searching for, you can use wildcards to help locate the records. **Wildcards** are special symbols that substitute for unknown characters. **CASE** *In response to a change in the bike trip from Ireland to Scotland, Kate needs to replace "Ireland" with "Scotland" in all of the tour names. She also wants to know how many Pacific Odyssey tours are scheduled for the year. You begin by searching for records with the text "Pacific Odyssey".*

STEPS

1. **Click cell A1 if necessary, click the HOME tab, click the Find & Select button in the Editing group, then click Find**

   The Find and Replace dialog box opens, as shown in **FIGURE G-11**. In the Find what text box, you enter criteria that specify the records you want to find. You want to search for records whose Tour field contains the label "Old Japan".

2. **Type Old Japan in the Find what text box, then click Find Next**

   A3 is the active cell because it is the first instance of Old Japan in the table.

3. **Click Find Next and examine the record for each Old Japan tour found until no more matching cells are found in the table and the active cell is A3 again, then click Close**

   There are four Old Japan tours.

4. **Return to cell A1, click the Find & Select button in the Editing group, then click Replace**

   The Find and Replace dialog box opens with the Replace tab selected and "Old Japan" in the Find what text box, as shown in **FIGURE G-12**. You will search for entries containing "Ireland" and replace them with "Scotland". To save time, you will use the asterisk (*) wildcard to help you locate the records containing Ireland.

QUICK TIP

You can also use the question mark (?) wildcard to represent any single character. For example, using "to?" as your search text would only find 3-letter words beginning with "to", such as "top" and "tot"; it would not find "tone" or "topography".

5. **Delete the text in the Find what text box, type Ir* in the Find what text box, click the Replace with text box, then type Scotland**

   The asterisk (*) wildcard stands for one or more characters, meaning that the search text "Ir*" will find words such as "iron", "hair", and "bird". Because you notice that there are other table entries containing the text "ir" with a lowercase "i" (in the Air Included column heading), you need to make sure that only capitalized instances of the letter "I" are replaced.

6. **Click Options >>, click the Match case check box to select it, click Options <<, then click Find Next**

   Excel moves the cell pointer to the cell containing the first occurrence of "Ireland".

7. **Click Replace All, click OK, then click Close**

   The dialog box closes. Excel made three replacements, in cells A27, A36, and A40. The Air Included field heading remains unchanged because the "ir" in "Air" is lowercase.

8. **Save the workbook**

FIGURE G-11: Find and Replace dialog box

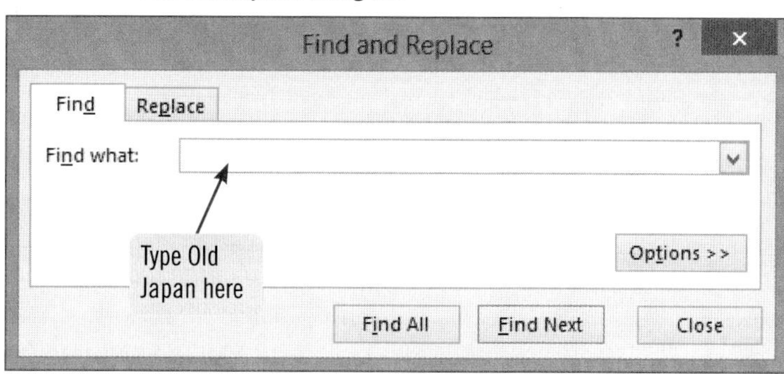

FIGURE G-12: The Replace tab in the Find and Replace dialog box

	A	B	C	D	E	F	G	H	I	J
1	Tour	Depart Date	Number of Days	Seat Capacity	Seats Reserved	Price	Air Included	Insurance Included	Seats Available	Visa Require
2	Pacific Odyssey	1/12/2016	14	50	50	$ 2,255	Yes	No		
3	Old Japan	1/13/2016	21	47	42	$ 1,984	Yes	No		
4	Costa Rica					$ 1,966	Yes	Yes		
5	Yellowstone					$ 1,850	Yes	Yes		
6	Yellowstone					$ 1,850	Yes	Yes		
7	Amazing Amazon					$ 2,134	No	No		
8	Hiking Patagonia					$ 2,812	Yes	No		
9	Pearls of the Orient					$ 2,350	Yes	No		
10	Silk Road Travels					$ 2,110	Yes	Yes		
11	Photographing France	/20/2016	7	20	20	$ 1,755	Yes	Yes		
12	Green Adventures in Ecuado	3/23/2016	18	25	22	$ 2,450	No	No		
13	African National Parks	4/8/2016	30	12	10	$ 3,115	Yes	Yes		
14	Experience Cambodia	4/11/2016	12	35	21	$ 2,441	Yes	No		
15	Old Japan	4/15/2016	21	47	30	$ 1,900	Yes	No		
16	Costa Rica	4/18/2016	10	30	20	$ 2,800	Yes	Yes		

Using Find and Select features

You can also use the Find feature to navigate to a specific place in a workbook by clicking the Find & Select button in the Editing group, clicking Go To, typing a cell address, then clicking OK. Clicking the Find & Select button also allows you to find comments and conditional formatting in a worksheet. You can use the Go to Special dialog box to select cells that contain different types of formulas or objects. Some Go to Special commands also appear on the Find & Select menu. Using this menu, you can also change the mouse pointer shape to the Select Objects pointer so you can quickly select drawing objects when necessary. To return to the standard Excel pointer, press [Esc].

Delete Table Data

Learning Outcomes
- Delete a table field
- Delete a table row
- Remove duplicate data from a table

To keep a table up to date, you need to be able to periodically remove records. You may even need to remove fields if the information stored in a field becomes unnecessary. You can delete table data using the Delete button in the Cells group or by dragging the sizing handle at the table's lower-right corner. You can also easily delete duplicate records from a table. **CASE** *Kate is canceling the Old Japan tour that departs on 1/13/2016 and asks you to delete the record from the table. You will also remove any duplicate records from the table. Because the visa requirements are difficult to keep up with, Kate asks you to delete the field with visa information.*

STEPS

1. **Click the left edge of cell A3 to select the table row data, click the Delete list arrow in the Cells group, then click Delete Table Rows**

   The Old Japan tour is deleted, and the Costa Rica tour moves up to row 3, as shown in **FIGURE G-13**. You can also delete a table row or a column using the Resize Table button in the Properties group of the TABLE TOOLS DESGIN tab, or by right-clicking the row or column, pointing to Delete on the shortcut menu, then clicking Table Columns or Table Rows. You decide to check the table for duplicate records.

2. **Click the TABLE TOOLS DESIGN tab, then click the Remove Duplicates button in the Tools group**

   The Remove Duplicates dialog box opens, as shown in **FIGURE G-14**. You need to select the columns that will be used to evaluate duplicates. Because you don't want to delete tours with the same destination but different departure dates, you will look for duplicate data in all of the columns.

3. **Make sure that "My data has headers" is checked and that all the Columns check boxes (column headers) are checked, then click OK**

   Two duplicate records are found and removed, leaving 62 records of data and a total of 63 rows in the table, including the header row. You want to remove the last column, which contains space for visa information.

4. **Click OK, scroll down until cell J63 is visible, drag the sizing handle of the table's lower-right corner one column to the left to remove column J from the table**

   The table range is now A1:I63, and the Visa Required field no longer appears in the table.

5. **Delete the contents of cell J1, return to cell A1, then save the workbook**

QUICK TIP

You can also remove duplicates from worksheet data by clicking the DATA tab, then clicking the Remove Duplicates button in the Data Tools group.

FIGURE G-13: **Table with row deleted**

	A	B	C	D	E	F	G	H	I	J
1	Tour	Depart Date	Number of Days	Seat Capacity	Seats Reserved	Price	Air Included	Insurance Included	Seats Available	Visa Require
2	Pacific Odyssey	1/12/2016	14	50	50	$ 2,255	Yes	No		
3	Costa Rica	1/19/2016	10	31	28	$ 1,966	Yes	Yes		
4	Yellowstone	1/21/2016	18	51	40	$ 1,850	Yes	Yes		
5	Yellowstone	1/28/2016	18	51	0	$ 1,850	Yes	Yes		
6	Amazing Amazon	2/22/2016	14	43	39	$ 2,134	No	No		
7	Hiking Patagonia	2/28/2016	7	20	15	$ 2,812	Yes	No		
8	Pearls of the Orient	3/13/2016	14	45	15	$ 2,350	Yes	No		
9	Silk Road Travels	3/19/2016	18	23	19	$ 2,110	Yes	Yes		
10	Photographing France	3/20/2016	7	20	20	$ 1,755	Yes	Yes		
11	Green Adventures in Ecuado:	3/23/2016	18	25	22	$ 2,450	No	No		
12	African National Parks	4/8/2016	30	12	10	$ 3,115	Yes	Yes		
13	Experience Cambodia	4/11/2016	12	35	21	$ 2,441	Yes	No		
14	Old Japan	4/15/2016	21	47	30	$ 1,900	Yes	No		
15	Costa Rica	4/18/2016	10	30	20	$ 2,800	Yes	Yes		
16	Yellowstone	4/20/2016	18	51	31	$ 1,652	Yes	Yes		

Row is deleted and tours move up one row

FIGURE G-14: **Remove Duplicates dialog box**

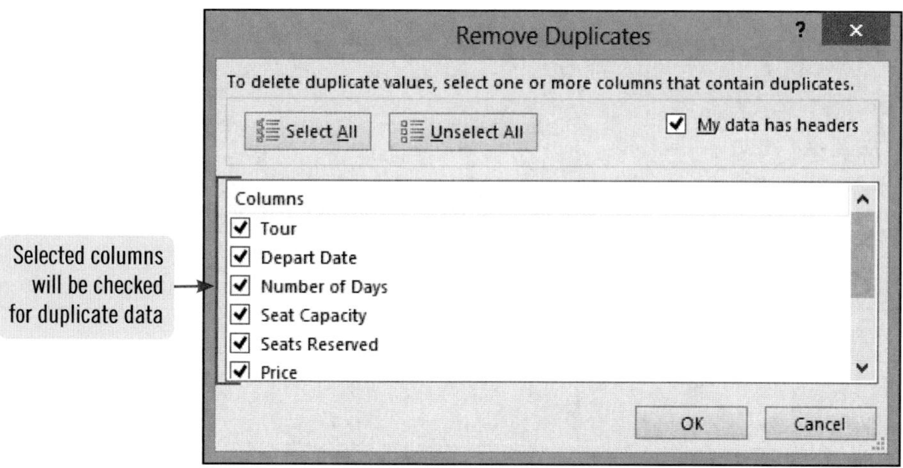

Excel 2013

Sort Table Data

Learning Outcomes
- Sort a table in ascending order
- Sort a table in descending order
- Sort a table using custom sort options

Usually, you enter table records in the order in which you receive information, rather than in alphabetical or numerical order. When you add records to a table, you usually enter them at the end of the table. You can change the order of the records any time using the Excel **sort** feature. Because the data is structured as a table, Excel changes the order of the records while keeping each record, or row of information, together. You can sort a table in ascending or descending order on one field using the filter list arrows next to the field name. In **ascending order**, the lowest value (the beginning of the alphabet or the earliest date) appears at the top of the table. In a field containing labels and numbers, numbers appear first in the sorted list. In **descending order**, the highest value (the end of the alphabet or the latest date) appears at the top of the table. In a field containing labels and numbers, labels appear first. TABLE G-2 provides examples of ascending and descending sorts. **CASE** *Kate wants the tour data sorted by departure date, displaying tours that depart the soonest at the top of the table.*

STEPS

QUICK TIP
Before you sort records, consider making a backup copy of your table or create a field that numbers the records so you can return them to their original order, if necessary.

1. **Click the Depart Date filter list arrow, then click Sort Oldest to Newest**
   Excel rearranges the records in ascending order by departure date, as shown in FIGURE G-15. The Depart Date filter list arrow has an upward pointing arrow indicating the ascending sort in the field. You can also sort the table on one field using the Sort & Filter button.

2. **Click the HOME tab, click any cell in the Price column, click the Sort & Filter button in the Editing group, then click Sort Largest to Smallest**
   Excel sorts the table, placing those records with the higher price at the top. The Price filter list arrow now has a downward pointing arrow next to the filter list arrow, indicating the descending sort order. You can also rearrange the table data using a **multilevel sort**. This type of sort rearranges the table data using more than one field, where each field is a different level, based on its importance in the sort. If you use two sort levels, the data is sorted by the first field, and the second field is sorted within each grouping of the first field. Since you have many groups of tours with different departure dates, you want to use a multilevel sort to arrange the table data by tours and then by departure dates within each tour.

QUICK TIP
You can also add a multilevel sort by clicking the DATA tab and then clicking the Sort button in the Sort & Filter group.

3. **Click the Sort & Filter button in the Editing group, then click Custom Sort**
   The Sort dialog box opens, as shown in FIGURE G-16.

QUICK TIP
You can include capitalization as a sort criterion by clicking Options in the Sort dialog box, then selecting the Case sensitive check box. When you choose this option, lowercase entries precede uppercase entries in an ascending order.

4. **Click the Sort by list arrow, click Tour, click the Order list arrow, click A to Z, click Add Level, click the Then by list arrow, click Depart Date, click the second Order list arrow, click Oldest to Newest if necessary, then click OK**
   FIGURE G-17 shows the table sorted alphabetically in ascending order (A–Z) by Tour and, within each tour grouping, in ascending order by the Depart Date.

5. **Save the workbook**

Sorting conditionally formatted data

If conditional formats have been applied to a table, you can sort the table using conditional formatting to arrange the rows. For example, if cells are conditionally formatted with color, you can sort a field on Cell Color, using the color with the order of On Top or On Bottom in the Sort dialog box. If the data is not in a table, you can select a cell in the column of conditionally formatted data you want to sort by, or select the range of cells to be sorted, right-click the selection, point to Sort, then select the font color, highlighted color, or icon that you want to appear on top.

FIGURE G-15: Table sorted by departure date

	A	B	C	D	E	F	G	H	I
1	Tour	Depart Date	Number of Days	Seat Capacity	Seats Reserved	Price	Air Included	Insurance Included	Seats Available
2	Pacific Odyssey	1/12/2016	14	50	[illegible]	[illegible]255	Yes	No	
3	Costa Rica	1/19/2016	10	31	[illegible]	[illegible]966	Yes	Yes	
4	Yellowstone	1/21/2016	18	51	[illegible]	[illegible]350	Yes	Yes	
5	Yellowstone	1/28/2016	18	51	[illegible]	[illegible]350	Yes	Yes	
6	Amazing Amazon	2/22/2016	14	43	[illegible]	[illegible],134	No	No	
	[illegible]ng Patagonia	2/28/2016	7	20	15	$ 2,812	Yes	No	
	[illegible]ls of the Orient	3/13/2016	14	45	15	$ 2,350	Yes	No	
	[illegible] Road Travels	3/19/2016	18	23	19	$ 2,110	Yes	Yes	
	[illegible]ographing France	3/20/2016	7	20	20	$ 1,755	Yes	Yes	
	[illegible]en Adventures in Ecuado[illegible]	3/23/2016	18	25	22	$ 2,450	No	No	
12	African National Parks	4/8/2016	30	12	10	$ 3,115	Yes	Yes	
13	Experience Cambodia	4/11/2016	12	35	21	$ 2,441	Yes	No	
14	Old Japan	4/15/2016	21	47	30	$ 1,900	Yes	No	
15	Costa Rica	4/18/2016	10	30	20	$ 2,800	Yes	Yes	
16	Yellowstone	4/20/2016	18	51	31	$ 1,652	Yes	Yes	

Up arrow indicates ascending sort in the field

Records are sorted by departure date in ascending order

FIGURE G-16: Sort dialog box

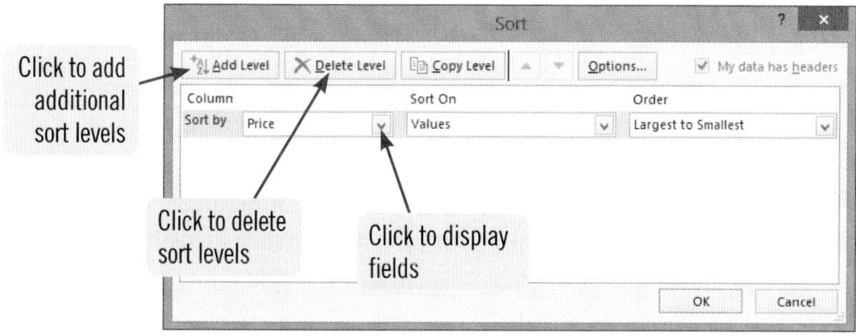

FIGURE G-17: Table sorted using two levels

	A	B	C	D	E	F	G	H	I
1	Tour	Depart Date	Number of Days	Seat Capacity	Seats Reserved	Price	Air Included	Insurance Included	Seats Available
2	African National Parks	4/8/2016	30	12	10	$ 3,115	Yes	Yes	
3	African National Parks	10/27/2016	30	12	8	$ 4,870	Yes	Yes	
4	Amazing Amazon	2/22/2016	14	43	39	$ 2,134	No	No	
5	Amazing Amazon	4/23/2016	14	43	30	$ 2,133	No	No	
6	Amazing Amazon	8/23/2016	14	43	18	$ 2,877	No	No	
7	Biking in France	5/23/2016	7	12	10	$ 1,635	No	No	
8	Biking in France	9/23/2016	7	12	7	$ 2,110	No	No	
9	Biking in Scotland	6/11/2016	10	15	10	$ 2,600	Yes	No	
10	Biking in Scotland	7/11/2[illegible]	[illegible]	[illegible]	9	$ 2,600	Yes	No	
11	Biking in Scotland	8/11/2[illegible]	[illegible]	[illegible]	6	$ 2,600	Yes	No	
12	Catalonia Adventure	5/9/2[illegible]	[illegible]	[illegible]	30	$ 2,587	Yes	No	
13	Catalonia Adventure	6/9/2[illegible]	[illegible]	[illegible]	15	$ 2,100	Yes	No	
14	Catalonia Adventure	10/9/2016	14	51	11	$ 2,100	Yes	No	
15	Corfu[illegible]	[illegible]10/2016	21	12	10	$ 2,190	Yes	No	
16	Corfu[illegible]	[illegible]9/2016	21	12	1	$ 2,190	Yes	No	

Second-level sort arranges records by departure date within each tour grouping

Top-level sort on Tour arranges records by tour name

TABLE G-2: Sort order options and examples

option	alphabetic	numeric	date	alphanumeric
Ascending	A, B, C	7, 8, 9	1/1, 2/1, 3/1	12A, 99B, DX8, QT7
Descending	C, B, A	9, 8, 7	3/1, 2/1, 1/1	QT7, DX8, 99B, 12A

Specifying a custom sort order

You can identify a custom sort order for the field selected in the Sort by box. Click the Order list arrow in the Sort dialog box, click Custom List, then click the desired custom order. Commonly used custom sort orders are days of the week (Sun, Mon, Tues, Wed, etc.) and months (Jan, Feb, Mar, etc.); alphabetic sorts do not sort these items properly.

Use Formulas in a Table

Learning Outcomes
- Build a table formula
- Use calculated columns to display formula results
- Use the table style options to add summary information to a table

Many tables are large, making it difficult to know from viewing them the "story" the table tells. The Excel table calculation features help you summarize table data so you can see important trends. After you enter a single formula into a table cell, the **calculated columns** feature fills in the remaining cells with the formula's results. The column continues to fill with the formula results as you enter rows in the table. This makes it easy to update your formulas because you only need to edit the formula once, and the change will fill in to the other column cells. The **structured reference** feature allows your formulas to refer to table columns by names that are automatically generated when you create the table. These names adjust as you add or delete table fields. An example of a table reference is =[Sales]–[Costs], where Sales and Costs are field names in the table. Tables also have a specific area at the bottom called the **table total row** for calculations using the data in the table columns. The cells in this row contain a dropdown list of functions that can be used for the column calculation. The table total row adapts to any changes in the table size. **CASE** *Kate wants you to use a formula to calculate the number of available seats for each tour. You will also add summary information to the end of the table.*

STEPS

1. **Click cell I2, then type =[**
   A list of the table field names appears, as shown in **FIGURE G-18**. Structured referencing allows you to use the names that Excel created when you defined your table to reference fields in a formula. You can choose a field by clicking it and pressing [Tab] or by double-clicking the field name.
2. **Click [Seat Capacity], press [Tab], then type]**
   Excel begins the formula, placing [Seat Capacity] in the cell in blue and framing the Seat Capacity data in a blue border.
3. **Type -[, double-click [Seats Reserved], then type]**
   Excel places [Seats Reserved] in the cell in red and outlines the Seats Reserved data in a red border.
4. **Press [Enter]**
   The formula result, 2, is displayed in cell I2. The table column also fills with the formula displaying the number of available seats for each tour.
5. **Click the AutoCorrect Options list arrow to view options for the column**
   Because the calculated columns option saves time, you decide to leave the feature on. You want to display the total number of available seats on all of the tours.
6. **Click any cell inside the table to close the menu, click the TABLE TOOLS DESIGN tab, then click the Total Row check box in the Table Style Options group to select it**
   A total row appears at the bottom of the table, and the sum of the available seats, 1088, is displayed in cell I64. You can select other formulas in the total row.
7. **Click cell C64, then click the cell list arrow on the right side of the cell**
   The list of available functions appears, as shown in **FIGURE G-19**. You want to find the average tour length.
8. **Click Average, then save your workbook**
   The average tour length, 13 days, appears in cell C64.

QUICK TIP
You can undo the calculated column results by clicking Undo Calculated Column in the AutoCorrect Options list. You can turn off the Calculated Columns feature by clicking Stop Automatically Creating Calculated Columns in the AutoCorrect Options list.

FIGURE G-18: Table field names

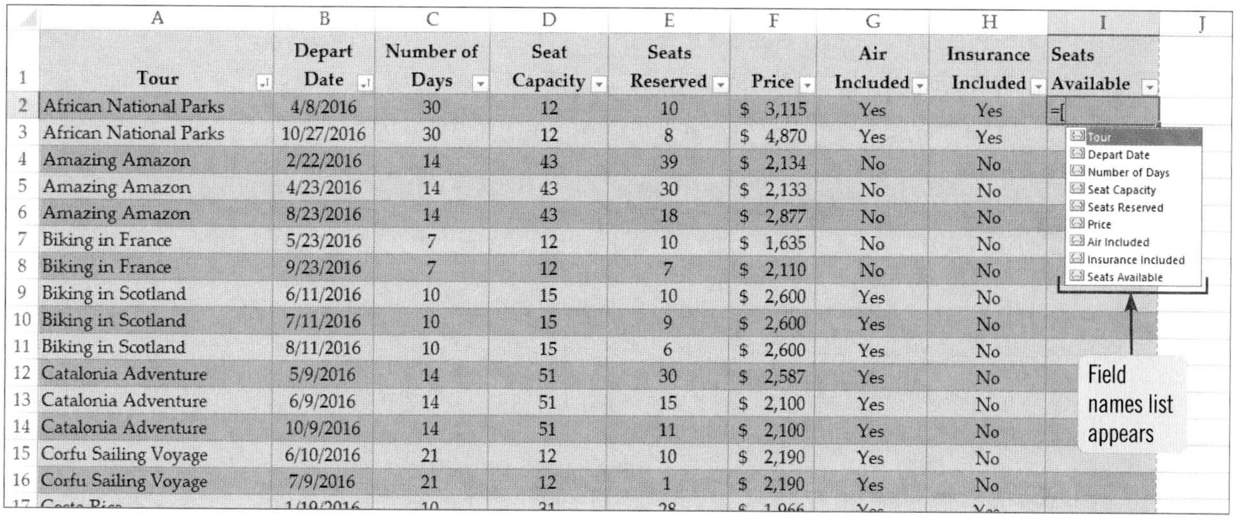

	A	B	C	D	E	F	G	H	I	J
1	Tour	Depart Date	Number of Days	Seat Capacity	Seats Reserved	Price	Air Included	Insurance Included	Seats Available	
2	African National Parks	4/8/2016	30	12	10	$ 3,115	Yes	Yes	=[	
3	African National Parks	10/27/2016	30	12	8	$ 4,870	Yes	Yes		
4	Amazing Amazon	2/22/2016	14	43	39	$ 2,134	No	No		
5	Amazing Amazon	4/23/2016	14	43	30	$ 2,133	No	No		
6	Amazing Amazon	8/23/2016	14	43	18	$ 2,877	No	No		
7	Biking in France	5/23/2016	7	12	10	$ 1,635	No	No		
8	Biking in France	9/23/2016	7	12	7	$ 2,110	No	No		
9	Biking in Scotland	6/11/2016	10	15	10	$ 2,600	Yes	No		
10	Biking in Scotland	7/11/2016	10	15	9	$ 2,600	Yes	No		
11	Biking in Scotland	8/11/2016	10	15	6	$ 2,600	Yes	No		
12	Catalonia Adventure	5/9/2016	14	51	30	$ 2,587	Yes	No		
13	Catalonia Adventure	6/9/2016	14	51	15	$ 2,100	Yes	No		
14	Catalonia Adventure	10/9/2016	14	51	11	$ 2,100	Yes	No		
15	Corfu Sailing Voyage	6/10/2016	21	12	10	$ 2,190	Yes	No		
16	Corfu Sailing Voyage	7/9/2016	21	12	1	$ 2,190	Yes	No		

Tour
Depart Date
Number of Days
Seat Capacity
Seats Reserved
Price
Air Included
Insurance Included
Seats Available

Field names list appears

FIGURE G-19: Functions in the Total Row

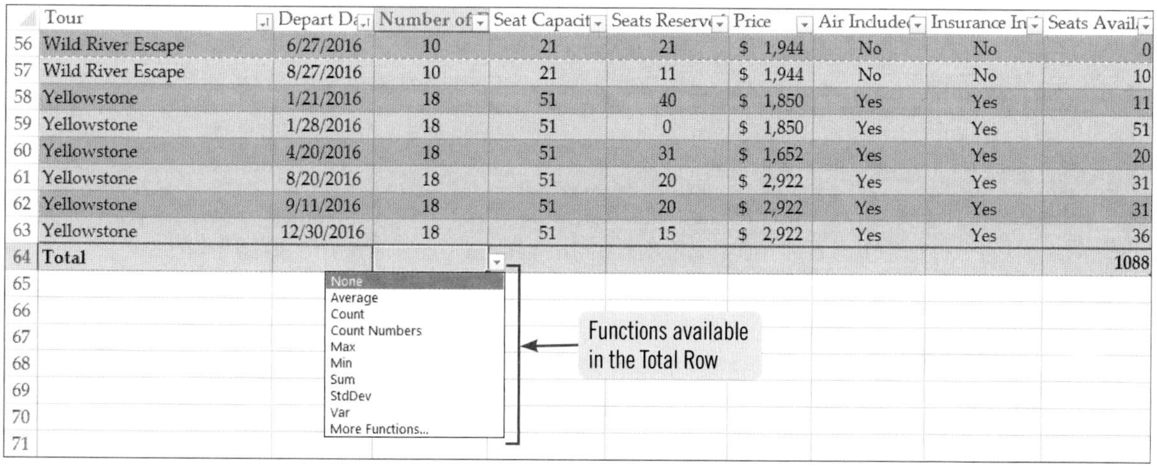

	Tour	Depart Da	Number of	Seat Capacit	Seats Reserv	Price	Air Include	Insurance In	Seats Avail
56	Wild River Escape	6/27/2016	10	21	21	$ 1,944	No	No	0
57	Wild River Escape	8/27/2016	10	21	11	$ 1,944	No	No	10
58	Yellowstone	1/21/2016	18	51	40	$ 1,850	Yes	Yes	11
59	Yellowstone	1/28/2016	18	51	0	$ 1,850	Yes	Yes	51
60	Yellowstone	4/20/2016	18	51	31	$ 1,652	Yes	Yes	20
61	Yellowstone	8/20/2016	18	51	20	$ 2,922	Yes	Yes	31
62	Yellowstone	9/11/2016	18	51	20	$ 2,922	Yes	Yes	31
63	Yellowstone	12/30/2016	18	51	15	$ 2,922	Yes	Yes	36
64	Total								1088

None
Average
Count
Count Numbers
Max
Min
Sum
StdDev
Var
More Functions...

Functions available in the Total Row

Excel 2013

Using structured references

When you create a table from worksheet data, Excel creates a default table name such as Table1. This table name appears in structured references. Structured references make it easier to work with formulas that use table data. You can reference the entire table, columns in the table, or specific data. Structured references are especially helpful to use in formulas because they automatically adjust as data ranges change in a table, so you don't need to edit formulas.

Print a Table

Learning Outcomes
- Preview a table
- Add print titles to a table

You can determine the way a table will print using the PAGE LAYOUT tab. Because tables often have more rows than can fit on a page, you can define the first row of the table (containing the field names) as the **print title**, which prints at the top of every page. Most tables do not have any descriptive information above the field names on the worksheet, so to augment the field name information, you can use headers and footers to add identifying text, such as the table title or the report date. **CASE** *Kate asks you for a printout of the tour information. You begin by previewing the table.*

STEPS

1. **Click the FILE tab, click Print, then view the table preview**
   Below the table you see 1 of 3.
2. **In the Preview window, click the Next Page button ▶ in the Preview area to view the second page, then click ▶ again to view the third page**
   All of the field names in the table fit across the width of page 1. Because the records on pages 2 and 3 appear without column headings, you want to set up the first row of the table, which contains the field names, as a repeating print title.
3. **Return to the worksheet, click the PAGE LAYOUT tab, click the Print Titles button in the Page Setup group, click inside the Rows to repeat at top text box under Print titles, in the worksheet scroll up to row 1 if necessary, click any cell in row 1 on the table, then compare your Page Setup dialog box to FIGURE G-20**
   When you select row 1 as a print title, Excel automatically inserts an absolute reference to the row that will repeat at the top of each page.
4. **Click the Print Preview button in the Page Setup dialog box, click ▶ in the preview window to view the second page, then click ▶ again to view the third page**
   Setting up a print title to repeat row 1 causes the field names to appear at the top of each printed page. The printout would be more informative with a header to identify the table information.
5. **Return to the worksheet, click the INSERT tab, click the Header & Footer button in the Text group, click the left header section text box, then type 2016 Tours**
6. **Select the left header section information, click the HOME tab, click the Increase Font Size button A in the Font group twice to change the font size to 14, click the Bold button B in the Font group, click any cell in the table, then click the Normal button ▦ in the status bar**
7. **Save the table, preview it, close the workbook, exit Excel, then submit the workbook to your instructor**
   Compare your printed table with **FIGURE G-21**.

QUICK TIP
You can hide or print headings and gridlines using the check boxes in the Sheet Options group on the PAGE LAYOUT tab.

QUICK TIP
You can also add a header or a footer by clicking the Page Layout button in the status bar and clicking in the header or footer area.

FIGURE G-20: Page Setup dialog box

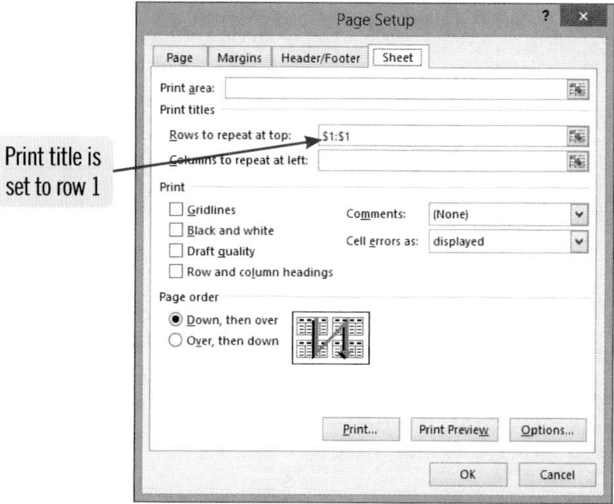

FIGURE G-21: Printed table

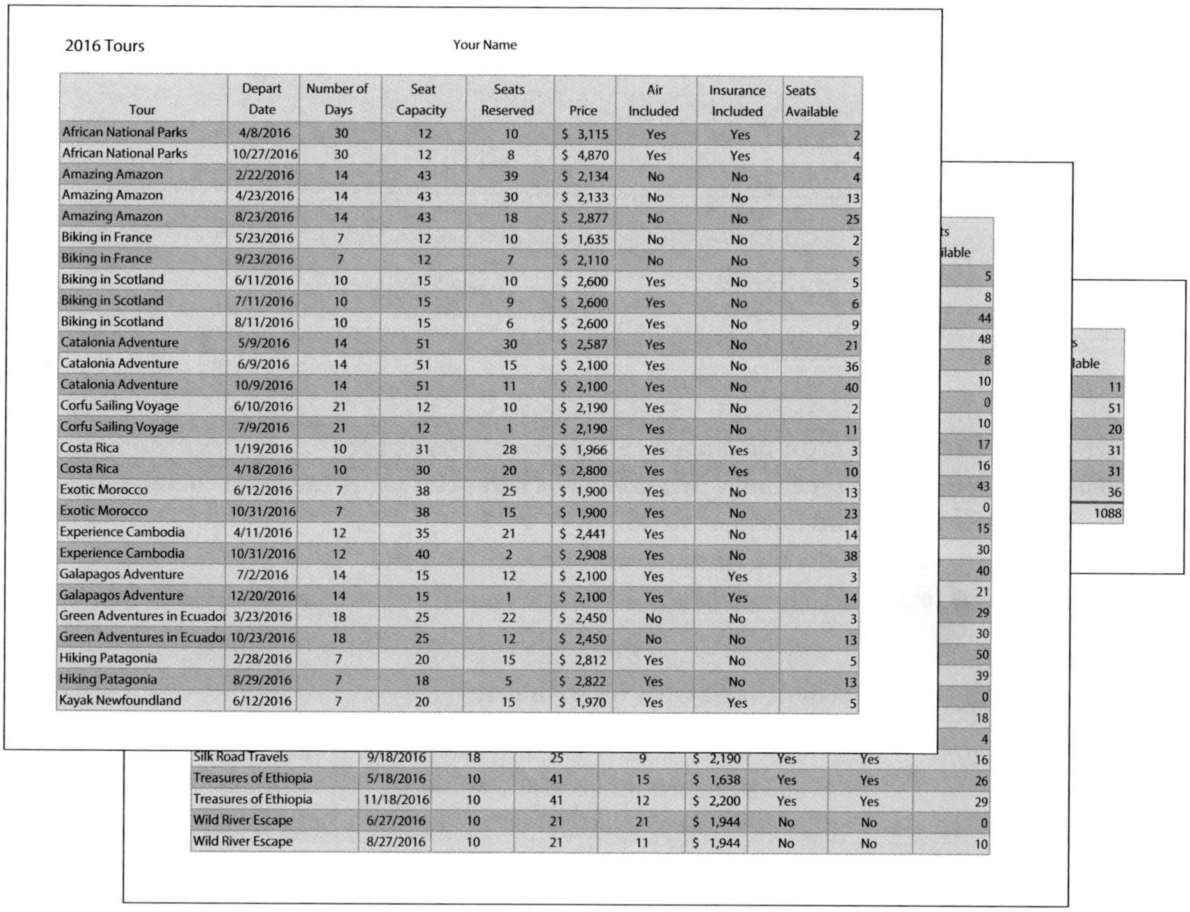

2016 Tours Your Name

Tour	Depart Date	Number of Days	Seat Capacity	Seats Reserved	Price	Air Included	Insurance Included	Seats Available
African National Parks	4/8/2016	30	12	10	$ 3,115	Yes	Yes	2
African National Parks	10/27/2016	30	12	8	$ 4,870	Yes	Yes	4
Amazing Amazon	2/22/2016	14	43	39	$ 2,134	No	No	4
Amazing Amazon	4/23/2016	14	43	30	$ 2,133	No	No	13
Amazing Amazon	8/23/2016	14	43	18	$ 2,877	No	No	25
Biking in France	5/23/2016	7	12	10	$ 1,635	No	No	2
Biking in France	9/23/2016	7	12	7	$ 2,110	No	No	5
Biking in Scotland	6/11/2016	10	15	10	$ 2,600	Yes	No	5
Biking in Scotland	7/11/2016	10	15	9	$ 2,600	Yes	No	6
Biking in Scotland	8/11/2016	10	15	6	$ 2,600	Yes	No	9
Catalonia Adventure	5/9/2016	14	51	30	$ 2,587	Yes	No	21
Catalonia Adventure	6/9/2016	14	51	15	$ 2,100	Yes	No	36
Catalonia Adventure	10/9/2016	14	51	11	$ 2,100	Yes	No	40
Corfu Sailing Voyage	6/10/2016	21	12	10	$ 2,190	Yes	No	2
Corfu Sailing Voyage	7/9/2016	21	12	1	$ 2,190	Yes	No	11
Costa Rica	1/19/2016	10	31	28	$ 1,966	Yes	Yes	3
Costa Rica	4/18/2016	10	30	20	$ 2,800	Yes	Yes	10
Exotic Morocco	6/12/2016	7	38	25	$ 1,900	Yes	No	13
Exotic Morocco	10/31/2016	7	38	15	$ 1,900	Yes	No	23
Experience Cambodia	4/11/2016	12	35	21	$ 2,441	Yes	No	14
Experience Cambodia	10/31/2016	12	40	2	$ 2,908	Yes	No	38
Galapagos Adventure	7/2/2016	14	15	12	$ 2,100	Yes	Yes	3
Galapagos Adventure	12/20/2016	14	15	1	$ 2,100	Yes	Yes	14
Green Adventures in Ecuador	3/23/2016	18	25	22	$ 2,450	No	No	3
Green Adventures in Ecuador	10/23/2016	18	25	12	$ 2,450	No	No	13
Hiking Patagonia	2/28/2016	7	20	15	$ 2,812	Yes	No	5
Hiking Patagonia	8/29/2016	7	18	5	$ 2,822	Yes	No	13
Kayak Newfoundland	6/12/2016	7	20	15	$ 1,970	Yes	Yes	5

Silk Road Travels	9/18/2016	18	25	9	$ 2,190	Yes	Yes	16
Treasures of Ethiopia	5/18/2016	10	41	15	$ 1,638	Yes	Yes	26
Treasures of Ethiopia	11/18/2016	10	41	12	$ 2,200	Yes	Yes	29
Wild River Escape	6/27/2016	10	21	21	$ 1,944	No	No	0
Wild River Escape	8/27/2016	10	21	11	$ 1,944	No	No	10

Setting a print area

Sometimes you will want to print only part of a worksheet. To do this, select any worksheet range, click the FILE tab, click Print, click the Print Active Sheets list arrow, then click Print Selection. If you want to print a selected area repeatedly, it's best to define a **print area**, the area of the worksheet that previews and prints when you use the Print command in Backstage view. To set a print area, select the range of data on the worksheet that you want to print, click the PAGE LAYOUT tab, click the Print Area button in the Page Setup group, then click Set Print Area. You can add to the print area by selecting a range, clicking the Print Area button, then clicking Add to Print Area. A print area can consist of one contiguous range of cells, or multiple areas in different parts of a worksheet.

Practice

Put your skills into practice with **SAM Projects**! SAM Projects for this unit can be found online. If you have a SAM account, go to www.cengage.com/sam2013 to download the most recent Project Instruction and Start Files.

Concepts Review

FIGURE G-22

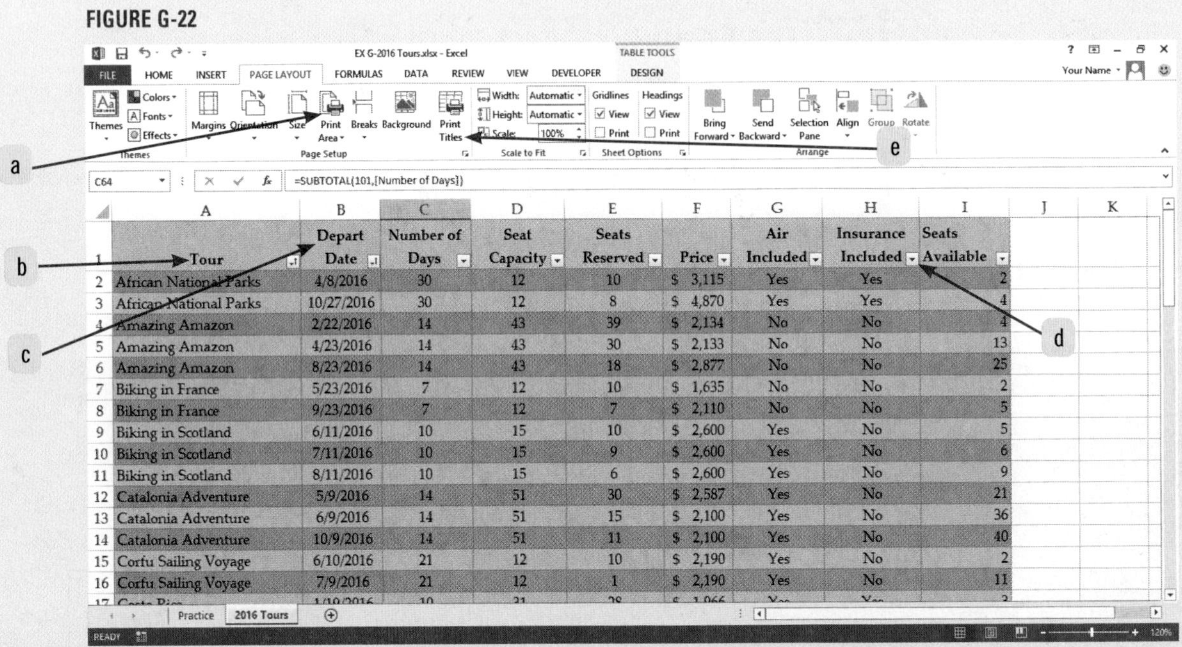

1. **Which element do you click to print field names at the top of every page?**
2. **Which element do you click to set a range in a table that will print using the Print command?**
3. **Which element points to a second-level sort field?**
4. **Which element do you click to sort field data on a worksheet?**
5. **Which element points to a top-level sort field?**

Match each term with the statement that best describes it.

6. Field	**a.** Organized collection of related information in Excel
7. Sort	**b.** Arrange records in a particular sequence
8. Record	**c.** Column in an Excel table
9. Table	**d.** First row of a table containing field names
10. Header row	**e.** Row in an Excel table

Select the best answer from the list of choices.

11. **Which of the following Excel sorting options do you use to sort a table of employee names in order from Z to A?**
    - **a.** Ascending
    - **b.** Absolute
    - **c.** Alphabetic
    - **d.** Descending

12. **Which of the following series appears in descending order?**
   a. 8, 6, 4, C, B, A
   b. 4, 5, 6, A, B, C
   c. 8, 7, 6, 5, 6, 7
   d. C, B, A, 6, 5, 4
13. **You can easily add formatting to a table by using:**
   a. Table styles.
   b. Print titles.
   c. Print areas.
   d. Calculated columns.
14. **When printing a table on multiple pages, you can define a print title to:**
   a. Include the sheet name in table reports.
   b. Include field names at the top of each printed page.
   c. Exclude from the printout all rows under the first row.
   d. Include gridlines in the printout.

Skills Review

1. **Create and format a table.**
   a. Start Excel, open the file EX G-2.xlsx from the location where you store your Data Files, then save it as **EX G-Employees**.
   b. Using the Practice sheet, enter the field names in the first row and the first two records in rows two and three, as shown in the table below, adjusting column widths as necessary to fit the text entries.

Last Name	First Name	Years Employed	Department	Full/Part Time	Training Completed
Diaz	Irina	3	Print Books	P	Y
Merril	Doreen	2	E-Books	F	N

   c. Create a table using the data you entered.
   d. On the Staff sheet, create a table with a header row. Adjust the column widths, if necessary, to display the field names. Enter your name in the center section of the worksheet footer, return to Normal view if necessary, then save the workbook.
   e. Apply a table style of Light 16 to the table.
   f. Enter your name in the center section of the worksheet footer, return to Normal view if necessary, then save the workbook.
2. **Add table data.**
   a. Add a new record in row seven for **Heather Walker**, a 5-year employee in the Print Books department. Heather works part time and has completed training. Adjust the height of the new row to match the other table rows.
   b. Insert a table row above Julie Kosby's record, and add a new record for **Sarah Allen**. Sarah works full time, has worked at the company for 2 years in E-Books, and has not completed training. Adjust the table formatting if necessary.
   c. Insert a new data field in cell G1 with a label **Weeks Vacation**. Adjust the column width, and wrap the label in the cell to display the field name with **Weeks** above **Vacation**. (*Hint*: Use the Wrap Text button in the Alignment group on the HOME tab.)
   d. Add a new column to the table by dragging the table's sizing handle, and give the new field a label of **Employee #**. Widen the column to fit the label.
   e. Save the file.
3. **Find and replace table data.**
   a. Return to cell A1.
   b. Open the Find and Replace dialog box and if necessary uncheck the Match case option. Find the first record that contains the text **Print Books**.
   c. Find the second and third records that contain the text **Print Books**.
   d. Replace all **Print Books** text in the table with **Books**, then save the file.

Skills Review (continued)

4. **Delete table data.**
   a. Go to cell A1.
   b. Delete the record for Irina Diaz.
   c. Use the Remove Duplicates button to confirm that the table does not have any duplicate records.
   d. Delete the Employee # table column, then delete its column header, if necessary.
   e. Save the file.
5. **Sort table data.**
   a. Sort the table by years employed in largest to smallest order.
   b. Sort the table by last name in A to Z order.
   c. Perform a multilevel sort: Sort the table first by Full/Part Time in A to Z order and then by last name in A to Z order.
   d. Check the table to make sure the records appear in the correct order.
   e. Save the file.
6. **Use formulas in a table.**
   a. In cell G2, enter the formula that calculates an employee's vacation time; base the formula on the company policy that employees working at the company less than 3 years have 2 weeks of vacation. At 3 years of employment and longer, an employee has 3 weeks of vacation time. Use the table's field names where appropriate. (*Hint*: The formula is: **=IF([Years Employed]<3,2,3)**.)
   b. Check the table to make sure the formula filled into the cells in column G and that the correct vacation time is calculated for all cells in the column.
   c. Add a Total Row to display the total number of vacation weeks.
   d. Change the function in the Total Row to display the maximum number of vacation weeks. Change the entry in cell A8 from Total to **Maximum**.
   e. Compare your table to **FIGURE G-23**, then save the workbook.

FIGURE G-23

	A	B	C	D	E	F	G
1	Last Name	First Name	Years Employed	Department	Full/Part Time	Training Completed	Weeks Vacation
2	Allen	Sarah	2	E-Books	F	N	2
3	Green	Jane	1	Books	F	N	2
4	Kosby	Julie	4	E-Books	F	Y	3
5	Merril	Doreen	2	E-Books	F	N	2
6	Ropes	Mark	1	E-Books	P	Y	2
7	Walker	Heather	5	Books	P	Y	3
8	Maximum						3

7. **Print a table.**
   a. Add a header that reads **Employees** in the left section, then format the header in bold with a font size of 16.
   b. Add column A as a print title that repeats at the left of each printed page.
   c. Preview your table to check that the last names appear on both pages.
   d. Change the page orientation to landscape, preview the worksheet, then save the workbook.
   e. Submit your workbook to your instructor. Close the workbook, then exit Excel.

Independent Challenge 1

You are the marketing director for a fitness equipment sales firm. Your administrative assistant created an Excel worksheet with customer data including the results of an advertising survey. You will create a table using the customer data, and analyze the survey results to help focus the company's advertising expenses in the most successful areas.

a. Start Excel, open the file EX G-3.xlsx from the location where you store your Data Files, then save it as **EX G-Customers**.
b. Create a table from the worksheet data, and apply Table Style Light 18.

Independent Challenge 1 (continued)

c. Add the two records shown in the table below:

Last Name	First Name	Street Address	City	State	Zip	Area Code	Ad Source
Riley	Cate	81 Apple St.	San Francisco	CA	94177	415	Fitness Center
Jenkins	Sam	307 7th St.	Seattle	WA	98001	206	Newspaper

d. Find the record for Mike Rondo, then delete it.

e. Click cell A1 and replace all instances of **TV** with **Social Media**. Compare your table to **FIGURE G-24**.

FIGURE G-24

	A	B	C	D	E	F	G	H
1	Last Name	First Name	Street Address	City	State	Zip	Area Code	Ad Source
2	Kahil	Kathy	14 South St.	San Francisco	CA	94177	415	Social Media
3	Johnson	Mel	17 Henley St.	Reading	MA	03882	413	Newspaper
4	Malone	Kris	1 South St.	San Francisco	CA	94177	415	Fitness Center
5	Worthen	Sally	2120 Central St.	San Francisco	CA	93772	415	Fitness Center
6	Herbert	Greg	1192 Dome St.	San Diego	CA	93303	619	Newspaper
7	Chavez	Jane	11 Northern St.	San Diego	CA	92208	619	Social Media
8	Chelly	Yvonne	900 Sola St.	San Diego	CA	92106	619	Fitness Center
9	Smith	Carolyn	921 Lopez St.	San Diego	CA	92104	619	Newspaper
10	Oren	Scott	72 Yankee St.	Brookfield	CT	06830	203	Health Website
11	Warner	Salvatore	100 Westside St.	Chicago	IL	60620	312	Newspaper
12	Roberts	Bob	56 Water St.	Chicago	IL	60618	771	Fitness Center
13	Miller	Hope	111 Stratton St.	Chicago	IL	60614	773	Newspaper
14	Duran	Maria	Galvin St.	Chicago	IL	60614	773	Health Website
15	Roberts	Bob	56 Water St.	Chicago	IL	60614	312	Newspaper
16	Graham	Shelley	989 26th St.	Chicago	IL	60611	773	Education Website
17	Kelly	Janie	9 First St.	San Francisco	CA	94177	415	Newspaper
18	Kim	Janie	9 First St.	San Francisco	CA	94177	415	Health Website
19	Williams	Tasha	1 Spring St.	Reading	MA	03882	413	Newspaper
20	Juarez	Manuel	544 Cameo St.	Belmont	MA	02483	617	Newspaper
21	Masters	Latrice	88 Las Puntas Rd.	Boston	MA	02205	617	Education Website
22	Kooper	Peter	671 Main St.	Cambridge	MA	02138	617	Social Media
23	Kelly	Shawn	22 Kendall St.	Cambridge	MA	02138	617	Education Website
24	Rodriguez	Virginia	123 Main St.	Boston	MA	02007	617	Radio
25	Frei	Carol	123 Elm St.	Salem	MA	01970	978	Newspaper
26	Stevens	Crystal	14 Waterford St.	Salem	MA	01970	508	Radio
27	Ichikawa	Pam	232 Shore Rd.	Boston	MA	01801	617	Newspaper
28	Paxton	Gail	100 Main St.	Woburn	MA	01801	508	Newspaper
29	Spencer	Robin	293 Serenity Dr.	Concord	MA	01742	508	Radio
30	Lopez	Luis	1212 City St.	Kansas City	MO	64105	816	Social Media
31	Nelson	Michael	229 Rally Rd.	Kansas City	MO	64105	816	Education Website

f. Remove duplicate records where all fields are identical.

g. Sort the list by Last Name in A to Z order.

h. Sort the list again by Area Code in Smallest to Largest order.

i. Sort the table first by State in A to Z order, then within the state, by Zip in Smallest to Largest order.

j. Enter your name in the center section of the worksheet footer.

k. Add a centered header that reads **Ad Survey** in bold with a font size of 16.

l. Add print titles to repeat the first row at the top of each printed page.

m. Save the workbook, preview it, then submit the workbook to your instructor.

n. Close the workbook, then exit Excel.

Independent Challenge 2

You manage Green Living, a store that sells environmentally friendly cleaning supplies in bulk online. Your customers purchase items in quantities of 10 or more. You decide to plan and build a table of sales information with eight records using the items sold.

a. Prepare a plan for a table that states your goal, outlines the data you need, and identifies the table elements.

b. Sketch a sample table on a piece of paper, indicating how the table should be built. Create a table documenting the table design including the field names, type of data, and description of the data. Some examples of items are glass cleaner, tile cleaner, carpet cleaner, stone cleaner, and paper towels.

Independent Challenge 2 (continued)

c. Start Excel, create a new workbook, then save it as **EX G-Store Items** in the location where you store your Data Files. Enter the field names shown in the table below in the designated cells:

cell	field name
A1	Customer Last
B1	Customer First
C1	Item
D1	Quantity
E1	Cost

d. Enter eight data records using your own data.
e. Create a table using the data in the range A1:E9. Adjust the column widths as necessary.
f. Apply the Table Style Light 11 to the table.
g. Add a field named **Total** in cell F1.
h. Enter a formula in cell F2 that calculates the total by multiplying the Quantity field by the Cost field. Check that the formula was filled down in the column.
i. Format the Cost and Total columns using the Accounting number format. Adjust the column widths as necessary.
j. Add a new record to your table in row 10. Add another record above row 4.
k. Sort the table in ascending order by Item.
l. Enter your name in the worksheet footer, then save the workbook.
m. Preview the worksheet, then submit your workbook to your instructor.
n. Close the workbook, then exit Excel.

Independent Challenge 3

You are a property manager at a firm that manages condominiums and apartments. You are managing your accounts using an Excel worksheet and have decided that a table will provide additional features to help you keep track of the accounts. You will use the table sorting features and table formulas to analyze your account data.

a. Start Excel, open the file EX G-4.xlsx from the location where you store your Data Files, then save it as **EX G-Accounts**.
b. Create a table with the worksheet data, and apply a table style of your choice. Adjust the column widths as necessary.
c. Sort the table on the Budget field using the Smallest to Largest order.
d. Sort the table using two fields, by Contact in A to Z order, then by Budget in Smallest to Largest order. Compare your table to **FIGURE G-25**. (Your table style may differ.)

FIGURE G-25

	A	B	C	D	E	F
1	Property	Type	Code	Budget	Expenses	Contact
2	South End	Apartment	SE	$ 250,000	$ 225,000	Cindy Boil
3	Northfield	Apartment	NF	$ 275,000	$ 215,000	Cindy Boil
4	Warren	Condominium	WR	$ 375,000	$ 250,000	Cindy Boil
5	Langley Place	Condominium	LP	$ 650,000	$ 550,000	Cindy Boil
6	River Place	Condominium	RP	$ 175,000	$ 150,000	Jane Smith
7	Deer Run	Condominium	DR	$ 250,000	$ 210,000	Jane Smith
8	Green Ridge	Condominium	GR	$ 350,000	$ 210,000	Jane Smith
9	Rangeley	Condominium	RG	$ 410,000	$ 320,000	Jane Smith
10	Northridge	Apartment	NR	$ 550,000	$ 525,000	Kathy Jenkins
11	West End	Apartment	WE	$ 750,000	$ 600,000	Kathy Jenkins

Independent Challenge 3 (continued)

e. Add the new field label **Balance** in cell G1, and adjust the column width as necessary.
f. Enter a formula in cell G2 that uses structured references to table fields to calculate the balance on an account as the Budget minus the Expenses.
g. Add a new record for a property named **Riverside** with a type of **Condominium**, a code of **RS**, a budget of **$350,000**, expenses of **$250,000**, and a contact of **Cindy Boil**.
h. Verify that the formula accurately calculated the balance for the new record.
i. Replace all of the Jane Smith data with **Jane Atkins**.
j. Find the record for the Green Ridge property and delete it.
k. Delete the Type field from the table.
l. Add a total row to the table and display the totals for appropriate columns. Adjust the column widths as necessary.
m. Enter your name in the center section of the worksheet footer, add a center section header of **Accounts** using formatting of your choice, change the page orientation to landscape, then save the workbook.
n. Preview your workbook, submit the workbook to your instructor, close the workbook, then exit Excel.

Independent Challenge 4: Explore

As the Vice President of Marketing at a design firm, you track the expense accounts of the associates in the department using a table in Excel. You decide to highlight accounts that are over budget for the monthly meeting.

a. Start Excel, open the file EX G-5.xlsx from the location where you store your Data Files, then save it as **EX G-Associates**.
b. Create a table with the worksheet data, and apply the table style of your choice. Adjust the column widths as necessary.
c. Sort the table on the Balance field using the Smallest to Largest order.
d. Use conditional formatting to format the cells of the table containing negative balances with a green fill with dark green text.
e. Sort the table using the Balance field with the order of no cell color on top.
f. Format the table to emphasize the Balance column, and turn off the banded rows. (*Hint*: Use the Table Style Options on the TABLE TOOLS DESIGN tab.)
g. Research how to print nonadjacent areas on a single page. (Excel prints nonadjacent areas of a worksheet on separate pages by default.) Enter the result of your research on Sheet2 of the workbook.
h. Return to Sheet1 and create a print area that prints only the Account Number, Associate, and Balance columns of the table on one page.
i. Compare your table with **FIGURE G-26**. Save the workbook.
j. Preview your print area to make sure it will print on a single page.
k. Enter your name in the worksheet footers, then save the workbook.
l. Submit the workbook to your instructor, close the workbook, then exit Excel.

FIGURE G-26

	A	B	F
1	Account Number	Associate	Balance
2	96634	Kris Lowe	$ 5,000
3	32577	George Well	$ 10,000
4	15334	Janet Colby	$ 19,790
5	98661	Judy Makay	$ 25,000
6	84287	Joe Wood	$ 345,000
7	78441	Nancy Allen	$ 600,000
8	41557	Judy Makay	$ (15,000)
9	21889	Nancy Allen	$ (10,000)
10	57741	George Well	$ (10,000)
11	38997	Janet Colby	$ (5,000)

Excel 2013

Visual Workshop

Start Excel, open the file EX G-6.xlsx from the location where you store your Data Files, then save it as **EX G-Products**. Create the table and sort the data as shown in **FIGURE G-27**. (*Hint*: The table is formatted using Table Style Medium 5.) Add a worksheet header with the sheet name in the center section that is formatted in bold with a size of 14. Enter your name in the center section of the worksheet footer. Save the workbook, preview the table, close the workbook, submit the workbook to your instructor, then exit Excel.

FIGURE G-27

	Order Number	Department	Amount	Shipping	Sales Rep
2	1111	Shoes	$ 52.31	Air	Ellie Cranson
3	1032	Home	$ 157.22	Air	Ellie Cranson
4	2187	Home	$ 157.33	Air	Ellie Cranson
5	1251	Food	$ 255.47	Air	Ellie Cranson
6	2357	Food	$ 287.66	Ground	Ellie Cranson
7	2113	Home	$ 109.66	Ground	Gene Coburn
8	2257	Shoes	$ 179.65	Air	Gene Coburn
9	1587	Children	$ 200.52	Ground	Gene Coburn
10	2588	Shoes	$ 333.74	Ground	Gene Coburn
11	1533	Children	$ 327.88	Ground	Neil Boxer
12	2001	Children	$ 532.44	Air	Neil Boxer

Analyzing Table Data

CASE The vice president of sales, Kate Morgan, asks you to display information from a table of the 2016 scheduled tours to help the sales representatives with customer inquiries. She also asks you to prepare summaries of the tour sales for a presentation at the international sales meeting. You will prepare these using various filters, subtotals, and Excel functions.

Unit Objectives

After completing this unit, you will be able to:

- Filter a table
- Create a custom filter
- Filter a table with the Advanced Filter
- Extract table data
- Look up values in a table
- Summarize table data
- Validate table data
- Create subtotals

Files You Will Need

EX H-1.xlsx
EX H-2.xlsx
EX H-3.xlsx
EX H-4.xlsx
EX H-5.xlsx
EX H-6.xlsx
EX H-7.xlsx

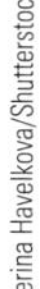

Filter a Table

Learning Outcomes
- Filter records using AutoFilter
- Filter records using search criteria

An Excel table lets you easily manipulate large amounts of data to view only the data you want, using a feature called **AutoFilter**. When you create a table, arrows automatically appear next to each column header. These arrows are called **filter list arrows**, **AutoFilter list arrows**, or **list arrows**, and you can use them to **filter** a table to display only the records that meet criteria you specify, temporarily hiding records that do not meet those criteria. For example, you can use the filter list arrow next to the Tour field header to display only records that contain Nepal Trekking in the Tour field. Once you filter data, you can copy, chart, and print the displayed records. You can easily clear a filter to redisplay all the records. **CASE** *Kate asks you to display only the records for the Yellowstone tours. She also asks for information about the tours that sell the most seats and the tours that depart in March.*

STEPS

1. **Start Excel, open the file EX H-1.xlsx from the location where you save your Data Files, then save it as EX H-Tours**

2. **Click the Tour list arrow**

   Sort options appear at the top of the menu, advanced filtering options appear in the middle, and at the bottom is a list of the tour data from column A, as shown in **FIGURE H-1**. Because you want to display data for only the Yellowstone tours, your **search criterion** (the text you are searching for) is Yellowstone. You can select one of the Tour data options in the menu, which acts as your search criterion.

> **QUICK TIP**
> You can also filter the table to display only the Yellowstone tour information by clicking the Tour list arrow, entering "Yellowstone" in the Search text box on the menu options below Text Filters, then clicking OK.

3. **In the list of tours for the Tour field, click Select All to clear the check marks from the tours, scroll down the list of tours, click Yellowstone, then click OK**

   Only those records containing "Yellowstone" in the Tour field appear, as shown in **FIGURE H-2**. The row numbers for the matching records change to blue, and the list arrow for the filtered field has a filter icon. : Both indicate that there is a filter in effect and that some of the records are temporarily hidden.

4. **Move the pointer over the Tour list arrow**

   The ScreenTip Tour: Equals "Yellowstone" describes the filter for the field, meaning that only the Yellowstone records appear. You decide to remove the filter to redisplay all of the table data.

5. **Click the Tour list arrow, then click Clear Filter From "Tour"**

   You have cleared the Yellowstone filter, and all the records reappear. You want to display the most popular tours, those that are in the top five percent of seats reserved.

> **QUICK TIP**
> You can also filter or sort a table by the color of the cells if conditional formatting has been applied.

6. **Click the Seats Reserved list arrow, point to Number Filters, click Top 10, select 10 in the middle box, type 5, click the Items list arrow, click Percent, then click OK**

   Excel displays the records for the top five percent in the number of Seats Reserved field, as shown in **FIGURE H-3**. You decide to clear the filter to redisplay all the records.

7. **On the HOME tab, click the Sort & Filter button in the Editing group, then click Clear**

   You have cleared the filter and all the records reappear. You can clear a filter using either the AutoFilter menu command or the Sort & Filter button on the HOME tab. The Sort & Filter button is convenient for clearing multiple filters at once. You want to find all of the tours that depart in March.

8. **Click the Depart Date list arrow, point to Date Filters, point to All Dates in the Period, then click March**

   Excel displays the records for only the tours that leave in March. You decide to clear the filter and display all of the records.

> **QUICK TIP**
> You can also clear a filter by clicking the Clear button in the Sort & Filter group on the DATA tab.

9. **Click the Sort & Filter button in the Editing group, click Clear, then save the workbook**

FIGURE H-1: Worksheet showing AutoFilter options

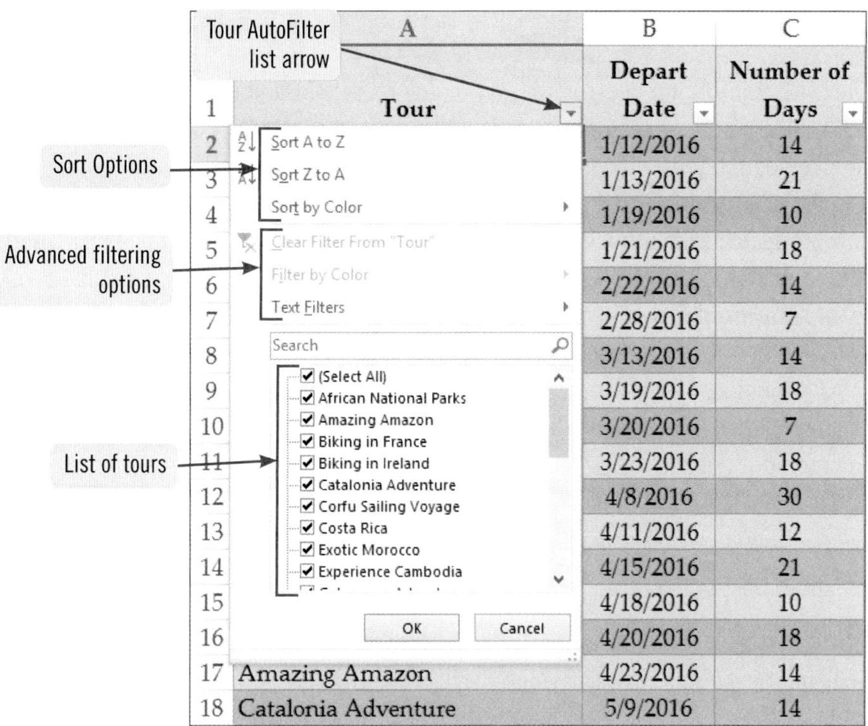

FIGURE H-2: Table filtered to show Yellowstone tours

	Tour	Depart Date	Number of Days	Seat Capacity	Seats Reserved	Price	Air Included	Insurance Included
5	Yellowstone	1/21/2016	18	51	40	$ 1,850	Yes	Yes
16	Yellowstone	4/20/2016	18	51	31	$ 1,652	Yes	Yes
41	Yellowstone	8/20/2016	18	51	20	$ 2,922	Yes	Yes
45	Yellowstone	9/11/2016	18	51	20	$ 2,922	Yes	Yes
63	Yellowstone	12/30/2016	18	51	15	$ 2,922	Yes	Yes
65								

Matching row numbers are blue and sequence indicates that not all rows appear

Filter displays only Yellowstone tours

List arrow changed to filter icon

FIGURE H-3: Table filtered with top 5% of Seats Reserved

	Tour	Depart Date	Number of Days	Seat Capacity	Seats Reserved	Price	Air Included	Insurance Included
2	Pacific Odyssey	1/12/2016	14	50	50	$ 2,255	Yes	No
3	Old Japan	1/13/2016	21	47	42	$ 1,984	Yes	No
5	Yellowstone	1/21/2016	18	51	40	$ 1,850	Yes	Yes
65								

Table filtered with top 5% in this field

Create a Custom Filter

Learning Outcomes
- Filter records with multiple criteria
- Determine when to use AND and OR logical conditions

While AutoFilter lists can display records that are equal to certain amounts, you will often need more detailed filters. You can use more complex filters with the help of options in the Custom AutoFilter dialog box. For example, your criteria can contain comparison operators such as "greater than" or "less than" that let you display values above or below a certain amount. You can also use **logical conditions** like And and Or to narrow a search even further. You can have Excel display records that meet a criterion in a field *and* another criterion in that same field. This is often used to find records between two values. For example, by specifying an **And logical condition**, you can display records for customers with incomes between $40,000 *and* $70,000. You can also have Excel display records that meet either criterion in a field by specifying an Or condition. The **Or logical condition** is used to find records that satisfy either of two values. For example, in a table of book data you can use the Or condition to find records that contain either Beginning *or* Introduction in the title name. **CASE** *Kate wants to locate tours for customers who like active vacations. She also wants to find tours that depart between February 15, 2016, and April 15, 2016. She asks you to create custom filters to find the tours satisfying these criteria.*

STEPS

1. **Click the Tour list arrow, point to Text Filters, then click Contains**
   The Custom AutoFilter dialog box opens. You enter your criteria in the text boxes. The left text box on the first line currently displays "contains." You want to display tours that contain the word "sailing" in their names.
2. **Type sailing in the right text box on the first line**
   You want to see entries that contain either sailing or biking.
3. **Click the Or option button to select it, click the left text box list arrow on the second line, scroll to and select contains, then type biking in the right text box on the second line**
   Your completed Custom AutoFilter dialog box should match **FIGURE H-4**.
4. **Click OK**
   The dialog box closes, and only those records having "sailing" or "biking" in the Tour field appear in the worksheet. You want to find all tours that depart between February 15, 2016 and April 15, 2016.
5. **Click the Tour list arrow, click Clear Filter From "Tour", click the Depart Date list arrow, point to Date Filters, then click Custom Filter**
   The Custom AutoFilter dialog box opens. The word "equals" appears in the left text box on the first line. You want to find the departure dates that are between February 15, 2016 and April 15, 2016 (that is, after February 15 *and* before April 15).
6. **Click the left text box list arrow on the first line, click is after, then type 2/15/2016 in the right text box on the first line**
   The And condition is selected, which is correct.
7. **Click the left text box list arrow on the second line, select is before, type 4/15/2016 in the right text box on the second line, then click OK**
   The records displayed have departure dates between February 15, 2016, and April 15, 2016. Compare your records to those shown in **FIGURE H-5**.
8. **Click the Depart Date list arrow, click Clear Filter From "Depart Date", then add your name to the center section of the footer**
   You have cleared the filter, and all the tour records reappear.

QUICK TIP
When specifying criteria in the Custom Filter dialog box, you can use the (?) wildcard to represent any single character and the (*) wildcard to represent any series of characters.

FIGURE H-4: Custom AutoFilter dialog box

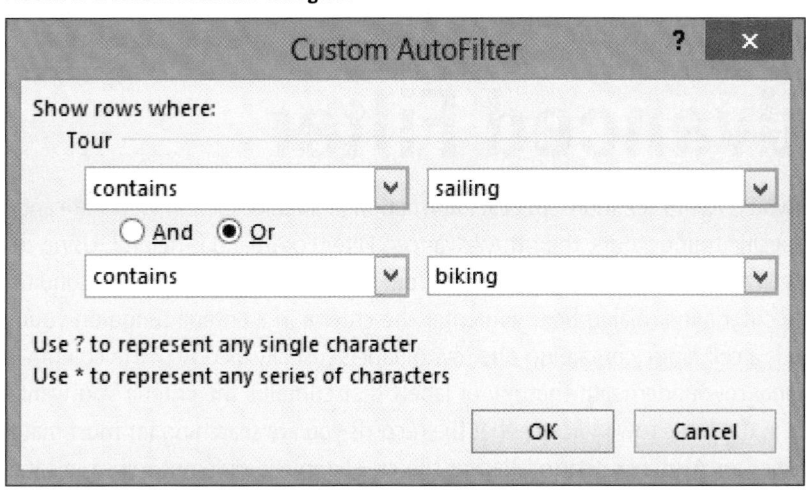

FIGURE H-5: Results of custom filter

	A	B	C	D	E	F	G	H
1	Tour	Depart Date	Number of Days	Seat Capacity	Seats Reserved	Price	Air Included	Insurance Included
6	Amazing Amazon	2/22/2016	14	43	39	$ 2,134	No	No
7	Hiking Patagonia	2/28/2016	7	20	15	$ 2,812	Yes	No
8	Pearls of the Orient	3/13/2016	14	45	15	$ 2,350	Yes	No
9	Silk Road Travels	3/19/2016	18	23	19	$ 2,110	Yes	Yes
10	Photographing France	3/20/2016	7	20	20	$ 1,755	Yes	Yes
11	Green Adventures in Ecuador	3/23/2016	18	25	22	$ 2,450	No	No
12	African National Parks	4/8/2016	30	12	10	$ 3,115	Yes	Yes
13	Experience Cambodia	4/11/2016	12	35	21	$ 2,441	Yes	No
65								

Departure dates are between 2/15 and 4/15

Excel 2013

Using more than one rule when conditionally formatting data

You can apply conditional formatting to table cells in the same way that you can format a range of worksheet data. You can add multiple rules by clicking the HOME tab, clicking the Conditional Formatting button in the Styles group, then clicking New Rule for each additional rule that you want to apply. You can also add rules using the Conditional Formatting Rules Manager, which displays all of the rules for a data range. To use the Rules Manager, click the HOME tab, click the Conditional Formatting button in the Styles group, click Manage Rules, then click New Rule for each rule that you want to apply to the data range. After you have applied conditional formatting such as color fills, icon sets, or color scales to a numeric table range, you can use AutoFilter to sort or filter based on the colors or symbols.

Filter a Table with the Advanced Filter

Learning Outcomes
- Filter records using a criteria range and the And condition
- Filter records using a criteria range and the Or condition

If you would like to see more specific information in a table, such as view date and insurance information for a specific tour or tours, then the Advanced Filter command is helpful. Using the Advanced Filter, you can specify data that you want to display from the table using And and Or conditions. Rather than entering the criteria in a dialog box, you enter the criteria in a criteria range on your worksheet. A **criteria range** is a cell range containing one row of labels (usually a copy of the column labels) and at least one additional row underneath the row of labels that contains the criteria you want to match. Placing the criteria in the same row indicates that the records you are searching for must match both criteria; that is, it specifies an **And condition**. Placing the criteria in the different rows indicates that the records you are searching for must match only one of the criterion; that is, it specifies an **Or condition**. With the criteria range on the worksheet, you can easily see the criteria by which your table is sorted. You can also use the criteria range to create a macro using the Advanced Filter feature to automate the filtering process for data that you filter frequently. Another advantage of the Advanced Filter is that you can move filtered table data to a different area of the worksheet or to a new worksheet, as you will see in the next lesson. **CASE** *Kate wants to identify tours that depart after 6/1/2016 and that cost less than $2,000. She asks you to use the Advanced Filter to retrieve these records. You begin by defining the criteria range.*

STEPS

1. **Select table rows 1 through 6, click the Insert list arrow in the Cells group, click Insert Sheet Rows; click cell A1, type Criteria Range, then click the Enter button ✓ on the Formula bar**

   Six blank rows are added above the table. Excel does not require the label "Criteria Range", but it is useful to see the column labels as you organize the worksheet and use filters.

2. **Select the range A7:H7, click the Copy button in the Clipboard group, click cell A2, click the Paste button in the Clipboard group, then press [Esc]**

   Next, you want to insert criteria that will display records for only those tours that depart after June 1, 2016 and that cost under $2,000.

3. **Click cell B3, type >6/1/2016, click cell F3, type <2000, then click ✓**

   You have entered the criteria in the cells directly beneath the Criteria Range labels, as shown in **FIGURE H-6**.

4. **Click any cell in the table, click the DATA tab, then click the Advanced button in the Sort & Filter group**

   The Advanced Filter dialog box opens, with the table (list) range already entered. The default setting under Action is to filter the table in its current location ("in-place") rather than copy it to another location.

5. **Click the Criteria range text box, select the range A2:H3 in the worksheet, then click OK**

   You have specified the criteria range and used the filter. The filtered table contains eight records that match both criteria—the departure date is after 6/1/2016 and the price is less than $2,000, as shown in **FIGURE H-7**. You'll filter this table even further in the next lesson.

QUICK TIP
You can apply multiple criteria by using AutoFilter a second time on the results of the previously filtered data. Each additional filter builds on the results of the filtered data and filters the data further.

TROUBLE
If your filtered records don't match **FIGURE H-7**, make sure there are no spaces between the > symbol and the 6 in cell B3 and the < symbol and the 2 in cell F3.

FIGURE H-6: Criteria in the same row indicating an and condition

	A	B	C	D	E	F	G	H
1	Criteria Range							
2	Tour	Depart Date	Number of Days	Seat Capacity	Seats Reserved	Price	Air Included	Insurance Included
3		>6/1/2016				<2000		
4								
5								
6								
7	Tour	Depart Date	Number of Days	Seat Capacity	Seats Reserved	Price	Air Included	Insurance Included
8	Pacific Odyssey	1/12/2016	14	50	50	$ 2,255	Yes	No
9	Old Japan	1/13/2016	21	47	42	$ 1,984	Yes	No
10	Costa Rica	1/19/2016	10	31	28	$ 1,966	Yes	Yes

Filtered records will match these criteria

FIGURE H-7: Filtered table

	A	B	C	D	E	F	G	H
1	Criteria Range							
2	Tour	Depart Date	Number of Days	Seat Capacity	Seats Reserved	Price	Air Included	Insurance Included
3		>6/1/2016				<2000		
4								
5								
6								
7	Tour	Depart Date	Number of Days	Seat Capacity	Seats Reserved	Price	Air Included	Insurance Included
33	Exotic Morocco	6/12/2016	7	38	25	$ 1,900	Yes	No
34	Kayak Newfoundland	6/12/2016	7	20	15	$ 1,970	Yes	Yes
37	Wild River Escape	6/27/2016	10	21	21	$ 1,944	No	No
42	Kayak Newfoundland	7/12/2016	7	20	15	$ 1,970	Yes	Yes
44	Magnificent Montenegro	7/27/2016	10	48	0	$ 1,890	No	No
46	Kayak Newfoundland	8/12/2016	7	20	12	$ 1,970	Yes	Yes
49	Wild River Escape	8/27/2016	10	21	11	$ 1,944	No	No
61	Exotic Morocco	10/31/2016	7	38	15	$ 1,900	Yes	No
71								

Depart dates are after 6/1/2013

Prices are less than $2000

Excel 2013

Using advanced conditional formatting options

You can emphasize top- or bottom-ranked values in a field using conditional formatting. To highlight the top or bottom values in a field, select the field data, click the Conditional Formatting button in the Styles group on the HOME tab, point to Top/Bottom Rules, select a Top or Bottom rule, if necessary enter the percentage or number of cells in the selected range that you want to format, select the format for the cells that meet the top or bottom criteria, then click OK. You can also format your worksheet or table data using icon sets and color scales based on the cell values. A **color scale** uses a set of two, three, or four fill colors to convey relative values. For example, red could fill cells to indicate they have higher values and green could signify lower values. To add a color scale, select a data range, click the HOME tab, click the Conditional Formatting button in the Styles group, then point to Color Scales. On the submenu, you can select preformatted color sets or click More Rules to create your own color sets. **Icon sets** let you visually communicate relative cell values by adding icons to cells based on the values they contain. An upward-pointing green arrow might represent the highest values, and downward-pointing red arrows could represent lower values. To add an icon set to a data range, select a data range, click the Conditional Formatting button in the Styles group, then point to Icon Sets. You can customize the values that are used as thresholds for color scales and icon sets by clicking the Conditional Formatting button in the Styles group, clicking Manage Rules, clicking the rule in the Conditional Formatting Rules Manager dialog box, then clicking Edit Rule.

Extract Table Data

Learning Outcomes
- Extract filtered records to another worksheet location
- Clear filtered records

Whenever you take the time to specify a complicated set of search criteria, it's a good idea to extract the matching records, rather than filtering it in place. When you **extract** data, you place a copy of a filtered table in a range that you specify in the Advanced Filter dialog box. This way, you won't accidentally clear the filter or lose track of the records you spent time compiling. To extract data, you use an Advanced Filter and enter the criteria beneath the copied field names, as you did in the previous lesson. You then specify the location where you want the extracted data to appear. **CASE** *Kate needs to filter the table one step further to reflect only the Wild River Escape or Kayak Newfoundland tours in the current filtered table. She asks you to complete this filter by specifying an Or condition, which you will do by entering two sets of criteria in two separate rows. You decide to save the filtered records by extracting them to a different location in the worksheet.*

STEPS

1. **In cell A3, enter Wild River Escape, then in cell A4, enter Kayak Newfoundland**
   The new sets of criteria need to appear in two separate rows, so you need to copy the previous filter criteria to the second row.
2. **Copy the criteria in B3:F3 to B4:F4**
   The criteria are shown in **FIGURE H-8**. When you use the Advanced Filter this time, you indicate that you want to copy the filtered table to a range beginning in cell A75, so that Kate can easily refer to the data, even if you use more filters later.
3. **If necessary, click the DATA tab, then click Advanced in the Sort & Filter group**
4. **Under Action, click the Copy to another location option button to select it, click the Copy to text box, then type A75**
   The last time you filtered the table, the criteria range included only rows 2 and 3, and now you have criteria in row 4.
5. **Edit the contents of the Criteria range text box to show the range $A$2:$H$4, click OK, then if necessary scroll down until row 75 is visible**
   The matching records appear in the range beginning in cell A75, as shown in **FIGURE H-9**. The original table, starting in cell A7, contains the records filtered in the previous lesson.
6. **Press [Ctrl][Home], then click the Clear button in the Sort & Filter group**
   The original table is displayed starting in cell A7, and the extracted table remains in A75:H80.
7. **Save the workbook**

QUICK TIP
Make sure the criteria range in the Advanced Filter dialog box includes the field names and the number of rows underneath the names that contain criteria. If you leave a blank row in the criteria range, Excel filters nothing and shows all records.

FIGURE H-8: Criteria in separate rows

	A	B	C	D	E	F	G
1	Criteria Range						
2	Tour	Depart Date	Number of Days	Seat Capacity	Seats Reserved	Price	Air Included
3	Wild River Escape	>6/1/2016				<2000	
4	Kayak Newfoundland	>6/1/2016				<2000	
5							

FIGURE H-9: Extracted data records

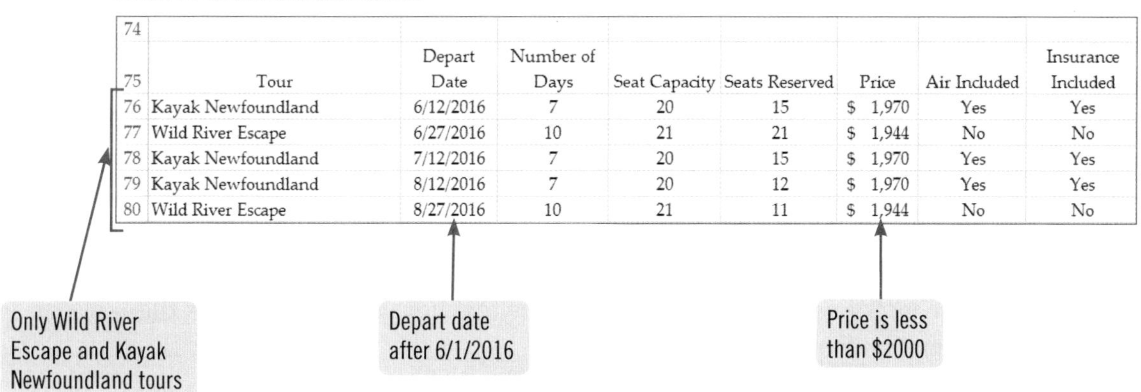

	Tour	Depart Date	Number of Days	Seat Capacity	Seats Reserved	Price	Air Included	Insurance Included
74								
75	Tour	Depart Date	Number of Days	Seat Capacity	Seats Reserved	Price	Air Included	Insurance Included
76	Kayak Newfoundland	6/12/2016	7	20	15	$ 1,970	Yes	Yes
77	Wild River Escape	6/27/2016	10	21	21	$ 1,944	No	No
78	Kayak Newfoundland	7/12/2016	7	20	15	$ 1,970	Yes	Yes
79	Kayak Newfoundland	8/12/2016	7	20	12	$ 1,970	Yes	Yes
80	Wild River Escape	8/27/2016	10	21	11	$ 1,944	No	No

Understanding the criteria range and the copy-to location

When you define the criteria range and the copy-to location in the Advanced Filter dialog box, Excel automatically creates the range names Criteria and Extract for these ranges in the worksheet. The Criteria range includes the field names and any criteria rows underneath them. The Extract range includes just the field names above the extracted table. You can select these ranges by clicking the Name box list arrow, then clicking the range name. If you click the Name Manager button in the Defined Names group on the FORMULAS tab, you will see these new names and the ranges associated with each one.

Look Up Values in a Table

Learning Outcomes
- Use table references in a VLOOKUP formula
- Find table information using VLOOKUP

The Excel VLOOKUP function helps you locate specific values in a table. VLOOKUP searches vertically (V) down the far left column of a table, then reads across the row to find the value in the column you specify, much as you might look up a number in a name and address list: You locate a person's name, then read across the row to find the phone number you want. **CASE** *Kate wants to be able to find a tour destination by entering the tour code. You will use the VLOOKUP function to accomplish this task. You begin by viewing the table name so you can refer to it in a lookup function.*

STEPS

QUICK TIP
You can change table names to better represent their content so they are easier to use in formulas. Click the table in the list of names in the Name Manager text box, click Edit, type the new table name in the Name text box, then click OK.

1. **Click the Lookup sheet tab, click the FORMULAS tab in the Ribbon, then click the Name Manager button in the Defined Names group**
   The named ranges for the workbook appear in the Name Manager dialog box, as shown in **FIGURE H-10**. The Criteria and Extract ranges appear at the top of the range name list. At the bottom of the list is information about the three tables in the workbook. Table1 refers to the table on the Tours sheet, Table2 refers to the table on the Lookup sheet, and Table3 refers to the table on the Subtotals worksheet. The Excel structured reference feature automatically created these table names when the tables were created.
2. **Click Close**
   You want to find the tour represented by the code 830L. The VLOOKUP function lets you find the tour name for any trip code. You will enter a trip code in cell M1 and a VLOOKUP function in cell M2.
3. **Click cell M1, enter 830L, click cell M2, click the Lookup & Reference button in the Function Library group, then click VLOOKUP**
   The Function Arguments dialog box opens, with boxes for each of the VLOOKUP arguments. Because the value you want to find is in cell M1, M1 is the Lookup_value. The table you want to search is the table on the Lookup sheet, so its assigned name, Table2, is the Table_array.

QUICK TIP
If you want to find only the closest match for a value, enter TRUE in the Range_lookup text box. However, this can give misleading results if you are looking for an exact match. If you use FALSE and Excel can't find the value, you see an error message.

4. **With the insertion point in the Lookup_value text box, click cell M1, click the Table_array text box, then type Table2**
   The column containing the information that you want to find and display in cell M2 is the second column from the left in the table range, so the Col_index_num is 2. Because you want to find an exact match for the value in cell M1, the Range_lookup argument is FALSE.
5. **Click the Col_index_num text box, type 2, click the Range_lookup text box, then enter FALSE**
   Your completed Function Arguments dialog box should match **FIGURE H-11**.
6. **Click OK**
   Excel searches down the far-left column of the table until it finds a trip code that matches the one in cell M1. It then looks in column 2 of the table range and finds the tour for that record, Old Japan, and displays it in cell M2. You use this function to determine the tour for one other trip code.
7. **Click cell M1, type 325B, then click the Enter button ✓ on the formula bar**
   The VLOOKUP function returns the value of Biking In France in cell M2.
8. **Press [Ctrl][Home], then save the workbook**

Finding records using the DGET function

You can also use the DGET function to find a record in a table that matches specified criteria. For example, you could use the criteria of L1:L2 in the DGET function. When using DGET, you need to include [#All] after your table name in the formula to include the column labels that are used for the criteria range. Unlike VLOOKUP, you do not have the option of using a Range_Lookup value of TRUE to find an approximate match.

FIGURE H-10: Named ranges in the workbook

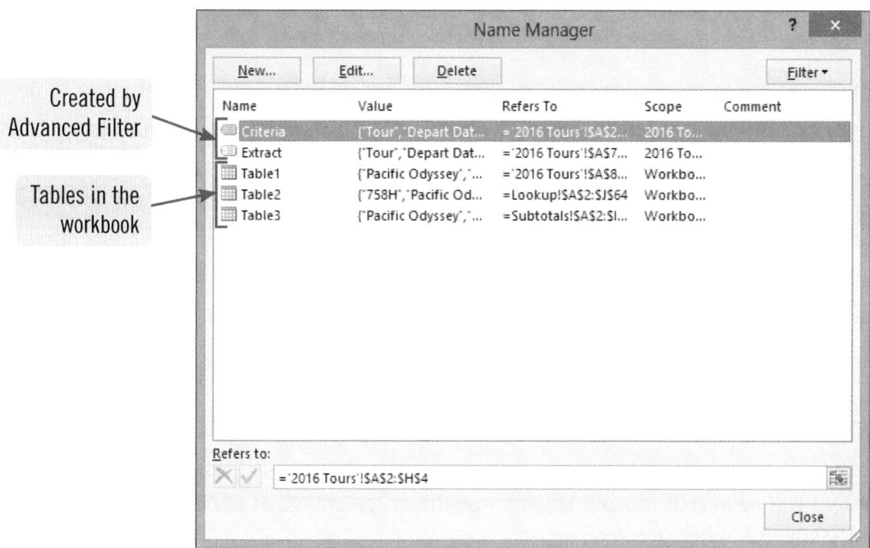

FIGURE H-11: Completed Function Arguments dialog box for VLOOKUP

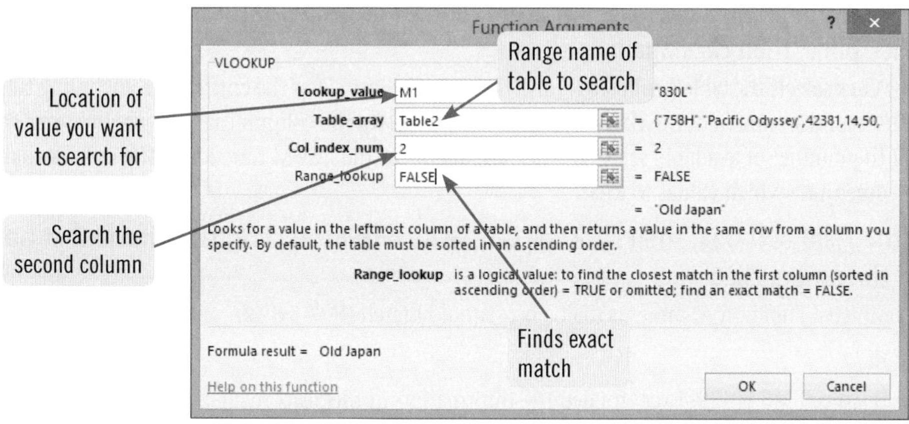

Using the HLOOKUP and MATCH functions

The VLOOKUP (Vertical Lookup) function is useful when your data is arranged vertically, in columns. When your data is arranged horizontally in rows, use the HLOOKUP (Horizontal Lookup) function. HLOOKUP searches horizontally across the upper row of a table until it finds the matching value, then looks down the number of rows you specify. The arguments for this function are identical to those for the VLOOKUP function, with one exception. Instead of a Col_index_number, HLOOKUP uses a Row_index_number, which indicates the location of the row you want to search. For example, if you want to search the fourth row from the top of the table range, the Row_index_number should be 4. You can use the MATCH function when you want the position of an item in a range. The MATCH function uses the syntax: MATCH (lookup_value,lookup_array,match_ type) where the lookup_value is the value you want to match in the lookup_array range. The match_type can be 0 for an exact match, 1 for matching the largest value that is less than or equal to lookup_value, or –1 for matching the smallest value that is greater than or equal to the lookup_value.

Summarize Table Data

Learning Outcomes
- Summarize table data using DSUM
- Summarize table data using DCOUNT or DCOUNTA

Because a table acts much like a database, database functions allow you to summarize table data in a variety of ways. When working with a sales activity table, for example, you can use Excel to count the number of client contacts by sales representative or to total the amount sold to specific accounts by month. TABLE H-1 lists database functions commonly used to summarize table data. **CASE** *Kate is considering adding tours for the 2016 schedule. She needs your help in evaluating the number of seats available for scheduled tours.*

STEPS

1. **Review the criteria range for the Yellowstone tour in the range L5:L6**

   The criteria range in L5:L6 tells Excel to summarize records with the entry "Yellowstone" in the Tour column. The functions will be in cells M8 and M9. You use this criteria range in a DSUM function to sum the seats available for only the Yellowstone tours.

2. **Click cell M8, click the Insert Function button in the Function Library group, in the Search for a function text box type database, click Go, scroll to and click DSUM under Select a function, then click OK**

   The first argument of the DSUM function is the table, or database.

> **QUICK TIP**
> Because the DSUM formula uses the column headings to locate and sum the table data, the header row needs to be included in the database range.

3. **In the Function Arguments dialog box, with the insertion point in the Database text box, move the pointer over the upper-left corner of cell A1 until the pointer becomes ↘, click once, then click again**

   The first click selects the table's data range, and the second click selects the entire table, including the header row. The second argument of the DSUM function is the label for the column that you want to sum. You want to total the number of available seats. The last argument for the DSUM function is the criteria that will be used to determine which values to total.

> **QUICK TIP**
> You can move the Function Arguments dialog box if it overlaps a cell or range that you need to click. You can also click the Collapse Dialog Box button, select the cell or range, then click the Expand Dialog Box button to return to the Function Arguments dialog box.

4. **Click the Field text box, then click cell G1, Seats Available; click the Criteria text box and select the range L5:L6**

   Your completed Function Arguments dialog box should match FIGURE H-12.

5. **Click OK**

   The result in cell M8 is 129. Excel totaled the information in the Seats Available column for those records that meet the criterion of Tour equals Yellowstone. The DCOUNT and the DCOUNTA functions can help you determine the number of records meeting specified criteria in a database field. DCOUNTA counts the number of nonblank cells. You will use DCOUNTA to determine the number of tours scheduled.

6. **Click cell M9, click the Insert Function button on the formula bar, in the Search for a function text box type database, click Go, select DCOUNTA from the Select a function list, then click OK**

7. **With the insertion point in the Database text box, move the pointer over the upper-left corner of cell A1 until the pointer becomes ↘, click once, click again to include the header row, click the Field text box and click cell B1, click the Criteria text box and select the range L5:L6, then click OK**

   The result in cell M9 is 5, and it indicates that there are five Yellowstone tours scheduled for the year. You also want to display the number of seats available for the Old Japan tours.

8. **Click cell L6, type Old Japan, then click the Enter button on the formula bar**

   FIGURE H-13 shows that 67 seats are available in the four Old Japan tours, and there are four tours scheduled.

FIGURE H-12: Completed Function Arguments dialog box for DSUM

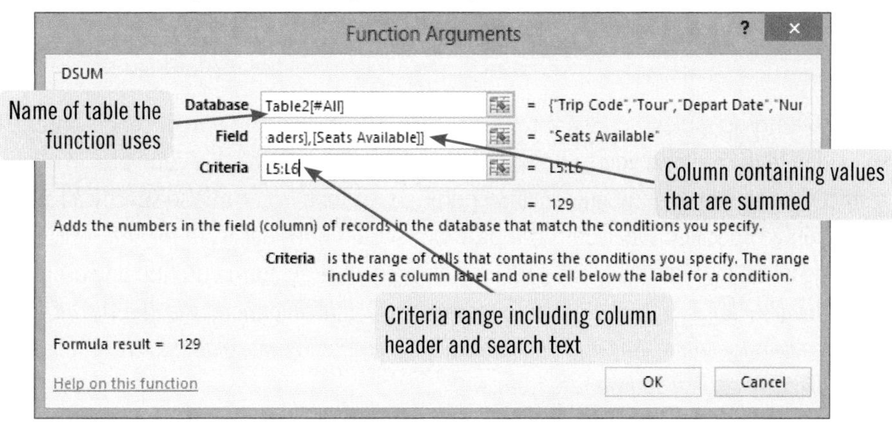

FIGURE H-13: Result generated by database functions

	G	H	I	J	K	L	M
1	Seats Available	Price	Air Included	Insurance Included		Trip Code	325B
2	0	$ 2,255	Yes	No		Tour	Biking in France
3	5	$ 1,984	Yes	No			
4	3	$ 1,966	Yes	Yes		Tour Information	
5	11	$ 1,850	Yes	Yes		Tour	
6	4	$ 2,134	No	No		Old Japan	
7	5	$ 2,812	Yes	No			
8	30	$ 2,350	Yes	No		Seats Available	67
9	4	$ 2,110	Yes	Yes		Number of tours scheduled	4
10	0	$ 1,755	Yes	Yes			
11	3	$ 2,450	No	No			

Information for Old Japan tours

TABLE H-1: Common database functions

function	result
DGET	Extracts a single record from a table that matches criteria you specify
DSUM	Totals numbers in a given table column that match criteria you specify
DAVERAGE	Averages numbers in a given table column that match criteria you specify
DCOUNT	Counts the cells that contain numbers in a given table column that match criteria you specify
DCOUNTA	Counts the cells that contain nonblank data in a given table column that match criteria you specify

Validate Table Data

Learning Outcomes
- Use data validation to restrict data entry to specified values
- Insert table data using data validation

When setting up tables, you want to help ensure accuracy when you or others enter data. The Excel data validation feature allows you to do this by specifying what data users can enter in a range of cells. You can restrict data to whole numbers, decimal numbers, or text. You can also specify a list of acceptable entries. Once you've specified what data the program should consider valid for that cell, Excel displays an error message when invalid data is entered and can prevent users from entering any other data that it considers to be invalid. **CASE** *Kate wants to make sure that information in the Air Included column is entered consistently in the future. She asks you to restrict the entries in that column to two options: Yes and No. First, you select the table column you want to restrict.*

STEPS

1. **Click the top edge of the Air Included column header**
   The column data is selected.
2. **Click the DATA tab, click the Data Validation button in the Data Tools group, click the Settings tab if necessary, click the Allow list arrow, then click List**
   Selecting the List option lets you type a list of specific options.
3. **Click the Source text box, then type Yes, No**
   You have entered the list of acceptable entries, separated by commas, as shown in **FIGURE H-14**. You want the data entry person to be able to select a valid entry from a drop-down list.
4. **Click the In-cell dropdown check box to select it if necessary, then click OK**
   The dialog box closes, and you return to the worksheet.
5. **Click the HOME tab, click any cell in the last table row, click the Insert list arrow in the Cells group, click Insert Table Row Below, click the last cell in the Air Included column, then click its list arrow to display the list of valid entries**
   The drop-down list is shown in **FIGURE H-15**. You could click an item in the list to have it entered in the cell, but you want to test the data restriction by entering an invalid entry.
6. **Click the list arrow to close the list, type Maybe, then press [Enter]**
   A warning dialog box appears and prevents you from entering the invalid data, as shown in **FIGURE H-16**.
7. **Click Cancel, click the list arrow, then click Yes**
   The cell accepts the valid entry. The data restriction ensures that records contain only one of the two correct entries in the Air Included column. The table is ready for future data entry.
8. **Delete the last table row, add your name to the center section of the footer, then save the workbook**

QUICK TIP
To specify a long list of valid entries, type the list in a column or row elsewhere in the worksheet, then type the list range in the Source text box.

TROUBLE
If you get an invalid data error, make sure that cell I1 is not included in the selection. If I1 is included, open the Data Validation dialog box, click Clear All, click OK, then begin with Step 1 again.

Restricting cell values and data length

In addition to providing an in-cell drop-down list for data entry, you can use data validation to restrict the values that are entered into cells. For example, if you want to restrict cells in a selected range to values less than a certain number, date, or time, click the DATA tab, click the Data Validation button in the Data Tools group, and on the Settings tab, click the Allow list arrow, select Whole number, Decimal, Date, or Time, click the Data list arrow, select less than, then in the bottom text box, enter the maximum value. You can also limit the length of data entered into cells by choosing Text length in the Allow list, clicking the Data list arrow and selecting less than, then entering the maximum length in the Maximum text box.

FIGURE H-14: Creating data restrictions

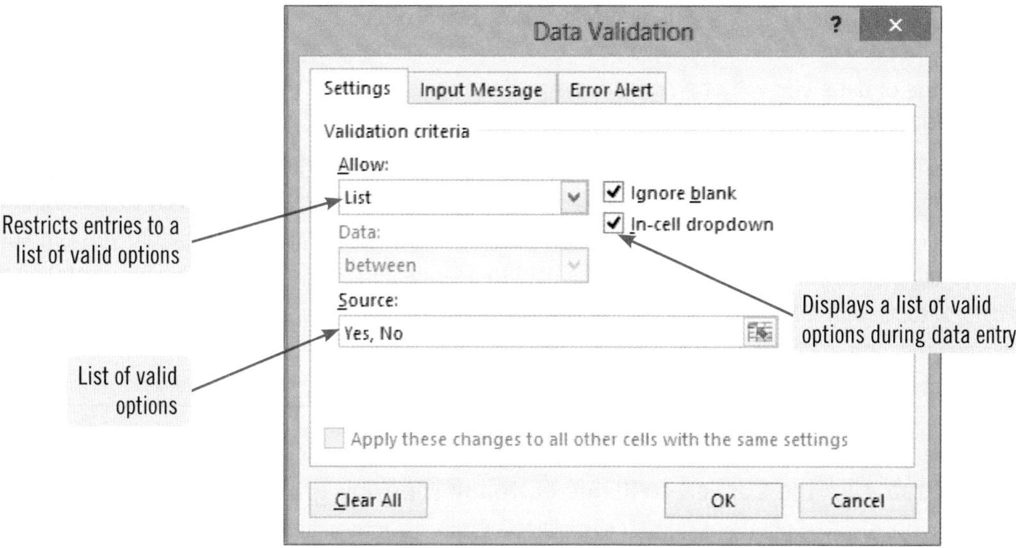

FIGURE H-15: Entering data in restricted cells

54	666B	Nepal Trekking	10/29/2016	14	18	8	10	$ 4,200	Yes	Yes
55	557N	Exotic Morocco	10/31/2016	7	38	15	23	$ 1,900	Yes	No
56	524Z	Experience Cambodia	10/31/2016	12	40	2	38	$ 2,908	Yes	No
57	509V	Treasures of Ethiopia	11/18/2016	10	41	12	29	$ 2,200	Yes	Yes
58	397S	Panama Adventure	12/18/2016	10	50	21	29	$ 2,204	Yes	Yes
59	621R	Panama Adventure	12/18/2016	10	50	21	29	$ 2,204	Yes	Yes
60	592D	Galapagos Adventure	12/20/2016	14	15	1	14	$ 2,100	Yes	Yes
61	793T	Galapagos Adventure	12/20/2016	14	15	1	14	$ 2,100	Yes	Yes
62	307R	Pacific Odyssey	12/21/2016	14	50	10	40	$ 2,105	Yes	No
63	927F	Yellowstone	12/30/2016	18	51	15	36	$ 2,922	Yes	Yes
64	448G	Old Japan	12/31/2016	21	47	4	43	$ 2,100	Yes	No
65							0			
66									Yes No	

Dropdown list

FIGURE H-16: Invalid data warning

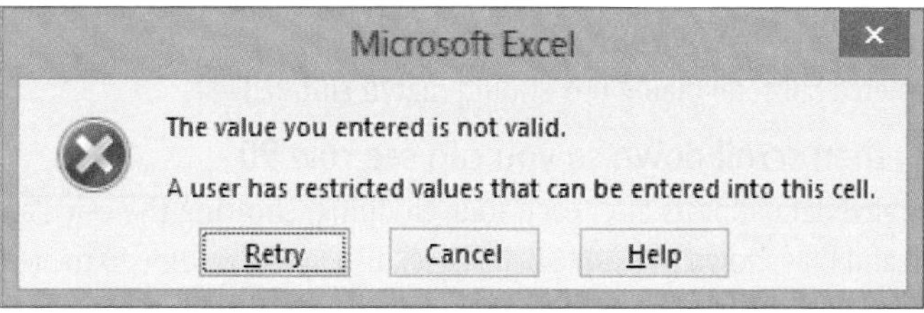

Adding input messages and error alerts

You can customize the way data validation works by using the two other tabs in the Data Validation dialog box: Input Message and Error Alert. The Input Message tab lets you set a message that appears when the user selects that cell. For example, the message might contain instructions about what type of data to enter. On the Input Message tab, enter a message title and message, then click OK. The Error Alert tab lets you set one of three alert levels if a user enters invalid data. The Information level displays your message with the information icon but allows the user to proceed with data entry. The Warning level displays your information with the warning icon and gives the user the option to proceed with data entry or not. The Stop level, which you used in this lesson, displays your message and only lets the user retry or cancel data entry for that cell.

Create Subtotals

Learning Outcomes
- Summarize worksheet data using subtotals
- Use outline symbols
- Convert a table to a range

In a large range of data, you will often need ways to perform calculations that summarize groups within the data. For example, you might need to subtotal the sales for several sales reps listed in a table. The Excel Subtotals feature provides a quick, easy way to group and summarize a range of data. It lets you create not only subtotals using the SUM function, but other statistics as well, including COUNT, AVERAGE, MAX, and MIN. However, subtotals cannot be used in an Excel table, nor can it rearrange data. Before you can add subtotals to table data, you must first convert the data to a range and sort it. **CASE** *Kate wants you to group data by tours, with subtotals for the number of seats available and the number of seats reserved. You begin by converting the table to a range.*

STEPS

1. **Click the Subtotals sheet tab, click any cell inside the table, click the TABLE TOOLS DESIGN tab, click the Convert to Range button in the Tools group, then click Yes**
   The filter list arrows and the TABLE TOOLS DESIGN tab no longer appear. Before you can add the subtotals, you must first sort the data. You decide to sort it in ascending order, first by tour and then by departure date.
2. **Click the DATA tab, click the Sort button in the Sort & Filter group, in the Sort dialog box click the Sort by list arrow, click Tour, click the Add Level button, click the Then by list arrow, click Depart Date, verify that the order is Oldest to Newest, then click OK**
   You have sorted the range in ascending order, first by tour, then by departure date within each tour grouping.
3. **Click any cell in the data range if necessary, then click the Subtotal button in the Outline group**
   The Subtotal dialog box opens. Here you specify the items you want subtotaled, the function you want to apply to the values, and the fields you want to summarize.
4. **Click the At each change in list arrow, click Tour if necessary, click the Use function list arrow, click Sum; in the "Add subtotal to" list, click the Seats Reserved and Seats Available check boxes to select them, if necessary, then click the Insurance Included check box to deselect it**
5. **If necessary, click the Replace current subtotals and Summary below data check boxes to select them**
   Your completed Subtotal dialog box should match **FIGURE H-17**.
6. **Click OK, then scroll down so you can see row 90**
   The subtotaled data appears after each tour grouping, showing the calculated subtotals and grand total in columns E and F, as shown in **FIGURE H-18**. Excel displays an outline to the left of the worksheet, with outline buttons to control the level of detail that appears. The button number corresponds to the detail level that is displayed. You want to show the second level of detail, the subtotals and the grand total.
7. **Click the outline symbol [2]**
   Only the subtotals and the grand total appear.
8. **Add your name to the center section of the footer, preview the worksheet, click the No Scaling list arrow, click Fit Sheet on One Page to scale the worksheet to print on one page, then save the workbook**
9. **Close the workbook, exit Excel, then submit the workbook to your instructor**

QUICK TIP
You can click the [−] button to hide or the [+] button to show a group of records in the subtotaled structure.

QUICK TIP
You can remove subtotals in a worksheet by clicking the Subtotal button and clicking Remove All. The subtotals no longer appear, and the Outline feature is turned off automatically.

FIGURE H-17: Completed Subtotal dialog box

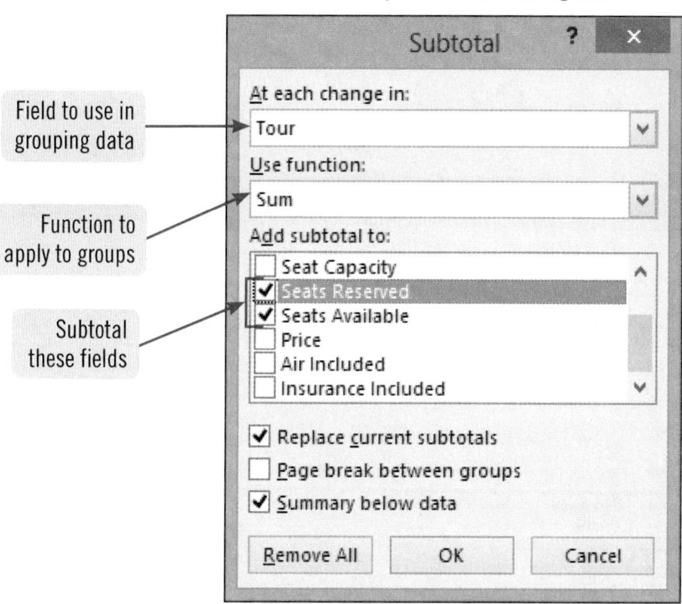

FIGURE H-18: Portion of subtotaled table

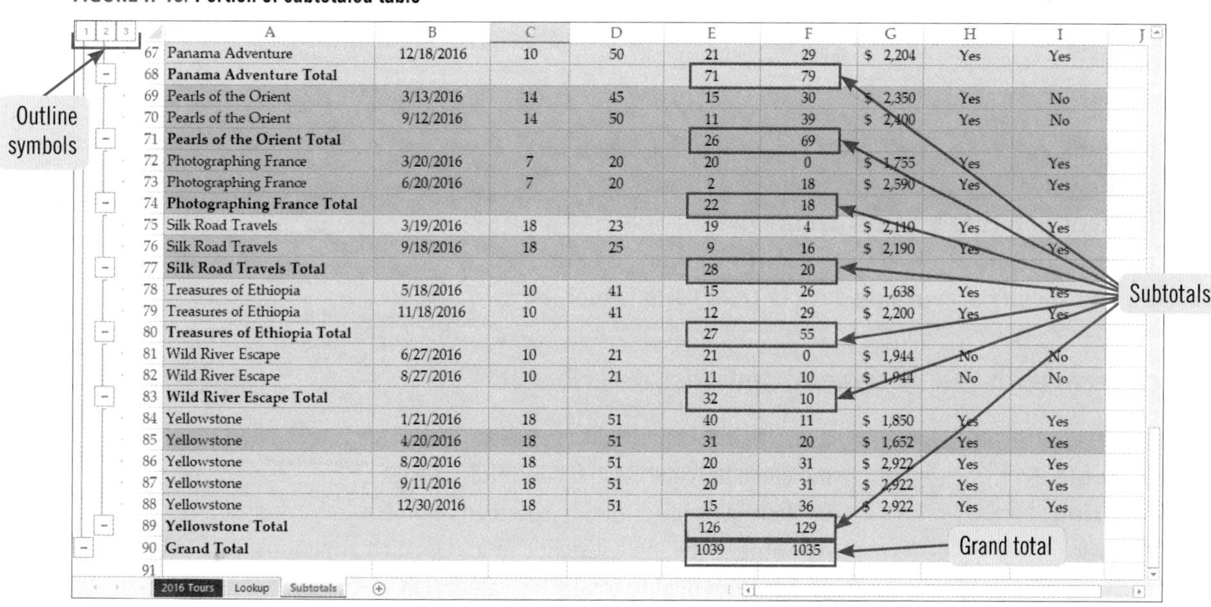

	A	B	C	D	E	F	G	H	I
67	Panama Adventure	12/18/2016	10	50	21	29	$ 2,204	Yes	Yes
68	**Panama Adventure Total**				71	79			
69	Pearls of the Orient	3/13/2016	14	45	15	30	$ 2,350	Yes	No
70	Pearls of the Orient	9/12/2016	14	50	11	39	$ 2,400	Yes	No
71	**Pearls of the Orient Total**				26	69			
72	Photographing France	3/20/2016	7	20	20	0	$ 1,755	Yes	Yes
73	Photographing France	6/20/2016	7	20	2	18	$ 2,590	Yes	Yes
74	**Photographing France Total**				22	18			
75	Silk Road Travels	3/19/2016	18	23	19	4	$ 2,110	Yes	Yes
76	Silk Road Travels	9/18/2016	18	25	9	16	$ 2,190	Yes	Yes
77	**Silk Road Travels Total**				28	20			
78	Treasures of Ethiopia	5/18/2016	10	41	15	26	$ 1,638	Yes	Yes
79	Treasures of Ethiopia	11/18/2016	10	41	12	29	$ 2,200	Yes	Yes
80	**Treasures of Ethiopia Total**				27	55			
81	Wild River Escape	6/27/2016	10	21	21	0	$ 1,944	No	No
82	Wild River Escape	8/27/2016	10	21	11	10	$ 1,944	No	No
83	**Wild River Escape Total**				32	10			
84	Yellowstone	1/21/2016	18	51	40	11	$ 1,850	Yes	Yes
85	Yellowstone	4/20/2016	18	51	31	20	$ 1,652	Yes	Yes
86	Yellowstone	8/20/2016	18	51	20	31	$ 2,922	Yes	Yes
87	Yellowstone	9/11/2016	18	51	20	31	$ 2,922	Yes	Yes
88	Yellowstone	12/30/2016	18	51	15	36	$ 2,922	Yes	Yes
89	**Yellowstone Total**				126	129			
90	**Grand Total**				1039	1035			
91									

Practice

Put your skills into practice with **SAM Projects!** SAM Projects for this unit can be found online. If you have a SAM account, go to www.cengage.com/sam2013 to download the most recent Project Instruction and Start Files.

Concepts Review

FIGURE H-19

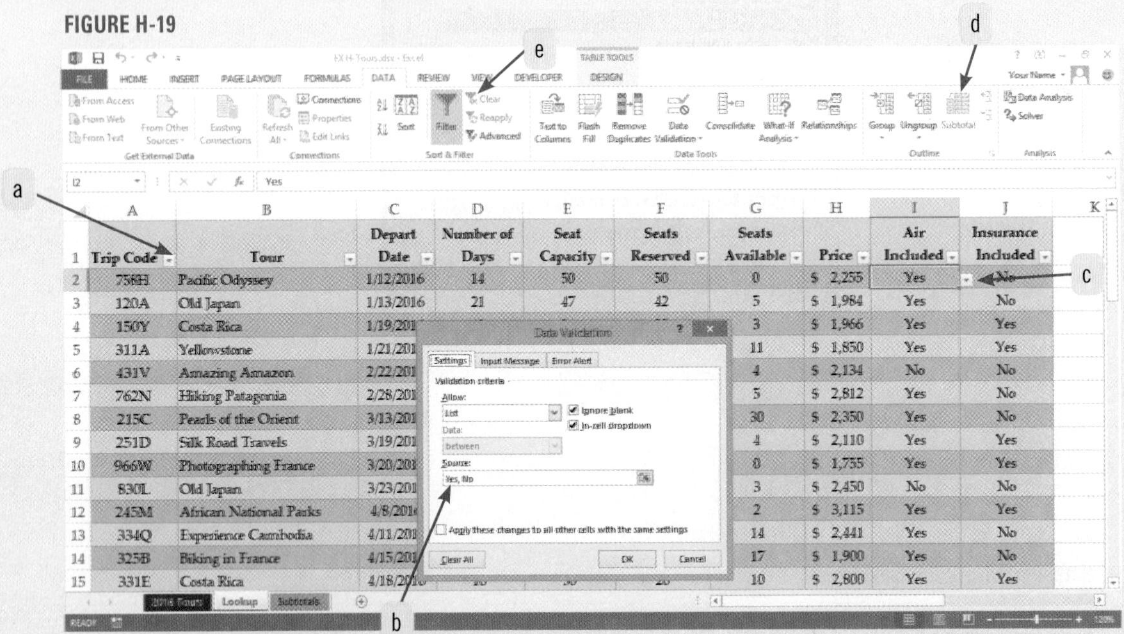

1. Which element points to an in-cell drop-down list arrow?

2. Which element would you click to remove a filter?

3. Which element points to a field's list arrow?

4. Which element do you click to group and summarize data?

5. Where do you specify acceptable data entries for a table?

Match each term with the statement that best describes it.

6. Table_array

7. Extracted table

8. Data validation

9. Criteria range

10. DSUM

a. Cell range when Advanced Filter results are copied to another location

b. Range in which search conditions are set

c. Restricts table entries to specified options

d. Name of the table searched in a VLOOKUP function

e. Function used to total table values that meet specified criteria

Select the best answer from the list of choices.

11. The ________ logical condition finds records matching both listed criteria.

a. True

b. Or

c. And

d. False

12. What does it mean when you select the Or option when creating a custom filter?

a. Both criteria must be true to find a match.

b. Neither criterion has to be 100% true.

c. Either criterion can be true to find a match.

d. A custom filter requires a criteria range.

13. **What must a data range have before subtotals can be inserted?**
    - **a.** Enough records to show multiple subtotals
    - **b.** Sorted data
    - **c.** Formatted cells
    - **d.** Grand totals
14. **Which function finds the position of an item in a table?**
    - **a.** VLOOKUP
    - **b.** MATCH
    - **c.** DGET
    - **d.** HLOOKUP

Skills Review

1. **Filter a table.**
    - **a.** Start Excel, open the file EX H-2.xlsx from the location where you store your Data Files, then save it as **EX H-Compensation**.
    - **b.** With the Compensation sheet active, filter the table to list only records for employees in the Boston branch.
    - **c.** Clear the filter, then add a filter that displays the records for employees in the Boston and Philadelphia branches.
    - **d.** Redisplay all employees, then use a filter to show the three employees with the highest annual salary.
    - **e.** Redisplay all the records.
2. **Create a custom filter.**
    - **a.** Create a custom filter showing employees hired before 1/1/2013 or after 12/31/2013.
    - **b.** Create a custom filter showing employees hired between 1/1/2013 and 12/31/2013.
    - **c.** Enter your name in the worksheet footer, then preview the filtered worksheet.
    - **d.** Redisplay all records.
    - **e.** Save the workbook.
3. **Filter and extract a table with the Advanced Filter.**
    - **a.** You want to retrieve a list of employees who were hired before 1/1/2014 and who have an annual salary of more than $75,000 a year. Define a criteria range by inserting six new rows above the table on the worksheet and copying the field names into the first row.
    - **b.** In cell D2, enter the criterion **<1/1/2014**, then in cell G2 enter **>75000**.
    - **c.** Click any cell in the table.
    - **d.** Open the Advanced Filter dialog box.
    - **e.** Indicate that you want to copy to another location, enter the criteria range **A1:J2**, verify that the List range is $A$7:$J$17, then indicate that you want to place the extracted list in the range starting at cell **A20**.
    - **f.** Confirm that the retrieved list meets the criteria as shown in **FIGURE H-20**.
    - **g.** Save the workbook, then preview the worksheet.

FIGURE H-20

	A	B	C	D	E	F	G	H	I	J
1	Employee Number	First Name	Last Name	Hire Date	Branch	Monthly Salary	Annual Salary	Annual Bonus	Benefits Dollars	Annual Compensation
2				<1/1/2014			>75000			
3										
4										
5										
6										
7	Employee Number	First Name	Last Name	Hire Date	Branch	Monthly Salary	Annual Salary	Annual Bonus	Benefits Dollars	Annual Compensation
8	1211	Mary	Lane	2/12/2013	New York	$ 4,650	$ 55,800	$ 1,370	$ 12,834	$ 70,004
9	4515	Leanne	Waters	4/1/2014	Boston	$ 5,970	$ 71,640	$ 5,725	$ 16,477	$ 93,842
10	4187	Debbie	Davie	5/6/2012	Philadelphia	$ 7,550	$ 90,600	$ 6,525	$ 20,838	$ 117,963
11	2599	Martha	Macky	12/10/2013	Boston	$ 8,450	$ 101,400	$ 7,550	$ 23,322	$ 132,272
12	2213	Jake	Green	2/15/2015	Boston	$ 2,950	$ 35,400	$ 680	$ 8,142	$ 44,222
13	6588	Paul	Early	3/25/2013	New York	$ 2,750	$ 33,000	$ 630	$ 7,590	$ 41,220
14	2120	Ellen	Meeb	6/23/2012	New York	$ 4,225	$ 50,700	$ 1,320	$ 11,661	$ 63,681
15	4450	Mark	Mollen	8/3/2015	Philadelphia	$ 6,750	$ 81,000	$ 5,900	$ 18,630	$ 105,530
16	9887	Hank	Randal	9/29/2014	Philadelphia	$ 8,500	$ 102,000	$ 7,650	$ 23,460	$ 133,110
17	3955	Jen	Richards	5/12/2013	Boston	$ 3,750	$ 45,000	$ 795	$ 10,350	$ 56,145
18										
19										
20	Employee Number	First Name	Last Name	Hire Date	Branch	Monthly Salary	Annual Salary	Annual Bonus	Benefits Dollars	Annual Compensation
21	4187	Debbie	Davie	5/6/2012	Philadelphia	$ 7,550	$ 90,600	$ 6,525	$ 20,838	$ 117,963
22	2599	Martha	Macky	12/10/2013	Boston	$ 8,450	$ 101,400	$ 7,550	$ 23,322	$ 132,272
23										

Excel 2013

Skills Review (continued)

4. Look up values in a table.

- **a.** Click the Summary sheet tab. Use the Name Manager to view the table names in the workbook, then close the dialog box.
- **b.** You will use a lookup function to locate an employee's annual compensation; enter the Employee Number **2213** in cell A17.
- **c.** In cell B17, use the VLOOKUP function and enter **A17** as the Lookup_value, **Table2** as the Table_array, **10** as the Col_index_num, and **FALSE** as the Range_lookup; observe the compensation displayed for that employee number, then check it against the table to make sure it is correct.
- **d.** Replace the existing Employee Number in cell A17 with **4187**, and view the annual compensation for that employee.
- **e.** Format cell B17 with the Accounting format with the $ symbol and no decimal places.
- **f.** Save the workbook.

5. Summarize table data.

- **a.** You want to enter a database function to average the annual salaries by branch, using the New York branch as the initial criterion. In cell E17, use the DAVERAGE function, and click the upper-left corner of cell A1 twice to select the table and its header row as the Database, select cell G1 for the Field, and select the range D16:D17 for the Criteria. Verify that the average New York salary is 46500.
- **b.** Test the function further by entering the text **Philadelphia** in cell D17. When the criterion is entered, cell E17 should display 91200.
- **c.** Format cell E17 in Accounting format with the $ symbol and no decimal places.
- **d.** Save the workbook.

6. Validate table data.

- **a.** Select the data in column E of the table, and set a validation criterion specifying that you want to allow a list of valid options.
- **b.** Enter a list of valid options that restricts the entries to **New York**, **Boston**, and **Philadelphia**. Remember to use a comma between each item in the list.
- **c.** Indicate that you want the options to appear in an in-cell drop-down list, then close the dialog box.
- **d.** Add a row to the table. Go to cell E12, then select Boston in the drop-down list.
- **e.** Select the data in column F in the table, and indicate that you want to restrict the data entered to only whole numbers. In the Minimum text box, enter **1000**; in the Maximum text box, enter **10000**. Close the dialog box.
- **f.** Click cell F12, enter **15000**, then press [Enter]. You should get an error message.
- **g.** Click Cancel, then enter **7000**.
- **h.** Complete the new record by adding an Employee Number of **1119**, a First Name of **Cate**, a Last Name of **Smith**, a Hire Date of **2/1/2016**, and an Annual Bonus of **$5000**. Format the range F12:J12 as Accounting with no decimal places and using the $ symbol. Compare your screen to **FIGURE H-21**.
- **i.** Add your name to the center section of the footer, save the worksheet, then preview the worksheet.

FIGURE H-21

	A	B	C	D	E	F	G	H	I	J
1	Employee Number	First Name	Last Name	Hire Date	Branch	Monthly Salary	Annual Salary	Annual Bonus	Benefits Dollars	Annual Compensation
2	1211	Mary	Lane	2/12/2013	New York	$ 4,650	$ 55,800	$ 1,370	$ 12,834	$ 70,004
3	4515	Leanne	Waters	4/1/2014	Boston	$ 5,970	$ 71,640	$ 5,725	$ 16,477	$ 93,842
4	4187	Debbie	Davie	5/6/2012	Philadelphia	$ 7,550	$ 90,600	$ 6,525	$ 20,838	$ 117,963
5	2599	Martha	Macky	12/10/2013	Boston	$ 8,450	$101,400	$ 7,550	$ 23,322	$ 132,272
6	2213	Jake	Green	2/15/2015	Boston	$ 2,950	$ 35,400	$ 680	$ 8,142	$ 44,222
7	6588	Paul	Early	3/25/2013	New York	$ 2,750	$ 33,000	$ 630	$ 7,590	$ 41,220
8	2120	Ellen	Meeb	6/23/2012	New York	$ 4,225	$ 50,700	$ 1,320	$ 11,661	$ 63,681
9	4450	Mark	Mollen	8/3/2015	Philadelphia	$ 6,750	$ 81,000	$ 5,900	$ 18,630	$ 105,530
10	9887	Hank	Randal	9/29/2014	Philadelphia	$ 8,500	$102,000	$ 7,650	$ 23,460	$ 133,110
11	3955	Jen	Richards	5/12/2013	Boston	$ 3,750	$ 45,000	$ 795	$ 10,350	$ 56,145
12	1119	Cate	Smith	2/1/2016	Boston	$ 7,000	$ 84,000	$ 5,000	$ 19,320	$ 108,320
13										
14										
15										
16	Employee Number	Annual Compensation		Branch	Average Annual Salary					
17	4187	$ 117,963		Philadelphia	$ 91,200					
18										

Skills Review (continued)

7. Create subtotals.

- **a.** Click the Subtotals sheet tab.
- **b.** Use the Branch field list arrow to sort the table in ascending order by branch.
- **c.** Convert the table to a range.
- **d.** Group and create subtotals of the Annual Compensation data by branch, using the SUM function.
- **e.** Click the 2 outline button on the outline to display only the subtotals and the grand total. Compare your screen to **FIGURE H-22**.
- **f.** Enter your name in the worksheet footer, save the workbook, then preview the worksheet.
- **g.** Save the workbook, close the workbook, exit Excel, then submit your workbook to your instructor.

FIGURE H-22

	A	B	C	D	E	F	G	H	I	J
1	Employee Number	First Name	Last Name	Hire Date	Branch	Monthly Salary	Annual Salary	Annual Bonus	Benefits Dollars	Annual Compensation
6					Boston Total					$ 326,481
10					New York Total					$ 174,905
14					Philadelphia Total					$ 356,603
15					Grand Total					$ 857,989
16										

Independent Challenge 1

As the manager of Miami Dental, a dental supply company, you spend a lot of time managing your inventory. To help with this task, you have created an Excel table that you can extract information from using filters. You also need to add data validation and summary information to the table.

- **a.** Start Excel, open the file EX H-3.xlsx from the location where you store your Data Files, then save it as **EX H-Dental**.
- **b.** Using the table data on the Inventory sheet, create a filter to display information about only the product bond refill. Clear the filter.
- **c.** Use a Custom Filter to generate a list of products with a quantity greater than 15. Clear the filter.
- **d.** Copy the labels in cells A1:F1 into A16:F16. Type **Retention Pins** in cell A17, and type **Small** in cell C17. Use the Advanced Filter with a criteria range of A16:F17 to extract a table of small retention pins to the range of cells beginning in cell A20. Enter your name in the worksheet footer, save the workbook, then preview the worksheet.
- **e.** On the Summary sheet tab, select the table data in column B. Open the Data Validation dialog box, then indicate you want to use a validation list with the acceptable entries of **Barnes**, **Blake**, **Lyon**, **Maxwell**. Make sure the In-cell dropdown check box is selected.
- **f.** Test the data validation by trying to change a cell in column B of the table to **Lane**.
- **g.** Using **FIGURE H-23** as a guide, enter a function in cell E18 that calculates the total quantity of bond refill available in your inventory. Enter your name in the worksheet footer, preview the worksheet, then save the workbook.
- **h.** On the Subtotals sheet, sort the table in ascending order by product. Convert the table to a range. Insert subtotals by product using the Sum function, then select Quantity in the "Add Subtotal to" box. Remove the check box for the Total field, if necessary. Use the appropriate button on the outline to display only the subtotals and grand total. Save the workbook, then preview the worksheet.
- **i.** Submit the workbook to your instructor. Close the workbook, then exit Excel.

FIGURE H-23

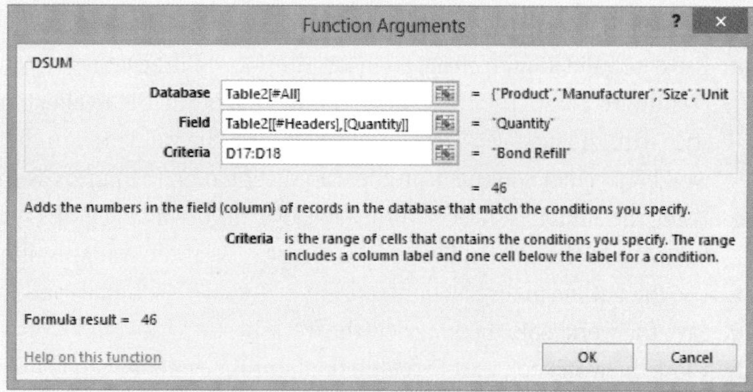

Excel 2013

Independent Challenge 2

As the senior accountant at Cambridge Electrical Supply you are adding new features to the company's accounts receivables workbook. The business supplies both residential and commercial electricians. You have put together an invoice table to track sales for the month of June. Now that you have this table, you would like to manipulate it in several ways. First, you want to filter the table to show only invoices over a certain amount with certain order dates. You also want to subtotal the total column by residential and commercial supplies. To prevent data entry errors you will restrict entries in the Order Date column. Finally, you would like to add database and lookup functions to your worksheet to efficiently retrieve data from the table.

a. Start Excel, open the file EX H-4.xlsx from the location where you store your Data Files, then save it as **EX H-Invoices**.

b. Use the Advanced Filter to show invoices with amounts more than $100.00 ordered before 6/15/2016, using cells A27:B28 to enter your criteria and extracting the results to cell A33. (*Hint*: You don't need to specify an entire row as the criteria range.) Enter your name in the worksheet footer.

c. Use the Data Validation dialog box to restrict entries to those with order dates between 6/1/2016 and 6/30/2016. Test the data restrictions by attempting to enter an invalid date in cell B25.

d. Enter **23698** in cell G28. Enter a VLOOKUP function in cell H28 to retrieve the total based on the invoice number entered in cell G28. Make sure you have an exact match with the invoice number. Format H28 using Accounting format with two decimal places. Test the function with the invoice number 23720.

e. Enter the date **6/1/2016** in cell J28. Use the database function, DCOUNT, in cell K28 to count the number of invoices for the date in cell J28. Save the workbook, then preview the worksheet.

f. On the Subtotals worksheet, sort the table in ascending order by Type, then convert the table to a range. Create subtotals showing the totals for commercial and residential invoices. Display only the subtotals for the commercial and residential accounts along with the grand total.

g. Save the workbook, preview the worksheet, close the workbook, then exit Excel. Submit the workbook to your instructor.

Independent Challenge 3

You are the manager of Nest, a paint and decorating store. You have created an Excel table that contains your order data, along with the amounts for each item ordered and the date the order was placed. You would like to manipulate this table to display product categories and ordered items meeting specific criteria. You would also like to add subtotals to the table and add database functions to total orders. Finally, you want to restrict entries in the Category column.

a. Start Excel, open the file EX H-5.xlsx from the location where you store your Data Files, then save it as **EX H-Nest**.

b. Create an advanced filter that extracts records with the following criteria to cell A42: orders greater than $1500 having dates either before 9/10/2016 or after 9/19/2016. (*Hint*: Recall that when you want records to meet one criterion or another, you need to place the criteria on separate lines.)

c. Use the DSUM function in cell H2 to let worksheet users find the total order amounts for the category entered in cell G2. Format the cell containing the total order using the Accounting format with the $ symbol and no decimals. Test the DSUM function using the Paint category name. (The sum for the Paint category should be $11,558.) Preview the worksheet.

d. Use data validation to create an in-cell drop-down list that restricts category entries to "Paint", "Wallpaper", "Hardware", and "Tile". Use the Error Alert tab of the Data Validation dialog box to set the alert level to the Warning style with the message "Data is not valid." Test the validation in the table with valid and invalid entries. Save the workbook, enter your name in the worksheet footer, then preview the worksheet.

e. Using the Subtotals sheet, sort the table by category in ascending order. Convert the table to a range, and add Subtotals to the order amounts by category. Widen the columns, if necessary.

f. Use the outline to display only category names with subtotals and the grand total.

g. Save the workbook, then preview the worksheet.

h. Close the workbook, exit Excel, then submit the workbook to your instructor.

Independent Challenge 4: Explore

You are an inventory manager at American Eyewear, an eyewear distributor. You track your inventory of eye products in an Excel worksheet. You would like to use conditional formatting in your worksheet to help track the products that need to be reordered as well as your inventory expenses. You would also like to prevent data entry errors using data validation. Finally, you would like to add an area to quickly lookup prices and quantities for customers.

a. Start Excel, open the file EX H-6.xlsx from the location where you store your Data Files, then save it as **EX H-Eyewear**.

b. Use conditional formatting to add icons to the quantity field using the following criteria: quantities greater than or equal to 300 are formatted with a green circle, quantities greater than or equal to 100 but less than 300 are formatted with a yellow circle, and quantities less than 100 are formatted with a red circle. If your icons are incorrect, select the data in the Quantity field, click the Conditional Formatting button in the Styles group of the HOME tab, click Manage Rules, click the Show formatting for list arrow, select Current Selection, then double click Icon Set and compare your formatting rule to **FIGURE H-24**. (*Hint*: You may need to click in the top Value text box for the correct value to display for the red circle.)

FIGURE H-24

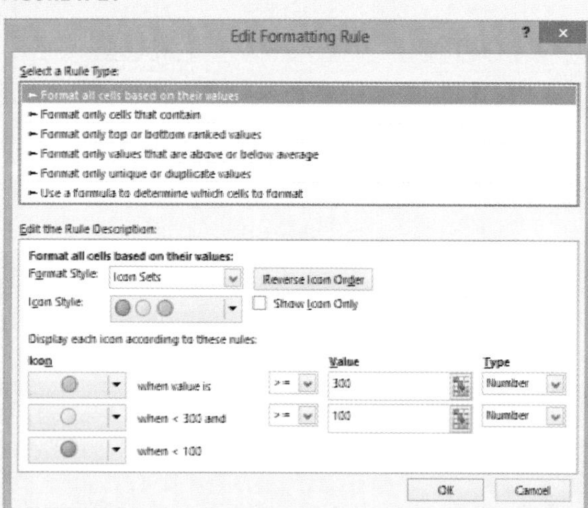

c. Conditionally format the Total data using Top/Bottom Rules to emphasize the cells containing the top 30 percent with red text.

d. Add another rule to format the bottom 20 percent in the Total column with purple text.

e. Restrict the Wholesale Price field entries to decimal values between 0 and 100. Add an input message of **Prices must be less than $100**. Add a Warning-level error message of **Please check price**. Test the validation entering a price of $105 in cell D3 and allow the new price to be entered.

f. Below the table, create a product lookup area with the following labels in adjacent cells: **Product Number**, **Wholesale Price**, **Quantity**.

g. Enter 1544 under the label Product Number in your products lookup area.

h. In the product lookup area, enter lookup functions to locate the wholesale price and quantity information for the product number that you entered in the previous step. Make sure you match the product number exactly. Format the wholesale price with the Accounting format with the $ symbol and two decimal places.

i. Enter your name in the center section of the worksheet header, save the workbook then preview the worksheet comparing it to **FIGURE H-25**.

j. Close the workbook, exit Excel, then submit the workbook to your instructor.

FIGURE H-25

Your Name

American Eyewear

Product Number	Category	Vendor	Wholesale Price	Quantity	Total
1122	Reading Glasses	Berkley	$105.00	125	$13,125.00
1132	Reading Glasses	Mallory	$10.66	68	$724.88
1184	Sports Eyewear	Bromen	$18.21	187	$3,405.27
1197	Sunglasses	Lincoln	$32.22	210	$6,766.20
1225	Frames	Berkley	$33.99	87	$2,957.13
1267	Frames	Mallory	$34.19	240	$8,205.60
1298	Sports Eyewear	Berkley	$21.97	375	$8,238.75
1345	Reading Glasses	Lincoln	$21.88	105	$2,297.40
1367	Safety Goggles	Lincoln	$17.18	168	$2,886.24
1398	Sports Eyewear	Bromen	$30.39	97	$2,947.83
1422	Sunglasses	Lincoln	$25.19	157	$3,954.83
1436	Cases	Mallory	$5.12	81	$414.72
1445	Sunglasses	Rand	$45.20	150	$6,780.00
1456	Custom	Berkley	$82.33	377	$31,038.41
1498	Safety Goggles	Rand	$19.22	51	$980.22
1521	Cases	Lincoln	$7.84	87	$682.08
1531	Lenses	Lincoln	$40.34	197	$7,946.98
1544	Reading Glasses	Bromen	$23.01	472	$10,860.72
1556	Frames	Bromen	$45.06	12	$540.72
1569	Sports Eyewear	Rand	$17.36	178	$3,090.08
1578	Sunglasses	Mallory	$63.22	35	$2,212.70
1622	Reading Glasses	Mallory	$25.33	874	$22,138.42
1634	Cases	Berkley	$18.47	501	$9,253.47
1657	Sunglasses	Bromen	$34.55	10	$345.50
1688	Safety Goggles	Rand	$18.66	73	$1,362.18
1723	Reading Glasses	Rand	$8.64	534	$4,613.76
1736	Sports Eyewear	Bromen	$25.66	15	$384.90
1798	Sports Eyewear	Mallory	$32.78	640	$20,979.20
1822	Cases	Mallory	$17.44	86	$1,499.84

Product Number	Wholesale Price	Quantity
1544	$ 23.01	472

Excel 2013

Visual Workshop

Open the file EX H-7.xlsx from the location where you save your Data Files, then save it as **EX H-Schedule**. Complete the worksheet as shown in **FIGURE H-26**. An in-cell drop-down list has been added to the data entered in the Room field. The range A18:G21 is extracted from the table using the criteria in cells A15:A16. Add your name to the worksheet footer, save the workbook, preview the worksheet, then submit the workbook to your instructor.

FIGURE H-26

	A	B	C	D	E	F	G
1	Spring 2016 Schedule of Yoga Classes						
2							
3	Class Code	Class	Time	Day	Room	Fee	Instructor
4	YOG100	Basics	7:30 AM	Monday	Mat Room	$15	Malloy
5	YOG101	Power	8:00 AM	Tuesday	Equipment Room	$20	Gregg
6	YOG102	Hatha	9:00 AM	Wednesday	Mat Room	$15	Malloy
7	YOG103	Kripalu	10:00 AM	Monday	Mat Room	$15	Brent
8	YOG104	Basics	11:00 AM	Friday	Mat Room	$15	Paulson
9	YOG105	Power	12:00 PM	Saturday	Equipment Room	$20	Dally
10	YOG106	Hatha	12:00 PM	Tuesday	Mat Room	$15	Rand
11	YOG107	Power	2:00 PM	Monday	Equipment Room	$20	Walton
12	YOG108	Basics	4:00 PM	Tuesday	Mat Room	15	Malloy
13					Please select Mat Room or Equipment Room		
14							
15	Class						
16	Basics						
17							
18	Class Code	Class	Time	Day	Room	Fee	Instructor
19	YOG100	Basics	7:30 AM	Monday	Mat Room	$15	Malloy
20	YOG104	Basics	11:00 AM	Friday	Mat Room	$15	Paulson
21	YOG108	Basics	4:00 PM	Tuesday	Mat Room	$15	Malloy
22							

Automating Worksheet Tasks

CASE Kate Morgan, the North America regional vice president of sales at Quest, wants you to automate a task in the sales workbooks by creating a macro for the sales division. Kate sees this as a timesaver for the sales group. The macro will automatically insert text that identifies the worksheet as a sales division document.

Unit Objectives

After completing this unit, you will be able to:

- Plan a macro
- Enable a macro
- Record a macro
- Run a macro
- Edit a macro
- Assign keyboard shortcuts to macros
- Use the Personal Macro Workbook
- Assign a macro to a button

Files You Will Need

EX I-1.xlsx
EX I-2.xlsm
EX I-3.xlsx

Plan a Macro

Learning Outcomes
- Plan a macro
- Determine the storage location for a macro

A **macro** is a named set of instructions you can create that performs tasks automatically, in an order you specify. You create macros to automate Excel tasks that you perform frequently. For example, you can create a macro to enter and format text or to save and print a worksheet. To create a macro, you record the series of actions using the macro recorder built into Excel, or you write the instructions in a special programming language. Because the sequence of actions in a macro is important, you need to plan the macro carefully before you record it. **CASE** *Kate wants you to create a macro for the sales division that inserts the text "Quest Sales" in the upper-left corner of any worksheet. You work with her to plan the macro.*

DETAILS

To plan a macro, use the following guidelines:

- **Assign the macro a descriptive name**
  The first character of a macro name must be a letter; the remaining characters can be letters, numbers, or underscores. Letters can be uppercase or lowercase. Spaces are not allowed in macro names; use underscores in place of spaces. Press [Shift][-] to enter an underscore character. Kate wants you to name the macro "DivStamp". See **TABLE I-1** for a list of macros that could be created to automate other tasks at Quest.
- **Write out the steps the macro will perform**
  This planning helps eliminate careless errors. Kate writes a description of the macro she wants, as shown in **FIGURE I-1**.
- **Decide how you will perform the actions you want to record**
  You can use the mouse, the keyboard, or a combination of the two. Kate wants you to use both the mouse and the keyboard.
- **Practice the steps you want Excel to record, and write them down**
  Kate has written down the sequence of actions she wants you to include in the macro.
- **Decide where to store the description of the macro and the macro itself**
  Macros can be stored in an active workbook, in a new workbook, or in the **Personal Macro Workbook**, a special workbook used only for macro storage. Kate asks you to store the macro in a new workbook.

FIGURE I-1: Handwritten description of planned macro

Macro to create stamp with the division name

Name: DivStamp

Description: Adds a stamp to the top left of the worksheet, identifying it as a Quest sales worksheet

Steps:

1. Position the cell pointer in cell A1.
2. Type Quest Sales, then click the Enter button.
3. Click the Format button, then click Cells.
4. Click the Font tab, under Font style, click Bold; under Underline, click Single; under Color, click Blue; then click OK.

TABLE I-1: Possible macros and their descriptive names

description of macro	descriptive name for macro
Enter a frequently used proper name, such as "Kate Morgan"	KateMorgan
Enter a frequently used company name, such as Quest	Company_Name
Print the active worksheet on a single page, in landscape orientation	FitToLand
Add a footer to a worksheet	FooterStamp
Add totals to a worksheet	AddTotals

Enable a Macro

Learning Outcomes
- Create a macro-enabled workbook
- Enable macros by changing a workbook's security level

Because a macro may contain a **virus**—destructive software that can damage your computer files—the default security setting in Excel disables macros from running. Although a workbook containing a macro will open, if macros are disabled, they will not function. You can manually change the Excel security setting to allow macros to run if you know a macro came from a trusted source. When saving a workbook with a macro, you need to save it as a macro-enabled workbook with the extension .xlsm. **CASE** *Kate asks you to change the security level to enable all macros. You will change the security level back to the default setting after you create and run your macros.*

STEPS

QUICK TIP
If the DEVELOPER tab is displayed on your Ribbon, skip steps 2 and 3.

1. **Start Excel, open a blank workbook, click the Save button on the Quick Access toolbar, navigate to the location where you store your Data Files, in the Save As dialog box click the Save as type list arrow, click Excel Macro-Enabled Workbook (*.xlsm), in the File name text box type EX I-Macro Workbook, then click Save**
   The security settings that enable macros are available on the DEVELOPER tab. The DEVELOPER tab does not appear by default, but you can display it by customizing the Ribbon.
2. **Click the FILE tab, click Options, then click Customize Ribbon in the category list**
   The Customize the Ribbon options open in the Excel Options dialog box, as shown in **FIGURE I-2**.
3. **Click the Developer check box, if necessary, in the Main Tabs area on the right side of the screen to select it, then click OK**
   The DEVELOPER tab appears on the Ribbon. You are ready to change the security settings.
4. **Click the DEVELOPER tab, then click the Macro Security button in the Code group**
   The Trust Center dialog box opens.
5. **Click Macro Settings if necessary, click the Enable all macros (not recommended; potentially dangerous code can run) option button to select it as shown in FIGURE I-3, then click OK**
   The dialog box closes. Macros remain enabled until you disable them by deselecting the Enable all macros option. As you work with Excel, you should disable macros when you are not working with them.

FIGURE I-2: Excel Options dialog box

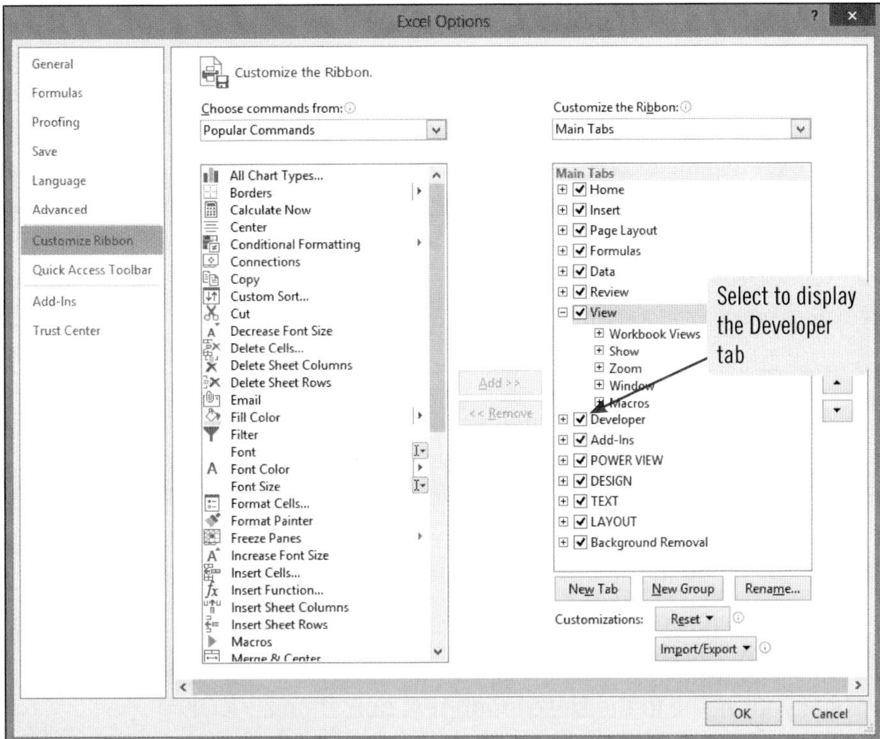

FIGURE I-3: Trust Center dialog box

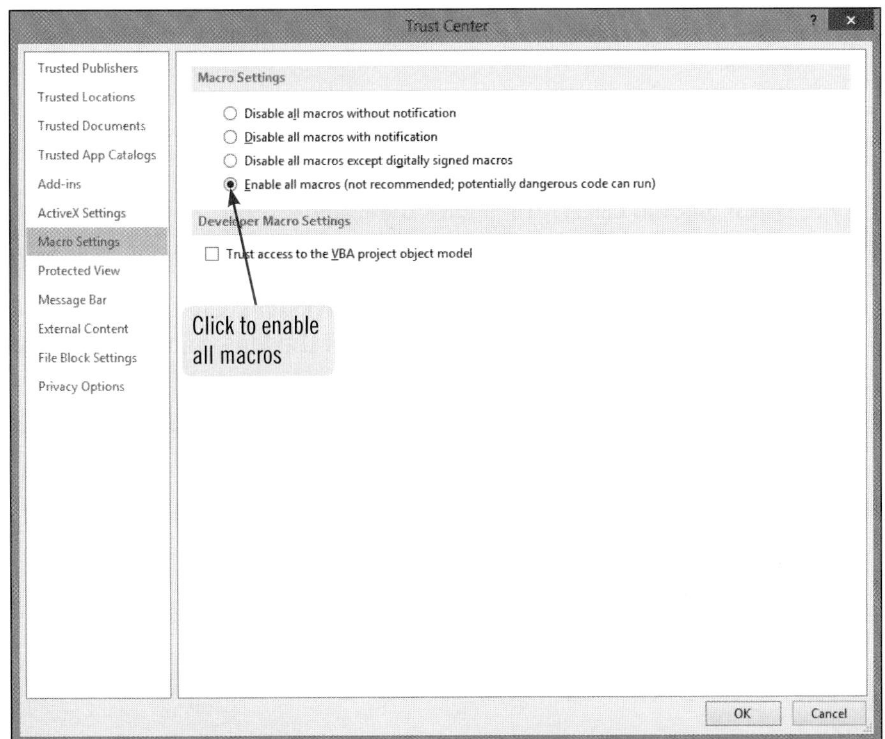

Disabling macros

To prevent viruses from running on your computer, you should disable all macros when you are not working with them. To disable macros, click the DEVELOPER tab, then click the Macro Security button in the Code group. Clicking any of the first three options disables macros. The first option disables all macros without notifying you. The second option notifies you when macros are disabled, and the third option allows only digitally signed macros to run.

Record a Macro

Learning Outcomes
- Choose a macro storage location
- Create a macro by recording steps

The easiest way to create a macro is to record it using the Excel Macro Recorder. You turn the Macro Recorder on, name the macro, enter the keystrokes and select the commands you want the macro to perform, then stop the recorder. As you record the macro, Excel automatically translates each action into program code that you can later view and modify. You can take as long as you want to record the macro; a recorded macro contains only your actions, not the amount of time you took to record it. **CASE** *Kate wants you to create a macro that enters a division "stamp" in cell A1 of the active worksheet. You create this macro by recording your actions.*

STEPS

QUICK TIP
You can also click the Record Macro button in the Code group on the DEVELOPER tab, or the Macros button in the Macros group of the VIEW tab to record a new macro.

1. **Click the Record Macro button on the left side of the status bar**
   The Record Macro dialog box opens, as shown in FIGURE I-4. The default name Macro1 is selected. You can either assign this name or enter a new name. This dialog box also lets you assign a shortcut key for running the macro and assign a storage location for the macro.
2. **Type DivStamp in the Macro name text box**
3. **If the Store macro in list box does not display "This Workbook", click the list arrow and select This Workbook**
4. **Type your name in the Description text box, then click OK**
   The dialog box closes, and the Record Macro button on the status bar is replaced with a Stop Recording button. Take your time performing the steps below. Excel records every keystroke, menu selection, and mouse action that you make.
5. **Press [Ctrl][Home]**
   When you begin an Excel session, macros record absolute cell references. By beginning the recording with a command to move to cell A1, you ensure that the macro includes the instruction to select cell A1 as the first step, in cases where A1 is not already selected.
6. **Type Quest Sales in cell A1, then click the Enter button on the formula bar**
7. **Click the HOME tab, click the Format button in the Cells group, then click Format Cells**
8. **Click the Font tab, in the Font style list box click Bold, click the Underline list arrow and click Single, click the Color list arrow and click the Blue color in the Standard Colors row, then compare your dialog box to FIGURE I-5**
9. **Click OK, click the Stop Recording button on the left side of the status bar, click cell D1 to deselect cell A1, then save the workbook**
   FIGURE I-6 shows the result of recording the macro.

QUICK TIP
You can also click the Stop Recording button in the Code group on the DEVELOPER to stop recording a macro.

FIGURE I-4: Record Macro dialog box

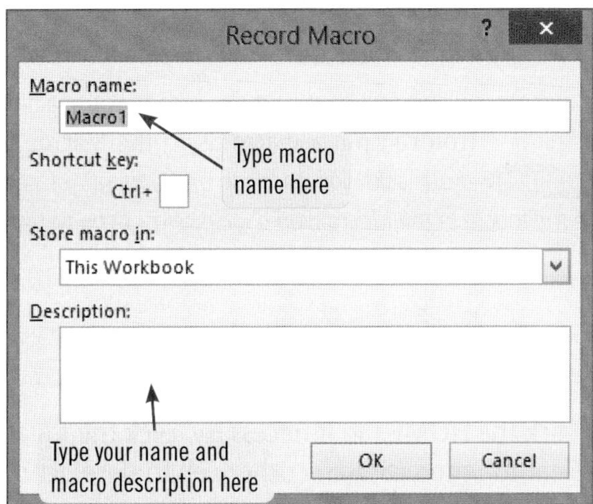

FIGURE I-5: Font tab of the Format Cells dialog box

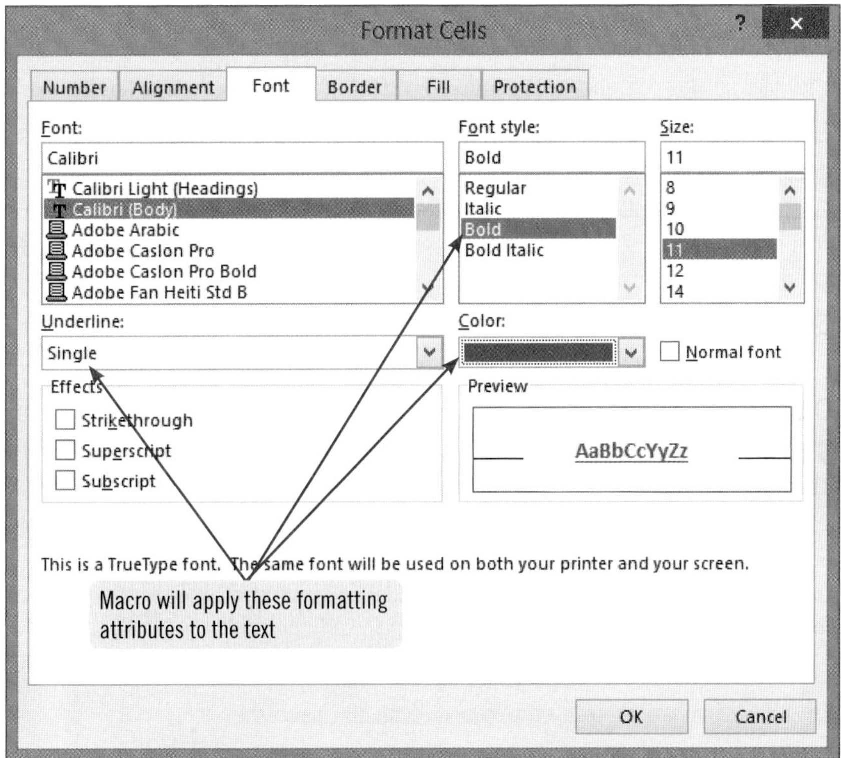

FIGURE I-6: Sales Division stamp

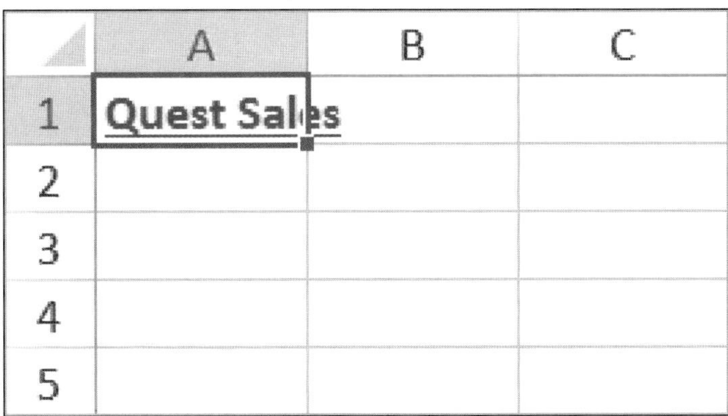

Excel 2013

Run a Macro

Learning Outcomes
- Display selected macros
- Run a macro using the Macro dialog box

Once you record a macro, you should test it to make sure that the actions it performs are correct. To test a macro, you **run** (play) it. You can run a macro using the Macros button in the Code group of the DEVELOPER tab. **CASE** *Kate asks you to clear the contents of cell A1, and then test the DivStamp macro. After you run the macro in the Macro workbook, she asks you to test the macro once more from a newly opened workbook.*

STEPS

1. **Click cell A1, click the HOME tab if necessary, click the Clear button in the Editing group, click Clear All, then click any other cell to deselect cell A1**
   When you delete only the contents of a cell, any formatting still remains in the cell. By using the Clear All option you can be sure that the cell is free of contents and formatting.
2. **Click the DEVELOPER tab, click the Macros button in the Code group, click the Macros in list arrow, then click This Workbook**
   The Macro dialog box, shown in **FIGURE I-7**, lists all the macros contained in the workbook.
3. **Click DivStamp in the Macro name list if necessary, as you watch cell A1 click Run, then deselect cell A1**
   The macro quickly plays back the steps you recorded in the previous lesson. When the macro is finished, your screen should look like **FIGURE I-8**. As long as the workbook containing the macro remains open, you can run the macro in any open workbook.
4. **Click the FILE tab, click New, then click Blank workbook**
   Because the EX I-Macro Workbook.xlsm is still open, you can use its macros.
5. **Deselect cell A1, click the DEVELOPER tab, click the Macros button in the Code group, click the Macros in list arrow, then click All Open Workbooks, click 'EX I-Macro Workbook.xlsm'!DivStamp, click Run, then deselect cell A1**
   When multiple workbooks are open, the macro name in the Macro dialog box includes the workbook name between single quotation marks, followed by an exclamation point which is an **external reference indicator**, indicating that the macro is outside the active workbook. Because you only used this workbook to test the macro, you don't need to save it.
6. **Close Book2 without saving changes**
   The EX I-Macro Workbook.xlsm workbook remains open.

QUICK TIP
To create a custom button on the Quick Access toolbar that will run a macro, right-click the Ribbon, click Customize Quick Access Toolbar, click the Choose commands from list arrow, select Macros, select the macro to assign to a custom button in the macro list on the left, click Add to move the macro to the list of buttons on the Quick Access Toolbar, then click OK.

FIGURE I-7: Macro dialog box

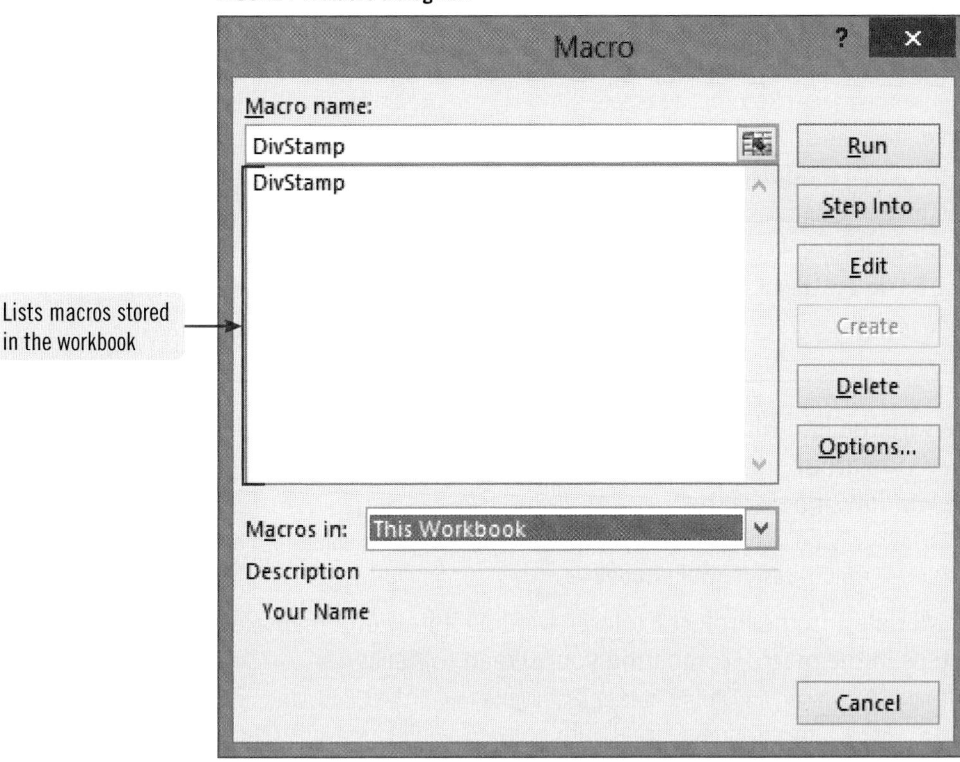

FIGURE I-8: Result of running DivStamp macro

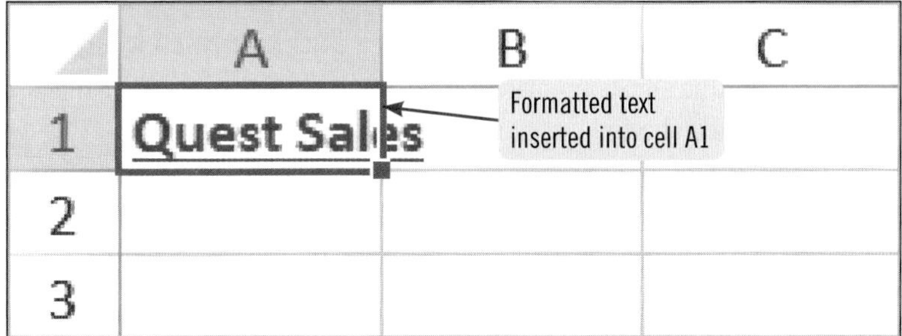

Running a macro automatically

You can create a macro that automatically performs certain tasks when the workbook in which it is saved is opened. This is useful for actions you want to do every time you open a workbook. For example, you may import data from an external data source into the workbook or format the worksheet data in a certain way. To create a macro that will automatically run when the workbook is opened, you need to name the macro Auto_Open and save it in that workbook.

Excel 2013
UNIT I

Edit a Macro

Learning Outcomes
- Edit a macro using VBA
- Add comments to Visual Basic Code

When you use the Macro Recorder to create a macro, the program instructions, called **program code**, are recorded automatically in the **Visual Basic for Applications (VBA)** programming language. Each macro is stored as a **module**, or program code container, attached to the workbook. After you record a macro, you might need to change it. If you have a lot of changes to make, it might be best to record the macro again. But if you need to make only minor adjustments, you can edit the macro code directly using the **Visual Basic Editor**, a program that lets you display and edit your macro code. **CASE** *Kate wants you to modify the DivStamp macro to change the point size of the department stamp to 12.*

STEPS

1. **Make sure the EX I-Macro Workbook.xlsm workbook is open, click the Macros button in the Code group, make sure DivStamp is selected, click Edit, then maximize the Code window, if necessary**
   The Visual Basic Editor starts, showing three windows: the Project Explorer window, the Properties window, and the Code window, as shown in **FIGURE I-9**.

2. **Click Module 1 in the Project Explorer window if it's not already selected, then examine the steps in the macro, comparing your screen to FIGURE I-9**
   The name of the macro and your name appear at the top of the Code window. Below this area, Excel has translated your keystrokes and commands into macro code. When you open and make selections in a dialog box during macro recording, Excel automatically stores all the dialog box settings in the macro code. For example, the line .FontStyle = "Bold" was generated when you clicked Bold in the Format Cells dialog box. You also see lines of code that you didn't generate directly while recording the DivStamp macro, for example, .Name = "Calibri".

TROUBLE
If the Properties window does not appear in the lower-left portion of your screen, click the Properties Window button on the Visual Basic Standard toolbar, then resize it as shown in the figure if necessary.

3. **In the line .Size = 11, double-click 11 to select it, then type 12**
   Because Module1 is attached to the workbook and not stored as a separate file, any changes to the module are saved automatically when you save the workbook.

4. **Review the code in the Code window**

5. **Click File on the menu bar, then click Close and Return to Microsoft Excel**
   You want to rerun the DivStamp macro to make sure the macro reflects the change you made using the Visual Basic Editor. You begin by clearing the division name from cell A1.

QUICK TIP
You can return to Excel without closing the module by clicking the View Microsoft Excel button on the Visual Basic Editor toolbar.

6. **Click cell A1, click the HOME tab, click the Clear button in the Editing group, then click Clear All**

7. **Click any other cell to deselect cell A1, click the DEVELOPER tab, click the Macros button in the Code group, make sure DivStamp is selected, click Run, then deselect cell A1**
   The department stamp is now in 12-point type, as shown in **FIGURE I-10**.

QUICK TIP
Another way to start the Visual Basic Editor is to click the DEVELOPER tab, then click the Visual Basic button in the Code group.

8. **Save the workbook**

FIGURE I-9: Visual Basic Editor showing Module1

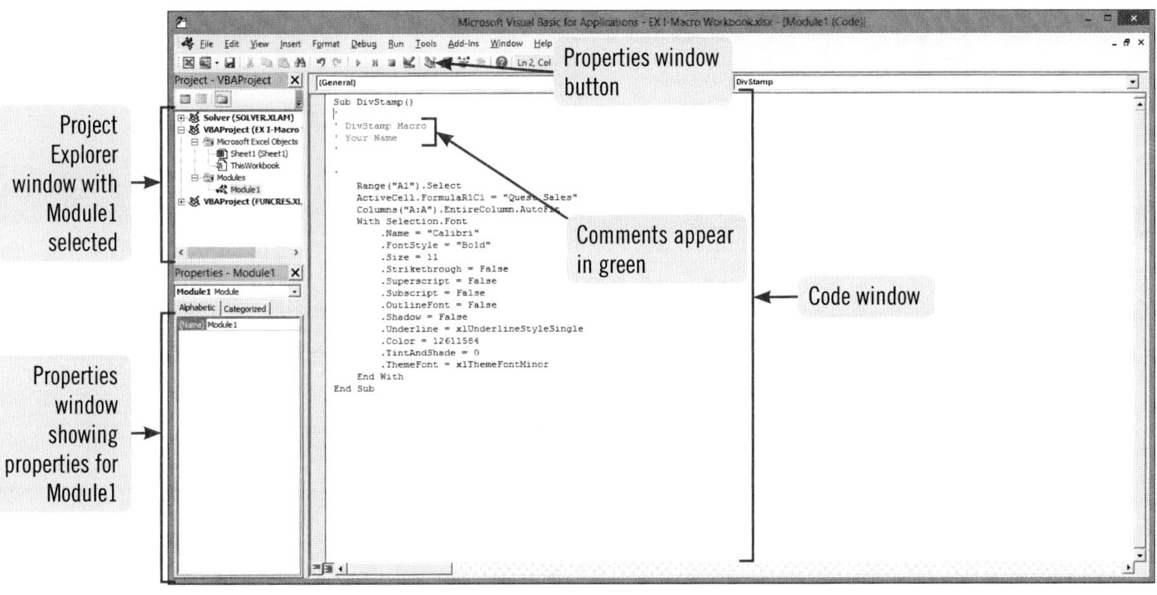

FIGURE I-10: Result of running edited DivStamp macro

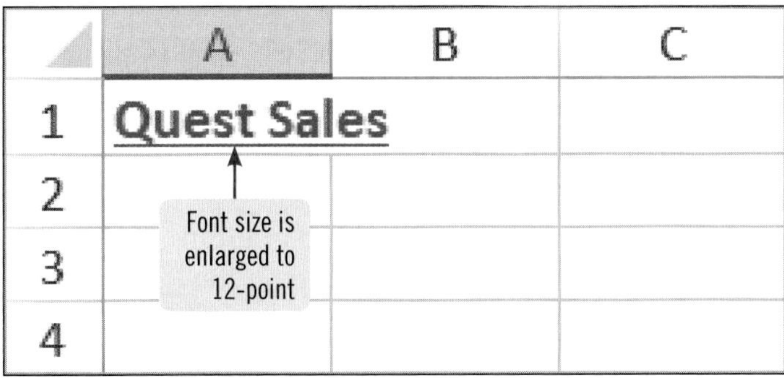

Adding comments to Visual Basic code

With practice, you will be able to interpret the lines of macro code. Others who use your macro, however, might want to review the code to, for example, learn the function of a particular line. You can explain the code by adding comments to the macro. **Comments** are explanatory text added to the lines of code. When you enter a comment, you must type an apostrophe (') before the comment text. Otherwise, the program tries to interpret it as a command. On the screen, comments appear in green after you press [Enter], as shown in **FIGURE I-9**. You can also insert blank lines as comments in the macro code to make the code more readable. To do this, type an apostrophe, then press [Enter].

Excel 2013
UNIT I

Learning Outcomes
- Run a macro using shortcut key combinations

Assign Keyboard Shortcuts to Macros

For macros that you run frequently, you can run them by using shortcut key combinations instead of the Macro dialog box. You can assign a shortcut key combination to any macro. Using shortcut keys saves you time by reducing the number of actions you need to take to run a macro. You assign shortcut key combinations in the Record Macro dialog box. **CASE** *Kate also wants you to create a macro called Region to enter the company region into a worksheet. You assign a shortcut key combination to run the macro.*

STEPS

1. **Click cell B2**

   You want to record the macro in cell B2, but you want the macro to enter the region of North America anywhere in a worksheet. Therefore, you do not begin the macro with an instruction to position the cell pointer, as you did in the DivStamp macro.

2. **Click the Record Macro button on the status bar**

   The Record Macro dialog box opens. Notice the option Shortcut key: Ctrl+ followed by a blank box. You can type a letter (A–Z) in the Shortcut key text box to assign the key combination of [Ctrl] plus that letter to run the macro. Because some common Excel shortcuts use the [Ctrl][*letter*] combination, such as [Ctrl][C] for Copy, you decide to use the key combination [Ctrl][Shift] plus a letter to avoid overriding any of these shortcut key combinations.

> **QUICK TIP**
> Be careful when choosing letters for a keyboard shortcut. The letters entered in the shortcut key text box are case sensitive.

3. **With the default macro name selected, type Region in the Macro name text box, click the Shortcut key text box, press and hold [Shift], type C, then in the Description box type your name**

   You have assigned the shortcut key combination [Ctrl][Shift][C] to the Region macro. After you create the macro, you will use this shortcut key combination to run it. Compare your screen with **FIGURE I-11**. You are ready to record the Region macro.

4. **Click OK to close the dialog box**

5. **Type North America in cell B2, click the Enter button on the formula bar, press [Ctrl][I] to italicize the text, click the Stop Recording button on the status bar, then deselect cell B2**

   North America appears in italics in cell B2. You are ready to run the macro in cell A5 using the shortcut key combination.

6. **Click cell A5, press and hold [Ctrl][Shift], type C, then deselect the cell**

   The region appears in cell A5, as shown in **FIGURE I-12**. The macro played back in the selected cell (A5) instead of the cell where it was recorded (B2) because you did not begin recording the macro by clicking cell B2.

FIGURE I-11: Record Macro dialog box with shortcut key assigned

FIGURE I-12: Result of running the Region macro

	A	B	C	D	E	F	G
1	Quest Sales						
2		*North America*	Result of recording macro in cell B2				
3							
4							
5	*North America*	Result of running macro in cell A5					
6							
7							

Using relative referencing when creating a macro

By default, Excel records absolute cell references in macros. You can record a macro's actions based on the relative position of the active cell by clicking the Use Relative References button in the Code group prior to recording the action. For example, when you create a macro using the default setting of absolute referencing, bolding the range A1:D1 will always bold that range when the macro is run. However, if you click the Use Relative References button when recording the macro before bolding the range, then running the macro will not necessarily result in bolding the range A1:D1. The range that will be bolded will depend on the location of the active cell when the macro is run. If the active cell is A4, then the range A4:D4 will be bolded. Selecting the Use Relative References button highlights the button name, indicating it is active, as shown in **FIGURE I-13**. The button remains active until you click it again to deselect it. This is called a toggle, meaning that it acts like an off/on switch: it retains the relative reference setting until you click it again to turn it off or you exit Excel.

FIGURE I-13: Use Relative References button selected

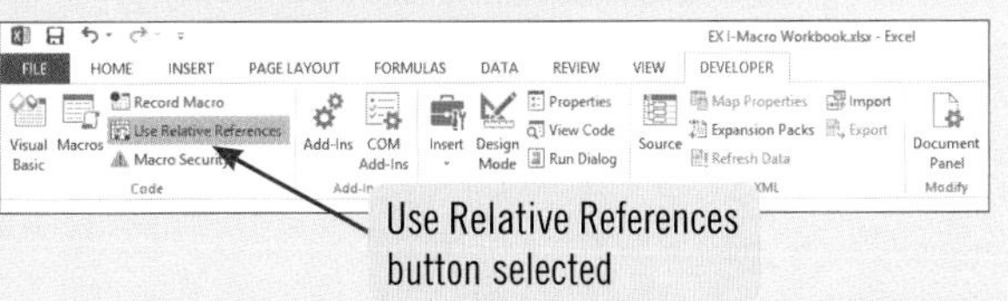

Excel 2013

Use the Personal Macro Workbook

Learning Outcomes
- Determine when when to use the Personal Macro Workbook
- Save a macro in the Personal Macro Workbook

When you create a macro, it is automatically stored in the workbook in which you created it. But if you wanted to use that macro in another workbook, you would have to copy the macro to that workbook. Instead, it's easier to store commonly used macros in the Personal Macro Workbook. The **Personal Macro Workbook** is an Excel file that is always available, unless you specify otherwise, and gives you access to all the macros it contains, regardless of which workbooks are open. The Personal Macro Workbook file is automatically created the first time you choose to store a macro in it, and is named PERSONAL.XLSB. You can add additional macros to the Personal Macro Workbook by saving them in the workbook. By default, the PERSONAL.XLSB workbook opens each time you start Excel, but you don't see it because Excel designates it as a hidden file. **CASE** *Kate often likes to print her worksheets in landscape orientation with 1" left, right, top, and bottom margins. She wants you to create a macro that automatically formats a worksheet for printing this way. Because she wants to use this macro in future workbooks, she asks you to store the macro in the Personal Macro Workbook.*

STEPS

1. **Click the Record Macro button on the status bar**
   The Record Macro dialog box opens.
2. **Type FormatPrint in the Macro name text box, click the Shortcut key text box, press and hold [Shift], type F, then click the Store macro in list arrow**
   You have named the macro FormatPrint and assigned it the shortcut combination [Ctrl][Shift][F]. The "This Workbook" storage option is selected by default, indicating that Excel automatically stores macros in the active workbook, as shown in **FIGURE I-14**. You can also choose to store the macro in a new workbook or in the Personal Macro Workbook.
3. **Click Personal Macro Workbook, in the Description text box enter your name, then click OK**
   The recorder is on, and you are ready to record the macro keystrokes.
4. **Click the PAGE LAYOUT tab, click the Orientation button in the Page Setup group, click Landscape, click the Margins button in the Page Setup group, click Custom Margins, then enter 1 in the Top, Left, Bottom, and Right text boxes**
   Compare your margin settings to **FIGURE I-15**.
5. **Click OK, then click the Stop Recording button on the status bar**
   You want to test the macro.
6. **Add a new worksheet, in cell A1 type Macro Test, press [Enter], press and hold [Ctrl][Shift], then type F**
   The FormatPrint macro plays back the sequence of commands.
7. **Preview Sheet2 and verify in the Settings that the orientation is landscape and the Last Custom Margins are 1" on the left, right, top, and bottom**
8. **Click the Back button then save the workbook**

TROUBLE
If a dialog box appears saying that a macro is already assigned to this shortcut combination, choose another letter for a keyboard shortcut. If a dialog box appears with the message that a macro named FormatPrint already exists, click Yes to replace it.

TROUBLE
You may have to wait a few moments for the macro to finish. If you are using a different letter for the shortcut key combination, type that letter instead of the letter F.

FIGURE I-14: Record Macro dialog box showing macro storage options

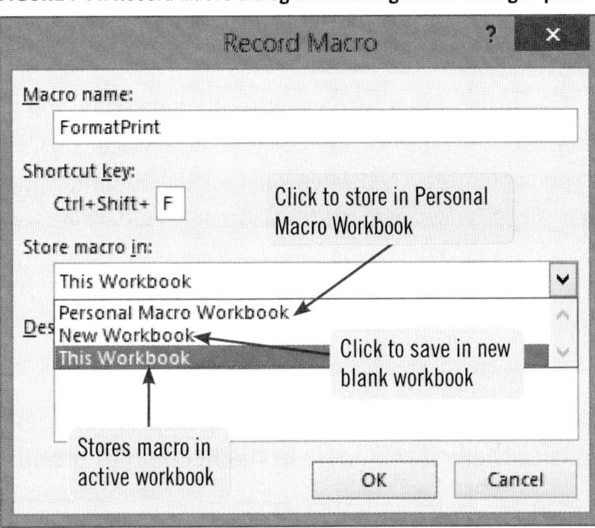

FIGURE I-15: Margin settings for the FormatPrint macro

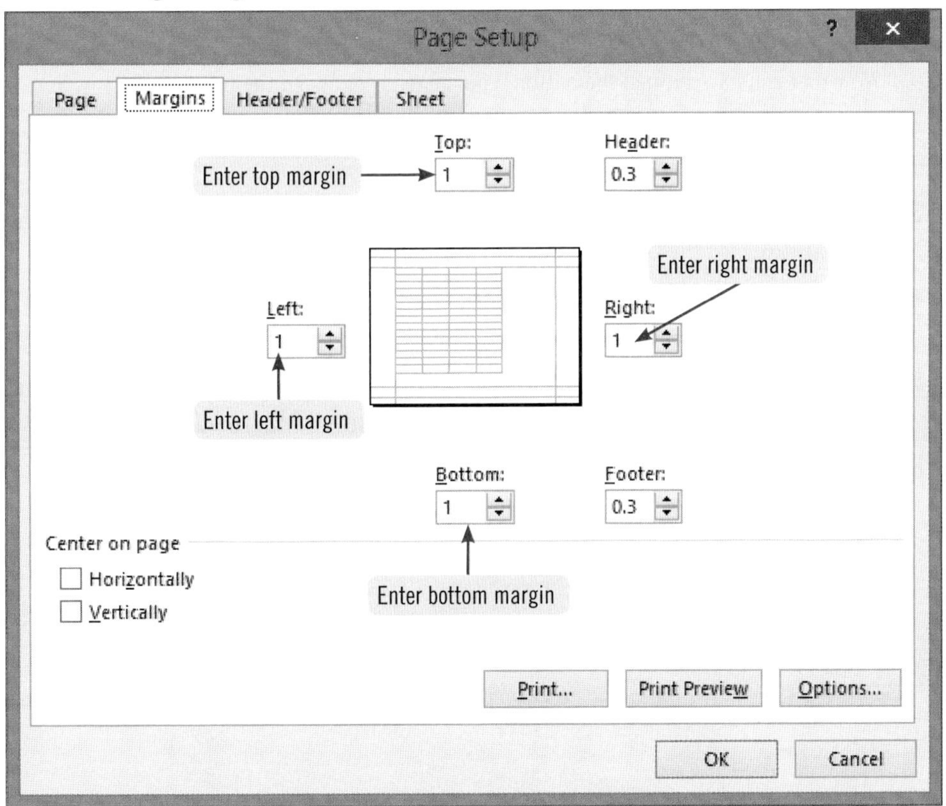

Working with the Personal Macro Workbook

Once you use the Personal Macro Workbook, it opens automatically each time you start Excel so you can add macros to it. By default, the Personal Macro Workbook is hidden in Excel as a precautionary measure so you don't accidentally delete anything from it. If you need to delete a macro from the Personal Macro Workbook, click the VIEW tab, click Unhide in the Window group, click PERSONAL.XLSB, then click OK. To hide the Personal Macro Workbook, make it the active workbook, click the VIEW tab, then click Hide in the Window group. If you should see a message that Excel is unable to record to your Personal Macro Workbook, check to make sure it is enabled: Click the FILE tab, click Options, click Add-ins, click the Manage list arrow, click Disabled Items, then click Go. If your Personal Macro Workbook is listed in the Disabled items dialog box, click its name, then click Enable.

Assign a Macro to a Button

Learning Outcomes
- Create a button shape in a worksheet
- Assign a macro to a button

When you create macros for others who will use your workbook, you might want to make the macros more visible so they're easier to use. In addition to using shortcut keys, you can run a macro by assigning it to a button on your worksheet. Then when you click the button the macro will run. **CASE** *To make it easier for people in the sales division to run the DivStamp macro, Kate asks you to assign it to a button on the workbook. You begin by creating the button.*

STEPS

1. **Add a new worksheet, click the INSERT tab, click the Shapes button in the Illustrations group, then click the first rectangle in the Rectangles group**
   The mouse pointer changes to a + symbol.
2. **Click at the top-left corner of cell A8, and drag the pointer to the lower-right corner of cell B9**
   Compare your screen to **FIGURE I-16**.
3. **Type Division Macro to label the button**
   Now that you have created the button, you are ready to assign the macro to it.
4. **Right-click the new button, then on the shortcut menu click Assign Macro**
   The Assign Macro dialog box opens.
5. **Click DivStamp under "Macro name", then click OK**
   You have assigned the DivStamp macro to the button.
6. **Click any cell to deselect the button, then click the button**
   The DivStamp macro plays, and the text Quest Sales appears in cell A1, as shown in **FIGURE I-17**.
7. **Save the workbook, preview Sheet3, close the workbook, then exit Excel, clicking Don't Save when asked to save changes to the Personal Macro Workbook**
8. **Submit the workbook to your instructor**

QUICK TIP
To format a macro button using 3-D effects, clip art, photographs, fills, and shadows, right-click it, select Format Shape from the shortcut menu, then select features such as Fill, Line Color, Line Style, Shadow, Reflection, Glow and Soft Edges, 3-D Format, 3-D Rotation, Picture Color, and Text Box in the Format Shape pane.

FIGURE I-16: Button shape

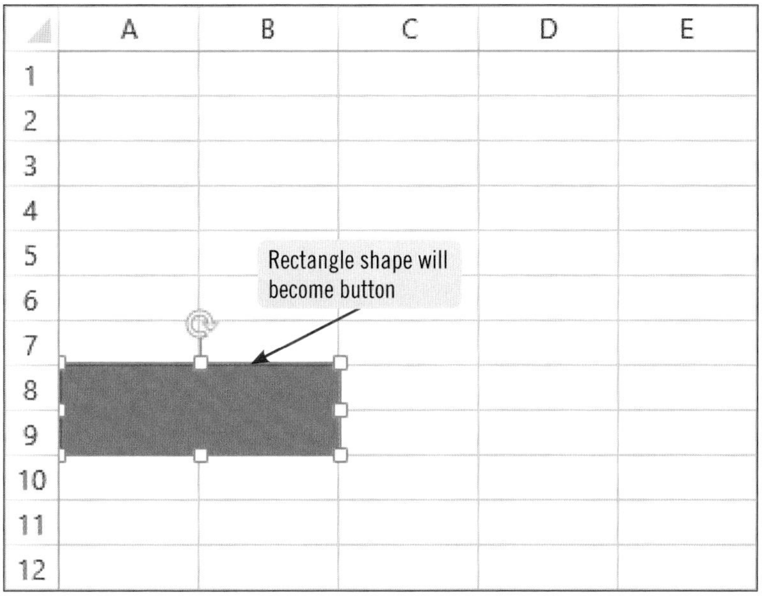

Rectangle shape will become button

FIGURE I-17: Sheet3 with the Sales Division text

Creating and formatting a form control

You can add an object called a **form control** to an Excel worksheet to make it easier for users to enter or select data. Click the DEVELOPER tab on the Ribbon, click the Insert button in the Controls group, click the desired control in the Form Controls area of the Insert gallery, then draw the shape on the worksheet. After adding a control to a worksheet, you need to link it to a cell or cells in the worksheet. To do this, right-click it, select Format Control, then click the Control tab. For example, if you add a list box form control, the input range is the location of the list box selections and the cell link is the cell with the numeric value for the current position of the list control. To edit the form control's positioning properties (such as moving, sizing, and printing) right-click the form control, select Format Control and click the Properties tab. See **FIGURE I-18**.

FIGURE I-18: Properties tab of the Format Control dialog box

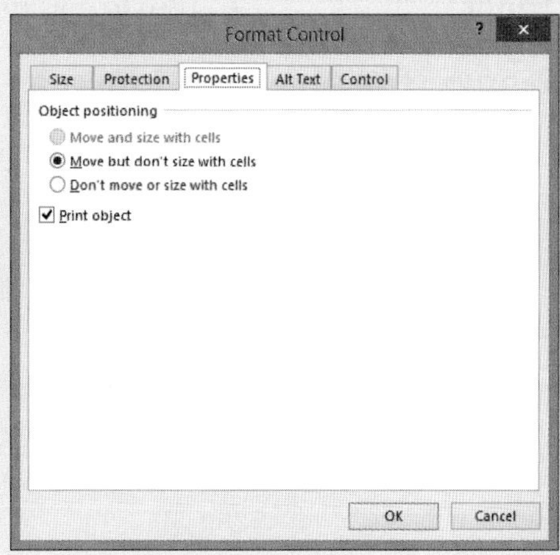

Excel 2013

Practice

Put your skills into practice with SAM! If you have a SAM account, go to www.cengage.com/sam2013 to access SAM assignments for this unit.

Concepts Review

FIGURE I-19

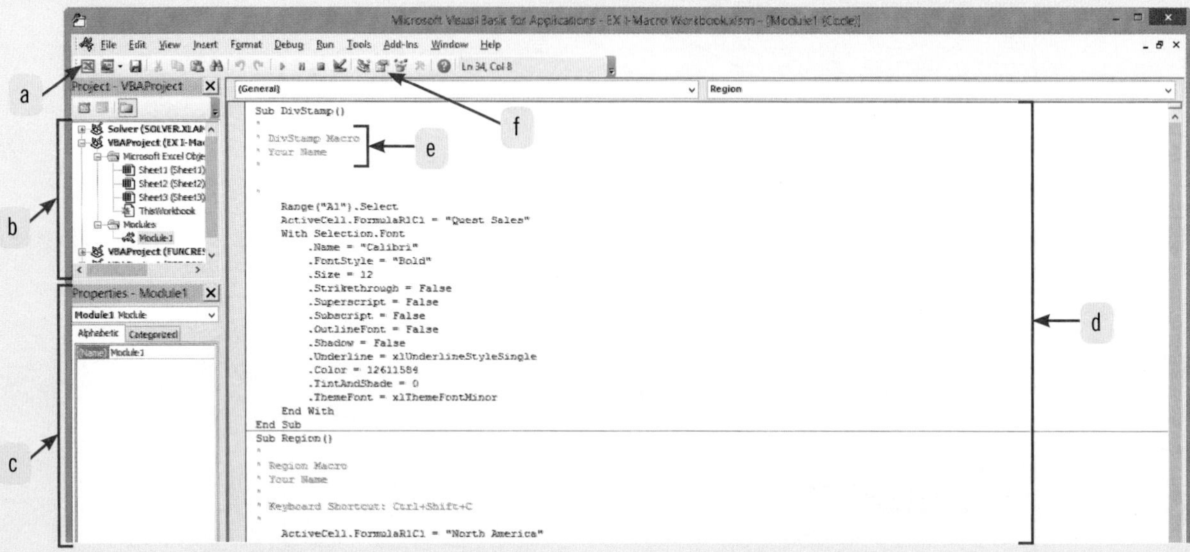

1. **Which element points to comments?**
2. **Which element do you click to return to Excel without closing the module?**
3. **Which element points to the Code window?**
4. **Which element points to the Properties Window button?**
5. **Which element points to the Project Explorer window?**
6. **Which element points to the Properties window?**

Match each term or button with the statement that best describes it.

7. **Macro**
8. **Virus**
9. **Comments**
10. **Personal Macro Workbook**
11. **Visual Basic Editor**

a. Set of instructions that performs a task in a specified order
b. Statements that appear in green explaining the macro
c. Destructive software that can damage computer files
d. Used to make changes to macro code
e. Used to store frequently used macros

Select the best answer from the list of choices.

12. **Which of the following is the best candidate for a macro?**
    a. Often-used sequences of commands or actions
    b. Nonsequential tasks
    c. Seldom-used commands or tasks
    d. One-button or one-keystroke commands
13. **You can open the Visual Basic Editor by clicking the ______________ button in the Macro dialog box.**
    a. Edit
    b. Programs
    c. Modules
    d. Visual Basic Editor
14. **A Macro named ______________ will automatically run when the workbook it is saved in opens.**
    a. Default
    b. Auto_Open
    c. Macro1
    d. Open_Macro

15. Which of the following is *not* true about editing a macro?

- **a.** You edit macros using the Visual Basic Editor.
- **b.** A macro cannot be edited and must be recorded again.
- **c.** You can type changes directly in the existing program code.
- **d.** You can make more than one editing change in a macro.

16. Why is it important to plan a macro?

- **a.** Macros can't be deleted.
- **b.** Planning helps prevent careless errors from being introduced into the macro.
- **c.** It is impossible to edit a macro.
- **d.** Macros won't be stored if they contain errors.

17. Macros are recorded with relative references:

- **a.** Only if the Use Relative References button is selected.
- **b.** In all cases.
- **c.** By default.
- **d.** Only if the Use Absolute References button is not selected.

18. You can run macros:

- **a.** From the Macro dialog box.
- **b.** From shortcut key combinations.
- **c.** From a button on the worksheet.
- **d.** Using all of the above.

19. Macro security settings can be changed using the ______________ tab.

- **a.** Home
- **b.** Developer
- **c.** Security
- **d.** Review

Skills Review

1. Plan and enable a macro.

- **a.** You need to plan a macro that enters and formats your name and e-mail address in a worksheet.
- **b.** Write out the steps the macro will perform.
- **c.** Write out how the macro could be used in a workbook.
- **d.** Start Excel, open a new workbook, then save it as a Macro-Enabled workbook named **EX I-Macros** in the location where you store your Data Files. (*Hint*: The file will have the file extension .xlsm.)
- **e.** Use the Excel Options feature to display the DEVELOPER tab if it is not showing in the Ribbon.
- **f.** Using the Trust Center dialog box, enable all macros.

2. Record a macro.

- **a.** You want to record a macro that enters and formats your name and e-mail address in the range A1:A2 in a worksheet using the steps below.
- **b.** Name the macro **MyEmail**, store it in the current workbook, and make sure your name appears in the Description text box as the person who recorded the macro.
- **c.** Record the macro, entering your name in cell A1 and your e-mail address in cell A2. (*Hint*: You need to press [Ctrl][Home] first to ensure cell A1 will be selected when the macro runs.)
- **d.** Resize column A to fit the information entirely in that column.
- **e.** Add an outside border around the range A1:A2 and format the font using Green from the Standard Colors.
- **f.** Add bold formatting to the text in the range A1:A2.
- **g.** Stop the recorder and save the workbook.

3. Run a macro.

- **a.** Clear cell entries and formats in the range affected by the macro, resize the width of column A to 8.43, then select cell B3.
- **b.** Run the MyEmail macro to place your name and e-mail information in the range A1:A2.
- **c.** On the worksheet, clear all the cell entries and formats generated by running the MyEmail macro. Resize the width of column A to 8.43.
- **d.** Save the workbook.

Skills Review (continued)

4. Edit a macro.

- **a.** Open the MyEmail macro in the Visual Basic Editor.
- **b.** Change the line of code above the last line from Selection.Font.Bold = True to Selection.Font.Bold = False.
- **c.** Use the Close and Return to Microsoft Excel command on the File menu to return to Excel.
- **d.** Test the macro on Sheet1, and compare your worksheet to **FIGURE I-20** verifying that the text is not bold.
- **e.** Save the workbook.

FIGURE I-20

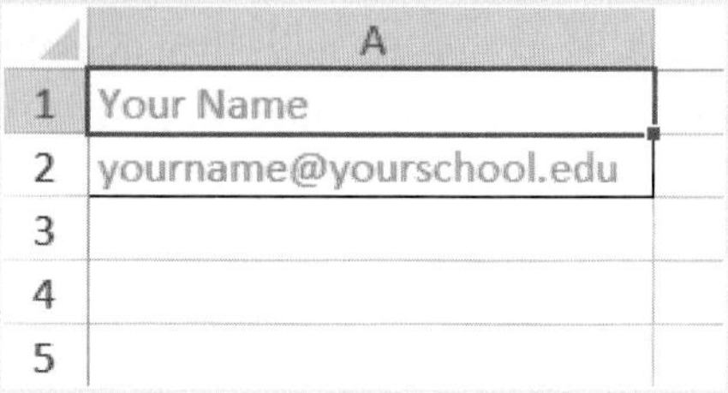

5. Assign keyboard shortcuts to macros.

- **a.** Create a macro named **EmailStamp** in the current workbook, assign your macro the shortcut key combination [Ctrl][Shift][Q], enter your name in the description. (*Hint*: If you get an error when trying to use [Ctrl][Shift][Q], select another key combination.)
- **b.** Begin recording, enter your e-mail address, format it in italics with a font color of red, without underlining, in the selected cell of the current worksheet. Stop recording.
- **c.** After you record the macro, clear the contents and formats from the cell containing your e-mail address that you used to record the macro.
- **d.** Use the shortcut key combination to run the EmailStamp macro in a cell other than the one in which it was recorded. Compare your macro result to **FIGURE I-21**. Your e-mail address may appear in a different cell.
- **e.** Save the workbook.

FIGURE I-21

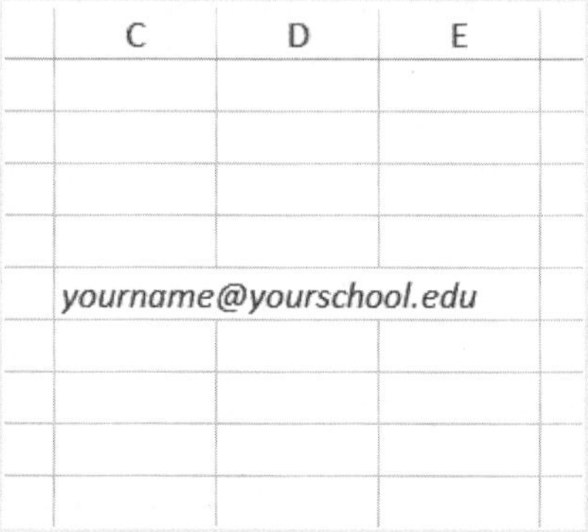

6. Use the Personal Macro Workbook.

- **a.** Using Sheet1, record a new macro called **FitToLand** and store it in the Personal Macro Workbook with your name in the Description text box. If you already have a macro named FitToLand replace that macro. The macro should set the print orientation to landscape.
- **b.** After you record the macro, Add a new worksheet, and enter **Test data for FitToLand macro** in cell A1.
- **c.** Preview Sheet2 to verify that the orientation is set to portrait.
- **d.** Run the FitToLand macro. (You may have to wait a few moments.)
- **e.** Add your name to the Sheet2 footer, then preview Sheet2 and verify that it is now in Landscape orientation.
- **f.** Save the workbook.

7. Assign a macro to a button.

- **a.** Add a new worksheet and enter **Button Test** in cell A1.
- **b.** Using the rectangle shape, draw a rectangle in the range A7:B8.
- **c.** Label the button with the text **Landscape**. Compare your worksheet to **FIGURE I-22**.
- **d.** Assign the macro PERSONAL.XLSB!FitToLand to the button.
- **e.** Verify that the orientation of Sheet3 is set to portrait.
- **f.** Run the FitToLand macro using the button.
- **g.** Preview the worksheet, and verify that it is in landscape view.
- **h.** Add your name to the Sheet3 footer, then save the workbook.
- **i.** Close the workbook, exit Excel without saving the FitToLand macro in the Personal Macro Workbook, then submit your workbook to your instructor.

FIGURE I-22

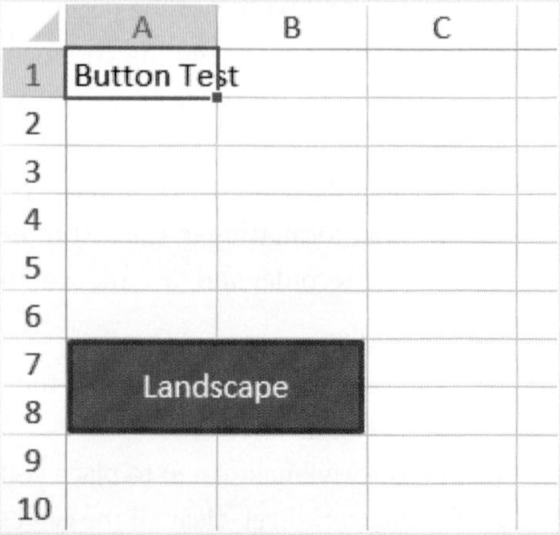

Independent Challenge 1

As the office manager of Ocean Point Consulting Group, you need to develop ways to help your fellow employees work more efficiently. Employees have asked for Excel macros that can do the following:

- Adjust the column widths to display all column data in a worksheet.
- Place the company name of Ocean Point Consulting Group in the header of a worksheet.

a. Plan and write the steps necessary for each macro.

b. Start Excel, open the Data File EX I-1.xlsx from the location where you store your Data Files, then save it as a macro-enabled workbook called **EX I-Consulting**.

c. Check your macro security on the DEVELOPER tab to be sure that macros are enabled.

d. Create a macro named **ColumnFit**, save it in the EX I-Consulting.xlsm workbook, assign the ColumnFit macro a shortcut key combination of [Ctrl][Shift][X], and add your name in the description area for the macro. Record the macro using the following instructions:

- Record the ColumnFit macro to adjust a worksheet's column widths to display all data. (*Hint*: Select the entire sheet, click the HOME tab, click the Format button in the Cells group, select AutoFit Column Width, then click cell A1 to deselect the worksheet.)
- End the macro recording.

e. Format the widths of columns A through G to 8.43, then test the ColumnFit macro with the shortcut key combination [Ctrl][Shift][X].

f. Create a macro named **CompanyName**, and save it in the EX I-Consulting.xlsm workbook. Assign the macro a shortcut key combination of [Ctrl][Shift][Y], and add your name in the description area for the macro.

g. Record the CompanyName macro. The macro should place the company name of Ocean Point Consulting Group in the center section of the worksheet header.

h. Enter **CompanyName test data** in cell A1 of Sheet2, and test the CompanyName macro using the shortcut key combination [Ctrl][Shift][Y]. Preview Sheet2 to view the header.

i. Edit the CompanyName macro in the Visual Basic Editor to change the company name from Ocean Point Consulting Group to **Shore Consulting Group**. Close the Visual Basic Editor and return to Excel.

j. Add a rectangle button to Sheet3 in the range A6:B7. Label the button with the text **Company Name**.

k. Assign the CompanyName macro to the button.

l. Enter **New CompanyName Test** in cell A1. Compare your screen to **FIGURE I-23**. Use the button to run the CompanyName macro. Preview the worksheet, checking the header to be sure it is displaying the new company name.

m. Enter your name in the footers of all three worksheets. Save the workbook, close the workbook, then submit the workbook to your instructor and exit Excel.

FIGURE I-23

New CompanyName Test

Company Name

Independent Challenge 2

You are an assistant to the VP of Sales at Twin Cities Beverage Company, a distributor of juices, water, and soda to 'supermarkets. As part of your work, you create spreadsheets with sales projections for different regions of the company. You frequently have to change the print settings so that workbooks print in landscape orientation with custom margins of 1" on the top and bottom. You also add a header with the company name on every worksheet. You have decided that it's time to create a macro to streamline this process.

a. Plan and write the steps necessary to create the macro.

b. Check your macro security settings to confirm that macros are enabled.

Independent Challenge 2 (continued)

c. Start Excel, create a new workbook, then save it as a macro-enabled file named **EX I-Sales Macro** in the location where you store your Data Files.

d. Create a macro that changes the page orientation to landscape, adds custom margins of 1" on the top and bottom of the page, adds a header of **Twin Cities Beverage Company** in the center section formatted as Bold with a font size of 14 points. Name the macro **Format**, add your name in the description, assign it the shortcut key combination [Ctrl][Shift][W], and store it in the current workbook.

e. Add a new worksheet and enter the text **Format Test** in cell A1. Test the macro using the shortcut key combination of [Ctrl][Shift][W]. Preview Sheet2 to check the page orientation, margins, and the header.

f. Add a new worksheet, enter the text **Format Test** in cell A1 add a rectangular button with the text **Format Worksheet** to run the Format macro, then test the macro using the button.

g. Preview the Visual Basic code for the macro.

h. Save the workbook, close the workbook, exit Excel, then submit the workbook to your instructor.

Independent Challenge 3

You are the Northeast regional sales manager of New England Technology, a technology consulting firm. You manage the New England operations and frequently create workbooks with data from the office locations. It's tedious to change the tab names and colors every time you open a new workbook, so you decide to create a macro that will add the office locations and colors to the three office location worksheet tabs, as shown in **FIGURE I-24**.

FIGURE I-24

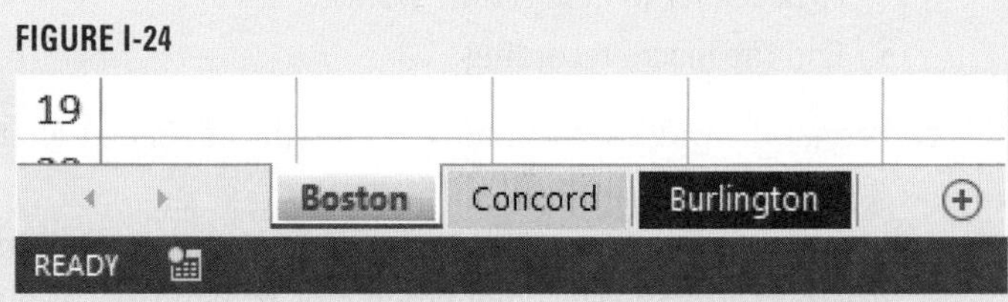

a. Plan and write the steps to create the macro described above.

b. Start Excel and open a new workbook.

c. Create the macro using the plan you created in Step a, name it **SheetFormat**, assign it the shortcut key combination [Ctrl][Shift][Q], store it in the Personal Macro Workbook, and add your name in the description area.

d. After recording the macro, close the workbook without saving it. Save the changes to the Personal Macro workbook.

e. Open a new workbook, then save it as a macro-enabled workbook named **EX I-Office Test** in the location where you store your Data Files. Use the shortcut key combination of [Ctrl][Shift][Q] to test the macro in the new workbook.

f. Unhide the PERSONAL.XLSB workbook. (*Hint*: Click the VIEW tab, click the Unhide button in the Window group, click PERSONAL.XLSB, then click OK.)

g. Edit the SheetFormat macro using **FIGURE I-25** as a guide, changing the Burlington sheet name to Portland. (*Hint*: There are three instances of Burlington that need to be changed.)

h. Open a new workbook, then save it as a macro-enabled workbook named **EX I-Office Test New** in the location where you store your Data Files. Test the edited macro using the shortcut key combination of [Ctrl][Shift][Q].

i. Add a new sheet in the workbook, and name it **Code**. Copy the SheetFormat macro code from the Personal Macro Workbook, and paste it in the Code sheet beginning in cell A1. Save the workbook, close the workbook, then submit the EX I-Office Test New workbook to your instructor.

FIGURE I-25

```
Sub SheetFormat()
'
' SheetFormat Macro
' Your Name
'
' Keyboard Shortcut: Ctrl+Shift+Q
'
    Sheets("Sheet1").Select
    Sheets("Sheet1").Name = "Boston"
    Sheets("Boston").Select
    With ActiveWorkbook.Sheets("Boston").Tab
        .Color = 12611584
        .TintAndShade = 0
    End With
    Sheets("Sheet2").Select
    Sheets("Sheet2").Name = "Concord"
    Sheets("Concord").Select
    With ActiveWorkbook.Sheets("Concord").Tab
        .Color = 65535
        .TintAndShade = 0
    End With
    Sheets("Sheet3").Select
    Sheets("Sheet3").Name = "Portland"
    Sheets("Portland").Select
    With ActiveWorkbook.Sheets("Portland").Tab
        .Color = 10498160
        .TintAndShade = 0
    End With
End Sub
```

Independent Challenge 3 (continued)

j. Hide the PERSONAL.XLSB workbook. (*Hint*: With the PERSONAL.XLSB workbook active, click the VIEW tab, then click the Hide button in the Window group.)
k. Close the workbook without saving changes to the PERSONAL.XLSB workbook, then exit Excel.

Independent Challenge 4: Explore

As the owner of a yoga studio you manage your courses using an Excel workbook. You have created a macro that will display available classes when a type of class is entered. You have been manually entering the class name and then running the macro. You have hired an assistant and would like to simplify the process of displaying class information by adding a form control to help select the data in the worksheet and then run the macro. Specifically, you will ask your assistant to use a list box which will return a numeric value for the current position of the control. That numeric value can be used with an Index function to insert the selected data in the necessary location for the macro which will use it as criteria to filter your data to return the requested course information.

a. Start Excel, open the Data File EX I-2.xlsm from the location where you store your Data Files, then save it as **EX I-Classes**.
b. Test the macro FindClass by entering **Power** in cell A20 and running the macro. Scroll down to cell A23 to see the results.
c. Insert a button form control in cells B19:C20 and assign the FindClass macro to the form control button. Label the button with the text **Find Classes**.
d. Enter **Basics** in cell A20 and test the button.
e. On the Controls sheet create a list for a List Box form control by entering **Basics** in cell A1, **Power** in cell A2, **Hatha** in cell A3, and **Kripalu** in cell A4.
f. On the Yoga Classes sheet enter **Select Class** in cell A1. Insert a list box form control in cells B1:B4. Format the control to set the Input range to A1:A4 of the Controls sheet and the Cell link to cell B1 in the Controls sheet. Compare your controls to **FIGURE I-26**.
g. Test the list box by clicking different classes and viewing the position in the list displayed in cell B1 of the Controls sheet, the cell link used in the previous step.
h. Replace the class in cell A20 with the index formula **=INDEX(Controls!A1:A4,Controls!B1,0)**. This will use the list position displayed in cell B1 of the Controls sheet to find the class in the range A1:A4 of the Controls sheet and display the class name in cell A20. Test the index formula by selecting different classes in the list box and verifying cell A20 matches the selection.
i. Delete the form control button in cells B19:C20.
j. Assign the FindClass macro to the list box form control.
k. Select a class from the list box and verify the macro is working properly.
l. Enter your name in the footers of both worksheets. Save the workbook, close the workbook, then submit the workbook to your instructor and exit Excel.

FIGURE I-26

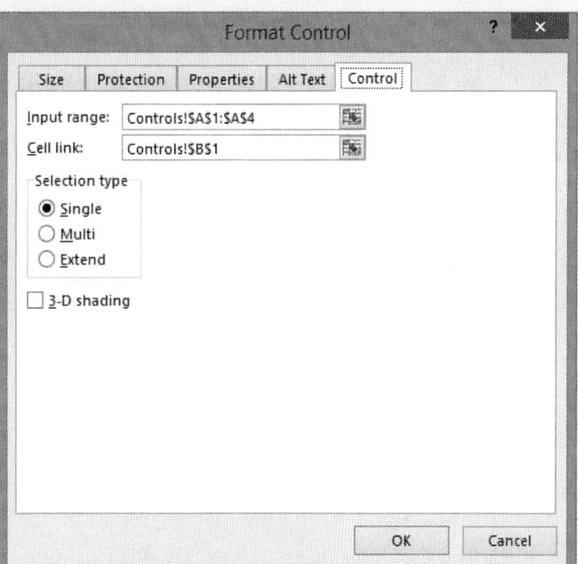

Excel 2013

Visual Workshop

Start Excel, open the Data File EX I-3.xlsx from the location where you store your Data Files, then save it as a macro-enabled workbook called **EX I-Payroll**. Create a macro with the name **TotalHours**, save the macro in the EX I-Payroll workbook that does the following:

- Totals the weekly hours for each employee by totaling the hours for the first employee and copying that formula for the other employees
- Adds a row at the top of the worksheet and inserts a label of **Hours** in a font size of 14 point, centered across all columns
- Adds your name in the worksheet footer

Test the TotalHours macro by opening the Data File EX I-3.xlsx from the location where you store your Data Files and running the macro. Compare your macro results to **FIGURE I-27**. Close the Data File EX I-3 without saving it, then save the EX I-Payroll workbook. Submit the EX I-Payroll workbook to your instructor.

FIGURE I-27

	A	B	C	D	E	F	G	H	I
1				Hours					
2		Monday	Tuesday	Wednesday	Thursday	Friday	Saturday	Sunday	Total
3	Mary Jacobs	7	8	6	8	5	0	1	35
4	John Malone	5	7	8	7	7	6	2	42
5	Ken Duffy	6	5	7	6	3	5	0	32
6	Sally Landry	8	7	6	5	5	1	0	32
7	Kathy Bane	8	7	5	8	7	7	0	42
8	Jacki Rand	8	7	5	5	7	8	0	40
9	Cindy Healy	7	5	2	6	8	5	3	36
10	Randy Thomas	2	7	8	6	7	2	0	32
11	Ken Yang	0	4	4	4	4	4	1	21
12	Linda Regan	7	8	2	8	8	1	0	34
13									

Using What-if Analysis

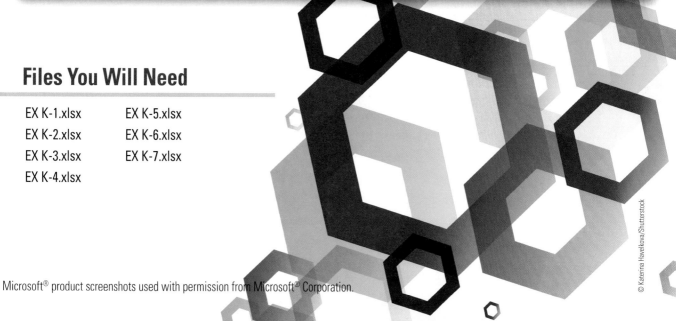

CASE Kate Morgan, the vice president of sales at Quest, is meeting with the U.S. region manager to discuss sales projections for the first half of the year. In preparation for her meeting, Kate asks you to help analyze the U.S. sales data using what-if scenarios, data tables, goal seek, Solver and the Analysis ToolPak.

Unit Objectives

After completing this unit, you will be able to:

- Define a what-if analysis
- Track a what-if analysis with Scenario Manager
- Generate a scenario summary
- Project figures using a data table
- Use Goal Seek
- Set up a complex what-if analysis with Solver
- Run Solver and summarize results
- Analyze data using the Analysis ToolPak

Files You Will Need

EX K-1.xlsx
EX K-2.xlsx
EX K-3.xlsx
EX K-4.xlsx
EX K-5.xlsx
EX K-6.xlsx
EX K-7.xlsx

Define a What-if Analysis

Learning Outcomes
- Develop guidelines for performing what-if analysis
- Define what-if analysis terminology

By performing a what-if analysis in a worksheet, you can get immediate answers to questions such as "What happens to profits if we sell 25 percent more of a certain product?" or "What happens to monthly payments if interest rates rise or fall?". A worksheet you use to produce a what-if analysis is often called a **model** because it acts as the basis for multiple outcomes or sets of results. To perform a what-if analysis in a worksheet, you change the value in one or more **input cells** (cells that contain data rather than formulas), then observe the effects on dependent cells. A **dependent cell** usually contains a formula whose resulting value changes depending on the values in the input cells. A dependent cell can be located either in the same worksheet as the changing input value or in another worksheet. **CASE** *Kate Morgan has received projected sales data from regional managers. She has created a worksheet model to perform an initial what-if analysis, as shown in* **FIGURE K-1**. *She thinks the U.S. sales projections for the month of January should be higher. You first review the guidelines for performing a what-if analysis.*

DETAILS

When performing a what-if analysis, use the following guidelines:

- **Understand and state the purpose of the worksheet model**
  Identify what you want to accomplish with the model. What problem are you trying to solve? What questions do you want the model to answer for you? Kate's Quest worksheet model is designed to total Quest sales projections for the first half of the year and to calculate the percentage of total sales for each Quest region. It also calculates the totals and percentages of total sales for each month.

- **Determine the data input value(s) that, if changed, affect the dependent cell results**
  In a what-if analysis, changes in the content of the data input cells produces varying results in the output cells. You will use the model to work with one data input value: the January value for the U.S. region, in cell B3.

- **Identify the dependent cell(s) that will contain results**
  The dependent cells usually contain formulas, and the formula results adjust as you enter different values in the input cells. The results of two dependent cell formulas (labeled Total and Percent of Total Sales) appear in cells H3 and I3, respectively. The total for the month of January in cell B7 is also a dependent cell, as is the percentage in cell B8.

- **Formulate questions you want the what-if analysis to answer**
  It is important that you know the questions you want your model to answer. In the Quest model, you want to answer the following question: What happens to the U.S. regional percentage if the sales amount for the month of January is increased to $109,667?

- **Perform the what-if analysis**
  When you perform the what-if analysis, you explore the relationships between the input values and the dependent cell formulas. In the Quest worksheet model, you want to see what effect an increase in sales for January has on the dependent cell formulas containing totals and percentages. Because the sales amounts for this month is located in cell B3, any formula that references that cell is directly affected by a change in this sales amount—in this case, the total formula in cell H3. Because the formula in cell I3 references cell H3, a change in the sales amount affects this cell as well. The percentage formulas will also change because they reference the total formulas. **FIGURE K-2** shows the result of the what-if analysis described in this example.

FIGURE K-1: Worksheet model for a what-if analysis

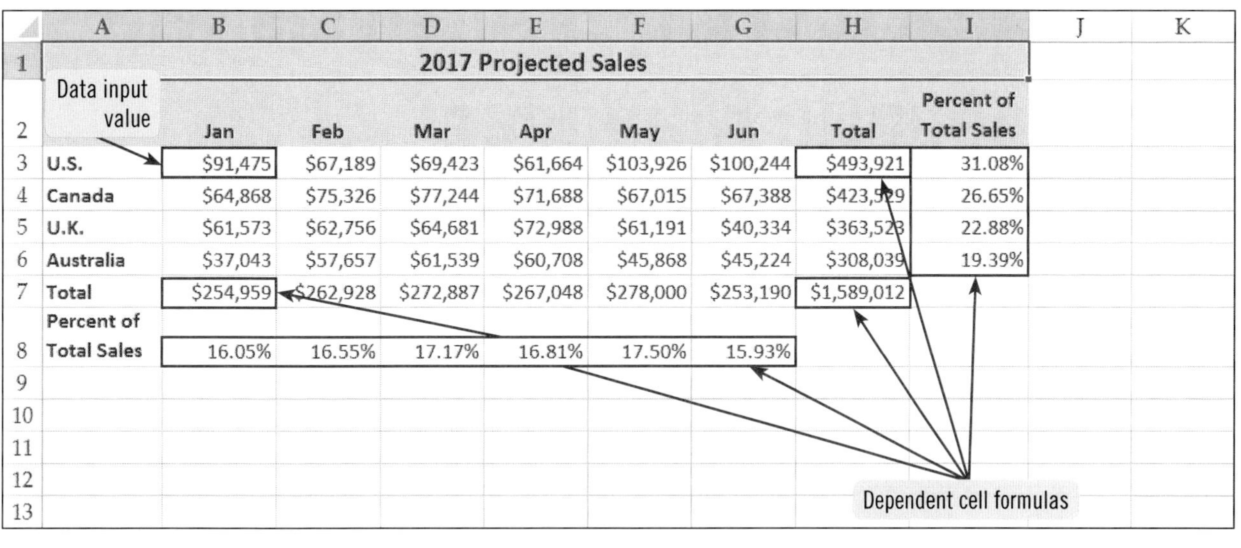

	A	B	C	D	E	F	G	H	I	J	K
1	2017 Projected Sales										
2		Jan	Feb	Mar	Apr	May	Jun	Total	Percent of Total Sales		
3	U.S.	$91,475	$67,189	$69,423	$61,664	$103,926	$100,244	$493,921	31.08%		
4	Canada	$64,868	$75,326	$77,244	$71,688	$67,015	$67,388	$423,529	26.65%		
5	U.K.	$61,573	$62,756	$64,681	$72,988	$61,191	$40,334	$363,523	22.88%		
6	Australia	$37,043	$57,657	$61,539	$60,708	$45,868	$45,224	$308,039	19.39%		
7	Total	$254,959	$262,928	$272,887	$267,048	$278,000	$253,190	$1,589,012			
8	Percent of Total Sales	16.05%	16.55%	17.17%	16.81%	17.50%	15.93%				
9											
10											
11											
12											
13											

FIGURE K-2: Changed input values and dependent formula results

	A	B	C	D	E	F	G	H	I	J
1	2017 Projected Sales									
2		Jan	Feb	Mar	Apr	May	Jun	Total	Percent of Total Sales	
3	U.S.	$109,667	$67,189	$69,423	$61,664	$103,926	$100,244	$512,113	31.86%	
4	Canada	$64,868	$75,326	$77,244	$71,688	$67,015	$67,388	$423,529	26.35%	
5	U.K.	$61,573	$62,756	$64,681	$72,988	$61,191	$40,334	$363,523	22.62%	
6	Australia	$37,043	$57,657	$61,539	$60,708	$45,868	$45,224	$308,039	19.17%	
7	Total	$273,151	$262,928	$272,887	$267,048	$278,000	$253,190	$1,607,204		
8	Percent of Total Sales	17.00%	16.36%	16.98%	16.62%	17.30%	15.75%			
9										
10										
11										
12										
13										
14										
15										

Changed input value

Changed formula results

Learning Outcomes
- Create scenarios to analyze Excel data
- Analyze scenarios using Scenario Manager

Track a What-if Analysis with Scenario Manager

A **scenario** is a set of values you use to observe different worksheet results. For example, you might plan to sell 100 of a particular item, at a price of $5 per item, producing sales results of $500. But what if you reduced the price to $4 or increased it to $6? Each of these price scenarios would produce different sales results. A changing value, such as the price in this example, is called a **variable**. The Excel Scenario Manager simplifies the process of what-if analysis by allowing you to name and save multiple scenarios with variable values in a worksheet. **CASE** *Kate asks you to use Scenario Manager to create scenarios showing how a U.S. sales increase can affect total Quest sales over the 3-month period of February through April.*

STEPS

1. **Start Excel, open the file EX K-1.xlsx from the location where you store your Data Files, then save it as EX K-Sales**

   The first step in defining a scenario is choosing the changing cells. **Changing cells** are those that will vary in the different scenarios.

2. **With the Projected Sales sheet active, select range C3:E3, click the DATA tab, click the What-If Analysis button in the Data Tools group, then click Scenario Manager**

   You want to be able to easily return to your original worksheet values, so your first scenario contains those figures.

3. **Click Add, drag the Add Scenario dialog box to the right if necessary until columns A and B are visible, then type Original Sales Figures in the Scenario name text box**

   The range in the Changing cells box shows the range you selected, as shown in **FIGURE K-3**.

4. **Click OK to confirm the scenario range**

   The Scenario Values dialog box opens, as shown in **FIGURE K-4**. The existing values appear in the changing cell boxes. Because you want this scenario to reflect the current worksheet values, you leave these unchanged.

5. **Click OK**

   You want to create a second scenario that will show the effects of increasing sales by $5,000.

6. **Click Add; in the Scenario name text box type Increase Feb, Mar, Apr by 5000; verify that the Changing cells text box reads C3:E3, then click OK; in the Scenario Values dialog box, change the value in the $C$3 text box to 72189, change the value in the $D$3 text box to 74423, change the value in the $E$3 text box to 66664, then click Add**

   You are ready to create a third scenario. It will show the effects of increasing sales by $10,000.

7. **In the Scenario name text box, type Increase Feb, Mar, Apr by 10000 and click OK; in the Scenario Values dialog box, change the value in the $C$3 text box to 77189, change the value in the $D$3 text box to 79423, change the value in the $E$3 text box to 71664, then click OK**

   The Scenario Manager dialog box reappears, as shown in **FIGURE K-5**. You are ready to display the results of your scenarios in the worksheet.

8. **Make sure the Increase Feb, Mar, Apr by 10000 scenario is still selected, click Show, notice that the percent of U.S. sales in cell I3 changes from 31.08% to 32.36%; click Increase Feb, Mar, Apr by 5000, click Show, notice that the U.S. sales percent is now 31.73%; click Original Sales Figures, click Show to return to the original values, then click Close**

9. **Save the workbook**

QUICK TIP
You can delete a scenario by selecting it in the Scenario Manager dialog box and clicking Delete.

QUICK TIP
To edit a scenario, select it in the Scenario Manager dialog box, click the Edit button, then edit the Scenario.

FIGURE K-3: Add Scenario dialog box

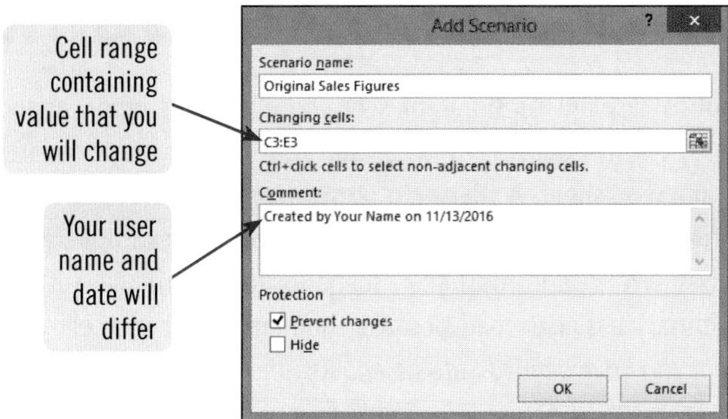

FIGURE K-4: Scenario Values dialog box

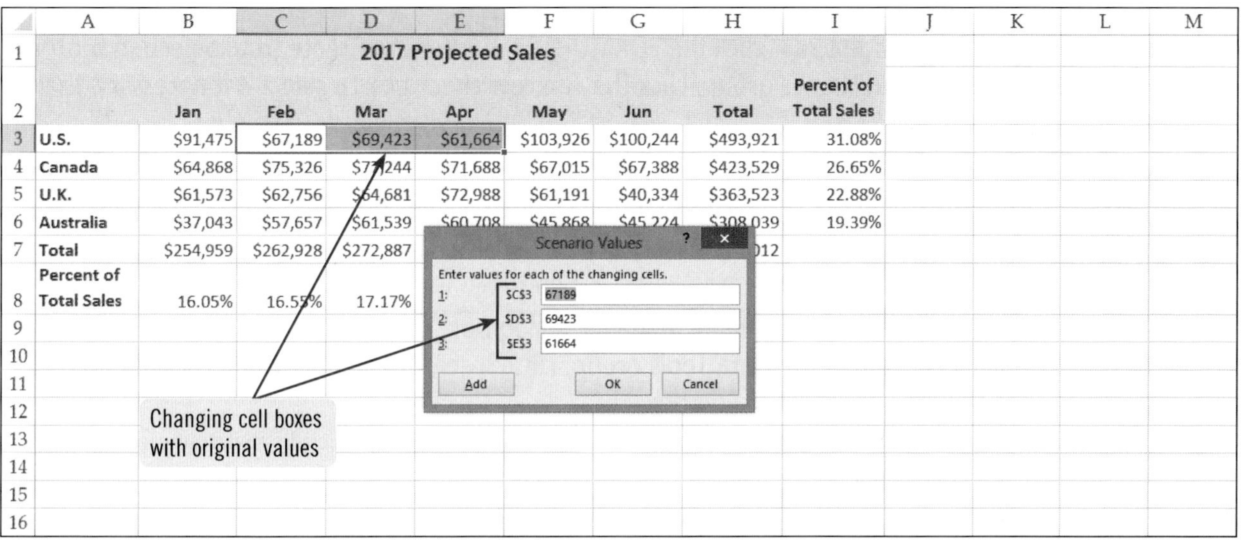

FIGURE K-5: Scenario Manager dialog box with three scenarios listed

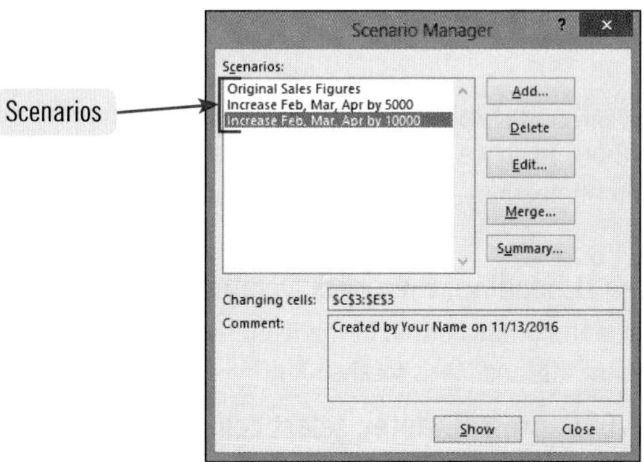

Merging scenarios

Excel stores scenarios in the workbook and on the worksheet in which you created them. To apply scenarios from another worksheet or workbook into the current worksheet, click the Merge button in the Scenario Manager dialog box. The Merge Scenarios dialog box opens, letting you select scenarios from other locations. When you click a sheet name in the sheet list, the text under the sheet list tells you how many scenarios exist on that sheet. To merge scenarios from another workbook, such as those sent to you in a workbook by a coworker, open the other workbook file, click the Book list arrow in the Merge Scenarios dialog box, then click the workbook name. When you merge workbook scenarios, it's best if the workbooks have the same structure, so that there is no confusion of cell values.

Excel 2013

Generate a Scenario Summary

Learning Outcomes
- Display scenarios in a scenario summary report
- Format a scenario summary report

Although it may be useful to display the different scenario outcomes when analyzing data, it can be difficult to keep track of them. In most cases, you will want to refer to a single report that summarizes the results of all the scenarios in a worksheet. A **scenario summary** is an Excel table that compiles data from the changing cells and corresponding result cells for each scenario. For example, you might use a scenario summary to illustrate the best, worst, and most likely scenarios for a particular set of circumstances. Using cell naming makes the summary easier to read because the names, not the cell references, appear in the report. **CASE** *Now that you have defined Kate's scenarios, she needs you to generate and print a scenario summary report. You begin by creating names for the cells in row 3 based on the labels in row 2, so that the report will be easier to read.*

STEPS

1. **Select the range B2:I3, click the FORMULAS tab, click the Create from Selection button in the Defined Names group, click the Top row check box to select it if necessary, then click OK**

   Excel creates the names for the data in row 3 based on the labels in row 2. You decide to review them.

QUICK TIP
You can also click the Name box list arrow on the formula bar to view cell names.

2. **Click the Name Manager button in the Defined Names group**

   The eight labels appear, along with other workbook names, in the Name Manager dialog box, confirming that they were created, as shown in **FIGURE K-6**. Now you are ready to generate the scenario summary report.

3. **Click Close to close the Name Manager dialog box, click the DATA tab, click the What-If Analysis button in the Data Tools group, click Scenario Manager, then click Summary in the Scenario Manager dialog box**

   Excel needs to know the location of the cells that contain the formula results that you want to see in the report. You want to see the results for U.S. total and percentage of sales, and on overall Quest sales.

4. **With the Result cells text box selected, click cell H3 on the worksheet, type , (a comma), click cell I3, type , (a comma), then click cell H7**

   With the report type and result cells specified, as shown in **FIGURE K-7**, you are now ready to generate the report.

QUICK TIP
To see the Comments for each scenario, which by default contain the creator name and creation date, click the plus sign to the left of row 3.

5. **Click OK**

   A summary of the worksheet's scenarios appears on a new sheet titled Scenario Summary. The report shows outline buttons to the left of and above the worksheet so that you can hide or show report details. Because the Current Values column shows the same values as the Original Sales Figures column, you decide to delete column D.

6. **Right-click the column D heading, then click Delete in the shortcut menu**

   Next, you notice that the notes at the bottom of the report refer to the column that no longer exists. You also want to make the report title and labels for the result cells more descriptive.

7. **Select the range B13:B15, press [Delete], select cell B2, edit its contents to read Scenario Summary for U.S. Sales, click cell C10, then edit its contents to read Total U.S. Sales**

QUICK TIP
The scenario summary is not linked to the worksheet. If you change the values in the worksheet, you must generate a new scenario summary.

8. **Click cell C11, edit its contents to read Percent U.S. Sales, click cell C12, edit its contents to read Total Quest Sales, then click cell A1**

   The completed scenario summary is shown in **FIGURE K-8**.

9. **Add your name to the center section of the Scenario Summary sheet footer, change the page orientation to landscape, then save the workbook and preview the worksheet**

FIGURE K-6: Name Manager dialog box displaying new names

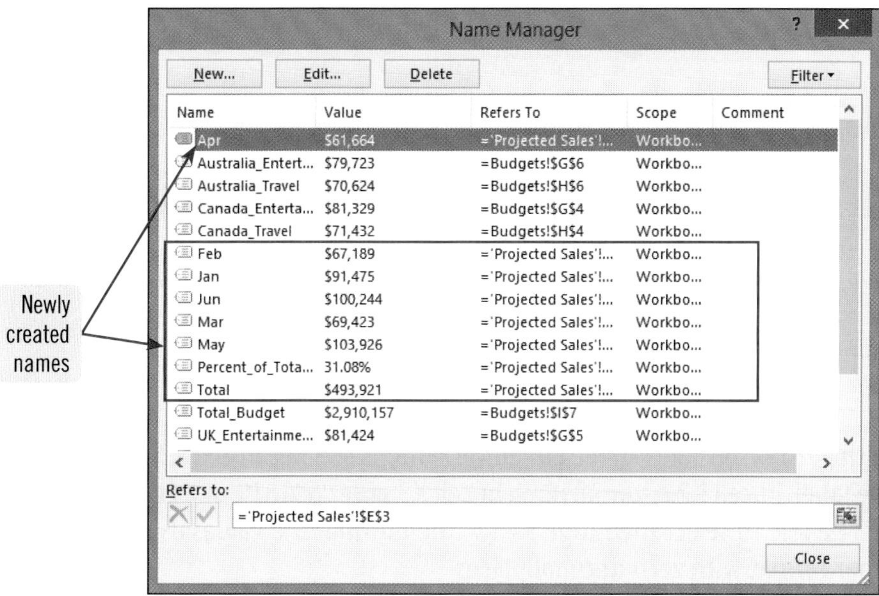

FIGURE K-7: Scenario Summary dialog box

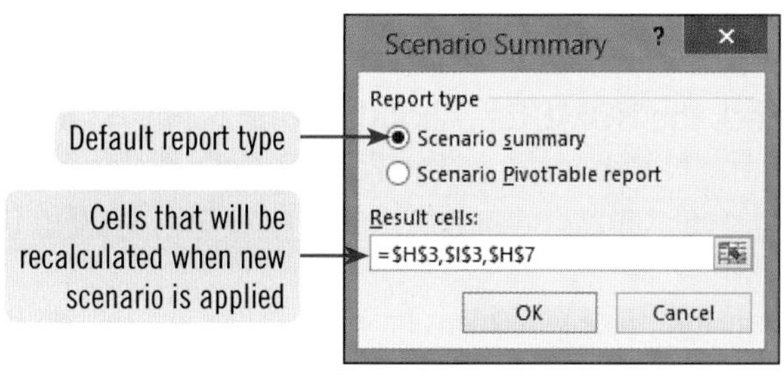

FIGURE K-8: Completed Scenario Summary report

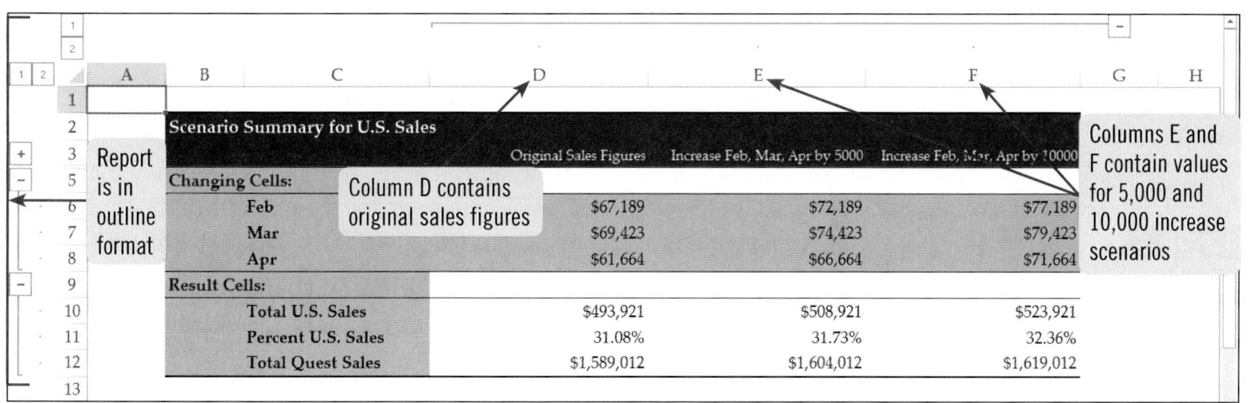

Project Figures Using a Data Table

Learning Outcomes
- Develop a data table structure
- Analyze options using a data table

Another way to answer what-if questions in a worksheet is by using a data table. A **data table** is a range of cells that simultaneously shows the varying resulting values when you change one or more input values in a formula. A **one-input data table** is a table that shows the result of varying one input value, such as the interest rate. **CASE** *Now that you have completed Kate's analysis, she wants you to find out how the U.S. sales percentage would change as U.S. total sales increased.*

STEPS

1. **Click the Projected Sales sheet tab, enter Total U.S. Sales in cell K1, widen column K to fit the label, in cell K2 enter 481819, in cell K3 enter 531819, select the range K2:K3, drag the fill handle to select the range K4:K6, then format the values using the Accounting number format with zero decimal places**

   You begin setting up your data table by entering total U.S. sales lower and higher than the total in cell H3 in increasing amounts of $50,000. These are the **input values** in the data table. With the varying input values listed in column K, you enter a formula reference to cell I3 that you want Excel to use in calculating the resulting percentages (the **output values**) in column L, based on the possible sales levels in column K.

2. **Click cell L1, type =, click cell I3, click the Enter button ✓ on the formula bar, then format the value in cell L1 using the Percentage format with two decimal places**

   The value in cell I3, 31.08%, appears in cell L1, and the cell name =Percent_of_Total_Sales appears in the formula bar, as shown in **FIGURE K-9**. Because it isn't necessary for users of the data table to see the value in cell L1, you want to hide the cell's contents from view.

> **QUICK TIP**
> You can create your own custom format by clicking a format that resembles the one you want and customizing it in the Type text box.

3. **With cell L1 selected, click the HOME tab, click the Format button in the Cells group, click Format Cells, click the Number tab in the Format Cells dialog box if necessary, click Custom under Category, select any characters in the Type box, type ;;; (three semicolons), then click OK**

   Applying the custom cell format of three semicolons hides the values in a cell. With the table structure in place, you can now generate the data table showing percentages for the varying sales amounts.

> **TROUBLE**
> If you receive the message "Selection not valid", repeat Step 4, taking care to select the entire range K1:L6.

4. **Select the range K1:L6, click the DATA tab, click the What-If Analysis button in the Data Tools group, then click Data Table**

   The Data Table dialog box opens, as shown in **FIGURE K-10**. Because the percentage formula in cell I3 (which you just referenced in cell L1) uses the total sales in cell H3 as input, you enter a reference to cell H3. You place this reference in the Column input cell text box, rather than in the Row input cell text box, because the varying input values are arranged in a column in your data table structure.

5. **Click the Column input cell text box, click cell H3, then click OK**

   Excel completes the data table by calculating percentages for each sales amount.

6. **Format the range L2:L6 with the Percentage format with two decimal places, then click cell A1**

   The formatted data table is shown in **FIGURE K-11**. It shows the sales percentages for each of the possible levels of U.S. sales. By looking at the data table, Kate determines that if she can increase total U.S. sales to over $700,000, the U.S. division will then comprise about 40% of total Quest sales for the first half of 2017.

> **QUICK TIP**
> You cannot delete individual output values in a data table; you must delete all output values.

7. **Add your name to the center section of the worksheet footer, change the worksheet orientation to landscape, then save the workbook and preview the worksheet**

FIGURE K-9: One-input data table structure

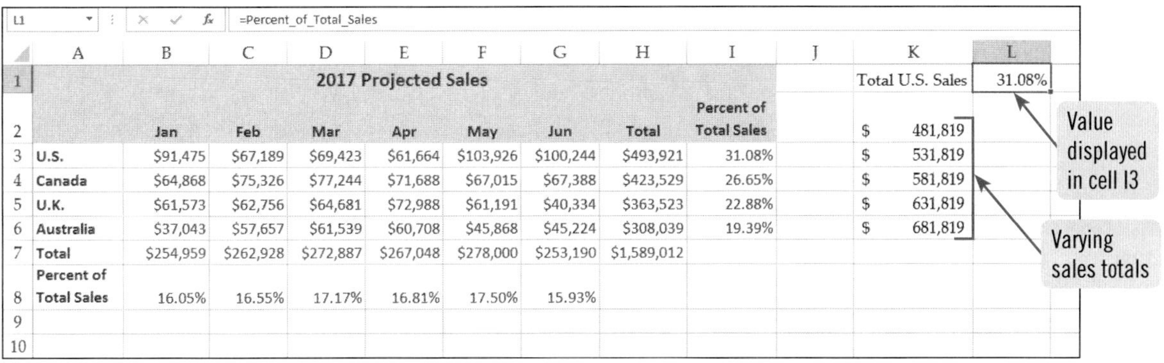

L1 =Percent_of_Total_Sales

	A	B	C	D	E	F	G	H	I	J	K	L
1	2017 Projected Sales										Total U.S. Sales	31.08%
2		Jan	Feb	Mar	Apr	May	Jun	Total	Percent of Total Sales		$ 481,819	
3	U.S.	$91,475	$67,189	$69,423	$61,664	$103,926	$100,244	$493,921	31.08%		$ 531,819	
4	Canada	$64,868	$75,326	$77,244	$71,688	$67,015	$67,388	$423,529	26.65%		$ 581,819	
5	U.K.	$61,573	$62,756	$64,681	$72,988	$61,191	$40,334	$363,523	22.88%		$ 631,819	
6	Australia	$37,043	$57,657	$61,539	$60,708	$45,868	$45,224	$308,039	19.39%		$ 681,819	
7	Total	$254,959	$262,928	$272,887	$267,048	$278,000	$253,190	$1,589,012				
8	Percent of Total Sales	16.05%	16.55%	17.17%	16.81%	17.50%	15.93%					
9												
10												

FIGURE K-10: Data Table dialog box

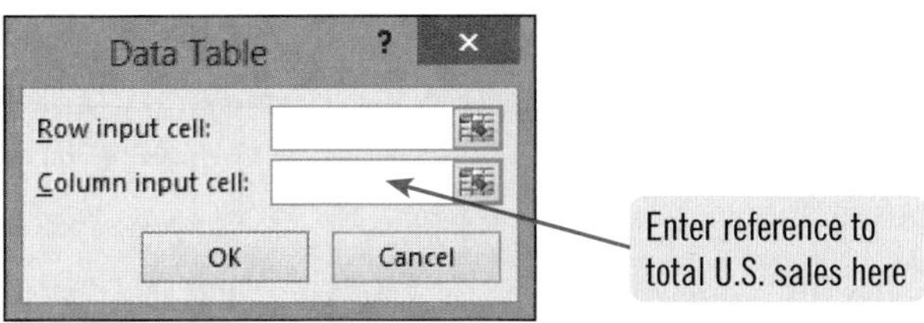

FIGURE K-11: Completed data table with resulting values

	A	B	C	D	E	F	G	H	I	J	K	L
1	2017 Projected Sales										Total U.S. Sales	
2		Jan	Feb	Mar	Apr	May	Jun	Total	Percent of Total Sales		$ 481,819	30.55%
3	U.S.	$91,475	$67,189	$69,423	$61,664	$103,926	$100,244	$493,921	31.08%		$ 531,819	32.69%
4	Canada	$64,868	$75,326	$77,244	$71,688	$67,015	$67,388	$423,529	26.65%		$ 581,819	34.70%
5	U.K.	$61,573	$62,756	$64,681	$72,988	$61,191	$40,334	$363,523	22.88%		$ 631,819	36.59%
6	Australia	$37,043	$57,657	$61,539	$60,708	$45,868	$45,224	$308,039	19.39%		$ 681,819	38.37%
7	Total	$254,959	$262,928	$272,887	$267,048	$278,000	$253,190	$1,589,012				
8	Percent of Total Sales	16.05%	16.55%	17.17%	16.81%	17.50%	15.93%					
9												
10												
11												
12												
13												

Input values in column K

Percentages (output values) in column L

Completed data table

Creating a two-input data table

A **two-input data table** shows the resulting values when two different input values are varied in a formula. You could, for example, use a two-input data table to calculate your monthly car payment based on varying interest rates and varying loan terms, as shown in **FIGURE K-12**. In a two-input data table, different values of one input cell appear across the top row of the table, while different values of the second input cell are listed down the left column. You create a two-input data table the same way that you created a one-input data table, except you enter both a row and a column input cell. In the example shown in **FIGURE K-12**, the two-input data table structure was created by first entering the number of payments in the range B6:D6 and rates in the range A7:A15. Then the data table values were created by first selecting the range A6:D15, clicking the DATA tab, clicking the What-If Analysis button in the Data Tools group, then clicking Data Table. In the Data Table dialog box, the row input value is the term in cell C2. The column input value is the interest rate in cell B2. You can check the accuracy of these values by cross-referencing the values in the data table with those in row 2 where you can see that an interest rate of 4.5% for 36 months has a monthly payment of $594.94.

FIGURE K-12: Two-input data table

	A	B	C	D	E
1	Loan Amount	Interest Rate	# Payments	Monthly Payment	
2	$20,000.00	4.50%	36	$594.94	
3					
4		Car Payment for $20,000 Loan			
5			Term		
6		36	48	60	
7	4.00%	$590.48	$451.58	$368.33	
8	4.25%	$592.71	$453.82	$370.59	
9	4.50%	$594.94	$456.07	$372.86	
10	4.75%	$597.18	$458.32	$375.14	
11	5.00%	$599.42	$460.59	$377.42	
12	5.25%	$601.67	$462.85	$379.72	
13	5.50%	$603.92	$465.13	$382.02	
14	5.75%	$606.18	$467.41	$384.34	
15	6.00%	$608.44	$469.70	$386.66	
16					
17					

Use Goal Seek

Learning Outcomes
- Determine input values for a desired result using goal seek
- Answer questions about data using goal seek

You can think of goal seeking as a what-if analysis in reverse. In a what-if analysis, you might try many sets of values to achieve a certain solution. To **goal seek**, you specify a solution, then ask Excel to find the input value that produces the answer you want. "Backing into" a solution in this way, sometimes referred to as **backsolving**, can save a significant amount of time. For example, you can use Goal Seek to determine how many units must be sold to reach a particular sales goal or to determine what expense levels are necessary to meet a budget target. **CASE** *After reviewing her data table, Kate has a follow-up question: What January U.S. sales target is required to bring the January Quest sales percentage to 17%, assuming the sales for the other regions don't change? You use Goal Seek to answer her question.*

STEPS

1. **Click cell B8**

   The first step in using Goal Seek is to select a goal cell. A **goal cell** contains a formula in which you can substitute values to find a specific value, or goal. You use cell B8 as the goal cell because it contains the percent formula.

2. **Click the DATA tab, click the What-If Analysis button in the Data Tools group, then click Goal Seek**

   The Goal Seek dialog box opens. The Set cell text box contains a reference to cell B8, the percent formula cell you selected in Step 1. You need to indicate that the figure in cell B8 should equal 17%.

3. **Click the To value text box, then type 17%**

   The value 17% represents the desired solution you want to reach by substituting different values in the By changing cell.

4. **Click the By changing cell text box, then click cell B3**

   You have specified that you want cell B3, the U.S. January amount, to change to reach the 17% solution, as shown in FIGURE K-13.

5. **Click OK**

   The Goal Seek Status dialog box opens with the following message: "Goal Seeking with Cell B8 found a solution." By changing the sales amount in cell B3 to $109,667, Goal Seek achieves a January percentage of 17.

6. **Click OK, then click cell A1**

   Changing the sales amount in cell B3 changes the other dependent values in the worksheet (B7, H3, I3, and H7) as shown in FIGURE K-14.

7. **Save the workbook, then preview the worksheet**

QUICK TIP
Before you select another command, you can return the worksheet to its status prior to the Goal Seek by pressing [Ctrl][Z].

FIGURE K-13: Completed Goal Seek dialog box

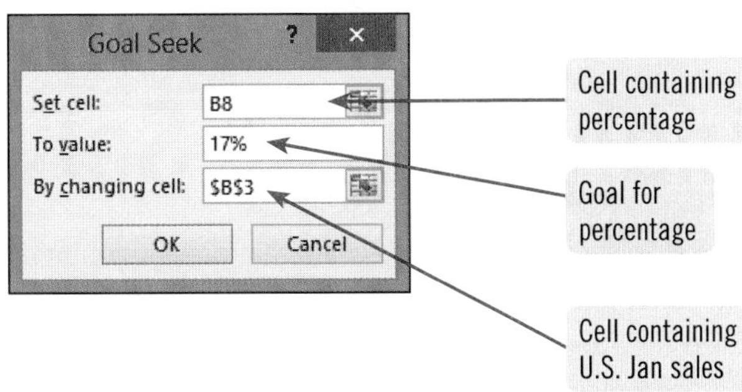

FIGURE K-14: Worksheet with new dependent values

	A	B	C	D	E	F	G	H	I	J
1	2017 Projected Sales									
2		Jan	Feb	Mar	Apr	May	Jun	Total	Percent of Total Sales	
3	U.S.	$109,667	$67,189	$69,423	$61,664	$103,926	$100,244	$512,113	31.86%	
4	Canada	$64,868	$75,326	$77,244	$71,688	$67,015	$67,388	$423,529	26.35%	
5	U.K.	$61,573	$62,756	$64,681	$72,988	$61,191	$40,334	$363,523	22.62%	
6	Australia	$37,043	$57,657	$61,539	$60,708	$45,868	$45,224	$308,039	19.17%	
7	Total	$273,151	$262,928	$272,887	$267,048	$278,000	$253,190	$1,607,204		
8	Percent of Total Sales	17.00%	16.36%	16.98%	16.62%	17.30%	15.75%			
9										
13										
14										
15										

New target values calculated by Goal Seek

New dependent values

Excel 2013

Set up a Complex What-if Analysis with Solver

Learning Outcomes
- Develop an understanding of the solver terminology
- Set up a worksheet analysis using the Solver Parameters dialog box

The Excel Solver is an **add-in** program that provides optional features. It must be installed before you can use it. Solver finds the best solution to a problem that has several inputs. The cell containing the formula is called the **target cell**, or **objective**. As you learned earlier, cells containing the values that vary are called "changing cells." Solver is helpful when you need to perform a complex what-if analysis involving multiple input values or when the input values must conform to specific limitations or restrictions called **constraints.** CASE *Kate decides to fund each region with the same amount, $775,000, to cover expenses. She adjusts the travel and entertainment allocations to keep expenditures to the allocated amount of $775,000. You use Solver to help Kate find the best possible allocation.*

STEPS

TROUBLE
If Solver is not on your DATA tab, click the FILE tab, click Options, click Add-Ins, click Go, in the Add-Ins dialog box click the Solver Add-in check box to select it, then click OK.

1. **Click the Budgets sheet tab**

   This worksheet is designed to calculate the travel, entertainment, and other budget categories for each region. It assumes fixed costs for communications, equipment, advertising, salaries, and rent. You use Solver to change the entertainment and travel amounts in cells G3:H6 (the changing cells) to achieve your target of a total budget of $3,100,000 in cell I7 (the target cell). You want your solution to include a constraint on cells G3:H6 specifying that each region is funded $775,000. Based on past budgets, you know there are two other constraints: the travel budgets must include at least $83,000, and the entertainment budgets must include at least $95,000. It is a good idea to enter constraints on the worksheet for documentation purposes, as shown in **FIGURE K-15**.

2. **Click the DATA tab, then click the Solver button in the Analysis group**

   If the Solver Parameters dialog box opens, you indicate the target cell with its objective, the changing cells, and the constraints under which you want Solver to work. You begin by entering your total budget objective.

QUICK TIP
If your Solver Parameters dialog box has entries in the By Changing Variable Cells box or in the Subject to the Constraints box, click Reset All, click OK, then continue with Step 3.

3. **With the insertion point in the Set Objective text box, click cell I7 in the worksheet, click the Value Of option button, double-click the Value Of text box, then type 3,100,000**

   You have specified an objective of $3,100,000 for the total budget. In typing the total budget figure, be sure to type the commas.

4. **Click the By Changing Variable Cells text box, then select the range G3:H6 on the worksheet**

   You have told Excel which cells to vary to reach the goal of $3,100,000 total budget. You need to specify the constraints on the worksheet values to restrict the Solver's answer to realistic values.

5. **Click Add, with the insertion point in the Cell Reference text box in the Add Constraint dialog box, select the range I3:I6 in the worksheet, click the list arrow in the dialog box, click =, then with the insertion point in the Constraint text box click cell C9**

   As shown in **FIGURE K-16**, the Add Constraint dialog box specifies that cells in the range I3:I6, the total region budget amounts, should be equal to the value in cell C9. Next, you need to add the constraint that the budgeted entertainment amounts should be at least $95,000.

QUICK TIP
If your solution needs to be an integer, you can select it in the Add Constraint dialog box.

6. **Click Add, with the insertion point in the Cell Reference text box select the range G3:G6 in the worksheet, click the list arrow, select >=, with the insertion point in the Constraint text box click cell C11**

   Next, you need to specify that the budgeted travel amounts should be greater than or equal to $83,000.

7. **Click Add, with the insertion point in the Cell Reference text box select the range H3:H6, select >=, with the insertion point in the Constraint text box click cell C10, then click OK**

   The Solver Parameters dialog box opens with the constraints listed, as shown in **FIGURE K-17**. In the next lesson, you run Solver and generate solutions to the budget constraints.

FIGURE K-15: Worksheet set up for a complex what-if analysis

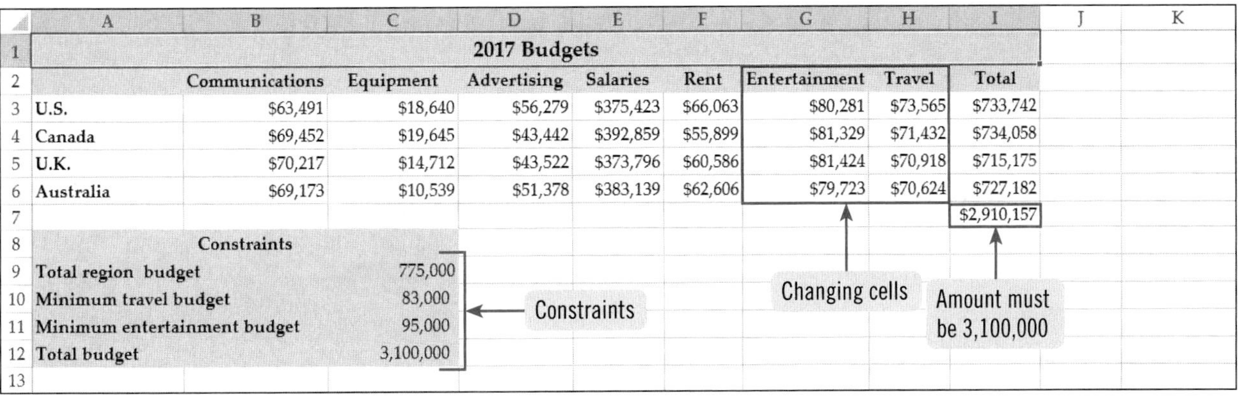

	A	B	C	D	E	F	G	H	I	J	K
1	2017 Budgets										
2		Communications	Equipment	Advertising	Salaries	Rent	Entertainment	Travel	Total		
3	U.S.	$63,491	$18,640	$56,279	$375,423	$66,063	$80,281	$73,565	$733,742		
4	Canada	$69,452	$19,645	$43,442	$392,859	$55,899	$81,329	$71,432	$734,058		
5	U.K.	$70,217	$14,712	$43,522	$373,796	$60,586	$81,424	$70,918	$715,175		
6	Australia	$69,173	$10,539	$51,378	$383,139	$62,606	$79,723	$70,624	$727,182		
7									$2,910,157		
8	Constraints										
9	Total region budget		775,000								
10	Minimum travel budget		83,000								
11	Minimum entertainment budget		95,000								
12	Total budget		3,100,000								
13											

FIGURE K-16: Adding constraints

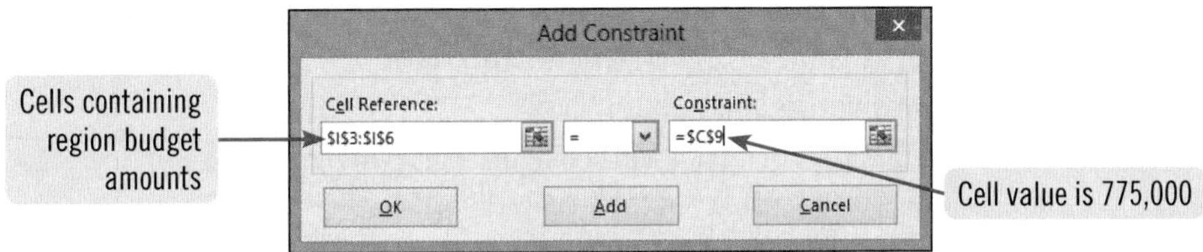

FIGURE K-17: Completed Solver Parameters dialog box

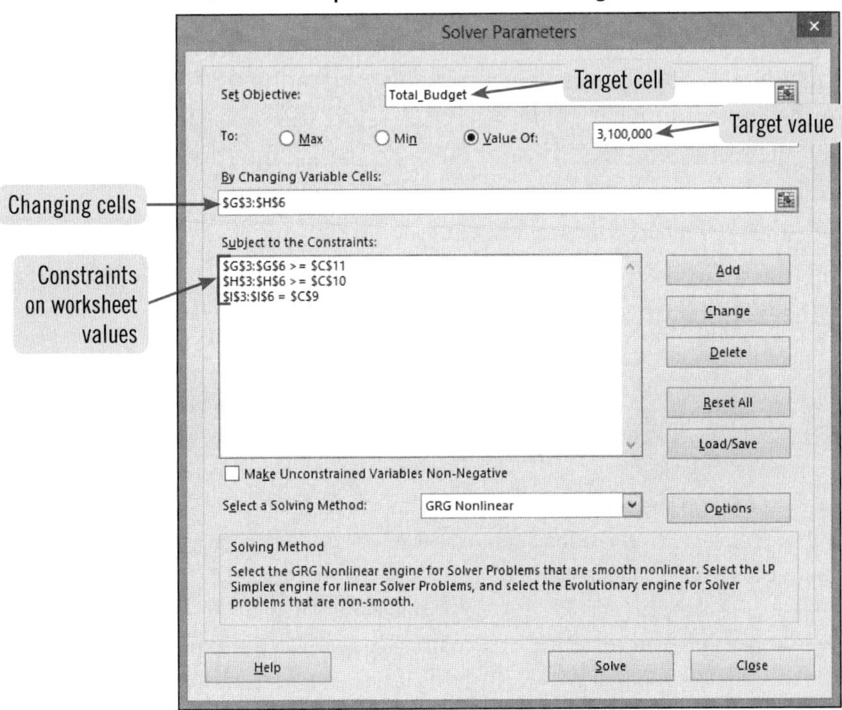

Excel 2013

Run Solver and Summarize Results

Learning Outcomes
- Run solver using the parameters in the Solver Parameters dialog box
- Create an answer report using solver

After entering all the parameters in the Solver Parameters dialog box, you can run Solver to find a solution. In some cases, Solver may not be able to find a solution that meets all of your constraints. Then you would need to enter new constraints and try again. **CASE** *You have finished entering the parameters in the Solver Parameters dialog box. Kate wants you to run Solver and create a summary of the solution on a separate worksheet.*

STEPS

1. **Make sure your Solver Parameters dialog box matches FIGURE K-17 in the previous lesson**
2. **Click Solve**

   The Solver Results dialog box opens, indicating that Solver has found a solution, as shown in **FIGURE K-18**. The solution values appear in the worksheet, but you decide to save the solution values in a summary worksheet and display the original values in the worksheet.
3. **Click Save Scenario, enter Adjusted Budgets in the Scenario Name text box, click OK, in the Solver Results dialog box click the Restore Original Values option button, then click OK to close the Solver Results dialog box**

   The Solver Results dialog box closes, and the original values appear in the worksheet. You will display the Solver solution values on a separate sheet.
4. **Click the What-If Analysis button in the Data Tools group, click Scenario Manager, with the Adjusted Budgets scenario selected in the Scenario Manager dialog box click Summary, then click OK**

   The Solver results appear on the Scenario Summary 2 worksheet, as shown in **FIGURE K-19**. You want to format the solution values on the worksheet.
5. **Select Column A, click the HOME tab if necessary, click the Delete button in the Cells group, right-click the Scenario Summary 2 sheet tab, click Rename on the shortcut menu, type Adjusted Budgets, then press [Enter]**
6. **Select the range A16:A18, press [Delete], select the range A2:D3, click the Fill Color list arrow in the Font group, click Blue, Accent 2, select the range A5:D15, click the Fill Color list arrow, click Blue, Accent 2, Lighter 80%, right-click the row 1 header to select the row, click Delete, select cell A1, then enter Solver Solutions**

   The formatted Solver solution is shown in **FIGURE K-20**.
7. **Enter your name in the center section of the worksheet footer, save the workbook, then preview the worksheet**

Understanding Answer Reports

Instead of saving Solver results as a scenario, you can select from three types of answer reports in the Solver Results window. One of the most useful is the Answer Report, which compares the original values with the Solver's final values. The report has three sections. The top section has the target cell information; it compares the original value of the target cell with the final value. The middle section of the report contains information about the adjustable cells. It lists the original and final values for all cells that were changed to reach the target value. The last report section has information about the constraints. Each constraint you added into Solver is listed in the Formula column, along with the cell address and a description of the cell data. The Cell Value column contains the Solver solution values for the cells. The Status column contains information on whether the constraints were binding or not binding in reaching the solution.

FIGURE K-18: Solver Results dialog box

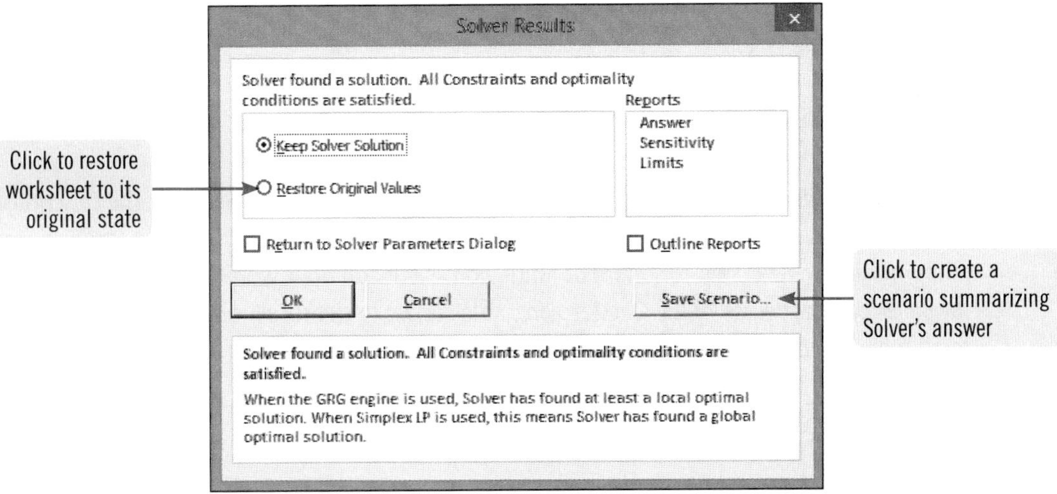

FIGURE K-19: Solver Summary

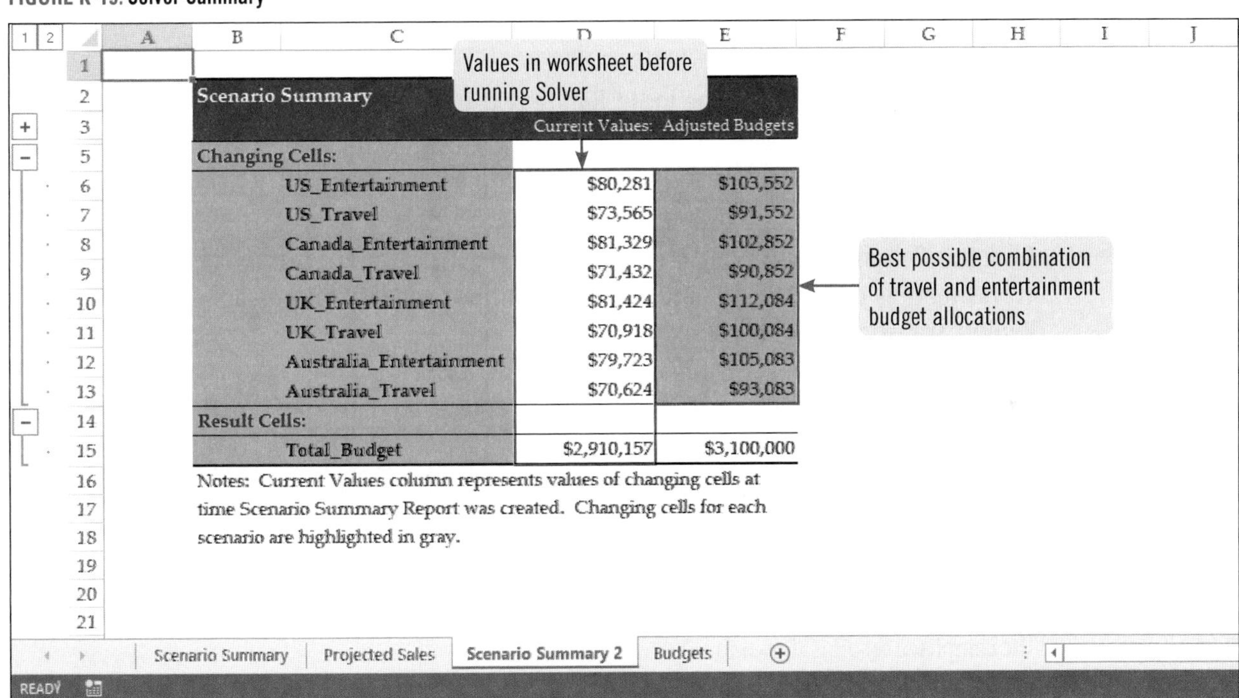

	Current Values:	Adjusted Budgets
Changing Cells:		
US_Entertainment	$80,281	$103,552
US_Travel	$73,565	$91,552
Canada_Entertainment	$81,329	$102,852
Canada_Travel	$71,432	$90,852
UK_Entertainment	$81,424	$112,084
UK_Travel	$70,918	$100,084
Australia_Entertainment	$79,723	$105,083
Australia_Travel	$70,624	$93,083
Result Cells:		
Total_Budget	$2,910,157	$3,100,000

FIGURE K-20: Formatted Solver Summary

Solver Solutions	Current Values:	Adjusted Budgets
Changing Cells:		
US_Entertainment	$80,281	$103,552
US_Travel	$73,565	$91,552
Canada_Entertainment	$81,329	$102,852
Canada_Travel	$71,432	$90,852
UK_Entertainment	$81,424	$112,084
UK_Travel	$70,918	$100,084
Australia_Entertainment	$79,723	$105,083
Australia_Travel	$70,624	$93,083
Result Cells:		
Total_Budget	$2,910,157	$3,100,000

Analyze Data Using the Analysis ToolPak

Learning Outcomes
- Create a summary statistics worksheet
- Analyze worksheet data using descriptive statistics

The Analysis ToolPak is an Excel add-in that contains many statistical analysis tools. The Descriptive Statistics tool in the Data Analysis dialog box generates a statistical report including mean, median, mode, minimum, maximum, and sum for an input range you specify on your worksheet. **CASE** *After reviewing the projected sales figures for the Quest regions, Kate decides to statistically analyze the projected regional sales totals submitted by the managers. You use the Analysis ToolPak to help her generate the sales statistics.*

STEPS

TROUBLE
If Data Analysis is not on your DATA tab, click the FILE tab, click Options, click Add-Ins, click Go, in the Add-Ins dialog box click the Analysis ToolPak check box to select it, then click OK.

1. **Click the Projected Sales sheet tab, click the DATA tab, then click the Data Analysis button in the Analysis group**
   The Data Analysis dialog box opens, listing the available analysis tools.
2. **Click Descriptive Statistics, then click OK**
   The Descriptive Statistics dialog box opens, as shown in **FIGURE K-21**.
3. **With the insertion point in the Input Range text box, select the range H3:H6 on the worksheet**
   You have told Excel to use the total projected sales cells in the statistical analysis. You need to specify that the data is grouped in a column and the results should be placed on a new worksheet named Region Statistics.

QUICK TIP
Selecting the New Worksheet Ply option places the statistical output on a new worksheet in the workbook.

4. **Click the Columns option button in the Grouped By: area if necessary, click the New Worksheet Ply option button in the Output options section if necessary, then type Region Statistics in the text box**
   You want to add the summary statistics to the new worksheet.
5. **Click the Summary statistics check box to select it, then click OK**
   The statistics are generated and placed on the new worksheet named Region Statistics. **TABLE K-1** describes the statistical values provided in the worksheet. Column A is not wide enough to view the labels, and the worksheet needs a descriptive title.

QUICK TIP
If there are fewer than four data values, the Kurtosis will display the DIV/0! error value.

6. **Widen column A to display the row labels, then edit the contents of cell A1 to read Total Projected Sales Jan – Jun**
   The completed report is shown in **FIGURE K-22**.
7. **Enter your name in the center section of the Region Statistics footer, preview the report, save the workbook, close the workbook, then exit Excel**
8. **Submit the workbook to your instructor**

Choosing the right tool for your data analysis

The Analysis ToolPak offers 19 options for data analysis. Anova, or the analysis of variance, can be applied to one or more data samples. The Regression option creates a table of statistics from a least-squares regression. The Correlation choice measures how strong of a linear relationship exists between two random variables. A Moving Average is often calculated for stock prices or any other data that is time sensitive. Moving averages display long-term trends by smoothing out short-term changes. The Random Number Generation option creates a set of random numbers between values that you specify. The Rank and Percentile option creates a report of the ranking and percentile distribution.

FIGURE K-21: Descriptive Statistics dialog box

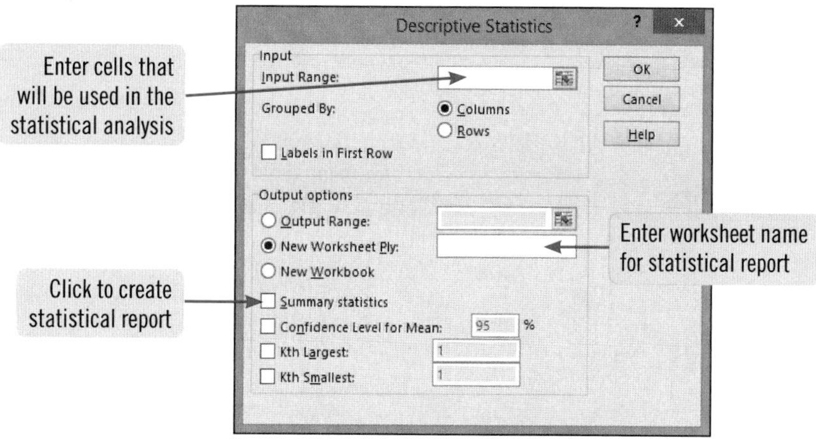

FIGURE K-22: Completed report

Total Projected Sales Jan - Jun	
Mean	401801
Standard Error	43681.95
Median	393526
Mode	#N/A
Standard Deviatior	87363.9
Sample Variance	7.63E+09
Kurtosis	-0.46892
Skewness	0.472144
Range	204074
Minimum	308039
Maximum	512113
Sum	1607204
Count	4

TABLE K-1: Descriptive statistics

statistic	definition
Mean	The average of a set of numbers
Standard Error	The deviation of the mean of your data from the overall population
Median	The middle value of a set of numbers
Mode	The most common value in a set of numbers
Standard Deviation	The measure of how widely spread the values in a set of numbers are; if the values are all close to the mean, the standard deviation is close to zero
Sample Variance	The measure of how scattered the values in a set of numbers are from an expected value
Kurtosis	The measure of the peakedness or flatness of a distribution of data
Skewness	The measure of the asymmetry of the values in a set of numbers
Range	The difference between the largest and smallest values in a set of numbers
Minimum	The smallest value in a set of numbers
Maximum	The largest value in a set of numbers
Sum	The total of the values in a set of numbers
Count	The number of values in a set of numbers

Practice

Put your skills into practice with SAM! If you have a SAM account, go to www.cengage.com/sam2013 to access SAM assignments for this unit.

Concepts Review

FIGURE K-23

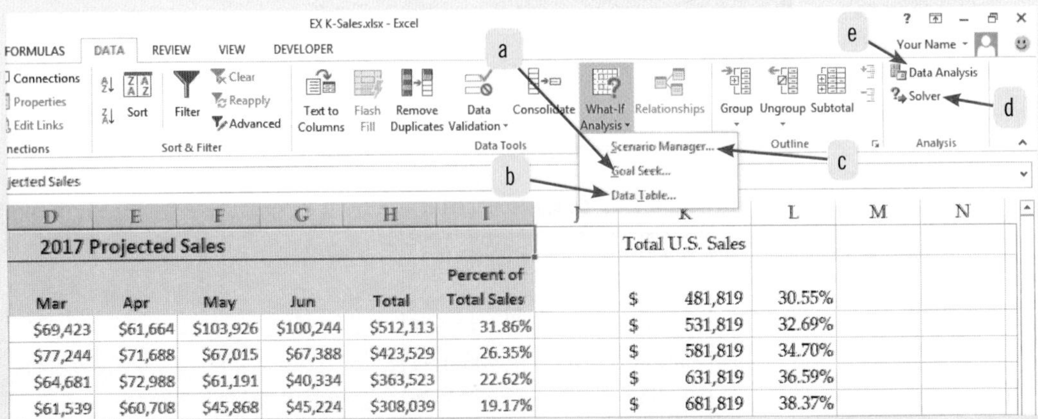

1. **Which element do you click to create a range of cells showing the resulting values with varied formula input?**
2. **Which element do you click to perform a statistical analysis on worksheet data?**
3. **Which element do you click to name and save different sets of values to forecast worksheet results?**
4. **Which element do you click to perform a what-if analysis involving multiple input values with constraints?**
5. **Which element do you click to find the input values that produce a specified result?**

Match each term with the statement that best describes it.

6. **Solver**
7. **One-input data table**
8. **Scenario summary**
9. **Goal Seek**
10. **Two-input data table**

- **a.** Add-in that helps you solve complex what-if scenarios with multiple input values
- **b.** Separate sheet with results from the worksheet's scenarios
- **c.** Generates values resulting from varying two sets of changing values in a formula
- **d.** Helps you backsolve what-if scenarios
- **e.** Generates values resulting from varying one set of changing values in a formula

Select the best answer from the list of choices.

11. **To hide the contents of a cell from view, you can use the custom number format:**
    - **a.** —
    - **b.** ;;;
    - **c.** Blank
    - **d.** " "
12. **The __________ button in the Scenario Manager dialog box allows you to bring scenarios from another workbook into the current workbook.**
    - **a.** Combine
    - **b.** Add
    - **c.** Merge
    - **d.** Import
13. **When you use Goal Seek, you specify a ____________, then find the values that produce it.**
    - **a.** Row input cell
    - **b.** Column input cell
    - **c.** Changing value
    - **d.** Solution

14. In Solver, the cell containing the formula is called the:

a. Target cell.

b. Changing cell.

c. Input cell.

d. Output cell.

15. Which of the following Excel add-ins can be used to generate a statistical summary of worksheet data?

a. Solver

b. Lookup Wizard

c. Conditional Sum

d. Analysis ToolPak

Skills Review

1. Define a what-if analysis.

a. Start Excel, open the file EX K-2.xlsx from the location where you store your Data Files, then save it as **EX K-Repair**.

b. Examine the Auto Repair worksheet to determine the purpose of the worksheet model.

c. Locate the data input cells.

d. Locate any dependent cells.

e. Examine the worksheet to determine problems the worksheet model can solve.

2. Track a what-if analysis with Scenario Manager.

a. On the Auto Repair worksheet, select the range B3:B5, then use the Scenario Manager to set up a scenario called **Most Likely** with the current data input values.

b. Add a scenario called **Best Case** using the same changing cells, but change the Labor cost per hour in the $B$3 text box to **70**, change the Parts cost per job in the $B$4 text box to **65**, then change the Hours per job value in cell $B$5 to **2.5**.

c. Add a scenario called **Worst Case**. For this scenario, change the Labor cost per hour in the $B$3 text box to **95**, change the Parts cost per job in the $B$4 text box to **80**, then change the Hours per job in the $B$5 text box to **3.5**.

d. If necessary, drag the Scenario Manager dialog box to the right until columns A and B are visible.

e. Show the Worst Case scenario results, and view the total job cost.

f. Show the Best Case scenario results, and observe the job cost. Finally, display the Most Likely scenario results.

g. Close the Scenario Manager dialog box.

h. Save the workbook.

3. Generate a scenario summary.

a. Create names for the input value cells and the dependent cell using the range A3:B7.

b. Verify that the names were created.

c. Create a scenario summary report, using the Cost to complete job value in cell B7 as the result cell.

d. Edit the title of the Summary report in cell B2 to read **Scenario Summary for Auto Repair**.

e. Delete the Current Values column.

f. Delete the notes beginning in cell B11. Compare your worksheet to **FIGURE K-24**.

g. Return to cell A1, enter your name in the center section of the Scenario Summary sheet footer, save the workbook, then preview the Scenario Summary sheet.

4. Project figures using a data table.

a. Click the Auto Repair sheet tab.

b. Enter the label **Labor $** in cell D3.

FIGURE K-24

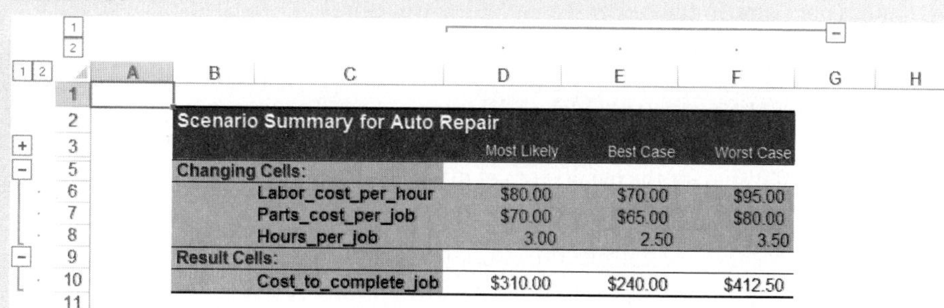

	Most Likely	Best Case	Worst Case
Scenario Summary for Auto Repair			
Changing Cells:			
Labor_cost_per_hour	$80.00	$70.00	$95.00
Parts_cost_per_job	$70.00	$65.00	$80.00
Hours_per_job	3.00	2.50	3.50
Result Cells:			
Cost_to_complete_job	$310.00	$240.00	$412.50

Excel 2013

Skills Review (continued)

c. Format the label so that it is boldfaced and right-aligned.
d. In cell D4, enter **75**; then in cell D5, enter **80**.
e. Select the range D4:D5, then use the fill handle to extend the series to cell D8.
f. In cell E3, reference the job cost formula by entering **=B7**.
g. Format the contents of cell E3 as hidden, using the ;;; Custom formatting type on the Number tab of the Format Cells dialog box.
h. Generate the new job costs based on the varying labor costs. Select the range D3:E8 and create a data table. In the data table dialog box, make cell B3 (the labor cost) the column input cell.
i. Format the range E4:E8 as currency with two decimal places. Compare your worksheet to **FIGURE K-25**.
j. Enter your name in the center section of the worksheet footer, save the workbook, then preview the worksheet.

5. Use Goal Seek.

a. Click cell B7, and open the Goal Seek dialog box.
b. Assuming the labor rate and the hours remain the same, determine what the parts would have to cost so that the cost to complete the job is $290. (*Hint*: Enter a job cost of **290** as the To value, and enter **B4** (the Parts cost) as the By changing cell. Write down the parts cost that Goal Seek finds.
c. Click OK, then use [Ctrl][Z] to reset the parts cost to its original value.
d. Enter the cost of the parts that you found in step 5b into cell A14.
e. Assuming the parts cost and hours remain the same, determine the fee for the labor so that the cost to complete the job is $250. Use [Ctrl][Z] to reset the labor cost to its original value. Enter the labor cost in cell A15.
f. Save the workbook, then preview the worksheet.

FIGURE K-25

	A	B	C	D	E
1	Auto Repair Model				
2					
3	Labor cost per hour	$80.00		Labor $	
4	Parts cost per job	$70.00		75	$295.00
5	Hours per job	3.00		80	$310.00
6				85	$325.00
7	Cost to complete job:	$310.00		90	$340.00
8				95	$355.00
9					
10					

6. Set up a complex what-if analysis with Solver.

a. With the Brake Repair sheet active, open the Solver Parameters dialog box.
b. Make B14 (the total repair costs) the objective cell, with a target value of 16,000.
c. Use cells B6:D6 (the number of scheduled repairs) as the changing cells.
d. Specify that cells B6:D6 must be integers. (*Hint*: Select int in the Add Constraint dialog box.)
e. Specify a constraint that cells B6:D6 must be greater than or equal to 10.

7. Run Solver and summarize results.

a. Use Solver to find a solution.
b. Save the solution as a scenario named **Repair Solution**, and restore the original values to the worksheet.
c. Create a scenario summary using the Repair Solution scenario, delete the notes at the bottom of the solution, and rename the worksheet **Repair Solution**. Compare your worksheet to **FIGURE K-26**.
d. Enter your name in the center section of the worksheet footer, save the workbook, then preview the worksheet.

FIGURE K-26

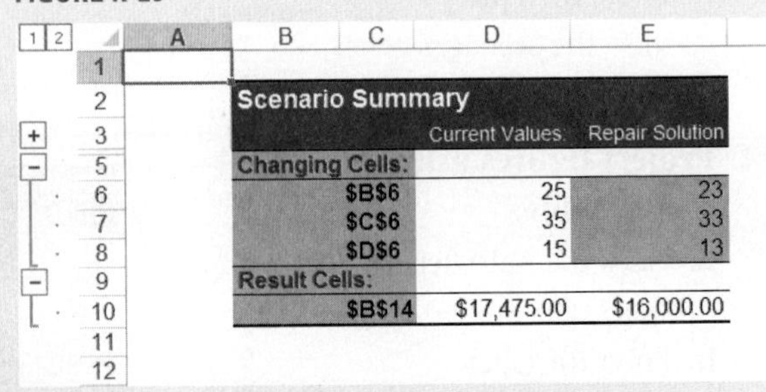

Scenario Summary
Current Values
Repair Solution
Changing Cells:
$B$6
25
23
$C$6
35
33
$D$6
15
13
Result Cells:
$B$14
$17,475.00
$16,000.00

8. Analyze data using the Analysis ToolPak.

a. With the Brake Repair sheet active, generate summary descriptive statistics for the repair cost per model, using cells B10:D10 as the input range. (*Hint*: The input is grouped in a row.) Place the new statistics on a worksheet named **Repair Cost Statistics**.
b. Widen columns as necessary to view the statistics.

c. Change the contents of cell A1 to **Repair Cost Per Model**. Delete row 9 containing the kurtosis error information. (This was generated because you only have three data values.) Compare your worksheet to **FIGURE K-27**.

d. Add your name to the center section of the worksheet footer, then preview the worksheet.

e. Save and close the workbook, submit the workbook to your instructor, then exit Excel.

FIGURE K-27

	A	B
1	*Repair Cost Per Model*	
2		
3	Mean	5825
4	Standard Error	1517.467737
5	Median	6500
6	Mode	#N/A
7	Standard Deviation	2628.33122
8	Sample Variance	6908125
9	Skewness	-1.0794537
10	Range	5125
11	Minimum	2925
12	Maximum	8050
13	Sum	17475
14	Count	3
15		

Independent Challenge 1

You are the manager for Stern & Jones, an environmental consulting firm based in Boston. You are planning a computer hardware upgrade for the engineers in the company. The vice president of finance at the company has asked you to research the monthly cost for a $200,000 equipment loan to purchase the new hardware. You will create a worksheet model to determine the monthly payments based on several different interest rates and loan terms, using data from the company's bank. Using Scenario Manager, you will create the following three scenarios: a 4-year loan at 6.8 percent; a 3-year loan at 5.75 percent; and a 2-year loan at 5.5 percent. You will also prepare a scenario summary report outlining the payment details.

a. Start Excel, open the file EX K-3.xlsx from the location where you store your Data Files, then save it as **EX K-Hardware Loan**.

b. Create cell names for the cells B4:B11 based on the labels in cells A4:A11, using the Create Names from Selection dialog box.

c. Use Scenario Manager to create scenarios that calculate the monthly payment on a $200,000 loan under the three sets of loan possibilities listed below. (*Hint*: Create three scenarios using cells B5:B6 as the changing cells.)

Scenario Name	Interest Rate	Term
6.8% 4 Yr	.068	48
5.75% 3 Yr	.0575	36
5.5% 2 Yr	.055	24

d. Show each scenario to make sure it performs as intended, then display the 6.8% 4 Yr scenario.

e. Generate a scenario summary titled **Scenario Summary for Hardware Purchase**. Use cells B9:B11 as the Result cells.

f. Delete the Current Values column in the report, and delete the notes at the bottom of the report. Rename the sheet **Hardware Purchase**.

g. Enter your name in the center section of the Hardware Purchase sheet footer. Save the workbook, then preview the scenario summary.

h. Close the workbook, exit Excel, then submit the workbook to your instructor.

Independent Challenge 2

You are a CFO at Bay City Digital, an interactive media consulting company based in Michigan. The company president has asked you to prepare a loan summary report for a business expansion. You need to develop a model to show what the monthly payments would be for a $750,000 loan with a range of interest rates. You will create a one-input data table that shows the results of varying interest rates in 0.2% increments, then you will use Goal Seek to specify a total payment amount for this loan application.

a. Start Excel, open the file EX K-4.xlsx from the location where you store your Data Files, then save it as **EX K-Capital Loan Payment Model**.

Independent Challenge 2 (continued)

b. Use **FIGURE K-28** as a guide to enter the data table structure. Reference the monthly payment amount from cell B9 in cell E4, then format the contents of cell E4 as hidden.

FIGURE K-28

	A	B	C	D	E
1	Bay City Digital				
2					
3				Interest Rate	
4	Loan Amount	$750,000.00			
5	Annual Interest Rate	7.80%		7.00%	
6	Term in Months	60		7.20%	
7				7.40%	
8				7.60%	
9	Monthly Payment:	$15,135.61		7.80%	
10	Total Payments:	$908,136.58		8.00%	
11	Total Interest:	$158,136.58		8.20%	
12				8.40%	
13				8.60%	

c. Using cells D4:E13, create a one-input data table with varying interest rates for the loan.

d. Generate the data table that shows the effect of varying interest rates on the monthly payments. Use cell B5, the Annual Interest Rate, as the column input cell. Format the range E5:E13 as currency with two decimal places.

e. Select cell B10 and use Goal Seek to find the interest rate necessary for a total payment amount of $850,000. Use cell B5, the Annual Interest Rate, as the By changing cell. Note the interest rate, then cancel the solution found by Goal Seek. Enter the interest rate in cell B16.

f. Select cell B9 and use Goal Seek to find the interest rate necessary for a monthly payment amount of $13,000. Use cell B5, the Annual Interest Rate, as the By changing cell. Note the interest rate, then cancel the solution found by Goal Seek. Enter the interest rate in cell B17.

g. Enter your name in the center section of the worksheet footer, save the workbook, then preview the worksheet.

h. Close the workbook, exit Excel, then submit the workbook to your instructor.

Independent Challenge 3

You are the owner of Cape Medical, a home medical products company based in Boston. You are considering a purchase of vans, sedans, and compact cars to provide local delivery service. You want to use Goal Seek to look at how the interest rate affects the monthly payments for two of each type of vehicle. Next you want to look at options for expanding the delivery service by purchasing a combination of vans, sedans, and compact cars that can deliver a total of 1500 cubic feet of products. As you review your expansion options, you need to keep the total monthly payments for all of the vehicles at or below $6,500. You use Solver to help find the best possible combination of vehicles.

a. Start Excel, open the file EX K-5.xlsx from the location where you store your Data Files, then save it as **EX K-Vehicle Purchase**.

b. Use Goal Seek to find the interest rate that produces a monthly payment for the van purchase of $1,800, and write down the interest rate that Goal Seek finds. Reset the interest rate to its original value, record the interest rate in cell A19, then enter **Interest rate for $1800 van payment** in cell B19.

c. Use Goal Seek to find the interest rate that produces a monthly payment for the sedan purchase of $1000. Reset the interest rate to its original value, record the interest rate in cell A20, then enter **Interest rate for $1000 sedan payment** in cell B20.

Independent Challenge 3 (continued)

d. Use Goal Seek to find the interest rate that produces a monthly payment for the compact purchase of $650. Reset the interest rate to its original value, record the interest rate in cell A21, then enter **Interest rate for $650 compact payment** in cell B21.

e. Assign cell B8 the name **Quantity_Van**, name cell C8 **Quantity_Sedan**, name cell D8 **Quantity_Compact**, and name cell B15 **Total_Monthly_Payments**. Use Solver to set the total delivery capacity of all vehicles to 1500. Use the quantity to purchase, cells B8:D8, as the changing cells. Specify that cells B8:D8 must be integers. Make sure that the total monthly payments amount in cell B15 is less than or equal to $6,500.

f. Generate a scenario named **Delivery Solution** with the Solver values, and restore the original values in the worksheet. Create a scenario summary using the Delivery Solution scenario and the Total Monthly Payments as the result cells, delete the notes at the bottom of the solution, and edit cell B2 to contain **Total Capacity of 1500**.

g. Enter your name in the center footer section of both worksheets. Preview both worksheets, then save the workbook.

h. Close the workbook, then submit the workbook to your instructor.

Independent Challenge 4: Explore

You are researching various options for financing a new car loan. You haven't decided whether to finance the car for 3, 4, or 5 years. Each loan term carries a different interest rate. To help with the comparison, you will create a two-input data table using interest rates and terms available at your credit union.

a. Start Excel, open the file EX K-6.xlsx from the location where you store your Data Files, then save it as **EX K-Car Loan**.

b. Using **FIGURE K-29** as a guide, enter the input values for a two-input data table with varying interest rates for 3-, 4-, and 5-year terms.

c. Reference the monthly payment amount from cell B9 in cell A13, and format the contents of cell A13 as hidden.

d. Generate the data table, using cells A13:D22, that shows the effect of varying interest rates and loan terms on the monthly payments. (*Hint*: Use cell B6, Term in Months, as the row input cell, and cell B5, the Annual Interest Rate, as the column input cell.)

e. Format the range B14:D22 as currency with two decimal places.

f. Enter your name in the center section of the Loan sheet footer, then preview the Loan sheet.

g. Save the workbook, close the workbook, then exit Excel and submit the workbook to your instructor.

FIGURE K-29

	A	B	C	D
1	Car Financing Options			
2				
3				
4	Loan Amount	$20,000.00		
5	Annual Interest Rate	3.50%		
6	Term in Months	60		
7				
8				
9	Monthly Payment:	$363.83		
10	Total Payments:	$21,830.09		
11	Total Interest:	$1,830.09		
12				
13		36	48	60
14	3.00%			
15	3.25%			
16	3.50%			
17	3.75%			
18	4.00%			
19	4.25%			
20	4.50%			
21	4.75%			
22	5.00%			
23				
24				

Visual Workshop

Open the file EX K-7.xlsx from the location where you store your Data Files, then save it as **EX K-Columbus Manufacturing**. Create the worksheet shown in FIGURE K-30. (*Hint*: Use Goal Seek to find the Hourly labor cost to reach the total profit in cell H11 in the figure and accept the solution.) Then generate descriptive statistics for the products' total profits on a worksheet named **Manufacturing Profits**, as shown in FIGURE K-31. Add your name to the center footer section of each sheet, change the orientation of the Profit sheet to landscape, then preview and print both worksheets.

FIGURE K-30

	A	B	C	D	E	F	G	H
1	Columbus Manufacturing							
2	December Production							
3	Hourly Labor Cost	$51.76						
4								
5								
6	Product Number	Hours	Parts Cost	Cost to Produce	Retail Price	Unit Profit	Units Produced	Total Profit
7	NA425	9	$473	$ 938.85	$1,522.00	$ 583.15	425	$ 247,838.73
8	CX877	7	$230	$ 592.33	$ 974.00	$ 381.67	387	$ 147,707.14
9	QA287	2	$421	$ 524.52	$ 776.00	$ 251.48	127	$ 31,937.68
10	TQ894	11	$187	$ 756.37	$1,322.00	$ 565.63	305	$ 172,516.46
11	Total Profit							$ 600,000.00
12								
13								

FIGURE K-31

	A	B
1	*Profit Statistics*	
2		
3	Mean	150000
4	Standard Error	44743.1
5	Median	160112
6	Mode	#N/A
7	Standard Deviation	89486.3
8	Sample Variance	8E+09
9	Kurtosis	1.376
10	Skewness	-0.64908
11	Range	215901
12	Minimum	31937.7
13	Maximum	247839
14	Sum	600000
15	Count	4
16		

Glossary

3-D reference A worksheet reference that uses values on other sheets or workbooks, effectively creating another dimension to a workbook.

Absolute cell reference In a formula, a cell address that refers to a specific cell and does not change when you copy the formula; indicated by a dollar sign before the column letter and/or row number. *See also* Relative cell reference.

Accessories Simple Windows application programs (apps) that perform specific tasks, such as the Calculator accessory for performing calculations. Also called Windows accessories.

Active The currently available document, program, or object; on the taskbar, when more than one program is open, the button for the active program appears slightly lighter.

Active cell The cell in which you are currently working.

Active window The window you are currently using; if multiple windows are open, the window with the darker title bar.

Add-in An extra program, such as Solver and the Analysis ToolPak, that provides optional Excel features. To activate an add-in, click the File tab, click Options, click Add-Ins, then select or deselect add-ins from the list.

Address A sequence of drive and folder names that describes a folder's or file's location in the file hierarchy; the highest hierarchy level is on the left, with lower hierarchy levels separated by the ▸ symbol to its right.

Address bar In a window, the area just below the title bar that shows the file hierarchy, or address of the files that appear in the file list below it; the address appears as a series of links you can click to navigate to other locations on your computer.

Alignment The placement of cell contents in relation to a cell's edges; for example, left-aligned, centered, or right-aligned.

And logical condition A filtering feature that searches for records by specifying that all entered criteria must be matched.

App An application program; Windows 8 apps are designed to occupy the full screen and are available on the Start screen and at the Windows store. Desktop apps, such as Microsoft Office, open in resizable windows, and are available from many software companies.

App window The window that opens after you start an app, showing you the tools you need to use the program and any open program documents.

Application program Any program that lets you work with files or create and edit files such as graphics, letters, financial summaries, and other useful documents, as well as view Web pages on the Internet and send and receive e-mail. Also called an app.

Apply (a template) To open a document based on an Excel template.

Argument Information necessary for a formula or function to calculate an answer. In the Visual Basic for Applications (VBA) programming language, variable used in procedures that a main procedure might run. *See also* Main procedure.

Arithmetic operators In a formula, symbols that perform mathematical calculations, such as addition (+), subtraction (–), multiplication (*), division (/), or exponentiation (^).

Ascending order In sorting an Excel field (column), the lowest value (the beginning of the alphabet, or the earliest date) appears at the beginning of the sorted data.

ASCII file A text file that contains data but no formatting; instead of being divided into columns, ASCII file data are separated, or delimited, by tabs or commas.

Attributes Styling characteristics such as bold, italic, and underlining that you can apply to change the way text and numbers look in a worksheet or chart. In XML, the components that provide information about the document's elements.

Auditing An Excel feature that helps track errors and check worksheet logic.

AutoComplete In the Visual Basic for Applications (VBA) programming language, a list of words that appears as you enter code; helps you automatically enter elements with the correct syntax.

AutoFill Feature activated by dragging the fill handle; copies a cell's contents or continues a series of entries into adjacent cells.

AutoFill Options button Button that appears after using the fill handle to copy cell contents; enables you to choose to fill cells with specific elements (such as formatting) of the copied cell if desired.

AutoFilter A table feature that lets you click a list arrow and select criteria by which to display certain types of records; also called filter.

AutoFilter list arrows *See* Filter List arrows.

AutoFit A feature that automatically adjusts the width of a column or the height of a row to accommodate its widest or tallest entry.

Backsolving A problem-solving method in which you specify a solution and then find the input value that produces the answer you want; sometimes described as a what-if analysis in reverse. In Excel, the Goal Seek feature performs backsolving.

Backstage view Appears when then FILE tab is clicked. The navigation bar on the left side contains commands to perform actions common to most Office programs, such as opening a file, saving a file, and closing the file.

Backup A duplicate copy of a file that is stored in another location.

Backward-compatible Software feature that enables documents saved in an older version of a program to be opened in a newer version of the program.

Banding Worksheet formatting in which adjacent rows and columns are formatted differently.

Blog Web log, or a personal commentary on a website.

Border A window's edge; you can drag to resize the window.

Bug In programming, an error that causes a procedure to run incorrectly.

Button A small rectangle you can click in order to issue a command to an application program.

Calculated columns In a table, a column that automatically fills in cells with formula results, using a formula entered in only one other cell in the same column.

Calculation operators Symbols in a formula that indicate what type of calculation to perform on the cells, ranges, or values.

Call statement A Visual Basic statement that retrieves a procedure that you want to run, using the syntax Call *procedurename*.

Canvas In the Paint accessory, the area in the center of the app window that you use to create drawings.

Case sensitive An application program's (app's) ability to differentiate between uppercase and lowercase letters; usually used to describe how an operating system evaluates passwords that users type to gain entry to user accounts.

Category axis Horizontal axis in a chart, usually containing the names of data categories; in a 2-dimensional chart, also known as the x-axis.

Cell The intersection of a column and a row in a worksheet or table.

Cell address The location of a cell, expressed by cell coordinates; for example, the cell address of the cell in column A, row 1 is A1.

Cell comments Notes you've written about a workbook that appear when you place the pointer over a cell.

Cell pointer Dark rectangle that outlines the active cell.

Cell styles Predesigned combinations of formats based on themes that can be applied to selected cells to enhance the look of a worksheet.

Change history A worksheet containing a list of changes made to a shared workbook.

Changing cells In what-if analysis, cells that contain the values that change in order to produce multiple sets of results.

Charms bar A set of buttons that appear on the right side of the Windows 8 screen that let you find and send information, change your machine settings, and turn off your computer. When you display the Charms bar, the time and date appear on the left side of the screen.

Chart animation The movement of a chart element after the relevant worksheet data changes.

Chart elements Parts of a chart, such as its title or its legend, which you can add, remove, or modify.

Chart sheet A separate sheet in a workbook that contains only a chart, which is linked to the workbook data.

Charts Pictorial representations of worksheet data that make it easier to see patterns, trends, and relationships; *also called* graphs.

Check box A box that turns an option on when checked or off when unchecked.

Click To quickly press and release the left button on the pointing device; also called single-click.

Clip A media file, such as a graphic, sound, animation, or movie.

Clip art A graphic image, such as a corporate logo, a picture, or a photo, that can be inserted into a document.

Clipboard A temporary Windows storage area that holds the selections you copy or cut.

Close button In a Windows title bar, the rightmost button; closes the open window, app, and/or document.

Cloud-based Refers to applications that are stored online, or "in the cloud," and not installed on your computer.

Cloud computing Work done in a virtual environment using data, applications, and resources stored on servers and accessed over the Internet or a company's internal network rather than on users' computers.

Cloud storage File storage locations on the World Wide Web, such as Windows SkyDrive or Dropbox.

Code *See* Program code.

Code window In the Visual Basic Editor, the window that displays the selected module's procedures, written in the Visual Basic programming language.

Color scale In conditional formatting, a formatting scheme that uses a set of two, three, or four fill colors to convey relative values of data.

Column heading A box that appears above each column in a worksheet; identifies the column letter, such as A, B, etc.

Combination chart Two charts in one, such as a column chart combined with a line chart, that together graph related but dissimilar data.

Command An instruction to perform a task, such as opening a file or emptying the Recycle Bin.

Command button A button you click to issue instructions to modify applicaton program (app) objects.

Comments In a Visual Basic procedure, notes that explain the purpose of the macro or procedure; they are preceded by a single apostrophe and appear in green. *See also* Cell comments.

Comparison operators In a formula, symbols that compare values for the purpose of true/false results.

Compatibility The ability of different programs to work together and exchange data.

Complex formula A formula that uses more than one arithmetic operator.

Conditional formatting A type of cell formatting that changes based on the cell's value or the outcome of a formula.

Consolidate To combine data on multiple worksheets and display the result on another worksheet.

Constraints Limitations or restrictions on input data in what-if analysis.

Contextual tab A tab that is displayed only when a specific task can be performed: they appear in an accent color and close when no longer needed.

Copy To make a duplicate copy of a file, folder, or other object that you want to store in another location.

Criteria range In advanced filtering, a cell range containing one row of labels (usually a copy of column labels) and at least one additional row underneath it that contains the criteria you want to match.

Custom chart type A specially formatted Excel chart.

D

Data entry area The unlocked portion of a worksheet where users are able to enter and change data.

Data label Descriptive text that appears above a data marker in a chart.

Data marker A graphical representation of a data point in a chart, such as a bar or column.

Data point Individual piece of data plotted in a chart.

Data series The selected range in a worksheet whose related data points Excel converts into a chart.

Data source Worksheet data used to create a chart or a PivotTable.

Data table A range of cells that shows the resulting values when one or more input values are varied in a formula; when one input value is changed, the table is called a one-input data table, and when two input values are changed, it is called a two-input data table. In a chart, it is a grid containing the chart data.

Data validation A feature that allows you to specify what data is allowable (valid) for a range of cells.

Database An organized collection of related information. In Excel, a database is called a table.

Database program An application, such as Microsoft Access, that lets you manage large amounts of data organized in tables.

Database table A set of data organized using columns and rows that is created in a database program.

Debug In programming, to find and correct an error in code.

Declare In the Visual Basic programming language, to assign a type, such as numeric or text, to a variable.

Default In an app window or dialog box, a value that is automatically set; you can change the default to any valid value.

Delimiter A separator such as a space, comma, or semicolon between elements in imported data.

Dependent cell A cell, usually containing a formula, whose value changes depending on the values in the input cells. For example, a payment formula or function that depends on an input cell containing changing interest rates is a dependent cell.

Descending order In sorting an Excel field (column), the order that begins with the letter Z, the highest number, or the latest date of the values in a field.

Desktop apps Application programs (apps), such as Microsoft Office, that open in resizeable windows that you can move and resize to view alongside other app windows; also called traditional apps.

Destination program In a data exchange, the program that will receive the data.

Device A hardware component that is part of your computer system, such as a disk drive, a pointing device, or a touch screen device.

Dialog box A window with controls that lets you tell Windows how you want to complete an application program's (app's) command.

Dialog box launcher An icon you can click to open a dialog box or task pane from which to choose related commands.

Document To make notes about basic worksheet assumptions, complex formulas, or questionable data. In a macro, to insert comments that explain the Visual Basic code.

Document window Most of the screen in any given program, where you create a document, slide, or worksheet.

Double-click To quickly press and release or click the left button on the pointing device twice.

Drag To point to an object, press and hold the left button on the pointing device, move the object to a new location, and then release the left button.

Drag and drop To use a pointing device to move or copy a file or folder directly to a new location instead of using the Clipboard.

Drive A physical location on your computer where you can store files.

Drive name A name for a drive that consists of a letter followed by a colon, such as C: for the hard disk drive.

Dropbox A free online storage site that lets you transfer files that can be retrieved by other people you invite. *See also* Cloud storage.

Dynamic page breaks In a larger workbook, horizontal or vertical dashed lines that represent the place where pages print separately. They also adjust automatically when you insert or delete rows or columns, or change column widths or row heights.

E

Edit To make a change to the contents of a file or an active cell.

Edit Link A link to a workbook on a SkyDrive that can be edited by users.

Electronic spreadsheet A computer program used to perform calculations and analyze and present numeric data.

Element An XML component that defines the document content.

Embed To insert a copy of data into a destination document; you can double-click the embedded object to modify it using the tools of the source program.

Embedded chart A chart displayed as an object in a worksheet.

Encrypted data Data protected by use of a password, which encodes it in a form that only authorized people with a password can decode.

Exploding Visually pulling a slice of a pie chart away from the whole pie chart in order to add emphasis to the pie slice.

Extensible Markup Language (XML) A system for defining languages using tags to structure data.

External reference indicator In a formula or macro name, an exclamation point (!) that indicates that a macro is outside the active workbook.

Extract To place a copy of a filtered table in a range you specify in the Advanced Filter dialog box.

Field In a table (an Excel database) or PivotTable, a column that describes a characteristic about records, such as first name or city. In a PivotTable, drag field names to PivotTable row, column, data, or report filter areas to explore data relationships.

Field name A column label that describes a field.

File A stored collection of data.

File Explorer A Windows accessory that allows you to navigate your computer's file hierarchy and manage your files and folders.

File extension A three- or four-letter sequence, preceded by a period, at the end of a filename that identifies the file as a particular type of document; for example, documents in the Rich Text Format have the file extension .rtf.

File hierarchy The tree-like structure of folders and files on your computer.

File list A section of a window that shows the contents of the folder or drive currently selected in the Navigation pane.

File management The ability to organize folders and files on your computer.

Filename A unique, descriptive name for a file that identifies the file's content.

Filter list arrows List arrows that appear next to field names in an Excel table; used to display portions of your data. Also called AutoFilter list arrows.

Flash Fill An Excel feature that automatically fills in column or row data based on calculations you enter.

Folder An electronic container that helps you organize your computer files, like a cardboard folder on your desk; it can contain subfolders for organizing files into smaller groups.

Folder name A unique, descriptive name for a folder that helps identify the folder's contents.

Font The typeface or design of a set of characters (letters, numbers, symbols, and punctuation marks).

Font size The size of characters, measured in units called points.

Font style Format such as bold, italic, and underlining that can be applied to change the way characters look in a worksheet or chart.

Form control An object that can be added to a worksheet to help users enter data. An example is a list box form control.

Format The appearance of a cell and its contents, including font, font styles, font color, fill color, borders, and shading. *See also* Number format.

Formula A set of instructions used to perform one or more numeric calculations, such as adding, multiplying, or averaging, on values or cells.

Formula bar The area above the worksheet grid where you enter or edit data in the active cell.

Formula prefix An arithmetic symbol, such as the equal sign (=), used to start a formula.

Forum Electronic gathering place where anyone can add questions and answers on computer issues.

Freeze To hold in place selected columns or rows when scrolling in a worksheet that is divided in panes. *See also* Panes.

Function (Excel) A built-in formula that includes the information necessary to calculate an answer; for example, SUM (for calculating a sum) or FV (for calculating the future value of an investment) (Visual Basic) In the Visual Basic for Applications (VBA) programming language, a predefined procedure that returns a value, such as the InputBox function that prompts the user to enter information.

Gallery A visual collection of choices you can browse through to make a selection. Often available with Live Preview.

Gesture An action you take with your fingertip directly on the screen, such as tapping or swiping, to make a selection or perform a task.

Goal cell In backsolving, a cell containing a formula in which you can substitute values to find a specific value, or goal.

Goal Seek A problem-solving method in which you specify a solution and then find the input value that produces the answer you want; sometimes described as a what-if analysis in reverse; also called backsolving.

Gridlines Evenly spaced horizontal and/or vertical lines used in a worksheet or chart to make it easier to read.

Groups Each tab on the Ribbon is arranged into groups to make features easy to find.

Hard disk A built-in, high-capacity, high-speed storage medium for all the software, folders, and files on a computer. Also called a hard drive.

Header row In an Excel table, the first row; it contains field (column) names.

Highlighted Describes the changed appearance of an item or other object, usually a change in its color, background color, and/or border; often used for an object on which you will perform an action, such as a desktop icon.

HTML (Hypertext Markup Language) The format of pages that a Web browser can read.

Hyperlink An object (a filename, a word, a phrase, or a graphic) in a worksheet that, when you click it, displays another worksheet or a Web page called the target. *See also* Target.

Hypertext Markup Language *See* HTML.

Icon A small image that represents an item, such as the Recycle Bin on your computer; you can rearrange, add, and delete desktop icons.

Icon sets In conditional formatting, groups of images that are used to visually communicate relative cell values based on the values they contain.

If...Then...Else statement In the Visual Basic programming language, a conditional statement that directs Excel to perform specified actions under certain conditions; its syntax is "If *condition* Then *statements* Else [*elsestatements*]".

Inactive window An open window you are not currently using; if multiple windows are open, the window(s) with the dimmed title bar.

Input cells Spreadsheet cells that contain data instead of formulas and that act as input to a what-if analysis; input values often change to produce different results. Examples include interest rates, prices, or other data.

Input values In a data table, the variable values that are substituted in the table's formula to obtain varying results, such as interest rates.

Insertion point A blinking vertical line that appears when you click in the formula bar or in an active cell; indicates where new text will be inserted.

Instance A worksheet in its own workbook window.

Integrate To incorporate a document and parts of a document created in one program into another program; for example, to incorporate an Excel chart into a PowerPoint slide, or an Access table into a Word document.

Integration A process in which data is exchanged among Excel and other Windows programs; can include pasting, importing, exporting, embedding, and linking.

Interface The look and feel of a program; for example, the appearance of commands and the way they are organized in the program window.

Intranet An internal network site used by a group of people who work together.

Keyword (Excel) Terms added to a workbook's Document Properties that help locate the file in a search. (Macros) In a macro procedure, a word that is recognized as part of the Visual Basic programming language. (Windows) A word or phrase you enter to obtain a list of results that include that word or phrase.

Labels Descriptive text or other information that identifies data in rows, columns, or charts, but is not included in calculations.

Landscape Page orientation in which the contents of a page span the length of a page rather than its width, making the page wider than it is tall.

Launch To open or start a program on your computer.

Layout An arrangement of files or folders in a window, such as Large icons or Details. There are eight layouts available.

Legend In a chart, information that identifies how data is represented by colors or patterns.

Library A window that shows files and folders stored in different storage locations; default libraries in Windows 8 include the Documents, Music, Pictures, and Videos libraries.

Linear trendline In an Excel chart, a straight line representing an overall trend in a data series.

Link To insert an object into a destination program; the information you insert will be updated automatically when the data in the source document changes. (Windows) Also called a hyperlink, text or an image you click to display another location.

Linking The dynamic referencing of data in the same or in other workbooks, so that when data in the other location is changed, the references in the current location are automatically updated.

List arrows *See* AutoFilter list arrows.

List box A box that displays a list of options from which you can choose (you may need to scroll and adjust your view to see additional options in the list).

Live Preview A feature that lets you point to a choice in a gallery or palette and see the results in the document without actually clicking the choice.

Live tile Updated, "live" content that appears on some apps' tiles on the Windows Start screen, including the Weather app and the News app.

Load To copy and place an app into your computer's memory in preparation for use.

Lock To secure a row, column, or sheet so that data in that location cannot be changed.

Lock screen The screen that appears when you first start your computer, or after you leave it unattended for a period of time, before the sign-in screen.

Log in To select a user account name when a computer starts up, giving access to that user's files. Also called sign in.

Logical conditions Using the operators And and Or to narrow a custom filter criteria.

Logical formula A formula with calculations that are based on stated conditions.

Logical test The first part of an IF function; if the logical test is true, then the second part of the function is applied; if it is false, then the third part of the function is applied.

Macro A named set of instructions, written in the Visual Basic programming language, that performs tasks automatically in a specified order.

Main procedure A macro procedure containing several macros that run sequentially.

Major gridlines In a chart, the gridlines that represent the values at the tick marks on the value axis.

Manual calculation An option that turns off automatic calculation of worksheet formulas, allowing you to selectively determine if and when you want Excel to perform calculations.

Map An XML schema that is attached to a workbook.

Map an XML element A process in which XML element names are placed on an Excel worksheet in specific locations.

Maximize button On the right side of a window's title bar, the center button of three buttons; used to expand a window so that it fills the entire screen. In a maximized window, this button changes to a Restore button.

Maximized window A window that fills the desktop.

Menu A list of related commands.

Metadata Information that describes data and is used in Microsoft Windows document searches.

Microsoft Community Website A Microsoft Help feature that lets you search forums (electronic gathering places where anyone can add questions and answers on computer issues), Microsoft help files, and even on-screen video demonstrations about selected topics. (Formerly the Microsoft Answers website.)

Microsoft SkyDrive *See* SkyDrive.

Microsoft Windows 8 An operating system.

Minimize button On the right side of a window's title bar, the leftmost button of three buttons; use to reduce a window so that it only appears as an icon on the taskbar.

Minimized window A window that is visible only as an icon on the taskbar.

Minor gridlines In a chart, the gridlines that represent the values between the tick marks on the value axis.

Mixed reference Cell reference that combines both absolute and relative cell addressing.

Mode In dialog boxes, a state that offers a limited set of possible choices.

Mode indicator An area on the left end of the status bar that indicates the program's status. For example, when you are changing the contents of a cell, the word 'Edit' appears in the mode indicator.

Model A worksheet used to produce a what-if analysis that acts as the basis for multiple outcomes.

Modeless Describes dialog boxes that, when opened, allow you to select other elements on a chart or worksheet to change the dialog box options and format, or otherwise alter the selected elements.

Module In Visual Basic, a module is stored in a workbook and contains macro procedures.

Mouse pointer A small arrow or other symbol on the screen that you move by manipulating the pointing device; also called a pointer.

Move To change the location of a file, folder, or other object by physically placing it in another location.

Multilevel sort A reordering of table data using more than one column (field) at a time.

My Documents folder The folder on your hard drive used to store most of the files you create or receive from others; might contain subfolders to organize the files into smaller groups.

Name box Box to the left of the formula bar that shows the cell reference or name of the active cell.

Navigate To move around in a worksheet; for example, you can use the arrow keys on the keyboard to navigate from cell to cell, or press [Page Up] or [Page Down] to move one screen at a time.

Navigate down To move to a lower level in your computer's file hierarchy.

Navigate up To move to a higher level in your computer's file hierarchy.

Navigation pane A pane in a window that contains links to folders and libraries; click an item in the Navigation pane to display its contents in the file list or click the or symbols to display or hide subfolders in the Navigation pane.

Normal view Default worksheet view that shows the worksheet without features such as headers and footers; ideal for creating and editing a worksheet, but may not be detailed enough when formatting a document.

Notification area An area on the right side of the Windows 8 taskbar that displays the current time as well as icons representing apps; displays pop-up messages when a program on your computer needs your attention.

Number format A format applied to values to express numeric concepts, such as currency, date, and percentage.

Object A chart or graphic image that can be moved and resized and contains handles when selected. In object linking and embedding (OLE), the data to be exchanged between another document or program. In Visual Basic, every Excel element, including ranges.

Object Linking and Embedding (OLE) A Microsoft Windows technology that allows you to transfer data from one document and program to another using embedding or linking.

Objective *See* Target cell.

Office App Applications that can be added to a worksheet to help manage and personalize the data. Examples are maps, dictionaries, and calendars.

Office Web Apps Versions of the Microsoft Office applications with limited functionality that are available online. Users can view documents online and then edit them in the browser using a selection of functions. Office Web Apps are available for Word, PowerPoint, Excel, and One Note.

OLE *See* Object Linking and Embedding.

One-input data table A range of cells that shows resulting values when one input value in a formula is changed.

Online collaboration The ability to incorporate feedback or share information across the Internet or a company network or intranet.

Operating system A program that manages the complete operation of your computer and lets you interact with it.

Option button A small circle in a dialog box that you click to select only one of two or more related options.

Or logical condition A filtering feature that searches for records by specifying that only one entered criterion must be matched.

Order of precedence Rules that determine the order in which operations are performed within a formula containing more than one arithmetic operator.

Outline symbols In outline view, the buttons that, when clicked, change the amount of detail in the outlined worksheet.

Output values In a data table, the calculated results that appear in the body of the table.

Page Break Preview A worksheet view that displays a reduced view of each page in your worksheet, along with page break indicators that you can drag to include more or less information on a page.

Page Layout view Provides an accurate view of how a worksheet will look when printed, including headers and footers.

Panes Sections into which you can divide a worksheet when you want to work on separate parts of the worksheet at the same time; one pane freezes, or remains in place, while you scroll in another pane until you see the desired information.

Password A special sequence of numbers and letters that users can use to control who can access the files in their user account area; keeping the password private helps keep users' computer information secure.

Paste To place a copied item from the Clipboard to a location in a document.

Paste Options button Button that appears onscreen after pasting content; enables you to choose to paste only specific elements of the copied selection, such as the formatting or values, if desired.

Path An address that describes the exact location of a file in a file hierarchy; shows the folder with the highest hierarchy level on the left and steps through each hierarchy level toward the right. Locations are separated by small triangles or by backslashes.

Personal macro workbook A workbook that can contain macros that are available to any open workbook. By default, the personal macro workbook is hidden.

Photos app A Windows 8 app that lets you view and organize your pictures.

PivotChart report An Excel feature that lets you summarize worksheet data in the form of a chart in which you can rearrange, or "pivot," parts of the chart structure to explore new data relationships. Also called a PivotChart.

PivotTable Field List A window containing fields that can be used to create or modify a PivotTable.

PivotTable Report An Excel feature that allows you to summarize worksheet data in the form of a table in which you can rearrange, or "pivot," parts of the table structure to explore new data relationships; also called a PivotTable.

Plot The Excel process that converts numerical information into data points on a chart.

Plot area In a chart, the area inside the horizontal and vertical axes.

Point A unit of measure used for font size and row height. One point is equal to 1/72nd of an inch.

Point To position the tip of the mouse pointer over an object, option, or item.

Pointer *See* Mouse pointer.

Pointing device A device that lets you interact with your computer by controlling the movement of the mouse pointer on your computer screen; examples include a mouse, trackball, touchpad, pointing stick, on-screen touch pointer, or a tablet.

Pointing device action A movement you execute with your computer's pointing device to communicate with the computer; the five basic pointing device actions are point, click, double-click, drag, and right-click.

Populate The process of importing an XML file and filling the mapped elements on the worksheet with data from the XML file. Also the process of adding data or fields to a table, PivotTable, or a worksheet.

Portrait Page orientation in which the contents of a page span the width of a page, so the page is taller than it is wide.

Power button The physical button on your computer that turns your computer on.

Presentation graphics program A program such as Microsoft PowerPoint that you can use to create slide show presentations.

Preview pane A pane on the right side of a window that shows the actual contents of a selected file without opening an app; might not work for some types of files.

Previewing Prior to printing, seeing onscreen exactly how the printed document will look.

Primary key The field in a database that contains unique information for each record.

Print area A portion of a worksheet that you can define using the Print Area button on the Page Layout tab; after you select and define a print area, the Quick Print feature prints only that worksheet area.

Print title In a table that spans more than one page, the field names that print at the top of every printed page.

Procedure A sequence of Visual Basic statements contained in a macro that accomplishes a specific task.

Procedure footer In Visual Basic, the last line of a Sub procedure.

Procedure header The first line in a Visual Basic procedure, it defines the procedure type, name, and arguments.

Program A set of instructions written for a computer, such as an operating system program or an application program; also called an application or an app.

Program code Macro instructions, written in the Visual Basic for Applications (VBA) programming language.

Project In the Visual Basic Editor, the equivalent of a workbook; a project contains Visual Basic modules.

Project Explorer In the Visual Basic Editor, a window that lists all open projects (or workbooks) and the worksheets and modules they contain.

Properties File characteristics, such as the author's name, keywords, or the title, that help others understand, identify, and locate the file.

Properties window In the Visual Basic Editor, the window that displays a list of characteristics, or properties, associated with a module.

Property In Visual Basic, an attribute of an object that describes its character or behavior.

Publish To place an Excel workbook or worksheet on a Web site or an intranet in HTML format so that others can access it using their Web browsers.

Quick Access toolbar A small toolbar on the left side of a Microsoft application program window's title bar, containing icons that you click to quickly perform common actions, such as saving a file.

Quick Analysis tool An icon that is displayed below and to the right of a range that lets you easily create charts and other elements.

RAM (Random Access Memory) The storage location that is part of every computer, that temporarily stores open apps and document data while a computer is on.

Range A selection of two or more cells, such as B5:B14.

Range object In Visual Basic, an object that represents a cell or a range of cells.

Read-only format Describes cells that display data but that cannot be changed in a protected worksheet.

Record In a table (an Excel database), data about an object or a person.

Recycle Bin A desktop object that stores folders and files you delete from your hard drive(s) and enables you to restore them.

Reference operators In a formula, symbols which enable you to use ranges in calculations.

Refresh To update a PivotTable so it reflects changes to the underlying data.

Regression analysis A way of representing data with a mathematically-calculated trendline showing the overall trend represented by the data.

Relative cell reference In a formula, a cell address that refers to a cell's location in relation to the cell containing the formula and that automatically changes to reflect the new location when the formula is copied or moved; default type of referencing used in Excel worksheets. *See also* Absolute cell reference.

Removable storage Storage media that you can easily transfer from one computer to another, such as DVDs, CDs, or USB flash drives.

Report filter A feature that allows you to specify the ranges you want summarized in a PivotTable.

Restore Down button On the right side of a maximized window's title bar, the center of three buttons; use to reduce a window to its last non-maximized size. In a restored window, this button changes to a Maximize button.

Return In a function, to display a result.

Ribbon Appears beneath the title bar in every Office program window, and displays commands you're likely to need for the current task.

Rich Text Format (RTF) The file format that the WordPad app uses to save files.

Right-click To press and release the right button on the pointing device; use to display a shortcut menu with commands you issue by left-clicking them.

Roaming setting A computer setting, such as your account name or picture, that you can access from any connected device.

RTF *See* Rich Text Format.

Run To play, as a macro.

Scenario A set of values you use to forecast results; the Excel Scenario Manager lets you store and manage different scenarios.

Scenario summary An Excel table that compiles data from various scenarios so that you can view the scenario results next to each other for easy comparison.

Schema In an XML document, a list of the fields, called elements or attributes, and their characteristics.

Scope In a named cell or range, the worksheet(s) in which the name can be used.

Screen capture An electronic snapshot of your screen, as if you took a picture of it with a camera, which you can paste into a document.

Screenshot An image of an open file that is pasted into an Excel document; you can move, copy, and edit the image.

ScreenTip A small box containing informative text that appears when you position the mouse over an object; identifies the object when you point to it.

Scroll To adjust your view to see portions of the app window that are not currently in a window.

Scroll arrow A button at each end of a scroll bar for adjusting your view in a window in small increments in that direction.

Scroll bars Bars on the right edge (vertical scroll bar) and bottom edge (horizontal scroll bar) of the document window that allow you to move around in a document that is too large to fit on the screen at once.

Scroll box A box in a scroll bar that you can drag to display a different part of a window.

Search criterion In a workbook or table search, the text you are searching for.

Search Tools tab A tab that appears in the File Explorer window after you click the Search text box; lets you specify a specific search location, limit your search, repeat previous searches, save searches, and open a folder containing a found file.

Secondary axis In a combination chart, an additional axis that supplies the scale for one of the chart types used.

Select To change the appearance of an item by clicking, double-clicking, or dragging across it, to indicate that you want to perform an action on it.

Select pointer The mouse pointer shape that looks like a white arrow pointing toward the upper-left corner of the screen.

Share *See* Shared workbook.

Shared workbook An Excel workbook that several users can open and modify.

Sheet tabs Identify the sheets in a workbook and let you switch between sheets; located below the worksheet grid.

Sheet tab scrolling buttons Allow you to navigate to additional sheet tabs when available; located to the left of the sheet tabs.

Shortcut An icon that acts as a link to an app, file, folder, or device that you use frequently.

Shortcut menu A menu of context-appropriate commands for an object that opens when you right-click that object.

Shut down To exit the operating system and turn off your computer.

Sign in To select a user account name when a computer starts up, giving access to that user's files. Also called log in.

Single-click *See* Click.

Sizing handles Small series of dots at the corners and edges of a chart indicating that the chart is selected; drag to resize the chart.

SkyDrive A Microsoft Web site where you can obtain free file storage space, using your own account, that you can share with others; you can access SkyDrive from a laptop, tablet computer, or smartphone.

Slicer A graphic object used to filter a PivotTable.

SmartArt graphic Predesigned diagram types for the following types of data: List, Process, Cycle, Hierarchy, Relationship, Matrix, and Pyramid.

Snap feature For desktop application programs, the Windows 8 feature that lets you drag a window to the left or right side of the screen, where it "snaps" to fill that half of the screen; also, for Windows 8 apps, the feature that lets you position one of two open apps so it occupies one- or two-thirds of the screen.

Sort Change the order of, such as the order of files or folders in a window, based on criteria such as date, file size, or alphabetical by filename.

Source program In a data exchange, the program used to create the data you are embedding or linking.

Sparklines Miniature charts that show data trends in a worksheet range, such as increases or decreases.

Spin box A text box with up and down arrows; you can type a setting in the text box or click the arrows to increase or decrease the setting.

Start screen The screen you see after you sign in to Windows 8; contains controls, such as tiles, that let you interact with the Windows 8 operating system.

Stated conditions In a logical formula, criteria you create.

Statement In Visual Basic, a line of code.

Status bar Bar at the bottom of the Excel window that provides a brief description about the active command or task in progress.

Strong password A password that is difficult to guess and that helps to protect your workbooks from security threats; has at least 14 characters that are a mix of upper- and lowercase letters, numbers, and special characters.

Structured reference Allows table formulas to refer to table columns by names that are automatically generated when the table is created.

Sub procedure A series of Visual Basic statements that performs an action but does not return a value.

Subfolder A folder within another folder.

Suite A group of programs that are bundled together and share a similar interface, making it easy to transfer skills and program content among them.

Summary function In a PivotTable, a function that determines the type of calculation applied to the PivotTable data, such as SUM or COUNT.

Synced Short for synchronized; refers to when you add, change, or delete files on one computer and the same files on your other devices are also updated.

Syntax In the Visual Basic programming language, the formatting rules that must be followed so that the macro will run correctly.

T

Tab A page in an application program's Ribbon, or in a dialog box, that contains a group of related commands and settings.

Table An organized collection of rows and columns of similarly structured data on a worksheet.

Table styles Predesigned formatting that can be applied to a range of cells or even to an entire worksheet; especially useful for those ranges with labels in the left column and top row, and totals in the bottom row or right column. *See also* Table.

Table total row A row you can add to the bottom of a table for calculations using the data in the table columns.

Target The location that a hyperlink displays after you click it.

Target cell In what-if analysis (specifically, in Excel Solver), the cell containing the formula. Also called objective.

Taskbar The horizontal bar at the bottom of the Windows 8 desktop; displays icons representing apps, folders, and/or files on the left, and the Notification area, containing the date and time and special program messages, on the right.

Template A predesigned, formatted file that serves as the basis for a new workbook; Excel template files have the file extension .xltx.

Text annotations Labels added to a chart to draw attention to or describe a particular area.

Text concatenation operators In a formula, symbols used to join strings of text in different cells.

Text file *See* ASCII file.

Theme A predefined set of colors, fonts, line and fill effects, and other formats that can be applied to an Excel worksheet and give it a consistent, professional look.

Tick marks Notations of a scale of measure on a chart axis.

Tile A shaded rectangle on the Windows 8 Start screen that represents an app. *See also* App and Application program.

Title bar Appears at the top of every Office program window: displays the document name and program name.

Toggle A button with two settings, on and off.

Toolbar In an application program, a set of buttons, lists, and menus you can use to issue program commands.

Touch pointer A pointer on the screen for performing pointing operations with a finger if touch input is available on your computer.

Tracer arrows In Excel worksheet auditing, arrows that point from cells that might have caused an error to the active cell containing an error.

Track To identify and keep a record of who makes which changes to a workbook.

Traditional apps Application programs (apps), such as Microsoft Office, that open in windows that you can move and resize to view alongside other app windows; also called desktop apps.

Trendline A series of data points on a line that shows data values that represent the general direction in a series of data.

Two-input data table A range of cells that shows resulting values when two input values in a formula are changed.

USB flash drive A removable storage device for folders and files that you plug into a USB port on your computer; makes it easy to transport folders and files to other computers. Also called a pen drive, flash drive, jump drive, keychain drive, or thumb drive.

User account A special area in a computer's operating system where users can store their own files and preferences.

User interface A collective term for all the ways you interact with a software program.

Username The name that appears in the User name text box of the Excel Options dialog box. This name is displayed at the beginning of comments added to a worksheet.

Validate A process in which an XML schema makes sure the XML data follows the rules outlined in the schema.

Validation *See* Data Validation.

Value axis In a chart, the axis that contains numerical values; in a 2-dimensional chart, also known as the y-axis.

Values Numbers, formulas, and functions used in calculations.

Variable In the Visual Basic programming language, an area in memory in which you can temporarily store an item of information; variables are often declared in Dim statements such as *DimNameAsString*. In an Excel scenario or what-if analysis, a changing input value, such as price or interest rate, that affects a calculated result.

VBA *See* Visual Basic for Applications.

View A method of displaying a document window to show more or fewer details or a different combination of elements that makes it easier to complete certain tasks, such as formatting or reading text. (Windows) A set of appearance choices for folder contents, such as Large icons view or Details view.

View Link A link to a workbook on a SkyDrive that can be viewed by users.

Virus Destructive software that can damage your computer files.

Visual Basic Editor A program that lets you display and edit macro code.

Visual Basic for Applications (VBA) A programming language used to create macros in Excel.

Watermark A translucent background design on a worksheet that is displayed when the worksheet is printed. A watermark is a graphic file that is inserted into the document header.

Web query An Excel feature that lets you obtain data from a Web, Internet, or intranet site and places it in an Excel workbook for analysis.

What-if analysis A decision-making tool in which data is changed and formulas are recalculated in order to predict various possible outcomes.

Wildcard A special symbol that substitutes for unknown characters in defining search criteria in the Find and Replace dialog box. The most common types of wildcards are the question mark (?), which stands for any single character, and the asterisk (*), which represents any group of characters.

Window A rectangular-shaped work area that displays an app or a collection of files, folders, and Windows tools.

Window control icons The set of three buttons on the right side of a window's title bar that let you control the window's state, such as minimized, maximized, restored to its previous open size, or closed.

Windows 8 apps Apps (application programs) for Windows 8 that have a single purpose, such as Photos, News, or SkyDrive.

Windows 8 UI The Windows 8 user interface. *See also* User interface.

Windows accessories Application programs (apps), such as Paint or WordPad, that come with the Windows 8 operating system.

Windows desktop An electronic work area that lets you organize and manage your information, much like your own physical desktop.

Windows Search The Windows feature that lets you look for files and folders on your computer storage devices; to search, type text in the Search text box in the title bar of any open window, or click the Search charm in the Charms bar and type search text.

Windows Website A link in the Windows Help app that lets you find Windows 8 resources such as blogs, video tours, and downloads.

WordArt Specially formatted text, created using the WordArt styles on the Format tab.

Workbook A collection of related worksheets contained within a single file which has the file extension xlsx.

Worksheet A single sheet within a workbook file; also, the entire area within an electronic spreadsheet that contains a grid of columns and rows.

Worksheet window Area of the program window that displays part of the current worksheet; the worksheet window displays only a small fraction of the worksheet, which can contain a total of 1,048,576 rows and 16,384 columns.

Write access The ability to make changes to a workbook; with read access, a user can only read the workbook contents and cannot make changes.

X-axis The horizontal axis in a chart; because it often shows data categories, such as months or locations, also called Category axis.

XML (Extensible Markup Language) A system for defining languages using tags to structure, store, and send data.

Y-axis The vertical axis in a chart; because it often shows numerical values, also called Value axis.

Z-axis The third axis in a true 3-D chart; lets you compare data points across both categories and values.

Zooming in A feature that makes a document appear larger but shows less of it on screen at once; does not affect actual document size.

Zooming out A feature that shows more of a document on screen at once but at a reduced size; does not affect actual document size.

Index

C

D

E

F

G

H

I

L

M

N

P

Q

R

S

T

U

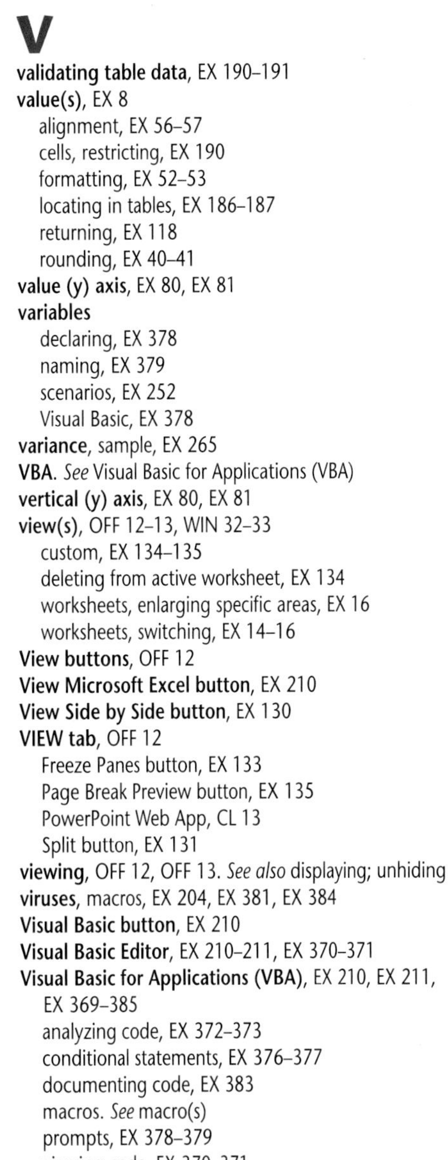

V

W

Y

Z